CFA Institute

CW01649370

FIXED INCOME

CFA® Program Curriculum

2026 • LEVEL I • VOLUME 6

WILEY

ISBN 978-1-961409-88-0

May 2025

Please visit our website at
www.WileyGlobalFinance.com.

WILEY

SKY14E3B9DA-5F0F-4927-AA56-37780D53C79D_022725

CONTENTS

How to Use the CFA Program Curriculum

The CFA® Program exams measure your mastery of the core knowledge, skills, and abilities required to succeed as an investment professional. These core competencies are the basis for the Candidate Body of Knowledge (CBOK™). The CBOK consists of four components:

A broad outline that lists the major CFA Program topic areas (www.cfainstitute.org/programs/cfa/curriculum/cbok/cbok)

Topic area weights that indicate the relative exam weightings of the top-level topic areas (www.cfainstitute.org/en/programs/cfa/curriculum)

Learning outcome statements (LOS) that tell you the specific knowledge, skills, and abilities you should gain from each curriculum topic area. You will find these statements at the start of each learning module and lesson. We encourage you to review the information about the LOS on our website (www.cfainstitute.org/programs/cfa/curriculum/study-sessions), including the descriptions of LOS "command words" on the candidate resources page at www.cfainstitute.org/-/media/documents/support/programs/cfa-and-cipm-los-command-words.ashx.

The CFA Program curriculum that candidates receive access to upon exam registration.

Therefore, the key to your success on the CFA exams is studying and understanding the CBOK. You can learn more about the CBOK on our website: www.cfainstitute.org/programs/cfa/curriculum/cbok.

The curriculum, including the practice questions, is the basis for all exam questions. The curriculum is selected/developed specifically to provide candidates with the knowledge, skills, and abilities reflected in the CBOK.

CFA INSTITUTE LEARNING ECOSYSTEM (LES)

Your exam registration fee includes access to the CFA Institute Learning Ecosystem (LES). This digital learning platform provides access to all the curriculum content and practice questions. The LES is organized as a series of learning modules consisting of short online lessons and associated practice questions. This tool is your source for all study materials, including practice questions and mock exams. The LES is the primary method by which CFA Institute delivers your curriculum experience. Here, you will find additional practice questions to test your knowledge, including some interactive questions.

DESIGNING YOUR PERSONAL STUDY PROGRAM

An orderly, systematic approach to exam preparation is critical. You should dedicate a consistent block of time every week to reading and studying. Review the LOS both before and after you study curriculum content to ensure you can demonstrate the knowledge, skills, and abilities described by the LOS and the assigned learning module. Use the LOS as a self-check to track your progress and highlight areas of weakness for later review.

Successful candidates report an average of more than 300 hours preparing for each exam. Your preparation time will vary based on your prior education and experience, and you will likely spend more time on some topics than on others.

ERRATA

The curriculum development process is rigorous and involves multiple rounds of reviews by content experts. Despite our efforts to produce a curriculum that is free of errors, we must make corrections in some instances. Curriculum errata are periodically updated and posted by exam level and test date on the Curriculum Errata webpage (www.cfainstitute.org/en/programs/submit-errata). If you believe you have found an error in the curriculum, you can submit your concerns through our curriculum errata reporting process found at the bottom of the Curriculum Errata webpage.

OTHER FEEDBACK

Please send any comments or suggestions to info@cfainstitute.org, and we will review your feedback thoughtfully.

Fixed Income

LEARNING MODULE

1

Fixed-Income Instrument Features

LEARNING OUTCOMES

Mastery	*The candidate should be able to:*
☐	describe the features of a fixed-income security
☐	describe the contents of a bond indenture and contrast affirmative and negative covenants

INTRODUCTION

1

Fixed-income instruments, such as loans and bonds, are the most common means of financing. Fixed-income issuers include businesses, governments, and not-for-profits that promise to pay interest and repay borrowed principal to investors. Loans are commonly used between an individual or company and a bank. Bonds are more standardized fixed-income instruments designed to be more easily tradeable than loans and are commonly issued by larger companies, governments, and special purpose issuers. Bonds are a core holding for many investors, including mutual funds, pension plans, insurance companies, and central banks. This module introduces the features of fixed-income instruments and the legal contracts that govern them.

LEARNING MODULE OVERVIEW

- Fixed-income instruments are debt instruments, such as loans and bonds, that represent a contractual agreement under which an issuer borrows money from investors in exchange for interest and future repayment of principal.
- Key features of fixed-income instruments include the issuer (borrower), time to maturity, principal amount, coupon rate and frequency, seniority, and contingency provisions. These features in turn define the cash flow structure of the instrument.
- A fixed-income investor (lender) receives a return or yield based on the periodic cash flows paid by the bond issuer and the change in price of the bond. A bond's price and yield vary inversely with one another.

- Fixed-income investors are exposed to credit risk, the risk of loss resulting from the issuer failing to make full and timely payments of interest and/or to repay principal. Investors expect to earn the lowest yield on bonds that carry little or no credit risk and expect higher yields on lower-credit-quality instruments.
- A fixed-income instrument's credit quality is affected by the underlying source of repayment, its seniority, credit provisions such as collateral backing, and the issuer's willingness to pay.
- The legal contract describing the features and other terms of a fixed-income security is known as an indenture.
- Indentures often contain covenants, or legally enforceable terms, agreed to at the time of issuance. These may either require the bond issuer to take an action or prohibit the issuer from performing some action.

LEARNING MODULE SELF-ASSESSMENT

These initial questions are intended to help you gauge your current level of understanding of this learning module.

1. The annual coupon amount for a fixed-rate bond is calculated by:

   A. multiplying its yield by the par value of the bond.

   B. Multiplying its coupon rate by the price of the bond.

   C. Multiplying its coupon rate by the par value of the bond.

   Solution:

   C is correct. On each interest payment date, a fixed-rate bond issuer pays investors a coupon payment equal to the bond's coupon rate times its par value. For periods shorter than a year, the annual coupon amount is divided into smaller equal periodic payments. For example, a bond with a par value of 100 and a coupon rate of 6% paid quarterly would pay coupon payments of $0.06 \times 100 = 60/4 = 15$ four times per year.

2. Match each bond type in the left column with a description in the right column.

A. Fixed-coupon bond	I. The difference between its issuance price and par value at maturity represents a cumulative interest payment at maturity.
B. Floating-rate note	II. Usually involves uniform payments that occur at monthly, quarterly, semi-annual, or annual intervals.
C. Zero-coupon bond	III. Involves interest payments that reset periodically based on market factors.

Solution:

A. II is correct. Fixed-coupon bonds usually involve uniform payments that occur at monthly, quarterly, semi-annual, or annual intervals.

B. III is correct. Floating-rate notes (FRNs) involve interest payments that reset periodically based on market factors.

C. I is correct. Zero-coupon bonds are typically issued at a discount to par; the difference between the issuance price and par value represents a cumulative interest payment at maturity.

3. The coupon rate for a floating rate note (FRN) is composed of a market reference rate and:

   A. a credit rating.

   B. an issuer-specific spread.

   C. The yield on a fixed-rate benchmark bond.

   Solution:

   B is correct. An FRN coupon rate comprises a market reference rate (MRR) and an issuer-specific spread that is usually constant and set at the time of issuance, while the MRR resets periodically based on market factors. As the MRR changes, the FRN coupon rate and interest payment change accordingly.

   A is incorrect. While the issuer's credit rating may be a determinant of an FRN's spread over the MRR, a credit rating is a letter-grade assessment of credit risk and is not directly involved in the calculation of the coupon rate.

   C is incorrect. The yield on a fixed-rate benchmark bond would reflect top-down factors that determine interest rates, such as real growth and expected inflation, which are already considered in the MRR.

4. A sovereign bond is usually a safer investment than a corporate bond of similar maturity issued within a country because:

   A. corporate bonds are subject to inflation risk.

   B. sovereign bonds are backed by taxation and fiscal power of the issuing government.

   C. sovereign bonds are secured by high-quality collateral, such as property and equipment.

   Solution:

   B is correct. Sovereign bonds are backed by a national government's taxation and fiscal power and thus usually represent the highest-credit-quality bonds in each geographic market.

   A is incorrect because sovereign bonds, unless specifically indexed to inflation, are also subject to inflation risk.

   C is incorrect because sovereign bonds are typically not secured by collateral; this is more commonly a feature of corporate bonds and asset-backed securities.

5. Which of the following is the appropriate order of claims in liquidation, by type of bond, in order of highest to lowest?

   A. Junior, senior secured, senior unsecured

   B. Senior unsecured, senior secured, junior

   C. Senior secured, senior unsecured, junior

   Solution:

   C is correct. Senior secured debts would be the highest-priority claims to be satisfied. Senior unsecured debts would be the next to receive allocations of the liquidated asset value, and junior debts would be the lowest-priority claims to be satisfied.

6. Describe the purpose of a pari passu clause in a bond indenture.

   Solution:

   A pari passu ("equal footing") clause ensures that a debt obligation is treated the same as the borrower's other senior debt instruments.

2 FEATURES OF FIXED-INCOME SECURITIES

☐ describe the features of a fixed-income security

Fixed-income instruments are debt instruments, such as loans and bonds. **Loans** are debt instruments formed and governed by a private agreement usually between an individual or company and a financial intermediary, such as a bank. **Bonds** or **fixed-income securities** are more standardized contractual agreements between larger issuers and investors. A bond issuer borrows money most often to fund operations or capital expenditures. Bond investors are lenders who provide funds to the issuer in exchange for interest payments and future repayment of principal. While corporate issuers tend to have, at most, one or two types of equity securities outstanding, they often have many types of debt obligations outstanding, each with distinct features, such as time to maturity, seniority, and currency.

WHICH LIABILITIES ARE FIXED-INCOME INSTRUMENTS?

Earlier modules in corporate issuers and financial statement analysis discussed the balance sheets of corporate issuers composed of assets and the liabilities and equity that finance them. Liabilities are broadly defined by accounting standards as present obligations to transfer economic resources as a result of past events. This definition encompasses many types of obligations, including amounts that an issuer owes to suppliers, customers, employees, governments, retirees, lessors, and so on.

Not all liabilities are fixed-income instruments (or "debt"), but all fixed-income instruments are liabilities. In these modules on fixed income, from the perspective of a corporate issuer, we are focused only on loans and bonds: instruments that can be settled in cash and for which the counterparty is an investor or a bank. Other liabilities, particularly leases and pension obligations, share some characteristics with fixed-income instruments but are outside the scope of these modules.

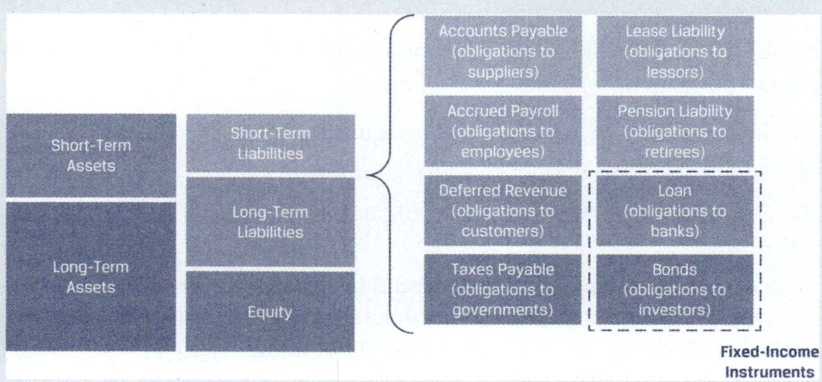

Note that government issuers tend to be financed by bonds, not by loans, though some exceptions exist—for example, loans from supranational organizations such as the International Monetary Fund (IMF).

The committed periodic cash flows of a bond distinguish it from equity securities. Exhibit 1 shows the cash flows of a fixed-rate bond issued by Bright Wheels Automotive (BRWA) Corporation.

Exhibit 1: BRWA Corporation Bond Cash Flows

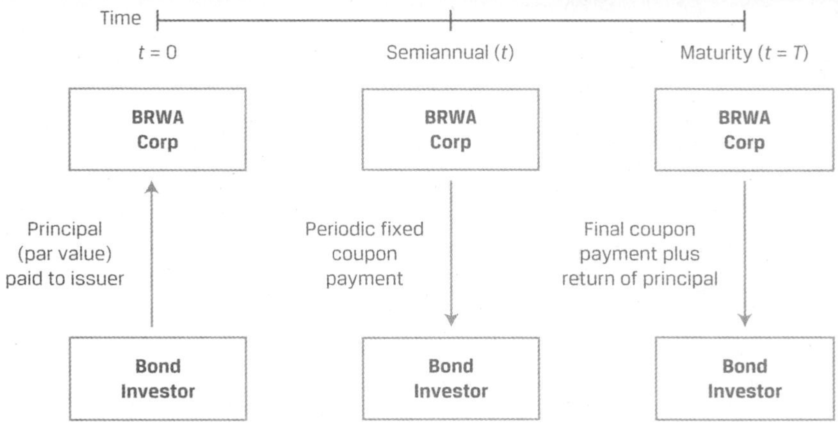

At issuance, investors purchased the BRWA bond in exchange for cash equal to the bond **principal** or the amount borrowed, which is also referred to as the bond's **par value**. On each interest payment date, BRWA commits to pay bond investors an interest or **coupon** payment equal to the coupon rate times the par value of the bond. For periods shorter than a year, the annual coupon amount is divided into smaller equal periodic payments. On the bond's maturity date, BRWA pays the final fixed coupon and the principal amount to investors.

The key features of each bond issue are usually summarized in a prospectus. Exhibit 2 outlines the terms of BRWA Corporation's bond issue.

Exhibit 2: BRWA Corporation Bond: Brief Summary of Terms

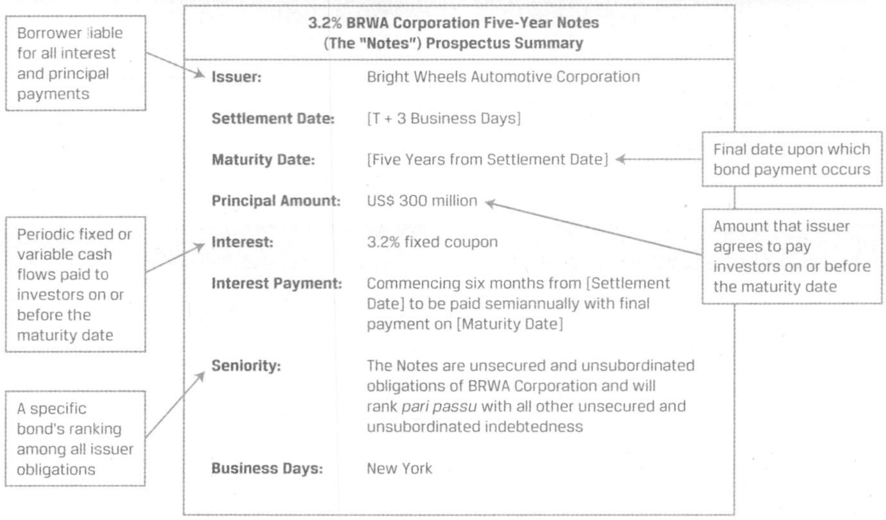

Key bond features include the issuer, time to maturity, principal amount, coupon rate and frequency, seniority, and contingency provisions.

Issuer

A bond issuer can be any legal entity and is liable for all interest and principal payments. Government sector issuers include national (also termed sovereign) or local governments, supranational organizations (such as the World Bank), and quasi-government entities (agencies owned or sponsored by governments, such as postal services or national railways). Because sovereign bonds are backed by the taxation and fiscal power of the issuing government, they usually represent the lowest-credit-risk bond in each region. Private sector issuers include corporate issuers and special purpose entities created to take ownership in such assets as loans or receivables, financed by **asset-backed securities (ABS)** issued to investors, which will be discussed in detail in later lessons.

Maturity

A bond's **maturity** is the date of the final payment the issuer makes to investors, and the **tenor** refers to the remaining time to maturity. Fixed-income securities with a tenor one year or less at issuance are known as **money market securities**, examples of which include government Treasury bills and commercial paper issued by corporations. Bonds with tenors longer than one year at issuance are called **capital market securities**. **Perpetual bonds** are a less common bond type with no stated maturity. Public sector entities were the first issuers of perpetual bonds, and current examples include local governments and local authorities, as well as certain bonds issued by banks to meet regulatory capital requirements. Perpetual bonds are still distinct from equities, however, in that they have contractually defined cash flows, no voting rights, and greater seniority in the capital structure.

AIRPORT AUTHORITY HONG KONG'S PERPETUAL BONDS

Airport Authority Hong Kong (AAHK) is a statutory body responsible for operating and developing Hong Kong International Airport, one of the world's busiest cargo airports and a major passenger hub connecting to over 200 global destinations. In late 2020, following a sharp decline in passenger volume during the COVID-19 pandemic, AAHK announced a two-part, USD1.5 billion perpetual bond issue to fund construction of a third runway and for general corporate purposes. Asian and European investors demonstrated confidence in the airport's recovery of passenger volume, placing orders totaling more than 10× the offer amount.

Principal (Par or Face Value)

The principal, par value, or **face value** is the amount an issuer agrees to repay to investors at maturity. In the BRWA Corporation example, the principal amount of USD300 million is repaid at maturity, which is five years from issuance. Certain instruments may repay the principal in equal or variable increments over time. A common example is a mortgage loan, for which borrowers make a monthly payment composed of both principal repayment and interest. The principal is repaid over time and not in a lump sum at maturity.

Coupon Rate and Frequency

A bond's interest can be paid as

- a fixed coupon paid on specified dates,
- a variable coupon determined and paid on specified dates, or
- part of a single payment with the principal at maturity.

Fixed-coupon bond payments usually involve uniform payments at monthly, quarterly, semi-annual, or annual intervals. Corporate bonds tend to pay semiannually.

Bonds with variable interest payments are called **floating-rate notes** (FRNs). An FRN coupon is determined as a combination of a **market reference rate** (MRR) and an issuer-specific spread referred to as the **credit spread**. The MRR is a standard borrowing or lending rate for issuers with the highest creditworthiness or lowest default risk for different currencies and maturities. MRRs were historically determined by a poll of lenders (Libor) but transitioned to an average of observed market transaction rates.

The credit spread is set at the time of FRN issuance, is usually constant over the bond's life, and is expressed in basis points (bps), or hundredths of a percentage point. The higher an issuer's credit quality, the lower the spread. In contrast, the MRR resets periodically throughout the bond's life based on market factors. As the MRR changes, the FRN coupon rate and interest payment change accordingly.

Bonds that do not pay periodic interest and instead pay interest as part of a single payment with principal at maturity are termed **zero-coupon bonds** or **pure discount bonds**. Zero-coupon bonds are typically issued at a discount to par; the difference between the issuance price and par value represents a cumulative interest payment at maturity.

Seniority

A debt issue's **seniority** or priority of repayment among all issuer obligations is an important determinant of risk. **Senior debt** has priority over other debt claims in the case of bankruptcy or liquidation. **Junior debt**, or **subordinated debt**, claims have a lower priority than senior debt and are paid only once senior claims are satisfied. The BRWA Corporation bonds are senior debt and would be repaid before any BRWA subordinated debt in the event of bankruptcy.

Contingency Provisions

A **contingency provision** is a clause in a legal agreement that allows for an action if an event or circumstance occurs. The most common contingency provision for bonds involves **embedded options**—specifically, call, put, and conversion to equity options. These resemble option contracts but cannot be traded separately from the bond itself. However, the value of these embedded options may be established by comparing the value of a bond with a contingency provision with that of an otherwise similar standard bond from the same issuer. The BRWA bond does not contain any contingency provisions, but this feature will be explored in depth in later lessons.

We can use the features of a bond issue to model its cash flows. Exhibit 3 illustrates the cash flows over the life of the five-year, fixed-coupon BRWA Corporation bond described earlier.

Exhibit 3: BRWA Corporation Bond Cash Flows

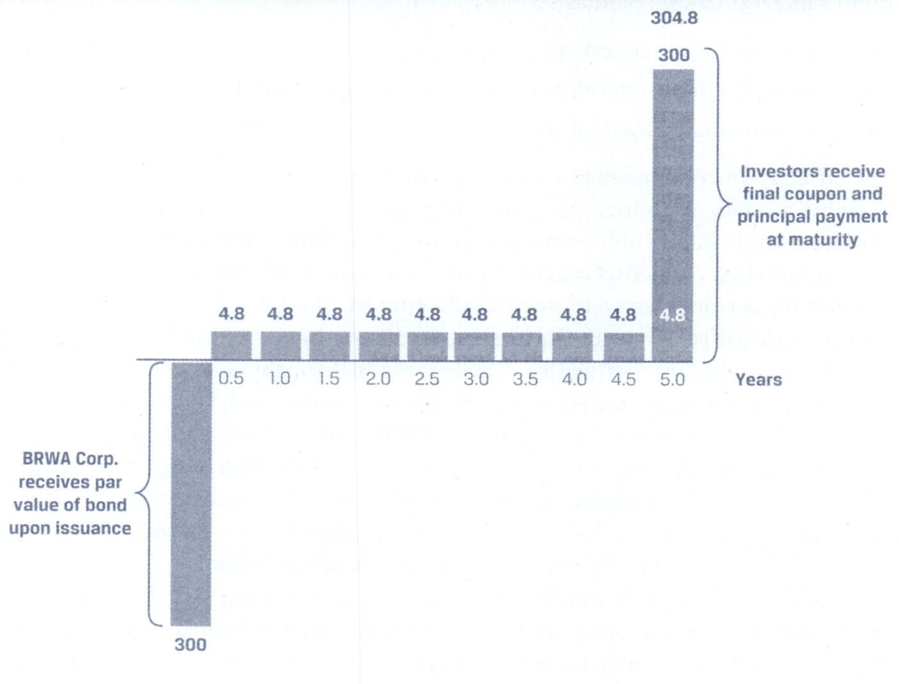

At the time of issuance, investors purchase the bond and pay cash to BRWA Corporation equal to the USD300 million in par value. BRWA investors receive periodic interest payments as follows:

Annual interest expense = Bond par value × Coupon rate.

Annual interest expense = USD300,000,000 × 3.2%.

Annual interest expense = USD9,600,000.

Semiannual interest expense = USD9,600,000/2 = USD4,800,000.

At the end of the fifth year on the maturity date, BRWA Corporation pays investors the final semiannual coupon payment plus the par value of USD300 million for a total of USD304.8 million.

Yield Measures

Given a bond's expected cash flows and its price, return or yield measures can be calculated. One simple measure is the **current yield** (CY), equal to the bond's annual coupon divided by the bond's price and expressed as a percentage. For example, if the five-year BRWA bond were trading at a price of USD101 per USD100 in face value at time *t*, its current yield would be

CY_t = Annual $coupon_t$/Bond $price_t$ = 3.2%/1.01 = 3.168%.

The current yield is analogous to the dividend yield for an equity security.

A more complex but far more common yield measure is the **yield-to-maturity** (YTM), which is the internal rate of return (IRR) calculated using the bond's price and its expected cash flows to maturity. YTM is usually quoted as an annual rate. An investor's rate of return on a bond will equal the bond's YTM at the time of purchase as long as the investor

1. receives all promised interest and principal payments as scheduled (i.e., no default),
2. holds the bond until maturity, and
3. reinvests all periodic cash flows at the YTM.

Notice that these are the same IRR assumptions discussed in earlier modules. If any of these assumptions do not hold, the investor's rate of return on the bond investment will differ from the YTM. If the five-year BRWA bond were trading at a price of USD101 per USD100 in face value immediately after issuance, its YTM is the rate, *r*, in the following equation (recall that the 3.2% coupon is paid semiannually, or 1.6 in each of 10 periods per USD100 in face value):

$$101 = 1.6/(1 + r)^1 + 1.6/(1 + r)^2 + \ldots + 101.6/(1 + r)^{10}.$$

r = 1.49% on a semiannual basis, or 1.49% × 2 = 2.98% annualized.

The YTM calculation is covered in depth in later modules.

Yield Curves

Most fixed-income issuers have many debt instruments outstanding. A useful way of evaluating the YTM on one issue is to graph all an issuer's debt instruments with identical features by their YTM and times to maturity. This graphical depiction results in a **yield curve**. BRWA has six bond issues outstanding, shown in Exhibit 4. The 3.2%, five-year bond is the third point from the left.

Exhibit 4: BRWA Corporation Bond Yield Curve

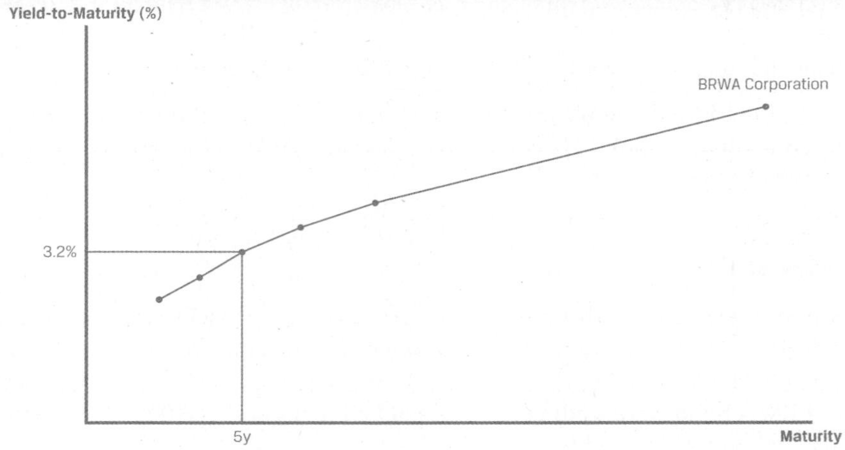

In this example, the BRWA bonds with longer maturities have higher YTMs, indicating that investors are demanding higher expected returns to compensate for higher risk associated with longer-maturity bonds of the same issuer. A way to measure the credit risk (one type of investment risk of fixed-income securities) for a bond is to compare an issuer's yield curve to that of comparable sovereign bonds, which have little or no credit risk. Exhibit 5 shows the yield curve for BRWA bonds versus the yield curve for comparable sovereign bonds in the United States, which are US Treasuries.

Exhibit 5: BRWA Corporation Yield Curve vs. Treasuries

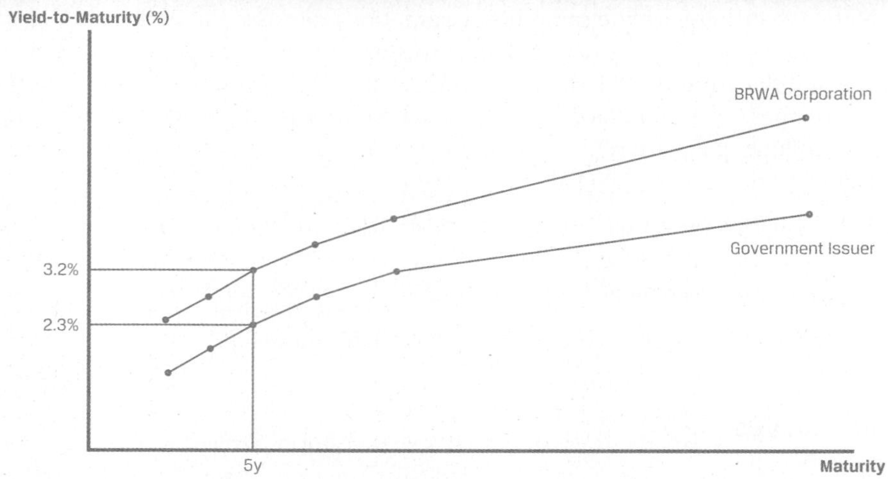

The yield-to-maturity difference between the five-year BRWA bond and the five-year US Treasury bond is 90 bps (= 3.2% – 2.3%), which reflects compensation that investors demand for taking the additional credit risk associated with the BRWA bonds.

QUESTION SET

1. Match the fixed-income instrument type in the left column with its description in the right column.

A. Money market securities	I. Public and private bonds with a time to maturity of greater than one year
B. Capital market securities	II. Fixed-income instruments with maturities of less than one year, such as commercial paper
C. Perpetual bonds	III. Bonds that have no stated maturity date

Solution:

A. II is correct. Money market securities are fixed-income instruments with maturities of less than one year, such as commercial paper.

B. I is correct. Capital market securities are public and private bonds with a time to maturity of greater than one year.

C. III is correct. Perpetual bonds have no stated maturity date.

2. Calculate the coupon payment on a 2.5% coupon bond with GBP100,000 par value and a semiannual payment frequency.

Solution:

The correct answer is GBP1,250.

The annual coupon on a bond is calculated by multiplying the coupon rate and the par value. For this bond, the coupon rate of 2.5% and par value of GBP100,000 results in a GBP2,500 annual coupon. However, since the payment frequency is semiannual (twice a year), each coupon payment is GBP1,250.

3. Determine the appropriate FRN coupon and interest payable in the following example: A European corporation issues a EUR10 million FRN that pays quarterly interest equal to the three-month MRR plus 125 bps. If three-month MRR is –0.50%, what is the corporation's FRN coupon interest payable on the FRN for the period?

Solution:

The answer is EUR18,750.

An FRN coupon comprises MRR plus the issuer-specific spread.

FRN coupon = MRR + Spread.

FRN coupon = –0.50% + 1.25%.

FRN coupon = 0.75%.

Annual interest = Principal × FRN coupon.

Annual interest = €10,000,000 × 0.75%.

Annual interest = €75,000, or €18,750 on a quarterly basis.

4. Fill in the blanks. The current yield is equal to a bond's annual _____ divided by the bond's price expressed as a percentage. If the bond's price were to fall, we would expect the current yield to ____.

   Solution:

   The current yield is equal to a bond's annual *coupon* divided by the bond's price expressed as a percentage. If the bond's price were to fall, we would expect the current yield to *rise.*

5. Fill in the blanks. A downward-sloping yield curve indicates that yields-to-maturity on an issuer's longer-term bonds are __________ than yields-to-maturity on that issuer's shorter-term bonds.

   Solution:

   A downward-sloping yield curve indicates that yields-to-maturity on an issuer's longer-term bonds are *lower* than yields-to-maturity on that issuer's shorter-term bonds.

3 BOND INDENTURES AND COVENANTS

☐ describe the contents of a bond indenture and contrast affirmative and negative covenants

Bond Indentures

Fixed-income security features outlined in the prior lesson are included in a legal contract that describes the form of the bond, the obligations of the issuer, and the rights of the bondholders. This legal contract is referred to as the bond **indenture**. In addition to specifying a bond's features, an indenture identifies the issuer's sources of repayment, any commitments made by the issuer to bondholders, as well as any provisions that support or enhance the issuer's ability to repay its debt in full.

Sources of Repayment

The sources of bond repayment vary among issuers and are a key factor in determining a bond's relative risk. For example, national governments have the sovereign right to tax economic activity (and, in some cases, print currency), which results in their bonds often holding the highest credit quality in a given region. Sovereign bonds in developed markets are often considered to have no default risk and are used as the benchmark for relative bond market risk.

Local or regional governments may either use their taxing authority as the source of bond repayment or consider fees from infrastructure projects, such as bridges, toll roads or public transit systems, to repay interest and principal on an associated bond issue.

Investors in corporate bonds usually rely on the operating cash flows of the firm as their primary source for interest and principal payments. As shown in later lessons, investors use such factors as profitability and leverage to gauge the expected variability of corporate cash flows available to service debt. Corporate bonds for issuers of higher credit quality are usually **unsecured**, which means these cash flows are the *sole* source of repayment, as in the earlier BRWA Corporation example. Corporate issuers with less stable operating cash flows usually face more credit provisions and restrictions and may offer investors a legal claim (or **lien** or **pledge**) on specific assets as a secondary source of debt repayment in what are referred to as **secured** bonds. In liquidation, the secured debtholders may receive the value of the designated assets while unsecured debtholders would only receive any funds remaining after this allocation. A junior unsecured bondholder would be the last creditor in line to receive the asset value of an issuer in default, because all secured debts and senior unsecured debts would have higher-priority claims.

Investors evaluate operating cash flows as well as these secondary claims (referred to as **collateral**) when assessing an issuer's credit quality, which may include physical assets; cash flows, such as licensing fees; or financial guarantees from a third party. Issuers must weigh the benefit of providing these credit enhancements (lower borrowing costs) with the costs in terms of reduced operating flexibility.

Exhibit 6: Sovereign Bond and Corporate Bond Sources of Repayment

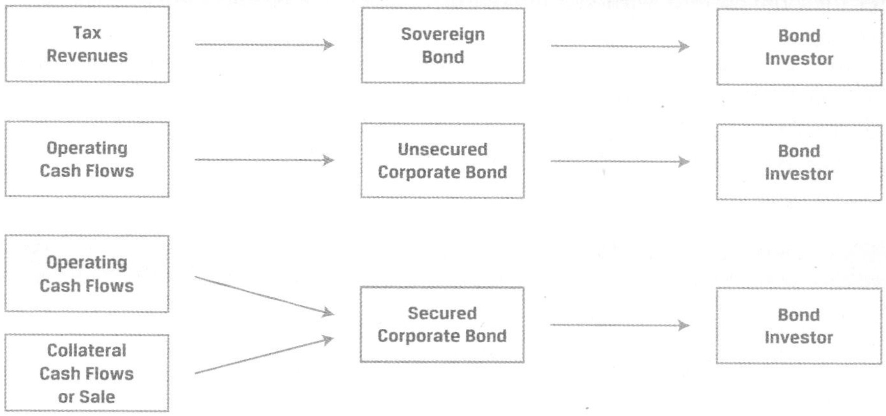

As the name suggests, the source of repayment for asset-backed securities (ABS) are the cash flows from a group of loans or receivables owned by the special purpose issuer. A later module will show in detail how an ABS transaction recreates an entire capital structure of asset-based cash flow claims across investor classes with different priority claims to these cash flows. These different classes shown in Exhibit 7 are referred to as **tranches**.

Exhibit 7: Asset-Backed Security Sources of Repayment

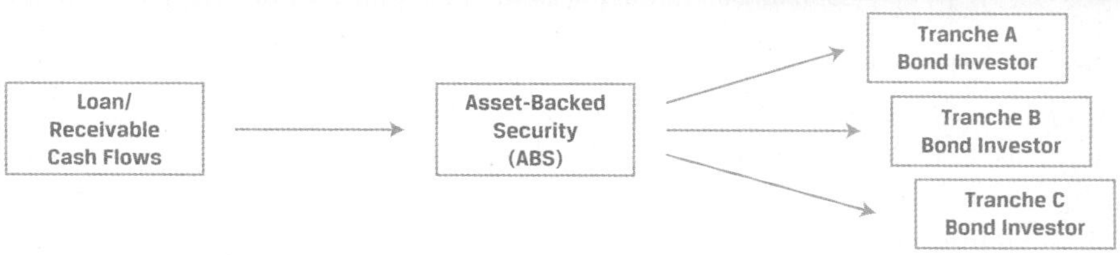

For example, Tranche A notes might have a priority claim to periodic cash flows followed by Tranche B. Tranche C investors would receive cash flows only after Tranche A and B investors.

Bond Covenants

Bondholders have limited influence over an issuer as compared to equity investors, who have voting rights. One exception to this is legally enforceable rules or bond **covenants** that borrowers and lenders agree on at the time a bond is issued or a loan is made. Affirmative covenants specify what issuers are required to do, whereas negative covenants specify what issuers are prohibited from doing.

Affirmative covenants are typically administrative in nature. For example, common affirmative covenants include the use of proceeds from the bond issue, the provision of timely financial reports, and permitting bondholders to redeem their bonds at a premium to par if the issuer is acquired.

Other affirmative covenant examples include a **pari passu clause** (or "equal footing" clause), which ensures that a debt obligation is treated the same as the borrower's other debt obligations with similar seniority. A **cross-default clause** specifies that borrowers are considered in default if they default on another debt obligation. These covenants typically neither impose additional costs on an issuer nor materially constrain the issuer's discretion in operating its business.

Exhibit 8 provides the covenants faced by BRWA Corporation for its senior unsecured bonds from the prior example.

Exhibit 8: BRWA Bond: Brief Summary of Indenture Terms

3.2% BRWA Corporation Five-Year Notes Prospectus Summary (Continued)	
Issuer:	Bright Wheels Automotive Corporation
Use of Proceeds:	We will use the net proceeds from the Notes for general corporate purposes
Seniority:	The Notes are unsecured and unsubordinated obligations of BRWA Corporation and will rank pari passu with all other unsecured and unsubordinated indebtedness.
Limitation on Liens:	The Indenture restricts our ability to pledge some of our assets as security for other debt.
Limitation on Sales and Leasebacks:	The Indenture prohibits us from selling and leasing back any plant for a term of more than [X] years
Merger and Consolidation:	The Indenture prohibits us from merging or consolidating with any company or selling all or substantially all of our assets to any company if after doing so the surviving company would violate the limitation on liens or sales and leasebacks discussed above.

As a senior unsecured issuer, BRWA's use of proceeds is broadly defined, and it faces few negative covenants limiting its business decisions. The limitations of liens and sale and leaseback, as well as merger and consolidation restrictions, all protect bondholders from the dilution of their claims as senior bondholders.

Issuers of lower credit quality often face additional covenants established to protect bondholders if an issuer's financial condition deteriorates. For example, consider the case of Vivivyu Inc., a digital media corporation that has issued senior secured callable bonds, as shown in Exhibit 9.

Exhibit 9: Vivivyu Inc. Summary of Bond and Indenture Terms

6.5% Vivivyu Inc. (VIVU) Seven-Year Callable Notes (The "Notes")
Prospectus Summary

Issuer:	Vivivyu Incorporated
Settlement Date:	[T + 3 Business Days]
Maturity Date:	[Seven Years from Settlement Date]
Principal Amount:	USD400 million
Interest:	6.5% fixed coupon
Interest Payment:	Starting six months from [Settlement Date] to be paid semiannually with final payment on [Maturity Date]
Seniority:	The Notes are secured and unsubordinated obligations of VIVU and rank pari passu with all other secured and unsubordinated debt
Call Provision:	The Issuer may redeem some or all of the Notes on any Business Day before [Maturity] starting three years after [Settlement] based on the Call Price Schedule as a percentage of the Principal Amount plus accrued interest
Call Price Schedule:	103.25% [Three to Four Years after Settlement] 102.50% [Four to Five Years after Settlement] 101.75% [Five to Six Years after Settlement] 101.00% [Six to Seven Years after Settlement]

In the case of Vivivyu, bondholders are protected by a set of covenants which closely monitor certain financial ratios and restrict its ability to pay dividends to shareholders, repurchase shares, and / or take on additional debt unless tighter financial restrictions are met under what is referred to as an **incurrence test** (see Exhibit 10).

Exhibit 10: VIVU Bond: Brief Summary of Indenture Terms

6.5% Vivivyu Inc. (VIVU) Seven-Year Callable Notes (The "Notes")
Prospectus Summary (continued)

Issuer:	Vivivyu Incorporated
Transaction Security:	The Notes are secured by a pledge of certain assets as identified in the Indenture.
Restriction on Additional Debt:	Unless the Incurrence Test is met, the Issuer shall not issue additional debt unless it is (a) subordinated or (b) a working capital facility up to 20% of the Principal Amount of Notes outstanding.
Restrictions on Dividends and Distributions:	The Issuer shall not (i) pay any dividend in respect of its shares, (ii) repurchase any of its own shares, or (iii) reduce share capital with repayment to shareholders unless the Incurrence Test is met.
Debt Restriction Test:	Issuer must maintain (a) Net Interest Bearing Debt to EBITDA not greater than 5.00× and (b) Interest Coverage Ratio greater than 2.50× for each financial reporting period.
Incurrence Test:	Test is met if issuer has (a) Net Interest Bearing Debt to EBITDA not greater than 4.50× and (b) Interest Coverage Ratio greater than 3.0× for each financial reporting period.

Other negative covenants include limitations on investments, the disposal of assets, or issuance of debt senior to existing obligations under what is known as a **negative pledge clause**. Negative covenants seek to ensure that an issuer maintains the ability to make interest and principal payments. Highly restrictive covenants may not be in the bondholders' best interest if they force an issuer to default when it may be avoided. For example, strict debt restrictions may prevent an issuer from raising new funds necessary to meet contractual obligations. Covenant violations can provide bondholders recourse in several possible ways, including a change in financial terms, such as an increase in a bond's interest rate, accelerated debt payments, or termination of the debt agreement.

QUESTION SET

1. Explain the difference in the sources of repayment for a secured and an unsecured corporate bond.

   Solution:

   The sole source of repayment for unsecured corporate bonds is typically operating cash flows of the issuer, while secured corporate bonds also include specific assets as a secondary source of debt repayment in addition to the issuer's operating cash flows.

2. Describe the source of repayment for asset-backed securities.

   Solution:

   The source of repayment for asset-backed securities are cash flows from the group of loans or receivables owned by the special purpose issuer.

3. Match the bond covenant type in the left column with the examples in the right column.

A. Affirmative Covenant	I. Additional Debt Restriction
B. Negative Covenant	II. Cross-Default Clause
	III. Interest Coverage Minimum

   Solution:

   A. II is correct. A cross-default clause specifies that borrowers are considered in default if they default on another debt obligation and is an affirmative covenant.

   B. I and III are correct. An additional debt restriction clause limits an increase in issuer debt and is a negative covenant. An interest coverage minimum limits the amount of leverage relative to an issuer's operating income or EBITDA.

4. Describe the difference between affirmative and negative bond covenants.

   Solution:

   Affirmative covenants specify what issuers are required to do, whereas negative covenants specify what issuers are prohibited from doing.

5. Fill in the blanks. Covenant violations provide bondholders recourse in several possible ways, including a change in _________ terms, such as an

increase in a bond's interest rate or security, ___________ debt payments, or ___________ of the debt agreement.

Solution:

Covenant violations provide bondholders recourse in several possible ways, including a change in *financial* terms, such as an increase in a bond's interest rate or security, *accelerated* debt payments, or *termination* of the debt agreement.

PRACTICE PROBLEMS

The following information relates to questions 1-5

Antelas AG is a German emerging technology company focused on manufacturing process design. The firm has developed several valuable patents related to micromachining and metal 3D printing technology and derives its revenue through licensing royalties and consultation services. Antelas recently issued the following debt instrument:

Antelas AG Four-Year Floating-Rate Notes (The "Notes")
Prospectus Summary

Issuer:	Antelas AG
Settlement Date:	[T + 5 Business Days]
Maturity Date:	[Four Years from Settlement Date]
Principal Amount:	EUR250 million
Interest:	MRR plus 250 bps p.a.
Interest Payment:	Commencing three months from [Settlement Date] to be paid quarterly with final payment on [Maturity Date]
Seniority:	The Notes are secured and unsubordinated obligations of Antelas AG and will rank pari passu with all other secured and unsubordinated indebtedness.
Business Days:	Frankfurt

1. "Four years" and "MRR plus 250 bps p.a." refer, respectively, to which bond features as of the settlement date?
   - **A.** Time to maturity and coupon rate
   - **B.** Coupon frequency and current yield
   - **C.** Time to maturity and contingency provision

2. Which of the following statements *best* describes the source(s) of repayment for the Antelas AG floating-rate notes?
   - **A.** Since the notes are secured (or backed) by Antelas AG's assets, the floating-rate notes would be considered asset-backed securities.
   - **B.** The Antelas AG notes rely on the operating cash flows of the firm as their *sole* source for interest and principal payments.
   - **C.** The Antelas AG notes rely on the operating cash flows of the firm as their *primary* source for interest and principal payments.

3. Antelas AG's issuer-specific credit spread rises by 25 bps p.a. one year after the FRN issuance. Which of the following *best* describes how Antelas AG's FRN cou-

pon would change as a result?

A. Antelas AG's FRN coupon payment to investors will *immediately* increase by 25 bps p.a.

B. Antelas AG's FRN coupon payment to investors will increase by 25 bps p.a. but will not become effective until the next full debt coupon period begins.

C. Antelas AG's FRN coupon will remain unchanged.

4. Calculate the value of Antelas's payment to bondholders on the maturity date if the MRR is 0.25% p.a. for the final interest period.

A. EUR1,718,750

B. EUR251,718,750

C. EUR256,875,000

5. Antelas decides to raise new secured, unsubordinated debt. Which of the following best describes the priority of payments between the issuer's new debt and its existing debt?

A. Because the Antelas AG notes have a pari passu (or "equal footing") clause, this debt obligation will be treated the same as any other secured, unsubordinated debt from this borrower.

B. Because the existing debt was issued earlier, it would receive priority over the new debt in terms of the payment of interest and principal.

C. We do not have enough information to answer this question; the necessary information would be provided in the indenture for new secured, unsubordinated notes.

SOLUTIONS

1. A is correct. The notes mature (the date Antelas AG will pay the final coupon and principal amount) four years after the trade settlement date, and the coupon rate is variable, determined by the MRR plus a fixed 250 bp spread.

2. C is correct. Secured corporate bonds rely on the operating cash flows of the firm as their primary source for interest and principal payments and a legal claim on assets as a secondary source of payment.

   A is incorrect because asset-backed securities (ABS) are issued by special-purpose entities created to take ownership in loans or receivables, the cash flows from which are used to pay interest and principal to investors.

   B is incorrect because it describes *unsecured*, not secured, corporate debt.

3. C is correct. For the Antelas AG FRN, the spread is fixed at 250 bps and the coupon will only change with changes in the MRR.

4. B is correct. On the maturity date, Antelas AG pays investors the final FRN coupon payment plus the bond's principal amount. The FRN coupon comprises MRR plus the issuer-specific spread.

   - **FRN coupon rate:** MRR plus spread, or 0.25% + 2.50%= 2.75%
   - **Annual interest expense:** Principal × FRN coupon, or €EUR250,000,000 × 2.75% = EUR6,875,000
   - **Quarterly interest expense:** Annual interest expense/4, or EUR6,875,000/4 = EUR1,718,750
   - **Principal Amount:** EUR250,000,000
   - **Total Payment** = EUR250,000,000 + EUR1,718,750 = 251,718,750

5. A is correct. Antelas AG's existing secured, unsubordinated debt has a pari passu (or "equal footing") clause, which ensures that this debt obligation will be treated the same as any other secured, unsubordinated debt from this borrower.

   B is incorrect because the priority of payments is unrelated to the timing of issuance.

   C is incorrect because the pari passu clause ensures equal footing for similar new debt.

LEARNING MODULE

2

Fixed-Income Cash Flows and Types

LEARNING OUTCOMES

Mastery	The candidate should be able to:
☐	describe common cash flow structures of fixed-income instruments and contrast cash flow contingency provisions that benefit issuers and investors
☐	describe how legal, regulatory, and tax considerations affect the issuance and trading of fixed-income securities

INTRODUCTION

1

A fixed-income instrument's cash flows are determined by its features. In this module, we discuss common fixed-income instrument cash flow structures and their implications for issuers and investors. The module's final lesson discusses the legal, regulatory, and tax considerations across jurisdictions faced by fixed-income issuers and investors.

LEARNING MODULE OVERVIEW

- In contrast to standard bullet bonds with full principal repayment at maturity, amortizing bonds have a payment schedule that involves early repayment of principal. Sinking funds and waterfall structures represent special cases of amortizing bonds.
- Other coupon payment structures include index-linked bonds that offer payments adjusted for changes in price indices and bonds with step-up coupons, with coupons that increase by specific amounts in the future based on a schedule or subject to specific provisions.
- Fixed-income contingency provisions include call, put, and conversion features. A call feature grants an issuer the right to buy bonds back early at a fixed price, while a put feature grants an investor the right to sell bonds to the issuer at a fixed price prior to maturity. Convertible bonds grant investors the right to convert the bond into shares of the issuer's stock at a pre-determined price.

- Bonds can be classified as domestic, foreign, or Eurobonds. Domestic bonds are those issued in a country by an issuer incorporated in that same country, while foreign bonds are issued by entities incorporated elsewhere.
- Eurobonds are issued internationally in a currency different from that country's domestic currency (e.g. US dollar bonds issued in London) and are subject to fewer listing, disclosure, and regulatory requirements than domestic or foreign bonds.
- Bond interest earned by an investor is usually taxed as ordinary income, although some bonds offer tax advantages. Some countries also apply a capital gains tax. Specific tax provisions often apply for bonds issued at a discount or purchased at a premium.

LEARNING MODULE SELF-ASSESSMENT

These initial questions are intended to help you gauge your current level of understanding of this learning module.

1. An investor that is more sensitive to an issuer's credit risk than to reinvesting risk would most likely invest in a:

   A. bullet bond.

   B. partially amortizing bond.

   C. fully amortizing bond.

   Solution:

   C is correct. Investors receive higher near-term cash flows on amortizing debt versus bullet bonds and face lower credit risk because the borrower's liability is reduced over time. However, investors also face the risk of reinvesting the higher near-term cash flows at prevailing market interest rates, which can fluctuate. This effect is larger for fully amortizing bonds versus partially amortizing bonds.

2. Match the term in the left column with its description in the right column.

A. Bullet bond	I. A bond with a fixed periodic payment schedule that reduces the bond's outstanding principal to a portion of the principal to be repaid on the maturity date
B. Partially amortizing bond	II. A bond with a coupon rate that increases by specified margins at one or more specified dates
C. Step-up coupon bond	III. A bond that pays its face value and final interest payment at maturity

   Solution:

   A. III is correct. A bullet bond pays 100% of its face value plus a final interest payment at the bond's maturity.

   B. I is correct. A bond characterized by a fixed periodic payment schedule that reduces the bond's outstanding principal to a portion of the principal to be repaid on the maturity date is known as a partially amortizing bond.

C. II is correct. A bond with a coupon rate that increases by specified margins at one or more specified dates is known as a step-up coupon bond.

3. A call provision embedded in a fixed-income security:

   A. is a benefit to the issuer.

   B. gives the bondholder the right but not an obligation to sell the bond.

   C. grants the bondholder some degree of inflation protection.

Solution:

A is correct. A call provision gives the issuer the right to redeem all or part of the bond at a pre-determined price on specified dates. It is a benefit to the issuer because if market interest rates fall, the issuer can replace the callable bond with one with a lower interest rate. It also gives the issuer added flexibility if it has excess cash or wishes to change its capital structure in the future.

B is incorrect. This describes a putable bond, not a callable bond. If a callable bond is called, the bondholder is obliged to sell it to the issuer according to the specified terms.

C is incorrect. A call provision does not grant the bondholder inflation protection. A call would be exercised by the issuer if interest rates fall.

4. A put provision embedded in a fixed-income security:

   A. is a benefit to the bondholders.

   B. leads to a lower value compared to a bullet bond.

   C. increases the likelihood that its issuer will be acquired.

Solution:

A is correct. A put provision gives bondholders the right to sell the bonds back to the issuer at a pre-determined price on specified dates. The put provision is a benefit to bondholders because it can protect them from the risk of the price of the bond falling from, for example, rising interest rates.

B is incorrect. As put provisions are beneficial to investors, putable bonds are priced at a premium, not a discount, relative to option-free counterparts.

C is incorrect. Put provisions can deter acquirers because the exercise of putable bonds results in an immediate claim on cash, making the acquisition more expensive. Issuing bonds with put provisions is a strategy employed by some firms to deter unfriendly takeovers known as a "poison puts."

5. Match the term in the left column with its description in the right column.

A. Eurobond	I. A bond issued outside the jurisdiction of any single country
B. Global bond	II. A bond issued simultaneously in the Eurobond market and in at least one domestic bond market

Solution:

A. I is correct. Eurobonds are issued outside the jurisdiction of any single country, are usually unsecured, and may be denominated in any currency, including the issuer's domestic currency.

B. II is correct. A global bond is a bond issued simultaneously in the Eurobond market and in at least one domestic bond market, ensuring sufficient demand for large bond issues and access to all fixed-income investors regardless of location.

6. Compared to a bond with an original issue discount (OID) tax provision, an otherwise identical bond without this provision would *most likely* have:

A. lower taxes due at maturity.

B. the same taxes due at maturity.

C. higher taxes due at maturity.

Solution:

C is correct. Under the OID tax provision, the investor will recognize a prorated portion of the OID as taxable income each year and pay no capital gains tax upon maturity. Investors without an OID tax provision will recognize no taxable income until maturity, upon which they will face capital gains tax on the OID (provided there is capital gains tax in their jurisdiction).

2 FIXED-INCOME CASH FLOW STRUCTURES

☐ describe common cash flow structures of fixed-income instruments and contrast cash flow contingency provisions that benefit issuers and investors

The most common bond cash flow structure is that of a standard fixed-coupon bond, often referred to as a **bullet bond**. The bond issuer receives the principal at settlement, makes periodic, fixed coupon payments, and repays the principal at maturity. Most government and corporate issuers use bullet bonds as their primary means of debt financing, and investors often prefer the associated fixed income stream and set maturity to fund known cash flows. Exhibit 1 shows the bullet bond structure of the five-year, USD300 million, 3.2% semiannual coupon BRWA bond introduced in the prior module.

Exhibit 1: BRWA Corporation Bullet Bond Cash Flows

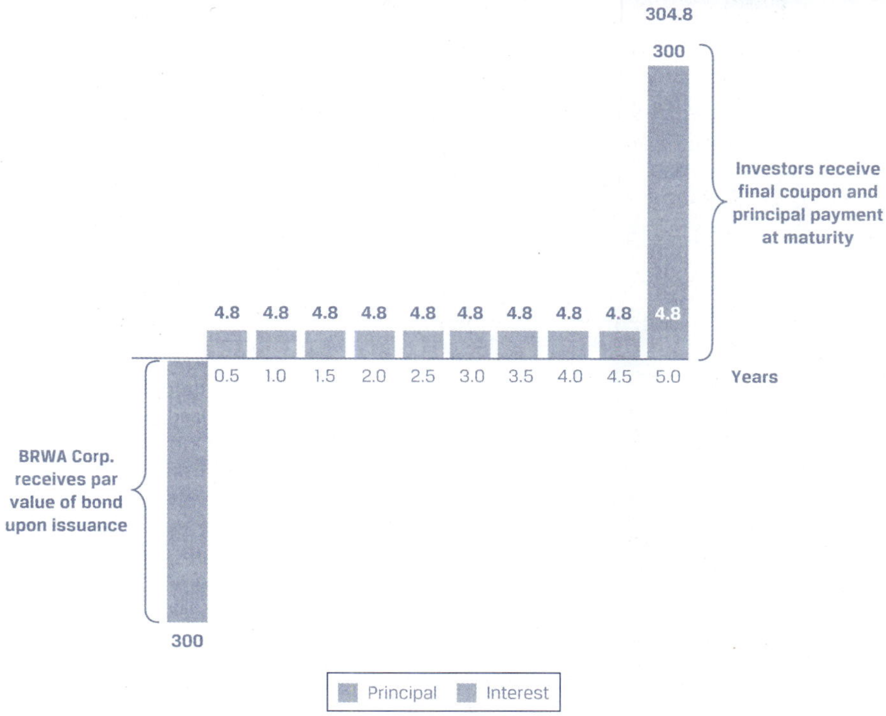

Some instruments, including most loans, have cash flow structures that differ from that of the bullet bond. For example, some instruments have principal repayments distributed over the life of the instrument. In the case of interest payments, most loans pay periodic interest at a rate that changes as short-term market rates change, while others change based on credit or other provisions. Finally, zero-coupon bonds are sold at a discount with no cash flow during their life until repayment of par at maturity. These bonds pay no periodic interest, but the difference between the discount price and par at maturity represents a cumulative interest payment at maturity.

Amortizing Debt

Fixed-income instruments that periodically retire a portion of principal outstanding prior to maturity offer a borrower the ability to spread payments more evenly over the life of the instrument. Examples include commercial or residential real estate mortgage loans. Investors receive higher near-term cash flows on this **amortizing debt** relative to bullet bonds and face lower credit risk because the borrower's liability is reduced over time. However, investors also face the risk of reinvesting the higher cash flows at prevailing market interest rates over the life of the instrument, which could decline.

Let us consider the opposite of the BRWA five-year bullet bond, a **fully amortizing loan** for the same term and at the same interest rate. As shown in Exhibit 2, principal amortization begins on the first interest payment date and continues through maturity.

Exhibit 2: BRWA Corporation Fully Amortizing Loan Cash Flows

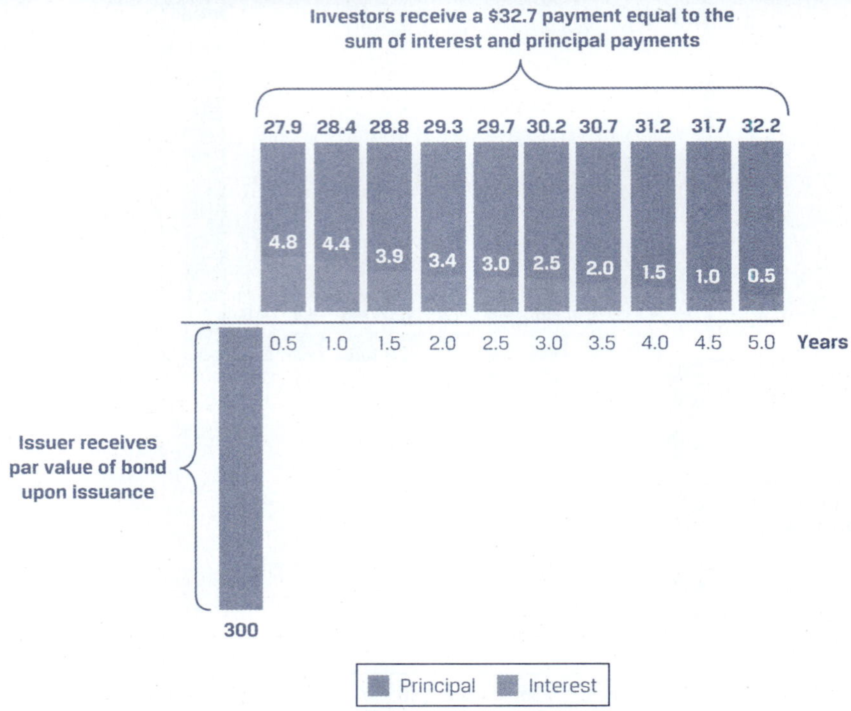

Note that while the first interest payment, USD4.8, is identical to that of the bullet bond, instead of interest-only coupons each period followed by the final coupon and principal at maturity, investors receive a uniform USD32.7 periodic cash flow until maturity, which in the first period includes USD27.9 of principal amortization. Over time, the interest portion of the payment declines while the principal repayment portion increases.

Let us assume instead that BRWA issues a bond with the same maturity and at the same rate but repays a *portion* of the principal each period, with a final lump sum payment (or **balloon payment**) at maturity equal to half of the principal amount. The interest and principal payments for this **partially amortizing bond** are shown in Exhibit 3.

Exhibit 3: BRWA Corporation Partially Amortizing Bond Cash Flows

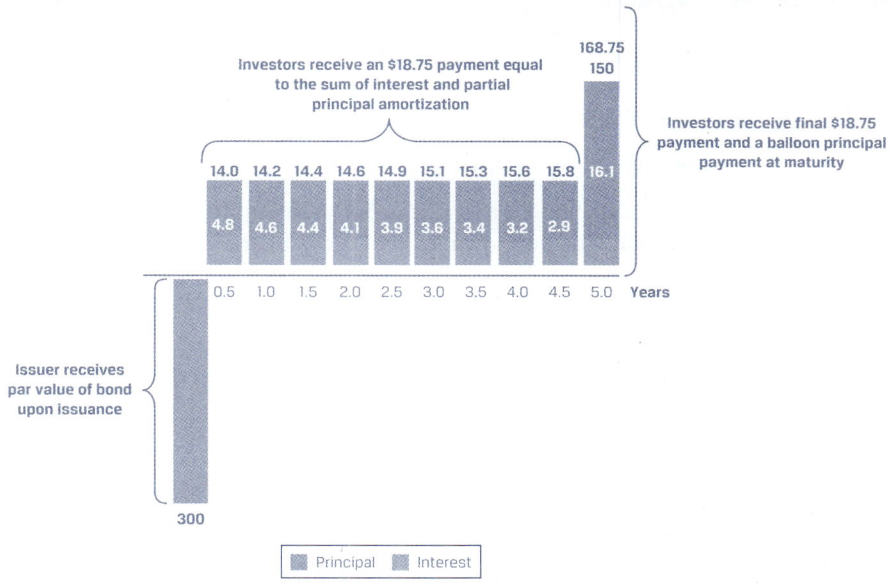

The cash flows for the partially amortizing bond combine elements of the bullet and fully amortizing examples. Cash flow schedules from the perspective of the investor for the bullet bond, partially amortizing bond, and fully amortizing loan with the same principal, maturity, and fixed coupon rate are shown in Exhibit 4.

Exhibit 4: Investor Perspective: BRWA Bond/Loan Cash Flow Summary (USD millions)

Year	Bullet Bond	Partially Amortizing Bond	Fully Amortizing Loan
0	−300	−300	−300
0.5	4.8	18.75	32.7
1	4.8	18.75	32.7
1.5	4.8	18.75	32.7
2	4.8	18.75	32.7
2.5	4.8	18.75	32.7
3	4.8	18.75	32.7
3.5	4.8	18.75	32.7
4	4.8	18.75	32.7
4.5	4.8	18.75	32.7
5	304.8	168.75	32.7

The fully amortizing loan has a level semiannual payment equal to the sum of interest and principal repayment. We may calculate the periodic payment (A) as follows:

$$A = \frac{r \times \text{Principal}}{1 - (1 + r)^{-N}}, \tag{1}$$

where

A = Periodic payment amount

r = Market interest rate per period

$Principal$ = Principal amount of loan or bond

N = Number of payment periods

The fully amortized BRWA bond is a five-year, 3.2% semiannual coupon bond with a par value of USD300 million. The periodic payment is calculated as follows, in millions:

$$A = \frac{r \times \text{Principal}}{1 - (1 + r)^{-N}}.$$

r = 3.2%/2 = 1.6% on a semiannual basis.

Principal = USD300 million.

$N = 5 \times 2 = 10$ semiannual periods.

$$A = \frac{0.016 \times \text{USD300}}{1 - (1.016)^{-10}}.$$

A = USD32.70.

Therefore, the semiannual payment is a constant USD32.70, as shown in Exhibit 2, but the principal and interest amounts vary each period as follows:

- First semiannual interest payment: USD300 × 3.2%/2 = USD4.80.
- Initial principal repayment: USD32.7 – USD4.8 = USD27.90.
- Outstanding principal after first period: USD300 – USD27.90 = USD272.10.

The USD272.10 outstanding principal becomes the basis for the calculation of the interest and principal payment in the second period:

- Second semiannual interest payment: USD272.10 × 3.2%/2 = USD4.35.
- Second principal repayment: USD32.70 – USD4.35 = 28.35.
- Outstanding principal after second period: USD272.10 – USD28.35 = USD243.75.

Note that the periodic payment is constant, but over time, the interest payment decreases while the principal repayment increases.

The partially amortized bond in Exhibit 3 with the USD150 balloon principal payment paid at maturity combines two elements:

1. a five-year fully amortizing loan with USD150 notional and
2. a USD150 balloon payment at maturity.

The sum of the present values of these two elements is equal to the bond price of USD300. The present value (*PV*) of the USD150 balloon payment is calculated as

$$\text{PV of balloon payment} = \frac{\text{USD150}}{(1.016)^{10}} = \text{USD127.98}.$$

Subtracting the present value of the balloon payment from the USD300 price of the bond gives us USD172 in principal repayment to amortize over 10 semiannual periods to leave a remaining principal of USD150 at maturity. Using this USD172 principal amount, we can compute the periodic payment amount as

$$A = \frac{0.016(\text{USD172})}{1 - (1.016)^{-10}} = \text{USD18.75}.$$

The periodic payment is USD18.75, as shown in Exhibit 3. The final semiannual payment of USD168.75 is the sum of the final constant USD18.75 payment and the outstanding principal amount of USD150. Since the principal amount is not fully amortized, interest payments are higher for the partially amortized bond in each period than for the fully amortized bond, except the first period when they are equal.

Commercial and residential mortgages are common examples of fully amortizing loans. Mortgage borrowers usually prefer the constant cash flows of fully amortizing loans, because they are better able to match rental or lease income in the case of commercial borrowers or personal income for households. In the United States, these mortgage loans often back bonds known as **mortgage-backed securities** with cash flows similar to those of the loan shown in Example 1.

EXAMPLE 1

30-Year Fixed-Rate Residential Mortgage Loan

A borrower agrees to purchase a home and enters into a mortgage loan with a financial intermediary based on the following terms:

Home price: USD500,000

Loan amount: USD400,000

Annual interest rate: 3.50%

Loan term: 360 months

Noting that the borrower's monthly interest rate is 0.29167% (= 3.50%/12), we can use Equation 1 to calculate the homeowner's monthly mortgage payment on the USD400,000 loan as follows:

$$A = \frac{0.0029167(\text{USD}400,000)}{1-(1.0029167)^{-360}} = \text{USD}1,796.18.$$

As in the case of BRWA, we can calculate the interest and principal components of each periodic payment, with the first five and final five monthly payments of the 30-year mortgage shown below.

Month	Total Monthly Payment	Monthly Interest Payment	Monthly Principal Payment	Remaining Principal
1	USD1,796.18	USD1,166.67	USD629.51	USD399,370.49
2	USD1,796.18	USD1,164.83	USD631.35	USD398,739.14
3	USD1,796.18	USD1,162.99	USD633.19	USD398,105.95
4	USD1,796.18	USD1,161.14	USD635.04	USD397,470.91
5	USD1,796.18	USD1,159.29	USD636.89	USD396,834.03
356	USD1,796.18	USD25.97	USD1,770.21	USD7,132.63
357	USD1,796.18	USD20.80	USD1,775.38	USD5,357.26
358	USD1,796.18	USD15.63	USD1,780.55	USD3,576.70
359	USD1,796.18	USD10.43	USD1,785.75	USD1,790.96
360	USD1,796.18	USD5.22	USD1,790.96	USD0.00

Two additional bond amortization arrangements commonly encountered are **sinking funds**, used primarily by government and some corporate issuers, and **waterfall structures**, which are commonly used in asset-backed securities (ABS) and mortgage-backed securities (MBS).

A sinking fund arrangement is used by issuers to periodically retire a bond's principal outstanding. The term *sinking fund* refers to an issuer's plans to set aside funds over time in an escrow account to retire the bond early based on terms agreed upon issuance. For example, an issuer may direct the bond trustee to redeem a predetermined principal amount selected from among investors at random. Alternatively, the issuer may have the right to repurchase bonds prior to maturity at a predetermined fixed price under a contingency feature addressed later in this lesson. Like amortization, sinking funds reduce credit risk while increasing reinvestment risk due to a reduction of principal outstanding prior to maturity.

Another structure for principal repayment is a waterfall. This approach is used to determine the timing of cash flows to investor classes with different priority claims to the same cash flows. In the most common form, interest or coupon payments are paid to all classes with no preference, but the repayment of principal occurs sequentially so that the most senior investor class with the highest ranking in the capital structure receives principal payments first, followed by the second-highest ranked investors once the most senior class has been fully repaid. Exhibit 5 shows a typical waterfall structure based on the three-tranche example from the prior module.

Exhibit 5: Typical ABS Waterfall Structure

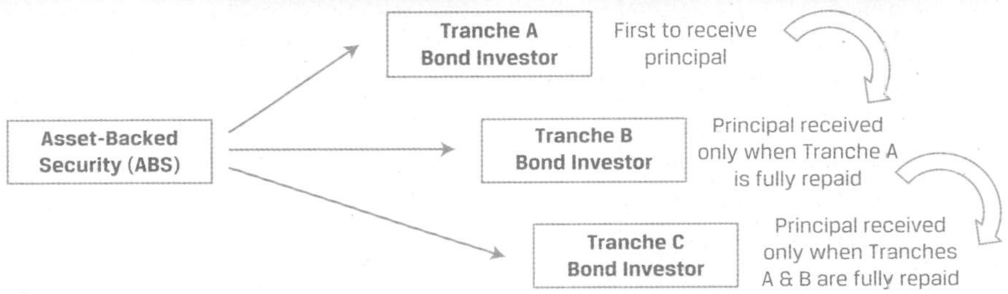

Payment shortfalls are borne by the more junior tranches since the senior tranches are paid first, so Tranche A faces the lowest credit risk, followed by Tranches B and C.

Variable Interest Debt

Some bonds and most loans have variable interest payments, calculated using a market reference rate (MRR) and a credit spread. Financial intermediaries, such as banks, prefer floating-rate loan assets since they match their variable-rate liabilities, such as deposits. Loans or floating-rate notes (FRN) are also attractive to investors seeking to benefit from rising interest rates.

Recall that a variable-rate loan or FRN coupon consists of a periodically resetting MRR plus an issuer-specific credit spread.

FRN coupon = MRR + Credit spread.

For example, practice problems in the prior module highlighted the four-year, EUR250 million Antelas AG FRN issued at an interest rate of MRR + 250 bps p.a. paid quarterly. Exhibit 6 shows the final four Antelas AG FRN cash flows, including principal repayment at maturity similar to a fixed-rate bullet bond.

Exhibit 6: Antelas AG FRN Cash Flows

Note Principal Amount (EUR)	250,000,000
Credit Spread over MRR	2.50%

Quarter	MRR	Coupon Rate	Quarterly Interest Payment	Principal Payment
13	−0.50%	2.00%	1,250,000	
14	0.15%	2.65%	1,656,250	
15	0.25%	2.75%	1,718,750	
16	0.50%	3.00%	1,875,000	250,000,000

For example, in Quarter 15, the coupon rate is 2.75% (= 0.25% + 2.50%) and the quarterly interest payment is calculated as follows:

(2.75% × EUR250,000,000)/4 = EUR1,718,750.

Investors face less interest rate risk with variable-rate instruments because coupon payments adjust with interest rates, unlike fixed-coupon bonds. However, like fixed-coupon bonds, variable-rate instruments still have credit risk: If an issuer's likelihood of missing payments increases, investors will seek a higher yield as compensation for lower credit quality, causing their price to fall, irrespective of any changes in the MRR.

In addition to changing cash flows based on variations in MRR, other adjustment mechanisms exist, which can be either predetermined or tied to an event. In the case of predetermined adjustments, a bond coupon increases by specified margins at specified dates. These bonds are referred to as **step-up bonds** and are used to protect investors against rising rates and, in some cases, to provide an incentive for issuers to take advantage of a contingency provision, as addressed later. An example of cash flow changes based on an event are higher coupons in the event of a deterioration in an issuer's credit quality. This provides investors with greater comfort that they will be compensated for adverse credit changes and allows less creditworthy issuers to obtain debt financing for longer and/or at lower spreads than may be possible at a fixed coupon. This is most common with **leveraged loans**, or loans to issuers of lower credit quality. Coupon changes may also be linked to financial covenants or credit ratings, which are sometimes used in what are referred to as **credit-linked notes**.

For example, say that Antelas AG experiences a decline in its credit quality as the FRN matures. It must therefore adequately address investor credit concerns by revising the terms of its debt. Exhibit 7 shows how Antelas might achieve this by entering a loan agreement arranged by a bank with a credit spread that adjusts based on leverage and interest coverage ratios.

Exhibit 7: Antelas AG Leveraged Loan Term Sheet

	Antelas AG Five-Year Leveraged Loan Term Sheet
Issuer:	Antelas AG
Settlement Date:	[T + 3 Business Days]
Maturity Date:	[Five Years from Settlement Date]
Principal Amount:	EUR250 million
Interest:	MRR Plus Credit Spread

Antelas AG Five-Year Leveraged Loan Term Sheet

Interest Payment:	Commencing three months from [Settlement Date] to be paid quarterly with final payment on [Maturity Date]
Credit Spread:	Based on Issuer's Total Leverage Ratio (TLR) at the end of each quarter as follows: 325 bps p.a. if TLR ≥ 3.5× 300 bps p.a. if 3.5× > TLR ≥ 3.0× 275 bps p.a. if 3.0× > TLR ≥ 2.5× 250 bps p.a. if TLR ≤ 2.5×
Seniority:	The Loan is a secured, unsubordinated obligation of Antelas AG.
Debt Restriction Test:	Issuer must maintain (a) Total Leverage Ratio (Net Interest Bearing Debt to EBITDA) not greater than 5.00× and (b) Interest Coverage Ratio greater than 2.50× for each financial reporting period.

Antelas maintains its current credit spread only if its total leverage ratio remains below 2.5×, with a higher spread if leverage increases. An issuer concerned about potential cash flow problems in the future might seek to add a **payment-in-kind** (PIK) feature to a loan or bond. PIK features allow an issuer to pay periodic interest in the form of an increase in the bond or loan principal outstanding rather than as a cash payment. This feature is most frequently used by firms with relatively high reliance on debt financing and are usually associated with a higher interest rate to compensate investors assuming greater principal risk.

As the following box example shows, the use of variable bond coupon provisions is not limited to issuers with credit quality or cash flow issues.

PUBLIC POWER CORPORATION (PPC) SUSTAINABILITY-LINKED BOND

Fixed-income markets have rapidly adapted to the growing importance of environmental, social, and governance (ESG) factors among issuers and investors. For example, **green bonds** are fixed-income instruments usually issued by governments or private companies that are created to fund projects with a positive environmental impact.

Public Power Corporation (PPC) is a publicly traded company that is 51% owned by the Greek government and is Greece's largest electricity utility. PPC announced plans to close most of its coal power capacity to sharply reduce carbon emissions, increase renewable energy production, and modernize and partially privatize its power grid. In order to attract a broader investor base to provide debt financing for its ambitious plans, PPC issued sustainability-linked bonds in early 2021 based on the following terms:

Public Power Corporation Five-Year Sustainability-Linked Bonds Key Terms

Issuer:	Public Power Corporation S.A.
Settlement Date:	March 18, 2021
Maturity Date:	March 30, 2026
Principal Amount:	EUR775 million
Interest:	3.875% p.a.
Step-Up Margin:	50 bps p.a. if a Step-Up Event occurs

Public Power Corporation Five-Year Sustainability-Linked Bonds Key Terms	
Step-Up Event:	Issuer fails to reduce CO_2 emissions by 40% by December 2022 versus 2019 base year
Interest Payment:	Commencing 9/30/21 to be paid semiannually with final payment on the Maturity Date
Seniority:	The Notes are senior unsecured obligations of the Issuer

PPC's sustainability-linked bonds were the first of its kind for a European high-yield issuer. The CO_2-related step-up margin feature in PPC's bonds was a significant factor in attracting widespread investor demand in a transaction that exceeded the original EUR500 million planned size.

Index-linked bonds have interest and/or principal payments linked to a specified index. Although a bond may be linked to any variable, in practice, **inflation-linked bonds** (sometimes referred to as linkers) tied to a broad consumer price index are by far the most common type of index-linked bonds. The fixed interest and principal payments of a standard bond are nominal cash flows whose purchasing power declines with inflation. The interest rate a bondholder receives net of inflation is the real interest rate, which is approximately equal to the nominal interest rate minus the rate of inflation. Investors often use inflation-linked bonds to protect against rising prices by receiving inflation-adjusted cash flows. Most inflation-linked bonds are issued by sovereign governments. Examples include **Treasury Inflation-Protected Securities (TIPS)** in the United States, which address investor demand for inflation-indexed cash flows. There is also growing demand for inflation-linked emerging market bonds due to investor concerns over high inflation. The following example demonstrates how TIPS cash flows are adjusted for inflation.

EXAMPLE 2

TIPS Cash Flow

An investor purchases TIPS with the following terms:

Principal amount:	USD115,000,000
Semiannual coupon:	1.00% p.a.
Time to maturity:	9.5 years
Inflation protection:	Based on the change in the Consumer Price Index for All Urban Consumers: All Items in U.S. City Average, Not Seasonally Adjusted (CPI)

If the CPI rises from 265.00 to 267.25 over the next semiannual interest period, the next coupon payment is calculated as follows:

- Inflation adjustment: (267.25 – 265) / 265 = 0.849%.
- Inflation-adjusted principal = Principal amount × (1 + Inflation adjustment)

  = USD115,976,350 = USD115,000,000 × 1.00849.
- Annual interest expense = Coupon rate × Inflation-adjusted principal, or

  = 1.00% × USD115,976,350 = USD1,159,764.
- Semiannual interest paid = USD1,159,764/2 = USD579,882.

TIPS, which have a periodic principal adjustment based on a price index, are an example of a **capital-indexed bond**. This approach protects the real value of debt principal. Capital-indexed bonds are also issued by other sovereign governments, including those of Australia, Canada, and the United Kingdom. Note that while deflation causes the principal to decline over time, investors usually receive the greater of the inflation-adjusted principal or par at maturity.

Unlike capital-indexed bonds, **interest-indexed bonds** pay a fixed nominal principal amount at maturity. Only the coupon is index linked and pays an inflation adjustment. These bonds are essentially an FRN in which the MRR is the rate of inflation. Interest-indexed bonds are more commonly issued by private financial intermediaries than by governments.

Zero-Coupon Structures

Zero-coupon bonds repay principal at maturity but have no coupon payments. Zero-coupon bonds are often referred to as discount bonds, since they are priced below par if interest rates are positive. An investor's sole source of return is the difference between the price paid and the principal, which represents a cumulative interest payment at maturity. Zero-coupon bonds are commonly issued by governments with tenors less than 12 months. As sovereign interest rates fell to (or below) zero in the wake of global financial crisis in 2008, zero-coupon bonds also became more common at longer maturities. Zero-coupon bonds are also created by financial intermediaries that sell individual interest or principal payments separated (or stripped) from sovereign bullet bonds.

Zero-coupon bonds are useful for funding fixed future obligations. If interest rates fall, a standard fixed-rate bond may fall short of meeting the obligation because falling interest rates reduce reinvestment income (in other words, the investor's rate of return will fall below the original YTM because the reinvestment assumption at the YTM does not hold). Since zero-coupon bonds require no coupon reinvestment, investors in these bonds do not face this risk.

Deferred Coupon Structures

Deferred coupon bonds pay no interest for the first few years and have a higher coupon paid later through maturity. Issuers of deferred coupon bonds usually seek to conserve cash immediately following the bond issue, which may indicate lower credit quality or that the issuer is financing a construction project that does not generate income until completion. Similar to zero-coupon bonds, which may be considered an extreme form of deferred coupon bond, deferred coupon bonds are typically priced at a discount to par since the higher coupon is not usually sufficient to offset the forgone interest in earlier periods.

Exhibit 8 summarizes the common types of cash flow structures for fixed-income instruments.

Exhibit 8: Fixed-Income Instrument Cash Flow Structures

Standard, Fixed-Rate Bond ("bullet bond")	- Fixed coupon rate - Coupons are interest only - Par value or principal paid at maturity - Example: most long-term corporate and government bonds
Amortizing Principal	- Often uniform periodic payments, composed of both interest and principal - Principal paid over life of the instrument - Example: mortgage loans
Variable Interest	- Cash flows change based on specified market interest rate, index, inflation rate, etc. - Example: floating rate notes, most bank loans
Zero Coupon	- Fixed 0% coupon rate - Par value or principal paid at maturity - Typically sold at a discount - Example: short-term government bonds

QUESTION SET

1. Compared to a bullet bond, an otherwise identical amortizing bond would *most likely* have:

   A. lower credit risk.

   B. lower reinvestment risk.

   C. lower near-term cash flows.

   Solution:

   A is correct. Compared to a bullet bond, an otherwise identical amortizing bond would have early principal repayments each period instead of all principal paid at maturity, lowering exposure to the issuers credit risk. However, larger periodic payments increase reinvestment risk.

2. Calculate the periodic payment and the interest and principal components of the first payment for a fully amortizing bond based on the following:

   - Loan amount: USD10,000,000
   - Annual interest rate: 2.75%
   - Loan term: 10 semiannual periods (5 years)

   Solution:

   Using Equation 1:

$$A = \frac{r \times \text{Principal}}{1 - (1 + r)^{-N}},$$

where

r = 1.375% (= 2.75%/2)

Principal = USD10,000,000

N = 10

Solve for the periodic payment (A) as follows:

$$\text{USD}1,077,174 = \frac{(0.01375) \times (10,000,000)}{1 - (1.01375)^{-10}}.$$

The initial USD1,077,174 periodic payment comprises the following:

- Initial interest payment: USD10,000,000 × 1.375% = USD137,500.
- Initial principal repayment: USD1,077,174 – USD137,500 = USD939,674.

3. Describe how a decrease in the consumer price index would affect the next coupon payment of a capital-indexed inflation-linked bond.

Solution:

The principal of capital-indexed inflation-linked bonds is adjusted using a price index, with coupon payments calculated using a fixed coupon rate and the adjusted principal. A decrease in the consumer price index (or deflation) will cause the principal of a capital-indexed inflation-linked bond to be adjusted downward in the next period and result in a lower coupon payment.

4. Match the term in the left column with its description in the right column.

A. Payment-in-kind	I. Coupon is based on a market reference rate plus a spread.
B. Floating-rate note	II. Interest coupon may be paid by increasing the principal.
C. Step-up coupon	III. Coupon increases by specified margins at specified dates.

Solution:

A. II is correct. A payment-in-kind feature allows an issuer to pay a bond or loan interest coupon by increasing principal.

B. I is correct. A floating-rate note coupon is based on a market reference rate plus a spread.

C. III is correct. A step-up coupon feature involves a coupon that increases by specified margins at specified dates.

FIXED-INCOME CONTINGENCY PROVISIONS

3

- [ ] describe common cash flow structures of fixed-income instruments and contrast cash flow contingency provisions that benefit issuers and investors

A contingency provision is a clause in a legal agreement that allows for an action if an event or circumstance occurs. The most common contingency provisions for bonds involve the right—but not the obligation—for an issuer or the bondholders to take an action specified in an indenture. These bond contingency provisions are often referred to as embedded options because they resemble option contracts but cannot be traded separately from the bond itself. The value of these embedded options may be established by comparing the value of a bond with a contingency provision with that of a bond from the same issuer without the provision. The most common bonds with contingency provisions include callable bonds, putable bonds, and convertible bonds.

Callable Bonds

An issuer of a **callable bond** has the right to redeem (or "call") all or part of the bond prior to the specified maturity date. An issuer considering callable versus non-callable bonds usually seeks the flexibility to refinance debt if market interest rates were to fall. **Fixed-price calls** grant an issuer the right to buy back the bond at a predetermined price in the future, as shown in Exhibit 9 for the Vivivyu Inc. bonds that were introduced in the prior module.

Exhibit 9: Vivivyu (VIVU) Callable Bond Terms

6.5% Vivivyu Inc. (VIVU) Seven-Year Callable Notes (the "Notes") Prospectus Summary	
Issuer:	Vivivyu Incorporated
Settlement Date:	[T + 3 Business Days]
Maturity Date:	[Seven Years from Settlement Date]
Principal Amount:	USD400 million
Interest:	6.5% fixed coupon
Interest Payment:	Starting six months from [Settlement Date] to be paid semiannually with final payment on [Maturity Date]
Seniority:	The Notes are secured and unsubordinated obligations of VIVU and rank pari passu with all other secured and unsubordinated debt.
Call Provision:	The Issuer may redeem some or all of the Notes on any Business Day before [Maturity] starting three years after [Settlement] based on the Call Price Schedule as a percentage of the Principal Amount plus accrued interest.
Call Price Schedule:	103.25% [Three to Four Years after Settlement] 102.50% [Four to Five Years after Settlement] 101.75% [Five to Six Years after Settlement] 101.00% [Six to Seven Years after Settlement]

Callable bonds typically specify a period over which the call feature cannot be used, known as a **call protection period**. During the **call period**, the period in which the call feature may be used, a schedule specifies the **call price**, or fixed price payable to bondholders if the issuer calls the bond.

For example, the VIVU bond may not be called for the first three years but during the following year may be called at a price of USD103.25 per USD100 in par value. VIVU has the right to call the bond during the final four years at a fixed price that declines over time. Investors face reinvestment risk starting in year three when the bond can be called, as well as limited bond price appreciation beyond the fixed call price.

The value of the call feature depends on the relationship between the YTM and the coupon of the bond. If the YTM rises above the coupon rate, there is little incentive for the issuer to use the call feature. The YTM provides an estimate of refinancing costs, which in this case exceeds the existing coupon. Therefore, the callable bond behaves much like a non-callable equivalent bond with respect to price movements due to interest rate changes. However, as a callable bond's YTM falls below its coupon rate, its price is effectively capped at the fixed call price, while the price of a non-callable bond will continue to rise. Investors expect to be compensated on callable bonds with a higher yield versus a similar non-callable bond given the uncertain maturity and limited price appreciation, known as **call risk**.

Some bonds have a call feature, different from the fixed-price call, under which the issuer compensates investors to buy bonds back known as a make-whole call. Make-whole calls are most common among highly rated bond issues and offer issuers greater flexibility to repurchase debt than purchases in the market. However, this provision usually requires an issuer to pay bondholders a high price based on the YTM of a sovereign bond of similar maturity. Because this is usually well above the bond's current market price, make-whole calls are rarely executed and have little economic impact on issuers or investors.

Putable Bonds

A put provision gives bondholders the right to sell the bond back to the issuer at a pre-determined price on specified dates. The put price is usually the par value of the bond. **Putable bonds** benefit bondholders by guaranteeing a pre-specified selling price at the redemption dates. If interest rates rise after issuance and bond prices fall, bondholders can sell or "put" the bond back to the issuer and reinvest the proceeds at higher market interest rates. The issuer will then be forced to refinance its debt earlier than planned at higher yields.

Since a put provision has value to bondholders, the price of a putable bond will be above the price of an otherwise similar non-putable bond. The yield on a bond with a put provision must therefore be lower than the yield on an otherwise similar non-putable bond. The lower yield compensates the issuer for the value of the put option to the investor.

If a putable bond's YTM is less than its coupon rate (so the price is higher than the put price), the put feature is less valuable, and the putable bond behaves like an option-free equivalent bond with respect to interest rate changes. However, if the putable bond's YTM increases above its coupon rate, the put price serves as a price floor for the bond.

Convertible Bonds

A **convertible bond** is a debt instrument with a contingency provision related to the issuer's outstanding common equity. It grants bondholders the right to exchange the issuer's bond for a number of its common shares in the future at an effective price per share known as the **conversion price**. The conversion feature rises in value to investors as the share price appreciates. Rather than a right to retire debt early in the case of callable and putable bonds, if exercised, the convertible feature replaces debt with equity.

Exhibit 10 shows a convertible bond for ZTG BioTech S.p.a., a publicly traded Italian company.

Exhibit 10: ZTG BioTech S.p.a. Convertible Bond Terms

1.25% ZTG Biotech (ZTGB) Five-Year Convertible Notes (the "Notes") Term Sheet	
Issuer:	ZTG Biotech S.p.a.
Settlement Date:	[T + 3 Business Days]
Maturity Date:	Five Years from Settlement Date unless the Notes are redeemed earlier in a Conversion
Principal Amount:	EUR300 million
Interest:	1.25% fixed coupon to be paid annually starting One Year from the Settlement Date with the final coupon paid at Maturity
Seniority:	The Notes are an unsecured obligation of ZTGB and rank pari passu with other unsecured debt
Conversion Provision:	An Investor has, at its sole option, the right to convert a portion or the full sum of the Principal Amount, or any part outstanding at any time at the Conversion Price during the Conversion Period
Current Share Price:	EUR28.00 per ZTGB common equity share
Conversion Price:	EUR42.00 per ZTGB common equity share
Conversion Period:	Any Business Day starting One Year from the Settlement Date through the Maturity Date

The 1.25% annual coupon on the ZTGB convertible bond is well below the YTM investors would expect for a standard ZTGB bond of the same maturity. Bondholders are often willing to accept a yield-to-maturity that is very low (or even zero) in exchange for conversion rights. ZTGB bond investors have the right to exchange debt for ZTGB common stock at a price of EUR42.00 per share, which represents a 50% premium over the current ZTGB price of EUR28.00 per share [= (42.00 − 28.00)/28.00]. The **conversion ratio** represents the number of common shares a bond may be converted into for a specific par value:

$$\text{Conversion ratio} = \text{Convertible bond par value/Conversion price.} \quad (2)$$

For example, if the ZTGB bond is traded in EUR1,000 face value units,

- the conversion ratio is equal to EUR1,000/EUR42, or 23.81, and
- an owner of one EUR1,000 unit of the ZTGB bond has the right to redeem the bond for 23.81 shares of ZTGB stock during the conversion period.

One way to estimate the value of the conversion feature at any time is to compare the convertible bond's price with its value if the bondholder were to convert the bonds today. This **conversion value** is calculated as follows:

$$\text{Conversion value} = \text{Conversion ratio} \times \text{Current share price.} \quad (3)$$

For example, assume that one year from ZTGB's issuance date, the issuer's shares are trading at EUR35.00. A ZTGB bondholder could therefore convert one EUR1,000 unit to a conversion value of EUR833.35 (= 23.81 × EUR35.00). If the convertible bond is trading at par (or a market price of EUR1,000 per unit), the investor will prefer to hold the bond and receive interest and principal rather than convert the bond to shares. In general, a convertible bond's price will vary with that of the issuer's shares. If the share price is well below the conversion price, the convertible bond's price will approach that of a standard non-convertible bond. If the issuer's share price far exceeds the conversion price, the bond's price will more closely track its conversion value.

The use of convertible debt is common among growth companies, which may have limited cash flow to pay interest and repay principal but are willing to raise equity at a higher conversion price in the future. Convertible bonds also often include additional features, such as a call provision, allowing issuers to limit bond investor gains from share price appreciation by redeeming bonds early.

Some issuers may issue warrants with bonds. A **warrant** is an "attached," rather than embedded, option entitling the bondholder to buy the issuer's stock at a fixed exercise price until the expiration date. Warrants are used as a yield enhancement to bond investors and are traded separately in financial markets, such as the Deutsche Börse and the Hong Kong Stock Exchange.

Several European banks have issued a type of convertible bond called **contingent convertible bonds** (CoCos), with contingent write-down provisions. While standard convertibles will be converted when the share price increases, CoCos are converted on the downside. This conversion is also not at the discretion of the investor but happens automatically if a specified event occurs—for example, if the bank's core Tier 1 capital ratio (a measure of the bank's proportion of core equity capital available to absorb losses) falls below a minimum regulatory requirement. If the bank experiences losses that reduce its equity capital below the minimum regulatory capital requirement, CoCos convert debt into equity to increase its capital and reduce the bank's likelihood of default. CoCos were introduced in order to limit systemic risk, or the risk of financial system failure. For this reason, CoCos offer investors a higher yield than otherwise similar bonds. Note that the conversion is triggered by a specific event, the breach of certain minimum regulatory capital requirements, and not by certain equity or debt price levels.

QUESTION SET

1. All else equal, the bond with the greatest benefit to the issuer is a bond with:

   A. no contingency provisions.

   B. a fixed-price call provision.

   C. a make-whole call provision.

   Solution:

   B is correct. Fixed-price calls grant the issuer the right to buy back the bond at a predetermined price in the future, which is a benefit to the issuer if interest rates fall.

   A is incorrect. A bond with no contingency provisions is an option-free bond and is not as beneficial to the issuer as a bond with a fixed-price call provision.

   C is incorrect. A make-whole call is a contingency feature under which issuers can buy bonds back at a price usually based on the yield-to-maturity of a sovereign bond of similar maturity plus a predetermined spread. Make-whole calls are rarely executed and have little economic impact on issuers or investors.

2. Callable and putable bond prices with the same coupon rate will behave most like an option-free equivalent bond when their YTMs are, respectively:

   A. above the coupon rate and below the coupon rate.

   B. below the coupon rate and above the coupon rate.

   C. both near the coupon rate.

   Solution:

   A is correct. If a callable bond's YTM rises above its coupon rate, the call feature is less valuable and a callable bond behaves much like a non-callable bond with respect to price movements due to interest rate changes. If a putable bond's YTM is less than its coupon rate, the put feature is less valuable and the putable bond's price behaves like an option-free equivalent bond with respect to interest rate changes.

   B is incorrect. This is the reverse of the correct relationship.

   C is incorrect. If their YTMs are both near the coupon rate, both bonds will be near their price limits where the call and put features would be exercised. Their price changes would be lower in magnitude relative to a non-callable bond.

3. A convertible bond will closely track its conversion value if the issuer's share price is:

   A. below the conversion price.

   B. equal to the conversion price.

   C. above the conversion price.

   Solution:

   C is correct. In general, a convertible bond's price will vary with that of the issuer's shares. If the issuer's share price far exceeds the conversion price, the bond's price will more closely track its conversion value.

   A is incorrect. If the share price is well below the conversion price, the convertible bond's price will approach that of a non-convertible bond.

   B is incorrect. In this case, the convertible bond would have a mix of price properties between that of a non-convertible bond and a convertible bond.

4. Match each description in the right column with the correct bond in the left column.

A. Convertible bond	I. Conversion occurs automatically
B. Contingent convertible (CoCo) bond	II. Conversion occurs at the discretion of the investor
	III. More likely to convert if share price increases
	IV. More likely to convert if share price decreases

   Solution:

   A. II and III are correct. A standard convertible bond grants the right to redeem a bond for an issuer's equity, occurs at the discretion of the investor, and is more likely if the issuer's share price increases.

B. I and IV are correct. Contingent convertible (CoCo) bonds are convertible on the downside and occur automatically if a specified event occurs, such as a decline in bank capital below a regulatory minimum level.

5. An issuer that would like to conserve near-term cash outflows would most likely issue a:

   A. putable bond.

   B. callable bond.

   C. convertible bond.

Solution:

C is correct. All else equal, an issuer would have the lowest interest payments on a convertible bond. Bondholders are often willing to accept a yield-to-maturity that is very low (or even zero) in exchange for conversion rights. Putable bonds offer lower yields than callable bonds because the put option is a benefit to the bondholder while the call option is a benefit to the issuer. However, the yields on callable and putable bonds are high compared to yields on convertibles.

4 LEGAL, REGULATORY, AND TAX CONSIDERATIONS

☐ describe how legal, regulatory, and tax considerations affect the issuance and trading of fixed-income securities

Fixed-income securities are subject to different legal and regulatory requirements depending on where they are issued and traded, as well as who holds them. Based on the jurisdictions of the issuer and the issuance, a bond can be classified as a domestic, foreign, or Eurobond. This classification has legal, tax, and regulatory implications for issuers and investors.

Legal and Regulatory Considerations

Bonds issued by entities incorporated in the same country are called **domestic bonds**, whereas bonds issued by entities incorporated in another country are called **foreign bonds**. Domestic bond markets vary widely across emerging and developed markets, and private and public issuers borrow outside the domestic market for various reasons. Corporate issuers often match the currency of their bond financing cash flows with that of their foreign operations using foreign bonds. Emerging market sovereign governments typically issue bonds in major foreign currencies to attract a broader set of investors and to diversify their investor base beyond the domestic bond market. In order to establish itself as a center for Islamic finance and attract shari'a-compliant investors, the UK government issued a sukuk, as described below.

UK SOVEREIGN SUKUK ISSUANCE

Sukuk are fixed-income instruments developed in accordance with Islamic law or *shari'a*, which prohibits the payment of interest and financing of non-shari'a-compliant sectors, such as alcohol or gambling. Instead of periodic interest, sukuk pay investors a periodic rental cash flow (or profit rate) from underlying assets, against which the investment company issuing the securities has an ownership claim for the life of the security.

Sukuk issuers were historically concentrated in predominately Muslim countries, including supranational entities, such as the Islamic Development Bank; sovereign issuers, including the Republic of Turkey; and corporate issuers, such as Saudi Aramco. In 2014, the United Kingdom became the first sovereign sukuk issuer outside the Muslim world with a GBP200 million, five-year sukuk issuance listed on the London Stock Exchange. These British pound–denominated sukuk were issued at a profit rate equivalent to the yield-to-maturity on a UK government benchmark security with a similar maturity, and the sukuk were backed by assets directly owned by the UK central government.

In smaller emerging markets with less financial intermediation (frontier markets), domestic bond issuance in frontier markets usually comprises domestic sovereign bonds and bonds of local financial intermediaries, such as banks. Corporate debt financing usually takes the form of a bank loan in these markets, and investors are limited to indirect fixed-income exposure to corporate issuers via bank bond purchases. Frontier market sovereign governments access local bond markets and use international bond markets to fund external debt in foreign currencies. For example, Romania's domestic bond market, denominated in the Romanian leu (RON), is limited in scope, while the Romanian government often issues debt in international bond markets. More established domestic bond markets in emerging markets may include state-owned or state-controlled enterprises and producers operating in a dominant domestic industry, such as basic commodities. Since many emerging market bonds are denominated in a restricted domestic currency with varying degrees of liquidity, the sovereign government and a select few domestic issuers may issue bonds in a major foreign currency, such as US dollars or euros. Developed market bond markets in major currencies, in contrast, reflect a high degree of both financial intermediation and specialization, attracting issuers from other jurisdictions and investors seeking returns in liquid markets denominated in freely floating currencies. Multinational corporate issuers may access several domestic bond markets to meet their funding needs. Recall the earlier example of BRWA Corporation's five-year US dollar fixed-rate bonds. Since BRWA is a US-based corporation issuing bonds denominated in US dollars in the United States, these bonds are considered domestic. If BRWA or a foreign subsidiary were to issue euro-denominated bonds in Germany or yuan-denominated bonds in China, these bonds would be considered foreign.

The Eurobond market was created in the 1960s primarily to bypass the legal, regulatory, and tax constraints imposed on bond issuers and investors, particularly in the United States. Bonds issued and traded in this cross-border market are called **Eurobonds**, and they are usually named for the currency in which they are denominated, such as Eurodollar and Euroyen bonds, or euro-denominated Eurobonds for the euro.

Eurobonds are issued outside the jurisdiction of any single country, are usually unsecured, and may be denominated in any currency, including the issuer's domestic currency. They are usually underwritten by a group of financial intermediaries from different jurisdictions and mostly sold to investors in Europe, the Middle East, and Asia. Eurobonds denominated in US dollars cannot be sold to US investors at the time of issue because they are not registered with the US Securities and Exchange Commission (SEC), with an exception for large qualified institutional investors. In the past, Eurobonds typically were **bearer bonds**, meaning that the trustee did not keep records of who owned the bonds; only the clearing system knew who the bond owners were. Eurobonds, domestic bonds, and foreign bonds are now **registered bonds** for which ownership is recorded by either name or serial number.

A global bond is a bond issued simultaneously in the Eurobond market and in at least one domestic bond market, ensuring sufficient demand and access to all fixed-income investors regardless of location. For example, the World Bank is a regular issuer of global bonds. Many market participants refer to foreign bonds, Eurobonds, and global bonds as *international bonds*, as opposed to domestic bonds.

For example, Exhibit 11 shows the terms of Romania's first ever 30-year euro-denominated bond issued in 2019.

Exhibit 11: 2019 Romanian EUR1.95 Billion, 30-Year Issuance

4.625% Romania Ministry of Finance Bonds Brief Summary of Terms	
Issuer:	Romania (Ministry of Finance)
Settlement Date:	April 3, 2019
Maturity Date:	April 3, 2049
Principal Amount:	EUR1.95 billion
Interest:	4.625% fixed annual coupon
Issuance Price:	99.488
Issuance Spread:	411.4 bps versus 1.25% Federal Republic of Germany bond maturing 8/15/48
Issuance and Trading:	Eurobond US Private Placement under Rule 144A DTC/Euroclear/Clearstream
Seniority:	Senior Unsecured
Exchanges:	Luxembourg

Note that the Romanian sovereign bonds were available to both Eurobond investors and investors in the United States under a private placement provision (Rule 144A) that limits bond sales to certain qualified investors. The bond was priced at a 4.11% spread over a German sovereign benchmark.

Cross-border issuance of public debt is not limited to sovereign governments. Many federal agencies, as well as state and local governments, seek fixed-income investors in foreign currencies and/or jurisdictions. For example, PT Indonesia Infrastructure Finance (IIF) is a quasi-government entity established by the Republic of Indonesia along with the World Bank and other multilateral institutions to provide infrastructure financing and advisory in Indonesia. IIF issued US dollar–denominated Eurobonds as outlined in Exhibit 12.

Exhibit 12: IIF US Dollar–Denominated Bonds

1.50% PT Indonesia Infrastructure Finance (IIF) Brief Summary of Terms	
Issuer:	PT Indonesia Infrastructure Finance
Settlement Date:	[T + Five Business Days]
Maturity Date:	Five Years from Settlement Date
Principal Amount:	USD150 million
Interest:	1.50% fixed semiannual
Issuance Price:	98.808
Issuance Spread:	+129 bps versus current 5-year US Treasury Note

1.50% PT Indonesia Infrastructure Finance (IIF) Brief Summary of Terms	
Issuance and Trading:	Eurobond (Medium Term Note)
Use of Proceeds:	Notes are sustainable in accordance with IIF's sustainable finance framework (ICMA compliant)
Seniority:	Senior Unsecured
Exchanges:	Singapore

Domestic bonds, foreign bonds, Eurobonds, and global bonds are subject to different legal, regulatory, and tax requirements in different jurisdictions. They also have different interest payment frequencies and calculation methods affecting bond cash flows and prices. Note, however, that the currency in which a bond is denominated has a stronger effect on its price than where the bond is issued or traded. This is because market interest rates have a strong influence on a bond's price, and the market interest rates that affect a bond are those associated with the currency in which the bond is denominated. For example, while IIF was able to issue five-year US dollar debt with a 1.50% coupon, its domestic Indonesian rupiah–denominated bonds of a similar tenor had a 6.97% yield-to-maturity.

Tax Considerations

The tax treatment of fixed-income securities is an important consideration for both issuers and investors. For corporate issuers weighing the relative cost of debt and equity capital, the tax deductibility of interest expense is an important factor in financing decisions, as discussed in an earlier module on corporate issuers. For investors, bond interest income is usually taxed at the ordinary income tax rate, which is typically the same tax rate that an individual would pay on wage or salary income.

Tax treatment for investors who purchase specific types of government bonds may also vary by jurisdiction. For example, UK citizens pay income tax on accrued and paid interest income but are exempt from capital gains tax arising when a bond is sold above its original purchase price. In the United States, investors in US Treasuries pay federal income tax on interest income but are exempt from state and local tax, while investors in US state and local government bonds (known as municipal bonds) are often exempt from federal income tax and from the income tax of the state in which the bonds are issued, thereby encouraging investors to purchase state and local bonds where they reside. The tax status of bond income may also depend on where the bond is issued and traded. For example, some domestic bonds pay their interest net of income tax. Other bonds, including some Eurobonds, make gross interest payments (i.e., no withholding), which may give some investors greater flexibility as to how and where they pay taxes on this interest income.

In addition to earnings from interest, a bond investment will generate a capital gain or loss if sold prior to maturity at a price different from the purchase price. Capital gains or losses usually face different tax treatment from taxable income, which often varies for long-term and short-term capital gains. For example, capital gains recognized over a year after the original bond purchase may be taxed at a lower long-term capital gains tax rate, whereas capital gains recognized within a year of bond purchase may be taxed as a short-term capital gain that equals the ordinary income tax rate. Exceptions exist, and not all countries have a separate capital gains tax or a distinction by holding period.

For bonds such as zero-coupon bonds issued at a discount, the tax status of the original issue discount (OID) is an additional tax consideration that varies by country. The OID is the difference between the par value and the original issue price. For example, the United States includes a prorated portion of the discount in interest income every tax year, while Japan does not. The following example illustrates the difference in tax treatment using a zero-coupon bond.

EXAMPLE 3

Zero-Coupon Bond Tax Treatment

Assume both a US-based investor and an investor based in a tax jurisdiction without an original discount tax provision purchase an identical zero-coupon US Treasury security based on the following terms:

- Principal amount: USD25,000,000
- Time to maturity: 5 years
- Issuance price: USD92.83 (per USD100 par value)

The original issue discount may be calculated as follows:

Original issue discount = Bond par value − Issuance price.

USD1,792,500 = USD25,000,000 − (0.9283 × USD25,000,000).

The USD1,792,500 original issue discount represents the interest that will accrue to both investors over five years. Under the original issue discount tax provision in the United States, the US-based investor will recognize a prorated portion of the USD1,792,500 OID as taxable income each year and pay no capital gains tax upon maturity. The non-US investor without an OID tax provision will recognize no taxable income until maturity, upon which it will face capital gains tax on the OID (provided there is capital gains tax in their jurisdiction).

Similarly, some jurisdictions also have tax provisions for bonds purchased at a premium. They may allow investors to deduct a prorated portion of the amount paid in excess of the bond's par value from their taxable income every tax year until maturity. This deduction may be a choice rather than a requirement, with an investor able to decide whether to deduct a prorated portion of the premium each year or to deduct nothing and declare a capital loss when the bond is redeemed at maturity.

QUESTION SET

1. Identify the following statement as true or false: A bond's coupon payment is most likely to be taxed as ordinary income.

   Solution:

   True. Bond interest is usually taxed at the ordinary income tax rate, which is typically the same tax rate that an individual would pay on wage or salary income.

2. Match the bond type in the left column to its correct description in the right column.

A. Foreign bond	I. Bonds issued outside the jurisdiction of any single country
B. Eurobond	II. Bonds issued by entities that are incorporated in that country
C. Domestic bond	III. Bonds sold in a country and denominated in that country's currency by an entity from another country

Solution:

A. III is correct. Bonds sold in a country and denominated in that country's currency by an entity from another country are known as foreign bonds.

B. I is correct. Bonds issued outside the jurisdiction of any single country are known as Eurobonds.

C. II is correct. Bonds issued by entities that are incorporated in that country are known as domestic bonds.

3. Fill in the blanks. An unregulated bond issued in domestic currency outside the issuer's national borders is known as a _______________. A bond issued simultaneously in the Eurobond market and in at least one domestic bond market is known as a ____________ bond.

Solution:

An unregulated bond issued in domestic currency outside the issuer's national borders is known as a *Eurobond*. A bond issued simultaneously in the Eurobond market and in at least one domestic bond market is known as a *global* bond.

4. Match the tax provision in the left column with the correct tax treatment in the right column.

A. Original issue discount (OID) tax provision	I. Pay tax on interest income each year
B. No original issue discount tax provision	II. Do not pay tax on interest income each year
	III. Pay capital gains tax at maturity
	IV. Do not pay capital gains tax at maturity

Solution:

A. I and IV are correct. Investors who face an original issue discount tax provision and purchase bonds issued at a discount must recognize a prorated portion of the OID in taxable income each year and pay no capital gains tax upon maturity.

B. II and III are correct. Investors in bonds issued at a discount who do not face an OID tax provision will recognize no interest income until maturity, when they face capital gains tax on the OID.

5. A bond issued by a South African company denominated in British pounds sold exclusively to investors who are legally domiciled in the United Kingdom would most likely be classified as:

   A. foreign.

   B. domestic.

   C. a Eurobond.

   Solution:

   A is correct. Bonds sold in a country (United Kingdom) and denominated in that country's currency (British pounds) by an entity from another country (South Africa) are referred to as foreign bonds.

6. A domestic corporate issuer seeking to finance operations in a foreign market would *most likely* issue:

   A. foreign bonds.

   B. domestic bonds.

   C. Treasury bonds.

   Solution:

   A is correct. Corporate issuers often match the currency of their bond financing cash flows with that of their foreign operations using foreign bonds.

   B is incorrect. The use of domestic bonds would not match the currency of the issuer's foreign operations. A second possibility would be to issue a domestic bond and then use a swap to obtain the desired foreign currency exposure. However, this method is beyond the scope of this lesson and will be introduced later.

   C is incorrect. Treasury bonds are issued by sovereign issuers.

PRACTICE PROBLEMS

The following information relates to questions 1-5

Digistrype Logistics (DILO) is a Canadian firm that generates a large portion of revenue in Europe. To finance its planned expansion into digital logistics, DILO is seeking to issue euro-denominated bonds to institutional investors in Germany. A term sheet for the proposed bond issue is presented below.

1.25% Digistrype Logistics (DILO) Seven-Year Convertible Notes (the "Notes") Term Sheet

Issuer:	Digistrype Logistics Inc.
Settlement Date:	[T + 3 Business Days]
Maturity Date:	Seven Years from Settlement Date unless the Notes are redeemed earlier in a Conversion
Principal Amount:	EUR250 million
Unit Size:	EUR1,000 per bond
Interest:	3.25% fixed coupon to be paid annually starting one Year from the Settlement Date with the final coupon paid at Maturity
Seniority:	The Notes are an unsecured obligation of DILO and rank pari passu with other unsecured debt.
Conversion Provision:	An Investor has, at its sole option, the right to convert a portion or the full sum of the Principal Amount, or any part outstanding at any time at the Conversion Price during the Conversion Period.
Current Share Price:	EUR60.00 per DILO common equity share
Conversion Price:	EUR75.00 per DILO common equity share
Conversion Period:	Any Business Day starting from the Settlement Date through the Maturity Date

Institutional investors have expressed concern about increased credit risk due to Digistrype's planned expansion outside of its core business. Digistrype's CFO would prefer to fund the expansion using debt, despite an expectation of lower market interest rates in the next few years. The CFO is also considering removing the conversion feature because of a concern about the possible share dilution if the bonds are converted to equity and a belief that DILO shares are significantly undervalued.

1. Which of the following statements *best* describes the *type* of bonds to be issued given the issuer's country and where the bonds will be issued and traded?

   A. Since Digistrype is planning to issue and sell euro-denominated bonds, its bonds would be considered Eurobonds.

   B. Since Digistrype is planning to issue and sell euro-denominated bonds to investors in Germany, its bonds would be considered foreign bonds.

   C. Since Digistrype is planning to issue and sell bonds to domestic investors in Germany, its bonds would be considered domestic bonds.

2. Which of the following modifications could Digistrype incorporate to *best* mitigate the investors' credit concerns?
   - **A.** Digistrype could consider deferred debt coupons and/or principal payments.
   - **B.** Digistrype could consider adding a call provision to its new debt.
   - **C.** Digistrype could consider accelerating principal repayment or linking debt coupon changes to financial covenants.

3. Which of the following is the *best* contingency feature Digistrype could add to mitigate its own concerns regarding lower interest rates?
   - **A.** Add a call provision to the proposed new debt.
   - **B.** Add a put provision to the proposed new debt.
   - **C.** Add a step-up coupon to the proposed new debt.

4. If DILO's share price on the Frankfurt Stock Exchange were to rise to EUR75, the bond's conversion value would be:
   - **A.** EUR1,000.
   - **B.** EUR15,000.
   - **C.** EUR75,000.

5. Which of the following statements *best* describes the implications of removing the conversion feature from the bond?
   - **A.** Removal of the conversion feature would likely result in a higher coupon.
   - **B.** Removal of the conversion feature would likely increase the bond price.
   - **C.** Removal of the conversion feature would likely reduce credit risk.

SOLUTIONS

1. B is correct. Digistrype, a Canadian firm, is planning to issue and sell euro-denominated bonds to investors in Germany. Bonds issued by entities that are incorporated in another country are called foreign bonds.

   A is incorrect because Eurobonds are cross-border bonds that are not necessarily denominated in euros.

   C is incorrect because domestic bonds refer to a domestic *issuer*, not investor.

2. C is correct. Principal repayment acceleration, such as full amortization, partial principal amortization, or a sinking fund arrangement, is a way to reduce credit risk. Alternatively, Digistrype could incorporate debt coupon changes linked to financial covenants and/or credit ratings in order to address investor concerns.

   A is incorrect because it would delay rather than accelerate repayment.

   B is incorrect because a call provision does not address credit concerns.

3. A is correct. A call provision gives Digistrype the right to redeem all or part of the bond prior to maturity if interest rates decline, so new debt could be issued at a lower cost.

   B is incorrect because a put provision grants investors, not issuers, the right to redeem debt prior to maturity but would not be exercised if interest rates fell, because a put provision is intended to limit investor's downside, not upside.

   C is incorrect; a step-up coupon is not a contingency provision.

4. A is correct. The conversion value of a bond equals its par value if the current share price and conversion price are equal.

   Conversion ratio = Convertible bond par value/Conversion price.

   We know that

   Conversion value = Conversion ratio × Current share price.

   Or, after rearranging,

   Conversion ratio = Conversion value/Current share price,

   which can be substituted into the lefthand side of the first equation:

   Conversion value/Current share price

   = Convertible bond par value/Conversion price.

   If Current share price = Conversion price, then Conversion value

   = Convertible bond par value.

5. A is correct. Because the conversion provision is valuable to bondholders, the convertible bond price is higher than the price of an otherwise similar bond without the conversion provision. Similarly, the yield on a convertible bond is lower than the yield on an otherwise similar non-convertible bond. Thus, should the Digistrype team elect to remove the conversion feature, it would likely have to increase the bond's coupon rate in order to attract investors.

   B is incorrect because removal of the conversion feature would decrease, not increase, the bond price.

   C is incorrect because removal of the conversion feature would not change the credit risk.

LEARNING MODULE

3

Fixed-Income Issuance and Trading

LEARNING OUTCOMES	
Mastery	***The candidate should be able to:***
☐	describe fixed-income market segments and their issuer and investor participants
☐	describe types of fixed-income indexes
☐	compare primary and secondary fixed-income markets to equity markets

INTRODUCTION

1

Fixed-income instruments and markets are often categorized by issuer type, credit quality, time to maturity, and, sometimes, additional features, such as currency, geography, and environmental, social, and governance (ESG) characteristics. Fixed-income indexes are categorized in a similar manner and serve important functions, like the role of equity market indexes in stock markets. Like other financial markets, fixed-income markets are composed of primary markets in which issuers raise financing from investors with new issues and secondary markets where investors trade existing instruments with other investors. Given bonds' finite maturities and other features, there are important distinctions in fixed-income markets from the primary and secondary markets for equities.

LEARNING MODULE OVERVIEW

- Fixed-income instruments and markets are typically categorized along three dimensions: issuer type (i.e., sector), credit quality, and time to maturity.
- Fixed-income investors have corresponding positions along the credit and maturity spectrum as they seek exposures to certain risks and attempt to match the cash flows of known future obligations.

- Similar to equity market indexes, fixed-income indexes track the returns of groups of securities that meet their inclusion criteria. Indexes are used to evaluate market performance, benchmark the performance of investments and investment managers, and form the basis of indexed investment strategies.
- Fixed-income indexes can be classified as broad-based, aggregate indexes with a vast number of constituents or narrower indexes that focus on criteria such as issuer type, credit quality, and time to maturity.
- Primary bond markets are markets in which an issuer sells a new bond or bonds to investors to raise financing, whereas secondary bond markets are markets in which existing bonds are traded among investors.

LEARNING MODULE SELF-ASSESSMENT

These initial questions are intended to help you gauge your current level of understanding of this learning module.

1. Discuss two ways that an investor could seek to increase her expected return on a fixed-income portfolio.

   Solution:

   Investors could increase *credit risk* with instruments with lower credit ratings. Second, provided that the yield curve is upward sloping, investors may also increase expected returns with *longer-term bonds*.

2. Which of the following statements about fixed-income and equity indexes is correct?

   A. There is more turnover in equity indexes than in fixed-income indexes.

   B. Fixed-income indexes often have more constituent securities than equity indexes.

   C. Fixed-income index constituents are typically equally weighted, while equity index constituents are typically weighted by issuers' market capitalization.

   Solution:

   B is correct. Fixed-income indexes often have more constituent securities than equity indexes because issuers tend to have many types of instruments outstanding, and governments issue large amounts of fixed-income securities but not equity securities. The finite maturity of bonds and the higher frequency of new issuance lead to far more turnover in fixed-income indexes than in equity indexes. Fixed-income index constituents are usually weighted by market value of debt outstanding, whereas equity indexes are weighted by issuers' market capitalizations.

3. The Bloomberg Barclays Global Aggregate Index includes:

   A. all issuer sizes.

   B. issuers in multiple currencies.

C. high-yield and unrated issuers.

Solution:

B is correct. The Bloomberg Barclays Global Aggregate Index includes fixed-coupon capital market securities from all major issuer types in 28 developed and emerging markets that meet the inclusion criteria. However, the index excludes high-yield and unrated debt instruments and those that do not meet minimum issuance size.

4. A debut issuer seeking to sell its bonds only to a select group of investors will *most likely* undertake a:

   A. public offering.

   B. shelf registration.

   C. private placement.

Solution:

C is correct. Bonds can be sold via a private placement, in which only a select group of investors or a single investor purchases the bonds. Bonds can also be sold in a public offering in which any member of the public may buy the bonds. Frequent bond issuers use a shelf registration, which is updated regularly and may be used for a range of future bond issuances.

5. A frequent bond issuer that seeks flexibility to issue bonds opportunistically when market conditions are favorable would *most likely* use a:

   A. reopening.

   B. shelf offering.

   C. private placement.

Solution:

B is correct. Frequent issuers of bonds have ready access to the bond market and often choose issuance timing on an opportunistic basis, when market conditions are most favorable. Frequent bond issuers use a shelf registration or a broad, all-encompassing offering circular that is updated regularly and may be used for a range of future bond issuances. A less common strategy is to increase the size of an *existing* bond with a price significantly *different* from par, which is referred to as the reopening of an existing bond. In a private placement, only a selected investor or group of investors may buy the bonds.

FIXED-INCOME SEGMENTS, ISSUERS, AND INVESTORS 2

☐ describe fixed-income market segments and their issuer and investor participants

Fixed-income instruments and markets are typically categorized along three dimensions: issuer type (often known as sector), credit quality, and time to maturity. Sometimes, instruments and markets are additionally classified by issuers' geography, currency, and ESG characteristics.

In contrast to equities, where issuers typically issue just one or two instruments, issuers often have *many* fixed-income instruments outstanding. For example, a corporate issuer may have loans or both loans and bonds, either on a short-term basis to finance working capital or a long-term basis for capital investment. Some large companies also issue commercial paper, a type of short-term bond to finance working capital needs that can be collateralized by specific assets. These debt instruments may be in varying currencies to hedge exposures and broaden access to investors. For example, at the end of 2021, Apple Inc. had over 80 fixed-income instruments but a single equity instrument (common stock) outstanding.

Exhibit 1 illustrates typical issuers and instrument types across credit and time-to-maturity segments.

Exhibit 1: Issuers across the Credit and Maturity Spectrums: Issuers and Instrument Types

Credit Quality / Years to Maturity	< 1y Short-Term	1y–10y Intermediate-Term	> 10y Long-Term
"Default Risk Free"	Treasury bills	Treasury notes	Treasury bonds
Investment Grade	Repo Commercial Paper ABCP	Unsecured Corporate bonds ABS	Unsecured Corporate bonds MBS
High Yield		Secured Corporate bonds Leveraged loans	

Note: ABCP is asset-backed commercial paper.

Fixed-income investors have corresponding positions along the credit and maturity spectrums as they seek to gain exposures to certain risks and to match the cash flows of known future obligations. Near-term obligations and the desire for liquid cash alternatives are often met with money market securities, while investors may assume greater interest rate risk with long-term bonds to meet obligations further in the future or pursue higher expected returns. Pension funds and insurance companies with long investment time horizons favor fixed-income instruments with fixed periodic coupon cash flows and a maturity profile that matches their long-term liabilities. Additionally, investors may take credit risk at any point on the maturity spectrum to augment returns. Exhibit 2 illustrates common investor positions across the credit and maturity spectrums.

Exhibit 2: Investors across the Credit and Maturity Spectrums: Investors

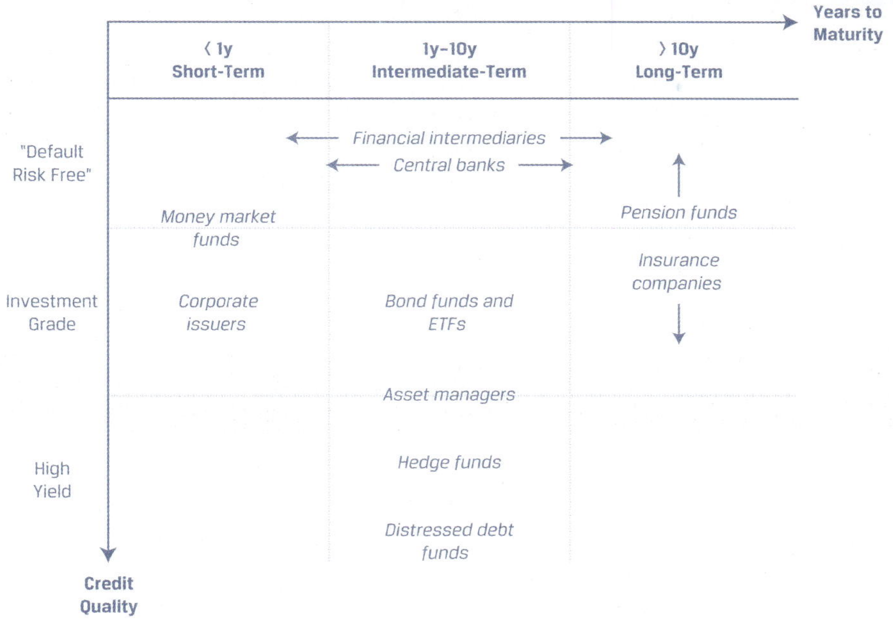

A common measure of credit quality is a **credit rating**. Credit ratings are letter-grade, qualitative measures of an issuer's ability to meet its debt obligations based on both the probability of default and the expected loss under a default scenario. Credit ratings are given and maintained by **credit rating agencies** for both short-term and long-term debt and for *issuers* and specific bond *issues*. Two of the largest credit rating agencies are Standard & Poor's (S&P) and Moody's. Many investors are restricted to instruments with credit ratings, with a limited percentage of their portfolio invested in unrated instruments. Credit risk and credit ratings will be discussed in detail in later lessons.

S&P CREDIT RATINGS

S&P ratings range from AAA for the highest credit quality to D for default, with ratings in descending order of credit quality as follows:

Investment Grade	AAA	Extremely strong capacity to meet financial commitments; highest rating
	AA	Very strong capacity to meet financial commitments
	A	Strong capacity to meet financial commitments but somewhat susceptible to adverse economic conditions and changes in circumstances
	BBB	Adequate capacity to meet financial commitments but more subject to adverse economic conditions
	BBB-	Considered lowest investment grade by market participants
Speculative Grade *or* High Yield	BB+	Considered highest speculative grade by market participants

BB	Less vulnerable in the near term but faces major ongoing uncertainties to adverse business, financial, and economic conditions
B	More vulnerable to adverse business, financial, and economic conditions but currently has the capacity to meet financial commitments
CCC	Currently vulnerable and dependent on favorable business, financial, and economic conditions to meet financial commitments
CC	Highly vulnerable; default has not yet occurred but is expected to be a virtual certainty
C	Currently highly vulnerable to non-payment, and ultimate recovery is expected to be lower than that of higher-rated obligations
D	Payment default on a financial commitment or breach of an imputed promise; also used when a bankruptcy petition has been filed or similar action taken

Source: S&P Global Ratings.

Developed market (DM) sovereign issuers usually represent the most creditworthy borrowers within a market and often carry a AAA rating. Because investors often assume they will receive all promised interest and principal payments on DM sovereign bonds, they comprise the "default risk free" category in Exhibit 1.

Issuers rated BBB- (Baa3 on Moody's scale) or higher are considered **investment grade**. Issuers rated BB+ (Ba1 on Moody's scale) or lower are referred to as **high yield**, speculative grade, or junk. High-yield issuers include new issuers for which investors are more likely to require collateral due to less stable operating cash flows, as well as formerly investment-grade issuers whose credit quality has deteriorated since the time of issuance (known as "**fallen angels**").

The participation of issuers and investors in heterogeneous fixed-income markets is illustrated in the following examples.

EXAMPLE 1

BRWA Corporation Debt Profile

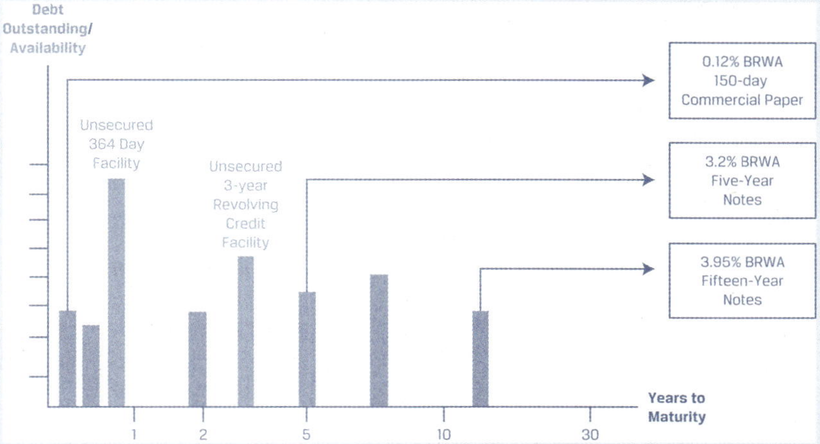

BRWA is an example of an investment-grade corporate issuer with ready access to unsecured debt across maturities and markets as well as in different currencies either directly or through its affiliates. It uses commercial paper to meet its short-term or seasonal working capital needs, intermediate-term debt to cover more permanent working capital or medium-term investments, and long-term debt to match the longer useful life of capital investments, such as new manufacturing equipment or factories. BRWA pays a fee to a group (or **syndicate**) of banks for two **credit facilities**, which are loan agreements with pre-specified terms and limits but with fluctuating balances based on borrower-specific needs at different points in time, analogous to a credit card. The first is a 364-day facility which backs the commercial paper program, and the second is a longer-term revolving credit facility.

The combination of domestic and cross-border operating, financing, and leasing activities in Example 1 leads many of BRWA's real-world industry peers to have *hundreds* of unique debt instruments outstanding across all affiliates. We may contrast the BRWA example with VIVU, the digital media company introduced in an earlier module that has fewer fixed assets, less stable operating cash flows, and, therefore, limited access to fixed-income markets.

EXAMPLE 2

VIVU Fixed-Income Issuance

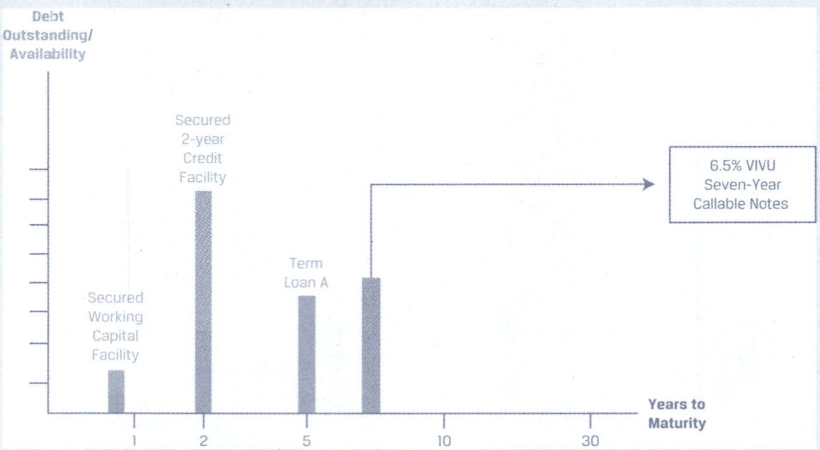

VIVU is an example of a high-yield corporate issuer that has limited access to secured debt across shorter maturities. VIVU has no access to the unsecured commercial paper market but, rather, relies on partially drawn secured working capital and credit facilities from banks to meet its short-term needs. VIVU has a fully drawn loan (Term Loan A) that has a floating-rate coupon equal to MRR plus a fixed credit spread. VIVU also has seven-year callable notes outstanding under which it has the right to redeem the notes at a fixed price starting three years from issuance.

Sovereign government issuers typically have the lowest credit risk (highest credit rating) in each market, due to sovereign governments' right to tax economic activity. Developed market sovereign bonds are often widely held by both foreign investors and foreign central banks seeking to hold reserves in the developed market's currency in the form of an interest-bearing asset. Sovereign bonds also serve important functions in the domestic financial system. Central banks often use domestic sovereign bonds to conduct monetary policy, borrowing or lending these securities to increase or decrease monetary reserves.

Investment-grade bond investors expect more stable cash flows, and defaults among investment-grade issuers are relatively rare. Expected returns are therefore lower than those for high-yield bonds and usually comparable or modestly higher than those of sovereign bonds. High-yield investors expect greater return for assuming a higher probability of default and often compare returns to those of equity investments.

EXAMPLE 3

Baywhite Financial's Bond Funds

Baywhite Financial manages its Core Bond Fund with the objectives of long-run capital appreciation with a relatively low tolerance for credit risk. The fund invests in investment-grade intermediate- and long-term bonds, including BRWA's 5- and 15-year notes. The composition of the fund's holdings, which include 3,601 positions, is as follows:

Baywhite Core Bond Fund Holdings by Credit Rating

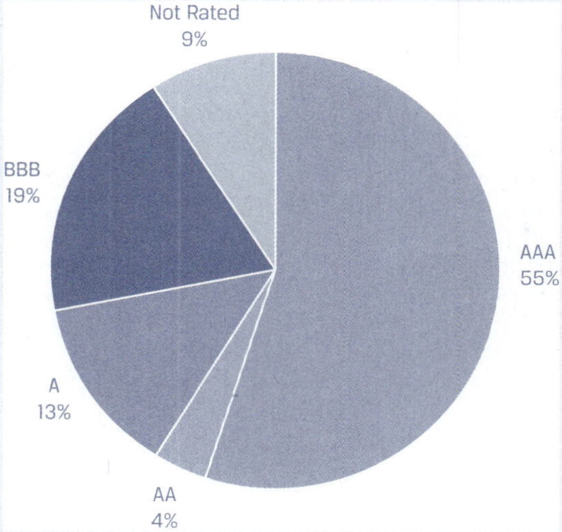

Baywhite Core Bond Fund Holdings by Issuer Type

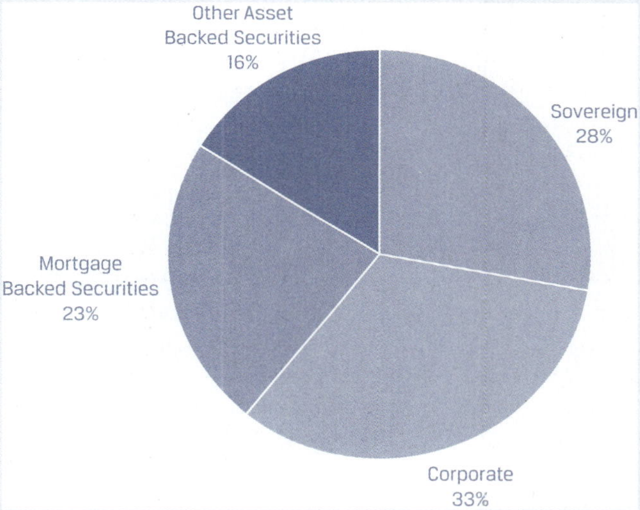

Baywhite Core Bond Fund Holdings by Time to Maturity

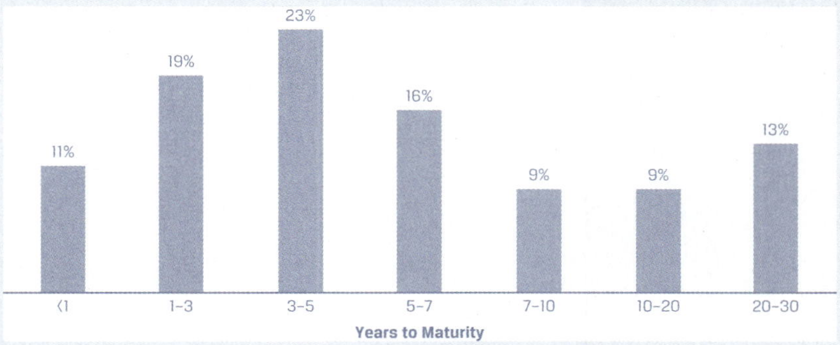

Baywhite also manages the Short-Term Bond Fund as a liquid cash alternative for investors, and it takes minimal credit and interest rate risk by investing in investment-grade, short-term bonds, such as BRWA's commercial paper. The composition of the Short-Term Bond Fund's holdings, which include 451 positions, is as follows:

Baywhite Short-Term Bond Fund Holdings by Credit Rating

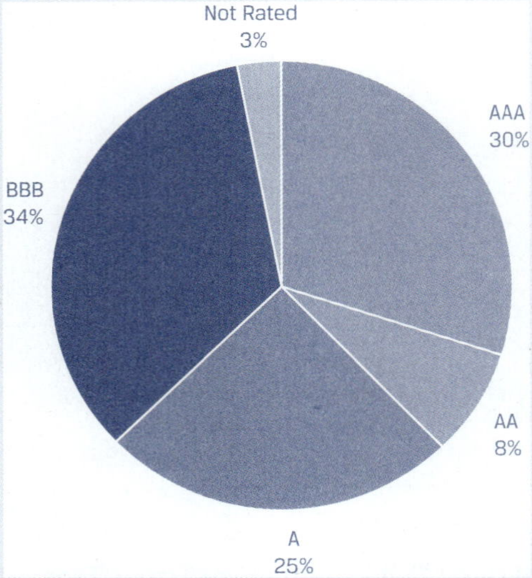

Baywhite Short-Term Bond Fund Holdings by Issuer Type

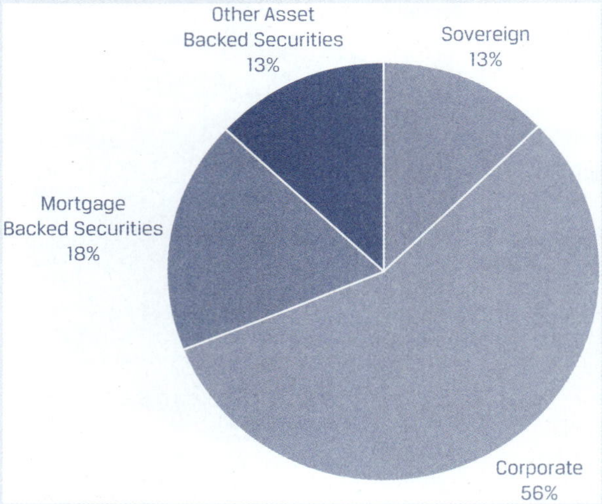

Baywhite Short-Term Bond Fund Holdings by Time to Maturity

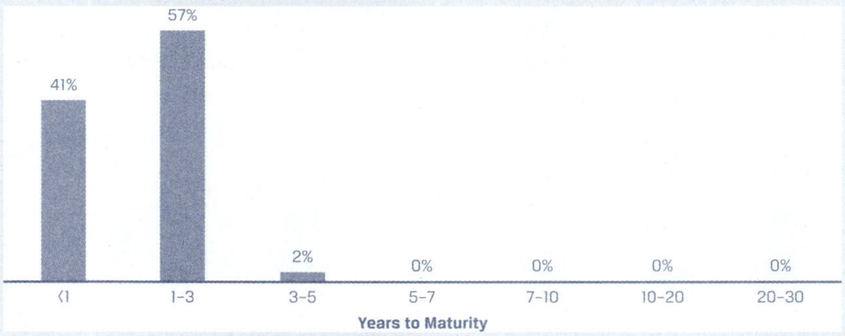

Neither of these funds would invest in VIVU's seven-year callable notes, because both are restricted to owning investment-grade debt.

QUESTION SET

1. A fixed-income mutual fund that is required to invest in only investment-grade bonds would *most likely* invest in:

   A. B rated bonds.

   B. BB+ rated bonds.

   C. BBB- rated bonds.

   Solution:

   C is correct. Both B and BB+ rated bonds are considered high-yield bonds. A BBB- rated bond is considered the lowest investment-grade bond.

2. New issuers for which investors are likely to require collateral due to more volatile operating cash flows are *best* categorized as:

   A. fallen angels.

   B. high-yield issuers.

   C. investment-grade issuers.

   Solution:

   B is correct. High-yield issuers (not investment-grade issuers) include new issuers for which investors are more likely to require collateral due to less stable operating cash flows. Investment-grade issuers whose credit quality has deteriorated since the time of issuance are known as fallen angels.

3. A corporate issuer seeking to fund working capital needs would *most likely* issue:

   A. commercial paper.

   B. intermediate-term debt.

   C. long-term debt.

   Solution:

   B is correct. A corporate issuer would use commercial paper to meet its short-term or seasonal working capital needs, intermediate-term debt to cover more medium-term investments, and long-term debt or equity to match the longer useful life of capital investments.

4. A high-yield corporate issuer would *most likely* finance its operations using:

   A. secured term loans.

   B. long-term callable bonds.

   C. unsecured commercial paper.

   Solution:

   A is correct. A high-yield corporate issuer has limited access to secured debt across shorter maturities but has no access to unsecured commercial paper or the long-term bond market. (See Example 2.)

5. Identify the following statement as true or false. Justify your answer.

   Foreign investors in emerging market debt have an expected return that is similar to that of developed market sovereign bonds.

   Solution:

   False. Foreign investors in emerging market debt expect a return above that of developed market sovereign bonds in exchange for holding bonds with lower credit quality and higher risk related to currency fluctuations.

3 FIXED-INCOME INDEXES

☐ describe types of fixed-income indexes

An earlier module highlighted the role of market indexes in tracking the broad risk and return of different security markets, which enable the evaluation of market performance, benchmarking the performance of investments and investment managers, and forming the basis for indexed investment strategies. Fixed-income indexes perform a similar function in bond markets as equity indexes in stock markets but differ in three important ways from their equity counterparts.

1. A single issuer may have many individual fixed-income securities outstanding. *All* bonds that meet index eligibility requirements are included in indexes, causing fixed-income indexes to have many more constituent securities than equity indexes have. Some indexes have over 10,000 constituents.
2. The finite maturity of bonds and the higher frequency of new issuance lead to far more changes in constituents (turnover) in fixed-income indexes than in equity indexes. Bond indexes are usually rebalanced each month to both add new issues and remove those that fall below a minimum maturity.
3. Analogous to equity indexes weighted by issuers' market capitalization, bond index constituents are usually weighted by market value of debt outstanding. Since bonds are issued by many types of issuers, broad bond indexes will reflect changes to bond market composition over time—for example, increases in public versus private issuer debt, longer maturities, and deterioration in credit quality. Government issuers are large bond issuers, so many broad bond indexes have high weights of government debt.

If a bond fund aims to match the returns of a specific index, it will typically hold a representative sample of constituent securities in order to match index returns because the complexity of bond indexes makes it impossible to purchase all the constituent securities.

Fixed-income indexes can be classified as aggregate indexes, with a vast number of constituents, or narrower indexes, based on criteria such as sector, credit quality, time to maturity, geography, and ESG considerations. The choice of index for investment manager performance evaluation is important and will be discussed in detail later in the curriculum, but generally speaking, the index chosen to evaluate an investment manager or fund should correspond to that manager's or fund's investment strategy. For example, Baywhite's Short-Term Bond Fund invests in short-term, investment-grade bonds. To evaluate the fund, its returns should be compared to an index of instruments with similar maturity and credit quality.

The following three exhibits illustrate fixed-income indexes and their use by investors.

Exhibit 3: Global Aggregate Bond Index

Bloomberg Barclays Global Aggregate Index
Brief Summary of Inclusion Criteria

Issuers:	Fixed-rate bonds from sovereign, government, corporate, and securitized issuers based in DM and EM markets
Currencies:	28 eligible currencies across the Americas, EMEA, and Asia Pacific
Credit Quality:	Investment-grade rating or equivalent
Coupon:	Fixed rate, zero coupon, and step-up coupon (if step-up dates are predetermined)
Amount Outstanding:	Minimum issuance size by market, for example: —CAD150 m —USD300 m, EUR300 m, CHF300 m, AUD300 m —CNY 5 bn (Treasury and bank debt) —RUB20 bn —JPY35 bn
Maturity:	At least one year to final maturity or average weighted maturity
Rebalancing Rules:	At each month end, the composition of the fixed set of bonds for the following monthly index return is established. Bonds that no longer meet maturity, rating, size, or other criteria are removed, and new issues where security reference information and pricing are available are included.
Reinvestment of Cash Flows:	Intra-month interest and principal payments contribute to monthly index returns and are reinvested into the index on the following rebalancing date.
Market of Issue:	Global and regional public markets
Seniority of Debt:	Senior and subordinated issues
Taxability:	Only fully taxable issues are eligible.

The Bloomberg Barclays Global Aggregate Index includes fixed-coupon capital market securities from all major issuer types in 28 developed and emerging markets that meet the above inclusion criteria. However, the index excludes high-yield and unrated debt instruments and those that do not meet minimum issuance size.

The index sponsor prices all bonds at a predetermined time each business day to calculate the index value. Mutual funds and ETFs that track this benchmark index offer *comprehensive* exposure to many fixed-income markets with *no* active security selection and portfolio turnover limited solely to either new issuance or issues no longer meeting inclusion criteria. Similar subindexes are available by market or region, and returns may include gains or losses due to currency fluctuations (unhedged returns) or may offset these currency-based changes using currency forwards on rebalancing dates (hedged returns).

The Bloomberg Barclays Global Aggregate Index might be appropriate to use to evaluate Baywhite Financial's Core Bond Fund since it includes investment-grade, longer-term bonds from a variety of sectors. However, if Baywhite invests in only a single market, such as Japan, a more appropriate benchmark would be the Bloomberg Barclays Japanese Aggregate Index.

The J.P. Morgan EMBI+ Index in Exhibit 4 is a more narrowly defined fixed-income index that includes US dollar–denominated debt of sovereign governments at or below a certain credit quality of a minimum issuance size and maturity. The focus on foreign debt of lower credit quality targets a higher US dollar–based return than for developed market sovereign bonds while assuming the external debt risk of issuer countries.

Exhibit 4: Emerging Markets Bond Index

J.P. Morgan Emerging Markets Bond Index Plus (EMBI+)
Brief Summary of Inclusion Criteria

Issuers:	Emerging market sovereign issuers of US dollar debt
Currencies:	Only US dollar–denominated bonds are included. Bonds with a coupon or redemption payment linked to an exchange rate are not eligible.
Credit Quality:	Sovereign rating of Baa1/BBB+/BBB+ or below by Moody's/S&P/ Fitch Ratings
Coupon:	Fixed rate, zero coupon, and step-up coupon (if step-up dates are predetermined)
Amount Outstanding:	Issues with a current face amount outstanding of USD500 million or more
Maturity:	Only instruments with at least 2.5 years until maturity are considered. At each month-end, instruments that will fall below 12 months to maturity during the upcoming month will be excluded.
Return Calculation:	Index total return is calculated as a weighted average of bond returns using bid side prices.
Rebalancing:	Occurs on the final US business day of each month
Reinvestment of Cash Flows:	All coupons received are immediately reinvested into the index

Bond investors seeking to incorporate ESG considerations into fixed-income investment decisions frequently use bond indexes that regularly screen for and exclude issuers that fail to meet certain minimum ESG criteria. For example, the Bloomberg Barclays MSCI Euro Corporate Sustainable SRI Index (see Exhibit 5) filters by sector, currency, credit quality, time to maturity, *and* ESG considerations, such as a minimum ESG rating and exclusion of issuers involved in certain business activities.

Exhibit 5: Corporate Sustainable Socially Responsible Investment (SRI) Bond Index

Bloomberg Barclays MSCI Euro Corporate Sustainable SRI Index
Brief Summary of Inclusion Criteria

Issuers:	Corporate (industrial, utility, and financial institution) issuers
Currencies:	Only euro-denominated bonds are included.
Credit Quality:	Security rating of Baa3/BBB-/BBB- or above by Moody's/S&P/ Fitch or equivalent
Coupon:	Fixed rate, zero coupon, and step-up coupon (if step-up dates are predetermined)
Amount Outstanding:	EUR300 million minimum par amount outstanding

Bloomberg Barclays MSCI Euro Corporate Sustainable SRI Index
Brief Summary of Inclusion Criteria

Maturity:	At least one year to final maturity, with fixed-to-floating perpetual bonds excluded one year prior to conversion. Fixed-rate perpetual bonds are excluded.
Return Calculation:	Index total return is calculated as a weighted average of bond returns using bid side prices.
Rebalancing:	Occurs on the final US business day of each month
Reinvestment of Cash Flows:	Intra-month interest and principal payments contribute to monthly index returns and are reinvested into the index on the following rebalancing date.
ESG Rules:	▪ Must have an MSCI ESG rating of BBB or higher ▪ Excludes issuers involved in the following business lines/activities: • Alcohol • Tobacco • Gambling • Adult Entertainment • Genetically Modified Organisms (GMOs) • Nuclear Power • Civilian Firearms • Military Weapons • Thermal Coal • Generation of Thermal Coal • Oil Sands ▪ Excludes issuers with a "Red" MSCI Controversies score measuring issuer involvement in major ESG controversies and adherence to international norms and principles

QUESTION SET

1. Which of the following indexes would be *most* suitable for evaluating Baywhite's Short-Term Bond Fund?

   An index composed primarily of:

   A. high-yield short-term bonds.

   B. investment-grade short-term bonds.

   C. investment-grade bonds with more than five years to maturity.

   Solution:

   B is correct. Baywhite's Short-Term Bond Fund invests in investment-grade, short-term bonds. To evaluate this fund, its returns should be compared to those of an index of similar maturity and credit instruments.

2. Match the characteristics on the right with the indexes on the left.

A. Broad equity index	I. Includes sovereign issuers
B. Broad bond index	II. Less frequent rebalancing

III. Easier to fully replicate
IV. Larger number of constituents

Solution:

A. II and III

B. I and IV

3. Relative to equity indexes, fixed-income indexes exhibit more turnover due to:

   A. annual rebalancing.

   B. the finite maturity of bonds.

   C. the lower frequency of new issues.

Solution:

B is correct. The finite maturity of bonds and the higher frequency of new issuance leads to far more turnover in fixed-income indexes than in equity indexes. Bond indexes are usually rebalanced each month to both add new issues and remove those that fall below a minimum maturity.

4. The composition of broad bond indexes will *most likely* change due to changes in:

   A. the maturity mix of issuers only.

   B. the proportion of public versus private issuers only.

   C. both the maturity mix of issuers and the proportion of public versus private issuers.

Solution:

C is correct. Since bonds are issued by many types of issuers, broad bond indexes will reflect changes to bond market composition over time—for example, increases in public versus private issuer debt, longer maturities, and deterioration in credit quality.

5. Identify the following statement as true or false. Justify your answer.

   The Bloomberg Barclays MSCI Euro Corporate Sustainable SRI Index requires an MSCI ESG rating of AAA and excludes all emerging market issuers.

Solution:

False. The Bloomberg Barclays MSCI Euro Corporate Sustainable SRI Index requires an MSCI ESG rating of BBB or higher and excludes certain business lines/activities, including alcohol, tobacco, gambling, and thermal coal. Emerging market issuers are not excluded.

PRIMARY AND SECONDARY FIXED-INCOME MARKETS 4

☐ compare primary and secondary fixed-income markets to equity markets

Primary Fixed-Income Markets

Primary bond markets are markets in which an issuer sells a new bond or bonds to investors to raise capital. In contrast, **secondary bond markets** are markets in which existing bonds are traded among investors. As in the case of an IPO for equity investors, an issuer approaching the bond market for the first time (often referred to as a **debut issuer**) represents the first opportunity for a fixed-income investor to purchase an issuer's bonds. Bonds can be sold via a public offering, in which any member of the public may buy the bonds, or via a private placement, in which only a selected investor or group of investors may buy the bonds. Similar to primary equity issuance, which typically involves a transfer from private to public ownership, a debut issuer is often replacing private debt, such as a bank loan, with bonds. Examples of debut bond issuers include

- new corporate legal entities formed after a merger, acquisition, or divestiture, which usually refinance *all* existing debt outstanding;
- companies that reach a more mature stage of the life cycle with more predictable cash flows and begin issuing debt; and
- sovereign governments that raise external foreign currency debt for the first time.

For debut issuers that must complete the respective domestic market or Eurobond registration process, the underwriters usually conduct roadshows and other information sessions for a period of several weeks prior to issuance to familiarize potential investors with the new entity and its uses of and sources for repayment for the new bond.

For *repeat* issuers of fixed-income securities, the process is far more abbreviated than for debut issuers and for follow-on offerings of equities. Whereas publicly traded companies that return to the equity market to increase their shares outstanding do so under an identical instrument, fixed-income issuers usually issue a new security priced at or close to par. A less common strategy is to increase the size of an *existing* bond with a price significantly *different* from par, which is referred to as the **reopening** of an existing bond.

For example, unsecured investment-grade issuance of new corporate bonds usually takes place within a several-hour period, as shown in the diagram and timeline in Exhibit 6.

Exhibit 6: Investment-Grade Corporate Bond Issuance Timeline

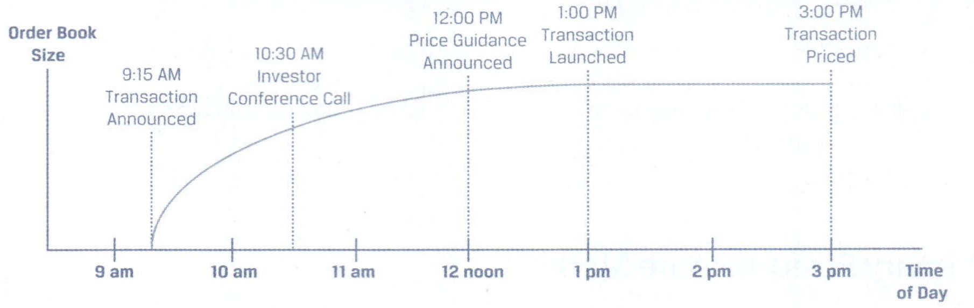

Illustrative Timeline:

9:00 a.m.	Underwriters and issuer agree to launch transaction
9:15 a.m.	Transaction announced (size, spread, and maturities TBD) Electronic roadshow released Order book opens to investors
10:30 a.m.	Investor conference call with issuer and underwriters
12:00 p.m.	Price guidance, size, and maturities subject to change Order book closed to investors
1:00 p.m.	Transaction launched with final size, pricing, and maturities
1:00–3:00 p.m.	Underwriters allocate transaction to investors
3:00 p.m.	Transaction priced (government benchmark and coupon set)
4:00 p.m.	Final term sheet delivered, bonds free to trade same or next day

Exhibit 6 is an example of an underwritten bond offering in which one or more financial intermediaries (or underwriters) guarantee the sale of the bond issue at an offering price that is negotiated with the issuer. Investors in such bonds (e.g., Baywhite) are usually very familiar with the bond indenture and financial statements of these frequent issuers. As in the case of BRWA earlier in this module, issuers of such bonds have ready access to the bond market and often choose issuance timing on an opportunistic basis when market conditions are most favorable. Underwriters seek to manage the bond order book to ensure the greatest availability to large institutional investors at the lowest possible spread across maturities. Frequent bond issuers use a shelf registration or a broad, all-encompassing offering circular that is updated regularly and may be used for a range of future bond issuances.

Secured bond issuance among corporate high-yield, some special purpose entities, and other issuers (e.g., VIVU) is usually a longer and more involved process than for unsecured investment-grade bonds. Investors must familiarize themselves with unique and more complex covenants, as well as the use of *both* operating cash flows *and* collateral as sources of bond repayment. For bonds of lower credit quality, the financial intermediary does not guarantee the sale and may serve only as a broker in a best-efforts offering. That is, it tries to sell the bond issue on a commission basis at the negotiated price only if it can do so.

In instances where the bond size is small, the issuer is less well known, or the terms are more customized, a bond might take the form of a private placement or non-underwritten, unregistered offering of bonds sold only to a small group of investors.

Primary market issuance of sovereign debt usually takes the form of a public auction led by the national treasury or finance ministry, which are discussed in detail in a later module.

Secondary Fixed-Income Markets

While progress continues to be made by various electronic marketplace platforms, such as MarketAxess and Tradeweb, fixed-income markets are mostly quote-driven or over-the-counter (OTC) markets. Major participants in secondary bond market trading include institutional investors (such as the Baywhite funds introduced earlier), financial intermediaries, and central banks.

Secondary bond market liquidity varies widely across fixed-income market segments and even among bonds outstanding from a single issuer. The bid–offer spread or difference in price at which a dealer will buy (or bid) from a customer and sell (or offer) to a customer is a key liquidity measure. This spread is often quoted in basis points in fixed-income markets.

The most recently issued, or on-the-run, developed market sovereign bonds are typically the most liquid fixed-income securities, with primary dealers making active markets in large size with bid–offer spreads equal to a fraction of a basis point. In some markets, such as Australia, domestic sovereign government bonds are traded on an exchange. Among corporate issuers, recently issued corporate bonds from frequent issuers of higher credit quality usually exhibit the greatest liquidity and tightest bid–offer spreads. Underwriters and other dealers are more likely to hold trading inventory in recent issues and may therefore quote bid-offer spreads of a few basis points. Bonds of less frequent corporate issuers or more seasoned bonds of frequent issuers are rarely traded, leading dealers to quote bid–offer spreads of at least 10–20 basis points or more for small sizes. One exception that can increase trading frequency of a seasoned issue is a significant deterioration in a bond's credit quality, as in the following example.

EXAMPLE 4

Hertz Corporation

Hertz Global Holdings Inc. (Hertz) is a US-based car rental company that filed for Chapter 11 bankruptcy protection in May 2020 amid the initial outbreak of COVID-19 in the United States. Hertz's bonds maturing in 2022 and 2028 were trading at an average of less than 10% of par value, a decline of more than 90% from three months earlier. However, a year later, the bonds rose back to their pre-pandemic price as the company exited bankruptcy through a reorganization with outside investors that kept these bonds intact.

Source: Bloomberg News

Bonds of issuers believed to be very close to or in bankruptcy, as in the previous example, are referred to as **distressed debt**. Distressed debt typically trades in the secondary market at a price well below par, because bondholders are unlikely to receive all promised future interest and principal payments. Investors with policies limiting their bond investments to highly rated securities may be forced to sell distressed debt, while hedge funds and other opportunistic investors seeking more equity-like returns (from price appreciation) are often the buyers of distressed bonds. Distressed debt is traded until either the corporate issuer has liquidated its assets or its outstanding bonds have been restructured. In contrast, an equity security may be removed or delisted from secondary trading on an exchange if it fails to meet the listing requirements of the exchange, which often include minimum share prices, net worth, and free float. By the time an issuer's debt has become distressed, its equity securities will likely have already been delisted.

Finally, many bond issues do not trade at all on a regular basis. Price quotes from dealers or on platforms such as Bloomberg for illiquid bonds often rely on estimates derived from more liquid bonds of similar credit quality and maturity, a process covered in a later module.

QUESTION SET

1. A bond issuance by a company after it has reached a more mature stage of the life cycle with more predictable cash flows would be *best* considered a:

   A. private placement.

   B. primary fixed-income market transaction.

   C. secondary fixed-income market transaction.

   Solution:

   B is correct. Primary bond markets are markets in which an issuer sells a new bond or bonds to investors to raise capital. Secondary bond markets are markets in which existing bonds are traded among investors. Bonds can be sold via a private placement, in which only a selected investor or group of investors may buy the bonds.

2. Which of the following statements about debut issuers is *correct*?

   A. A debut issuer typically replaces bank loans with bonds.

   B. Debut issuers transfer ownership from public to private markets.

   C. Debut issuers offer bonds in a public offering, not a private placement.

   Solution:

   A is correct. Similar to primary equity issuance, which typically involves a transfer from private to public ownership, a first-time bond issuer is often replacing private debt, such as a bank loan, with bonds.

   B is incorrect. Fixed-income securities have no voting or control rights, and debut issues represent a private to public (not public to private) transition.

   C is incorrect. A debut issuer can offer bonds in either a public offering or a private placement.

3. Relative to unsecured issuers, secured issuers *most likely* experience an issuance timeline that is:

   A. shorter.

   B. the same.

   C. longer.

   Solution:

   C is correct. Secured bond issuance among corporate high-yield, some special purpose entities, and other issuers (e.g., VIVU) is usually a longer and more involved process than for unsecured investment-grade bonds. Investors must familiarize themselves with unique and more complex covenants, as well as the use of *both* operating cash flows *and* collateral as sources of bond repayment.

4. Identify the following statement as true or false. Justify your answer.

Secondary fixed-income markets consist mostly of quote-driven or over-the-counter markets, while secondary trading for listed equity markets primarily occurs on an electronic exchange.

Solution:

True. Unlike listed equities, for which secondary trading largely occurs on an electronic exchange, fixed-income markets consist mostly of quote-driven or over-the-counter markets.

5. For a firm in distress, its bonds will *most likely* stop trading:

A. before the firm's equity.

B. at the same time as the firm's equity.

C. after the firm's equity.

Solution:

C is correct. Distressed debt is traded until either the corporate issuer has liquidated its assets or its outstanding bonds have been restructured. In contrast, an equity security may be removed or delisted from secondary trading on an exchange if it fails to meet the listing requirements of the exchange, which often include minimum share prices, net worth, and free float. By the time an issuer's debt has become distressed, its equity securities will likely have already been delisted.

PRACTICE PROBLEMS

1. Match the instrument type on the left with its typical investor on the right.

A. Commercial paper	I. Insurance companies
B. Unsecured corporate bonds	II. Hedge funds
C. Secured corporate bonds	III. Money market funds

2. An issuer with a AAA credit rating would *most likely* be a:

   A. distressed issuer.

   B. high-yield issuer.

   C. sovereign issuer.

3. An index tracking the Bloomberg Barclays Global Aggregate Index would *most likely* have:

   A. limited security selection.

   B. modest turnover due to changes in market values.

   C. comprehensive exposure to fixed-income markets.

4. A firm that increases the size of an existing bond issue with a price significantly different from par is conducting a:

   A. reopening.

   B. private placement.

   C. distressed debt issuance.

5. The bond issue trading at the highest bid–offer spread is *most likely* a:

   A. recently issued sovereign bond.

   B. seasoned investment-grade corporate bond.

   C. recently issued investment-grade corporate bond.

SOLUTIONS

1.

   A. III

   B. I

   C. II

2. C is correct. Sovereign government issuers typically have the lowest credit risk (highest credit rating) in each market, due to sovereign governments' right to tax economic activity. High-yield issuers have below-investment-grade credit ratings (BBB- or below), while distressed issuers typically have high-yield ratings or are in default.

3. C is correct. Mutual funds and ETFs that track this benchmark index offer *comprehensive* exposure to many fixed-income markets with *no* active security selection and portfolio turnover limited solely to either new issuance or issues no longer meeting inclusion criteria.

4. A is correct. Increasing the size of an existing bond with a price significantly different from par is referred to as the reopening of an existing bond. A private placement refers to bonds being sold to a selected investor or group of investors, versus a sale to the public. Bonds of issuers believed to be very close to or in bankruptcy are referred to as distressed.

5. B is correct. Bonds of less frequent corporate issuers or more seasoned bonds of frequent issuers are rarely traded, leading dealers to quote bid–offer spreads of at least 10–20 basis points or more for small sizes. The most recently issued, or on-the-run, developed market sovereign bonds are typically the most liquid fixed-income securities, with primary dealers making active markets in large size with bid–offer spreads equal to a fraction of a basis point. Among corporate issuers, recently issued corporate bonds from frequent issuers of higher credit quality usually exhibit the greatest liquidity and tightest bid–offer spreads.

LEARNING MODULE

4

Fixed-Income Markets for Corporate Issuers

LEARNING OUTCOMES	
Mastery	***The candidate should be able to:***
☐	compare short-term funding alternatives available to corporations and financial institutions
☐	describe repurchase agreements (repos), their uses, and their benefits and risks
☐	contrast the long-term funding of investment-grade versus high-yield corporate issuers

INTRODUCTION

1

Previous modules described various types of fixed-income issuers and investors. In this module, we focus on the corporate fixed-income sector, composed of instruments issued by financial institutions and non-financial corporate issuers across the time-to-maturity and credit spectrums. These instruments account for a significant portion of total debt issuance and debt outstanding globally.

LEARNING MODULE OVERVIEW

- Non-financial corporations frequently use short-term external funding in the form of bank loans and securities, such as commercial paper to meet cash needs.
- Financial institutions rely on deposits, interbank markets, commercial paper, and repurchase agreements (repos) as primary sources of short-term funding.
- Commercial paper is a short-term unsecured promissory note issued by both financial institutions and non-financial corporations.
- A repurchase agreement (repo) is a form of short-term secured lending that involves the sale and simultaneous agreement to buy back a security at a pre-agreed future price.

- An investment-grade bond has a significant proportion of its yield-to-maturity (YTM) attributed to the government benchmark yield due to its strong ability to meet promised interest and principal obligations from operating cash flows.
- High-yield issuers are characterized by a higher expected likelihood of financial distress. Relative to investment-grade bonds, a higher proportion of their bonds' YTM is attributed to an issuer-specific spread over the government benchmark yield.

LEARNING MODULE SELF-ASSESSMENT

These initial questions are intended to help you gauge your current level of understanding of this learning module.

1. Which of the following financing instruments provides the *most* reliable source of short-term bank funding for a non-financial corporation?

   A. Revolving credit agreement

   B. Committed bank line of credit

   C. Uncommitted bank line of credit

   Solution:

   A is correct. Revolving credit agreements, also referred to as revolvers, are the most reliable source of short-term bank funding.

   B is incorrect. While committed lines of credit are a more reliable source of financing than uncommitted lines because they involve a formal written commitment, they are less reliable than revolvers. C is incorrect because uncommitted bank lines of credit are the least reliable form of bank borrowing for a company.

2. Identify the following statement as true or false. Justify your answer.

   In an unsecured loan, the lender requires the company to provide collateral in the form of an asset that is pledged against the loan.

   Solution:

   False. *Secured* loans are loans in which the lender requires the company to provide collateral in the form of an asset, such as a fixed asset that the company owns or high-quality receivables or inventory. These assets are pledged against the loan, and the lender files a security interest against them. This pledge or lien is added to the borrowing company's financial record and reflected on its credit report. Companies that lack sufficient credit quality to qualify for unsecured loans may attempt to obtain secured loans.

3. Relative to long-term debt and equity, repo funding provides which of the following benefits to a financial institution?

   A. Lower cost

   B. Longer-term financing

   C. Greater financial flexibility

   Solution:

   A is correct. Financial institutions must balance the low cost of repo funding with the greater financial flexibility of more costly longer-term financing alternatives, such as long-term debt and equity. B and C are incorrect because they are both benefits of long-term debt and equity.

4. Venus, Inc., a financial institution, and Bank A, a large regional bank, enter into a repurchase agreement in which Venus is the security seller and Bank A is the security buyer. The repo is subject to a 102% initial margin. Which of the following statements is correct?

   A. Bank A benefits from a long-term cash investment on a collateralized basis with minimal liquidity risk.

   B. Bank A could generate higher returns for longer repo terms and/or by accepting less liquid or lower-quality collateral.

   C. The repo transaction reduces Venus's funding requirement for the security to a fraction of the bond's purchase price.

   Solution:

   B is correct. Short-term repos with high-quality collateral (lowest risk) result in the lowest return; however, investors can expect higher returns for longer repo terms and/or by accepting less liquid or lower quality collateral.

   A is incorrect because Bank A benefits from a short-term (not long-term) cash investment on a collateralized basis with minimal liquidity risk.

   C is incorrect because the repo transaction reduces Bank A's (not Venus's) funding requirement for the security to a fraction of the bond's purchase price due to the 102% initial margin.

5. An investor is analyzing three bonds for a potential investment: a AA rated bond, a B rated bond, and a CCC rated bond. Which of the bonds is *most appropriate* if the investor is seeking safety with few issuer restrictions?

   A. AA rated bond

   B. B rated bond

   C. CCC rated bond

   Solution:

   A is correct. The AA rated bond is investment grade with low likelihood of default and minimal issuer restrictions. B and C are incorrect because the B rated and CCC rated bonds are considered high yield with equity-like risk attributes and often greater issuer restrictions.

6. A bond analyst would *most likely* consider the probability of default and loss given default for:

   A. an investment-grade bond because of its equity-like cash flow.

   B. a high-yield bond because of its higher expected likelihood of financial distress.

   C. an investment-grade bond because of the importance of financial ratios and credit ratings to determine the issuer's likelihood of default.

   Solution:

   B is correct. High-yield issuers are characterized by a higher expected likelihood of financial distress. Given the higher chance of default, these instruments are more equity-like in nature and analysts place a greater emphasis on the likelihood (probability) of default, potential loss given default, and the protections and secondary repayment sources that are available. A is incorrect because investment-grade bonds exhibit bond-like cash flows, for which there is a high probability of receiving the agreed-upon interest and principal payments. C is incorrect because investment-grade bond analysts use financial ratios and credit ratings to determine if and when an investment-grade issuer's likelihood of default will change and don't rely on probability of default or loss given default measures.

2 SHORT-TERM FUNDING ALTERNATIVES

☐ compare short-term funding alternatives available to corporations and financial institutions

Both non-financial corporations and financial institutions rely on borrowed capital to support their short-term activities. As discussed in an earlier module in the corporate issuers reading, corporations use external short-term financing to meet cash needs during their cash conversion cycle, preserve liquidity, and take advantage of supplier discounts.

Non-financial corporate sources and uses of short-term funding are summarized in Exhibit 1.

Exhibit 1: Sources and Uses of Short-Term Funding for Non-Financial Corporates

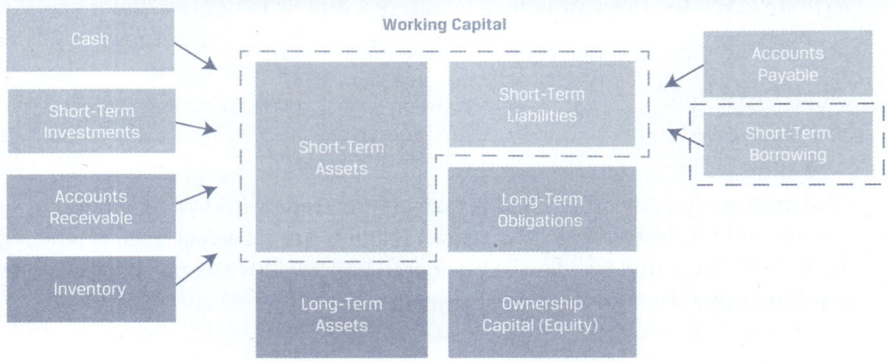

External Loan Financing

Non-financial corporations often rely on financial intermediaries for short-term financing. Common instruments include

- uncommitted bank lines of credit,
- committed bank lines of credit, and
- revolving credit agreements, or revolvers.

These can be unsecured or secured, depending on a company's financial strength, general credit situation, and jurisdiction. Uncommitted lines and revolvers are used more frequently in the United States, whereas regular committed lines are more common elsewhere. Credit lines typically offer the most flexible and immediate access to short-term funding.

Lines of Credit

Uncommitted lines of credit are the least reliable form of bank borrowing for a company, as the name suggests. A bank offers uncommitted credit lines up to a certain principal amount ("credit line") for a pre-determined maximum maturity, charging a base or market reference rate (MRR) plus an issuer-specific spread on only the principal outstanding for the period of use. Under normal business conditions, companies often find uncommitted bank credit lines to be the most flexible and least costly means of external funding. Banks usually offer these lines on an unsecured basis to clients who maintain stable cash deposits at the bank, allowing the banks to closely monitor and react to adverse borrower developments, such as declining account balances. Uncommitted credit lines require minimal capital reserves until they are drawn down and used, but banks reserve the right to refuse to honor any request for use of the line. Firms cannot therefore rely on uncommitted lines as a primary source of funding, because banks may choose not to lend if business or economic conditions deteriorate. Alternative funding sources may be difficult to obtain or are prohibitively expensive at times when uncommitted funding becomes unavailable. The primary attraction of uncommitted lines is that they do not require the company to pay any compensation other than interest on balances outstanding to the bank. From a bank perspective, these uncommitted lines of credit serve as valuable tools to maintain a long-term business relationship with the borrower through which the bank can monitor borrower activity. Funding for these lines often comes from stable deposits that the bank holds, allowing it to finance these lines using funds that depositors do not regularly touch.

Committed (regular) lines of credit are a more reliable source of financing than uncommitted lines because they involve a formal written commitment. Committed lines require more bank capital than uncommitted lines, although commitments of less than a year (usually 364 days) minimize a bank's capital requirement. For larger corporate borrowers, banks often further reduce the committed capital needed to support the line by forming a group of banks or a syndicate, which involves a mutual agreement to accept a pre-determined percentage of the total credit commitment and loan drawdown over time. When drawn, regular credit lines are short-term liabilities, usually classified as notes payable or the equivalent. Undrawn committed lines are sometimes used as a source of backup credit for other financing forms, such as short-term securities, as shown later.

Regular lines are unsecured and prepayable without penalty. Although they are a more reliable source of short-term funding than uncommitted lines, these commitments face the risk of renewal at maturity, particularly when heavily used and drawn by a borrower with weakening credit conditions. Unlike uncommitted lines, regular lines usually involve upfront costs in the form of a commitment fee (such as 0.50%) on either the full or unused amount of the line for the commitment period.

Revolving credit agreements, also referred to as "revolvers" (or "operating lines of credit"), are the most reliable source of short-term bank funding. These are multiyear credit commitments and lenders typically seek protections, such as covenants which require or restrict certain borrower actions as in the case of a bond indenture. Otherwise, revolvers have similar features to regular lines with respect to borrowing rates and commitment fees and may also include optional medium-term loan features.

Secured Loans and Factoring

Secured loans, also called asset-based loans, are loans in which the lender requires the company to provide collateral in the form of an asset, such as a fixed asset that the company owns or high-quality receivables, inventory, or marketable securities. These assets are pledged against the loan, and the lender files a security interest (or right to possess the asset until the loan is repaid) against them. This pledge or lien is added to the borrowing company's financial record and reflected on its credit report. Companies that lack sufficient credit quality to qualify for unsecured loans might arrange for secured loans.

A company can use its accounts receivable to generate cash flow through the assignment of accounts receivable, which is the use of receivables as collateral for a loan. Firms can also sell accounts receivable to a lender, called a factor, typically at a substantial discount. Under an assignment, the company remains responsible for the collection of the accounts, whereas in a **factoring arrangement**, the company shifts the credit-granting and collection process to the lender or factor. The cost of this credit (i.e., the amount of the discount) depends on the credit quality of the accounts and the collection costs. Similarly, inventory can be used in different ways as collateral for a loan.

External, Security-Based Financing

For some firms, loans can be more expensive than debt, secured or unsecured, issued in financial markets. Large, highly rated companies can issue short-term, unsecured notes known as **commercial paper** (CP) in the public market or via a private placement. Commercial paper issued by corporations typically matures in less than three months and can be used to fund working capital, seasonal demand for cash, or to provide **bridge financing** (i.e., interim financing that provides funds until permanent financing can be arranged).

In most cases, maturing commercial paper is paid with the proceeds of newly issued commercial paper (or "rolled over"). This practice raises the possibility that an issuer is unable to issue new paper at maturity, known as **rollover risk**. To minimize rollover risk, investors usually require a committed **backup line of credit** from banks, also referred to as a liquidity enhancement or backup liquidity lines. The purpose of the backup lines of credit is to ensure that the issuer can fully repay maturing commercial paper if a rollover is not possible. Given their short maturity, commercial paper markets adapt quickly to adverse credit events and defaults are relatively rare.

Apart from non-financial corporations, the largest commercial paper issuers include financial institutions, governments, and supranational agencies. Commercial paper issued in the international market is known as Eurocommercial paper (ECP). Although similar to United States commercial paper (USCP), typical ECP transaction sizes are much smaller and less liquid than the USCP market.

Short-Term Funding Alternatives for Financial Institutions

Common bank sources and uses of funding are shown in Exhibit 2. The short-term funding needs of financial institutions, such as banks, arise from their role as intermediaries between borrowers and depositors. In addition to cash and reserves, most bank assets are loans issued or securities purchased. Liabilities include deposits received from households and firms, securities sold, or short-term borrowing.

Exhibit 2: Bank Short-Term Funding Sources and Uses

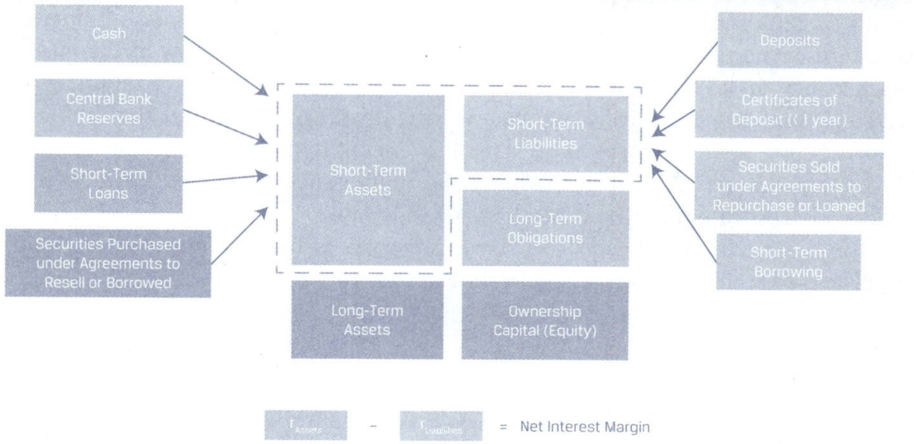

Deposits

Household (or retail) and commercial deposits are a primary source of short-term funding for most banks. These are usually in the form of **checking accounts**, or deposits with no stated maturity available for transactional purposes that pay little or no interest. Although these so-called demand deposit balances may be withdrawn at any time, fee rebates, uncommitted credit lines, and other services extended by banks under normal business conditions to their commercial customers allow them to rely on this stable source to meet both short-term and longer-term funding needs. For larger depositors, these so-called **operational deposits** generated by clearing, custody, and cash management activities are also a relatively stable source of funding, while rules requiring banks to maintain liquidity reserves against other less stable demand deposits make them a less attractive funding source.

Saving deposits are usually held for non-transactional purposes and often have a stated term. For example, a bank may accept a specific deposit with a pre-determined maturity and interest rate known as a **certificate of deposit** (CD). CDs typically have maturities shorter than one year and pay interest at maturity. A non-negotiable CD involves payment of principal and interest at maturity to the initial depositor, with a penalty for early withdrawal. Negotiable CDs allow a depositor to withdraw funds by selling the CD in the open market prior to maturity. A negotiable CD oriented toward the retail market is called a small-denomination CD, while large-denomination CDs are a common source of wholesale funding from institutional investors. As in the case of CP, CDs are traded in the Eurobond market.

Interbank Market

The **interbank market** involves short-term borrowing and lending among financial institutions on a secured or unsecured basis. Unsecured loans and deposits in the interbank market typically range from overnight to a one-year term at an interest rate closely tied to a market reference rate. Banks typically factor credit risk into the interest rate on these loans and deposits and impose counterparty limits as part of their credit risk management.

In most countries, banks and other financial institutions are required to maintain reserves at the central bank. While some banks may have excess funds over the minimum reserve requirement, others may run short of required reserves. This imbalance is solved through the **central bank funds market**, allowing banks with a surplus of funds to lend to others. The interest rate at which central bank funds are bought (i.e., borrowed) and sold (i.e., lent) is known as the **central bank funds rate**. Central banks target a specific rate or range of policy rates and use open market operations or interest paid on reserves to achieve it. A bank unable to borrow in the interbank market may do so directly from the central bank as a last resort (discount window lending), but this is typically associated with posting of collateral with the central bank and may lead to greater central bank oversight that can result in restrictions on the bank's activities to address the bank's liquidity issues. Such lending is offered at a higher interest rate than the central bank funds rate.

The most common form of secured interbank borrowing and lending involves repurchase agreements addressed in the next lesson.

Commercial Paper

Commercial paper issuance is dominated by large financial institutions, which use these *unsecured* notes to meet short-term borrowing needs and in some cases to fund longer-term balance sheet assets, such as loans. Approximately 60% of the annual issuance volume comes from financial institutions, and the remainder comes from non-financial corporate issuers. As in the case of non-financial corporations, banks also face rollover risk to the extent that their funding needs exceed the maturity of commercial paper outstanding.

Banks and other financial institutions also commonly use a *secured* form of commercial paper issuance known as **asset-backed commercial paper** (ABCP). Recall from an earlier lesson that in some cases, loans or receivables are sold to a special purpose entity (SPE) that issues debt and makes interest and principal payments from asset cash flows. Exhibit 3 shows an ABCP issuance in two simple steps (asset-backed securities will be covered in detail later). First, a bank agrees to transfer short-term loans to an SPE in exchange for cash. Second, the SPE issues ABCP to investors with a backup credit liquidity line provided by the bank.

Exhibit 3: Asset-Backed Commercial Paper Issuance

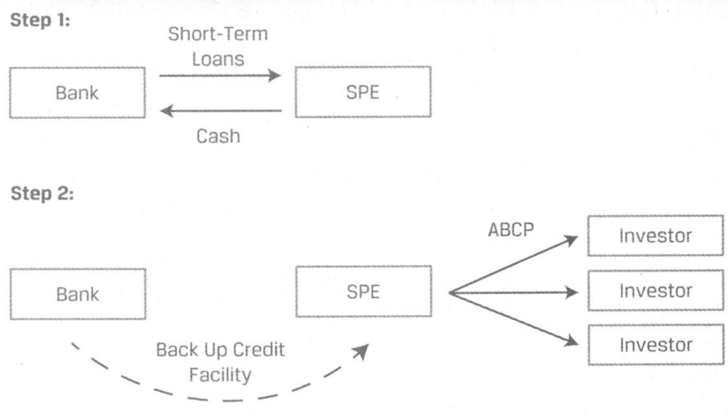

This financing is not recorded on the balance sheet of the issuer, and such off-balance-sheet financing benefits both the bank (as the SPE sponsor and backup credit provider) and investors. The bank receives cash when the commercial paper is issued and reduces its capital costs by providing undrawn backup liquidity instead of holding the short-term loans to maturity. Investors purchase a liquid, short-term note with interest and principal payments from a loan portfolio to which they would otherwise not have direct access.

The ABCP market experienced rapid growth prior to the Global Financial Crisis due in part to a significant increase in the funding of long-term assets using short-term notes. However, the inability of many issuers to roll ABCP at the height of the crisis caused numerous SPEs to fail. Following the crisis, the ABCP market reverted to primarily funding short-term, generally high-quality loans and receivables.

QUESTION SET

1. Pennington Corporation is a large pharmaceutical company with an investment-grade credit rating and uses Cavalier Bank for some of its financing needs. Pennington maintains stable cash deposits at Cavalier Bank and is seeking a short-term financing option with no upfront commitment fee. Which of the following financing options would be *most appropriate* for Pennington?

   A. Secured loan

   B. Committed bank line of credit

   C. Uncommitted bank line of credit

   Solution:

   C is correct. Banks offer uncommitted lines of credit on an unsecured basis to clients who maintain stable cash deposits at the bank, allowing the banks to closely monitor and react to adverse borrower developments, such as declining account balances. Uncommitted lines of credit also have no upfront commitment fee and are obtained by stronger companies, such as Pennington. A is incorrect because secured loans are obtained by companies that lack sufficient credit quality to qualify for unsecured loans. B is incorrect because committed lines of credit have upfront commitment fees.

2. Which of the following statements about revolvers is correct?

   A. Revolvers are the least reliable form of bank borrowing for a company.

   B. Revolvers are multiyear credit commitments where lenders typically seek covenants that require or restrict certain borrower actions.

   C. Revolvers usually involve upfront costs in the form of a commitment fee on either the full or the unused amount of the line for the commitment period.

   Solution:

   B is correct. Revolvers are multiyear credit commitments in which lenders typically seek protections, such as covenants, which require or restrict certain borrower actions, as in the case of a bond indenture. A is incorrect because uncommitted lines of credit are the least reliable form of bank borrowing for a company. C is incorrect because committed lines of credit, not revolvers, usually involve upfront costs in the form of a commitment fee on either the full or the unused amount of the line for the commitment period.

3. Which of the following would a commercial paper issuer *most likely* obtain to minimize rollover risk?

   A. Credit rating

   B. Bridge financing

C. Liquidity enhancement

Solution:

C is correct. To minimize rollover risk, investors usually require a liquidity enhancement to ensure that the issuer can fully repay maturing commercial paper if a rollover is not possible. B is incorrect because bridge financing, which is interim financing that provides funds until permanent financing can be arranged, would require additional issuance of commercial paper by the issuer, increasing rollover risk. A is incorrect because a credit rating does not affect rollover risk.

4. Which of the following statements about asset-backed commercial paper is correct?

   A. This financing is not recorded on the balance sheet of the issuer.

   B. The bank issues ABCP to investors with a backup credit liquidity line provided by the SPE.

   C. Investors purchase an illiquid, short-term note with interest and principal payments from the SPE.

Solution:

A is correct. This financing is not recorded on the balance sheet of the issuer. B is incorrect because the SPE (not the bank) issues ABCP to investors with a backup credit liquidity line provided by the bank. C is incorrect because investors purchase a *liquid*, short-term note from the SPE.

3 REPURCHASE AGREEMENTS

☐ describe repurchase agreements (repos), their uses, and their benefits and risks

An important source of *secured* short-term lending and borrowing is the repurchase agreement (repo) market. A **repurchase agreement**, or repo, involves the sale of a security with a simultaneous agreement by the seller to buy the same (or a similar) security back from the purchaser at an agreed-on **repurchase price** and future date called the **repurchase date**. Exhibit 4 shows the mechanics of a simple repurchase agreement.

Exhibit 4: Repurchase Agreement

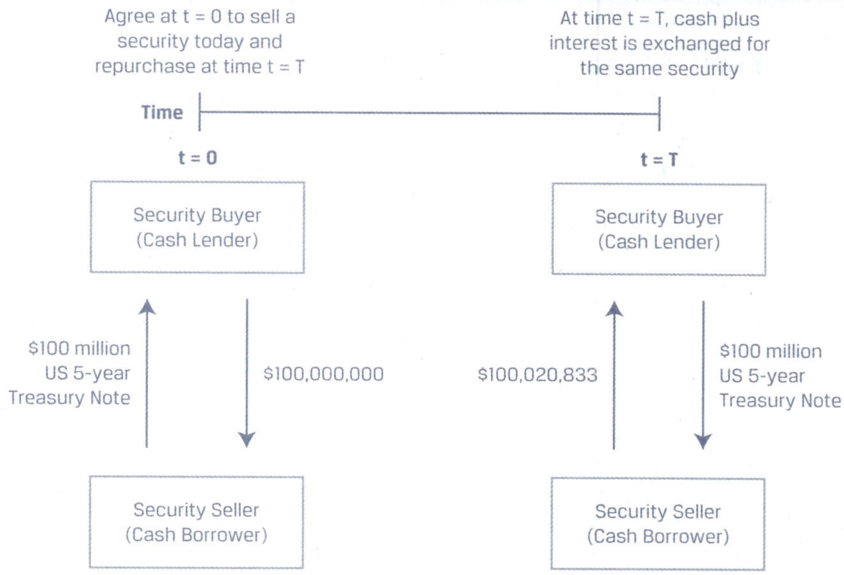

Assume that today ($t = 0$) the current US five-year Treasury note trades at a price equal to the bond's face value of USD100,000,000. The security *buyer* takes delivery of the US Treasury note today and pays the security *seller* USD100,000,000. If we assume a repo term of 30 days (and 360 days in a year) and an annual interest rate (or **repo rate**) of 0.25%, then the buyer agrees to return the Treasury note 30 days from today ($t = T$) to the seller at a repurchase price of USD100,020,833, calculated as follows:

$$\text{USD}100{,}000{,}000 \times [1 + (0.25\% \times 30/360)] = \text{USD}100{,}020{,}833.$$

In effect, the security seller borrows USD100,000,000 on a short-term basis at a low cost, with interest (USD20,833) paid at maturity, because the loan is collateralized by the US Treasury note.

The details of repo and other money market interest calculations are addressed in a later lesson. In a repo transaction, the seller of the security (cash borrower) retains ownership of the security over the repo term, as well as the interest and actual coupon paid by the security, while the security buyer (cash lender) receives the repo rate.

Because cash lenders in the repo market are primarily interested in both the liquidity and safety of their investments, most repos are typically very short-term transactions with the highest-quality securities (e.g., sovereign bonds) serving as collateral. Repo periods range from overnight to so-called **term repos**, those involving any maturity longer than one day. The underlying securities used in repo transactions are usually limited to the most liquid bonds with the lowest credit risk, such as sovereign bonds of various maturities. Rather than involving a specific security as in Exhibit 4, a repo transaction may instead reference a specific group of securities as eligible collateral (such as government bonds of a specific maturity) in what is known as a **general collateral repo** transaction. These transactions take place at the **general collateral repo rate**.

In addition to the high quality of underlying securities, repos include features designed to reduce the risk of a collateral shortfall over the contract life. One such feature is the provision of collateral in excess of the cash exchanged, known as **initial margin**, defined as the following ratio:

$$\text{Initial Margin} = \frac{\text{Security Price}_0}{\text{Purchase Price}_0}. \quad (1)$$

A 100% initial margin indicates a fully collateralized loan, while a higher margin indicates even greater initial collateral protection. This is alternatively considered a *reduction* or **haircut** of the underlying loan relative to the initial collateral value, which may be shown as follows:

$$\text{Haircut} = \frac{\text{Security Price}_0 - \text{Purchase Price}_0}{\text{Security Price}_0}. \quad (2)$$

The use of excess collateral is shown in the following repo example.

KNOWLEDGE CHECK

1. Assume the repurchase agreement in Exhibit 4 is subject to a 102% initial margin.

   Calculate the revised original purchase price (loan amount).

   Solution: Using an initial margin of 102%, we can solve for a revised purchase price using Equation 1:

   $$\text{Initial Margin} = \frac{\text{Security Price}_0}{\text{Purchase Price}_0}.$$

   $$102\% = \frac{\text{USD}100,000,000}{\text{Purchase Price}_0}.$$

   $$\text{Purchase Price}_0 = \text{USD}98,039,216.$$

   Note that security seller must finance the remaining USD1,960,784 from other sources.

2. Calculate the associated repo haircut.

   Solution: Using Equation 2, solve for the haircut as follows:

   $$\text{Haircut} = \frac{\text{Security Price}_0 - \text{Purchase Price}_0}{\text{Security Price}_0}.$$

   $$\text{Haircut} = \frac{\text{USD}100,000,000 - \text{USD}98,039,216}{\text{USD}100,000,000}.$$

   $$\text{Haircut} = 1.96\%.$$

3. Calculate the repurchase price using the same 30-day repo term and 0.25% repo rate.

   Solution: The repurchase price may be calculated as follows:

   $$\text{Repurchase price} = \text{USD}98,039,216 \times [1 + (0.25\% \times 30/360)].$$

   $$\text{Repurchase price} = \text{USD}98,059,641.$$

Repos address collateral value *changes* by granting contract participants the right to request additional collateral (or release existing collateral) to maintain a security interest equal to the original initial margin terms. This variable margin payment (referred to as **variation margin**) is equal to the difference between current margin required and the security's price at time *t*, as shown in Equation 3:

$$\text{Variation margin} = (\text{Initial margin} \times \text{Purchase price}_t) - \text{Security Price}_t. \quad (3)$$

For example, a security price *decline* requires a cash borrower (security seller) to provide additional collateral to the seller.

KNOWLEDGE CHECK

1. Assume the same repurchase agreement terms from Exhibit 4 and the previous Knowledge Check. Calculate the variation margin five days after trade inception if the price of the five-year US Treasury note rises to 103% of the security's USD100 million face value.

   Solution:

   Recall the original loan amount (or purchase price at $t = 0$) is equal to USD98,039,216, or USD100,000,000/1.02. We may solve for the purchase price when $t = 5$ as follows:

   $$\text{Purchase price} = \text{USD}98{,}039{,}216 \times [1 + (0.25\% \times 5/360)].$$

   $$\text{Purchase price} = \text{USD}98{,}042{,}620.$$

   To calculate the variation margin, we use Equation 3:

   $$\text{Variation margin} = (\text{Initial margin} \times \text{Purchase price}_t) - \text{Security price}_t.$$

   $$\text{Variation margin} = (102\% \times \text{USD}98{,}042{,}620) - \text{USD}103{,}000{,}000.$$

   $$\text{Variation margin} = -\text{USD}2{,}996{,}528.$$

   The security price increase to USD103,000,000 resulted in an overcollateralization of the loan by USD2,996,528, allowing the cash borrower (security seller) to request the release of five-year US Treasury notes with a face value of approximately USD2.91 million (= USD2,996,528/1.03).

Repo contract participants typically agree to margining and other terms, such as the substitutability of collateral and events of default, in a **master repurchase agreement** or similar legal document that governs all trades between parties.

Repurchase Agreement Applications and Benefits

Financial market participants use the repo market for three specific purposes:

- Finance the ownership of a security
- Earn short-term income by lending funds on a secured basis
- Borrow a security in order to sell it short

Financial institutions that trade securities often or hold securities inventory frequently participate in the repo market as security sellers or cash borrowers. For example, say an investor sells a bond to a bank's trading desk in exchange for cash. The bank must pay the investor immediately although it may intend to sell the security to another party at a later time. To do so, the bank may borrow the purchase price from another bank or an asset manager in exchange for delivering the bond just purchased. The repo transaction reduces the bank's funding requirement for the security to a fraction (equal to the initial margin) of the bond's purchase price.

From a security buyer's perspective, a repo offers a short-term cash investment on a collateralized basis with minimal liquidity or default risk. Overnight cash repos with high-quality collateral result in the lowest return; investors can generate higher returns for longer repo terms or by accepting less liquid or lower quality collateral.

These investors include banks and other institutions, such as mutual funds or pension funds. As shown in Equation 4, these short-term assets appear on a bank's balance sheet as "Securities Purchased under Agreements to Resell or Borrowed."

Central banks are also active participants in the repo market to conduct monetary policy. While reserve requirements and the outright purchase and sale of securities are more permanent means of influencing the money supply, repo contracts are frequently used for shorter-term, transitory policy measures. For example, a central bank may temporarily increase cash reserves in the banking system by borrowing securities and lending cash.

Sometimes, a security buyer enters a repo not only to lend cash for interest but also to use the security for another use. For instance, a hedge fund may take a short position in a security, with a view that its price will decline. The use of a repo transaction to facilitate this transaction is shown in Exhibit 5.

Exhibit 5: Reverse Repos and Short Security Positions

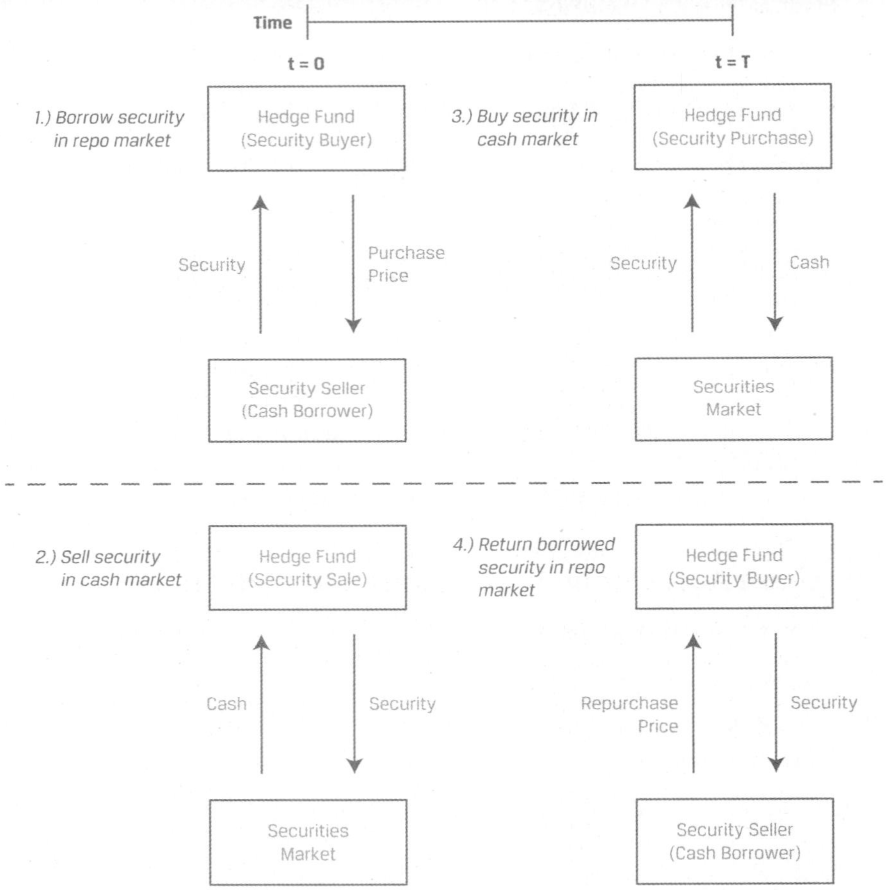

Exhibit 5 illustrates this transaction in four steps:

At time $t = 0$:

1. The hedge fund *borrows* the security in exchange for cash in a repo transaction.
2. The hedge fund simultaneously *sells* the security in the secondary market and receives cash.

At time $t = T$:

3. The hedge fund *purchases* the security in the secondary market and pays the current market price.
4. The hedge fund simultaneously *delivers* the security at the pre-agreed repurchase price for cash to settle the repo.

When viewed from the perspective of the security buyer (cash lender), a repo transaction is sometimes referred to as a **reverse repurchase agreement** or reverse repo.

KNOWLEDGE CHECK

1. Assume that a hedge fund enters the same repurchase agreement from Exhibit 4 as the security buyer (cash lender), sells the security short in the secondary market today, and buys back the security to deliver for repo settlement in 30 days. For purposes of this example, we exclude initial or variation margin.

   Calculate the hedge fund's return on the transaction if it is able to purchase the five-year US Treasury note in 30 days in the secondary market at a price equal to 99% of the face value.

   Solution:

   Follow the four steps in Exhibit 5:

   1. The hedge fund *borrows* the five-year US Treasury note priced at USD100,000,000 today and delivers USD100,000,000 in cash to the security seller in a repo transaction.

      As in Exhibit 4, the hedge fund (security buyer) agrees to return the five-year Treasury note 30 days from today to the seller at a repurchase price of USD100,020,833, calculated (using a 0.25% repo rate) as follows:

   $$\text{USD}100{,}000{,}000 \times [1 + (0.25\% \times 30)/360] = \text{USD}100{,}020{,}833.$$

   2. The hedge fund simultaneously *sells* the five-year US Treasury note in the secondary market today and receives USD100,000,000 in cash.
   3. In 30 days, the hedge fund purchases the five-year US Treasury note in the secondary market at the current market price of USD99,000,000.
   4. The hedge fund simultaneously *delivers* the five-year US Treasury note and receives the pre-agreed repurchase price of USD100,020,833 to settle the repo.

   The hedge fund has therefore earned a return of USD1,020,833 (= USD100,020,833 – USD99,000,000), ignoring transaction costs. The hedge fund's short position yields a profit because the price of the Treasury note fell over the time period.

Ignoring initial margin and other transaction costs, the hedge fund will earn a positive return if the short position gain exceeds the repo rate for the period. Note that such a repo transaction requires delivery of a particular security, known as a special trade, which occurs at a special collateral rate. When a particular security is subject to very high borrowing demand, this special repo rate may fall below the general collateral repo rate or even below zero. Under a negative repo rate, the security buyer *pays* interest on cash lent to the cash borrower.

Repo rates are influenced by several factors, including the following:

- Money market interest rates: Repo rates are correlated with other short-term interest rates. Central banks use secured repo markets to influence the unsecured central bank funds rate.
- Collateral quality: Higher collateral risk increases repo rates. Repo rates are usually higher for equity securities or emerging market bonds than for developed market government bonds.
- Repo term: Repo rates generally increase with maturity, because long-term rates exceed short-term rates under normal market conditions and a longer term increases credit risk.
- Collateral uniqueness: The higher the demand for a specific security, the lower the repo rate. The most recently issued or on-the-run developed market sovereign bonds typically have the lowest repo rates in a given market.
- Collateral delivery: Repo rates are usually higher when either the cash lent is undercollateralized or no collateral is provided to the funds lender.

Risks Associated with Repurchase Agreements

Repo markets are a widely used source of short-term funding, with relatively low borrowing costs relative to other financing available to banks and other financial institutions. However, repurchase agreements involve a number of structural risks, and excessive reliance on this form of secured financing under adverse market conditions can lead to financial distress or insolvency.

Each repo contract participant is exposed to the risk that the other party is unable to meet its obligations. While the secured nature of repo contracts reduces risk due to the value of the underlying collateral, several risks are important to consider:

- Default risk: Default risk is the primary exposure under a repo transaction, despite the existence of collateral. Collateral received from less creditworthy parties is more likely to be tested under a default scenario and may face illiquidity, adverse price changes, and legal or operational challenges.
- Collateral risk: In addition to minimizing liquidity and credit risks to ensure quick and efficient liquidation under a default, the collateral should have little or no correlation with the credit risk of the repo counterparty in order to diversify credit exposure.
- Margining risk: Proper and timely collateral valuation and transfer of variation margin to minimize collateral shortfalls in the event of liquidation following a default are important. Such adverse market conditions may also cause large changes in collateral value, increasing margin calls among market participants and forcing further liquidations.
- Legal risk: Addresses the ability to enforce legal rights under a repurchase agreement.
- Netting and settlement risk: Addresses the ability of repo contract participants to both offset or net the obligations of a non-defaulting party and take possession of collateral or cash in settlement of a trade.

In many cases, repo market participants manage these risks by engaging a third party. Repos executed directly between two parties are called bilateral repos; under a **triparty repo**, both parties agree to use a third-party agent for the transaction. While triparty agents do not change the credit risk relationship between repo participants in the event of default, they create cost efficiencies by providing access to a larger collateral pool and multiple counterparties, as well as specializing in the valuation and safekeeping of assets. The triparty agent (a custodian or clearinghouse) administers the transaction and is responsible for cash, securities, collateral valuation, and management, as well as collateral custody, as shown in Exhibit 6.

Exhibit 6: Bilateral versus Triparty Repo Agreements

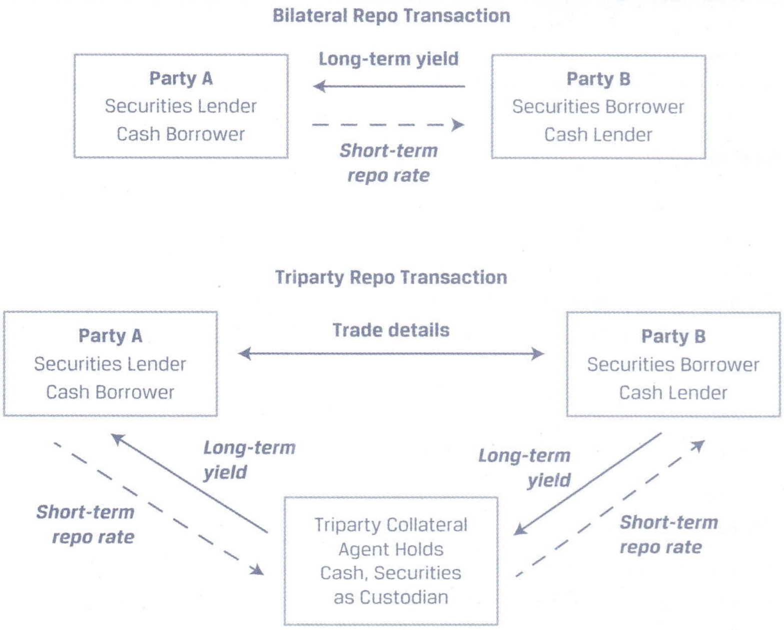

While the repo market represents a more stable funding source than short-term unsecured financing, both the uncommitted nature of repo markets and their very short (mostly overnight) maturity give rise to significant rollover and liquidity risks under adverse market conditions. Financial institutions must balance the low cost of repo funding with the greater financial flexibility of more costly longer-term financing alternatives, such as long-term debt and equity. In theory, the collateralized nature of repo transactions should provide cash lenders comfort to roll existing repo trades. In practice, financial firms that have lost the confidence of market participants have faced substantial losses and even bankruptcy during past financial crises due in part to their heavy reliance on repo financing.

THE FALL OF BEAR STEARNS AND THE REPO MARKET

Bear Stearns was the fifth-largest US investment bank, with USD350 billion in total assets at the end of 2006 and record revenue of over USD9 billion in that year. As a major underwriter of mortgage-backed securities (MBS) and subprime MBS, the firm faced challenges in 2007 as the MBS market deteriorated. The firm's losses mounted due to the failure of subprime mortgage hedge funds it had sponsored in July 2007 and the write-down of over USD2 billion in MBS it held later in the year, resulting in its first ever quarterly loss and a credit downgrade at the end of 2007.

At the same time, Bear Stearns significantly reduced its unsecured short-term funding (from USD25.8 billion at the end of 2006 to USD11.6 billion at the end of 2007) and specifically its commercial paper (USD20.7 billion to USD3.9 billion) in favor of secured funding–specifically, repo borrowing. As of 10 March

2008, Bear Stearns had USD18 billion in cash, but within two days, a loss of confidence due to the credit downgrade of related entities and market rumors caused this to fall to USD2 billion. Specifically, repo counterparties declined to roll over or renew repo trades, prime brokerage clients withdrew cash and securities, and other banks withdrew or refused to extend credit. On Friday, 14 March 2008, Bear Stearns received an emergency Federal Reserve loan against its securities collateral to prevent its failure, and on Monday, 17 March 2008, Bear Stearns agreed to be purchased by JPMorgan, which received a loan from the Federal Reserve.

QUESTION SET

1. Assume that today ($t = 0$) the current US five-year Treasury note trades at a price equal to the bond's face value of USD100,000,000. The security buyer takes delivery of the US Treasury note today and pays the security seller a purchase price based on an initial margin of 103%. The repo haircut is *closest* to:

   A. 0.00%.

   B. 2.91%.

   C. 3.00%.

   Solution:

   B is correct. Using an initial margin of 103%, the purchase price (loan amount) is calculated as USD100,000,000/1.03 = USD97,087,379.

   The repo haircut is then calculated as

   (USD100,000,000 − USD97,087,379)/USD100,000,000 = 2.91%.

2. Assume that today ($t = 0$) the current US five-year Treasury note trades at a price equal to the bond's face value of USD200,000,000. The security buyer takes delivery of the US Treasury note today and pays the security seller a purchase price based on an initial margin of 102%. Assume a repo term of 15 days (and 360 days in a year) and an annual interest rate (or repo rate) of 0.50%. If the buyer agrees to return the five-year Treasury note 15 days from today ($t = T$) to the seller, the repurchase price is closest to:

   A. USD196,119,281.

   B. USD196,160,130.

   C. USD200,041,667.

   Solution:

   A is correct. Using an initial margin of 102%, the purchase price (loan amount) is calculated as USD200,000,000/1.02 = USD196,078,431.

   The repurchase price is then calculated as follows:

   USD196,119,281 = USD196,078,431 × [1 + (0.50% × 15)/360].

   B is incorrect because it incorrectly uses a repo term of 30 days:

   USD196,160,130 = USD196,078,431 × [1 + (0.50% × 30)/360].

   C is incorrect because it does not incorporate the initial margin in calculating the purchase price:

   USD200,041,667 = USD200,000,000 × [1 + (0.50% × 15)/360].

3. Which of the following statements about repos is correct?

   A. Financial market participants use the repo market to earn short-term income by lending funds on a secured basis.

   B. Investors can generate higher returns for shorter repo terms.

   C. From a security buyer's perspective, a repo offers a short-term cash investment on a collateralized basis with significant liquidity or default risk.

   Solution:

   A is correct. Financial market participants use the repo market to earn short-term income by lending funds on a secured basis. B is incorrect because investors can generate higher returns for longer (not shorter) repo terms. C is incorrect because from a security buyer's perspective, a repo offers a short-term cash investment on a collateralized basis with minimal (not significant) liquidity or default risk.

4. Which of the following statements about repos is correct?

   A. Repo rates are correlated with other short-term interest rates.

   B. Repo rates are usually lower for equity securities or emerging market bonds than for developed market government bonds.

   C. Most recently issued or on-the-run developed market sovereign bonds typically have the highest repo rates in a given market.

   Solution:

   A is correct. Repo rates are correlated with other short-term interest rates. Central banks use secured repo markets to influence the unsecured central bank funds rate. B is incorrect because repo rates are usually higher for equity securities or emerging market bonds than for developed market government bonds. C is incorrect because the most recently issued or on-the-run developed market sovereign bonds typically have the lowest repo rates in a given market.

LONG-TERM CORPORATE DEBT

4

☐ contrast the long-term funding of investment-grade versus high-yield corporate issuers

Earlier lessons on corporate issuers addressed the uses of long-term debt, including more stable funding for short-term activities and long-term needs, such as capital investments. While corporate issuers face similar capital allocation and capital structure decisions when issuing long-term debt regardless of their credit quality, differences in credit give rise to different features and availability of long-term corporate funding. Recall that corporate issuers categorized as investment grade (IG) have a stronger capacity to meet future fixed obligations from cash flows, while the ability of high-yield (HY) issuers to meet debt interest and principal payments is considered more vulnerable. The relative credit quality of an issuer grows in importance for longer maturities as the likelihood of financial distress increases over time.

Similarities between Long-Term Investment-Grade and High-Yield Issuance

Both issuers and investors considering (non-callable) long-term debt of different maturities weigh the relative risk associated with a maturity choice against its costs or yield-to-maturity. Under normal market conditions, longer maturities are associated with both higher interest rates (yields-to-maturity on government bonds) and higher credit spreads for a given issuer. This is shown in Exhibit 7 by returning to the example of BRWA Corporation.

Exhibit 7: Maturity Choices of Long-Term Issuers and Investors

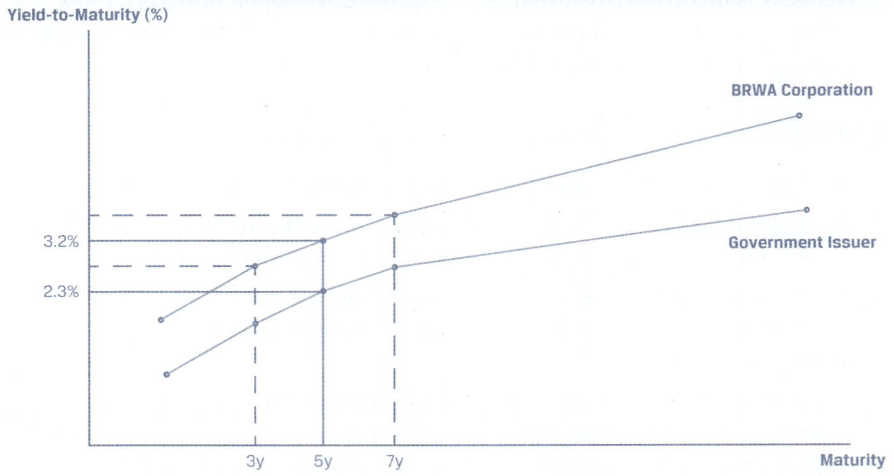

Exhibit 7 shows a partial yield curve for BRWA's bonds introduced earlier. Say an investor with a five-year investment horizon is instead attracted to the higher YTM of the seven-year BRWA bond. By investing in a bond whose maturity exceeds its planned investment horizon, the investor takes on the price risk of selling what will be a two-year bond in five years' time. Also note that the investor faces reinvestment risk, or the possibility that prevailing market interest rates at which the investor may invest funds received are lower than the original bond coupon rate. As an issuer, BRWA may, in contrast, be attracted to the lower YTM of a potential three-year issuance to fund a five-year project. However, in doing so, BRWA assumes rollover risk, or the possibility of having to refinance at higher interest rates when these bonds mature in three years. While these trade-offs for both investors and issuers exist for investment-grade and high-yield issuers alike, higher spreads associated with high-yield debt increase the risk-versus-return trade-off for issuers of lower credit quality. The change in a bond's price for a given change in yield for different maturities and investor returns over a specific horizon will be addressed in detail in later lessons.

Differences between IG and HY Issuance

The differences between investment-grade and high-yield corporate bonds go well beyond simply a difference in credit spreads to compensate investors for assuming more or less default risk. Exhibit 8 summarizes the differences between IG and HY bonds.

Exhibit 8: IG versus HY Bonds

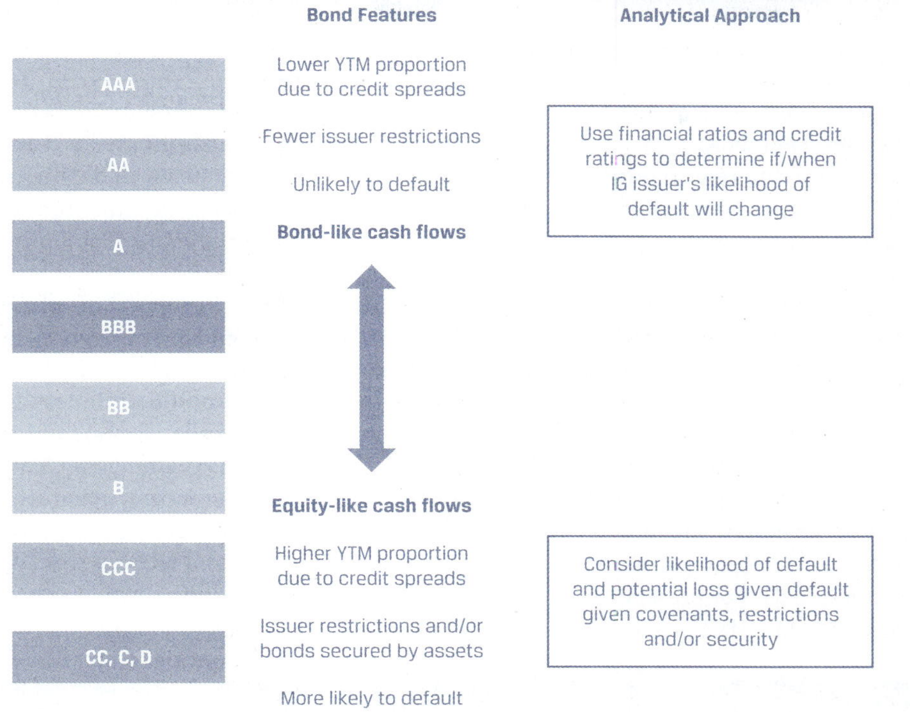

Given their strong ability to meet promised interest and principal obligations from operating cash flows, a significant proportion of the yield-to-maturity on an investment-grade bond is attributed to the government benchmark yield. High investor confidence that an IG issuer will be able to make debt service payments over time from operating cash flows typically allows these borrowers to issue debt with relatively little monitoring from bondholders throughout the debt term. Issuers are able to take advantage of a high degree of flexibility in choosing debt maturities (usually up to 30 years), which are accepted by investors with few or no restrictive covenants, as shown in Exhibit 9.

Exhibit 9: BRWA Restrictive Covenants

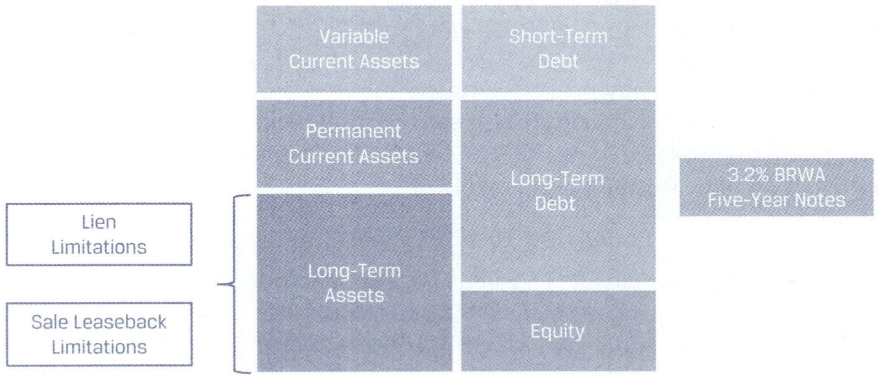

Because BRWA's senior unsecured notes rely solely on operating cash flows as a source of repayment, the restrictions on these investment-grade bonds are limited to those that broadly protect investor claims to the company's assets by preventing their sale and leaseback or pledge to a third party.

Investment-grade bonds are relatively standardized debt instruments, and issuers often have numerous general obligation unsecured bonds outstanding based on similar terms with different maturities at any given time. The most frequent IG debt issuers often minimize refinancing risk by staggering debt maturities over time, reducing rollover risk while preserving the ability to opportunistically raise more debt if market conditions allow.

High-yield issuers are characterized by a higher expected likelihood of financial distress, with a higher proportion of a bond's YTM attributed to an issuer-specific spread over the benchmark yield than for IG debt. Given the higher chance of default, these instruments are more equity-like in nature (i.e., uncertain cash flows) and analysts place a greater emphasis on the potential loss given default and the protections and secondary repayment sources that are available. As a result, investors generally impose more constraints on high-yield issuers. The debt covenants in a bond's indenture (or loan covenants in a loan agreement) establish the ability to monitor issuer financial performance based on predetermined criteria, allowing lenders to take actions to restructure debt or preserve creditor claims as needed. Exhibit 10 shows the restrictive covenants for VIVU's 6.5% seven-year callable bonds.

Exhibit 10: VIVU Restrictive Covenants

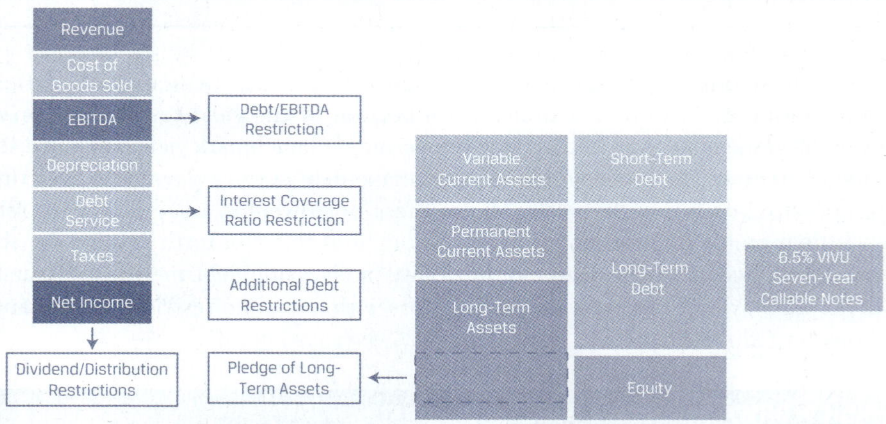

In contrast to BRWA's IG debtholders, who hold a general obligation unsecured bond and rely on operating cash flows as the source of repayment, as secured debtholders, VIVU investors hold a claim to specific pledged assets. This secondary repayment source aims to minimize losses in the more likely event of a default. The indenture also establishes limitations on additional debt and restrictions related to the level of debt versus operating cash flows and the distribution of net income to shareholders.

These investor restrictions and constraints result in far less HY issuer flexibility and market availability than for IG issuers. For example, VIVU's indenture introduced earlier prohibited the company from issuing additional debt under certain conditions unless the new debt is either subordinated or consists of short-term working capital up to 20% of the principal amount of notes outstanding. HY issuers also face limitations on debt maturities, which are typically shorter in maturity (10 years or less) and face greater fluctuations in both issuer-specific credit spreads and market availability over the economic cycle. Instead of financing opportunistically as market conditions allow, HY firms often must restructure debt and renegotiate covenants in order to take advantage of lower borrowing costs.

Issuers in the high-yield market often seek to retain financial flexibility by borrowing under leveraged loans with prepayment features or issuing bonds with contingency features. Recall that issuers of callable debt establish the right to redeem all or part of a bond prior to maturity at a fixed price. In the earlier VIVU example, the company issued 6.5% debt for seven years but owned the right to redeem bonds starting three years after issuance at an initial fixed price of 103.25% of principal. Borrowers who believe their creditworthiness will improve frequently choose to issue callable debt, because the value of this contingency feature rises as a firm's borrowing costs fall. Note that high-yield investors also benefit from higher bond prices (lower yields) as issuer-specific credit spreads fall, but in the case of callable debt, these gains are capped at the call price. For example, if VIVU were able to issue new debt in three years' time with financing cost savings that exceed the 3.25% call premium in present value terms, it would make sense for VIVU to call the bonds and issue new debt at a lower YTM. The relationship between the prices and yields of callable bonds and the different outcomes for high-yield issuers and investors are covered in detail later in the curriculum.

An important exception in the high-yield bond market is formerly investment-grade issuers known as "fallen angels," introduced earlier. While these borrowers' likelihood of financial distress is similar to that of other high-yield issuers, their outstanding debt has investment-grade features; that is, it is typically non-callable, with few restrictions and covenants and longer maturities. The reason for this is that the bonds were issued to investment-grade bond investors at a time when the borrower was highly rated. The subsequent deterioration in issuer credit quality results in losses to the original investors, many of whom must divest these bonds because they no longer meet minimum rating requirements for their portfolios. This can result in significant price deterioration because the market for high-yield bonds is a fraction of the size of the market for investment-grade bonds.

QUESTION SET

1. For a given issuer, longer maturities are typically associated with:

   A. lower interest rates and lower credit spreads.

   B. lower interest rates and higher credit spreads.

   C. higher interest rates and higher credit spreads.

   Solution:

   C is correct. Under normal market conditions, longer maturities are associated with both higher interest rates and higher credit spreads for a given issuer. A and B are incorrect because longer maturities are typically associated with higher interest rates and higher credit spreads.

2. Which of the following is a reason why a high-yield issuer may elect to issue equity as opposed to bonds?

   A. High-yield bond maturities are limited to 30 years or less.

   B. High-yield issuers face numerous restrictions when issuing debt.

C. High-yield bond analysts use financial ratios and credit ratings to determine when a high-yield issuer's credit rating is likely to change.

Solution:

B is correct. High-yield issuers face numerous restrictions when issuing debt; however, there are limited restrictions when issuing equity. A is incorrect because high-yield bond maturities tend to be limited to 10 years (not 30 years) or less whereas there is no maturity date on equity. C is incorrect because investment-grade bond analysts use financial ratios and credit ratings to determine when an investment-grade issuer's credit rating is likely to change.

3. Relative to investment-grade bonds, high-yield bonds exhibit:

   A. less market availability.

   B. more bond-like cash flows.

   C. fewer constraints by investors.

Solution:

A is correct. Investor restrictions and constraints on HY issuers lead to less market availability than for IG issuers. B is incorrect because high-yield bonds exhibit more equity-like cash flows. C is incorrect because high-yield bonds exhibit more restrictions and constraints by investors.

4. Which of the following statements about high-yield bonds relative to investment-grade bonds is correct?

   A. High-yield bonds have more bond-like cash flows.

   B. Investment-grade bonds have greater issuer restrictions.

   C. High-yield bonds have a higher proportion of YTM attributed to a credit spread.

Solution:

C is correct. High-yield bonds have a higher proportion of YTM attributed to a credit spread, while investment-grade bonds have a lower proportion of YTM attributed to a credit spread. A is incorrect because high-yield bonds have more equity-like cash flows while investment-grade bonds have more bond-like cash flows. B is incorrect because investment-grade bonds have fewer issuer restrictions than high-yield bonds.

5. Which of the following statements about fallen angels is correct?

   A. Their outstanding debt has high-yield bond features.

   B. Their likelihood of financial distress is similar to that of other high-yield issuers.

   C. The improvement in issuer credit quality results in gains to the original investors.

Solution:

B is correct. Fallen angels' likelihood of financial distress is similar to that of other high-yield issuers. A is incorrect because their outstanding debt has investment-grade (not high-yield) bond features; they are typically non-callable, with few restrictions and covenants and longer maturities. C is incorrect because the deterioration (not improvement) in issuer credit quality results in losses (not gains) to the original investors, many of whom must divest these bonds because they no longer meet minimum rating requirements. This can result in significant price deterioration because the high-yield bond market is a fraction of the size of the investment-grade bond market.

PRACTICE PROBLEMS

1. Which of the following is a benefit to a bank that makes short-term loans and issues asset-backed commercial paper?

   A. The bank receives commercial paper when the ABCP is issued.

   B. Capital costs are reduced by providing undrawn backup liquidity instead of holding the short-term loans to maturity.

   C. The bank purchases a liquid, short-term note with interest and principal payments from a short-term loan portfolio to which it would otherwise not have direct access.

2. Ewing Corp. is a large corporation that has an existing relationship with Sycamore Bank. Ewing is seeking short-term financing from a committed line of credit; however, Sycamore will offer only an uncommitted line of credit. Which of the following *best* supports Sycamore's decision?

   A. Sycamore will receive an upfront commitment fee on the uncommitted line of credit.

   B. Sycamore will require less bank capital for the uncommitted line than for the committed line of credit.

   C. Sycamore can form a syndicate to reduce the amount of committed capital needed under an uncommitted line of credit.

3. Assume that today ($t = 0$) the current US five-year Treasury note trades at a price equal to the bond's face value of USD50,000,000. The security buyer takes delivery of the US Treasury note today and pays the security seller USD50,000,000. Assume a repo term of 45 days (and 360 days in a year) and a repo rate of 0.375%. If the buyer agrees to return the five-year Treasury note 45 days from today ($t = T$) to the seller, the repurchase price is *closest* to:

   A. USD50,015,625.

   B. USD50,023,438.

   C. USD50,187,500.

4. A transaction where a hedge fund enters into a repo by taking a short position in a security with a view that its price will decline relative to the price of another security held is *best* described as:

   A. a reverse repo.

   B. a triparty repo.

   C. financing the ownership of a security.

5. Which of the following is *not* a reason why issuers elect to issue long-term debt as opposed to short-term debt?

   A. More stable funding for short-term activities

   B. Lower interest rates for longer maturities for a given issuer

C. More stable funding for long-term needs, such as capital investments

5. Which of the following statements about high yield is correct?

   A. High-yield investors benefit from higher bond prices as issuer-specific credit spreads fall, but in the case of callable debt, these gains are capped at the original purchase price.

   B. Issuers in the high-yield market seek to retain financial flexibility by borrowing under leveraged loans with prepayment features or issuing bonds with contingency features.

   C. Issuers who believe that their creditworthiness will decline frequently choose to issue callable debt, because the value of this contingency feature rises as a firm's borrowing costs rise.

SOLUTIONS

1. B is correct. The bank will reduce capital costs by providing undrawn back-up liquidity instead of holding the short-term loans to maturity. A is incorrect because the bank receives cash when the ABCP is issued, which increases the bank's return. C is incorrect because investors purchase a liquid, short-term note with interest and principal payments from a short-term loan portfolio to which it would otherwise not have direct access.

2. B is correct. Committed lines require more bank capital than uncommitted lines, although commitments of less than a year (usually 364 days) minimize a bank's capital requirement. A is incorrect because Sycamore will receive an upfront commitment fee on a committed line of credit. C is incorrect because Sycamore can form a syndicate to reduce the amount of committed capital needed under a committed line of credit.

3. B is correct. USD50,023,438 is calculated as:

   USD50,000,000 × [1 + (0.375% × 45/360)] = USD50,023,438.

   In effect, the security seller borrows USD50,000,000 on a short-term basis at a low cost, with interest (USD23,438) paid at maturity, because the loan is collateralized by the US Treasury note.

   A is incorrect because a repo term of 30 days, as opposed to 45 days, is incorrectly used:

   USD50,000,000 × [1 + (0.375% × 30/360)] = USD50,015,625.

   C is incorrect because the repo term and number of days in a year are not used:

   USD50,000,000 × (1 + 0.375%) = USD50,187,500.

4. A is correct. When viewed from the perspective of the security buyer (cash lender), a repo transaction is referred to as a reverse repurchase agreement or reverse repo. B is incorrect because under a triparty repo, both parties agree to use a third-party agent for the transaction. C is incorrect because financing the ownership of a security is not the purpose undertaken by the hedge fund.

5. B is correct. Under normal market conditions, longer maturities are associated with both higher interest rates (yields-to-maturity on government bonds) and higher credit spreads for a given issuer. A is incorrect because long-term debt provides more stable funding for short-term activities. C is incorrect because long-term debt provides more stable funding for long-term needs, such as capital investments.

6. B is correct. Issuers in the high-yield market often seek to retain financial flexibility by borrowing under leveraged loans with prepayment features or issuing bonds with contingency features, such as callable debt. A is incorrect because high-yield investors benefit from higher bond prices as issuer-specific credit spreads fall, but in the case of callable debt, these gains are capped at the call price and not the original purchase price. C is incorrect because issuers who believe that their creditworthiness will not decline frequently choose to issue callable debt, because the value of this contingency feature rises as a firm's borrowing costs fall.

LEARNING MODULE

5

Fixed-Income Markets for Government Issuers

LEARNING OUTCOMES

Mastery	The candidate should be able to:
☐	describe funding choices by sovereign and non-sovereign governments, quasi-government entities, and supranational agencies
☐	contrast the issuance and trading of government and corporate fixed-income instruments

INTRODUCTION

1

In this module, we complete the review of major fixed-income sectors by focusing on public sector issuers, including sovereign and non-sovereign governments, and how they differ from private sector issuers. Sovereign governments are distinguished by their right to tax within a jurisdiction, while non-sovereign, quasi-government, and supranational issuers may rely on local taxes, fee-based revenue, or other sources of repayment. Sovereign debt issuance is usually conducted through scheduled public auctions, with a different role for financial intermediaries than in private sector issuance. Sovereign debt securities are the most common benchmark securities used in pricing and valuation analyses for fixed-income instruments.

LEARNING MODULE OVERVIEW

- National or sovereign government issuers are distinguished by their legal authority to establish and maintain a country's public goods and services, as well as their ability to tax economic activity in their jurisdictions. Developed market sovereign issues are characterized by a strong, stable, well-diversified domestic economy, and emerging market sovereign issuers are usually characterized by higher growth but less stable and less well-diversified economies subject to greater fluctuations over the economic cycle.

- Sovereign debt issues include short-term securities (with maturities ranging from 1 to 12 months), medium- and long-term notes and bonds, and bonds that are guaranteed but not directly issued by the sovereign government.
- Issuance of sovereign debt usually takes the form of a public auction using standard procedures led by the national treasury or finance ministry, while corporate debt issuances are managed by investment bank underwriters on behalf of issuers. Sovereign governments designate a group of financial intermediaries as primary dealers that are required to participate in all auctions with competitive prices.
- Once a government debt auction is announced, prospective investors submit competitive or non-competitive bids. Once issued, sovereign debt is usually traded in a manner similar to private sector debt securities, primarily in OTC markets through financial intermediary broker/dealers.
- The level and type of non-sovereign government funding vary widely among countries, depending on whether specific goods and services are provided and financed at the national, regional, or local level.
- Agencies are quasi-government entities that issue debt in order to fund the government-sponsored provision of specific public goods or services based on sovereign or local law. Supranational organizations are created and supported by sovereign governments in pursuit of a common objective.

LEARNING MODULE SELF-ASSESSMENT

These initial questions are intended to help you gauge your current level of understanding of this learning module.

1. Complete the sentence by selecting the correct words from the options given.

   A nation's fiscal policy determines the (*level/composition*) of sovereign debt through central government spending, and government debt management policies address the (*level/composition*) of sovereign debt—that is, short term versus long term, as well as other features.

   Solution:

   A nation's fiscal policy determines the *level* of sovereign debt through central government spending, and government debt management policies address the *composition* of sovereign debt—that is, short term versus long term, as well as other features.

2. The issuer ranks bids by prices, choosing bids from highest to lowest until the desired issuance amount is reached, for:

   A. single-price auctions.

   B. multiple-price auctions.

C. single-price and multiple-price auctions.

Solution:

C is correct. For both a single-price and a multiple-price auction, the issuer ranks bids by prices, choosing bids from highest to lowest until the desired issuance amount is reached.

3. Compare the role of financial intermediaries when engaging with sovereign issuers versus corporate debt issuers.

Solution:

Sovereign issuers engage with financial intermediaries, like corporate debt issuers, but in a different form. Sovereign governments designate a group of financial intermediaries as primary dealers that are required to participate in all auctions with competitive prices, often serve as the central bank's counterparty for open market operations, and facilitate the purchase and sale of government debt by foreign central banks and other indirect bidders. Corporate debt issuances, in contrast, are managed by investment bank underwriters on behalf of issuers.

4. The ability of ________________________ government issuers to access funding across maturities is affected by the predictability and stability of sources of repayment.

A. Sovereign

B. Non-sovereign

C. Both sovereign and non-sovereign

Solution:

C is correct. Borrowing costs and access to financing for both sovereign and non-sovereign government issuers are affected by their credit quality.

5. Identify the following statement as true or false. Justify your answer.

Sovereign agencies, such as the Airport Authority of Hong Kong (AAHK) and the Government National Mortgage Association (Ginnie Mae), benefit from the full liquidity premium associated with sovereign debt.

Solution:

False. While each of these sovereign agencies is typically able to borrow at a yield-to-maturity near that of their sovereign guarantor, neither will benefit from the full liquidity premium associated with sovereign debt.

SOVEREIGN DEBT 2

☐ describe funding choices by sovereign and non-sovereign governments, quasi-government entities, and supranational agencies

National or sovereign government issuers are distinguished by their legal authority to establish and maintain a country's public goods and services and their ability to tax economic activity in their jurisdiction. Additional sources of repayment for their debt obligations include tariffs, usage fees, and cash flows from government-owned enterprises. The size and scope of public goods and services provided by national, versus regional or local, governments vary widely among markets, as does the degree of government involvement in the economy. Similar to private sector issuers, a government's "economic balance sheet" may be used to illustrate the sources and uses of funding, as shown in Exhibit 1, which also includes activities of the central bank.

Exhibit 1: Government "Balance Sheet"

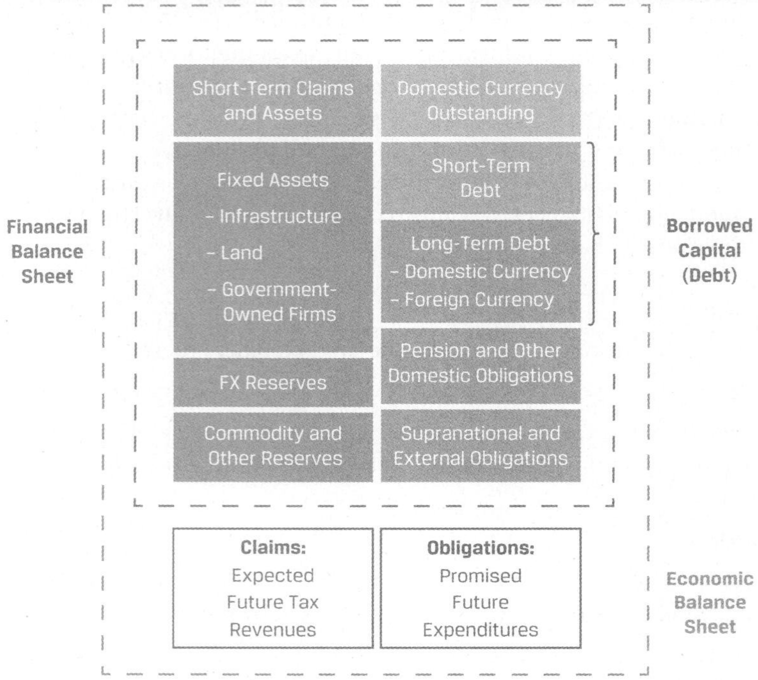

While private issuers prepare and file periodic financial statements in accordance with generally accepted accounting principles (GAAP), public sector financial accounting standards vary widely and are often prepared using cash, rather than accrual-based, principles, typically excluding such items as the depreciation of fixed public goods, such as federal highways, or the accrual of unfunded liabilities, such as government pension obligations. In contrast, the economic balance sheet in Exhibit 1 includes expected future claims and obligations and is therefore of greater relevance for public versus private sector issuers.

The relative size of the government sector as a proportion of the domestic economy varies widely among nations, and the allocation of these activities between the national government itself, quasi-government agencies, and local governments also differs among countries. As a result, this gives rise to non-sovereign issuers based in the same jurisdiction as the sovereign issuer, a topic discussed in Lesson 3.

A key distinction among national government issuers is the difference between developed market and emerging market sovereign issuers.

- *Developed market (DM) sovereign issuers:* DMs are characterized by a strong, stable, well-diversified domestic economy. DM national government budgets primarily comprise consistent, recurrent outlays financed with broad-based individual and business tax cash flows, resulting in stable and transparent fiscal policy. DM fixed-income securities are denominated in a major currency commonly held in reserve by foreign governments. These features allow DM sovereign governments to issue what is often referred to as default-risk-free debt with unconstrained market access across the maturity spectrum.

- *Emerging market (EM) sovereign issuers:* EMs are usually characterized by higher growth but less stable and less well-diversified economies subject to greater fluctuations over the economic cycle. EMs often depend on a dominant domestic industry or industries, such as commodities, and may involve more state-owned or state-controlled enterprises. Central government budget priorities may involve investments to expand economic and social infrastructure that exceed current domestic tax cash flows, giving rise to external or supranational funding. EM sovereign debt securities are often denominated in a **restricted domestic currency**, or one with limited convertibility into other currencies due to illiquidity. Currency restrictions may limit foreign investment and constrain access to longer-term maturities in domestic currency.

In the case of emerging market sovereign issuers, it is important to further distinguish between *domestic* debt issued in the domestic currency and **external debt**, or debt owed to foreign creditors. Sovereign bonds issued in domestic currency are often held mostly by domestic financial institutions and other domestic investors.

External debt of emerging and frontier market sovereign issuers comprises debt from supranational financial organizations and debt issuance denominated in a foreign currency held by foreign private investors. Earlier modules cited examples of emerging market sovereign Eurobond issuance, such as Romania's euro-denominated bond and the quasi-government PT Indonesia Infrastructure Finance US dollar–denominated bond. Investors based in developed markets who purchase these bonds do not face the same *direct* currency risk as for domestic currency emerging market sovereign debt. However, they face *indirect* exposure to currency fluctuations, because their returns depend on an issuer's ability to generate foreign currency revenue through international capital, goods, and services flows sufficient to meet foreign currency interest and principal payments. The following example highlights the case of the government of Sri Lanka's external debt.

GOVERNMENT OF SRI LANKA EXTERNAL DEBT

In May 2022, Sri Lanka became the first Asia-Pacific country in many years to default on its external debt when it failed to make USD78 million in foreign currency interest payments following a 30-day grace period. Sri Lanka's government debt rose sharply in the years preceding the default due in large part to infrastructure projects financed by global debt markets, supranational agencies, and major trading partners. Total government debt outstanding rose from 87% of Sri Lanka's GDP to over 100% in 2020, while both its economy and foreign currency reserves shrank during that year due to a collapse in tourism and declining remittances from citizens working abroad. Higher inflation and commodity prices in the wake of the 2022 war in Ukraine compounded the country's external debt problems and ultimately led to default.

Sri Lanka's External Debt, 2021

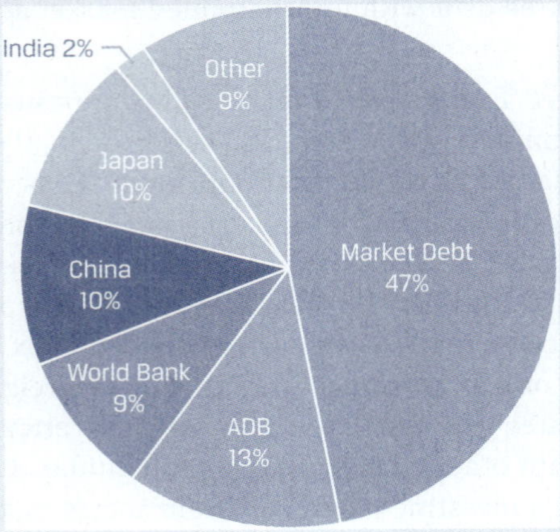

Note: "Market Debt" is primarily international sovereign bonds denominated in US dollars and owned by foreign private investors, including mutual funds.

Sources: Government of Sri Lanka, Department of External Resources (www.erd.gov.lk). Lilian Karunungan and Amelia Pollard, "Sri Lanka Falls into Default for the First Time Ever," Bloomberg (19 May 2022). Bank for International Settlements, "Debt Securities Statistics." "Infrastructure Financing in Sri Lanka: Lessons Learnt and Future Collaborations," European Institute for Asian Studies Policy Brief 16/2021.

A nation's fiscal policy determines the *level* of sovereign debt through central government spending, including both budgetary requirements and debt service costs, against tax receipts, fees, and revenue from government-owned enterprises or other sources. Government budget deficits increase the need for borrowing while surpluses reduce borrowing needs. Forecasts of sovereign debt levels must consider not only changes in fiscal policy but also the sensitivity of expenditures and revenues to changes in economic growth and inflation.

Government debt management policies address the *composition* of sovereign debt—that is, short term versus long term, as well as other features. Sovereign debt issues include the following:

- Short-term securities (with maturities ranging from 1 to 12 months), often known as Treasury bills, which are usually zero-coupon instruments sold at a discount to par.
- Medium- and long-term securities often known as Treasury notes and bonds. Fixed-rate coupon instruments in the domestic currency are most common, but sovereigns also issue floating-rate, inflation-linked, and foreign currency instruments.
- While not acting as the issuer, some sovereign governments guarantee certain other instruments that, in effect, make them a type of sovereign debt. The most prominent example is mortgage-backed securities, especially in the United States, that conform to certain criteria. Such instruments will be discussed in detail later.

Given the sovereign right to levy taxes on economic activity, national governments represent the lowest default risk among domestic currency issuers and are usually the largest bond issuer in a domestic market.

Recall from earlier in the corporate issuers reading that the Modigliani–Miller (MM) theorem stated that under certain strict conditions, a company's choice of capital structure is irrelevant in determining the present value of the firm's expected future cash flows. In the case of sovereign government debt, the Ricardian equivalence theorem introduced in an earlier economics lesson, which was based on similar simplified assumptions, gives an analogous result: a government's choice of debt maturity is irrelevant in determining the present value of future tax cash flows.

Under Ricardian equivalence, taxpayers expect government debt to be offset by higher future taxes, suggesting that a sovereign government should be indifferent between collecting taxes today or raising debt of any maturity based on the following assumptions:

- Taxpayers smooth consumption over time, saving expected future taxes today for future payment.
- Taxpayers form rational expectations that today's tax cuts will result in future tax increases.
- Capital markets are perfect with no transaction costs, and taxpayers can freely borrow and lend.
- Taxpayers are altruistic on an intergenerational basis; that is, they pass on tax savings to descendants.

The relaxation of these Ricardian equivalence assumptions to allow imperfect capital markets and friction costs between bond investors and taxpayers gives rise to debt management policies that offer liquidity benefits to investors and other issuers across the maturity spectrum.

For example, short-term government issuance provides investors with a high degree of liquidity and safety and often substitutes for bank deposits. Under normal market conditions, the prices of these very short-term government securities involve a liquidity premium; that is, their yields-to-maturity will tend to be *lower* than they otherwise would be in the absence of this liquidity benefit. While short-term sovereign debt is typically issued at regular intervals (discussed later) and standard maturities, government issuers have a high degree of flexibility to alter the size of these periodic auctions to manage uncertain cash flows, such as near-term tax receipts or unforeseen funding needs.

Strict adherence to Ricardian equivalence assumptions suggests that governments should fund themselves with the shortest possible maturity to minimize borrowing costs and avoid paying any term premium associated with longer-term interest rates. However, similar to the example of corporate bonds in the prior module, excessive government reliance on short-term funding introduces rollover risk, or uncertain refinancing costs, increasing the variability of budget costs and therefore tax rates. Since taxpayers are unable to perfectly smooth consumption over time nor do they form rational expectations about current versus future taxes across generations, fiscal instability creates uncertainty in future tax rates and threatens the stability of economic growth over time. Therefore, in practice, governments seek to minimize interest rate and rollover risks by distributing debt across maturities, while issuing debt in regular, predictable intervals.

Fiscal policies differ significantly across the 38 OECD member countries, but their sovereign debt maturity structures have shown far less variance. At the end of 2021, the weighted average maturity across the OECD was just over one year higher than the average at the end of 2007. Long-term debt represented 85% of total sovereign debt outstanding, largely unchanged since 2007, while annual issuance was evenly split between short and long term (short-term debt must be issued more frequently because it matures sooner). This time frame includes two major recessions and significant sovereign debt issuance.

Average Time to Maturity of OECD Nations' Sovereign Debt Outstanding (Years)

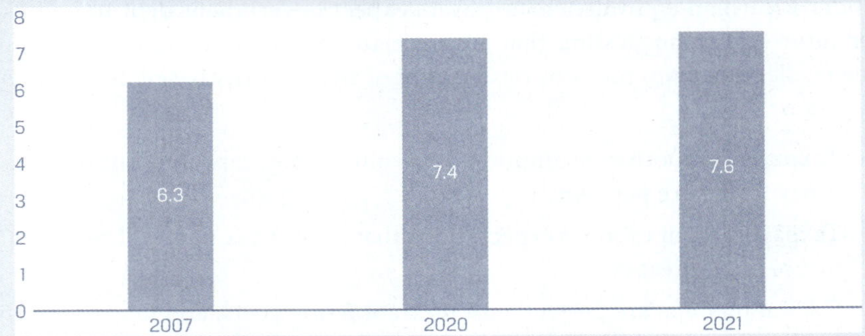

Maturity Structure of OECD Nations' Sovereign Government Debt Outstanding (Percent)

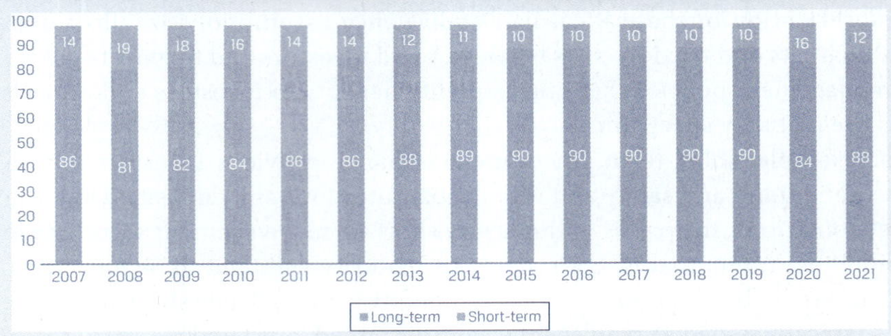

Source: OECD, "OECD Sovereign Borrowing Outlook 2022" (2022). https://doi.org/10.1787/b2d85ea7-en.

The use of medium- and long-term sovereign funding issuance must balance the trade-off of higher borrowing costs with greater fiscal stability, while considering liquidity or other benefits of issuing bonds with the lowest default risk across the maturity spectrum.

The benefits of issuing sufficient longer-term sovereign government securities to maintain liquidity across maturities include the following:

- *Establishment of a risk-free benchmark for all debt of specific maturities:* The first fixed-income module demonstrated the use of sovereign bond yields to calculate an issuer's credit risk premium. Government debt policies often mandate the regular issuance of benchmark securities across maturities to increase capital market efficiency and transparency for private issuers.
- *Use in managing and hedging market interest rate risk:* Market participants such as financial intermediaries and asset managers use medium- to long-term government securities and related derivatives to manage interest rate risk separately from credit risk.
- *Preferred use as collateral in repo and derivative transactions:* Longer-term government securities are the most common form of collateral for both repo and derivative transactions due to their high degree of liquidity and safety. Recall from the prior learning module that repurchase agreements offer security sellers a means of financing and offer security buyers a short-term collateralized investment with relatively little liquidity or default risk.
- *Government bond use in monetary policy and foreign exchange reserves:* Recall from an earlier lesson that central banks use government securities in fulfilling their monetary policy mandate, which includes the outright

purchase and sale of securities and repo contracts with government bonds as collateral. Given their high degree of liquidity and safety, foreign market participants often hold their foreign currency reserves in the form of liquid foreign government bonds.

While sovereign governments seek to maintain regular and predictable bond market access across maturities, changes in the amount of debt, the level of deficits, and the difference between short- and long-term interest rates lead to changes in debt management policy, as shown in the following example.

THE US TREASURY'S 30-YEAR BOND

In October 2001, the United States stopped issuing 30-year Treasury bonds due to cost concerns related to paying interest on the notes. At the time, Treasury officials saw a reduced need for future borrowing because the U government was posting a budget surplus. The move stunned the markets and resulted in the largest one-day price move in years due to supply concerns. In prior years, the Treasury Department suspended the three- and seven-year issues. The 10-year Treasury became the de facto benchmark for measuring the performance of long-term bonds during the suspension of the 30-year bond. Issuance of the 30-year US Treasury bond resumed in February 2006 to cover deficits created by tax cuts and war spending.

Sources: Wall Street Journal, "Yields Plunge after Treasury Halts Issue of 30-Year Bonds" (31 October 2001). www.wsj.com/articles/SB1004542963185681400
TSC Staff, "Treasury to Resume 30-Year Bond on Feb. 9," TheStreet (2 November 2005). www.thestreet.com/markets/rates-and-bonds/treasury-to-resume-30-year-bond-on-feb-9-10250971

QUESTION SET

1. Identify the following statement as true or false. Justify your answer.

   Emerging market external sovereign debt is denominated in a foreign currency.

   Solution:

   False. Although EM sovereigns do issue debt in foreign currencies to increase demand by foreign investors who desire less currency risk, many EM sovereigns have external debt denominated in their domestic currency as well, especially those with currencies that have exhibited exchange rate stability.

2. US-based investors of US dollar–denominated external sovereign debt can still face exposure to currency risk because:

   A. sovereign fixed-income securities are denominated in freely floating domestic currencies.

   B. the issuer's credit rating may be downgraded.

   C. the issuer must be able to generate foreign currency revenue.

   Solution:

   C is correct. Investors based in developed markets who purchase external debt of emerging and frontier market sovereign issuers face *indirect* exposure to currency fluctuations, because their returns depend on an issuer's ability to generate foreign currency revenue to meet foreign currency interest and principal payments through international capital, goods, and services flows.

3. Explain why national governments represent the lowest default risk among domestic currency issuers.

Solution:

National governments are distinguished by their sovereign right to generate tax cash flows from economic activity within a jurisdiction, unlike private sector issuers that rely on operating cash flows and secondary sources of repayment, such as asset sales, to service debt obligations.

4. Due to their high degree of liquidity and safety, the most common form of collateral for both repo and derivative transactions is:

   A. shorter-term government securities.

   B. medium-term government securities.

   C. longer-term government securities.

Solution:

C is correct. Longer-term government securities are the most common form of collateral for both repo and derivative transactions due to their high degree of liquidity and safety.

5. A sovereign government faced with growing deficits and concerns about rollover risk would *most likely*:

   A. lower tax rates.

   B. stop servicing the debt.

   C. issue medium- to long-term securities.

Solution:

C is correct. Government budget deficits increase the need for borrowing at a higher level while surpluses reduce borrowing needs. Excessive government reliance on short-term funding introduces rollover risk, or uncertain refinancing costs, increasing the variability of budget costs and therefore tax rates. Therefore, in practice, governments seek to minimize interest rate and rollover risks by distributing debt across maturities while issuing debt in regular, predictable intervals. A is incorrect because taxes should be raised, not lowered, in such a scenario. B is incorrect because such an action would put the government in default, with severe consequences for its credit standing and its ability to meet fiscal policy commitments.

3 SOVEREIGN DEBT ISSUANCE AND TRADING

☐ contrast the issuance and trading of government and corporate fixed-income instruments

In contrast to the opportunistic nature of corporate debt issuance managed by investment bank underwriters on behalf of issuers, issuance of sovereign debt usually takes the form of a public auction led by the national Treasury or finance ministry.

Once a government debt auction is announced, prospective investors submit competitive or non-competitive bids. A competitive bidder specifies an acceptable price and number of securities to be purchased. If the price determined at auction is above the bid, a competitive bidder will not be offered any securities. In contrast, a non-competitive bidder agrees to accept the price determined at auction and always receives securities.

A competitive bid process is either a **single-price auction** or **multiple-price auction**. In both cases, the issuer ranks bids by prices, choosing bids from highest to lowest until the desired issuance amount is reached. Under a single-price auction, *all* winning bidders pay the same price and receive the same coupon rate for the bonds regardless of their bid. In contrast, a multiple-price auction process generates different prices among bidders for the same bond issue. The single-price auction process may result in a lower cost of funds and broader distribution among investors, while multiple-price auctions may result in a narrower distribution of large bids because investors must accept bonds at their bid price.

A single-price auction process has four phases:

1. The auction is announced by the government debt management office, which includes information about the bond issue, such as the amount and type of securities being offered, the auction and issue dates, the maturity date of the bonds, and bidding times.
2. Dealers, institutional investors, and individuals make bids. Bids can be competitive or non-competitive.
3. All non-competitive bids are accepted while competitive bids are ranked starting at the lowest yield (highest bond price). The highest yield that fills the offering amount, counting from the bottom, is the "cut off." All securities are sold for a single price, using this stop yield. Competitive bidders who bid higher than this yield (lower price) do not purchase any securities. Results are announced publicly, as shown in Exhibit 2.
4. Securities are delivered to the non-competitive and winning competitive bidders in exchange for proceeds.

Exhibit 2: 30-Year Singapore Government Bond Auction Announcement and Results

On 8 September 2021, the Monetary Authority of Singapore announced an auction of SGD2.6 billion of 30-year Singapore government bonds.

The Monetary Authority of Singapore
21 September 2021
Application for Taxable Book-Entry Singapore Government Bonds

Tenor:	Approximately 30 Years
Total Amount Offered:	SGD2,600,000,000
Issue/Settlement Date:	1 October 2021
Maturity Date Amount:	1 October 2051
Coupon Rate:	To be determined based on the cut-off yield of successful applications
Yield and Price:	To be determined at the auction
Coupon Payment Dates:	1 October and 1 April

The Monetary Authority of Singapore
21 September 2021
Application for Taxable Book-Entry Singapore Government Bonds

Method of Sale:	Uniform-price auction
Bids must be submitted through primary dealers.	

The results were announced shortly after the auction on 28 September 2021.

The Monetary Authority of Singapore
28 September 2021
Results of Auction of Taxable Book-Entry Singapore Government Bonds to Be Issued 1 October 2021

Tenor:	Approximately 30 years
Total amount allotted:	SGD2,600,000,000
Amount allotted to non-competitive bids:	SGD207,355,000
Total amount of bids:	SGD4,105,487,000
Coupon rate:	1.875% p.a.
Cut-off yield and price:	1.95% p.a. and 98.303
Median yield and price:	1.89% p.a. and 99.658
Average yield and price:	1.84% p.a. and 100.804
Total amount of bids:	SGD4,105,487,000

The yield-to-maturity and price determined at this auction (the "Cut-off yield and price") was 1.95% and 98.303% of par. The Monetary Authority of Singapore's auction rules states that the bond coupon rate will be the cut-off yield rounded down to the nearest 0.125%, or 1.875%. This auction attracted bids totaling SGD4.1 billion, over 1.5× the offer amount.

GOVERNMENT OF INDIA SWITCHES FROM MULTIPLE-PRICE TO SINGLE-PRICE DEBT AUCTIONS

In July 2021, the central bank of India (Reserve Bank of India) moved from multiple- to single-price auctions for its 2-year, 3-year, 5-year, 10-year, 14-year, and floating-rate bonds. The 30-year and 40-year bonds continued to be auctioned via the multiple-price method. The Reserve Bank of India changed the methodology it uses for government bond issuance after it faced several partially failed auctions. Under the single-price auction, volatility in yields is reduced because all successful bidders receive the same rate.

Sources: BQ Prime, "RBI Tweaks Government Bond Auction Strategy amid Falling Sales" (2 July 2021). www.bloombergquint.com/business/rbi-tweaks-government-bond-auction-strategy-amid-falling-sales.
Subhadip Sircar, Suvashree Ghosh, and Ronojoy Mazumdar, "RBI Proposes Framework for Acceptable Bids at Auctions to Underwriters," Bloomberg (2 July 2021). www.bloomberg.com/news/articles/2021-07-02/rbi-said-to-propose-acceptable-bids-at-auctions-to-underwriters.

Sovereign issuers also engage with financial intermediaries, such as corporate debt issuers, but in a different form. Sovereign governments designate a group of financial intermediaries as **primary dealers** that are required to participate in all auctions with competitive prices, often serve as the central bank's counterparty for open market operations and facilitate the purchase and sale of government debt by foreign central banks and other indirect bidders. Investors may also participate directly in auctions—for example, through the UK Debt Management Office or TreasuryDirect in the United States.

Once issued, sovereign debt is usually traded in a manner similar to that of private sector debt securities primarily on OTC markets by financial intermediary broker/dealers, although in some markets, such as Australia, they are traded on an exchange. In each market, the sovereign issuer is often the largest borrower and their securities are the most liquid among fixed-income instruments. The most recently issued sovereign debt securities, known as **on-the-run securities**, are used for benchmark yield analyses because they are more liquid than previously issued **off-the-run securities**, which trade infrequently. Given their liquidity, some trading of on-the-run securities occurs electronically, on centralized marketplaces operated by private companies.

A significant difference in trading between sovereign and corporate debt is the presence of investors in sovereign debt with varying "non-economic" objectives. For example, major investors in US Treasuries include the Federal Reserve, which uses Treasuries in the conduct of monetary policy; major foreign governments, which hold the securities as US dollar reserves; state and local governments, which face restrictions on holding other types of securities; and banks and insurance companies that either must hold Treasuries or are incentivized to do so to meet regulatory requirements. These factors reduce sovereign borrowing costs versus the private sector and are most pronounced for sovereign issuers with a **reserve currency**, a currency held by global central banks in significant quantities and widely used to conduct international trade and financial transactions. In addition to the US dollar, the euro, Japanese yen, British pound, Swiss franc, Australian dollar, and Chinese renminbi are reserve currencies. However, the US dollar accounts for 60% of global foreign exchange reserves and about half of international trade, international loans, and global debt securities and is involved in nearly 90% of all FX market transaction.[1]

QUESTION SET

1. An advantage of a single-price auction versus a multiple-price auction is that a single-price auction may result in a:

   A. lower cost of funds and broader distribution among investors.

   B. narrower distribution of large bids because investors must accept bonds at their bid prices.

   C. ranking of bids by prices, where bids from highest to lowest are chosen until the desired issuance amount is reached.

   Solution:

   A is correct. The single-price auction process may result in a lower cost of funds and broader distribution among investors. B is incorrect because multiple-price auctions may result in a narrower distribution of large bids because investors must accept bonds at their bid price. C is incorrect because in both cases, the issuer ranks bids by prices, choosing bids from highest to lowest until the desired issuance amount is reached.

1 Congressional Research Service, "The U.S. Dollar as the World's Dominant Reserve Currency" (15 September 2022). https://crsreports.congress.gov/product/pdf/IF/IF11707.

2. Discuss how the type of auction (single price or multiple price) can impact the success of auctions and yield volatility.

Solution:

A multiple-price auction process generates different prices among bidders for the same bond issue. Under a single-price auction, volatility in yields is reduced because all successful bidders receive the same rate. The Reserve Bank of India changed the methodology it uses (from multiple price to single price) for government bond issuance after it faced a number of partially failed auctions.

3. A significant difference in trading between sovereign and corporate debt is:

A. the presence of investors in sovereign debt with varying "non-economic" objectives.

B. the opportunistic nature of sovereign debt issuance managed by investment bank underwriters on behalf of issuers.

C. that sovereign debt is usually traded on an exchange while private sector debt primarily trades on OTC markets mediated by broker/dealers.

Solution:

A is correct. A significant difference in trading between sovereign and corporate debt is the presence of investors in sovereign debt with varying "non-economic" objectives. For example, major investors in US Treasuries include the Federal Reserve, which uses Treasuries in the conduct of monetary policy; major foreign governments, which hold the securities as US dollar reserves; state and local governments, which face restrictions on holding other types of securities; and banks and insurance companies that either must hold Treasuries or are incentivized to do so to meet regulatory requirements. B is incorrect because in contrast to the opportunistic nature of *corporate debt issuance* managed by investment bank underwriters on behalf of issuers, sovereign auctions use standard procedures to ensure broad distribution among investors under a transparent price discovery process. C is incorrect because once issued, sovereign debt is usually traded in a manner similar to that of private sector debt securities: primarily on OTC markets mediated by broker/dealers, although in some markets, such as Australia, they are traded on an exchange.

4 NON-SOVEREIGN, QUASI-GOVERNMENT, AND SUPRANATIONAL AGENCY DEBT

☐ describe funding choices by sovereign and non-sovereign governments, quasi-government entities, and supranational agencies

The level and type of non-sovereign government funding vary widely among countries, depending on whether specific public goods and services are provided and financed at the national, regional, or local level. Some non-sovereign government issuers are similar to sovereign borrowers in that they can levy taxes to fund activities in their jurisdiction. Other non-sovereign issuers rely on national government budget allocations or user fees to meet interest and principal payments with or without the explicit financial support of a national or local government as a secondary repayment source. The ability of non-sovereign issuers to access funding across maturities is affected by the predictability and stability of these sources of repayment, which are key determinants of the issuer's credit quality.

Government Agencies

Government agencies are quasi-government entities that issue debt in order to fund the government-sponsored provision of specific public goods or services based on sovereign or local law. This may involve the financing of specific activities promoted by the government or the operation of necessary infrastructure as mandated by law. For example, the Airport Authority of Hong Kong (AAHK), introduced in an earlier module, is the statutory agency for operating and developing the Hong Kong International Airport. AAHK issues a combination of short- and long-term debt to meet the airport's specific working capital and capital investment needs. The primary source of repayment is cash flows from airport operations, while its sovereign government backing is a secondary source of repayment.

The Government National Mortgage Association (known as Ginnie Mae, not to be confused with Fannie Mae or Freddie Mac) securitizes and guarantees certain mortgage loans in the United States to subsidize and promote home ownership. Ginnie Mae issues callable agency debt securities to finance its operations with maturities matching the expected cash flows of its guaranteed mortgages. The primary source of repayment for the agency's debt are mortgage-based guaranty fees and other cash flows with its sovereign government backing as a secondary source of repayment.

Both AAHK and Ginnie Mae issue debt with maturities and structures consistent with their respective underlying activities. That said, while each of these sovereign agencies is typically able to borrow at a yield-to-maturity near that of their sovereign guarantor, neither will benefit from the full liquidity premium associated with sovereign debt outlined in the prior lesson.

Local and Regional Government Authorities

Non-sovereign government authorities may either issue debt for general purposes, which is repaid from local tax cash flows, or issue debt to fund specific projects or infrastructure, which is repaid from user fees or other cash flows directly derived from the project. The former are referred to as **general obligation bonds** (GO bonds), which are used to fund public goods and services in the non-sovereign's limited jurisdiction, such as the Province of Ontario green bond issue described in the term sheet below. These unsecured bonds are repaid with tax revenues from the provincial government, though their use of proceeds is limited to eligible green projects.

Province of Ontario 1.55% 2029 Global Green Bonds
Key Terms

Issuer:	Province of Ontario (Canada)
Settlement Date:	July 29, 2021
Maturity Date:	November 1, 2029
Principal Amount:	CAD2,750,000,000
Interest:	1.55% p.a.
Interest Payment:	Semi-annually on May 1 and November 1 of each year

Province of Ontario 1.55% 2029 Global Green Bonds
Key Terms

Other Relevant Features:	An amount equal to the net proceeds of the Bonds will be recorded in a designated account in the Province of Ontario's financial records. This designated account will be used to track the use of and allocation of proceeds to "Eligible Projects," which include projects in the following sectors: 1. Clean transportation 2. Energy efficiency and conservation 3. Clean energy and technology 4. Forestry, agriculture, and land management 5. Climate adaptation and resilience

Revenue bonds, in contrast, are issued for *specific* project financing (infrastructure such as roads, bridges, or tunnels) with the source of repayment often linked to a project's revenue stream (tolls, fees, etc.). Revenue bonds usually involve longer-dated funding, the maturity of which often matches the expected life of matching project cash flows.

Supranational Organizations

Supranational organizations, such as the World Bank, International Monetary Fund (IMF), and Asian Development Bank (ADB), are created and supported by sovereign governments as member states in pursuit of a common objective, such as fostering economic cooperation and development, promoting trade, or providing financing to emerging economies in pursuit of sustainable growth. Member states typically share decision-making authority and provide implicit and explicit financial support to these organizations, resulting in the highest credit quality among these issuers and a strong ability to access capital markets across maturities. In other cases, supranational and sovereign organizations partner to form quasi-government agencies that can issue debt at a lower cost than an emerging market sovereign government. For example, PT Indonesia Infrastructure Finance (IIF) was introduced in an earlier lesson as a US dollar–denominated issuer in the Eurobond market. IIF's ability to access this and similar markets is derived from indirect Indonesian government ownership and the strong financial support from a consortium of public sector entities, including the Asian Development Bank, the World Bank Group's International Finance Corporation (IFC), and the German sovereign government development bank (Kreditanstalt für Wiederaufbau, or KfW).

Supranational issuers target bond investors in major currencies using global bond markets. In the example bond issue below, the Asian Development Bank borrowed in Indonesian rupiah (IDR) but will pay interest and principal to investors in US dollars. The amounts are fixed in Indonesian rupiah, with the payments in US dollars determined using the spot USD/IDR rate two days prior to each payment date, so investors are still assuming currency risk.

Asian Development Bank 7.80% Global Medium-Term Notes due 15 March 2034
Key Terms

Issuer:	Asian Development Bank
Settlement Date:	18 March 2019
Maturity Date:	15 March 2034
Principal Amount:	IDR1,200,000,000,000 payable in US dollars
Interest:	7.80% p.a.

Asian Development Bank 7.80% Global Medium-Term Notes due 15 March 2034 Key Terms

Interest Payment:	Semi-annually on 15 March and 15 September each year
Listing:	Luxembourg Stock Exchange
Governing Law:	New York
Other Relevant Features:	The interest and principal amounts will be paid on each Interest Payment Date in US dollars converted from Indonesian rupiah at the applicable Reference Rate (as defined) on the Rate Fixing Date (as defined).

QUESTION SET

1. Which of the following features is typical of revenue bonds? Revenue bonds typically:

   A. provide shorter-dated funding.

   B. fund general local government spending.

   C. have maturities matching the expected life of matching project cash flows.

   Solution:

   C is correct. Revenue bonds usually involve longer-dated funding, the maturity of which often matches the expected life of matching project cash flows. A is incorrect because revenue bonds usually involve longer-dated funding. B is incorrect because revenue bonds fund specific projects while general obligation bonds fund local governments generally.

2. The Asian Development Bank is an example of a:

   A. government agency.

   B. non-sovereign government.

   C. supranational organization.

   Solution:

   C is correct. Supranational organizations, such as the World Bank, IMF, and ADB, are created by several sovereign governments in pursuit of a common objective, such as fostering economic cooperation and development, promoting trade, or providing financing to emerging economies in pursuit of sustainable growth. A is incorrect because government agencies are subunits of governments formed to carry out specific laws or objectives. B is incorrect because non-sovereign governments preside over subdivisions of countries (e.g., the province of Ontario in Canada) through constitutional or legislative authority.

3. Member states of a supranational organization typically share decision-making authority and provide implicit and explicit financial support to the organization, resulting in which of the following levels of credit quality among these issuers?

   A. Lowest

B. Average

C. Highest

Solution:

C is correct. Member states typically share decision-making authority and provide implicit and explicit financial support to these organizations, resulting in the highest credit quality among these issuers and a strong ability to access capital markets across maturities.

PRACTICE PROBLEMS

1. Balance sheets of government entities are unlikely to include:
   - **A.** FX reserves.
   - **B.** long-term debt.
   - **C.** accrual of unfunded liabilities.

2. In practice, which of the following applies as it relates to sovereign government financing?
   - **A.** Taxpayers smooth consumption over time, saving expected future taxes today for future payment.
   - **B.** Taxpayers form rational expectations that today's tax cuts will result in future tax increases and pass on tax savings to descendants.
   - **C.** Governments seek to minimize interest rate and rollover risks by distributing debt across maturities while issuing debt in regular, predictable intervals.

3. Which of the following is correct regarding the single-price auction process?
   - **A.** Bidders include only dealers and institutional investors.
   - **B.** Competitive bidders who bid higher than the stop yield are allocated securities.
   - **C.** All non-competitive bids are accepted, while competitive bids are ranked starting at the lowest yield (highest bond price).

4. On-the-run sovereign debt securities are:
   - **A.** used for benchmark yield analyses.
   - **B.** issued prior to off-the-run securities.
   - **C.** less liquid than off-the-run securities.

5. A non-sovereign bond issued to fund public goods and services in the non-sovereign's limited jurisdiction that is repaid from local tax cash flows is referred to as:
   - **A.** a GO bond.
   - **B.** a revenue bond.
   - **C.** an agency bond.

6. Government agencies issue debt that is:
   - **A.** at a yield-to-maturity equal to that of its sovereign guarantor.
   - **B.** primarily repaid by cash flows related to its underlying activities.
   - **C.** short term, only to meet working capital and capital investment needs.

SOLUTIONS

1. C is correct. Public sector financial accounting standards vary widely and are often prepared using cash, rather than accrual-based, principles, typically excluding such items as the depreciation of fixed public goods, such as federal highways, or the accrual of unfunded liabilities, such as government pension obligations. A and B are incorrect because balance sheets of government entities are likely to include FX reserves and long-term debt.

2. C is correct. Governments seek to minimize interest rate and rollover risks by distributing debt across maturities while issuing debt in regular, predictable intervals. A and B are incorrect because taxpayers are neither able to perfectly smooth consumption over time, nor do they form rational expectations about current versus future taxes across generations, leading to fiscal instability, creating uncertainty in future tax rates, and threatening the stability of economic growth over time.

3. C is correct. All non-competitive bids are accepted, while competitive bids are ranked starting at the lowest yield (highest bond price). A is incorrect because individuals can also bid, in addition to dealers and institutional investors. B is incorrect because competitive bidders who bid higher than the stop yield (lower price) do not purchase any securities. All securities are sold for a single price, using a stop yield.

4. A is correct. The most recently issued sovereign securities, known as on-the-run securities, are used for benchmark yield analyses. B is incorrect because off-the-run securities are issued prior to on-the-run securities. C is incorrect because on-the-run securities are not less liquid than off-the-run securities.

5. A is correct. General obligation bonds are used to fund public goods and services in the non-sovereign's limited jurisdiction and are repaid from local tax cash flows. B is incorrect because revenue bonds are issued for a specific project financing (infrastructure such as roads, bridges, or tunnels) with the source of repayment often linked to a project's revenue stream (tolls, fees, etc.). C is incorrect because government agencies are quasi-government entities that issue debt in order to fund the government-sponsored provision of specific public goods or services based on sovereign or local law, with the primary source of repayment related to the public good or service and the sovereign government backing as a secondary source of repayment.

6. B is correct. For the Airport Authority of Hong Kong, for example, the primary source of repayment is cash flows from airport operations, while its sovereign government backing is a secondary source of repayment. Similarly, the primary source of repayment for Ginnie Mae is mortgage-based guaranty fees and other cash flows, with its sovereign government backing as a secondary source of repayment. A is incorrect because while sovereign agencies typically borrow at a yield-to-maturity near that of their sovereign guarantor, they do not benefit from the full liquidity premium associated with sovereign debt. C is incorrect because agencies issue a combination of short- and long-term debt to meet specific working capital and capital investment needs.

LEARNING MODULE

6

Fixed-Income Bond Valuation: Prices and Yields

LEARNING OUTCOMES

Mastery	The candidate should be able to:
☐	calculate a bond's price given a yield-to-maturity on or between coupon dates
☐	identify the relationships among a bond's price, coupon rate, maturity, and yield-to-maturity
☐	describe matrix pricing

INTRODUCTION

1

We will now use discounted cash flow analysis to calculate bond prices and show how the discount rate used as well as a bond's features, such as its coupon rate and time-to-maturity, affect pricing. The price of a bond and its future cash flows can be used calculate an internal rate of return, known as the yield-to-maturity, which serves as a useful return measure for fixed-income investors under certain assumptions. One of these assumptions that applies to this learning module is that all bond interest and principal cash flows occur as promised. We will explore the relationship between bond prices and bond features, showing how different features affect a bond's price, and demonstrate pricing both on and between bond coupon dates. Finally, we will introduce matrix pricing, which uses comparable bonds to estimate a bond's price and yield-to-maturity when neither is known.

Most of the examples and exhibits used throughout the reading can be downloaded as a Microsoft Excel workbook. Each worksheet in the workbook is labeled with the corresponding example or exhibit number in the text.

LEARNING MODULE OVERVIEW

- Bond pricing is an application of discounted cash flow analysis. Bond prices are a function of a bond's features, including its cash flows and the interest rate(s) used to discount future cash flows.

- By comparing a bond's price to its face value or its coupon rate to the discount rate, we can identify whether a bond is trading at a discount, at par, or at a premium.
- If the market price of a bond is known, an internal rate of return on the cash flows can be calculated, known as the yield-to-maturity (YTM). The YTM is the single interest rate that equates the present value of future cash flows to the price of the bond.
- A bond investor's rate of return will equal the YTM if (1) the investor holds the bond to maturity, (2) the issuer makes full coupon and principal payments on the scheduled dates, and (3) the investor reinvests all coupon payments at the same YTM.
- When a bond is priced or traded in between coupon dates, an additional amount must be added for interest that has accrued since the last coupon payment, to compensate the seller, since the buyer will receive the entire next coupon payment.
- To calculate a bond's accrued interest on any date, we multiply the coupon by the fraction of days elapsed in the coupon period divided by the total days in the coupon period. There are various conventions for counting these days; two common conventions are actual/actual and 30/360.
- A bond's price changes inversely with changes in its YTM. A bond's features determine price sensitivity to changes in YTM.
- The lower the coupon rate on a fixed-coupon bond, the greater the percentage price change for a given change in the bond's yield-to-maturity. Generally, the longer a bond's time-to-maturity, the greater its percentage price change for a given change in its yield-to-maturity.
- Unlike listed equity securities, most bonds are thinly traded, which complicates price discovery.
- Matrix pricing is a price estimation process for new or illiquid bonds that uses yields on securities with the same or similar features. Matrix pricing is widely used in price quotations for bonds.

LEARNING MODULE SELF-ASSESSMENT

These initial questions are intended to help you gauge your current level of understanding of the learning module.

1. A corporate bond that matures on 1 January 2035 pays semiannual coupons of 3.25% per year and has a face value of 100. The market discount rate is 4.0%. For a trade settlement date of 1 January 2030, the price of the bond as a percentage of par value, assuming a 30/360 day count, is *closest* to:

   A. 96.632.

   B. 96.661.

   C. 103.436.

   Solution:

   A is correct. The bond price is the sum of the coupon and principal payments discounted at the market discount rate.

$PV = PMT_1/(1 + r)^1 + PMT_2/(1 + r)^2 + \ldots + (PMT_N + FV_N)/(1 + r)^N$,

where

$PMT = 1.625$

$r = 0.02$

$FV = 100$

$N = 10$

$$PV = \frac{1.625}{(1+0.02)^1} + \frac{1.625}{(1+0.02)^2} + \frac{1.625}{(1+0.02)^3} + \frac{1.625}{(1+0.02)^4} + \frac{1.625}{(1+0.02)^5} +$$

$$\frac{1.625}{(1+0.02)^6} + \frac{1.625}{(1+0.02)^7} + \frac{1.625}{(1+0.02)^8} + \frac{1.625}{(1+0.02)^9} + \frac{101.625}{(1-0.02)^{10}}$$

$PV = 96.632.$

Note: Quantities in the calculation are not rounded, though they are shown with three decimal places for presentation purposes. Solutions are rounded to three decimal places.

The calculation can also be done using the PV or PRICE functions in Microsoft Excel and Google Sheets:

```
=-PV(rate, nper, pmt, [FV], type)
```

=-PV(0.02,10,1.625,100,0)

= 96.632

```
=PRICE(settlement, maturity, rate, yield, redemp-
tion, frequency, [basis])
```

=PRICE(DATE(2030,1,1),DATE(2035,1,1),0.0325,0.04,100,2)

= 96.632

2. Which of the following is *not* required for a bond investor's rate of return on a bond investment to equal the bond's YTM?

   A. The bond is held to maturity.

   B. The issuer may default on one, but only one, coupon payment.

   C. Coupon payments are reinvested at the same rate as the YTM.

Solution:

B is correct. For a bond investor to earn the YTM, the issuer must make all coupon and principal payments on their scheduled dates.

A is incorrect because a bond investor does have to hold the bond to maturity to earn the YTM.

C is incorrect because a bond investor does have to reinvest coupons at the same rate as the YTM to earn the YTM.

3. A three-year sovereign bond issued on 1 January 2030 pays semiannual coupons of 1.5% per year on 30 June and 31 December each year and has a face value of 100. The market discount rate is 2.0%. For a trade settlement date

of 29 August 2031, the flat price of the bond as a percentage of par value, assuming an actual/actual day count, is *closest* to:

A. 99.343.

B. 99.587.

C. 99.832.

Solution:

A is correct. The flat price is the full price less accrued interest. The full price is the present value as of the trade settlement date, which involves partial payment periods because we're between coupon dates.

$$PV^{Full} = \frac{PMT}{(1+r)^{1-t/T}} + \frac{PMT}{(1+r)^{2-t/T}} + \cdots + \frac{PMT+FV}{(1+r)^{N-t/T}}.$$

Here,

$PMT = 0.75$

$r = 0.01$

$t = 60$ (days from 30 June 2031 to 29 August 2031)

$T = 184$ (days from 30 June 2031 to next coupon on 31 December 2031)

$FV = 100$

$N = 3$

$$PV_{Full} = \frac{0.75}{(1+0.01)^{1-60/184}} + \frac{0.75}{(1+0.01)^{2-60/184}} \frac{100.75}{(1+0.01)^{3-60/184}}$$

$$PV_{Full} = 99.587.$$

Accrued interest is the proportional share of the next coupon payment owed the seller.

$$AI = \frac{t}{T} \times PMT,$$

$$AI = \frac{60}{184} \times 0.75$$

$$AI = 0.245.$$

The flat price is 99.587 – 0.245 = 99.343.

The present value calculations can also be done easily on spreadsheet software. Additionally, the PRICE function in Microsoft Excel and Google Sheets can be used to directly solve for the flat price (note: *not* full prices).

```
=PRICE(settlement, maturity, rate, yield, redemp-
tion, frequency, [basis])
```

=PRICE(DATE(2031,8,29),DATE(2032,12,31),0.015,0.02,100,2)

= 99.343.

4. True or false: A bond's quoted price is also called its full price because it is the amount that the buyer pays the seller.

A. True

B. False

Solution:

False. A bond is quoted by its flat price. The full price is the amount paid by the buyer to the seller, and it includes accrued interest if settlement does not occur on a coupon payment date.

5. Assume that the Japanese government issues two non-callable fixed-coupon bonds on the same date with the same coupon rate. The bonds are identical except that one matures in 10 years and the other matures in 30 years. If the relevant market discount rates for both bonds rise by 65 bps, which of the following will be true?

   A. The 10-year bond will have a larger percentage price change than the 30-year bond.

   B. The 10-year bond will have a smaller percentage price change than the 30-year bond.

   C. The 10-year bond and the 30-year bond will have equal percentage price changes.

Solution:

B is correct. Generally, for the same coupon rate, a shorter-term bond will have a smaller percentage price change than a longer-term bond when their relevant market discount rates change by the same amount.

A is incorrect because generally a shorter-term bond will have a smaller percentage price change than a longer-term bond when their market discount rates change by the same amount.

C is incorrect because shorter-term bonds and longer-term bonds will not have the same percentage price changes when their market discount rates change by the same amount.

6. True or false. Justify your answer.

   Matrix pricing is an estimation process in which quotes from derivative markets (e.g., interest rates swaps) are used to determine the price of illiquid or new bonds for which transactional data are scarce.

   A. True

   B. False

Solution:

False. Matrix pricing is a process for estimating prices of illiquid or newly issued bonds using prices of comparable bonds, not from transactions in derivative markets. The comparable bonds have similar times-to-maturity, coupon rates, and credit quality as those of the bond under study.

BOND PRICING AND THE TIME VALUE OF MONEY 2

☐ calculate a bond's price given a yield-to-maturity on or between coupon dates

Bond Pricing with a Market Discount Rate

Bond pricing is an application of discounted cash flow analysis that depends on a bond's cash flow features and the rate (or rates) used for discounting. Recall from an earlier lesson that the price of the bond at issuance is the present value of the promised interest and principal cash flows. The market discount rate is used in the time-value-of-money calculation to obtain the present value. The **market discount rate** is the rate of return required by investors given the risk of the bond investment. It is also called the **required yield**, or the **required rate of return**.

The present value (PV) calculation for each bond coupon cash flow (PMT) that occurs in t periods with a market discount rate of r per period should be familiar from an earlier time-value-of-money lesson:

$$PV(\text{Bond coupon}) = PMT_t/(1 + r)^t. \quad (1)$$

Equation 2 extends this calculation in a general formula for calculating a bond price (PV) given the market discount rate on a coupon date:

$$PV = PMT_1/(1 + r)^1 + PMT_2/(1 + r)^2 + \ldots + (PMT_N + FV_N)/(1 + r)^N, \quad (2)$$

where FV is equal to the bond's face value and N is the number of periods to maturity.

Recall the Bright Wheels Automotive (BRWA) bond introduced in an earlier lesson. The bond's price was 100% of face or par value because the market discount rate, r, and the bond's fixed coupon rate, PMT, were equal (at 3.2% per annum, or 1.6% semiannually). We will now consider cases where the bond's coupon rate and the market discount rate are not equal.

EXAMPLE 1

BRWA Par, Discount, and Premium Bond

Period:	**1**	**2**	**3**	**4**	**5**	**6**	**7**	**8**	**9**	**10**
Cash Flow:	1.6	1.6	1.6	1.6	1.6	1.6	1.6	1.6	1.6	101.6
PV of Cash Flow at 1.2% periodic YTM:	1.6	1.6	1.5	1.5	1.5	1.5	1.5	1.5	1.4	90.2
Bond price (sum):	103.75									
PV of Cash Flow at 1.6% periodic YTM:	1.6	1.6	1.5	1.5	1.5	1.5	1.4	1.4	1.4	86.7
Bond price:	100.00									
PV of Cash Flow at 2.0% periodic YTM:	1.6	1.5	1.5	1.5	1.4	1.4	1.4	1.4	1.3	83.3
Bond price:	96.41									

Note: Please refer to the candidate learning ecosystem online for a spreadsheet of these calculations in the downloaded Microsoft Excel workbook.

If the market discount rate rises to 2% semiannually, new bonds to be issued at par must provide coupon rates that are also 2% semiannually. The previously issued BRWA bond pays coupons at a 1.6% rate, so it should have a lower price than a bond that pays 2%. We could say that the BRWA bond's 1.6% coupon rate is *deficient* relative to the higher 2% market discount rate. The market price of the BRWA bond, with its lower coupon, will therefore fall below 100% of par. Example 1 shows that when we discount the BRWA bond cash flows at a market discount rate of 2%, we calculate a price of 96.41. This lower price compensates for a coupon rate below the market discount rate. When a bond's price is less than 100, we say that the bond trades at a discount. (This use of "discount" when referring to the bond price is not connected to the use of "discount" in market discount rates). Exhibit 1 illustrates a bond trading at a discount.

Exhibit 1: Discount Bond Cash Flows

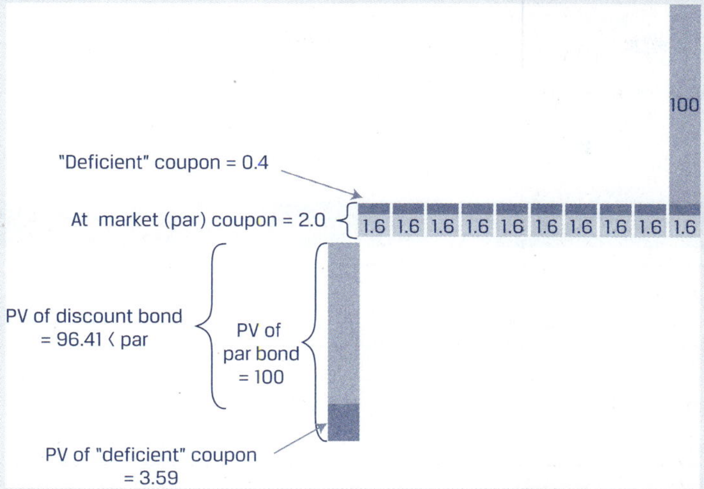

We now consider how the price of the existing BRWA bond will change if the market discount rate falls to 1.2%. A similar bond (five-year maturity, semi-annual coupon) issued when the five-year market discount rate is 1.2% semiannually will also have a semi-annual coupon rate of 1.2% so that its price will be 100% of par. Because the BRWA bond pays a higher coupon rate of 1.6%, its price should be higher than that of a bond that pays only 1.2%. We could say that the BRWA bond's 1.6% coupon rate is *excessive* relative to the lower 1.2% market discount rate. Therefore, the BRWA bond's price rises as the market discount rate falls. When we discount the cash flows of the BRWA bond at the market discount rate of 1.2% and then add them up, we calculate a bond price equal to 103.73% of par. It has a higher price than the 1.2% coupon bond because it pays a higher coupon. Exhibit 2 illustrates a bond trading at a premium.

Exhibit 2: Premium Bond Cash Flows

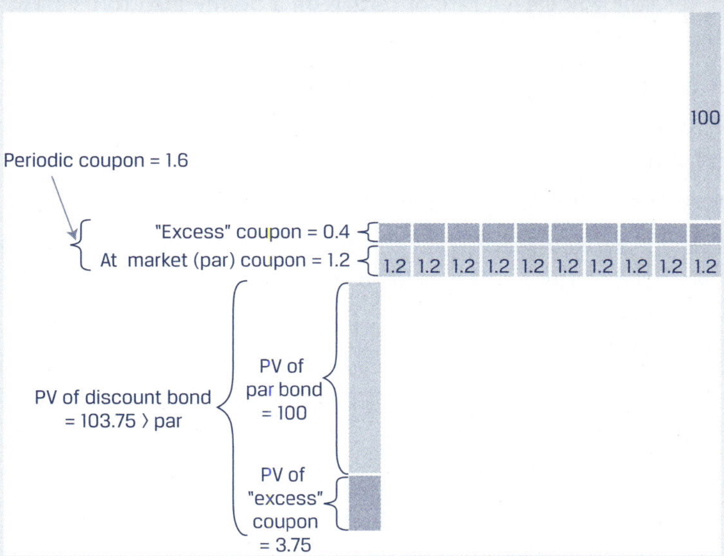

The PV function in Microsoft Excel or Google Sheets may also be used for the price calculation:

```
=PV(rate, nper, pmt, FV, type),
```

where

rate is the market discount rate per period
nper is the number of periods
pmt is the periodic coupon payment
FV is future or face value
type corresponds to payments made at the end (0) or beginning (1) of each period

The discount, premium, and par relationships are summarized in Exhibit 3.

Exhibit 3: Fixed-Rate Discount, Premium, and Par Bonds

Bond Price	Price vs. Future Value	Coupon vs. Market Discount Rate
Par	PV = FV	PMT = Market discount rate
Discount	PV < FV	PMT < Market discount rate
Premium	PV > FV	PMT > Market discount rate

The interest rates per period are annualized by multiplying the rate per period by the number of periods in a year. Therefore, an equivalent statement is that the BRWA bond is priced at a premium because its stated annual coupon rate of 3.2% is greater than the stated annual market discount rate of 2.4%. Unless stated otherwise, interest rates are typically quoted as annual rates.

Yield-to-Maturity

If the market price of a bond is known, Equation 2 can be used to calculate its yield-to-maturity. The **yield-to-maturity** is the internal rate of return on the cash flows—the uniform interest rate such that when the future cash flows are discounted at that rate, the sum of the present values equals the price of the bond. It is an *implied* or *observed* single market discount rate.

A bond investor will earn a rate of return on a bond equal to its YTM if each of the following is true:

1. The investor holds the bond to maturity.
2. The issuer makes full coupon and principal payments on scheduled dates. The YTM is the *promised* yield—that is, assuming no issuer default.
3. The investor reinvests all coupon payments at the same YTM.

For example, say we observe that the five-year 3.2% fixed-rate BRWA bond in Example 1 is priced at 108.15. The yield-to-maturity is the solution for the rate, *r*, in the following equation:

$$108.15 = 1.6/(1 + r)^1 + 1.6/(1 + r)^2 + \ldots + 101.6/(1 + r)^{10}.$$

The Microsoft Excel or Google Sheets YIELD function may be used for bonds that pay periodic interest:

`=YIELD(settlement, maturity, rate, pr, redemption, frequency, [basis])` where

settlement is the settlement date entered using the DATE function

maturity is the maturity date entered using the DATE function

rate is the semi-annual (or periodic) coupon

pr is the price per 100 face value

redemption is the future value at maturity

frequency is the number of coupons per year

[basis] is the day-count convention, typically 0 for US bonds (30/360 day count).

If we assume the BRWA bond settles and matures on 15 October 2025 and 15 October 2030, respectively, the appropriate entries are DATE(2025,10,15) and DATE(2030,10,15). The other entries are *rate* = 1.6%, *pr* = 108.15, *redemption* = 100, *frequency* = 2, and *basis* = 0, as follows:

=YIELD(DATE(2025,10,15),DATE(2030,10,15),1.6%,108.15,100,2,0)

Given a price of 108.15, the YIELD function calculates the annual yield-to- maturity for the BRWA bond to be 1.50%. Additionally, since the yield-to-maturity is an internal rate of return, we can also use the IRR function in Microsoft Excel or Google Sheets to get the same result.

Yield-to-maturity, commonly referred to as "yield," is often used interchangeably with the market discount rate or required yield and in place of discussing bond prices. For example, market participants will simply say "yields are rising" rather than "market discount rates are rising" or "bond prices are falling."

BONDS WITH NEGATIVE YIELDS-TO-MATURITY

The yield-to-maturity on a bond may be positive, zero, or negative. Yields on many sovereign bonds fell below zero following accommodative monetary policies introduced by central banks starting in 2012 in response to below-target inflation rates. Bonds with a negative yield-to-maturity include those issued at higher yields in the past that have experienced significant price appreciation and newly issued zero-coupon sovereign government bonds priced at a premium to par value. Bonds are generally not issued with negative coupons.

In 2020, China issued its first ever negative-yielding sovereign bond denominated in euros, with terms shown in Exhibit 4.

Exhibit 4: People's Republic of China Eurobond

People's Republic of China Zero-Coupon Bond Brief Summary of Terms	
Issuer:	People's Republic of China
Settlement Date:	November 25, 2020
Maturity Date:	November 25, 2025
Principal Amount:	EUR 750 million
Interest:	Zero coupon (ACT/ACT day count)
Issuance Price:	100.763
Issuance Spread:	+30 bps p.a. plus Mid Swaps

People's Republic of China Zero-Coupon Bond Brief Summary of Terms	
Issuance and Trading:	Eurobond Listed on Multiple Exchanges Euroclear/ Clearstream
Seniority:	Senior Unsecured
Exchanges:	Luxembourg

The Excel YIELD function cannot not be used for zero-coupon bonds. Instead, we solve for the annualized yield-to-maturity using Equation 1 for the single cash flow of par (PMT = 100) after five years (t = 5) at the original issuance price (PV = 100.763):

$$PV = \frac{PMT}{(1+r)^t}.$$

$$100.763 = \frac{100}{(1+r)^5}.$$

$$r = \left(\frac{100}{100.763}\right)^{\frac{1}{5}} - 1.$$

$$r = -0.15\%.$$

The *Financial Times* reported high demand for this negative-yielding Chinese bond since its yield was more than 50 bps above that of European sovereign bonds—the five-year German bund was at approximately –0.74% around the same time —and more generally because many investors sought portfolio exposure to China amid a relative scarcity of euro-denominated Chinese bonds at the time.

Flat Price, Accrued Interest, and the Full Price

When a bond is priced between coupon payment dates, its price has two components: the **flat price** (PV^{Flat}) and the **accrued interest** (AI). The sum of the parts is the **full price** (PV^{Full}), which also is known as the invoice or "dirty" price.

$$PV^{Full} = PV^{Flat} + AI. \tag{3}$$

The flat price, which is the full price minus the accrued interest, is also called the quoted or "clean" price and is the type of price usually quoted by bond dealers. If a trade takes place, the accrued interest is added to the flat price to obtain the full price paid by the buyer and received by the seller on the **trade settlement date**. The trade settles when the bond buyer pays and the seller delivers the security.

The flat price is used for quotations to avoid misleading investors about a bond's market price trend. If full prices were quoted by dealers, investors would see price rises each day even if the YTM did not change due to the accrual of interest. Once a coupon payment is made, the quoted price would drop significantly, as shown in Exhibit 5.

Exhibit 5: Flat Price, Accrued Interest, and Full Price

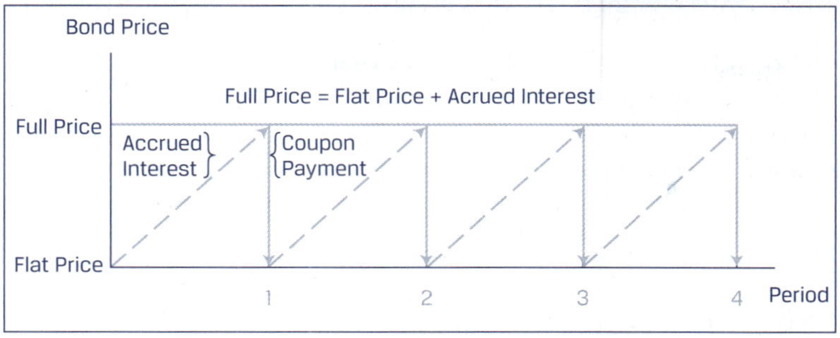

The accrued interest is the portion of the next coupon payment owed to the seller of a bond, because although the seller held the bond for a partial coupon period, the full coupon will be received by the buyer. To calculate accrued interest, we determine the fractional amount by counting the days in the period. If the coupon period has T days between payment dates and t days have passed since the last payment, the accrued interest is calculated using Equation 4:

$$AI = \frac{t}{T} \times PMT, \tag{4}$$

where

t = number of days from the prior coupon payment to the settlement date

T = number of days in the coupon period

t/T = fraction of coupon period that has passed since the prior payment

PMT = coupon payment per period

Note that the accrued interest portion of the full price does not depend on the yield-to-maturity. Therefore, it is only the flat price that is affected by a change in interest rates.

There are multiple approaches for day counting (or "day counts"). The day count is specified by two parameters: how days are counted within a given period and the number of days assumed per period. Two common day count conventions are 30/360 and actual/actual. The 30/360 day count assumes each month has exactly 30 days (although most don't) and each year has exactly 360 days (although none do). In contrast, the actual/actual day count convention assumes the actual number of days in each month and the actual number of days in a year.

EXAMPLE 2

Actual/Actual vs. 30/360 Day Count

Consider two otherwise identical bonds that pay 4.375% semiannual interest on 15 May and 15 November of each year. One is a government bond with an actual/actual day count and the other is a corporate bond with a 30/360 day count. The actual/actual method uses the actual number of days, including weekends, holidays, and leap days. The 30/360 method assumes 30 days in a month and 360 days in each year.

Calculate accrued interest for settlement on 27 June for both bonds.

Accrued interest for the actual/actual bond is the actual number of days between 15 May and 27 June (t = 43 days) divided by the actual number of days between 15 May and 15 November (T = 184 days), times the coupon payment.

For the 30/360 bond, we 42 days between 15 May and 27 June: 15 days between 15 May and 30 May and 27 days between 1 June and 27 June (31 May is not counted in the 30/360 convention). There are assumed to be 180 days in the six-month period between 15 May and 15 November.

	Actual/Actual Bond	30/360 Bond
Days (t)	43	42
Period (T)	184	180
t/T	0.233696	0.233333

Accrued interest is calculated as follows:

Actual/actual bond:AI = (43/184) × (4.375/2)

= 0.511209 per 100 of par value.

30/360 bond:AI = (42/180) × (4.375/2)

= 0.510417 per 100 of par value.

The full price of a fixed-rate bond between coupon payments given the market discount rate per period (r) is the present value of future cash flows as of the trade settlement date, as shown in Equation 5:

$$PV^{Full} = \frac{PMT}{(1+r)^{1-t/T}} + \frac{PMT}{(1+r)^{2-t/T}} + \cdots + \frac{PMT + FV}{(1+r)^{N-t/T}}. \quad (5)$$

This is very similar to Equation 2. The difference is that the next coupon payment (PMT) is discounted for the remainder of the coupon period, which is $1 - t/T$. The second coupon payment is discounted for that fraction plus another full period, $2 - t/T$.

Equation 5 is simplified by multiplying both the numerator and denominator by the expression $(1 + r)^{t/T}$. The result is Equation 6:

$$PV^{Full} = \left[\frac{PMT}{(1+r)^1} + \frac{PMT}{(1+r)^2} + \cdots + \frac{PMT + FV}{(1+r)^N}\right] \times (1+r)^{t/T}$$
$$= PV \times (1+r)^{t/T}. \quad (6)$$

An advantage of Equation 6 is that the expression in the brackets, PV, is easily obtained using the Excel YIELD function because there are N evenly spaced periods. PV here is the present value of future cash flows as of the last coupon date; it is identical to Equation 2 but is not the same as PV^{Flat}.

The next two examples demonstrate the calculation of a bond's flat price, accrued interest, and full price.

EXAMPLE 3

BRWA Bond—Flat and Full Price

Calculate the flat price and full price of the 3.2% fixed BRWA bond 90 days after the first coupon payment.

First, we calculate the bond's present value on the coupon date that begins the period during which settlement occurs, using Equation 2 or the PV function in Microsoft Excel or Google Sheets.

```
=-PV(rate, nper, pmt, [FV], type)
```

=-PV(0.02,9,1.60,100,0)

= 96.735

Next, we calculate the full price by counting the days using the specified day count convention and using Equation 6.

Number of days from beginning of period until settlement, $t = 90$

Number of days in the period containing settlement, $T = 180$

$$PV^{Full} = PV \times (1 + r)^{t/T}$$

$$PV^{Full} = 96.735 \times (1 + 0.02)^{90/180}$$

$$PV^{Full} = 97.698$$

Then we use Equation 4 to calculate accrued interest.

$$AI = \frac{t}{T} \times PMT$$

$$AI = \frac{90}{180} \times 1.60$$

$$AI = 0.80$$

Finally, we calculate the flat price using Equation 3 by subtracting the accrued interest from the full price.

$$PV^{Full} = PV^{Flat} + AI$$

$$PV^{Flat} = PV^{Full} - AI$$

$$PV^{Flat} = 97.698 - 0.80$$

$$PV^{Flat} = 96.898$$

Note: Quantities in the calculation are not rounded, though they are shown with three decimal places for presentation purposes. Solutions are rounded to three decimal places.

EXAMPLE 4

Romania Bond—Flat and Full Price

The 4.625% EUR annual, actual/actual fixed-coupon bond issued by Romania maturing 3 April 2049 was introduced in an earlier lesson. Calculate the full price (PV^{Full}), the accrued interest (AI), and the flat price (PV^{Flat}) for settlement on 15 December 2031 assuming an annual yield-to-maturity on that date of 3.50%.

Solution

Step 1 Calculate PV as of the beginning of the current coupon period for the settlement date:

```
=-PV(rate, nper, pmt, [FV], type)
```

=-PV(0.035,18,4.625,100,0)

= 114.838

Step 2 Calculate the actual number of days (t):

Days	Months
15	December
27	April
30	June, September, November
31	May, July, August, October
256	**Total**

Step 3 Calculate the actual number of days in the coupon period (T):

Date at beginning of period	4/3/2031
Date at end of period	4/3/2032
Actual number of days in period	**366**

Notice that 2032 is a leap year so it has an extra day.

Step 4 Use Equation 6 to solve for PV^{Full}:

$$PV^{Full} = PV \times (1 + r)^{\frac{t}{T}}.$$

$$PV^{Full} = 114.838 \times (1 + 0.035)^{\frac{256}{366}}.$$

$$PV^{Full} = 117.635.$$

Step 5 Use Equation 4 to solve for accrued interest:

$$AI = \frac{t}{T} \times PMT.$$

$$AI = \frac{256}{366} \times 4.625.$$

$$AI = 3.235.$$

Step 6 Use Equation 3 to solve for PV^{Flat}:

$$PV^{Full} = PV^{Flat} + AI.$$

$$PV^{Flat} = PV^{Full} - AI.$$

$$PV^{Flat} = 117.635 - 3.235.$$

$$PV^{Flat} = 114.400.$$

Note: Quantities in the calculation are not rounded, though they are shown with three decimal places for presentation purposes. Solutions are rounded to three decimal places.

KNOWLEDGE CHECK

1. Define yield-to-maturity.

Solution:

Yield-to-maturity is the internal rate of return on a bond's cash flows—the uniform interest rate such that when the future cash flows are discounted at that rate, the sum of the present values equals the price of the bond.

2. A non-callable fixed-coupon bond with a maturity in 10 years and a face value of 100 is issued with an annual coupon rate of 2.8% when the applicable market discount rate is also 2.8%. The price of this bond at issuance is:

   A. less than 100.

   B. exactly 100.

   C. more than 100.

   Solution:

   B is correct. When a bond is issued with a coupon rate that equals the market discount rate, it is priced at par.

3. A non-callable fixed-coupon bond with a maturity in 10 years and a face value of 100 has an annual coupon rate of 2.8%, while the market discount rate is 4.0%. The price of this bond at issuance is:

   A. less than 100.

   B. exactly 100.

   C. more than 100.

   Solution:

   A is correct. A bond with a coupon rate lower than the market discount rate will trade at a discount to par, to compensate for its "deficient" coupons relative to the market rate.

4. A sovereign bond that matures on 1 January 2030 pays an annual coupon of 1.2% and has a face value of 100. For a trade settlement date of 1 January 2020, the bonds are priced at 128. Calculate the yield-to-maturity as of the settlement date and price.

   Solution:

   –1.390%. We use the YIELD function in Microsoft Excel or Google Sheets:

```
=YIELD(settlement, maturity, rate, pr, redemption,
frequency, [basis])
```

   =YIELD(DATE(2020,1,1),DATE(2030,1,1),0.012,128,100,1)

   = -1.390%

5. A bond with a face value of 100 pays an annual coupon of 12% and matures on Ad14 August 2007. It uses the actual/actual day count convention. For a settlement date of 23 December 2002 and an annual YTM of 9.75%, calculate the full price, accrued interest, and flat price. Assume an actual/actual day count.

   Solution:

   Step 1 Calculate PV as of the beginning of the current coupon period for the settlement date:

```
=-PV(rate, nper, pmt, [FV], type)
```

   =-PV(0.0975,5,12,100,0)

   = 108.584

Step 2 Calculate the actual number of days (t):

Month	Days
August	17
September	30
October	31
November	30
December	23
Total	**131**

Step 3 Calculate the actual number of days in the coupon period (T):

Date at beginning of period	8/14/2002
Date at end of period	8/14/2003
Actual number of days in period	**365**

Step 4 Use Equation 6 to solve for PV^{Full}:

$$PV^{Full} = PV \times (1 + r)^{\frac{t}{T}}.$$

$$PV^{Full} = 108.584 \times (1 + 0.0975)^{\frac{131}{365}}.$$

$$PV^{Full} = 112.271.$$

Step 5 Use Equation 4 to solve for accrued interest:

$$AI = \frac{t}{T} \times PMT.$$

$$AI = \frac{131}{365} \times 12.$$

$$AI = 4.307.$$

Step 6 Use Equation 3 to solve for PV^{Flat}:

$$PV^{Full} = PV^{Flat} + AI.$$

$$PV^{Flat} = PV^{Full} - AI.$$

$$PV^{Flat} = 112.271 - 4.307.$$

$$PV^{Flat} = 107.964.$$

Note: Quantities in the calculation are not rounded, though they are shown with three decimal places for presentation purposes. Solutions are rounded to three decimal places.

6. Perform the same calculations for the same bond in Question 5, but use a 30/360 day count convention.

Solution:

Step 1 Calculate PV as of the beginning of the current coupon period for the settlement date:

```
=-PV(rate, nper, pmt, [FV], type)
```

=-PV(0.0975,5,12,100,0)

= 108.584

Step 2 Calculate the number of days (t):

Month	Days
August	16
September	30
October	30
November	30
December	23
Total	**129**

Step 3 Assume the number of days in the coupon period (T) is 360.

Step 4 Use Equation 6 to solve for PV^{Full}:

$$PV^{Full} = PV \times (1 + r)^{\frac{t}{T}}.$$

$$PV^{Full} = 108.584 \times (1 + 0.0975)^{\frac{129}{360}}.$$

$$PV^{Full} = 112.265.$$

Step 5 Use Equation 4 to solve for accrued interest:

$$AI = \frac{t}{T} \times PMT.$$

$$AI = \frac{129}{360} \times 12.$$

$$AI = 4.300.$$

Step 6 Use Equation 3 to solve for PV^{Flat}:

$$PV^{Full} = PV^{Flat} + AI.$$

$$PV^{Flat} = PV^{Full} - AI.$$

$$PV^{Flat} = 112.265 - 4.300.$$

$$PV^{Flat} = 107.965.$$

Note: Quantities in the calculation are not rounded, though they are shown with three decimal places for presentation purposes. Solutions are rounded to three decimal places.

RELATIONSHIPS BETWEEN BOND PRICES AND BOND FEATURES 3

☐ identify the relationships among a bond's price, coupon rate, maturity, and yield-to-maturity

Inverse Relationship

As seen in the prior lesson, the price of a fixed-rate bond will change as the interest rate used to discount future cash flows changes. For any time-value-of-money calculation, a higher discount rate results in a lower present value for any fixed future cash flow and a lower discount rate results in a higher present value. Therefore, bond yields-to-maturity and prices move in opposite directions.

Coupon Effect

The *size* of bond coupon cash flows affects how much a bond's price will change for a given yield change for bonds of the same maturity. The lower a bond's coupon, the higher the *proportion* of total cash flow that occurs at maturity. Discounting this final cash flow by the factor of $(1 + r)^N$ as shown in Equation 2 magnifies the impact of a given change in r relative to bonds whose final cash flow is a smaller proportion of the total. This coupon effect is best demonstrated by comparing the extreme case of a zero-coupon bond (with 100% of cash flows including cumulative interest paid at maturity) with an otherwise identical fixed-coupon bond, as in the following example.

EXAMPLE 5

Yield Change Effect for Zero-Coupon vs. Coupon Bond

Assume an investor has the choice between the 4.625% fixed-coupon 30-year Romania Eurobond priced at par and an otherwise identical zero-coupon bond from the same issuer at the same yield-to-maturity of 4.625%.

Calculate the percentage change in price for both bond alternatives if YTM rises or falls by 100 bps upon issuance.

Use Equation 1 (zero-coupon bond) and the Excel or Google Sheets PV function (4.625% coupon bond) to calculate and compare these changes. Please refer to the candidate learning ecosystem online for a spreadsheet of these calculations in the downloaded Microsoft Excel workbook.

Face Value	100
Periods / year	1
Number of periods	30
Coupon payment	4.625

Change	YTM	Prices		Price Changes		Percentage Price Changes	
		Coupon	Zero	Coupon	Zero	Coupon	Zero
--	0.04625	100.000	25.759	--	--	--	--
0.01	0.05625	85.665	19.364	−14.335	−6.395	−14.34%	−24.83%
−0.01	0.03625	118.107	34.361	18.107	8.601	18.11%	33.39%

For the same time-to-maturity, a lower-coupon (or zero-coupon) bond has a greater percentage price change than a higher-coupon bond when market discount rates change by the same amount.

Maturity Effect

The time-to-maturity of a bond also affects a bond's price/yield relationship. Generally, all else equal, a longer-term bond has a greater percentage price change than a shorter-term bond when the market discount rates change by the same amount. The maturity effect is the result of the higher N in Equation 2 for the longer-maturity bond.

EXAMPLE 6

Yield Change Effect for Different Maturities

Assume an investor has a choice between Bond A, with a 1.5% fixed coupon and a 30-year maturity priced at par, and Bond B, a 10-year, 1.5% fixed-coupon bond priced at par from the same issuer.

Calculate the percentage change in price for these if YTM rises or falls by 100 bps upon issuance.

Compare the price changes in the 10-year and 30-year bonds using the PV function to calculate and compare these changes. Please refer to the candidate learning ecosystem online for a spreadsheet of these calculations in the downloaded Microsoft Excel workbook.

Bond	A	B
Face Value	100	100
Price	100	100
Coupon Rate	0.015	0.015
Coupon Payment	1.50	1.50
Maturity	30	10
100 bps rise in YTM		
YTM	0.025	
Price	79.070	91.248
% change	−20.93%	−8.75%
100 bps fall in YTM		
YTM	0.005	
Price	127.794	109.730
% change	27.79%	9.73%

We see that the percentage price change for the longer-maturity bond is larger than that for the shorter-maturity bond. Also, we see that, in price terms, the change for a YTM *decrease* is larger than that for a YTM *increase*.

Exceptions to the maturity effect exist but are rare in practice. They occur only for low-coupon (but not zero-coupon), long-term bonds trading at a discount. The maturity effect always holds on zero-coupon bonds, as it does for bonds priced at par value or at a premium above par value.

Constant-Yield Price Trajectory

Bond prices change with the passage of time, even if the market discount rate remains the same. As time passes, so as N in Equation 2 approaches zero, the bondholder comes closer to receiving the par value at maturity, provided the issuer does not default. The **constant yield-price trajectory** in Exhibit 6 illustrates price changes of two 10-year bonds over time: a 2% coupon bond issued at a discount and an 8% coupon bond issued at a premium. At each time, the bond price is recalculated using a market discount rate of 5%.

Exhibit 6: Constant-Yield Price Trajectory

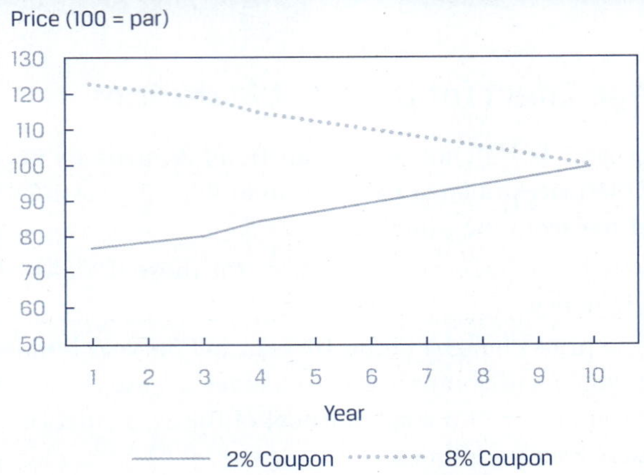

The 2% coupon bond's initial price is 76.835 per 100 of par value. The price increases each year and approaches par value as the maturity date nears. The 8% coupon bond's initial price is 123.165, and it decreases each year, approaching par value as the maturity date nears. Both prices are "pulled to par." Please refer to the candidate learning ecosystem online for a spreadsheet of these calculations in the downloaded Microsoft Excel workbook.

Convexity Effect

The *percentage* change in a bond's price will also vary depending on how the yield changes. The percentage price *increase* is greater, in absolute value, than the percentage price *decrease*. This implies that the relationship between bond prices and yields is not linear; instead, it is curved and "convex." Exhibit 7 shows this general relationship between a bond's price and its yield-to-maturity.

Exhibit 7: Convex Price–Yield Relationship

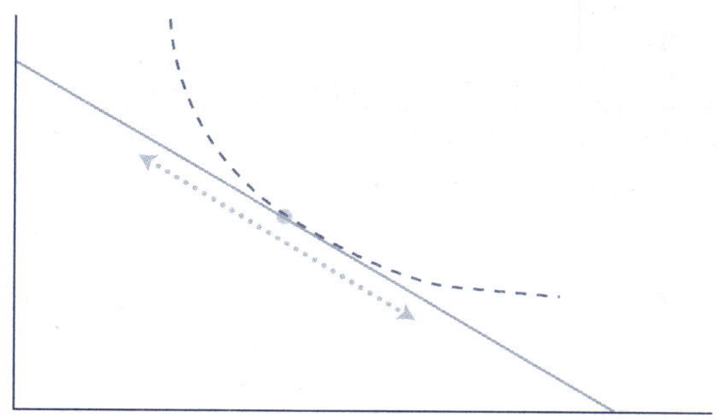

EXAMPLE 7

BRWA Bond: Convex Relationship

Despite a uniform increase and decrease in the BRWA bond's annual yield-to-maturity, notice how the resulting changes in price are different. Please refer to the candidate learning ecosystem online for a spreadsheet of these calculations in the downloaded Microsoft Excel workbook.

Face Value	100
Coupon payment	1.6
Number of periods	10

YTM Change	YTM	Price	% Price Change
--	0.016	100.00	--
0.004	0.020	96.41	−3.59%
−0.004	0.012	103.75	3.75%

A decrease in the yield-to-maturity from 160 bps to 120 bps results in a bond price increase of 3.75%, but an increase in the YTM from 160 bps to 200 bps results in a *smaller* bond price decrease. Based on this, we can say that the BRWA bond has *positive* convexity. Convexity will be discussed in greater detail in a later lesson.

KNOWLEDGE CHECK

1. Recall the Romania bond from Example 4. It pays annual coupons at a rate of 4.625% and has a face value of 100. Its issue date is 3 April 2019 and its maturity date is 3 April 2049. Calculate its original yield-to-maturity at issue if its issue price is 99.488.

   Solution:

   The original yield-to-maturity is 4.657%. The YIELD function arguments in Microsoft Excel or Google Sheets are as follows:

   ```
   =YIELD(settlement, maturity, rate, pr, redemption, frequency, [basis])
   ```

   =YIELD(DATE(2019,4,3),DATE(2049,4,3),0.04625,99.488,100,1)

   = 4.657%

2. Describe the coupon effect.

   Solution:

   Given two non-callable, fixed-coupon bonds that have different coupons but are otherwise identical, for a change in yield, the lower-coupon bond will have a greater percentage price change than the higher-coupon bond.

3. Describe the maturity effect.

   Solution:

   Generally, for two bonds that are identical except for their times-to-maturity, the longer-maturity bond will have a larger percentage price change than will the shorter-maturity bond when yields change by the same amount.

4. Two non-callable, fixed-coupon bonds have the same maturity date. One trades at a discount; the other trades at a premium. If the yield stays constant until the bonds mature and neither defaults, the two bonds' prices will, over time:

   A. converge.

   B. remain unchanged.

   C. diverge.

   Solution:

   A is correct. The prices will converge because of the "pull-to-par" effect. As the maturity date nears, the present values of future cash flows will fall or rise to the par value, provided that the issuer does not default.

4 MATRIX PRICING

☐ describe matrix pricing

Matrix Pricing Process

Unlike listed equity securities, most bonds are not actively traded, so there is often no current market price available to calculate yield-to-maturity. The same problem occurs for bonds that are not yet issued. In these situations, it is common to estimate price by using the prices of comparable but more frequently traded bonds. These comparable bonds have similar times-to-maturity, coupon rates, and credit quality. This estimation process, illustrated in Exhibit 8 and Exhibit 9, is called **matrix pricing**.

Exhibit 8: Matrix Pricing

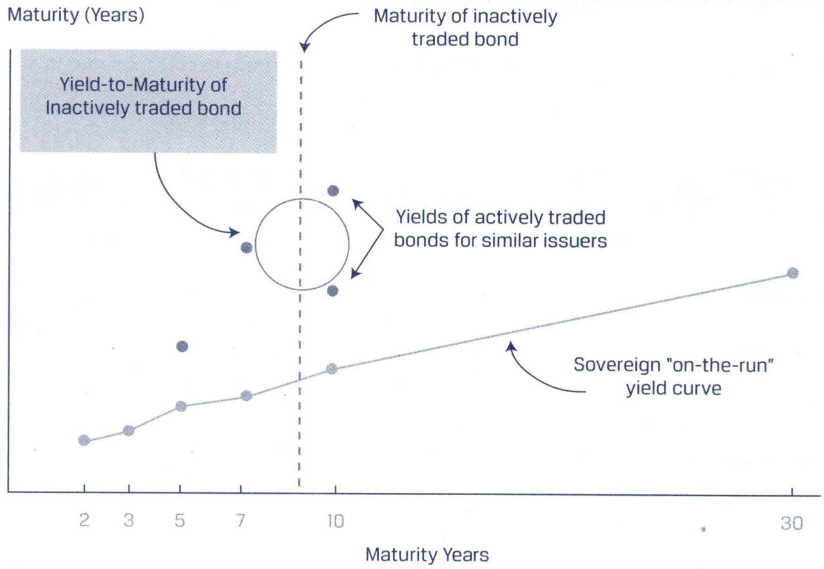

Exhibit 9: Determining Price of New or Illiquid Bond Using Matrix Pricing

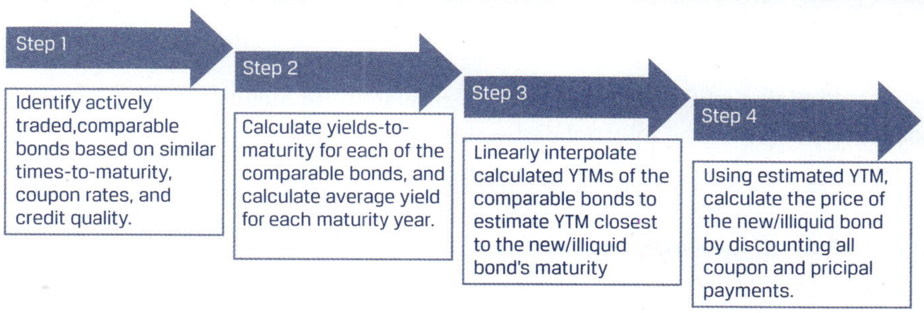

For example, suppose that an analyst needs to value a three-year, 4% semiannual coupon payment corporate bond, Bond X. Assume that Bond X is not actively traded and that there are no recent transactions reported for this particular security. Exhibit 10 and Exhibit 11 shows quoted prices and yields-to-maturity for four corporate bonds with very similar credit quality, in tabular and matrix form (by coupon rate and time-to-maturity).

Exhibit 10: Actively Traded Comparable Bonds

Bond	Tenor	Coupon (S/A)	Price	Yield-to-Maturity
A	2 years	3.00%	98.5	3.786%
B	2 years	5.00%	102.25	3.821%
C	5 years	2.00%	90.25	4.181%
D	5 years	4.00%	99.125	4.196%

Exhibit 11: Actively Traded Comparable Bonds Matrix

	2% Coupon	3% Coupon	4% Coupon	5% Coupon
Two Years		98.500 3.786%		102.250 3.821%
Three Years			Bond X	
Four Years				
Five Years	90.250 4.181%		99.125 4.196%	

Next, the analyst calculates the average yield for each year: 3.8035% for the two-year bonds and 4.1885% for the five-year bonds.

$$\frac{0.03786 + 0.03821}{2} = 3.8035\%$$

$$\frac{0.04181 + 0.04196}{2} = 4.1855\%$$

The estimated three-year yield for bonds of similar credit quality can be obtained with linear interpolation. The interpolated yield is 3.932%.

$$0.038035 + \left(\frac{3-2}{5-2}\right) \times (0.041885 - 0.038035) = 0.03932.$$

Using 3.9318% as the estimated three-year annual yield, the three-year, 4% semiannual coupon payment corporate bond has an estimated price of 100.191 per 100 of par value.

$$\frac{2}{(1.019659)^1} + \frac{2}{(1.019659)^2} + \frac{2}{(1.019659)^3} + \frac{2}{(1.019659)^4} + \frac{2}{(1.019659)^5} + \frac{102}{(1.019659)^6} = 100.191.$$

Calculation of yield-to-maturity can also be done with the Excel or Google Sheets YIELD function:

=YIELD(DATE(2025,10,1),DATE(2028,10,1),0.04,100.191,100,2,1)

Matrix pricing also is used in underwriting new bonds to get an estimate of the **required yield spread** over the benchmark rate, or the difference in yield-to-maturity between the bond and that of a government benchmark bond with the same or a similar time-to-maturity.

Suppose that a corporation is about to issue a five-year bond. The corporate issuer currently has a four-year, 3% annual coupon payment debt liability. The price of that bond is 102.400 per 100 of par value. This is the full price, which is the same as the flat price because the accrued interest is zero. This implies that the coupon payment has just been made and there are four full years to maturity. The four-year rate of return required by investors for this bond is 2.36%:

$$102.400 = \frac{3}{(1+r)^1} + \frac{3}{(1+r)^2} + \frac{3}{(1+r)^3} + \frac{103}{(1+r)^4};\ r = 0.0236.$$

This can also be calculated using the YIELD function in Microsoft Excel or Google Sheets:

=YIELD(DATE(2025,10,1),DATE(2029,10,1),0.03,102.401,100,2,1)

Suppose that there are no four-year government bonds to calculate the required yield spread on this security. However, there are three-year and five-year government bonds that have yields-to-maturity of 0.75% and 1.45%, respectively. The average of the two yields-to-maturity is 1.10%, which is the estimated yield for the four-year government bond. Therefore, the estimated required yield spread is 126 bps over the implied benchmark rate (0.0236 – 0.0110 = 0.0126).

The issuer now has an estimate of the four-year yield spread: 126 bps. This spread is a reference point for estimating the five-year spread for the newly issued bond.

QUESTION SET

1. True or false: Bond price quotes on such platforms as Bloomberg often represent the price at which the most recent trade for that bond was made.

   A. True

   B. False

   Solution:

   False. Most bonds are infrequently traded, so price quotes on such platforms as Bloomberg are often estimated using matrix pricing methods.

2. An analyst is estimating a price for an illiquid four-year, 4.5% annual coupon payment corporate bond. The analyst identifies two corporate bonds that have similar credit quality: One is a three-year, 5.50% annual coupon payment bond priced at 107.500 per 100 of par value, and the other is a five-year, 4.50% annual coupon payment bond priced at 104.750 per 100 of par value. Using matrix pricing, the estimated price of the illiquid bond per 100 of par value is *closest* to:

   A. 103.895.

   B. 104.991.

   C. 106.125.

   Solution:

   B is correct. The first step is to determine the yields-to-maturity on the observed bonds. The required yield on the three-year, 5.50% bond priced at 107.500 is 2.856%:

$$107.500 = \frac{5.50}{(1+r)^1} + \frac{5.50}{(1+r)^2} + \frac{105.50}{(1+r)^3};\ r = 0.02856.$$

The required yield on the five-year, 4.50% bond priced at 104.750 is 3.449%:

$$104.750 = \frac{4.50}{(1+r)^1} + \frac{4.50}{(1+r)^2} + \frac{4.50}{(1+r)^3} + \frac{4.50}{(1+r)^4} + \frac{104.50}{(1+r)^5};\ r = 0.03449.$$

The estimated yield for a four-year bond having the same credit quality is the average of two required yields:

$$\frac{0.02856 + 0.03449}{2} = 0.031525.$$

Given an estimated yield-to-maturity of 3.153%, the estimated price of the illiquid four-year, 4.50% annual coupon payment corporate bond is 104.991 per 100 of par value:

$$\frac{4.50}{(1.031525)^1} + \frac{4.50}{(1.031525)^2} + \frac{4.50}{(1.031525)^3} + \frac{104.50}{(1.031525)^4} = 104.991.$$

3. An analyst uses the matrix pricing approach to determine the price of an illiquid bond. Identify three bond features that could be used to compare frequently traded bonds with the illiquid one.

Solution:

Matrix pricing involves determining the price of a new or illiquid bond by comparing it to frequently traded bonds with similar

1. maturity,
2. coupon rates, and
3. credit quality.

PRACTICE PROBLEMS

1. A non-callable, fixed-coupon bond has a price of 106.0625 and a YTM of 2.8%. If the YTM were to increase instantaneously by 80 bps, the price of the bond would decrease by 11%. If the YTM were to decrease instantaneously by 80 bps, the price of the bond would increase by:

   A. less than 11%.

   B. exactly 11%.

   C. more than 11%.

2. Exceptions to the maturity effect exist for bonds that have:

   A. long maturities, make small coupon payments, and trade at a discount.

   B. short maturities, have high coupon rates, and trade at a discount.

   C. long maturities, have high coupon rates, and trade at a premium.

3. With a constant market discount rate, as a non-callable, fixed-coupon bond approaches maturity:

   A. the price–yield relationship will become more convex.

   B. a low-coupon bond trading at a discount will increase in price.

   C. a high-coupon bond trading at a premium will increase in price.

4. A fixed-income analyst is pricing a bond using the following equation.

$$PV = \frac{3}{(1+0.0275)^1} + \frac{3}{(1+0.0275)^2} + \dots + \frac{103}{(1+0.0275)^{40}}$$

   The bond's price, relative to par, is *most likely*:

   A. greater than 100.

   B. exactly 100.

   C. less than 100.

5. A four-year, 2.0% semiannual coupon bond that pays coupons semiannually is trading at a price of 102.581. The bond's annualized yield-to-maturity is *closest to*:

   A. 0.67%.

   B. 1.34%.

   C. 2.22%.

6. A bond is traded in between its coupon payment dates. Which of the following is true?

   A. The buyer must pay the full price plus the accrued interest.

   B. The bond's quoted price is greater than its flat price.

   C. Accrued interest is not included in the flat price.

7. An analyst is analyzing a bond that will soon be issued by XYZ Company. The new bond will have five years to maturity and a 2.25% coupon, paid semiannually. XYZ has never issued bonds before, so the analyst will use matrix pricing. The analyst has identified four similar bonds with the following characteristics.

Bond	Maturity	Coupon (S/A)	YTM
A	4 Years	2.250%	1.6995%
B	4 Years	1.750%	1.5438%
C	7 Years	2.250%	2.2671%
D	7 Years	1.500%	1.9576%

Using the information provided, create a pricing matrix for the analyst to estimate the price of the XYZ five-year bond by filling in the matrix below with Bonds A, B, C, and D:

	Coupon Rate			
	1.50%	1.75%	2.25%	2.25%
4 Years				
5 Years				
6 Years				
7 Years				

SOLUTIONS

1. C is correct. The absolute amount of the price increase would be more than the absolute amount of the price decrease for the same absolute change in YTM because of the convex relationship between bond price and yield.

   A is incorrect because of the positive convex relationship between bond price and yield. For a given level of yield change, the price rise for that given amount of yield decrease will be larger than the price decline for that amount of yield increase.

   B is incorrect because the relationship between bond price and yield is not linear.

2. A is correct. Exceptions to the maturity effect are rare and occur only for low-coupon (but not zero-coupon) long-term bonds trading at a discount.

   B is incorrect because the maturity effect holds for bonds that have short maturities and high coupons.

   C is incorrect because the maturity effect always holds on bonds priced at a premium above par value.

3. B is correct. Any bond trading at a discount will increase in price because of the pull-to-par effect.

   A is incorrect because the price–yield relationship generally becomes less convex as a bond approaches maturity.

   C is incorrect because a high-coupon bond trading at a premium will decrease in price as it approaches maturity.

4. A is correct. The bond's periodic coupon rate exceeds the periodic market discount rate, or its coupon rate is "excessive" relative to the market. Therefore, the bond will trade at a premium to par.

   B is incorrect. For the bond to trade at par, the coupon rate and market discount rate (yield-to-maturity) must be equal.

   C is incorrect. For the bond to trade at a discount, the yield-to-maturity would have to be higher than the coupon rate.

5. B is correct. Two approaches to calculating the yield-to-maturity are calculating an IRR or using the YIELD function in Microsoft Excel or Google Sheets. The periodic IRR is annualized by multiplying by two.

Period	Cash Flow	YIELD Function	
0	−102.581	Settlement date	1/1/2000
1	1	Maturity date	1/1/2004
2	1	Coupon	0.02
3	1	Price	102.581
4	1	Redemption	100
5	1	Coupon frequency	2
6	1	**Yield**	**1.34%**
7	1		
8	101		
Periodic IRR	**0.67%**		
Annualized IRR	**1.34%**		

   A is incorrect because 0.67% is the periodic, not annualized, yield-to-maturity.

C is incorrect. Note that this choice can be eliminated because the bond is trading at a premium; thus its yield-to-maturity is lower than its coupon rate of 2.0%.

Please refer to the candidate learning ecosystem online for a spreadsheet of these calculations in the downloaded Microsoft Excel workbook.

6. C is correct. The flat price, quoted by bond dealers, is the full price less accrued interest. Accrued interest is not included in the flat price.

   A is incorrect. The buyer must pay the full price, which already includes accrued interest.

   B is incorrect. The flat price is the quoted price.

7. To price the new XYZ bond, the analyst should group yields for comparable bonds in a matrix with maturities and coupon rates.

		Coupon Rate		
	1.50%	**1.75%**	**2.25%**	**2.25%**
4 Years		B		A
5 Years				
6 Years				
7 Years	D		C	

LEARNING MODULE

7

Yield and Yield Spread Measures for Fixed-Rate Bonds

LEARNING OUTCOMES

Mastery	*The candidate should be able to:*
☐	calculate annual yield on a bond for varying compounding periods in a year
☐	compare, calculate, and interpret yield and yield spread measures for fixed-rate bonds

INTRODUCTION

1

Earlier lessons demonstrated the relationship between bond prices and yields-to-maturity (YTMs), as well as other features, such as coupon rate and time-to-maturity. Two important considerations for interpreting and determining yields-to-maturity and other yield measures are the assumed frequency of compounding interest and the presence of embedded options that could affect cash flow amounts or timing. This module explores these considerations and extends the analysis of yields by introducing spread measures, which compare yields to benchmark rates to ascertain how much an investor would be compensated for taking certain risks.

Most of the examples and exhibits used throughout the reading can be downloaded as a Microsoft Excel workbook. Each worksheet in the workbook is labeled with the corresponding example or exhibit number in the text.

LEARNING MODULE OVERVIEW

- Yields-to-maturity allow analysts to use a single measure to compare bonds with varying maturities and coupons. An important factor in yield determination and interpretation is the frequency of compounding, known as periodicity.
- All else equal, more frequent compounding results in greater future values or returns. Therefore, compounding more frequently at a lower rate can be equivalent to compounding less frequently at a higher rate; the more frequent compounding makes up for the lower rate.

- Prices and yields of bonds with embedded options require adjustments to reflect the value of the option. The option-adjusted yield spread and yield-to-worst are measures that reflect option values.
- Yield measures for a bond, as well as changes in them, can be decomposed into a benchmark rate and a spread over the benchmark rate. Benchmark rates reflect macroeconomic, "top-down" conditions that affect all bonds in a market, while spreads capture issuer-specific, "bottom-up" factors, such as credit risk, liquidity, and taxation.
- Similar to how a yield curve graphically depicts the relationship between yields-to-maturity and times-to-maturity for securities with the same risk profile, benchmark rates and spreads can be graphed by time-to-maturity as well, to show the term structure of credit spreads.

LEARNING MODULE SELF-ASSESSMENT

These initial questions are intended to help you gauge your current level of understanding of the learning module.

1. Complete the sentences by filling in the blanks using the following words:

   annualized

   compounded

   standardized

   Both capital market securities' yields and money market rates with maturity dates shorter than one year are ________________. However, money market rates are not ________________.

   Solution:

   Both capital market securities' yields and money market rates with maturity dates shorter than one year are annualized. However, money market rates are not compounded.

2. A three-year sovereign non-callable bond is priced at 106.24 per 100. The bond pays a 2% semiannual coupon. The annual yield-to-maturity for the bond is closest to:

   A. 0.077%.

   B. 0.039%.

   C. 1.883%.

   Solution:

   A is correct. Given that the bond pays coupons semiannually, the semiannual yield-to-maturity is calculated by solving for *r* in the following equation. Additionally, the IRR or YIELD functions in Microsoft Excel and Google Sheets can be used.

$$106.24 = \frac{1}{(1+r)^1} + \frac{1}{(1+r)^2} + \frac{1}{(1+r)^3} + \frac{1}{(1+r)^4} + \frac{1}{(1+r)^5} + \frac{101}{(1+r)^6}.$$

$$r = -0.00038596.$$

Given that the yield is expressed in semiannual terms, it needs to be annualized by multiplying by 2, which results in –0.000772, or –0.077%.

B is incorrect because it is the semiannual, not annual, yield.

C is incorrect because 1.883% is the bond's current yield, not yield-to-maturity.

3. A fixed-income analyst obtains the following data for three corporate bonds with the same maturity dates. The relevant government bond benchmark rate, calculated on a semiannual bond equivalent basis, is 1.10%. Calculate the G-spread for each bond.

	Bond A	Bond B	Bond C
Yield-to-maturity	1.271%	1.213%	1.178%
Coupon frequency and assumed periodicity	Annual	Semiannual	Quarterly

Solution:

The G-spread for Bond B is (0.01213 – 0.011) = 11.3 bps.

Before computing the G-spreads for Bonds A and C, the yields-to-maturity must first be converted to a periodicity of two. The semiannual equivalent yield for Bond A is 1.267%:

$$\left(1 + \frac{APR_m}{m}\right)^m = \left(1 + \frac{APR_n}{n}\right)^n.$$

$$\left(1 + \frac{0.01271}{1}\right)^1 = \left(1 + \frac{APR_2}{2}\right)^2.$$

$$APR_2 = 0.01267 = 1.267\%.$$

Thus, its G-spread is (0.01267 – 0.011) = 167 bps.

The semiannual equivalent yield for Bond C is 1.1797%:

$$\left(1 + \frac{APR_m}{m}\right)^m = \left(1 + \frac{APR_n}{n}\right)^n.$$

$$\left(1 + \frac{0.01178}{4}\right)^4 = \left(1 + \frac{APR_2}{2}\right)^2.$$

$$APR_2 = 0.011797 = 1.1797\%.$$

Thus, its G-spread is (0.011797 – 0.011) = 8 bps.

4. If a bond has an embedded call option and the value of the call option is positive, the option-adjusted price, compared to the flat price of the bond, is most likely:

   A. lower.

   B. the same.

   C. higher.

Solution:

A is correct. The value of the call option is the price of the option-free bond minus the price of the callable bond. If the value of the call option is positive, then the option-adjusted price is lower compared to the flat price of the bond.

B is incorrect because if the value of the call option is positive, the option-adjusted price compared to the flat price of the bond is lower, not the same.

C is incorrect because if the value of the call option is positive, the option-adjusted price compared to the flat price of the bond is lower, not higher.

2 PERIODICITY AND ANNUALIZED YIELDS

☐ calculate annual yield on a bond for varying compounding periods in a year

Investors analyzing bonds with various cash flow and maturity profiles seek a *standardized* yield measure to compare across different choices. Yield measures are usually *annualized* in order to allow a direct comparison. For capital market securities maturing in more than one year, investors want an *annualized* and *compounded* yield-to-maturity. Conventions for instruments maturing in one year or less will be covered in a later lesson.

An annualized and compounded yield on a fixed-rate bond depends on the assumed number of interest periods in the year, which is called the **periodicity** of the annual rate. The periodicity typically matches the frequency of coupon payments. For example, the fixed-coupon five-year bond issued by Bright Wheels Automotive (BRWA) from earlier lessons pays semiannual coupons with a stated annual yield-to-maturity of 3.2% for a periodicity of 2—the rate per semiannual period (1.6%) times 2. A bond that pays quarterly coupons has a stated annual yield for a periodicity of 4—the rate per quarter times 4.

Exhibit 1 shows how a 5% stated annual yield-to-maturity generates different amounts in one year with annual, semiannual, quarterly, monthly compounding based on a fixed-rate par bond priced at 100.

Exhibit 1: Effective Annual Rate for Different Compounding Periods

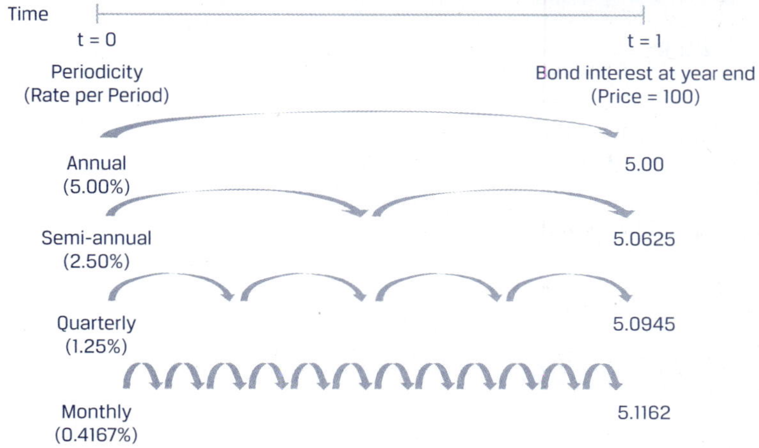

The bond interest amounts on the right-hand side of Exhibit 1 expressed as percentages are known as effective annual rates. An **effective annual rate** has a periodicity of 1 because there is just one compounding period in the year. For example, for a quarterly coupon bond that pays 1.25% per period, or an annual coupon rate of (1.25% × 4) = 5%, each coupon received is assumed to be reinvested at the periodic rate—here, 1.25%—for the remainder of the year. We can solve for the future value of these cash flows using the Excel or Google Sheets FV function:

```
=FV(rate, nper, pmt, [pv], [type]),
```

where

rate is the periodic reinvestment rate

nper is the number of periods in a year

pmt is the rate per period

[*pv*] is the present value

[*type*] indicates when payments occur, with 0 designating payment at the end of each period

For the quarterly coupon bond:

=FV(0.0125,4,1.25,0,0) = 5.0945.

Therefore, assuming each coupon is reinvested at 1.25% through the end of the year, a quarterly coupon bond with an annual stated rate of 5% generates the same interest as an annual coupon bond with a stated rate of 5.0945%. The Excel or Google Sheets EFFECT function may also be used to calculate the effective annual rate for a given number of compounding periods per year.

The most common periodicity in the United States, the United Kingdom, and several other fixed-income markets is 2 because most bonds in these jurisdictions make semiannual coupon payments. An annual rate having a periodicity of two is known as a **semiannual bond basis yield**, or **semiannual bond equivalent yield**. Therefore, a semiannual bond basis yield is the yield per semiannual period times 2. It is important to remember that "semiannual bond basis yield" and "yield per semiannual period" have different meanings. For example, if a bond yield is 2% per semiannual period, its annual yield is 4% when stated on a semiannual bond basis.

EXAMPLE 1

Periodicity of Zero-Coupon Bonds

The periodicity of the annual market discount rate for a zero-coupon bond is arbitrary because there are no coupon payments. Consider a five-year, zero-coupon bond priced at 80 per 100 of par value. Assuming annual compounding, or a periodicity of one, the yield-to-maturity is 4.564%.

$$80 = \frac{100}{(1+r)^5}; r = 0.045640; 4.564\%$$

Assuming quarterly compounding, or a periodicity of four, the annual yield-to-maturity for this same five-year, zero-coupon bond is 4.488%.

$$80 = \frac{100}{(1+r)^{20}}; r = 0.011220; \times 4 = 0.044880.$$

As shown in Exhibit 2, 2.2565% compounded 2 times a year, 1.1220% compounded 4 times a year, and 0.3726% compounded 12 times a year are all equivalent to an effective annual rate of 4.564%.

Exhibit 2: Periodicity of Annual Discount Rate for Zero-Coupon Bond

Column 1	*Column 2*	*Column 3: (Col. 2 × 5)*	*Column 4*	*Column 5: (Col. 2 × Col. 4)*	*Column 6: (1+Col. 4)^(Col. 2)*
Periodicity	**Number of Periods/ Year**	**Number of Compounding Periods**	**Periodic Yield-to-Maturity (%)**	**Annual Yield- to-Maturity (%)**	**Periodic YTM Compounded at Periods/ Year (%)**
Annual	1	5	0.045640	0.045640	0.045640
Semi-annual	2	10	0.022565	0.045130	0.045640
Quarterly	4	20	0.011220	0.044879	0.045640
Monthly	12	60	0.003726	0.044712	0.045640

The compounded total return is the same for each expression for the annual rate. They differ in terms of the number of compounding periods per year—that is, in terms of the *periodicity* of the annual rate. For a given pair of cash flows, the stated annual rate and the periodicity are inversely related.

An important tool in fixed-income analysis is the conversion of an annualized yield using one periodicity to another periodicity. These are called periodicity, or compounding, conversions. Equation 1 shows a general formula to convert an annual percentage rate (APR) for m periods per year, denoted APR_m, to an annual percentage rate for n periods per year, APR_n:

$$\left(1 + \frac{APR_m}{m}\right)^m = \left(1 + \frac{APR_n}{n}\right)^n. \quad (1)$$

For example, suppose that a three-year, 5% semiannual coupon payment corporate bond is priced at 104 per 100 of par value. Its yield-to-maturity is 3.582%, quoted on a semiannual bond basis for a periodicity of 2: 0.01791 × 2 = 0.03582.

$$104 = \frac{2.5}{(1+r)^1} + \frac{2.5}{(1+r)^2} + \frac{2.5}{(1+r)^3} + \frac{2.5}{(1+r)^4} + \frac{2.5}{(1+r)^5} + \frac{102.5}{(1+r)^6}; r = 0.01791.$$

To compare this bond with others, an analyst converts this annualized yield-to-maturity to quarterly and monthly compounding. Doing so entails using Equation 1 to convert from a periodicity of $m = 2$ to periodicities of $n = 4$ and $n = 12$.

$$\left(1+\frac{0.03582}{2}\right)^2 = \left(1+\frac{APR_4}{4}\right)^4; APR_4 = 0.03566.$$

$$\left(1+\frac{0.03582}{2}\right)^2 = \left(1+\frac{APR_{12}}{12}\right)^{12}; APR_{12} = 0.03556.$$

An annual yield-to-maturity of 3.582% for semiannual compounding provides the same rate of return as annual yields of 3.566% and 3.556% for quarterly and monthly compounding, respectively. A general rule for periodicity conversions is *compounding more frequently at a lower annual rate corresponds to compounding less frequently at a higher annual rate.* This rule can be used to check periodicity conversion calculations.

EXAMPLE 2

Comparing Strip Bonds to Coupon Bonds

Financial intermediaries can own coupon bonds and then issue individual zero-coupon bonds composed of coupon or principal payments from the coupon bonds. These zero-coupon bonds are known as strip bonds. Strip bonds are attractive to investors seeking to match known cash flows on a specific future date.

A 20-year government of Canada strip (zero-coupon) bond is priced at 69.4300 per 100. An analyst wants to compare the yield of the strip bond with that of a newly issued 20-year coupon bond. Both the strip bond and the coupon bond are non-callable. The 20-year coupon bond pays semiannual coupons of 2%, and its current price is 101.99 per 100, which corresponds to a semiannual bond equivalent yield of 1.880%.

The analyst will compute a semiannual bond equivalent yield for the strip bond and compare it to the semiannual bond equivalent yield of 1.880% of the 20-year coupon bond.

There are two approaches. The first involves calculating a yield-to-maturity assuming annual compounding for the strip bond and converting it to a semiannual equivalent bond yield. The second approach involves directly computing a semiannual yield-to-maturity for the strip bond and annualizing it by multiplying it by 2.

Approach 1

The 20-year strip bond does not pay any coupons, so as the first step, we assume annual compounding (periodicity of 1) to calculate an effective annual rate based on the current price and remaining years to maturity.

$$69.43 = \frac{100}{(1+r)^{20}}; r = 0.01840997 = 1.841\%.$$

The next step is to convert the effective annual rate to semiannual bond equivalent yield. This is done by using Equation 1 to convert from a periodicity of 1 to a periodicity of 2.

$$\left(1+\frac{APR_m}{m}\right)^m = \left(1+\frac{APR_n}{n}\right)^n.$$

$$\left(1+\frac{0.01841}{1}\right)^1 = \left(1+\frac{APR_2}{2}\right)^2.$$

$$APR_2 = 0.01832604 = 1.833\%.$$

Approach 2

Alternatively, we can assume that compounding happens semiannually (periodicity of two) and the effective rate calculated would be semiannual.

$$69.43 = \frac{100}{(1+r)^{40}}; r = 0.009163 = 0.916\%.$$

To annualize this, we multiply it by 2 and obtain the same result as the first approach: 1.833%.

EXAMPLE 3

Periodicity Conversion with Negative Yields

Assume the German government issues a five-year zero-coupon bond at a price of 103.72. Calculate the effective annual rate of the bond at issuance assuming annual, semiannual, and monthly compounding.

Solution:

First, we can calculate the German bond's yield-to-maturity as an effective annual rate assuming the periodicity of 1.

$$103.72 = \frac{100}{(1+r)^{5}}; r = -0.00727834 = -0.7278\%.$$

Converting that yield to semiannual and monthly compounding requires using Equation 1 to convert to from a periodicity of 1 to periodicities of 2 and 12, respectively.

Conversion of an annual yield (m = 1) to semiannual (n = 2):

$$\left(1+\frac{APR_m}{m}\right)^m = \left(1+\frac{APR_n}{n}\right)^n.$$

$$\left(1+\frac{-0.007278}{1}\right)^1 = \left(1+\frac{APR_2}{2}\right)^2.$$

$$APR_2 = -0.007291 = -0.7291\%.$$

Conversion of an annual yield (m = 1) to monthly (n = 12):

$$\left(1+\frac{APR_m}{m}\right)^m = \left(1+\frac{APR_n}{n}\right)^n.$$

$$\left(1+\frac{-0.007278}{1}\right)^1 = \left(1+\frac{APR_{12}}{12}\right)^{12}.$$

$$APR_2 = -0.007303 = -0.7303\%.$$

Note: Quantities in the calculation are not rounded, though they are shown with three decimal places for presentation purposes. Solutions are rounded to three decimal places.

QUESTION SET

1. A bond has a yield-to-maturity of –0.50% using annual compounding. If the yield is converted to monthly compounding, it will *most likely* be:

   A. greater than –0.50%.

   B. equal to –0.50%.

C. less than –0.50%.

Solution:

C is correct. A general rule for periodicity conversions is compounding more frequently within the year corresponds to a lower (or more negative) yield-to-maturity.

2. Convert a yield of 1.736% compounded monthly to an effective annual rate.

Solution:

The effective annual rate assumes only one compounding period in a year (periodicity of 1). Converting from monthly to annual compounding requires converting from a periodicity of 12 to 1:

$$\left(1+\frac{APR_m}{m}\right)^m = \left(1+\frac{APR_n}{n}\right)^n.$$

$$\left(1+\frac{0.01736}{12}\right)^{12} = \left(1+\frac{APR_1}{1}\right)^1.$$

$$APR_1 = 0.0175 = 1.75\%.$$

3. When calculating yield-to-maturity for a strip (zero-coupon) bond, the periodicity must be 1.

Justify your answer.

A. True

B. False

Solution

False. The periodicity of the annual market discount rate for a zero-coupon bond is arbitrary because there are no coupon payments. For example, a yield calculated using quarterly periodicity (4) can simply be converted to a yield with annual periodicity (1).

OTHER YIELD MEASURES, CONVENTIONS, AND ACCOUNTING FOR EMBEDDED OPTIONS

3

☐ compare, calculate, and interpret yield and yield spread measures for fixed-rate bonds

Other Yield Measures and Conventions

The current yield, a simple measure equal to a bond's annual coupon divided by the flat price, was introduced in an earlier lesson. For example, if the BRWA 3.2% semi-annual fixed-coupon five-year bond introduced earlier were trading at a price of 98.7 per $100 in face value at time *t*, its current yield would be

$$CY_t = \text{Annual coupon}_t/\text{Bond price}_t \quad (2)$$

$$= 3.2\%/0.987 = 3.242\%.$$

The current yield is a crude measure of return because it focuses solely on interest income, ignoring the frequency of coupon payments, interest on interest (time value of money), and accrued interest. In addition to collecting and reinvesting coupon payments, the investor has a gain if the bond is purchased at a discount and is redeemed at par value. The investor has a loss if the bond is purchased at a premium and is redeemed at par value.

In practice, the actual timing of cash flows is important for quoting and calculating bond yields-to-maturity. Consider from earlier the 30-year 4.625% annual coupon Romania eurobond maturing on 3 April 2049. Suppose that for settlement on 3 April 2026, the bond is priced at 97.3684 per 100 of par value to yield 4.75% quoted on an annual, actual/actual basis. Its coupon payment is scheduled for 3 April of each year. The yield calculation implicitly assumes that the payments are made on those exact dates. This calculation ignores the fact that several of those dates are not business days. For example, both 3 April 2027 and 3 April 2032 are Saturdays, so investors will receive coupon payments on the following Mondays, 5 April 2027 and 2032, respectively.

Yield measures that assume payments are made on scheduled dates and that do not account for weekends and holidays are quoted on what is called **street convention**. This assumption simplifies bond price and yield calculations and commonly is used in practice. A **true yield** that uses the actual payment dates (e.g., 5 April 2027 and 2032 in the Romania bond example), accounting for weekends and holidays, can also be computed. The true yield is never higher than the street convention yield because weekends and holidays delay the time to payment. The difference is typically small, no more than a basis point or two. Therefore, the true yield is not commonly used in practice.

Recall that corporate bond yields typically use the 30/360 day count convention. Sometimes, these yields are restated using an actual/actual day count, known as a **government equivalent yield**. The government equivalent yield on a corporate bond can be used to obtain the spread (difference) over a government bond yield.

EXAMPLE 4

Government Equivalent Yield for BRWA Five-Year Bond

In an earlier example, BRWA issued a 3.2% semiannual fixed-coupon five-year bond at par. As is standard for corporate bonds, the BRWA bond yield is calculated on a 30/360 day count basis. The comparable five-year US Treasury bond yields 2.3%, but as a government bond, the yield is calculated using the actual/actual day count basis. While the yield difference appears to be 90 bps (= 3.2% – 2.3%), the day count bases differ.

Calculate the government equivalent yield for the BRWA bond and show the yield difference between the BRWA and government bonds based on the same day count basis.

Solution:

A simple approximation for restating a corporate bond yield from the 30/360 day count basis to the actual/actual day count basis is to multiply the BRWA bond yield by 365/360.

$$Yield_{ACT/ACT} = \frac{365}{360} \times Yield_{30/360}.$$

$$Yield_{ACT/ACT} = \frac{365}{360} \times 0.032.$$

$$Yield_{ACT/ACT} = 3.244\%.$$

The bond equivalent yield for the BRWA bond is 3.2444%; hence, the yield-to-maturity difference between two bonds is 94.4 bps (= 3.2444% – 2.3%).

Sometimes the **simple yield** on a bond is quoted. It is the sum of the coupon payments plus the straight-line amortized share of the gain or loss, divided by the flat price. Simple yields are used mostly to quote Japanese government bonds, known as JGBs.

Exhibit 3: Summary of Yield Conventions

Convention	Meaning
Actual/Actual (Act/Act)	Actual number of days from prior coupon payment to settlement date/number of days in a coupon period, assuming the actual number of days in a year. Typically used with government bonds.
30/360	Number of days from prior coupon payment to settlement date, assuming 30 days in a month/number of days in a coupon period, assuming 360 days in a year. Typically used with corporate bonds.
Street Convention	Yield measure that does not account for weekends and bank holidays and thus assumes cash flows are paid on their scheduled dates.
True Yield	Yield measure that accounts for weekends and bank holidays and thus assumes cash flows are paid after their scheduled dates. True yield is never higher than street convention yield due to the delay in time to payment.
Government Equivalent Yield	Yield measure that restates a yield-to-maturity based on a 30/360 day count to one based on an actual/actual day count. It is used to restate the YTM on a corporate bond to obtain the spread over the government YTM.
Simple Yield	Yield measure that is the sum of coupon payments plus the straight-line amortized share of the gain or loss, divided by the flat price. It is used mostly to quote Japanese government bonds (JGBs).

EXAMPLE 5

Comparing Yields for Different Periodicities

An analyst observes the following reported statistics for two bonds.

	Antelas AG Bond	BRWA Bond
Annual Coupon Rate	3.20%	2.50%
Coupon Payment Frequency	Quarterly	Semiannually
Years to Maturity	5 Years	5 Years
Price (per 100 of par value)	94	98.70
Current Yield	3.40%	2.53%
Yield-to-Maturity	4.548%	2.780%

1. Confirm the calculation of the current yield and yield-to-maturity for the two bonds.

2. The analyst believes that the BRWA bond has less risk than the Antelas AG bond. How much additional compensation, in terms of basis points of yield-to-maturity, does a buyer of the Antelas AG bond receive for bearing this risk compared with the BRWA bond?

Solution to 1:

Recall that the current yield is the annual coupon expressed as a percentage of a bond's flat price.

$$\text{Current yield} = \frac{\text{Annual coupon}}{\text{Flat price}}.$$

Current yield for Antelas AG bond:

$$CY = \frac{3.20}{94}.$$

$$CY = 0.0340 = 3.40\%.$$

Current yield for BRWA bond:

$$CY = \frac{2.50}{98.70}.$$

$$CY = 0.0253 = 2.53\%.$$

Recall that the yield-to-maturity is an internal rate of return, the discount rate r that equates the price of a bond to the present value of future cash flows.

$$PV = PMT_1/(1 + r)^1 + PMT_2/(1 + r)^2 + \ldots + (PMT_N + FV_N)/(1 + r)^N.$$

The yield-to-maturity can also be calculated using the YIELD and IRR functions in Microsoft Excel or Google Sheets.

Antelas AG Bond		**BRWA Bond**	
Settlement date	1/1/2000	Settlement date	1/1/2000
Maturity date	1/1/2005	Maturity date	1/1/2005
Coupon	0.032	Coupon	0.025
Price	94	Price	98.7
Redemption	100	Redemption	100
Coupon frequency	4	Coupon frequency	2
YIELD	**4.548%**	**YIELD**	**2.780%**

Solution to 2:

The yields-to-maturity on the two bonds have different periodicity assumptions. Therefore, the difference in the yields is *not* 177 bps (0.04548 – 0.02780). It is essential to compare the yields for the same periodicity to make a statement about relative value.

The Antelas AG bond yield-to-maturity of 4.548% for a periodicity of 4 converts to 4.574% for a periodicity of 2:

$$\left(1 + \frac{APR_m}{m}\right)^m = \left(1 + \frac{APR_n}{n}\right)^n.$$

$$\left(1 + \frac{0.04548}{4}\right)^4 = \left(1 + \frac{APR_2}{2}\right)^2.$$

$$APR_2 = 0.04574 = 4.574\%.$$

When the yields-to-maturity for the Antelas AG and BRWA bonds are stated on a common periodicity, the additional yield that the buyer of the Antelas AG bond receives to compensate for its higher risk, compared to the BRWA bond, is (0.04574 – 0.02780) =179 bps.

Bonds with Embedded Options

If a fixed-rate bond contains an embedded option, other yield measures are used. Recall from an earlier lesson that these bond contingency provisions cannot be removed and traded separately from the bond. For example, a callable bond gives the issuer the right to buy the bond back from the investor. This occurs at specific prices on pre-determined dates after a call protection period during which the issuer is not allowed to exercise the call option.

For example, an earlier lesson on callable bonds introduced Vivivyu Inc. (VIVU) seven-year callable notes (see Exhibit 4).

Exhibit 4: 6.5% VIVU Seven-Year Callable Notes Term Sheet

6.5% Vivivyu Inc. (VIVU) Seven-Year Callable Notes (The "Notes")

Prospectus Summary

Issuer:	Vivivyu Incorporated
Settlement Date:	[T + 3 Business Days]
Maturity Date:	[Seven Years from Settlement Date]
Principal Amount:	US$ 400 million
Interest:	6.5% fixed coupon
Interest Payment:	Starting six months from [Settlement] to be paid semiannually with final payment on [Maturity]
Seniority:	The Notes are secured and unsubordinated obligations of VIVU and rank *pari passu* with all other secured and unsubordinated debt
Call Provision:	The Issuer may redeem some or all of the Notes on any Business Day before [Maturity] starting three years after [Settlement] based upon the Call Price Schedule as a percentage of the Principal Amount plus accrued interest
Call Price Schedule:	103.25% [Three to Four Years after Settlement]
	102.50% [Four to Five Years after Settlement]
	101.75% [Five to Six Years after Settlement]
	101.00% [Six to Seven Years after Settlement]

The VIVU bond may not be called for the first three years, but the following year it may be called at a price of $103.25 per $100 in face value. VIVU has the right to call the bond for the final four years based on a fixed price schedule. Investors facing call risk starting in Year 3 often estimate the lowest possible yield earned by calculating the sequence of yields corresponding to the bond's call dates.

Traditional yield-to-maturity measures assume that all cash flows occur as promised and therefore must be modified for callable bonds. Analysts must use alternative return measures that take the bond's call feature into account, such as the yield to the first call date, the second call date, and so on. The **yield-to-call** is calculated by modifying the general formula for calculating yield-to-maturity.

$$PV = \frac{PMT}{(1+r)^1} + \frac{PMT}{(1+r)^2} + \ldots + \frac{PMT + \text{Call price}}{(1+r)^N}, \quad (3)$$

where

PV = the price of the bond

PMT = coupon payment per period

Call price = price at which a bond can be called on a given date

r = yield per period or market discount rate

N = number of evenly spaced periods to the date when a bond can be called at the call price

EXAMPLE 6

Yields-to-Call for the VIVU Bond

Assuming the call price schedule for the VIVU bond, the calculation of yields-to-first, -second, -third, -fourth, and -worst call and yield-to-maturity are as follows:

Yield-to-first call:

$$106.50 = \frac{3.25}{(1+r)^1} + \frac{3.25}{(1+r)^2} + \frac{3.25}{(1+r)^3} + \frac{3.25}{(1+r)^4} + \frac{3.25}{(1+r)^5} + \frac{103.25 + 3.25}{(1+r)^6}.$$

$$r = 0.025748 \times 2 = 0.0515.$$

Alternatively, the YIELD function in Microsoft Excel or Google Sheets can be used.

Yield-to-second call:

$$106.50 = \frac{3.25}{(1+r)^1} + \frac{3.25}{(1+r)^2} + \frac{3.25}{(1+r)^3} + \frac{3.25}{(1+r)^4} + \frac{3.25}{(1+r)^5} + \frac{3.25}{(1+r)^6} + \frac{3.25}{(1+r)^7} + \frac{102.50 + 3.25}{(1+r)^8}.$$

$$r = 0.026237 \times 2 = 0.0525.$$

Yield-to-third call:

$$106.50 = \frac{3.25}{(1+r)^1} + \frac{3.25}{(1+r)^2} + \frac{3.25}{(1+r)^3} + \frac{3.25}{(1+r)^4} + \frac{3.25}{(1+r)^5} + \frac{3.25}{(1+r)^6} + \frac{3.25}{(1+r)^7} + \frac{3.25}{(1+r)^8} + \frac{3.25}{(1+r)^9} + \frac{101.75 + 3.25}{(1+r)^{10}}.$$

$$r = 0.02653 \times 2 = 0.0531.$$

Yield-to-fourth call:

$$106.50 = \frac{3.25}{(1+r)^1} + \frac{3.25}{(1+r)^2} + \frac{3.25}{(1+r)^3} + \frac{3.25}{(1+r)^4} + \frac{3.25}{(1+r)^5} + \frac{3.25}{(1+r)^6} + \frac{3.25}{(1+r)^7} + \frac{3.25}{(1+r)^8} + \frac{3.25}{(1+r)^9} + \frac{3.25}{(1+r)^{10}} + \frac{3.25}{(1+r)^{11}} + \frac{101.00 + 3.25}{(1+r)^{12}}.$$

$$r = 0.026811 \times 2 = 0.0536.$$

And finally, the yield-to-maturity assuming the bond is not called:

$$106.50 = \frac{3.25}{(1+r)^1} + \frac{3.25}{(1+r)^2} + \frac{3.25}{(1+r)^3} + \frac{3.25}{(1+r)^4} + \frac{3.25}{(1+r)^5} + \frac{3.25}{(1+r)^6} + \frac{3.25}{(1+r)^7} + \frac{3.25}{(1+r)^8} + \frac{3.25}{(1+r)^9} + \frac{3.25}{(1+r)^{10}} + \frac{3.25}{(1+r)^{11}} + \frac{3.25}{(1+r)^{12}} + \frac{3.25}{(1+r)^{13}} + \frac{100.00 + 3.25}{(1+r)^{14}}.$$

$r = 0.026868 \times 2 = 0.0537.$

In summary, the yield measures for the VIVU bond are as follows:

Yield-to-first call	5.149%
Yield-to-second call	5.247%
Yield-to-third call	5.313%
Yield-to-fourth call	5.362%
Yield-to-maturity	5.374%

The lowest of the sequence of yields-to-call and the yield-to-maturity is known as the **yield-to-worst**. For the VIVU bond, it is the yield-to-first call of 5.15%. The intent of this measure is to provide to the investor the most conservative measure for the rate of return.

The yield-to-worst is a commonly cited yield measure for fixed-rate callable bonds used by bond dealers and investors. However, a more precise approach is to use an option pricing model and an assumption about future interest rate volatility to value the embedded call option. The value of the embedded call option is added to the flat price of the bond to get the **option-adjusted price**. The investor bears the call risk (the bond issuer has the option to call), so the embedded call option reduces the value of the bond from the investor's perspective. The investor pays a lower price for the callable bond than if it were option-free. If the bond were non-callable, its price would be higher. The option-adjusted price is used to calculate the **option-adjusted yield**. The option-adjusted yield is the required market discount rate whereby the price is adjusted for the value of the embedded option. The value of the call option is the price of the option-free bond minus the price of the callable bond.

QUESTION SET

1. Identify which of the following yield measures corresponds to the characteristics listed below.

Yield Measure	Characteristic
A. Simple Yield	1. Yield measure assuming one compounding period per year
B. Effective Annual Rate	2. Yield measure that restates a yield based on a 30/360 day count to one based on an actual/actual day count
C. Street Convention Yield	3. Yield measure that is the sum of coupon payments plus the straight-line amortized share of the gain or loss, divided by the flat price
D. Government Equivalent Yield	4. Assumes cash flows are paid on their scheduled dates, without accounting for weekends and bank holidays

Solution:

Yield Measure	Characteristic
B. Effective Annual Rate	1. Yield measure assuming one compounding period in the year
D. Government Equivalent Yield	2. Yield measure that restates a yield-to-maturity based on a 30/360 day count to one based on an actual/actual day count
A. Simple Yield	3. Yield measure that is the sum of coupon payments plus the straight-line amortized share of the gain or loss, divided by the flat price
C. Street Convention Yield	4. Assumes cash flows are paid on their scheduled dates, without accounting for weekends and bank holidays

2. An analyst calculated the following yields for a four-year callable bond. Determine the yield-to-worst.

Yield Measure	Value
Yield-to-first call	0.000%
Yield-to-second call	0.157%
Yield-to-third call	0.939%
Yield-to-maturity	–0.385%

Solution:

–0.3852%. The yield-to-worst is the lowest of the sequence of yields-to-call and the yield-to-maturity. The intent of yield-to-worst is to provide to the investor the most conservative assumption for the rate of return.

Use the following information compiled by a fixed-income analyst for two bonds, on the day both were issued, to answer Questions 3 and 4.

	Corporate Bond	Sovereign Bond
Annual coupon rate	4.00%	1.00%
Coupon frequency	Semiannual	Quarterly
Years to maturity	3 Years	3 Years
Price (per 100 of par)	91	102
Day-count basis	30/360	Actual/actual
Call price schedule:	101.25 1–2 Years after settlement	-

3. The current yield of the sovereign bond is approximately:

A. 140 bps *lower* than the current yield of the corporate bond.

B. 340 bps *lower* than the current yield of the corporate bond.

C. 140 bps *higher* than the current yield of the corporate bond.

Solution:

B is correct. The current yield is the annual coupon expressed as a percentage of a bond's price. The current yield of the corporate bond is 440 bps, while the current yield of the sovereign bond is 98 bps, 342 bps lower.

4. The yield-to-first call of the corporate bond is closest to:

   A. 2.15%.

   B. 7.80%.

   C. 15.00%.

Solution:

C is correct. The yield-to-first call is the internal rate of return r for a callable bond assuming it is called at its earliest scheduled call date for its call price.

$$PV = \frac{PMT}{(1+r)^1} + \frac{PMT}{(1+r)^2} + \ldots + \frac{PMT + \text{Callprice}}{(1+r)^N}.$$

$$91 = \frac{2}{(1+r)^1} + \frac{101.5 + 2}{(1+r)^2}.$$

$$r = 0.0762 \times 2 = 0.1525.$$

The yield-to-first call for the bond is 15.25%.

YIELD SPREAD MEASURES FOR FIXED-RATE BONDS AND MATRIX PRICING 4

☐ compare, calculate, and interpret yield and yield spread measures for fixed-rate bonds

Yield Spreads over Benchmark Rates

In fixed-income security analysis, it is important to understand *why* bond prices and yields-to-maturity change. To do this, it is useful to decompose a yield-to-maturity into a base rate or **benchmark** and an issuer-specific **spread**. For example, an earlier lesson introduced government benchmark bonds as the most liquid securities with the lowest default risk for a specific time-to-maturity in each market. The **yield spread** is the difference between the yield-to-maturity and the benchmark yield.

These two components help investors distinguish between macroeconomic (top-down) and microeconomic (bottom-up) factors that affect the bond price and, therefore, its yield-to-maturity. The benchmark rate captures the top-down factors, while the spread captures the bottom-up factors, as shown in Exhibit 5.

Exhibit 5: Yield-to-Maturity Components

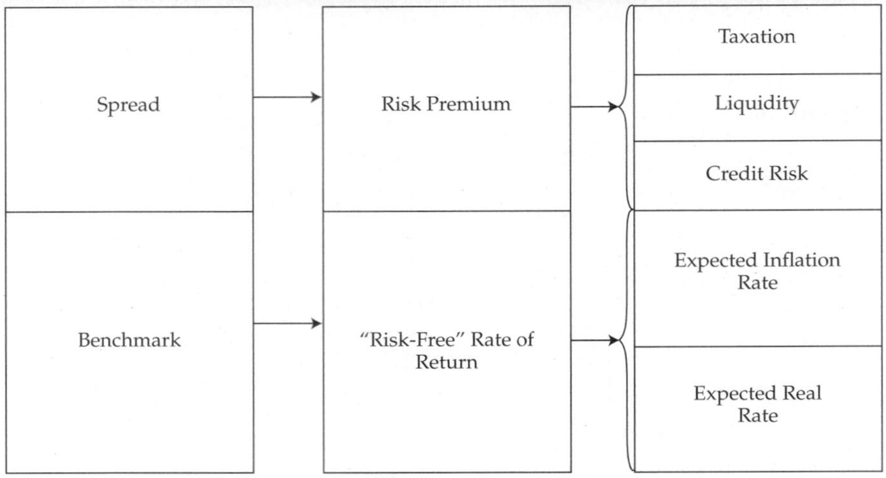

The most used benchmark rate is the most recently issued government bond, known as an **on-the-run** security. The on-the-run government bond is the most actively traded security and has a coupon rate closest to the current market discount rate for that maturity. That implies that it is priced close to par value. Seasoned government bonds are called **off-the-run**. On-the-run bonds typically trade at slightly lower yields-to-maturity than off-the-run bonds with the same or similar times-to-maturity because of differences in demand for the securities and, sometimes, differences in the cost of financing the government security in the repo market.

The yield spread over a specific benchmark is referred to as the **benchmark spread** and represents the risk premium for the credit and liquidity risks and possibly the tax impact of holding a specific bond. Exhibit 6 shows the relationship between yields-to-maturity for a specific issuer and a benchmark government yield curve.

Exhibit 6: Issuer and Government Yield Curves

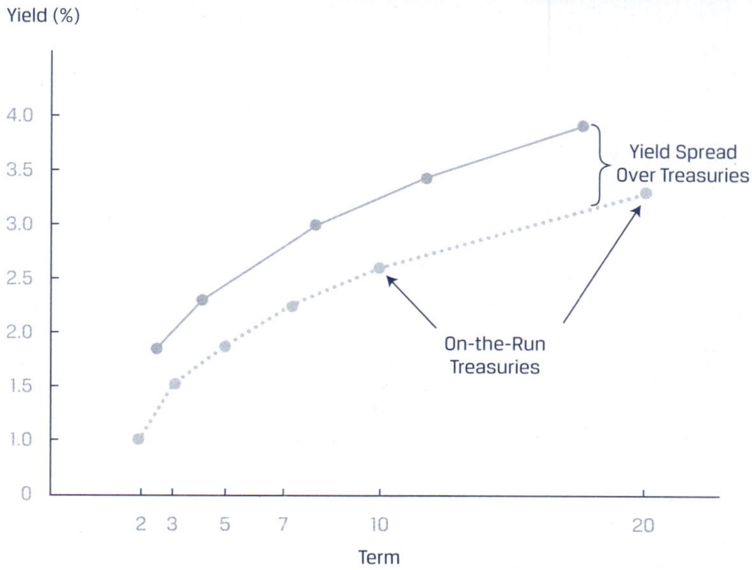

Spreads allow an analyst to better assess a bond's relative value on a historical and comparative basis by controlling for (excluding) macroeconomic factors, such as a broad increase or decrease in benchmark rates. An analyst might compare the current spread relative to its historical average and its past highs and lows and to other bonds to help identify whether a bond is under- or overpriced on a relative basis.

The yield spread in basis points over an actual or interpolated government bond yield is known as the **G-spread** and represents the return for bearing risks relative to the sovereign bond. If there is no sovereign benchmark bond that matches the maturity of the bond, an approximation process for finding the G-spread must be used, as illustrated in Exhibit 7 and shown in the following example.

Exhibit 7: Finding G-Spreads When a Comparable Benchmark Bond Does Not Exist

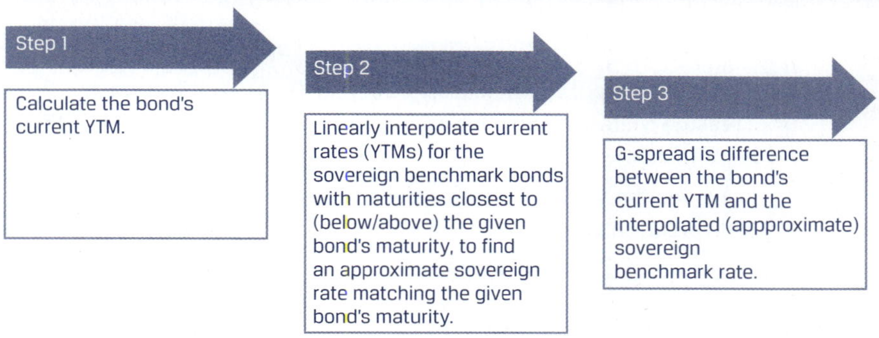

EXAMPLE 7

Calculating G-Spread without a Comparable Benchmark Bond

Assume that the Russian Federation has issued a 30-year US dollar–denominated sovereign bond based on the following terms:

5.25% Russian Federation Bonds	
Brief Summary of Terms	
Issuer:	Russian Federation
Settlement Date:	[T + 5 Business Days]
Maturity Date:	[30 Years from Settlement Date]
Principal Amount:	USD 750 million
Interest:	5.25% fixed semiannual 30/360 basis
Issuance Price:	99.625
Issuance Spread:	200 bp versus current US 30y Treasury
Issuance and Trading:	US Private Placement under Rule 144A
	DTC / Euroclear / Clearstream
Seniority:	Senior Unsecured
Exchanges:	Luxembourg

Six years after the original issuance date, on 15 March 2026, the bond is trading at a price of 123.5 per 100 face value, and an analyst observes that 20-year and 30-year US Treasury yields are currently 2.00% and 2.25%, respectively. Calculate the current G-spread of the Russian Federation bond.

Step 1 Calculate the current yield-to-maturity of the Russian Federation bond. We may solve for r using the general formula for bond price and yield:

$$PV = PMT_1/(1 + r)^1 + PMT_2/(1 + r)^2 + \ldots + (PMT_N + FV_N)/(1 + r)^N.$$

Or we can use the Excel or Google Sheets YIELD function assuming a settlement date of 15 March 2026:

=YIELD(DATE(2026,3,15),DATE(2050,3,15),5.25%,123.5,100,2,0)

= 3.756%.

Step 2 Linearly interpolate the current 20-year (r_{20y}) and 30-year (r_{30y}) US Treasury yields to solve for an approximate 24-year (r_{24y}) US Treasury benchmark:

1. Solve for the weights of the 20-year and the 30-year bonds in the interpolation calculation:

20-year bond weight = w_{20} = 60% [= (30 – 24)/(30 – 20)].

30-year bond weight = w_{30} = 40%, or (1 – w_{20}).

Note that (w_{20} × 20) + (w_{30} × 30) = 24.

2. The 24-year government rate is a weighted average of the 20-year bond rate and the 30-year US Treasury rate using the weights above.

$$r_{24y} = w_{20} \times r_{20y} + w_{30} \times r_{30y}$$

= (60% × 2.00%) + (40% × 2.25%) = 2.10%.

Step 3 The G-spread is the difference between the current Russian Federation bond yield-to-maturity and the 24-year US government rate:

1.656% = 3.756% – 2.10%, so the G-spread is 166 bps.

The yield spread for a bond over the standard swap rate in that currency of the same tenor is known as the **I-spread** or interpolated spread. This type of spread is a comparison against a short-term market-based reference rate and is common practice for pricing and quoting euro-denominated corporate bonds, using a euro interest rate swap as the benchmark. For example, the five-year zero-coupon euro bond issued by the Chinese government at a negative yield-to-maturity from a prior lesson was priced at a rate of "mid-swaps plus 30 bps," where "mid-swaps" is the average of the bid and offered swap rates.

Issuers will use the I-spread to determine the relative cost of fixed-rate bonds versus floating-rate alternatives, such as a bank loan or commercial paper, while investors use it as a measure of a bond's credit risk. Whereas a standard interest rate swap involves an exchange of fixed for floating cash flows based on a floating index, an asset swap converts the periodic fixed coupon of a specific bond to a market reference rate (MRR) plus or minus a spread. If the bond is priced close to par, this conversion approximates the price of a bond's credit risk over the MRR index.

EXAMPLE 8

Yield Spreads Using Bloomberg Fixed-Income Relative Value (FIRV)

The Bloomberg FIRV function for the 3.75% Apple bond that matures on 12 September 2047 shows the following. Identify the yield and yield spread measures.

FIRV Function for 3.75% AAPL Bond Maturing 12 September 2047

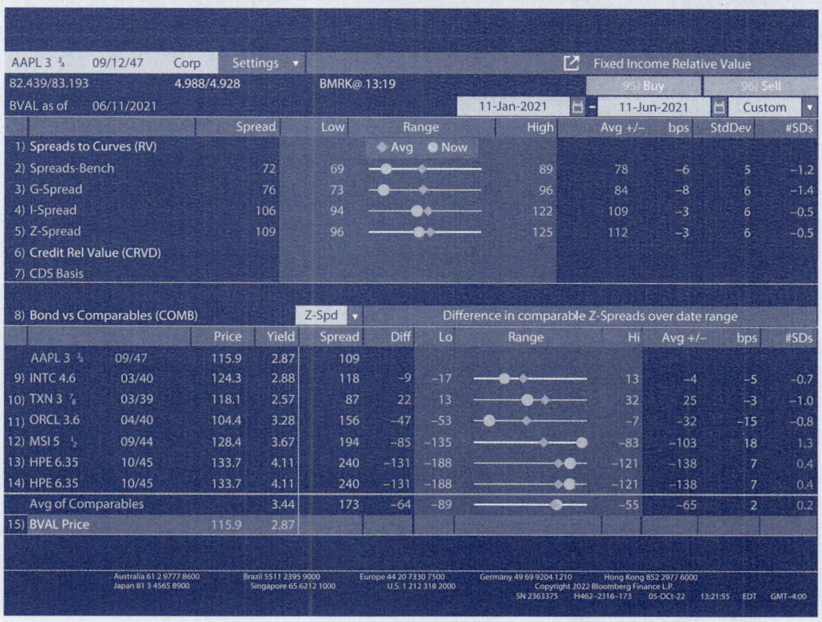

AAPL 3 ¾ 09/12/47 Corp Settings ▾ Fixed Income Relative Value

82.439/83.193 4.988/4.928 BMRK@ 13:19 95) Buy 96) Sell

BVAL as of 06/11/2021 11-Jan-2021 – 11-Jun-2021 Custom

	Spread	Low	Range (◆ Avg ● Now)	High	Avg +/–	bps	StdDev	#SDs
1) Spreads to Curves (RV)								
2) Spreads-Bench	72	69		89	78	–6	5	–1.2
3) G-Spread	76	73		96	84	–8	6	–1.4
4) I-Spread	106	94		122	109	–3	6	–0.5
5) Z-Spread	109	96		125	112	–3	6	–0.5
6) Credit Rel Value (CRVD)								
7) CDS Basis								

8) Bond vs Comparables (COMB) Z-Spd ▾ Difference in comparable Z-Spreads over date range

		Price	Yield	Spread	Diff	Lo	Range	Hi	Avg +/–	bps	#SDs
AAPL 3 ¾	09/47	115.9	2.87	109							
9) INTC 4.6	03/40	124.3	2.88	118	–9	–17		13	–4	–5	–0.7
10) TXN 3 ⅞	03/39	118.1	2.57	87	22	13		32	25	–3	–1.0
11) ORCL 3.6	04/40	104.4	3.28	156	–47	–53		–7	–32	–15	–0.8
12) MSI 5 ½	09/44	128.4	3.67	194	–85	–135		–83	–103	18	1.3
13) HPE 6.35	10/45	133.7	4.11	240	–131	–188		–121	–138	7	0.4
14) HPE 6.35	10/45	133.7	4.11	240	–131	–188		–121	–138	7	0.4
Avg of Comparables			3.44	173	–64	–89		–55	–65	2	0.2
15) BVAL Price		115.9	2.87								

Australia 61 2 9777 8600 Brazil 5511 2395 9000 Europe 44 20 7330 7500 Germany 49 69 9204 1210 Hong Kong 852 2977 6000
Japan 81 3 4565 8900 Singapore 65 6212 1000 U.S. 1 212 318 2000 Copyright 2022 Bloomberg Finance L.P.
SN 2363375 H462-2316-173 05-OCt-22 13:21:55 EDT GMT-4:00

Solution:

The yield spreads are in the top left corner. On the date of analysis:

- The yield spread over a particular Treasury benchmark was 72 bps.
- The G-spread over an interpolated government bond yield was 76 bps. The spread over the benchmark and the G-spread sometimes differ by a few basis points, especially if the benchmark maturity differs from that of the underlying bond.
- The bond's I-spread was 106 bps. An I-spread larger than the G-spread indicates that Treasury yields were slightly higher than swap rates at that time.

The use of these spreads in investment strategies will be covered in more detail later. In general, an analyst will track these spreads relative to their averages and historical highs and lows to identify relative value.

Yield Spreads over the Benchmark Yield Curve

Whereas the G-spread and I-spread are the difference between two single numbers and use the same discount rate (yield-to-maturity) for each cash flow, a different approach is to calculate a constant yield spread over a government (or interest rate swap) spot *curve*, or series of yields. This spread is known as the zero-volatility spread (**Z-spread**) of a bond over the benchmark rate. In other words, the Z-spread is what must be added to each benchmark spot rate to make the present value of a bond's cash flows equal its price. In Example 8, the Z-spread for the Apple bond, as quoted using the Bloomberg FIRV function, was 109 bps.

The Z-spread over the benchmark spot curve can be calculated with Equation 4:

$$PV = \frac{PMT}{(1+z_1+Z)^1} + \frac{PMT}{(1+z_2+Z)^2} + \cdots + \frac{PMT+FV}{(1+z_N+Z)^N}. \quad (4)$$

The benchmark spot or zero rates—$z_1, z_2, \ldots, z_N$—are derived from the government yield curve (or from fixed rates on interest rate swaps), as shown in detail in a later lesson. Z is the Z-spread per period and is the same for all time periods. In Equation 4 is an integer, so the calculation is on a coupon date when the accrued interest is zero. Sometimes, the Z-spread is called the "static spread" because it is constant (and has zero volatility). In practice, the Z-spread is usually calculated in a spreadsheet using a goal seek function or similar solver function.

The Z-spread is also used to calculate the **option-adjusted spread** (OAS) on a callable bond. The OAS, like the option-adjusted yield, is based on an option-pricing model and an assumption about future interest rate volatility. Then, the value of the embedded call option, which is stated in basis points per year, is subtracted from the yield spread.

$$\text{OAS} = \text{Z-spread} - \text{Option value in basis points per year.} \quad (5)$$

This important measure is covered in detail later.

Exhibit 8: Summary of Yield Spreads

Type	Description
G-spread	Government spread, the yield spread in basis points over an actual or interpolated government bond. Used in the US, the UK, Japan, and other jurisdictions.
I-spread	Interpolated spread, the yield spread of a bond over the standard swap rate in the same currency and with the same tenor. Euro-denominated corporate bonds are typically priced vs. a euro interest rate swap benchmark.
Z-spread	Zero-volatility spread, a constant yield spread over a government (or interest rate swap) spot curve used to derive the term structure of credit spreads for an issuer.
Option-adjusted spread	The Z-spread adjusted for the value of an embedded call option.

EXAMPLE 9

The G-Spread and Z-Spread

A 1.5% semiannual coupon, US dollar–denominated bond was issued by PT Indonesia Infrastructure Finance (IIF) three years ago. Currently, the bond has two years remaining to maturity and is trading at a price of 100.45. The two-year, 0.75% semiannual payment government benchmark bond is trading at a price of 100.750.

The government spot rates (stated as effective annual rates) are as follows:

Maturity	Spot Rate
6M	0.127%
12M	0.249%
18M	0.314%
24M	0.373%

1. Calculate the G-spread for the IIF bond.
2. Calculate the Z-spread for the IIF bond.

Solution to 1:

The G-spread is the yield spread in basis points over an actual or interpolated government bond. The yield-to-maturity for the IIF bond is 1.271%:

$$100.45 = \frac{0.75}{(1+r)^1} + \frac{0.75}{(1+r)^2} + \frac{0.75}{(1+r)^3} + \frac{100.75}{(1+r)^4}.$$

$r = 0.006357 \times 2 = 0.01271.$

The yield-to-maturity for the relevant government benchmark bond is 0.373%:

$$100.75 = \frac{0.375}{(1+r)^1} + \frac{0.375}{(1+r)^2} + \frac{0.375}{(1+r)^3} + \frac{100.375}{(1+r)^4}.$$

$r = 0.002618 \times 2 = 0.005235.$

Therefore, the G-spread is 0.01271 – 0.005235 = 75 bps.

Solution to 2:

The Z-spread is a constant yield spread over a government spot or interest rate swap curve.

The Z-spread for the IIF bond is the value of Z that solves the following equation, using the government spot rates provided:

$$PV = \frac{PMT}{(1 + z_1 + Z)^1} + \frac{PMT}{(1 + z_2 + Z)^2} + \cdots + \frac{PMT + FV}{(1 + z_N + Z)^N}.$$

$$100.45 = \frac{0.75}{(1 + 0.00127 + Z)^1} + \frac{0.75}{(1 + 0.00249 + Z)^2} + \frac{0.75}{(1 + 0.00314 + Z)^3} + \frac{100.75}{(1 + 0.00373 + Z)^4}.$$

The Solver add-in for Microsoft Excel finds $Z = 0.00268$, or 27 bps, by setting the price (sum of present values of cash flows) equal to 100.45 as the objective and Z as the change variable. Please refer to the candidate learning ecosystem online for a spreadsheet demonstrating the calculation in the downloadable Excel workbook.

QUESTION SET

1. Each of the five items below is a risk of investing in fixed-income instruments. For each, identify the component of yield-to-maturity that provides compensation for that risk: benchmark or spread.

   Credit

   Expected Real Rate

   Taxation

   Expected Inflation Rate

   Liquidity

Benchmark	Spread

Solution:

Benchmark	Spread
Expected Real Rate	Credit Risk
Expected Inflation Rate	Taxation Risk
	Liquidity Risk

The two components of yield—the benchmark and the spread—allow us to distinguish macroeconomic and microeconomic factors.

The benchmark yield captures the macroeconomic factors: the expected rate of inflation in the currency in which the bond is denominated, general economic growth and the business cycle, foreign exchange rates, and the impact of monetary and fiscal policy. Changes in those factors impact all bonds in the market.

The yield spread captures the microeconomic factors specific to the bond issuer and the bond itself: credit risk, liquidity and trading in comparable securities, and the tax status of the bond.

2. A Mexican corporate non-callable bond matures in three years and has an annual coupon of 5.5%. The government spot rates (stated as effective annual rates) are as follows:

Government Spot Rates

Maturity	Spot Rate
1Y	2.98%
2Y	3.48%
3Y	4.00%

Using the provided spot rates and a Z-spread of 378 bps, calculate the price of the Mexican corporate bond.

Solution:

The price of the bond is 94.20.

$$PV = \frac{PMT}{(1 + z_1 + Z)^1} + \frac{PMT}{(1 + z_2 + Z)^2} + \cdots + \frac{PMT + FV}{(1 + z_N + Z)^N}.$$

$$PV = \frac{5.5}{(1 + 0.0298 + 0.0378)^1} + \frac{5.5}{(1 + 0.0348 + 0.0378)^2} + \frac{105.5}{(1 + 0.04 + 0.0378)^3}.$$

$$PV = 94.20.$$

Use the information provided for Questions 3 and 4.

A fixed-income analyst has compiled the following statistics for three corporate bonds issued by companies domiciled in three different countries.

Bond	Yield-to-Maturity	Applicable Swap Rate
A	13.379%	12.419%
B	8.121%	6.527%
C	5.406%	4.184%

3. Which bond most likely has the greatest credit risk?

A. Bond A

B. Bond B

C. Bond C

Solution:

B is correct. As a "bottom-up" or issuer-specific risk factor, credit risk is a component of a yield spread. To estimate which bond most likely has the greatest credit risk, we calculate the I-spread, or the yield spread for a bond over a swap rate for the same currency and tenor.

Bond	Yield-to-Maturity	Applicable Swap Rate	I-Spread
A	13.379%	12.419%	96 bps
B	8.121%	6.527%	159 bps
C	5.406%	4.184%	122 bps

4. Assume that the issuers of Bonds A, B, and C are comparable in terms of credit risk and that the bonds have similar liquidity and tax characteristics. Based solely on the information provided, which bond might offer an investor the *least* relative value?

   A. Bond A

   B. Bond B

   C. Bond C

   Solution:

   A is correct. If the bonds are judged to be comparable in all material respects, then the least (most) relative value corresponds to the bond with the lowest (highest) spread. At 96 bps, Bond A has the lowest spread and thus the least attractive valuation to an investor.

5. Match the following characteristics to *on-the-run* and *off-the-run* bonds:

   - Seasoned government bonds
   - Most recently issued government bonds
   - Has a coupon rate below or above the current market discount rate for that maturity
   - Has a coupon rate closest to the current market discount rate for that maturity
   - Trades at slightly lower yields-to-maturity compared to bonds with the same or a similar time-to-maturity
   - Trades at slightly higher yields-to-maturity compared to bonds with the same or a similar time-to-maturity

   Solution:

On-the-Run	Off-the-Run
Most recently issued government bonds	Seasoned government bonds
Has a coupon rate closest to the current market discount rate for that maturity	Has a coupon rate below or above the current market discount rate for that maturity
Trades at slightly lower yields-to-maturity compared to bonds with the same or a similar time-to-maturity	Trades at slightly higher yields-to-maturity compared to bonds with the same or a similar time-to-maturity

PRACTICE PROBLEMS

1. A bond issued by RTR pays a quarterly coupon of 3.25%, has three years to maturity, and is currently trading at 97.28. The semiannual bond basis yield is closest to:

   A. 1.055%.

   B. 2.121%.

   C. 4.242%.

2. An analyst is analyzing a three-year, 2.25% annual coupon bond issued by QWE Company. Currently, the bond's yield-to-maturity is 2.707%. The three-year swap rate is 1.840%. The government spot rates are presented in the table.

Maturity	Government Spot Rate
1Y	0.899%
2Y	1.260%
3Y	1.904%

   The G-Spread (in basis points) for the QWE bond is closest to:

   A. 80.

   B. 87.

   C. 135.

3. The I-spread (in basis points) for the QWE bond is closest to:

   A. 46.

   B. 80.

   C. 87.

4. If the price of the QWE bond is 98.70% of par, its Z-spread (in basis points) is closest to:

   A. 80.

   B. 82.

   C. 87.

5. An analyst is analyzing a six-year callable bond with a semiannual coupon of 2.50% trading at a price of 98.90 per 100 par value and the following call schedule:

Call Schedule

Period	Call Price
4–5 Years	101.50
5–6 Years	101.00

   Match the yields below to the respective yield measures.

Yield	Yield Measure
2.6998%	Yield-to-first call
2.6998%	Yield-to-second call
2.9253%	Yield-to-maturity
3.1497%	Yield-to-worst

SOLUTIONS

1. C is correct. As a first step, we need to calculate the quarterly yield and annualize it:

$$PV = \frac{PMT}{(1+r)^1} + \frac{PMT}{(1+r)^2} + \ldots + \frac{PMT+FV}{(1+r)^N}.$$

$$97.28 = \frac{0.8125}{(1+r)^1} + \frac{0.8125}{(1+r)^2} + \ldots + \frac{100.8125}{(1+r)^{12}}.$$

$$r = 0.01055 \times 4 = 0.0422.$$

The next step is to convert the annualized quarterly yield to the semiannual bond basis yield.

$$\left(1 + \frac{APR_m}{m}\right)^m = \left(1 + \frac{APR_n}{n}\right)^n.$$

$$\left(1 + \frac{0.0422}{4}\right)^4 = \left(1 + \frac{APR_2}{2}\right)^2.$$

$$APR_2 = 0.04242 = 4.242\%.$$

A is incorrect because 1.0550% is the yield per quarter.
B is incorrect because 2.1100% is the yield per quarter (1.0550%) multiplied by 2.

2. A is correct. The G-spread is a yield spread above that of a government bond with the same maturity date. The yield-to-maturity for the corporate bond is 2.7070%. The yield-to-maturity for the government benchmark bond is 1.9036%.

G-spread = 2.707% – 1.904% = 0.8034% = 80.3 bps.

B is incorrect because 87 bps is the I-spread calculated as the yield spread of a bond over the standard swap rate in the same currency and with the same tenor.
C is incorrect because 135 bps is the spread calculated as the difference between the yield-to-maturity of the QWE bond and the average of government rates for all maturities.

3. C is correct. The I-spread is the yield spread of a bond over the standard swap rate in the same currency and with the same tenor. The yield-to-maturity for the corporate bond is 2.707%, and the swap rate for the same maturity is 1.840%.

I-spread = 2.707% – 1.840% = 0.867% = 87 bps.

A is incorrect because 46 bps is the difference between the bond's yield-to-maturity and coupon rate.

2.707% – 2.250% = 0.457% = 46 bps.

B is incorrect because 80 bps is the G-spread—the yield-to-maturity for the corporate bond less the yield-to-maturity for the government benchmark bond.

G-spread = 2.707% – 1.904% = 80 bps.

4. B is correct. To calculate the Z-spread, we must solve for Z in the following equation, given the spot rates and price of the bond:

$$PV = \frac{PMT}{(1+z_1+Z)^1} + \frac{PMT}{(1+z_2+Z)^2} + \cdots + \frac{PMT+FV}{(1+z_N+Z)^N}.$$

$$98.70 = \frac{2.25}{(1 + 0.00899 + Z)^1} + \frac{2.25}{(1 + 0.01260 + Z)^2} + \frac{102.25}{(1 + 0.01904 + Z)^3}.$$

The Solver add-in for Microsoft Excel finds Z = 0.0082, or 82 bps, by setting the price (sum of present values of cash flows) equal to 98.70 as the objective and Z as the change variable. Please refer to the candidate learning ecosystem online for a spreadsheet demonstrating the calculation in the downloadable Excel workbook.

A is incorrect because 80 bps is the value of the G-spread, not the Z-spread. The G-spread is calculated as the difference between the QWE bond yield and the yield of the government bond with the same maturity:

G-spread = 2.707% – 1.904% = 80 bps.

C is incorrect because 87 bps is the I-spread, not the Z-spread. The I-spread is calculated as a yield spread of a bond over the standard swap rate in the same currency and with the same tenor. The yield-to-maturity for the corporate bond is 2.707%, and the swap rate for the same maturity is 1.840%.

I-spread = 2.707% – 1.840% = 87 bps.

5. The correct yield values matched with the corresponding yield measures are presented in the following table:

Yield	Yield Measure
3.1497%	Yield-to-first call
2.9253%	Yield-to-second call
2.6998%	Yield-to-maturity
2.6998%	Yield-to-worst

Calculation of yield-to-first call:

$$PV = \frac{PMT}{(1 + r)^1} + \frac{PMT}{(1 + r)^2} + \ldots + \frac{PMT + \text{CallPrice}}{(1 + r)^N}.$$

$$PV = \frac{1.25}{(1 + r)^1} + \frac{1.25}{(1 + r)^2} + \ldots + \frac{1.25}{(1 + r)^7} + \frac{1.25 + 101.50}{(1 + r)^8}.$$

$r = 0.01548 \times 2 = 0.031497.$

Calculation of yield-to-second call:

$$PV = \frac{PMT}{(1 + r)^1} + \frac{PMT}{(1 + r)^2} + \ldots + \frac{PMT + \text{CallPrice}}{(1 + r)^N}.$$

$$PV = \frac{1.25}{(1 + r)^1} + \frac{1.25}{(1 + r)^2} + \ldots + \frac{1.25}{(1 + r)^9} + \frac{1.25 + 101.0}{(1 + r)^{10}}.$$

$r = 0.014626 \times 2 = 0.029253.$

Calculation of yield-to-maturity:

$$PV = \frac{PMT}{(1 + r)^1} + \frac{PMT}{(1 + r)^2} + \ldots + \frac{PMT + FV}{(1 + r)^N}.$$

$$PV = \frac{1.25}{(1 + r)^1} + \frac{1.25}{(1 + r)^2} + \ldots + \frac{1.25}{(1 + r)^{11}} + \frac{1.25 + 100.0}{(1 + r)^{12}}.$$

$r = 0.013499 \times 2 = 0.026998.$

LEARNING MODULE

8

Yield and Yield Spread Measures for Floating-Rate Instruments

LEARNING OUTCOMES

Mastery	*The candidate should be able to:*
☐	calculate and interpret yield spread measures for floating-rate instruments
☐	calculate and interpret yield measures for money market instruments

INTRODUCTION

1

Prior lessons covered pricing, yields, and spreads for bonds with fixed coupon rates and times-to-maturity of one year or longer. The next two lessons broaden the discussion to include instruments with variable rather than fixed coupons, known as floating-rate instruments, and those with original maturities of one year or less, known as money market instruments. Both types of instrument are important for investors and issuers. Floating-rate instruments, by adjusting cash flows to changes in interest rates, bear less price risk than fixed-rate instruments and are used to hedge certain exposures and to match asset and liability cash flows. Most loans are floating-rate instruments. Money market instruments are a significant source of short-term financing for many types of issuers. A short time-to-maturity means that investors can reinvest and issuers can refinance relatively quickly, which reduces interest rate risk.

Most of the examples and exhibits used throughout the reading can be downloaded as a Microsoft Excel workbook. Each worksheet in the workbook is labeled with the corresponding example or exhibit number in the text.

LEARNING MODULE OVERVIEW

- A floating-rate instrument is a debt instrument with interest determined by an observed market reference rate (MRR) plus a quoted margin. Interest payments are reset, capturing any change in the MRR, on predetermined dates.

- The quoted margin is a specified spread over or under the reference rate. The required margin, also known as the discount margin, is the spread required by investors.
- The required margin reflects "bottom-up" or issuer- and security-specific risks and is analogous to a yield spread for a fixed-rate bond discussed in prior lessons. If a floater trades at par, the quoted and required margins are equal.
- Money market instruments have original maturities of one year or less and are quoted using different conventions from those of longer-dated securities. Quotes are made on a discount rate or add-on rate basis.
- Money market discount rates are interest income divided by the face value (maturity value). They understate the investor's rate of return if the purchase price is below the face value and vice versa.
- Conventional money market measures can be converted to enhance comparability to longer-term securities.

LEARNING MODULE SELF-ASSESSMENT

These initial questions are intended to help you gauge your current level of understanding of the learning module.

1. The following information relates to three floating-rate notes (FRNs) issued at par value that have the three-month MRR as their reference rate.

Floating-Rate Note	Quoted Margin	Discount Margin
FRN 1	140 bps	128 bps
FRN 2	145 bps	145 bps
FRN 3	150 bps	165 bps

Based on the information provided, identify which FRN will be priced at a discount on the next reset date.

A. FRN 1

B. FRN 2

C. FRN 3

Solution:

C is correct. FRN 3 will be priced at a discount on the next reset date since its quoted margin of 150 bps is less than its discount margin of 165 bps. The discount amount is the present value of the deficient future interest payments of 15 bps per quarter (150 bps – 165 bps).

B is incorrect because FRN 2 will be priced at par value on the next reset date since its quoted margin is equal to its discount margin.

A is incorrect because FRN 1 will be priced at a premium because its quoted margin of 140 bps is greater than its discount margin of 128 bps. The premium amount is the present value of the extra, or "excess," interest payments of 12 bps each quarter (140 bps – 128 bps).

2. On a reset date, if the required margin falls to 30 bps because of a change in the issuer's credit risk, an FRN that has a quoted margin of 50 bps will be priced at a:

   A. discount.

   B. premium.

   C. discount or premium, depending on its duration.

   Solution:

   B is correct. The required margin reflects the credit risk of the issuer. It declined, meaning that the credit risk of the issuer improved; in other words, the market demands a lower spread. The required margin is below the quoted margin, so this floater will be priced at a premium.

3. A 365-day year bank certificate of deposit has an initial principal amount of USD96.5 million and a redemption amount due at maturity of USD100 million. The number of days between settlement and maturity is 270. The add-on rate of the certificate of deposit is closest to:

   A. 3.63%.

   B. 4.82%.

   C. 4.90%.

   Solution:

   C is correct. The add-on rate is closest to 4.90%. The add-on rate is calculated as

$$AOR = \frac{Year}{Days} \times \frac{FV - PV}{PV}.$$

$$AOR = \frac{365}{270} \times \frac{100 - 96.5}{96.5}.$$

$$AOR = 0.04903 = 4.90\%.$$

4. A 90-day commercial paper instrument is quoted at a discount rate of 0.120%, assuming a 360-day year. Given that the price of the instrument is paid 100 per face value, its bond equivalent yield rate is closest to:

   A. 0.107%.

   B. 0.120%.

   C. 0.135%.

   Solution:

   B is correct. The bond equivalent yield is closest to 0.120%. First, we need to calculate the price of the instrument. Then, we can calculate the AOR or its bond equivalent yield.

   The price (PV) of the commercial paper instrument is

$$PV = FV \times (1 - \frac{Days}{Year} \times DR).$$

$$PV = 100 \times (1 - \frac{90}{360} \times 0.0012).$$

$$PV = 99.97.$$

   PV is used to calculate the add-on rate or bond equivalent yield:

$$AOR = \frac{Year}{Days} \times \frac{FV - PV}{PV}.$$

$$AOR = \frac{360}{90} \times \frac{100 - 99.97}{99.97}.$$

$$AOR = 0.0012 = 0.12\%.$$

5. A fixed-income analyst is evaluating two instruments:

   - A 180-day Thai bank certificate of deposit (CD) quoted at a discount rate of 5.95%, assuming a 360-day year and a bond equivalent yield of 6.218%
   - A 180-day Thai corporate commercial paper (CP) quoted as an add-on rate of 6.10%, assuming a 365-day year and a bond equivalent yield of 6.100%.

   Assuming the six-month Thai T-bill is quoted at 4.36%, which instrument *most likely* has higher credit risk?

   Solution:

   The Thai CD. The spreads over the Thai T-bill for the CD and CP are 186 bps and 174 bps, respectively. We use the bond equivalent yield measure to compare the return of each instrument and derive the spread of each one over the Thai T-bill.

   The Thai bank CD has a spread of

   6.218% – 4.36% = 186 bps.

   And the Thai corporate CP has a spread of

   6.10% – 4.36% = 174 bps.

   Therefore, the Thai bank CD has a higher credit risk than the Thai corporate CP.

2 YIELD AND YIELD SPREAD MEASURES FOR FLOATING-RATE NOTES

☐ calculate and interpret yield spread measures for floating-rate instruments

Yield and Yield Spread Measures for Floating-Rate Instruments

Floating-rate instruments, including floating-rate notes (FRNs or floaters) and most loans, are different from fixed-rate bonds. Rather than fixed coupon payments, they vary from period to period depending on the current level of a reference interest rate. The intent is to both automatically adjust a borrower's base rate to market conditions and offer an investor or lender less price risk when market interest rates fluctuate. In principle, a floater has a stable price even in a period of volatile interest rates because cash flows adjust with changes in interest rates. With a traditional fixed-income security, constant future cash flows result in price changes in response to interest rate volatility.

Exhibit 1 shows the term sheet for four-year FRNs issued by Antelas AG, the German emerging technology company focused on manufacturing process design, introduced in an earlier lesson.

Exhibit 1: Antelas AG Floating-Rate Note Issue

Antelas AG Four-Year Floating-Rate Notes (the "Notes")
Prospectus Summary

Issuer:	Antelas AG
Settlement Date:	[T + 5 Business Days]
Maturity Date:	[Four Years from Settlement Date]
Principal Amount:	EUR250 million
Interest:	MRR plus 250 bps p.a.
Interest Payment:	MRR is reset quarterly and interest is paid quarterly Commencing three months from [Settlement Date] to be paid quarterly with final payment on [Maturity Date]
Seniority:	The Notes are secured and unsubordinated obligations of Antelas AG and will rank pari passu with all other secured and unsubordinated indebtedness
Business Days:	Frankfurt

Notice how the interest is stated "MRR plus 250 bps p.a." The market reference rate (MRR) on an FRN or loan usually is a short-term money market rate. Typically, the reference rate is determined at the beginning of the period, and the interest payment is made at the end of the period. This payment structure is called "in arrears." The most common day-count conventions for calculating accrued interest on floaters are actual/360 and actual/365. For the Antelas FRN, the MRR is reset quarterly and interest is paid quarterly.

For most FRNs and loans, a specified spread is added to or subtracted from the market reference rate. For the Antelas FRN, the spread over the MRR is 250 bps, and this is known as the **quoted margin** on the FRN. The role of the quoted margin is to compensate the investor for the difference in the credit risk of the issuer and that implied by the reference rate. Firms with very low credit risk may be able to obtain a negative quoted margin.

The **required margin** is the yield spread over or under the reference rate such that the FRN is priced at par value on a rate reset date. It is determined by the market. Suppose that a floater is issued at par value and pays MRR plus 0.50%. The quoted margin is 50 bps. If there is no change in the credit risk of the issuer, the required margin remains at 50 bps. On each quarterly reset date, the floater will be priced at par value. Between coupon dates, its flat price will be at a premium or discount to par value if MRR goes, respectively, down or up. However, if the required margin continues to be the same as the quoted margin, the flat price is "pulled to par" as the next reset date nears. At the reset date, any change in MRR is included in the interest payment for the next period.

Changes in the required margin usually come from changes in the issuer's credit risk. Changes in liquidity or tax status can also affect the required margin. Note that these are the same factors that affect the yield spread for fixed-rate bonds. Suppose that on a reset date, the required margin increases to 75 bps because of a downgrade in the issuer's credit rating. If the quoted margin is 50 bps, the issuer now pays its investors a "deficient" interest payment. This FRN will be priced at a discount below par value. The amount of the discount is the present value of the deficient future cash flows. That annuity is 25 bps per period for the remaining life of the bond. It is the difference between the required and quoted margins. If the required margin instead fell to 40 bps, perhaps from a decrease in the issuer's credit risk, the FRN would be priced at a premium. The amount of the premium is the present value of the 10 bp annuity for the "excess" interest payment each period.

Fixed-rate and floating-rate bonds are essentially the same with respect to changes in credit risk. With fixed-rate bonds, the premium or discount arises from a difference in the fixed coupon rate and the required yield-to-maturity. With floating-rate bonds, the premium or discount arises from a difference in the fixed quoted margin and the required margin. However, fixed-rate and floating-rate bonds are very different with respect to changes in benchmark interest rates.

The valuation of a floating-rate note requires a pricing model. Recall that the price for a fixed-rate bond given a market discount rate r and a coupon per period PMT is

$$PV = \frac{PMT}{(1+r)^1} + \frac{PMT}{(1+r)^2} + \ldots + \frac{PMT + FV}{(1+r)^N}.$$

For an FRN, PMT is a function of the MRR and the quoted margin and r is a function of the MRR and the discount margin. We can use this intuition to derive Equation 1, a simplified FRN pricing model.

$$PV = \frac{\frac{(MRR+QM)\times FV}{m}}{\left(1+\frac{MRR+DM}{m}\right)^1} + \frac{\frac{(MRR+QM)\times FV}{m}}{\left(1+\frac{MRR+DM}{m}\right)^2} + \ldots + \frac{\frac{(MRR+QM)\times FV}{m} + FV}{\left(1+\frac{MRR+DM}{m}\right)^N}, \quad (1)$$

where

PV = present value, or the price of the floating-rate note

MRR = the market reference rate, stated as an annual percentage rate (it is sometimes known generically as Index)

QM = the quoted margin, stated as an annual percentage rate

FV = the future value paid at maturity, or the par value of the bond

m = the periodicity of the floating-rate note, the number of payment periods per year

DM = the discount margin = required margin stated as an annual percentage rate

N = the number of evenly spaced periods to maturity

Notice that in Equation 1, because we are using annual rates for MRR, QM, and DM, we must divide by m periods in the year.

This is a simplified model for several reasons. First, PV is as of a rate reset date when there are N evenly spaced periods to maturity. There is no accrued interest, so the flat price is the full price. Second, the model assumes a 30/360 day-count convention, to make sure the periodicity, m, is an integer. However, in practice, most floaters use actual/360 day counts. Third, and most important, the same MRR is used for all cash flows. More complex FRN pricing models use projected future rates in the numerators and spot rates in the denominators. Therefore, the calculation for DM depends on the simplifying assumptions in the pricing model.

Suppose that we are pricing a two-year, semi-annual FRN that pays MRR plus 0.50%. Assume MRR is 1.25% and the yield spread required by investors is 40 bps. For Equation 1, we have the following inputs:

$MRR = 0.0125,$

$QM = 0.0050,$

$FV = 100,$

$m = 2,$

$DM = 0.0040,$ and

$N = 4.$

Using Equation 1 for $N = 4$, the FRN is priced at 100.196 per 100 of par value. This floater is priced at a premium above par value because the quoted margin is greater than the discount margin.

$$PV = \frac{\frac{(MRR + QM) \times FV}{m}}{\left(1 + \frac{MRR + DM}{m}\right)^1} + \frac{\frac{(MRR + QM) \times FV}{m}}{\left(1 + \frac{MRR + DM}{m}\right)^2} + \ldots + \frac{\frac{(MRR + QM) \times FV}{m} + FV}{\left(1 + \frac{MRR + DM}{m}\right)^N}.$$

$$PV = \frac{\frac{(0.0125 + 0.0050) \times 100}{2}}{\left(1 + \frac{0.0125 + 0.0040}{2}\right)^1} + \frac{\frac{(0.0125 + 0.0050) \times 100}{2}}{\left(1 + \frac{0.0125 + 0.0040}{2}\right)^2} + \frac{\frac{(0.0125 + 0.0050) \times 100}{2}}{\left(1 + \frac{0.0125 + 0.0040}{2}\right)^3} + \frac{\frac{(0.0125 + 0.0050) \times 100}{2} + 100}{\left(1 + \frac{0.0125 + 0.0040}{2}\right)^4}$$

$\text{PV} = 100.196$

If we have the market price of an FRN, we can also use Equation 1 to estimate the discount margin. Suppose that a two-year FRN pays MRR plus 0.75% on a semiannual basis. Currently, MRR is 1.10% and the price of the floater is 95.50 per 100 of par value, a discount to par, because of worsening credit risk. For Equation 1, we have the following inputs:

$PV = 95.50,$

$MRR = 0.0110,$

$QM = 0.0075,$

$FV = 100,$

$m = 2,$ and

$N = 4.$

Using the Solver add-in for Microsoft Excel, we find DM = 3.12%, or 312 bps, by setting the price (sum of present values of cash flows) equal to 95.50 as the objective and DM as the change variable. Please see the candidate learning ecosystem online for a spreadsheet demonstrating the calculation in the downloadable Excel workbook.

If this FRN was issued at par value, investors required at that time a spread of only 75 bps over MRR. Now, after the credit downgrade, investors require an *estimated* discount margin of 312 bps. The floater trades at a discount because the quoted margin remains fixed at 75 bps, so is "deficient" by 237 bps (312-75) per period The discount margin is an estimate because it is based on a simplified FRN pricing model.

The FRN pricing model in Equation 1 similarly applies to adjustable-rate loans made by banks and other fixed-income instruments based on MRR. Because a significant portion of bank funding comes from short-term deposits and other floating-rate sources, banks prefer to make floating-rate loans to businesses and individuals, as opposed to fixed-rate loans, to help maintain a match between assets and liabilities on the balance sheet.

EXAMPLE 1

Calculating the Discount Margin for a Floating-Rate Note

Suppose that the MRR for the Antelas AG four-year floating-rate note is on a three-month basis and the quoted margin is 250 bps. The floater is priced at 97 per 100 of par value. Calculate the discount margin for the floater assuming that three-month MRR is constant at –0.55%. Assume a 30/360 day-count convention and evenly spaced periods.

Solution:

We can use the Solver add-in in Microsoft Excel to quickly solve for *DM* = 3.29%, or 329 bps, in the same manner as in the prior example. Please see the candidate learning ecosystem online for a spreadsheet demonstrating the calculation in the downloadable Excel workbook.

Alternatively, we can use the RATE function in Microsoft Excel, Google Sheets, or a financial calculator by first solving for *PMT*, the numerators in Equation 1.

$$PMT = \frac{(MRR + QM) \times FV}{m}.$$

$$PMT = \frac{(-0.0055 + 0.0250) \times 100}{4}.$$

$$PMT = 0.4875.$$

Then, using $PV = -97$, $FV = 100$, $PMT = 0.4875$, and $N = 16$, we can solve for the discount rate per period of 0.686122%. We use this to solve for *DM*.

$$r = \frac{MRR + DM}{m}.$$

$$0.00686122 = \frac{-0.0055 + DM}{4}.$$

$$DM = 0.0329 = 3.29\%.$$

The quoted margin is 250 bps over the reference rate. Using the simplified FRN pricing model, the discount margin (the spread investors require for the floater to be priced at par) is 329 bps.

QUESTION SET

1. *Fill in the blanks using one of the words in each set of parentheses:*

   Floaters with longer reset periods may be __________ (more, less) exposed to interest rate and price volatility.

The __________ (shorter, longer) the reset period, the more a floater will behave similarly to a short-dated fixed-rate security and the __________ (less, more) its price will potentially fluctuate.

Solution:

Floaters with longer reset periods may be *more* exposed to interest rate and price volatility. The *longer* the reset period, the more a floater will behave similarly to a short-dated fixed-rate security and the *more* its price will potentially fluctuate.

2. For a five-year floating-rate security, if market interest rates change by 0.5%, the change in the price of the security will most likely be:

   A. zero.

   B. like an otherwise identical fixed-rate security.

   C. related to the security's coupon reset frequency.

Solution:

C is correct. The interest rate sensitivity of a floating-rate security comes typically from the time remaining until its next coupon reset date.

A is incorrect: when the interest rates changes, the discount rate of the floating rate security also changes, changing the present value of the security when discounting the cashflows.

B is incorrect: with a fixed-rate security, interest rates changes affect the price more than an identical (same-term) floating-rate security, due to its fixed coupon payments and a higher duration.

3. Identify the relationship between required margin and a floater's price at the reset date:

1. Required margin > Quoted margin	A. Floater priced at par
2. Required margin = Quoted margin	B. Floater priced at a discount
3. Required margin < Quoted margin	C. Floater priced at a premium

Solution:

1. Required margin > Quoted margin	B. Floater priced at a discount
2. Required margin = Quoted margin	A. Floater priced at par
3. Required margin < Quoted margin	C. Floater priced at a premium

For Required margin > Quoted margin, B is correct. Changes in the required margin usually come from changes in the issuer's credit risk. If the required margin increases and is above the quoted margin at the reset date, the floater pays a "deficient" interest payment. The floater will be priced at a discount below par value.

For Required margin = Quoted margin, A is correct. If the required margin continues to be the same as the quoted margin, the flat price is "pulled to par" as the next reset date nears.

For Required margin < Quoted margin, C is correct. If the required margin decreases and is below the quoted margin, the floater will be priced at a premium.

4. A two-year Italian floating-rate note pays three-month Euribor of –0.50% plus 250 bp. The floater is priced at 99 per 100 of par value. Assuming the 30/360 day-count convention and evenly spaced periods, the discount margin for the floater is closest to:

   A. 201 bps.

   B. 251 bps.

   C. 300 bps.

   Solution:

   C is correct. The discount margin for the floater is closest to 300 bps. Using the information provided, the periodic *PMT* is equal to

   $$\frac{(MRR + QM) \times FV}{m} = \frac{(-0.005 + 0.0025) \times 100}{4} = 0.5.$$

   Using the RATE function in Microsoft Excel, Google Sheets, or a financial calculator using $PV = -99$, $FV = 100$, $PMT = 0.5$, and $N = 8$, we solve for the discount rate per period of 0.628562%. The discount margin can be estimated by solving for *DM*:

   $$r = \frac{MRR + DM}{m}.$$

   $$0.00628562 = \frac{-0.005 + DM}{4}.$$

   $$DM = 0.03014 = 3.014\%.$$

5. The Antelas AG four-year floating-rate note pays three-month MRR of –0.55% plus 250 bps. The floater is priced at 102 per 100 of par value. Assuming the 30/360 day-count convention and evenly spaced periods, calculate the discount margin for the floating-rate note.

   Solution:

   The estimated discount margin is 199 bps.

   Using the information provided, the periodic *PMT* is equal to

   $$\frac{(MRR + QM) \times FV}{m} = \frac{(-0.0055 + 0.025) \times 100}{4} = 0.4875.$$

   Using the RATE function in Microsoft Excel, Google Sheets, or a financial calculator using $PV = -102$, $FV = 100$, $PMT = 0.4875$, and $N = 16$, we solve for the discount rate per period of 0.358655%. The discount margin can then be estimated by solving for *DM*:

   $$r = \frac{MRR + DM}{m}.$$

   $$0.00358655 = \frac{-0.0055 + DM}{4}.$$

   $$DM = 0.019846 = 1.99\%.$$

YIELD MEASURES FOR MONEY MARKET INSTRUMENTS

3

- [ ] calculate and interpret yield measures for money market instruments

Money market instruments are debt securities with original maturities of one year or less. There are many types, including overnight sale and repurchase agreements (repos), bank certificates of deposit, commercial paper, Treasury bills (government securities issued with a maturity of one year or less), bankers' acceptances, and time deposits based on market reference rates. There are mutual funds that invest solely in eligible money market securities, known as money market mutual funds, which are sometimes considered as an alternative to bank deposits.

There are several important differences in yield measures quoted for money market instruments versus bonds:

1. Bond yields-to-maturity are annualized and compounded. Yield measures in the money market are annualized but *not* compounded; the return on a money market instrument is stated on a simple interest basis.
2. Bond yields-to-maturity usually are stated for a common periodicity for all times-to-maturity. Money market instruments with different times-to-maturity have different periodicities for the annual rate.
3. Bond yields-to-maturity can be calculated using standard time-value-of-money analysis. Money market instruments are often quoted using non-standard interest rates and require different pricing equations than those used for bonds.

In general, quoted money market rates are either **discount rates** or **add-on rates**. Although market conventions vary around the world, commercial paper, Treasury bills, and bankers' acceptances often are quoted on a discount rate basis. Bank certificates of deposit, repos, and market reference rate indexes are quoted on an add-on rate basis. While *discount rate* usually means "interest rate used to calculate a present value," in the money market, the discount rate involves an instrument for which interest is included in the face value of the instrument. An add-on rate, in contrast, involves interest that is added to the principal or investment amount. Some examples will clarify this point.

Equation 2 is the pricing formula for money market instruments quoted on a discount rate basis.

$$PV = FV \times \left(1 - \frac{\text{Days}}{\text{Year}} \times DR\right), \tag{2}$$

where

PV = present value, or the price of the money market instrument

FV = the future value paid at maturity, or the face value of the money market instrument

Days = the number of days between settlement and maturity

Year = the number of days in the year

DR = the discount rate, stated as an annual percentage rate

Suppose that a 91-day Indian Treasury bill (T-bill) with a face value of INR10 million is quoted at a discount rate of 3.45% for an assumed 360-day year. The price of the Indian rupee T-bill is INR9,912,792.

$$PV = FV \times (1 - \frac{\text{Days}}{\text{Year}} \times DR).$$

$$PV = 10,000,000 \times (1 - \frac{91}{360} \times 0.0345).$$

$$PV = 9,912,791.67.$$

The unique characteristics of a money market discount rate can be examined with Equation 3, which transforms Equation 2 algebraically to isolate the *DR* term.

$$DR = \frac{\text{Year}}{\text{Days}} \times \frac{(FV - PV)}{FV}. \quad (3)$$

The first term, Year/Days, is the periodicity of the annual rate. The second term reveals the odd character of a money market discount rate. The numerator, $FV - PV$, is the interest earned on the rupee T-bill, INR87,208 (= 10,000,000 – 9,912,792), over the 91 days to maturity. However, the denominator is *FV*, not *PV*. In theory, an interest rate is the amount earned divided by the investment amount (*PV*), not the maturity value (*FV*), which includes the earnings. Therefore, by design, a money market discount rate *understates* the rate of return to the investor, and it *understates* the cost of borrowed funds to the issuer. That is because *PV* is less than *FV* if *DR* is greater than zero.

Equation 4 is the pricing formula for money market instruments quoted on an add-on rate basis.

$$PV = \frac{FV}{(1 + \frac{\text{Days}}{\text{Year}} \times AOR)}, \quad (4)$$

where

PV = present value, the principal amount, or the price of the money market instrument

FV = the future value, or the redemption amount paid at maturity including interest

Days = the number of days between settlement and maturity

Year = the number of days in the year

AOR = the add-on rate, stated as an annual percentage rate

EXAMPLE 2

Yield Measures on Bank Certificates of Deposit

Commercial Finance Partners AG (CFP Bank) issues 90-day certificates of deposit (CDs) to fund its floating-rate loans made to customers. The objective is to maintain a match between the bank's assets (floating-rate loans) and its funding sources. The quoted add-on rate for its 90-day CD is 0.12%, assuming a 365-day year. If the initial principal amount is EUR20 million, the redemption amount due at maturity is found by rearranging Equation 4 and entering PV = 20,000,000, Days = 90, Year = 365, and AOR = 0.0012.

$$FV = 20,000,000 + (20,000,000 \times \frac{90}{365} \times 0.0012).$$

$$FV = 20,005,918.$$

At maturity, CFP Bank pays EUR20,005,918, the principal of EUR20,000,000 plus interest of EUR5,918. The interest is calculated as the principal times the fraction of the year times the annual add-on rate. It is added to the principal to determine the redemption amount.

Suppose that after 45 days, the CD investor sells the CD to a dealer. At that time, the quoted add-on rate for a 45-day CD is 0.06%. The sale price for the CD can be calculated using Equation 4 for FV = 20,004,918, Days = 45, Year = 365, and AOR = 0.0012. The sale price is EUR20,002,958.

$$PV = \frac{FV}{(1 + \frac{\text{Days}}{\text{Year}} \times AOR)}.$$

$$PV = \frac{20,005,918}{(1 + \frac{45}{365} \times 0.0006)}.$$

$$PV = 20,003,438.$$

The characteristics of an add-on rate can be examined with Equation 5, which transforms Equation 4 algebraically to isolate the AOR term.

$$AOR = \frac{\text{Year}}{\text{Days}} \times \frac{FV - PV}{PV}. \tag{5}$$

The first term, Year/Days, is the periodicity of the annual rate. The second term is the interest earned ($FV - PV$) divided by the amount invested (PV).

CFP Bank's rate of return on its 45-day investment in the certificates of deposit can be calculated with Equation 5.

$$AOR = \frac{\text{Year}}{\text{Days}} \times \frac{FV - PV}{PV}.$$

$$AOR = \frac{365}{45} \times \frac{20,002,958 - 20,000,000}{20,000,000}.$$

$$AOR = 0.0012.$$

The rate of return, stated on a 365-day add-on rate basis, is 0.12%. This result is an annual rate for a periodicity of 8.11 (= 365/45). Implicitly, this assumes that the investment can be replicated 8.11 times over the year.

Investment analysis is more challenging for money market securities because (1) some instruments are quoted on a discount rate basis while others on an add-on rate basis and (2) some assume a 360-day year and others use a 365-day year. Another difference is that the "amount" of a money market instrument quoted by traders on a discount rate basis typically is the face value paid at maturity. However, the "amount" when quoted on an add-on rate basis usually is the price at issuance. Exhibit 2 summarizes these conventions.

Exhibit 2: Summary of Money Market Yield Measures

Conventions and Instruments	Description	
Quote Basis	Discount Rate (DR)	Add-on Rate (AOR)
Equation	DR = (Year/Days) × [(FV – PV)/FV].	AOR = (Year/Days) × [(FV – PV)/PV].

Conventions and Instruments	Description	
Quoted Amount	Face Value at Maturity (FV)	Price at Issuance (PV)
Typical Instruments	Commercial Paper, Treasury Bills, Bankers' Acceptances	Bank Certificates of Deposit, Repurchase Agreements (Repos), Market Reference Rates (MRRs)

To make money market investment decisions, it is essential to compare instruments on a common basis. The following example illustrates this point.

EXAMPLE 3

Yield Measures on Bank Certificates of Deposit

Suppose that an investor is comparing the following two money market instruments. Which offers the higher expected rate of return, assuming that credit risks are the same?

- A 90-day commercial paper (CP) issued by Bright Wheel Automotive Corporation (BRWA), quoted at a discount rate of 0.100% for a 360-day year
- A 90-day certificate of deposit issued by CFP Bank, quoted at an add-on rate of 0.120% for a 365-day year

The price of the commercial paper is 99.975 per 100 of face value, calculated using Equation 2 and entering FV = 100, Days = 90, Year = 360, and DR = 0.0010.

$$PV = FV \times \left(1 - \frac{\text{Days}}{\text{Year}} \times DR\right).$$

$$PV = 100 \times \left(1 - \frac{90}{360} \times 0.0010\right).$$

$$PV = 99.975.$$

Next, use Equation 5 to solve for AOR for a 365-day year, where Year = 365, Days = 90, FV = 100, and PV = 99.975.

$$AOR = \frac{\text{Year}}{\text{Days}} \times \frac{FV - PV}{PV}.$$

$$AOR = \frac{365}{90} \times \frac{100 - 99.975}{99.975}.$$

$$AOR = 0.00122.$$

The 90-day commercial paper discount rate of 0.10% converts to an add-on rate for a 365-day year of 0.1014%. This converted rate is called a bond equivalent yield, or sometimes just an "investment yield." A **bond equivalent yield** is a money market rate stated on a 365-day add-on rate basis. If the risks are the same, BRWA's CP offers 0.2 bps more in annual return than CFP Bank's CD.

Exhibit 3 summarizes the process just illustrated for comparing money market instruments on a common, bond equivalent yield basis.

Exhibit 3: Comparing Money Market Instruments on Bond Equivalent Yield Basis

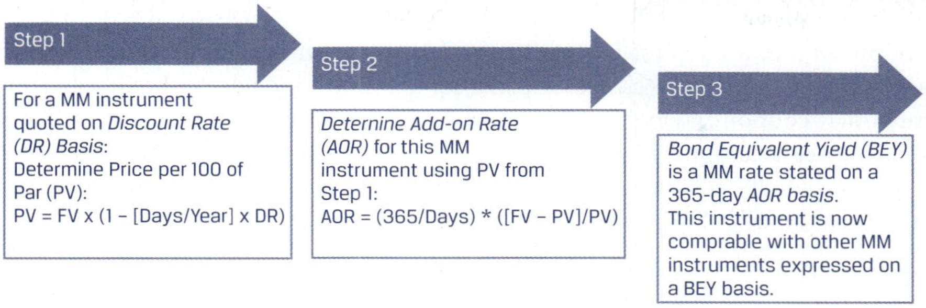

EXAMPLE 4

Comparing Money Market Instruments Based on Bond Equivalent Yields

A money market investor observes quoted rates on four 180-day money market instruments: A, B, C, and D.

Money Market Instrument	Quotation Basis	Assumed Number of Days in the Year	Quoted Rate
A	Discount Rate	360	4.33%
B	Discount Rate	365	4.36%
C	Add-On Rate	360	4.35%
D	Add-On Rate	365	4.45%

Using a spreadsheet, we can calculate the bond equivalent yield for each instrument so that rates of return can be compared. Bond A offers the highest rate of return (4.487%) and Bond C offers the lowest rate of return (4.410%) on a bond equivalent yield basis. Please refer to the candidate learning ecosystem online for a spreadsheet demonstrating the calculation in the downloadable Excel workbook.

	Money market Instrument	A	B	C	D
Input	Quotation Basis	Discount Rate	Discount Rate	Add-On Rate	Add-On Rate
	Number of Days in the Year	360	365	360	365
	Quoted Rated (%)	4.33%	4.36%	4.35%	4.45%
Output	PV/FV	97.835	97.850	102.175	102.195
	Add-On-Rate	0.04487	0.04456	0.04410	0.04450
	Bond Equivalent Yield (%)	4.487%	4.456%	4.410%	4.450%

Another important difference between yield measures in the money market and the bond market is the periodicity of the annual rate. Because bond yields-to-maturity are computed using interest rate compounding, there is a well-defined periodicity. For instance, bond yields-to-maturity for semiannual compounding are annualized for a periodicity of two. Money market rates are computed using simple interest without compounding. In the money market, the periodicity is the number of days in the year divided by the number of days to maturity. Therefore, money market rates for different times-to-maturity have different periodicities.

Suppose that an analyst prefers to convert money market rates to a semiannual bond basis so that the rates are directly comparable to yields on bonds that make semiannual coupon payments. The quoted rate for a 91-day Indian rupee T-bill is 3.50%, quoted as a bond equivalent yield, which means its periodicity is 365/91. We use the periodicity conversion formula covered in a previous lesson to convert from a periodicity m of 365/91 to n of 2:

$$\left(1+\frac{APR_m}{m}\right)^m = \left(1+\frac{APR_n}{n}\right)^n.$$

$$\left(1+\frac{0.035}{\frac{365}{91}}\right)^{\frac{365}{91}} = \left(1+\frac{APR_2}{2}\right)^2.$$

$$APR_2 = 0.03515 = 3.515\%.$$

Therefore, 3.50% for a periodicity of 365/91 corresponds to 3.515% for a periodicity of 2. The difference is –1.5 bps. In general, the difference depends on the level of the annual percentage rate. When interest rates are lower, the difference between the annual rates for any two periodicities is reduced.

QUESTION SET

1. Identify the correct relationship for a money market instrument quoted on a discount rate basis:

   A. $PV = FV \times (1 - \frac{Days}{Year} \times DR)$.

   B. $FV = PV \times (1 - \frac{Year}{Days} \times DR)$.

   C. $PV = \frac{FV}{(1 + DR)^{\frac{Days}{Year}}}$.

   Solution:

   A is correct. In the money market, the discount rate is a specific type of quoted rate. Hence, the price or the present value of a money market instrument is determined by

   $$PV = FV \times (1 - \frac{Days}{Year} \times DR),$$

   where

PV = present value, or the price of the money market instrument

FV = the future value paid at maturity, or the face value of the money market instrument

Days = the number of days between settlement and maturity

Year = the number of days in the year

DR = the discount rate, stated as an annual percentage rate

2. *True or false:* Yield measures in money market instruments are annualized and compounded.

   A. True

   B. False

   Solution:

   False. Bond yields-to-maturity are annualized and compounded. However, yield measures in money markets are annualized but not compounded.

3. *True or false:* Money market instruments use the standard time value of money, such as discount rates or add-on rates.

   A. True

   B. False

   Solution:

   False. Bond yields-to-maturity are calculated using the standard time value of money. Money market instruments are often quoted using non-standard interest rates, such as discount rates or add-on rates.

4. *True or false:* Money market instruments with different times-to-maturity have different periodicities.

   A. True

   B. False

   Solution:

   True. Money market instruments with different times-to-maturities have different periodicities. However, bond yields-to-maturity are given for a common periodicity for all times-to-maturity.

5. Explain the concept of a bond equivalent yield for a money market instrument.

   Solution:

   A bond equivalent yield is the rate of return on a money market instrument that is calculated with reference to the purchase price of the instrument based on a 365-day year. The converted rate or yield can be used to compare the return earned on the money market instrument with a similar return earned by a bond.

6. A portfolio manager has asked you to evaluate the following Thai baht–denominated 180 days money market instruments with equivalent credit risk.

Money Market Instrument	Quotation Basis	Number of Days in the Year	Quoted Rate
Short-Term Thai T-Bills	Discount Rate	360	4.78%
Thai Bank Certificate of Deposit	Discount Rate	365	4.81%
Thai Corporate Commercial Paper	Add-On Rate	365	4.85%

Which instrument has the highest rate of return on a bond equivalent yield basis?

A. Short-term Thai T-bills

B. Thai bank certificate of deposit

C. Thai corporate commercial paper

Solution:

A is correct. The bond equivalent yield for each instrument is most easily calculated using a spreadsheet. Please refer to the candidate learning ecosystem online for a spreadsheet demonstrating the calculations in the downloadable Excel workbook. The short-term Thai T-bills offer the highest return of 4.965% on a bond equivalent yield basis.

	Money Market Instrument	Short-Term Thai T-Bill	Thai Bank CD	Thai Corporate CP
Input	Quotation Basis	Discount Rate	Discount Rate	Add-On Rate
	Number of Days in the Year	360	365	365
	Quoted Rated (%)	4.78%	4.81%	4.85%
Output	PV/FV	97.610	97.628	102.392
	Add-On-Rate	0.04965	0.04927	0.04850
	Bond Equivalent Yield (%)	4.965%	4.927%	4.850%

The following information relates to questions 7-8

A German insurance company buys a 91-day certificate of deposit with a quoted add-on rate of 0.40% for a 365-day year.

7. If the initial payment amount is EUR20 million, calculate the redemption amount due at maturity.

Solution:

The redemption amount can be calculated using Equation 4:

$$PV = \frac{FV}{(1 + \frac{\text{Days}}{\text{Year}} \times AOR)}.$$

$$20{,}000{,}000 = \frac{FV}{(1 + \frac{91}{365} \times 0.0040)}.$$

$$FV = 20{,}019{,}945.$$

8. Suppose that after 31 days, the insurance company sells the CD. At the time of the sale, the quoted add-on rate for a 60-day CD is 0.21%. Calculate the sale price for the CD.

Solution:

After 31 days, the sale price of the certificate of deposit is also calculated using Equation 4:

$$PV = \frac{FV}{(1 + \frac{\text{Days}}{\text{Year}} \times AOR)}.$$

$$PV = \frac{20{,}019{,}945}{(1 + \frac{60}{365} \times 0.0021)}.$$

$$PV = 20,013,036.$$

PRACTICE PROBLEMS

1. A two-year floating-rate note issued by a French corporation pays the three-month MRR of –0.55% plus 160 bps. The floater is priced at 101.20 per 100 of par value. Assuming the 30/360 day-count convention and 90 days per period, the discount margin for the floater is closest to:

   A. 25 bps.

   B. 50 bps.

   C. 110 bps.

2. Changes in the required margin for a floater usually come from:

   A. shifts in the yield curve.

   B. changes in credit risk.

   C. increases or decrease in inflation.

The following information relates to questions 3-4

A fixed-income portfolio manager is looking to value a one-year US dollar–denominated floating-rate note that has quarterly payments based on 90-day MRR plus 80 bps. Assume the following information:

90-Day MRR: 2.5%

Quoted Margin: 80 bps

Discount Margin: 100 bps

Face Value: USD100

3. Without doing any calculation, this floating-rate note is priced at:

   A. a premium.

   B. a discount.

   C. par.

4. The price of the FRN is closest to:

   A. 98.804.

   B. 99.804.

   C. 100.804.

---

5. The bond equivalent yield of a 90-day European bank certificate of deposit quoted at a discount rate of 0.55% for a 360-day year is closest to:

   A. 0.21%.

B. 0.24%.

C. 0.56%.

6. A 91-day UK gilt (Treasury bill) has a face value of GBP2 million, a discount rate of 0.25%, and a price of GBP1.9 million. If a year has 366 days, the discount rate for the UK gilt is closest to:

   A. 0.1821.

   B. 0.2011.

   C. 0.2134.

7. Explain why a money market discount rate greater than zero understates the rate of return to an investor and understates the cost of borrowed funds for the issuer.

SOLUTIONS

1. B is correct.

   Using the information provided, the periodic *PMT* is equal to

   $$\frac{(MRR + QM) \times FV}{m} = \frac{(-0.055 + 0.016) \times 100}{4} = 0.2625.$$

   Using the RATE function in Microsoft Excel, Google Sheets, or a financial calculator and using $PV = -101.20$, $FV = 100$, $PMT = 0.275$, and $N = 8$, we solve for the discount rate per period of 12.4161%. The discount margin can then be estimated by solving for *DM*:

   $$r = \frac{MRR + DM}{m}.$$

   $$0.124161 = \frac{-0.005 + DM}{4}.$$

   $$DM = 0.4525.$$

   The estimated discount margin is 45.25 bps.

2. B is correct. The required margin is the yield spread over or under a reference rate, reflecting the credit risk of an issuer. Changes in the required margin typically come from a change in the issuer's credit risk.

   A and C are incorrect. Both risks, as "top-down" or macroeconomic risks, would be reflected in changes in the MRR, not in a spread such as the required margin.

3. B is correct. This FRN is priced at a discount, because the quoted margin is less than the discount (required) margin.

4. B is correct. The FRN is priced at 99.804 per 100 of par value. Using the information provided, the periodic *PMT* is equal to

   $$\frac{(MRR + QM) \times FV}{m} = \frac{(0.025 + 0.008) \times 100}{4} = 0.825.$$

   The assumed discount rate per period is equal to 0.875%.

   $$r = \frac{MRR + DM}{m}.$$

   $$r = \frac{0.025 + 0.01}{4}.$$

   $$r = 0.00875.$$

   To value this FRN, take the present value of each cash flow using the discount rate per period. The FRN is priced at 99.804 per 100 of par value.

   $$PV = \frac{0.825}{(1 + 0.00875)^1} + \frac{0.825}{(1 + 0.00875)^2} + \frac{0.825}{(1 + 0.00875)^3} + \frac{100.825}{(1 + 0.00875)^4}.$$

   $$PV = 99.804.$$

5. C is correct. The bond equivalent yield is closest to 0.56%.

   The present value of the banker's certificate of deposit is calculated as follows:

   $$PV = FV \times (1 - \frac{\text{Days}}{\text{Year}} \times DR).$$

   $$PV = 100 \times (1 - \frac{90}{360} \times 0.0055).$$

$PV = 99.865.$

The bond equivalent yield (AOR using a 365-day year) is calculated to be approximately 0.56%:

$$AOR = \frac{\text{Year}}{\text{Days}} \times \frac{FV - PV}{PV}.$$

$$AOR = \frac{365}{90} \times \frac{100 - 99.8625}{99.8625}.$$

$$AOR = 0.0056.$$

6. B is correct. The discount rate is closest to 0.2011.

$$DR = \frac{\text{Year}}{\text{Days}} \times \frac{(FV - PV)}{FV}.$$

$$DR = \frac{366}{91} \times \frac{(2,000,000 - 1,900,000)}{2,000,000}.$$

$$DR = 0.2011.$$

7. For a money market instrument, the discount rate is calculated as

$$DR = \frac{\text{Year}}{\text{Days}} \times \frac{(FV - PV)}{FV}.$$

The denominator for the second term is *FV*, not *PV*. In theory, an interest rate is the amount earned divided by the investment amount (*PV*), not the maturity value (*FV*), which includes the earnings. So long as *DR* is greater than zero, *FV* will be higher than *PV*. Therefore, by design, a money market discount rate *understates* the rate of return to the investor, and it *understates* the cost of borrowed funds to the issuer.

LEARNING MODULE

9

The Term Structure of Interest Rates: Spot, Par, and Forward Curves

LEARNING OUTCOMES

Mastery	The candidate should be able to:
☐	define spot rates and the spot curve, and calculate the price of a bond using spot rates
☐	define par and forward rates, and calculate par rates, forward rates from spot rates, spot rates from forward rates, and the price of a bond using forward rates
☐	compare the spot curve, par curve, and forward curve

INTRODUCTION

1

Prior lessons priced fixed-income instruments by discounting all future cash flows using a single interest rate, such as the yield-to-maturity or a market reference rate (MRR) plus a discount margin. The next three lessons relax this assumption by introducing the term structure of interest rates, or the fact that interest rates vary with time-to-maturity. The ideal data to use for term structure analysis are default-risk-free zero-coupon bonds, known as spot rates or the spot curve. Since these are generally not directly observable, various estimation techniques are used. The spot curve is used to derive two other important yield curves: the par curve and the forward curve. A par curve involves bond yields for hypothetical benchmark securities priced at par, while the forward curve involves rates for interest periods starting in the future. All three of these curves are fundamental to fixed-income analysis and other applications because they represent default-risk-free rates of return for time periods that start today and in the future. We show the pricing of bonds using these different rates and establish their relationships.

Most of the examples and exhibits used throughout the reading can be downloaded as a Microsoft Excel workbook. Each worksheet in the workbook is labeled with the corresponding example or exhibit number in the text.

LEARNING MODULE OVERVIEW

- Spot rates are market discount rates on default-risk-free zero-coupon bonds, sometimes referred to as zero rates. By using a sequence of spot rates in calculating bond prices, a no-arbitrage bond price is obtained.
- A par rate is the market discount rate for a specific maturity that would result in a bond priced at par. A par rate is derived from the spot rates up to and including the maturity date.
- Implied forward rates are calculated using spot rates and can be interpreted as an incremental, or marginal, return for extending the time-to-maturity for an additional time period. As such, they reflect a breakeven reinvestment rate.
- Since par and forward rates can be derived from spot rates, the shape of the spot curve is closely related to the shape of the par and forward curves.
- In upward-sloping term structures, par rates will be lower than their corresponding spot rates and forward rates will be greater than spot rates. In downward-sloping term structures, par rates will be greater than spot rates and forward rates will be lower than spot rates.

LEARNING MODULE SELF-ASSESSMENT

These initial questions are intended to help you gauge your current level of understanding of this learning module.

1. Calculate the price and yield-to-maturity (YTM) of a 1% coupon, three-year bond with par value of 100 given the following spot rates:

1-year	1.0%
2-year	1.5%
3-year	2.0%

Solution:

The price is 97.135:

$$PV = \frac{PMT}{(1+Z_1)^1} + \frac{PMT}{(1+Z_2)^2} + \cdots + \frac{PMT+FV}{(1+Z_N)^N}$$

$$PV = \frac{1}{(1+0.01)^1} + \frac{1}{(1+0.015)^2} + \frac{101}{(1+0.02)^3}$$

$$PV = 97.135$$

The YTM is 1.993%:

$$PV = \frac{PMT}{(1+r)^1} + \frac{PMT}{(1+r)^2} + \cdots + \frac{PMT+FV}{(1+r)^N}$$

$$97.135 = \frac{1}{(1+r)^1} + \frac{1}{(1+r)^2} + \frac{101}{(1+r)^3}$$

$$r = 0.01993 = 1.993\%$$

2. Define what a par rate represents in the context of bond pricing.

Solution:

The par rate is the yield-to-maturity that makes the present value of a bond's cash flows (i.e., its price) equal to its par or face value.

3. Calculate an implied one-year forward rate two years from now (i.e., 2y1y) given the following spot rates, assuming annual compounding:

1-year	1.0%
2-year	1.5%
3-year	2.0%

Solution:

$(1 + Z_A)^A \times (1 + IFR_{A,B-A})^{B-A} = (1 + Z_B)^B.$

$(1 + 0.01)^1 \times (1 + IFR_{2,1})^2 = (1 + 0.02)^3.$

$IFR_{2,1} = 2.50\%.$

4. Explain the economic meaning of the forward rate result calculated in Question 3.

Solution:

The one-year forward rate two years from now (2y1y) of 3.01% implies that investors expect the one-year interest rate to be 3.01% at the end of two years. This reflects the rate at which reinvestment would yield the same results over a three-year horizon regardless of whether the investor initially bought a two-year bond versus a three-year bond.

5. Contrast spot and forward rates.

Solution:

Spot rates reflect borrowing and investing rates for funds immediately (or in the next few days) over the specified tenor, while forward rates reflect rates applicable to agreements to borrow or invest beginning on a future date for a specified tenor.

6. True or false: One-year forward rates are higher compared to their corresponding spot rates when the spot rate curve is downward sloping.

A. True

B. False

Solution:

False. When the spot curve is downward sloping, the one-year forward rate curve will lie below the spot rate curve. Declining spot rates for longer maturities imply that investors should expect lower rates of reinvestment in future years, and the forward curve reflects these expectations.

2 MATURITY STRUCTURE OF INTEREST RATES AND SPOT RATES

- [ ] define spot rates and the spot curve, and calculate the price of a bond using spot rates

Maturity Structure of Interest Rates

Suppose that the yield-to-maturity is higher on one bond compared to another bond. There are several possible reasons for the difference, including credit risk, different currencies, liquidity, tax differences, and the periodicity assumption used in the yield calculation. Credit risk and currency differences were demonstrated in earlier lessons where Romania's (Ministry of Finance) 30-year euro-denominated bonds were issued at a 4.657% yield-to-maturity, a 411 bp spread over Federal Republic of Germany bonds. Another reason bonds may have different yields-to-maturity is that they have different times-to-maturity. This factor explaining the differences in yields is called the **maturity structure of interest rates** or **term structure of interest rates**.

Term structure is best analyzed using bonds that have all the same properties *other than* time-to-maturity; that is, the bonds should be denominated in the same currency and have the same credit risk, liquidity, tax status, and periodicity assumption and they should have the same coupon rate so that they each have the same degree of coupon reinvestment risk. This ideal dataset would be yields-to-maturity on a series of default-risk-free *zero-coupon* bonds, known as **spot rates**, for a full range of maturities. Developed market sovereign bonds are typically used for this purpose, because they represent the lowest default risk among issuers in a given market. Collectively, this dataset is the government bond **spot curve**, sometimes called the zero or "strip" curve (because the coupon payments are "stripped" off the bonds).

The government bond spot curve is ideal for analyzing maturity structure because it best meets the "other things being equal" assumption. These government bonds presumably have the same currency, credit risk, liquidity, and tax status. Most importantly, as zero-coupon bonds, they have no coupon reinvestment risk. A government bond spot curve is illustrated in Exhibit 1 for maturities ranging from 1 to 30 years. The annual yields are stated on a semiannual bond basis, which facilitates comparison to coupon-bearing bonds that make semiannual payments, like corporate bonds in many markets.

Exhibit 1: Government Bond Spot (Zero) Curve

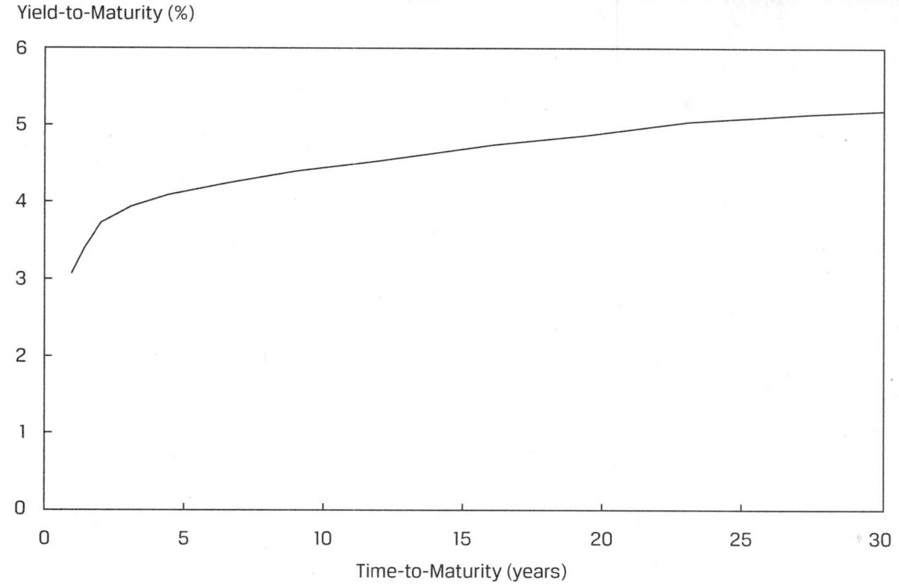

The spot curve in Exhibit 1 is upward sloping and flattens for longer times-to-maturity, meaning that the longer-term government bonds have higher yields than the shorter-term bonds. This pattern is typical under normal market conditions. Sometimes, a spot curve is downward sloping in that shorter-term yields are higher than longer-term yields. Such downward-sloping spot curves are called inverted yield curves. Theories that attempt to explain the shape of the yield curve and its implications for future financial market conditions are covered later.

While a spot curve comprised of zero-coupon government bonds is ideal for analysis, there are several practical issues to contend with. First, most actively traded government bonds make coupon payments. These coupon bonds might not have the same liquidity and tax status. Older ("seasoned") bonds tend to be less liquid than newly issued debt because they are owned by "buy-and-hold" institutional and retail investors. Governments issue new debt for regular times-to-maturity—for instance, 5-year and 10-year bonds. The current 6-year bond could be a 10-year bond that was issued four years ago. Also, because interest rates fluctuate, older bonds can be priced at a discount or premium to par value, which can lead to tax differences because some tax jurisdictions distinguish capital gains and losses from interest income.

In practice, therefore, only the most recently issued and actively traded government bonds are used to build a yield curve. These bonds have similar liquidity, and because they are priced closer to par value, they have fewer tax effects. Additionally, because there are limited data for the full range of maturities, interpolation is used to complete the curve. Exhibit 2 illustrates a yield curve for a government that issues 2-year, 3-year, 5-year, 7-year, 10-year, and 30-year bonds that make semiannual coupon payments. Straight-line interpolation is used between those points on the yield curve.

Exhibit 2: Government Coupon Bond Yield Curve

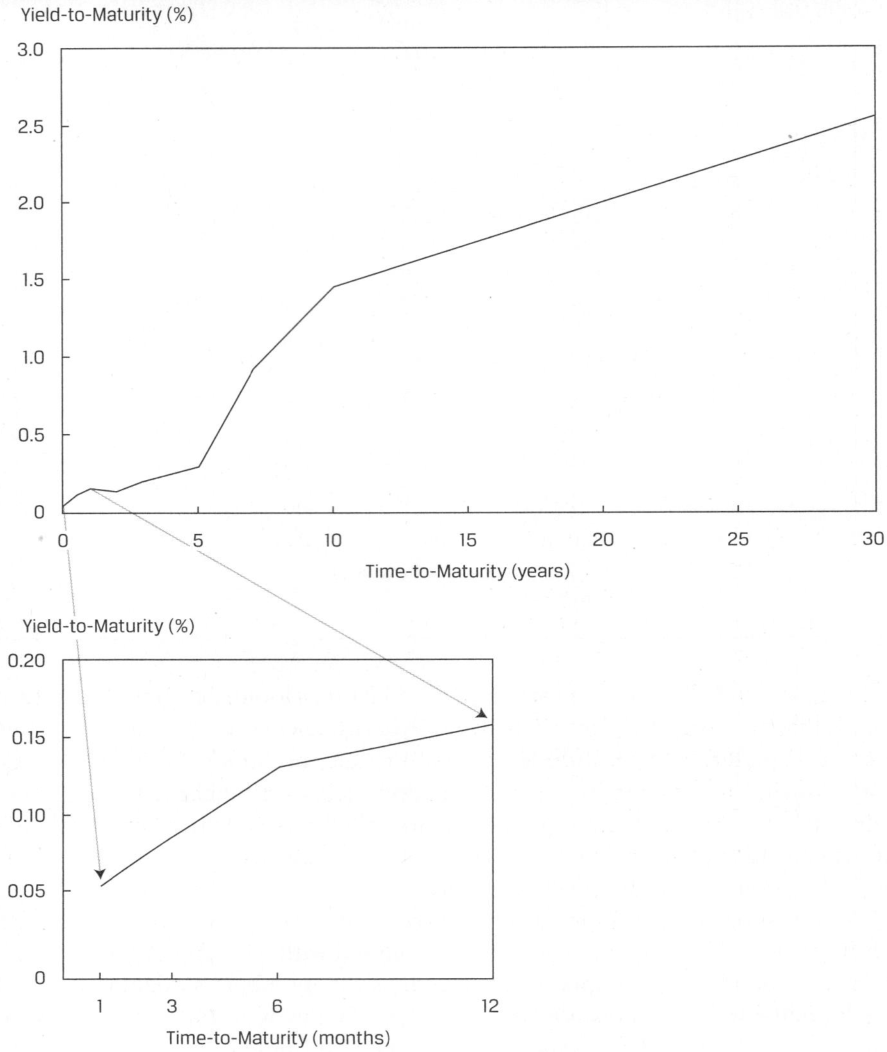

Exhibit 2 also includes yields for short-term government securities having 1 month, 3 months, 6 months, and 12 months to maturity. Although these money market instruments are issued and traded on a discount rate basis, they are converted to bond equivalent yields (i.e., add-on rates with a 365-day year). All bonds on the yield curve should also be converted to the same periodicity in order to facilitate comparisons across times-to-maturity. Conversion from discount rates to bond equivalent yields and across periodicities was demonstrated in prior lessons.

Bond Pricing Using Spot Rates

Since interest rates vary by maturity and have a term structure, we can price bonds using a sequence of discount rates that correspond to the cash flow dates. One such sequence, representing default-risk-free rates, is the spot curve. Bond prices determined using spot rates establish "no-arbitrage" prices; if a bond's price differs from its no-arbitrage value, an arbitrage opportunity exists in the absence of transaction costs.

Suppose that the one-year spot rate is 2%, the two-year spot rate is 3%, and the three-year spot rate is 4%. Then, the price of a three-year bond that makes a 5% annual coupon payment is 102.960:

$$\frac{5}{(1.02)^1} + \frac{5}{(1.03)^2} + \frac{105}{(1.04)^3} =$$

$$4.902 + 4.713 + 93.345 = 102.960.$$

This three-year bond is priced at a premium, so its yield-to-maturity must be less than its 5% coupon rate. Using the basic bond pricing formula, the yield-to-maturity is 3.935%:

$$102.960 = \frac{5}{(1+r)^1} + \frac{5}{(1+r)^2} + \frac{105}{(1+r)^3};\ r = 0.03935.$$

If the cash flows are discounted using the yield-to-maturity, the same price is obtained:

$$\frac{5}{(1.03935)^1} + \frac{5}{(1.03935)^2} + \frac{105}{(1.03935)^3} =$$

$$4.811 + 4.629 + 93.520 = 102.960.$$

Notice that the present values of the individual cash flows discounted using spot rates differ from those discounted using the yield-to-maturity. The present value of the first coupon payment is 4.902 when discounted at 2%, but it is 4.811 when discounted at 3.935%. The present value of the final cash flow, which includes the redemption of principal, is 93.345 at 4% and 93.520 at 3.935%. Nevertheless, the sum of the present values using either approach is 102.960.

Equation 1 is a general formula for calculating a bond price given the sequence of spot rates. Note that for pricing a bond with a different risk profile than the spot curve (such as credit risk, as for corporate bonds, for example), a spread would have to be added to the spot rates.

$$PV = \frac{PMT}{(1+Z_1)^1} + \frac{PMT}{(1+Z_2)^2} + \cdots + \frac{PMT+FV}{(1+Z_N)^N}, \quad (1)$$

where

Z_1 is the spot rate, or zero-coupon yield or zero rate, for period 1

Z_2 is the spot rate, or zero-coupon yield or zero rate, for period 2

Z_N is the spot rate, or zero-coupon yield or zero rate, for period N

We'll use spot rates on Canadian and Australian government bonds to demonstrate bond pricing with spot rates.

Exhibit 3: Government Bond Spot Rates: Canada and Australia

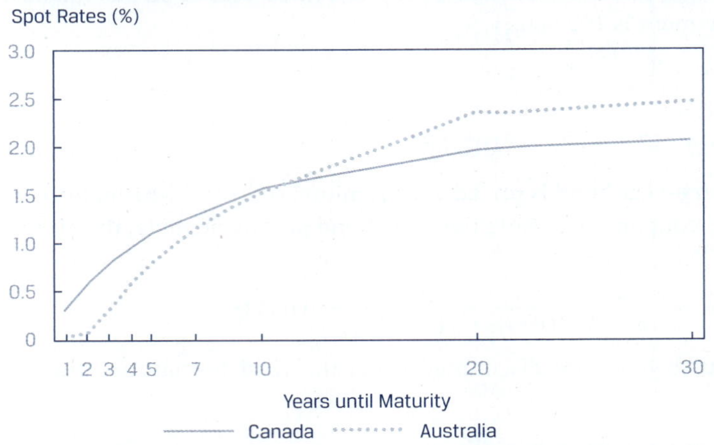

Maturity (Years)	1	2	3	4	5	7	10	20	30
Canada	0.31%	0.57%	0.80%	0.96%	1.11%	1.30%	1.58%	1.98%	2.06%
Australia	0.03%	0.07%	0.30%	0.59%	0.81%	1.17%	1.52%	2.35%	2.47%

EXAMPLE 1

Bond Prices and Yields-to-Maturity Based on Spot Rates

1. Calculate the price (per 100 par value) of a five-year Canadian government bond with a 1.00% coupon given the spot rates shown in Exhibit 3.

Solution:

99.50. To calculate the price of the bond, we use Equation 1 and the spot rates provided for each cash flow.

$$PV = \frac{PMT}{(1+Z_1)^1} + \frac{PMT}{(1+Z_2)^2} + \dots + \frac{PMT+FV}{(1+Z_N)^N}.$$

$$PV = \frac{1}{(1+0.0031)^1} + \frac{1}{(1+0.0057)^2} + \frac{1}{(1+0.0080)^3} + \frac{1}{(1+0.0096)^4} + \frac{101}{(1+0.0111)^5}.$$

$PV = 99.50.$

2. Calculate the price (per 100 par value) of a five-year Australian government bond with a 0.80% coupon given the spot rates shown in Exhibit 3.

Solution:

99.99. To calculate the price of the bond, we use Equation 1 and the spot rates provided for each cash flow.

$$PV = \frac{PMT}{(1+Z_1)^1} + \frac{PMT}{(1+Z_2)^2} + \dots + \frac{PMT+FV}{(1+Z_N)^N}.$$

$$PV = \frac{0.80}{(1+0.0003)^1} + \frac{0.80}{(1+0.0007)^2} + \frac{0.80}{(1+0.0030)^3} + \frac{0.80}{(1+0.0059)^4} + \frac{100.80}{(1+0.0081)^5}.$$

$PV = 99.99$

3. Calculate the YTM of the five-year Canadian government bond, using the price obtained in Question 1.

Solution:

1.104%. Instead of solving for the price, we use Equation 1 to solve for the YTM, the IRR that equates the price computed in Question 1 with the present value of future cash flows. In Microsoft Excel or Google Sheets, the RATE or IRR function can be used to solve for *r*.

$$PV = \frac{PMT}{(1+r)^1} + \frac{PMT}{(1+r)^2} + \cdots + \frac{PMT + FV}{(1+r)^N}$$

$$=$$

$$99.50 = \frac{1}{(1+r)^1} + \frac{1}{(1+r)^2} + \frac{1}{(1+r)^3} + \frac{1}{(1+r)^4} + \frac{101}{(1+r)^5}$$

$r = 0.011036 = 1.104\%$

Notice that the yield of the coupon bond is slightly below the five-year spot rate.

QUESTION SET

1. True or false: In practice, a spot curve is created by calculating the yields-to-maturity on recently issued coupon-paying government bonds of varying maturities.

   A. True

   B. False

Solution:

True. While zero-coupon government risk-free bonds would be preferable, in practice, the spot curve is created using yields on recently issued coupon-paying government bonds and linear interpolation. These bonds best satisfy the conditions for term structure analysis.

2. Determine the missing word in the following sentence: Because there are usually limited data to calculate yields for the full range of maturities, it is usually necessary to __________ between observed yields to complete curve data.

Solution:

Because there are usually limited data to calculate yields for the full range of maturities, it is usually necessary to <u>interpolate</u> between observed yields to complete curve data.

3. Calculate the price and yield-to-maturity of a 2.5% coupon, five-year bond given the following spot rates. Assume annual compounding.

1-year	3.000%
2-year	2.800%
3-year	2.600%

4-year	2.400%
5-year	2.200%

Solution:

The price is 101.314.

$$PV = \frac{PMT}{(1+Z_1)^1} + \frac{PMT}{(1+Z_2)^2} + \cdots + \frac{PMT+FV}{(1+Z_N)^N}.$$

$$PV = \frac{2.50}{(1+0.03)^1} + \frac{2.50}{(1+0.028)^2} + \frac{2.50}{(1+0.026)^3} + \frac{2.50}{(1+0.024)^4} + \frac{102.50}{(1+0.022)^5}.$$

$PV = 101.34$

The YTM is 2.22%.

$$PV = \frac{PMT}{(1+r)^1} + \frac{PMT}{(1+r)^2} + \cdots + \frac{PMT+FV}{(1+r)^N}$$

$$101.34 = \frac{2.50}{(1+r)^1} + \frac{2.50}{(1+r)^2} + \frac{2.50}{(1+r)^3} + \frac{2.50}{(1+r)^4} + \frac{102.50}{(1+r)^5}$$

$r = 0.022195 = 2.22\%$

4. Suppose we observed the following term structure for Canadian government bonds. Calculate the price of a 0.50% coupon, three-year Canadian government bond.

Maturity	Yield-to-maturity
1-Year	1.1000%
2-Year	0.9500%
3-Year	0.7951%
4-Year	0.5700%
5-Year	0.3100%

Solution:

The price is 99.126.

$$PV = \frac{PMT}{(1+Z_1)^1} + \frac{PMT}{(1+Z_2)^2} + \cdots + \frac{PMT+FV}{(1+Z_N)^N}.$$

$$PV = \frac{0.50}{(1+0.011)^1} + \frac{0.50}{(1+0.095)^2} + \frac{100.50}{(1+0.007951)^3}$$

$PV = 99.126$

5. Example 1 includes a question for a 0.50% coupon, three-year Canadian government bond, in which the bond's price is the same as the 99.126 price in Question 4 above. Contrast the Canadian spot curves in Example 1 and Question 4 and explain why these two different yield curves produced the same pricing result.

Solution:

Example 1 has an upward-sloping term structure, while in Question 4, the term structure is downward sloping. An important similarity is that, despite the vast difference in starting points (i.e., the one-year spot rates) between the two examples, the three-year spot rates are similar. In Example 1, the three-year rate is 0.7977%, and the three-year rate in Question 4 is 0.7951%. As a result of the similarity of the spot rates in the upward- and downward-sloping term structure examples, it is possible to exhibit the same price (and YTM) in upward- and downward-sloping term structure environments.

PAR AND FORWARD RATES

3

☐ define par and forward rates, and calculate par rates, forward rates from spot rates, spot rates from forward rates, and the price of a bond using forward rates

Par Rates from Spot Rates

An important use of spot rates is determining par rates. A **par rate** is a yield-to-maturity that makes the present value of a bond's cash flows equal to par (100% of face value). Par rates derived for *hypothetical* government bonds with different times-to-maturity are commonly used for term structure analysis because they control for tax, trading, and other potential distortions associated with actual bonds priced at either a discount or premium. The widely cited US Treasury yield curve published each day by the US Department of the Treasury, for example, is composed of par rates. The most recently issued or on-the-run government securities introduced in an earlier lesson, however, are *actual* bonds whose yields-to-maturity are close to but not equal to par rates.

On a coupon payment date, the following equation can be used to calculate a par rate by solving for *PMT* given a sequence of spot rates $Z_1, Z_2, \ldots, Z_n$. Between coupon dates, we set the flat price, rather than the full price, equal to 100.

$$100 = \frac{PMT}{(1+z_1)^1} + \frac{PMT}{(1+z_2)^2} + \cdots + \frac{PMT+100}{(1+z_N)^N}. \tag{2}$$

This equation is very similar to Equation 1, except $PV = FV = 100$. Recall that for a bond to trade at par, its coupon rate and yield-to-maturity must be equal. So, by solving for *PMT*, we also solve for the yield-to-maturity for the bond to trade at par. This single rate, divided by 100, is the par rate *per period.*

An example illustrates the calculation of par rates given spot rates. Suppose the current one-, two-, three-, and four- year spot rates on government bonds are 5.263%, 5.616%, 6.359%, and 7.008%, respectively. These are effective annual rates.

The one-year par rate is 5.263%:

$$100 = \frac{PMT+100}{(1.05263)^1};\ PMT = 5.263.$$

The two-year par rate is 5.606%.

$$100 = \frac{PMT}{(1.05263)^1} + \frac{PMT+100}{(1.05616)^2};\ PMT = 5.606.$$

The three-year and four-year par rates are 6.306% and 6.899%, respectively.

$$100 = \frac{PMT}{(1.05263)^1} + \frac{PMT}{(1.05616)^2} + \frac{PMT+100}{(1.06359)^3};\ PMT = 6.306.$$

$$100 = \frac{PMT}{(1.05263)^1} + \frac{PMT}{(1.05616)^2} + \frac{PMT}{(1.06359)^3} + \frac{PMT+100}{(1.07008)^4};\ PMT = 6.899.$$

We can confirm that these are the par rates through the pricing formula. Using these par rates as the coupon and yield-to-maturity, the price of the two-year bond is 100:

$$5.606/(1.05606)^1 + 105.606/(1.05606)^2 = 100.$$

Likewise, the price of the four-year bond is also 100:

$$6.899/(1.06899)^1 + 6.899/(1.06899)^2 + 6.899/(1.06899)^3 + 106.899/(1.06899)^4 = 100.$$

EXAMPLE 2

Bond Prices and Yields-to-Maturity Based on Par Rates

1. The par rate for a bond may be calculated from the set of spot rates reflecting maturities up to and including the maturity of the desired par rate. Using the spot rate data shown in Exhibit 1, calculate the par rate for a three-year Canadian government bond. In this example (and subsequent examples), annual payments and compounding are assumed.

   Solution:

   Use Equation 2 to solve for *PMT*, as follows:

   $$100 = \frac{PMT}{(1+z_1)^1} + \frac{PMT}{(1+z_2)^2} + \cdots + \frac{PMT + 100}{(1+z_N)^N}.$$

   $$100 = \frac{PMT}{(1+0.003117)^1} + \frac{PMT}{(1+0.00568)^2} + \frac{PMT + 100}{(1+0.007977)^3}.$$

   We can factor out *PMT* and then solve for it:

   $$100 = PMT \times \left(\frac{1}{(1+0.003117)^1} + \frac{1}{(1+0.00568)^2} + \frac{1}{(1+0.007977)^3}\right) + \frac{100}{(1+0.007977)^3}.$$

   $$PMT = 0.7952.$$

   To convert the coupon payment to a par rate per period, we divide by 100 (i.e., 0.7952/100). Thus, the par rate equals 0.7952%.

Forward Rates from Spot Rates

Spot rates can also be used to calculate **implied forward rates** (also known as forward yields), which are breakeven reinvestment rates. They link the return on an investment in a shorter-term zero-coupon bond to the return on an investment in a longer-term zero-coupon bond.

Suppose that the yields-to-maturity on three-year and four-year zero-coupon bonds are 3.65% and 4.18%, respectively. An analyst would like to know how much extra return is implied by these rates for investing for four rather than three years (i.e., an incremental year). This would be the implied one-year forward yield three years into the future, depicted in Exhibit 4.

Exhibit 4: The One-Year Implied Rate, Three Years from Today

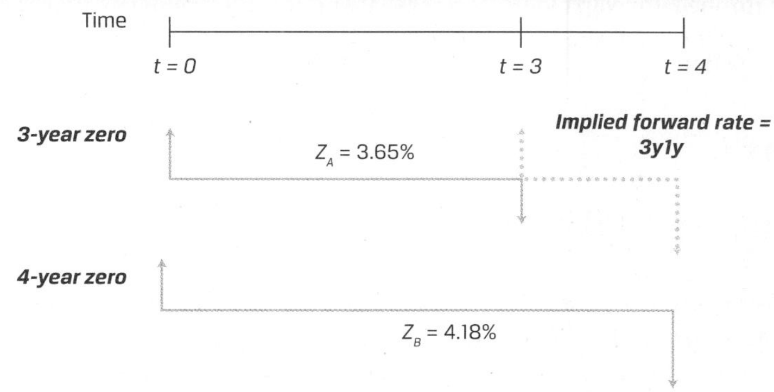

The most common market practice is to name this forward rate the "3y1y," pronounced "three-year into one-year rate," or simply "3's, 1's." The first number refers to the length of the forward period in years from today, and the second number refers to the **tenor** of the underlying bond, or its remaining time-to-maturity. In the money market, the forward rate is usually expressed in months.

If the investor's view on future bond yields is that the one-year yield in three years' time is likely to be lower than the 3y1y, it might be better to simply invest in the four-year zero-coupon bond. However, if the investor's view is that the one-year yield will be more than the implied forward rate, the investor might prefer the three-year bond and then reinvest at the expected higher rate for an additional one year. That explains why an implied forward rate is the *breakeven reinvestment rate.*

Equation 3 is a general formula for the implied forward rate, $IFR_{A,B-A}$, for a security begins at $t = A$ and matures at $t = B$ (tenor B – A). To solve for it, we need the spot rate, z_A, and the longer-term spot rate, z_B. This is illustrated in Exhibit 5.

$$(1 + Z_A)^A \times (1 + IFR_{A,B-A})^{B-A} = (1 + Z_B)^B. \quad (3)$$

Exhibit 5: Implied Forward Rates

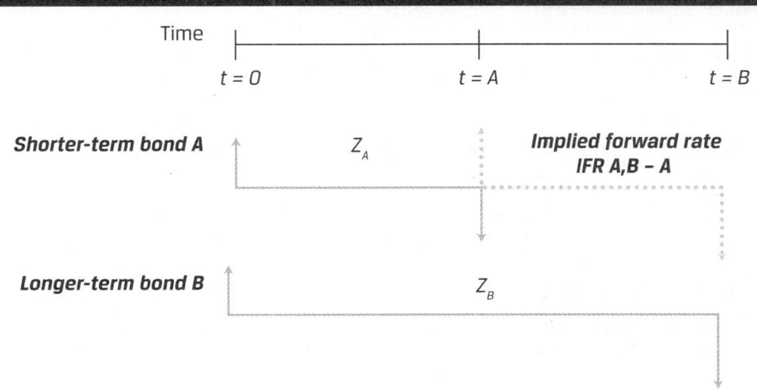

Using Equation 3, let's solve for the 3y1y since we know that the yields-to-maturity on three-year and four-year zero-coupon bonds are 3.65% and 4.18%, respectively:

$$(1 + Z_A)^A \times (1 + IFR_{A,B-A})^{B-A} = (1 + Z_B)^B.$$

$$(1 + 0.0365)^3 \times (1 + IFR_{3,1})^1 = (1 + 0.0418)^4.$$

$IFR_{3,1} = 0.057863 = 5.79\%$

The "3y1y" implied forward yield is 5.79%. If the investor believes that the one-year yield will be higher than that in three years, she should invest in the three-year bond rather than the four-year bond (and vice versa).

EXAMPLE 3

Deriving Forward Rates from Spot Rates

1. Let's return to the spot rates shown in Exhibit 1. In the following example, we will assume annual compounding (i.e., periodicity of 1). Calculate the 2y1y implied forward rate on Canadian government bonds.

   Solution:

   To calculate the 2y1y implied forward rate, we recognize that we are estimating the one-year rate at a point two years from Time 0. Therefore, $A = 2$, $B = 3$, Z_A is the two-year spot rate, and Z_B is the three-year spot rate:

   $$(1 + Z_A)^A \times (1 + IFR_{A,B-A})^{B-A} = (1 + Z_B)^B.$$

   $$(1 + 0.0188) \times (1 + 0.0277) = (1 + Z2)^2.$$

   $$\text{IFR}_{2,1} = 0.0126.$$

   Thus, the implied forward rate for a one-year bond two years from now is 1.26%.

Spot Rates from Forward Rates and Bond Pricing with Forward Rates

While forward rates can be calculated from spot rates, spot rates can also be calculated from forward rates, and either can be used for pricing because they are interconnected. An example will illustrate this process.

Suppose the current sequence of one-year rates today and the one-year rate one, two, and three years from now are as follows:

Time Period	Forward Rate
0y1y	1.88%
1y1y	2.77%
2y1y	3.54%
3y1y	4.12%

These are annual rates stated for a periodicity of 1. They are effective annual rates. The first rate, the 0y1y, is the one-year spot rate. The others are one-year forward rates. Spot rates can be calculated using Equation 3. The two-year implied spot rate is 2.324%:

$$(1 + Z_A)^A \times (1 + IFR_{A,B-A})^{B-A} = (1 + Z_B)^B.$$

$$(1 + 0.0188)^2 \times (1 + 0.0277)^1 = (1 + Z_2)^3.$$

$$Z_2 = 0.023240 = 2.324\%$$

Notice how the product of the 0y1y and 1y1y is the two-year spot rate. This property holds in general, because the spot curve can be calculated by taking the geometric average of the forward rates. This is evident if we solve for the implied three- and four-year spot rates. Using Equation 3, we can use the implied two-year spot rate we just found to solve for the three-year spot rate:

$$(1 + Z_A)^A \times (1 + IFR_{A,B-A})^{B-A} = (1 + Z_B)^B.$$

$$(1 + 0.023240)^2 \times (1 + 0.0277)^1 = (1 + Z_3)^3.$$

$$Z_3 = 0.027278 = 2.73\%$$

Or since the two-year spot rate is the product of the 0y1y and 1y1y rates, we can simply multiply across the forward curve for three- and four-year spot rates:

$$(1.0188 \times 1.0277 \times 1.0354) = (1+ Z_3)^3;\ Z_3 = 0.27278$$

$$(1.0188 \times 1.0277 \times 1.0354 \times 1.0412) = (1 + Z_4)^4;\ Z_4 = 0.030741$$

Suppose that an analyst needs to value a four-year 3.75% annual coupon payment bond that has the same risks as the bonds used to obtain the forward curve. Using the implied spot rates, the value of the bond is 102.637 per 100 of par value.

$$\frac{3.75}{(1.0188)^1} + \frac{3.75}{(1.023240)^2} + \frac{3.75}{(1.027278)^3} + \frac{103.75}{(1.030741)^4} = 102.637.$$

The bond also can be valued using the forward rates as follows:

$$\frac{3.75}{(1.0188)} + \frac{3.75}{(1.0188 \times 1.0277)} + \frac{3.75}{(1.0188 \times 1.0277 \times 1.0354)}$$
$$+ \frac{103.75}{(1.0188 \times 1.0277 \times 1.0354 \times 1.0412)} = 102.637.$$

EXAMPLE 4

Deriving Spot Rates from Forward Rates and Pricing Bonds Using Forward Rates

Suppose we have the following forward rates for Canadian government bonds:

Forward tenor	Rates
0y1y	0.3117%
1y1y	0.8250%
2y1y	1.2587%
1y2y	1.0416%

1. Calculate a three-year spot rate on Canadian government bonds using the forward rate information.

   Solution:

   The three-year spot rate is calculated using three of the one-year forward rates above: the 0y1y, 1y1y, and 2y1y.

   $$(1.003117 \times 1.008250 \times 1.012587) = (1 + z_3)^3.$$

   $$z_3 = 0.7977\%.$$

2. Calculate the value of a three-year Canadian government bond paying a 0.50% coupon using forward rates.

   Solution:

$$PV = \frac{0.5}{1.003117} + \frac{0.5}{(1.003117 \times 1.008250)} + \frac{100.50}{(1.003117 \times 1.008250 \times 1.0012587)}$$

   PV = 99.126

   This example corresponds to Question 4 in the earlier Lesson Question Set. A review of the solution to that problem indicates that we have shown that the value of the three-year 0.50% coupon Canadian government bond is equal to 99.126 regardless of whether we use spot rates or forward rates.

QUESTION SET

1. Contrast a par rate and a yield-to-maturity.

   Solution:

   A par rate is the YTM and coupon rate assuming a bond is priced at par value and cash flows are discounted using spot rates, while the yield-to-maturity is the internal rate of return on a bond's cash flows using a bond's current price.

2. Calculate a three-year par rate given the following spot rates. Assume annual compounding:

1-year	3.0000%
2-year	2.8000%
3-year	2.6000%

   Solution:

   2.607%.

$$100 = \frac{PMT}{(1 + z_1)^1} + \frac{PMT}{(1 + z_2)^2} + \ldots + \frac{PMT + 100}{(1 + z_N)^N}$$

$$100 = \frac{PMT}{(1 + 0.03)^1} + \frac{PMT}{(1 + 0.028)^2} + \frac{PMT}{(1 + 0.026)^3} + \frac{PMT + 100}{(1 + 0.026)^3}$$

$$100 = PMT \times \left(\frac{1}{(1 + 0.03)^1} + \frac{1}{(1 + 0.028)^2} + \frac{1}{(1 + 0.026)^3}\right) + \frac{100}{(1 + 0.026)^3}$$

   $PMT = 2.607\%$

3. Match the implied forward rate to the spot rates necessary to calculate it.

1. 1y2y	A. Three-year and two-year spot rates
2. 3y2y	B. Three-year and one-year spot rates
3. 2y1y	C. Five-year and three-year spot rates

   Solution:

   1. B. The 1y2y is a two-year forward rate in one year. Thus, we start with the three-year spot rate and use the one-year spot rate to find an implied two-year forward rate.

2. C. The 3y2y is a two-year forward rate in three years. Thus, we start with the five-year spot rate and use the three-year spot rate to find an implied two-year forward rate.

3. A. The 2y1y is a one-year forward rate in two years. Thus, we start with the three-year spot rate and use the two-year spot rate to find an implied one-year forward rate.

4. Determine the missing words in the following sentence: An implied forward rate represents a ____________ reinvestment rate such that no arbitrage opportunities exist between spot and forward rates.

Solution:

An implied forward rate represents a breakeven reinvestment rate such that no arbitrage opportunities exist between spot and forward rates.

5. Calculate the implied forward rate 2y3y given the following spot rates. Assume annual compounding.

Tenor	Spot Rate
1-year	2.0%
2-year	2.3%
3-year	2.5%
4-year	2.6%
5-year	2.4%

Solution:

2.467%.

$$(1 + Z_A)^A \times (1 + IFR_{A,B-A})^{B-A} = (1 + Z_B)^B$$

$$(1 + 0.023)^2 \times (1 + IFR_{2,3})^3 = (1 + 0.024)^5$$

$$Z_3 = 2.467\%$$

6. Calculate the price of a 2% coupon bond with 100 par value maturing in three years given the following forward rates, and demonstrate that this price is equivalent regardless of whether spot rates or forward rates are used as discount rates. Assume annual compounding and the following forward rates.

Tenor	Forward Rate
0y1y	1.5%
1y1y	2.5%
2y1y	3.5%

Solution:

The price is 98.619.

Forward rate approach:

$$PV = \frac{2}{(1.015)} + \frac{2}{(1.015 \times 1.025)} + \frac{102}{(1.015 \times 1.025 \times 1.035)}.$$

$PV = 98.6190.$

The implied one-, two-, and three-year spot rates are as follows:

One-year = 1.5%.

Two-year = $(1.015 \times 1.025)^{(1/2)} - 1 = 1.999\%$.

Three-year = $(1.015 \times 1.025 \times 1.035)^{(1/3)} - 1 = 2.4967\%$.

Using the spot prices to price the bond gives the following:

$$PV = \frac{2}{(1.015)^1} + \frac{2}{(1.01999)^2} + \frac{102}{(1.024967)^3}.$$

$PV = 98.6190.$

7. Demonstrate how an investor with a five-year investment horizon would optimally decide between the two following strategies:

- Buy a three-year government bond at the 3% spot rate, and then reinvest for two years at the expected future two-year rate.
- Buy a five-year government bond at the 4% spot rate.

Solution:

Calculate the implied two-year forward rate in three years:

$$(1 + Z_A)^A \times (1 + IFR_{A,B-A})^{B-A} = (1 + Z_B)^B.$$

$$(1 + 0.03)^3 \times (1 + \mathrm{IFR}_{3,2})^2 = (1 + 0.04)^5.$$

$IFR_{3,2} = 5.52\%$

If the investor believes that the two-year rate in three years will be greater than 5.52%, then the better strategy is to buy the three-year government bond and reinvest at a higher rate. If the investor believes that the two-year rate in three years will be less than 5.52%, then the five-year bond should be purchased. The implied forward rate represents the breakeven reinvestment rate.

4 SPOT, PAR, AND FORWARD YIELD CURVES AND INTERPRETING THEIR RELATIONSHIP

☐ compare the spot curve, par curve, and forward curve

Because spot, par, and forward rates are interconnected, so are the shapes of the spot, par, and forward curves. This analysis is best illustrated through an example. In an earlier lesson, we used spot rates to compute par rates and forward rates for Canadian and Australian government bonds. We can use these rates to build yield curves across a range of maturities, shown in Exhibit 1.

Spot, Par, and Forward Curves (Canada and Australia)

A. Spot, Par, and Forward Curves: Canadian Government Bonds

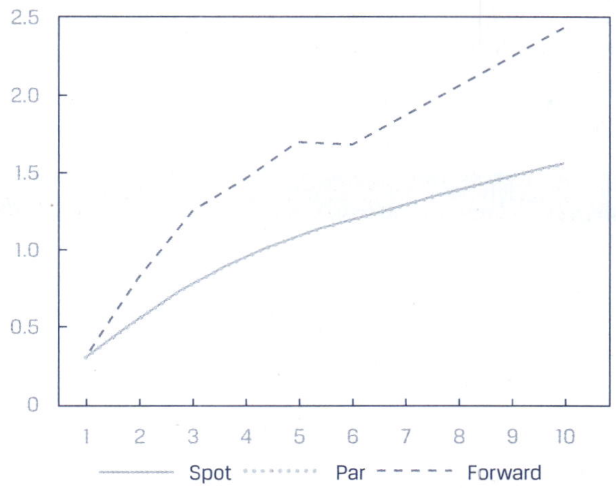

B. Spot, Par, and Forward Curves: Australian Government Bonds

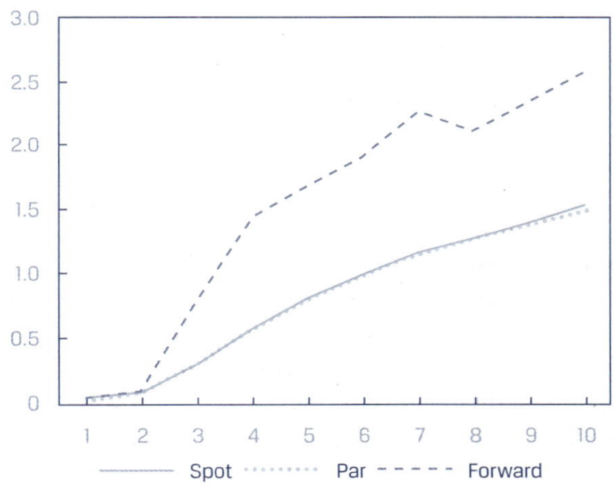

We can make the following general observations:

1. The spot rates are positive, and the spot curve is upward sloping.
2. The spot and par curves are nearly identical; the par rates are slightly lower than the spot rates, and the (slight) difference between the spot and par curves is greater at longer maturities.
3. Forward rates are greater than the spot and par rates.

These observations stem from general relationships between the shapes of the curves. If the spot curve is upward sloping, par rates will be near—but below—spot rates, particularly at the long end of the curve. This is because the low short-term spot rates result in higher bond prices, particularly for longer-term bonds, which results in low par rates when we do the calculation that assumes the price is 100% of par. Forward rates being above spot rates, if the spot curve is upward sloping, follows from the prior lesson, which established forward rates as incremental rates of return.

Exhibit 6 shows the spot, par, and forward curves if the spot curve is flat, assumed to be 2.50% for all maturities. When the spot rate is constant across all maturities, the par and forward rates will equate to the spot rate across all maturities as well. In short, a flat spot rate curve reflects no expectations of changes in future interest rates; thus forward rates equal spot rates. In this particular example, government bonds would pay a 2.5% coupon rate, and the bonds would be priced at par value (thus, the par rate is also 2.5%).

Exhibit 6: Flat Term Structure

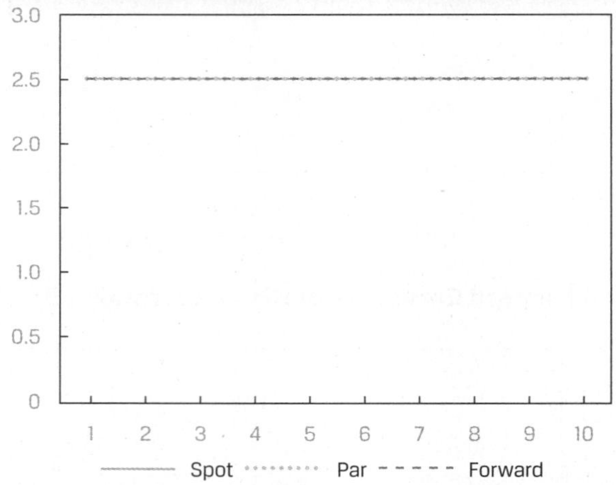

Exhibit 7 shows the spot, par, and forward curves for a downward-sloping (inverted) spot curve or falling spot rates as maturities lengthen. Starting from a 4% 1-year spot rate, rates fall to 1.90% for a maturity of 10 years. As in the previous examples, the par rates are similar to the spot rates. The inverted term structure of spot rates reflects expectations of significantly lower one-year rates in future years, and this is shown by the forward curve. In this example, the spot rate term structure implies a one-year rate of 0.1175% expected in nine years.

Exhibit 7: Inverted Term Structure

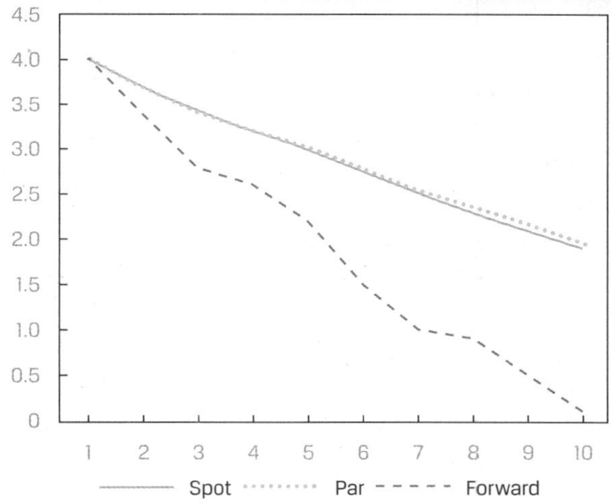

We conclude with Exhibit 8, which summarizes the general relationship between the spot, par, and forward curves for different spot curve shapes.

Exhibit 8: Spot, Par, and Forward Curve Relationship

Spot Curve Shape	Par Curve	Forward Curve
Upward Sloping	Below spot curve	Above spot curve
Flat	Equal to spot curve	Equal to spot curve
Downward Sloping (Inverted)	Above spot curve	Below spot curve

QUESTION SET

1. The chart below shows a spot curve and its implied forward curve. Identify the forward curve, and justify your choice.

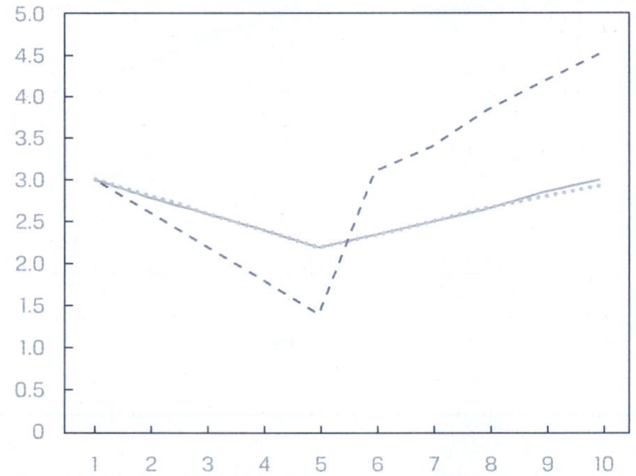

Solution:

The forward curve is represented by the line that moves from 3.0% to approximately 1.5% in Year 5 and then slopes dramatically higher from Year 5 to 6, ending at about 4.5% in Year 10.

When the spot curve is sloping downward (Years 1–5), forward rates will be below spot rates. When the spot curve is sloping upward (Years 6–10), forward rates will be above spot rates.

For Questions 2 and 3, refer to the spot rate data shown in Exhibit 9. It is important to note that some bonds will trade at negative yield. This was prevalent among developed market sovereign bonds in the wake of the financial crisis as central banks pursued accommodative monetary policy in response to below-target inflation. Negative rates do not change the fundamental mathematics used in bond pricing.

Exhibit 9: Negative Spot Rates (Germany and Switzerland)

Maturity	Germany	Switzerland
1-year	−0.6965%	−0.7882%
2-year	−0.7034%	−0.7133%
3-year	−0.7021%	−0.6435%
4-year	−0.6418%	−0.5615%
5-year	−0.5578%	−0.4757%
6-year	−0.4796%	−0.4080%
7-year	−0.4014%	−0.3402%
8-year	−0.3269%	−0.2673%
9-year	−0.2524%	−0.1945%
10-year	−0.1779%	−0.1216%

2. Calculate the implied one-year forward rate in nine years in Switzerland.

Solution:

The question is requesting the 9y1y forward rate. This is calculated from the 10-year and 9-year spot rates, as follows:

$$(1 + Z_A)^A \times (1 + IFR_{A,B-A})^{B-A} = (1 + Z_B)^B$$

$$(1 + -0.001945)^9 \times (1 + IFR_{9,1})^1 = (1 + -0.001216)^{10}$$

$$IFR_{9,1} = 0.537\%$$

Thus, the implied one-year forward rate in nine years for Swiss government bonds is 0.537%.

3. Explain why a country with negative spot rates, such as Switzerland, may have positive forward rates.

Solution:

As shown in earlier examples, an upward-sloping spot curve (which Switzerland has) will be characterized by forward rates that are greater than spot rates. As the negative rates become less negative and move closer to zero, the more likely that forward rates will be positive with an upward-sloping spot curve.

4. The following chart shows spot and forward curves for German sovereign bonds. Explain why the forward curve is close to identical to the spot curve for two and three-year maturities.

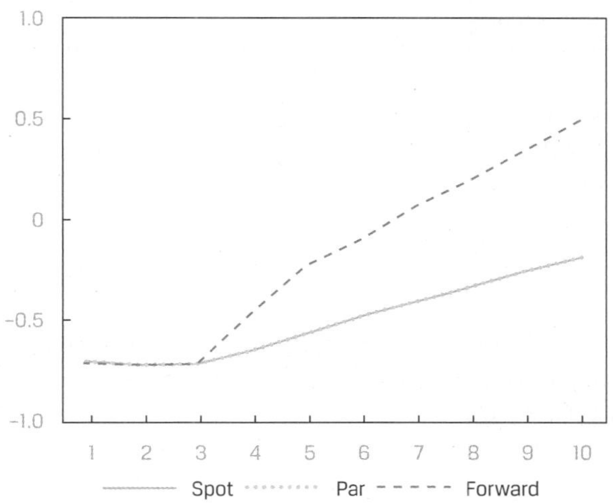

Solution:

In flat term structure environments, forward rates equal spot rates. The spot rates in Germany for two and three-year maturities appear to be approximately equivalent to the one-year spot rate. Thus, Germany's term structure is flat for the first three years, and forward rates should be approximately equal to spot rates.

PRACTICE PROBLEMS

The following information relates to questions 1-9

Use the spot rates provided to answer the following questions.

Government Bond Spot Rates

Maturity	Canada	Australia	Germany	Switzerland
1-year	0.3117%	0.0272%	−0.6965%	−0.7882%
2-year	0.5680%	0.0675%	−0.7034%	−0.7133%
3-year	0.7977%	0.3003%	−0.7021%	−0.6435%
4-year	0.9640%	0.5853%	−0.6418%	−0.5615%
5-year	1.1105%	0.8052%	−0.5578%	−0.4757%
6-year	1.2052%	0.9877%	−0.4796%	−0.4080%
7-year	1.2998%	1.1702%	−0.4014%	−0.3402%
8-year	1.3935%	1.2878%	−0.3269%	−0.2673%
9-year	1.4872%	1.4054%	−0.2524%	−0.1945%
10-year	1.5809%	1.5230%	−0.1779%	−0.1216%

1. Which level of coupon would the Swiss government choose if its goal is to minimize the premium over par value for a five-year debt issue?

   A. 1.0%

   B. 0.5%

   C. 0.0%

2. The Australian government is considering issuing three-year bonds with a 3.0% coupon with annual payments. Given the spot rates in Australia, the price is *closest* to:

   A. 108.05.

   B. 108.07.

   C. 108.69.

3. Suppose the one-year and two-year spot rates in Canada move upward by 20 bps but the three-year Canadian spot rate remains unchanged. Which of the following best reflects the updated three-year Canadian par rate?

   A. Increases by approximately 13 bps

   B. Increases by approximately 7 bps

   C. Increases by approximately 0.16 bps

4. Match the spot rates needed to calculate the corresponding implied forward rates.

1. Two-year and five-year spot rates	A. Two-year implied forward rate in five years
2. Two-year and seven-year spot rates	B. Three-year implied forward rate in two years
3. Five-year and seven-year spot rates	C. Five-year implied forward rate in two years

5. Which of the following choices is the closest to the implied five-year forward rate in two years for Swiss government bonds?

   A. −0.191%

   B. −0.001%

   C. −0.317%

6. Match the sequence of forward rates and the corresponding spot rate that the forward rates will calculate.

Forward rates	**Spot rate calculation**
1. 0y1y x 1y1y x 2y1y	A. Four-year spot rate
2. 0y1y x 1y2y x 3y3y	B. Three-year spot rate
3. 0y1y x 1y1y x 2y1y x 3y1y	C. Six-year spot rate

7. Which of the following statements about yield curves is true?

   A. Spot curves are derived from par rates.

   B. Par curves are derived from forward rates.

   C. Forward curves are derived from spot rates.

8. Match the following statements about forward rate curves with corresponding statements about spot rate curves.

1. The forward rate curve lies above the spot rate curve.	A. The spot rate curve is downward sloping (i.e., inverted).
2. The forward rate curve lies below the spot rate curve.	B. The spot rate curve is upward sloping (i.e., normal).
3. The forward rate curve is equivalent to the spot rate curve.	C. The spot rate curve is flat across all maturities.

9. Match the following statements about par rate curves with corresponding state-

ments about spot rate curves.

1. The par rate curve lies above the spot rate curve.	A. The spot rate curve is upward sloping (i.e., normal), and spot rates are negative.
2. The par rate curve lies below the spot rate curve.	B. The spot rate curve is upward sloping (i.e., normal), and spot rates are positive.
3. The par rate curve is equivalent to the spot rate curve.	C. The spot rate curve is flat across all maturities.

SOLUTIONS

1. C is correct. Given that Switzerland's current five-year spot (and par) rate is negative, any non-negative coupon will cause the Swiss government to issue debt at a premium to par. Issuance of debt without a coupon will minimize the size of the premium.

2. B is correct.

$$PV = \frac{PMT}{(1+Z_1)^1} + \frac{PMT}{(1+Z_2)^2} + \cdots + \frac{PMT + FV}{(1+Z_N)^N}.$$

$$PV = \frac{3}{(1+0.000272)^1} + \frac{3}{(1+0.000675)^2} + \frac{103}{(1+0.003003)^3}.$$

$PV = 108.07.$

3. C is correct. In Example 2, we calculated the three-year Canadian par rate. The par rate of 0.7952% approximates the spot rate of 0.7977%, so the most important change affecting the three-year par rate is the change in the three-year spot rate. Because it does not change, the only change will be a slight move in the par rate toward the spot rate (to approximately 0.7968%).

4. 1. B. By using two-year and five-year rates, the difference represents the tenor of the implied forward rate of three years, and the shorter tenor rate reflects the beginning of the forward in two years.

   2. C. By using two-year and seven-year rates, the difference represents the tenor of the implied forward rate of five years, and the shorter tenor rate reflects the beginning of the forward in two years.

   3. A. By using five-year and seven-year rates, the difference represents the tenor of the implied forward rate of two years, and the shorter tenor rate reflects the beginning of the forward in five years.

5. The correct answer is A. The implied five-year forward rate in two years is the 2y5y rate. To calculate, we use the seven-year Swiss government rate and the two-year Swiss government rate, as follows:

   2y5y IFR $= [(1 - 0.003402)^7/(1 - 0.007133)^2]^{(1/5)} - 1 = 0.191\%$.

   Choice B represents the 5y2y implied forward rate, and Choice C represents the 2y3y implied forward rate.

6. 1. B. This is a series of three one-year forwards, thus providing the information for a three-year spot rate.

   2. C. This sequence is a one-year spot rate, followed by a two-year forward rate in one year, followed by a three-year forward rate in three years.

   3. A. This sequence is a series of four one-year forwards.

7. The correct answer is C. The forward rates used to construct forward curves are derived from spot rates. Statement A is not true, because par rates are derived from spot rates. Statement B is not true, because par curves are derived from spot rates.

8. 1. B. In a normal interest rate environment with an upward-sloping yield curve, forward interest rates will be greater than their corresponding spot rates across

all maturities.

2. A. In an inverted spot rate environment, forward interest rates will be below their corresponding spot rates.

3. C. A flat maturity structure of interest rates is sometimes assumed. In such an environment in which spot rates are constant, this implies that future expectations are for interest rates to remain at a constant level. Thus, forward rates equal spot rates in a flat term structure environment.

9. 1. A. This situation is illustrated in the German and Swiss government interest rate data in which spot rates are negative while the spot rate curve is upward sloping. In such instances, par rates lie above spot rates.

   2. B. This situation is illustrated in the Canadian and Australian government interest rate data in which spot rates are positive and the spot curve is normal.

   3. C. This is a hypothetical case but can be seen by creating a flat spot rate curve.

LEARNING MODULE

10

Interest Rate Risk and Return

LEARNING OUTCOMES

Mastery	The candidate should be able to:
☐	calculate and interpret the sources of return from investing in a fixed-rate bond;
☐	describe the relationships among a bond's holding period return, its Macaulay duration, and the investment horizon;
☐	define, calculate, and interpret Macaulay duration.

INTRODUCTION

1

Prior lessons on yield measures established that a fixed-income investor's rate of return will equal a bond's yield-to-maturity (YTM) under certain assumptions. In these lessons, we explore the sources of return for fixed-income investments and demonstrate investment returns in different scenarios, including the one embedded in the YTM calculations. Prior lessons also established interest rate risk. We show how investment horizon, in relation to a bond's features, is a key determinant of interest rate risk for investors and how different investors in the same fixed-income investment can have different returns and views on risk. Finally, we introduce Macaulay duration, a weighted-average measure of the time to receipt for a bond's cash flows, and demonstrate how holding a bond for its Macaulay duration balances reinvestment and price risks.

LEARNING MODULE OVERVIEW

- There are three sources of return for fixed-rate bond investors: (1) coupon and principal payments, (2) reinvestment of coupons, and (3) gain or loss on the sale of the bond if the bond is sold prior to maturity.
- The rate of return on a fixed-rate bond investment is found by using the holding period, the future value of coupons received, the sale price, and the purchase price to calculate a compounded, annualized rate of return.

- If all cash flows are received at scheduled dates, coupons are reinvested at the same rate as a bond's YTM, and the bond is held to maturity, an investor's annualized compounded rate of return will equal the bond's YTM. If any of those assumptions do not hold, the investor's rate of return will vary.
- Reinvestment risk and price risk are types of interest rate risk and have an inverse relationship. Reinvestment risk is the risk of decreasing reinvestment returns on cash flows, which occurs when interest rates fall. Price risk refers to declining prices and occurs when interest rates rise.
- The longer the investment horizon, the more important reinvestment risk is relative to price risk. If an investor's investment horizon equals the Macaulay duration of a bond, the risks equally offset each other.
- Macaulay duration is the weighted-average time to receipt of a bond's cash flows, where the weights of each cash flow in the calculation are each cash flow's share of the bond's full price (i.e., present value).
- When the investment horizon is greater than (less than, equal to) a bond's Macaulay duration, coupon reinvestment risk is higher than (lower than, equal to) the bond's price risk.

LEARNING MODULE SELF-ASSESSMENT

These initial questions are intended to help you gauge your current level of understanding of the learning module.

1. A source of risk for a buy-and-hold fixed-income investor, ignoring credit risk, is from:

   A. capital gain/loss on sale only.

   B. coupon reinvestment only.

   C. neither capital gain/loss on sale nor coupon reinvestment.

   Solution:

   B is correct. Changes in interest rates during the holding period of the bond will impact returns from reinvestment of coupons.

   A is incorrect because for a buy-and-hold investor, there is no risk of capital gain or loss since the investor is not selling the bond prior to maturity and will get the par value of the bond at the maturity date.

   C is incorrect because a buy-and-hold investor's returns are impacted by the rate earned on the reinvestment of coupons, or reinvestment risk.

2. A family office purchases a six-year, 5.8% annual coupon eurobond priced at par for settlement on 15 December 2031. The bond matures on 15 December 2037. Immediately after the purchase of the bond, interest rates rise to 6.5%. The family office sells the bond after three years. The family office's total annualized return on the investment was *closest* to:

   A. 5.28%.

   B. 5.80%.

C. 6.50%.

Solution:

A is correct. The total annualized return is composed of the (1) coupon payments, (2) reinvestment of coupons, and (3) gain/loss on the sale. This is equal to 5.28%, as shown below.

The future value of the coupons including reinvestment is

= –*FV*(0.065, 3, 5.8, 0, 0) = 18.556.

The sale price of the bond after three years is

= –*PV*(0.065, 3, 5.8, 100, 0) = 98.146.

The realized return, r, is

$$r = \left(\frac{FV}{PV}\right)^{\frac{1}{T}} - 1.$$

$$r = \left(\frac{18.556 + 98.146}{100}\right)^{\frac{1}{3}} - 1.$$

$r = 0.0528 = 5.28\%$

B is incorrect because it would be the return if interest rates remained at 5.8%.

C is incorrect because 6.5% is the interest rate at which the coupons will be reinvested, not the rate of return for the family office on the investment.

3. The risk to an investor who buys a bond at par value and intends to sell it before the receipt of the first coupon payment, ignoring credit risk, is *most likely* from:

   A. price risk.

   B. reinvestment risk.

   C. neither price risk nor reinvestment risk.

Solution:

A is correct. Changes in interest rates can affect the price of the bond and, therefore, the returns for the investor.

B is incorrect because if the investor intends to sell the bond before the receipt of the first coupon, then reinvestment risk is irrelevant because no coupons will be reinvested.

C is incorrect because the investor faces price risk.

4. Reinvestment risk and price risk of a bond offset one another if an investor's investment horizon is:

   A. equal to the bond's time-to-maturity.

   B. equal to the bond's Macaulay duration.

   C. less than the bond's Macaulay duration.

Solution:

B is correct. When the investment horizon is equal to the Macaulay duration, the gain (loss) from coupon reinvestment is offset by the loss (gain) in the price of the bond from changes in interest rates.

A is incorrect because if an investor holds a bond to maturity (ignoring credit risk), the investor faces no price risk but does face reinvestment risk. Therefore, reinvestment risk will dominate price risk.

C is incorrect because if the investment horizon is less than the Macaulay duration, price risk dominates reinvestment risk.

5. Hightest Capital purchases a 15-year, 6.8% annual coupon bond and has an investment horizon of 7.0 years. The Macaulay duration of the bond is 9.85 years. The duration gap at the time of purchase is *closest* to:

   A. 2.85.

   B. 5.15.

   C. 8.00.

Solution:

A is correct. The duration gap for a bond is the difference between its Macaulay duration and the investor's investment horizon: 9.85 – 7.0 = 2.85.

B is incorrect because it is the difference between the bond's maturity and its Macaulay duration (15 – 9.85 = 5.15).

C is incorrect because it is the difference between the bond's maturity and the investor's investment horizon (15 – 7 = 8.00).

6. Consider a bond that has two years remaining to maturity, a coupon of 4% paid semiannually, and a yield-to-maturity of 4.60%. Assuming it is 63 days into the first coupon period and a 30/360 basis, the bond's annualized Macaulay duration is *closest* to:

   A. 0.9419 years.

   B. 1.7666 years.

   C. 1.9416 years.

Solution:

B is correct.

Period	Time to Receipt	Cash Flow	*PV*	Weight	Time to Receipt × Weight
1.0000	0.6500	2.0000	1.9707	0.0198	0.0129
2.0000	1.6500	2.0000	1.9264	0.0193	0.0319
3.0000	2.6500	2.0000	1.8830	0.0189	0.0501
4.0000	3.6500	102.0000	93.8759	0.9420	3.4383
			99.6559	1.0000	3.5331
				Annualized MacDur	1.7666

The first cash flow's time-to-receipt is (180-63)/180 = 0.65 periods from now as it is 63 days into the period. Each subsequent cash flow is received one period later after the first, so time-to-receipt = 0.65 + 1, 0.65 + 2, and so on.

7. Consider a bond that has five years remaining to maturity, a coupon of 0% paid annually, and a yield-to-maturity of –0.38%. Assuming it is the issuance

date and a 30/360 basis, the bond's annualized Macaulay duration is *closest* to:

A. 3.5361 years.

B. 5.0000 years.

C. 6.3412 years.

Solution:

B is correct. No calculation is required, because the Macaulay duration of a zero-coupon bond is its time-to-maturity unless it is between coupon dates. To demonstrate, however, see the following table:

Period	Time to Receipt	Cash Flow	*PV*	Weight	Time to Receipt × Weight
1.0000	1.0000	0.0000	0.0000	0.0000	0.0000
2.0000	2.0000	0.0000	0.0000	0.0000	0.0000
3.0000	3.0000	0.0000	0.0000	0.0000	0.0000
4.0000	4.0000	0.0000	0.0000	0.0000	0.0000
5.0000	5.0000	100.0000	100.9554	1.0000	5.0000
			100.9554	1.0000	5.0000

SOURCES OF RETURN FROM INVESTING IN A FIXED-RATE BOND

2

☐ calculate and interpret the sources of return from investing in a fixed-rate bond;

Fixed-rate bond investors have three sources of return: (1) receipt of promised coupon and principal payments on the scheduled dates, (2) reinvestment of coupon payments, and (3) potential capital gains or losses on the sale of the bond prior to maturity. We now focus on how interest rate changes affect the reinvestment of coupon payments and a bond's market price if sold *prior to* maturity.

We start with two investors buying BRWA's new 10-year, 6.2% (annual) coupon eurobond, but each investor has a different time horizon for holding it. Initially, interest rates are unchanged. Then, we demonstrate the impact of higher interest rates on investors' total return. Finally, we show the effect of lower interest rates.

EXAMPLE 1

The first investor, Viswan Family Office (VFO), is a "buy-and-hold" investor, purchasing BRWA's new 10-year, 6.2% (annual) coupon eurobond priced at par (settlement: 15 October 2025; maturity: 15 October 2035) and holds it to maturity. If the coupon payments are reinvested at 6.2%, the yield-to-maturity, the future value of the coupons on the bond's maturity date, is found using Microsoft Excel's FV function:

= -*FV*(*Rate*, *Nper*, *Pmt*, *Pv*, *Type*),

where *Type* indicates payment at the end (0) or beginning (1) of the period. For this bond,

$$= -FV(0.062, 10, 6.2, 0, 0) = 82.493 \text{ per 100 of par value.}$$

While 62 (= 6.2 × 10) in total coupons is received, the excess amount, 20.493 (= 82.493 – 62), is the "interest-on-interest" gain from reinvesting and compounding. The investor's rate of return, expressed as a compound annual growth rate, is 6.20%.

$$r = \left(\frac{FV}{PV}\right)^{\frac{1}{T}} - 1.$$

$$r = \left(\frac{82.493 + 100}{100}\right)^{\frac{1}{10}} - 1.$$

$$r = 0.0620 = 6.20\%.$$

Example 1 demonstrates that yield-to-maturity at the time of purchase equals the investor's rate of return under three assumptions: (1) the investor holds the bond to maturity, (2) there is no default by the issuer, and (3) the coupon interest payments are reinvested at that same rate of interest.

Example 2 considers the second investor, Baywhite Financial (Baywhite), which also buys the 10-year, 6.2% annual coupon payment bond and pays the same price. However, Baywhite has a four-year investment horizon, so coupon interest is reinvested for four years, and the bond is sold immediately after receiving the fourth coupon payment.

EXAMPLE 2

Baywhite buys BRWA's 10-year, 6.2% eurobond but sells after four years. If the coupon payments are reinvested at 6.2% for four years, the future value of the reinvested coupons is 27.20321 per 100 of par value.

$$= -FV(0.062, 4, 6.2, 0, 0) = 27.203.$$

Interest-on-interest gain from reinvesting and compounding is 2.403 (= 27.203 – 24.800). When the bond is sold, it has six years remaining to maturity. Assuming yield-to-maturity remains 6.2%, the sale price is still 100% of par.

Baywhite's annualized rate of return is 6.20%:

$$r = \left(\frac{FV}{PV}\right)^{\frac{1}{T}} - 1.$$

$$r = \left(\frac{27.203 + 100}{100}\right)^{\frac{1}{4}} - 1.$$

$$r = 0.0620 = 6.20\%.$$

Horizon yield is an investor's IRR based on the total return (reinvested coupon payments plus sale price or redemption amount) and the purchase price of the bond. The horizon yield on a bond investment is the annualized holding-period rate of return.

In Example 2, Baywhite's horizon yield is 6.2%, which matches the original yield-to-maturity even though Baywhite did not hold the bond until maturity. This example shows that the realized horizon yield matches the original yield-to-maturity if (1) coupon payments are reinvested at the same interest rate as the original yield-to-maturity and (2) the bond is sold at a price on the constant-yield price trajectory, implying there is no capital gain or loss when the bond is sold. Importantly, capital gains (losses) arise if a bond is sold at a price above (below) its constant-yield price trajectory, as shown in a prior lesson.

A point on the trajectory represents the **carrying value** of the bond at that time. The carrying value is the purchase price plus (minus) the amortized amount of the discount (premium) if the bond is purchased at a price below (above) par value. The constant-yield price trajectory for the investors in Example 1 and Example 2 is a flat curve at a price of 100 as the bonds were purchased and sold at par.

We now demonstrate the impact of *higher* interest rates on VFO and Baywhite by increasing interest rates by 100 basis points (bps) immediately after investment. The yield on the bond increases from 6.20% to 7.20%, and coupon reinvestment rates go up by 100 bps as well.

EXAMPLE 3

VFO, the buy-and-hold investor, purchases BRWA's new 10-year, 6.2% (annual) coupon eurobond at par, and then interest rates immediately increase to 7.20%. The future value of the reinvested coupons at 7.20% for 10 years is

$$= -FV(0.072, 10, 6.2, 0, 0) = 86.475.$$

And VFO's realized rate of return (horizon yield) is 6.43%:

$$r = \left(\frac{FV}{PV}\right)^{\frac{1}{T}} - 1.$$

$$r = \left(\frac{86.475 + 100}{100}\right)^{\frac{1}{10}} - 1.$$

$$r = 0.0643 = 6.43\%.$$

VFO benefits from the higher coupon reinvestment rate. The realized horizon yield is 6.43%, 23 bps higher than the outcome in Example 1, when interest rates were constant. Importantly, VFO does not incur a capital gain or loss because it holds the bond until maturity.

EXAMPLE 4

Baywhite buys the same BRWA eurobond at par, interest rates immediately rise to 7.2%, and it sells the bonds four years later. The future value of the reinvested coupons at 7.2% is

$$= -FV(0.072, 4, 6.2, 0, 0) = 27.609.$$

We must also calculate the sale price of the bond because the change in interest rates affects the bond's price and, unlike VFO, Baywhite is selling it before maturity. We calculate the sale price after four years as

$$= -PV(0.072, 6, 6.2, 100, 0) = 95.263,$$

resulting in a realized four-year horizon yield of 5.28%:

$$r = \left(\frac{FV}{PV}\right)^{\frac{1}{T}} - 1.$$

$$r = \left(\frac{27.609 + 95.263}{100}\right)^{\frac{1}{4}} - 1.$$

$r = 0.0528 = 5.28\%.$

While Baywhite also benefits from the higher coupon reinvestment rate, it is more than offset by the capital loss from the sale of the bonds at the higher yield (lower price). Thus, Baywhite's rate of return is lower than in Example 2, where the interest rate remained at 6.2%.

We now examine the rates of return for these two investors if interest rates *decline* by 100 bps; the yield on the BRWA bonds fall from 6.20% to 5.20% immediately after they are purchased.

KNOWLEDGE CHECK

Immediately after VFO, the buy-and-hold investor, purchases BRWA's 10-year eurobonds at par, interest rates fall to 5.20%.

1. Calculate the future value of reinvested coupons.

   Solution:

   The future value of reinvesting the coupon payments at 5.20% for 10 years is

   $= -FV(0.052, 10, 6.2, 0, 0) = 78.715.$

2. Calculate VFO's horizon yield (realized rate of return).

   Solution:

   VFO's horizon yield is 5.98%:

   $$r = \left(\frac{FV}{PV}\right)^{\frac{1}{T}} - 1.$$

   $$r = \left(\frac{78.715 + 100}{100}\right)^{\frac{1}{10}} - 1.$$

   $r = 0.0598 = 5.98\%.$

3. Contrast VFO's investment outcome in this scenario to Example 1 and Example 3.

   Solution:

   VFO suffers from the lower coupon reinvestment rate. The realized horizon yield of 5.98% is 22 bps lower than the result in Example 1, when interest rates were unchanged, and 45 bps lower than the result in Example 3. There is no capital gain or loss, because the bonds are held until maturity. VFO's experience indicates that interest rate risk for a buy-and-hold investor arises entirely from reinvestment risk.

Baywhite buys BRWA's 10-year Eurobonds at par, and interest rates fall immediately to 5.20%. Baywhite sells the bonds after four years.

4. Calculate the future value of the reinvested coupons.

   Solution:

   The future of the reinvested coupons is

   $= -FV(0.052, 4, 6.2, 0, 0) = 26.802.$

5. Calculate Baywhite's horizon yield (realized rate of return).

   Solution:

   The sale price of the bond after four years is

   $= -PV(0.052, 6, 6.2, 100, 0) = 105.043$,

   resulting in a realized four-year horizon yield of 7.16%:

   $$r = \left(\frac{FV}{PV}\right)^{\frac{1}{T}} - 1.$$

   $$r = \left(\frac{26.802 + 105.043}{100}\right)^{\frac{1}{4}} - 1.$$

   $r = 0.0716 = 7.16\%$

6. Contrast Baywhite's investment outcome in this scenario to Example 2 and Example 4.

   Solution:

   The reduction in the future value of the coupons is more than offset by Baywhite's capital gain from the sale. Consequently, Baywhite's horizon yield is higher than in both Example 2 and Example 4.

As just demonstrated, interest income is the return associated with the *passage of time*, so it includes the receipt of coupon interest, the reinvestment of those coupons, and the amortization of the discount (or premium) from purchase at a price below (or above) par value to realign the return with the market discount rate. A capital gain or loss is the investor's return associated with the *change in the value* of the security, which for a fixed-rate bond arises from a change in the yield-to-maturity (i.e., the implied market discount rate).

This series of examples illustrates an important point about fixed-rate bonds: an investor's *investment horizon* is at the heart of understanding interest rate risk and return. There are two offsetting types of interest rate risk that affect the bond investor: reinvestment risk and price risk. The future value of reinvested coupon payments *increases* when interest rates rise and *decreases* when rates fall. The sale price on a bond that matures after the horizon date *decreases* when interest rates rise and *increases* when rates fall.

Reinvestment risk matters more when the investor has a long-term investment horizon. A buy-and-hold investor only has reinvestment risk. Price risk matters more when the investor has a short-term investment horizon. An investor who sells before the first coupon is received has only price risk. Thus, two investors holding the same bond can have different exposures to interest rate risk if they have different investment horizons.

QUESTION SET

1. *Fill in the blanks using the two words below:*

   Reinvestment risk

   Price risk

An investor who has a long-term investment horizon is more concerned about ____________, while the investor with a short-term investment horizon is more concerned about ____________.

Solution:

An investor who has a long-term investment horizon is more concerned about reinvestment risk, while the investor with a short-term investment horizon is more concerned about price risk.

2. What is the carrying value of a bond?

Solution:

The carrying value of a bond is the total value of the price at which the bond was purchased plus (minus) the adjustment for amortization of the discount (premium) if the bond is purchased at a price below (above) par value.

3. *Match the following*

Future value of coupons	Interest rates
A. Increase	Decrease
B. Decrease	Increase

Solution:

The answer to A is increase. The future value of coupons has a direct relationship with interest rates. Rising interest rates mean coupons are reinvested at a higher rate, increasing their future value.

The answer to B is decrease. The future value of coupons has a direct relationship with interest rates. Falling interest rates mean coupons are reinvested at a lower rate, decreasing their future value.

4. An investor purchases a five-year, 5.6% (annual) coupon priced at par (settlement: 15 December 2031; maturity: 15 December 2036) and sells it after two years. Immediately after the purchase of the bond, interest rates rise to 5.9%. The investor's total return at the end of two years is *closest* to:

A. 5.23%.

B. 5.60%.

C. 5.75%.

Solution:

A is correct. The investor's total return is composed of the (1) coupons, (2) reinvestment of coupons, and (3) gain/loss on sale prior to maturity.

The future value of the coupons assuming reinvestment at 5.90% is

$= -FV(0.059, 2, 5.6, 0, 0) = 11.5304.$

The sale price of the bond after two years, when three years remain to maturity, is

$= -PV(0.059, 3, 5.6, 100, 0) = 99.1966.$

The realized rate of return is 5.23%:

$$r = \left(\frac{FV}{PV}\right)^{\frac{1}{T}} - 1.$$

$$r = \left(\frac{11.530 + 99.197}{100}\right)^{\frac{1}{2}} - 1.$$

$r = 0.0523 = 5.23\%.$

B is incorrect because it is the rate of return if interest rates remain at 5.60%.

C is incorrect because it is the average of the two rates (i.e., the coupon rate, 5.6%, and the new, higher interest rate, 5.9%).

5. An investor purchases a seven-year, 6.7% (annual) coupon eurobond priced at par (settlement: 15 December 2031; maturity: 15 December 2038) and sells it after four years. Immediately after the purchase of the bond, interest rates fall to 6.3%. The investor's annualized rate of return at the end of four years is *closest* to:

   A. 6.50%.

   B. 6.66%.

   C. 6.89%.

   Solution:

   C is correct. The future value of the coupon and its reinvestment at 6.30% is

   $= -FV(0.063, 4, 6.7, 0, 0) = 29.441.$

   The sale price of the bond after four years is

   $= -PV(0.063, 3, 6.7, 100, 0) = 101.063.$

   The investor's rate of return is 6.89%:

$$r = \left(\frac{FV}{PV}\right)^{\frac{1}{T}} - 1.$$

$$r = \left(\frac{29.441 + 101.063}{100}\right)^{\frac{1}{4}} - 1.$$

   $r = 0.0689 = 6.89\%.$

   A is incorrect because this is the average of the annual coupon rate and the prevailing interest rate.

   B is incorrect because this calculation does not account for the appreciation in the bond price after interest rates fall.

INVESTMENT HORIZON AND INTEREST RATE RISK 3

- ☐ describe the relationships among a bond's holding period return, its Macaulay duration, and the investment horizon;
- ☐ define, calculate, and interpret Macaulay duration.

We now extend the prior discussion by introducing a third investor in BRWA's 10-year, 6.2% annual eurobonds: Hightest Capital, which has an 8-year time horizon. If interest rates remain at 6.20%, the future value of reinvested coupon interest is

$= -FV(0.062, 8, 6.2, 0, 0) = 61.807.$

When the bond is sold, it has two years remaining to maturity. Assuming yield-to-maturity remains at 6.2% and the sale price is 100, Hightest's horizon yield (realized rate of return) is 6.20%:

$$r = \left(\frac{FV}{PV}\right)^{\frac{1}{T}} - 1.$$

$$r = \left(\frac{61.807 + 100}{100}\right)^{\frac{1}{8}} - 1.$$

$$r = 0.0620 = 6.20\%.$$

If interest rates immediately rose to 7.20% after the purchase, the future value of coupons would increase:

$= -FV(0.072, 8, 6.2, 0, 0) = 64.071.$

And the price of the bond at the time of sale would fall:

$= -PV(0.072, 2, 6.2, 100, 0) = 98.197.$

Hightest's realized eight-year horizon yield is now 6.24%:

$$r = \left(\frac{FV}{PV}\right)^{\frac{1}{T}} - 1.$$

$$r = \left(\frac{64.071 + 98.197}{100}\right)^{\frac{1}{8}} - 1.$$

$$r = 0.0624 = 6.24\%.$$

Notice that the capital loss from the bond sale of 1.803 (= 98.197 – 100.00) is roughly matched by the additional coupon reinvestment income of 2.265 from the increase in interest rates. Therefore, Hightest's total return is nearly the same as in the stable rate scenario (6.24%, compared with 6.20%).

Now assume instead that market interest rates *fall* by 100 bps, to 5.20%. The future value of coupons decreases while the price of the bond at the time of sale increases:

$= -FV(0.052, 8, 6.2, 0, 0) = 59.630.$

$= -PV(0.052, 2, 6.2, 100, 0) = 101.854.$

Hightest's realized eight-year horizon yield is now 6.17%:

$$r = \left(\frac{FV}{PV}\right)^{\frac{1}{T}} - 1.$$

$$r = \left(\frac{59.630 + 101.854}{100}\right)^{\frac{1}{8}} - 1.$$

$$r = 0.0617 = 6.17\%.$$

Notice that the capital gain from the bond sale of 1.854 is roughly matched by the decrease in coupon reinvestment income. Again, Hightest's total return is nearly the same as in the stable rate scenario (6.17%, compared to 6.20%).

Hightest's investment results, along with those of VFO and Baywhite, are summarized in Exhibit 1. They reveal an important outcome for Hightest with the eight-year horizon: *Total returns and horizon yields are nearly the same regardless of interest rates.*

Exhibit 1

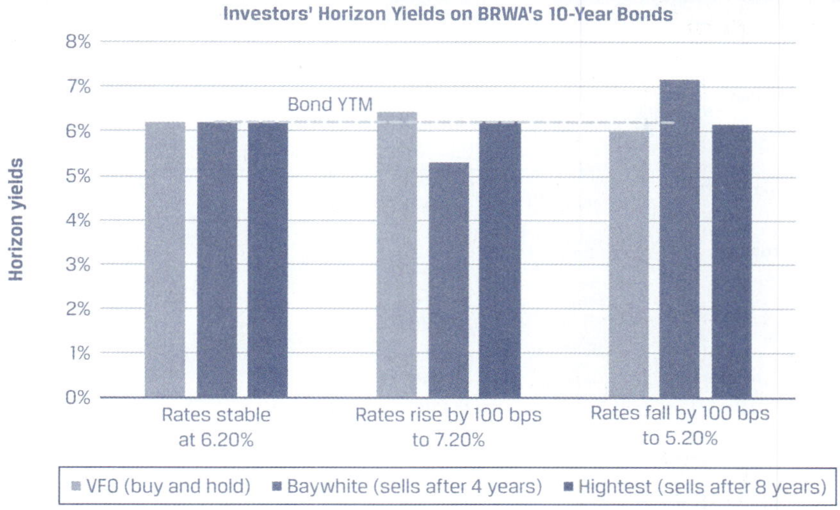

Hightest's investment horizon of eight years was chosen to illustrate an important quantity for the BRWA bond and fixed-income instruments generally: **Macaulay duration**, a holding period for a bond that balances coupon reinvestment gain (loss) and price loss (gain) for a one-time instantaneous "parallel" shift in the yield curve once the bond purchase is settled. It is named after Frederick Macaulay, the Canadian economist who introduced the concept in 1938. Given the result for Hightest, we know that the Macaulay duration of this BRWA bond is close to eight years.

Exhibit 2 illustrates Macaulay duration for a bond initially priced at par value.

Exhibit 2: Interest Rate Risk, Macaulay Duration, and Investment Horizon

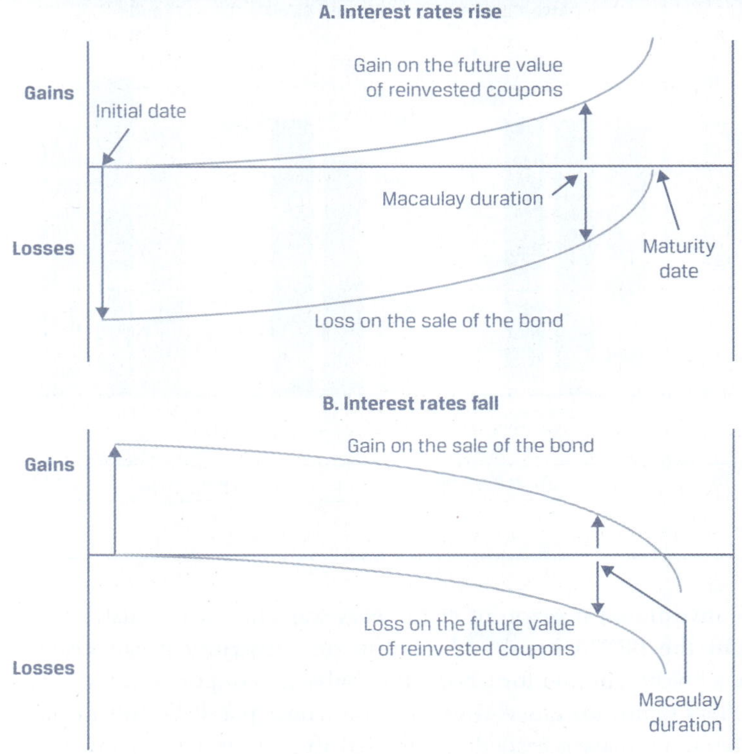

As shown in Panel A, when interest rates rise, there is an immediate drop in price. Then, as time passes, the bond price is "pulled to par." The increase in the future value of reinvested coupons starts small but builds over time, and the curve indicates the added future value of reinvested coupons due to the higher interest rate. At the Macaulay duration, the two effects offset each other: the gain on reinvested coupons is equal to the loss from the increase in interest rates.

The same pattern is shown in Panel B, when interest rates fall. There is an immediate increase in price, but then the "pull-to-par" effect brings the price down as time passes. The impact from reinvesting at a lower rate starts small but becomes significant over time. Again, the Macaulay duration indicates the point when the two effects offset each other, so the gain from the decrease in interest rates equally offsets the loss from coupon reinvestment at lower rates.

The foregoing discussion allows for statements about the general relationships among interest rate risk, the Macaulay duration, and the investment horizon shown in Exhibit 3:

Exhibit 3: Macaulay Duration, Investment Horizon, and Interest Rate Risk

	Dominant Risk	Source of Interest Rate Risk
Investment Horizon > Macaulay Duration	Reinvestment Risk	Falling Interest Rates
Investment Horizon = Macaulay Duration	Price Risk = Reinvestment Risk	—
Investment Horizon < Macaulay Duration	Price Risk	Rising Interest Rates

The Macaulay duration of the BRWA bond is 7.7429 years (the calculation will be demonstrated in the next lesson). So, Statement 1 reflects VFO's situation with its 10-year horizon; Statement 2, Hightest, the investor with the 8-year horizon; and Statement 3, Baywhite, the investor with the 4-year horizon.

As shown in Equation 1, the **duration gap** for a bond is the difference between its Macaulay duration and the investor's investment horizon.

$$\text{Duration gap} = \text{Macaulay duration} - \text{Investment horizon}. \quad (1)$$

VFO, with a 10-year horizon, has a negative duration gap. Therefore, the primary risk it faces is lower interest rates. Hightest, with the eight-year horizon, has a duration gap of approximately zero, so it is nearly hedged against interest rate risk. Baywhite, with the four-year horizon, has a positive duration gap and is at risk of higher rates. Importantly, as time passes, the investment horizon is reduced and the Macaulay duration of the bond also falls.

KNOWLEDGE CHECK

Three investors, Rook Point Investors, Fyleton Investments, and Amy Investments, purchase a 5.61%, 30-year Romanian eurobond at par value. The bond's Macaulay duration is 15.16 years. Rook Point's investment horizon is five years, while Fyleton and Amy have investment horizons of 15 and 30 years, respectively.

1. Calculate the returns for the three investors for three scenarios:

   Scenario 1: Interest rates fall by 50 bps immediately after the purchase.

   Scenario 2: Interest rates stay stable at 5.61%.

   Scenario 3: Interest rates rise by 50 bps immediately after the purchase.

   Solution:

   The total returns under the various scenarios for each investor are shown in the table below.

   The key point to note is that when an investor's investment horizon is almost equal to the bond's Macaulay duration, the returns under various interest rate scenarios remain the same. The gain (loss) from coupon reinvestment risk is offset by the loss (gain) from the price risk.

Rates Stable at 5.61%			Rates Rise to 6.11%			Rates Fall to 5.11%		
Rook Point	Fyleton	Amy	Rook Point	Fyleton	Amy	Rook Point	Fyleton	Amy
Investment Horizon			Investment Horizon			Investment Horizon		

Rates Stable at 5.61%			Rates Rise to 6.11%			Rates Fall to 5.11%		
5	15	30	5	15	30	5	15	30
MacDur > Horizon	MacDur ≅ Horizon	MacDur < Horizon	MacDur > Horizon	MacDur ≅ Horizon	MacDur < Horizon	MacDur > Horizon	MacDur ≅ Horizon	MacDur < Horizon
Future Value of Coupons			Future Value of Coupons			Future Value of Coupons		
31.379	126.765	414.223	31.694	131.678	452.199	31.067	122.063	379.840
Redemption Value or Sale Price			Redemption Value or Sale Price			Redemption Value or Sale Price		
100.000	100.000	100.000	93.675	95.179	100.000	106.970	105.152	100.000
Horizon Yield			Horizon Yield			Horizon Yield		
5.610%	5.610%	5.610%	4.626%	5.613%	5.861%	6.659%	5.624%	5.367%

QUESTION SET

1. Match the following:

Duration Gap	Risk Source
A. Negative	Rising interest rates
B. Positive	Falling interest rates

Solution:

The answer to A is falling interest rates. A negative duration gap means that the bond's Macaulay duration is lower than the investor's investment horizon, which means that reinvestment risk is the dominant source of interest rate risk, from falling interest rates.

The answer to B is rising interest rates. A positive duration gap means that the bond's Macaulay duration is higher than the investor's investment horizon, which means that price risk is the dominant source of interest rate risk, from rising interest rates.

2. Complete the equation below with the following terms:

Macaulay duration

Investment horizon

Time-to-maturity

Duration gap = __________ – __________.

Solution:

Duration gap = Macaulay duration – Investment horizon.

3. An investor intends to hold a bond with eight years remaining to maturity for eight years. The bond's Macaulay duration is 6.841. The investor is *primarily* exposed to which of the following interest rate risks:

A. Price risk

B. Reinvestment risk

C. Neither price nor reinvestment risk

Solution:

B is correct. A buy-and-hold investor is not exposed to price risk, because she does not intend to sell the bond prior to maturity. However, her rate of return is impacted by the rate at which she can reinvest coupons.

Alternatively, the investor's investment horizon is eight years, whereas the bond's Macaulay duration is 6.841. When the investment horizon exceeds the Macaulay duration, reinvestment risk dominates.

MACAULAY DURATION 4

☐ define, calculate, and interpret Macaulay duration.

The prior lesson established Macaulay duration as a holding period for a bond that balances reinvestment and price risk. We now turn to its calculation.

The most straightforward way to understand the Macaulay duration of a traditional fixed-rate bond is that it is the weighted average of the *time to receipt* of the bond's cash flows, where the weights of each cash flow in the calculation are each cash flow's share of the bond's full price (i.e., present value). Before we introduce the general equation, let's take a specific example to demonstrate the calculation of Macaulay duration: BRWA's 10-year, 6.2% (annual) coupon eurobond used in the previous lessons.

Exhibit 4 illustrates the calculation of Macaulay duration at issuance, assuming the bond was issued at par, settled on 15 October 2025, and matures on 15 October 2035. Because this is a corporate bond, we assume a 30/360 day-count basis.

Exhibit 4: Macaulay Duration of BRWA Corp. 10-Year, 6.2% Annual Eurobond at Issuance

Coupon	6.20%
Coupon frequency per year	1
Price per 100 par value	100
Yield-to-maturity	6.20%
Settlement date	15 October 2025
Maturity	15 October 2035
Years to maturity	10

(1)	(2)	(3)	(4)	(5)	(6)
				(4) ÷ Sum of present values	(1) × (5)
Period	**Time to receipt**	**Cash flow**	**Present value**	**Weight**	**Time to receipt × weight**
1	1	6.2	5.8380	0.0584	0.0584
2	2	6.2	5.4972	0.0550	0.1099
3	3	6.2	5.1763	0.0518	0.1553
4	4	6.2	4.8741	0.0487	0.1950
5	5	6.2	4.5895	0.0459	0.2295
6	6	6.2	4.3216	0.0432	0.2593
7	7	6.2	4.0693	0.0407	0.2849
8	8	6.2	3.8317	0.0383	0.3065
9	9	6.2	3.6080	0.0361	0.3247
10	10	106.2	58.1942	0.5819	5.8194
			100.0000	1.0000	7.7429

- Columns 1 and 2 show the number of periods and the time to receipt of the cash flow, respectively. If the calculation is done at issuance or on a coupon date, they are equal.
- Column 3 is the cash flow per 100 of par value, and column 4 is the present value of that cash flow.
- The fifth column is the weight, or each cash flow's share of total PV. Notice that the final payment, $PMT_N + FV_N$, of 106.2 accounts for 58% of the bond's PV.
- The sixth column is the time to receipt of the cash flow (Column 2) multiplied by the weight (Column 5). The sum of this column is the Macaulay duration, 7.7429. This is close to Hightest Capital's investment horizon of eight years from the prior lesson, which means that Hightest has balanced its reinvestment and price risk.

Macaulay duration is often quoted as an annualized statistic. Since this bond pays coupons annually, no adjustment is needed. If the bond were a semiannual coupon bond, we would divide the Macaulay duration by 2 (two semiannual periods per year) to obtain an annualized Macaulay duration. When quoted as an annualized statistic, the units for Macaulay duration is years.

Notice how 7.7429 years is less than 10, the time-to-maturity of the bond. This is because Macaulay duration is a present value–weighted average of the time to receipt of the cash flows, while time-to-maturity is the time to receipt of the final cash flow.

The general calculation of Macaulay duration, *MacDur*, that also accounts for partial coupon periods if the calculation is done between coupon dates is shown in Equation 2.

$$\text{MacDur} = \left\{ \begin{array}{l} (1 - t/T)\left[\dfrac{\frac{PMT}{(1+r)^{1-t/T}}}{PV^{Full}}\right] + (2 - t/T)\left[\dfrac{\frac{PMT}{(1+r)^{2-t/T}}}{PV^{Full}}\right] + \cdots + \\ (N - t/T)\left[\dfrac{\frac{PMT + FV}{(1+r)^{N-t/T}}}{PV^{Full}}\right] \end{array} \right\}, \quad (2)$$

where

t is the number of days from the last coupon payment to the settlement date;

T is the number of days in the coupon period;

t/T is the fraction of the coupon period that has passed since the last payment;

PMT is the coupon payment per period;

FV is the future value paid at maturity, or the par value of the bond;

r is the yield-to-maturity per period; and

N is the number of evenly spaced periods to maturity as of the beginning of the current period.

EXAMPLE 5

Macaulay Duration between Coupon Dates

Now let's compute the Macaulay duration for the BRWA bond *between* coupon dates—specifically, on 11 December 2025, 57 days after issuance. The only difference from the prior example is that we are 57 days in the future, so rather than $t/T = 0$ like at issuance, $t/T = 57/360$, and each cash flow's time to receipt is 57 days earlier.

Macaulay Duration of BRWA Corp. 10-Year, 6.2% Annual Eurobond Settling 57 Days after Issuance

Coupon	6.20%
Coupon frequency per year	1
Price per 100 par value	100
Yield-to-maturity	6.20%
Settlement date	11 December 2025
Maturity	15 October 2035
Years to maturity	10

(1)	(2)	(3)	(4)	(5)	(6)
				(4) ÷ Sum of present values	(1) × (5)
Period	**Time to receipt**	**Cash flow**	**Present value**	**Weight**	**Time to receipt × weight**
1	0.8417	6.2	5.8939	0.0584	0.0491
2	1.8417	6.2	5.5498	0.0550	0.1012
3	2.8417	6.2	5.2258	0.0518	0.1471
4	3.8417	6.2	4.9207	0.0487	0.1872
5	4.8417	6.2	4.6335	0.0459	0.2222
6	5.8417	6.2	4.3630	0.0432	0.2525
7	6.8417	6.2	4.1082	0.0407	0.2784
8	7.8417	6.2	3.8684	0.0383	0.3005

Period	Time to receipt	Cash flow	Present value	Weight	Time to receipt × weight
9	8.8417	6.2	3.6426	0.0361	0.3190
10	9.8417	106.2	58.7511	0.5819	5.7273
			100.9570	1.0000	7.5845

Comparing this example to the prior example, we see that the time to receipt of each flow is lower, reflecting the fact that we are 57 days later, which increases the present value of each cash flow. However, the present value weight of each cash flow remains the same. The Macaulay duration (7.5845) is lower than in the prior example (7.7429), reflecting the lower times to receipt.

This example demonstrates an important property of Macaulay duration: it is not static; it falls as time elapses and the time to receipt of each cash flow falls.

Besides a spreadsheet, Macaulay duration also can be calculated using the DURATION function in Microsoft Excel or Google Sheets:

=DURATION(*Settlement*, *Maturity*, *Coupon*, *Yld*, *Frequency*, [*Basis*])

where

Settlement is the date of settlement, in DATE form

Maturity is the maturity date, in DATE form

Coupon is the annual coupon rate

Yld is the annualized yield-to-maturity

Frequency is the periodicity, typically the number of coupon payments per year; it is 1 for annual, 2 for semiannual, 4 for quarterly

[*Basis*] is the day-count convention; 0 or omitted is 30/360, 1 is act/act, 2 is act/360, 3 is act/365

Finally, another approach to calculating Macaulay duration is to use a closed-form equation derived using calculus and algebra, shown as Equation 3:

$$MacDur = \left\{\frac{1+r}{r} - \frac{1+r+[N\times(c-r)]}{c\times\left[(1+r)^N-1\right]+r}\right\} - \frac{t}{T} \quad (3)$$

where

r is the yield-to-maturity per period;

N is the number of evenly spaced periods to maturity as of the beginning of the current period;

c is the coupon rate per period;

t is the number of days from the last coupon payment to the settlement date; and

T is the number of days in the coupon period.

QUESTION SET

1. Consider a bond that has three years remaining to maturity and a coupon of 4% paid semiannually and is priced at 100. The bond's annualized Macaulay duration is *closest* to:

   A. 2.801 years.

   B. 2.857 years.

   C. 3.000 years.

   Solution:

   B is correct.

Period	Time to receipt	Cash flow	Present value	Weight	Time to receipt × weight
1	1	2	1.961	0.0196	0.01961
2	2	2	1.922	0.0192	0.03845
3	3	2	1.885	0.0189	0.05654
4	4	2	1.848	0.0185	0.07391
5	5	2	1.811	0.0181	0.09057
6	6	102	90.573	0.9057	5.43438
			100.00000	1.00000	5.71346
Annualized Macaulay duration (years)					2.857

2. An investor with a three-year investment horizon purchases a bond with four years remaining to maturity, a coupon of 1% paid semiannually, and a yield-to-maturity of 0.90%. With respect to interest rate risk, the investor is *primarily* concerned about:

   A. rising interest rates.

   B. falling interest rates.

   C. neither rising nor falling interest rates.

   Solution:

   A is correct. The Macaulay duration of the bond is 3.9312 years.

Period	Time to Receipt	Cash Flow	PV	Weight	Time to Receipt × Weight
1.0000	1.0000	0.5000	0.4978	0.0050	0.0050
2.0000	2.0000	0.5000	0.4955	0.0049	0.0099
3.0000	3.0000	0.5000	0.4933	0.0049	0.0147
4.0000	4.0000	0.5000	0.4911	0.0049	0.0196
5.0000	5.0000	0.5000	0.4889	0.0049	0.0243
6.0000	6.0000	0.5000	0.4867	0.0048	0.0291
7.0000	7.0000	0.5000	0.4845	0.0048	0.0338
8.0000	8.0000	100.5000	96.9542	0.9658	7.7260

Period	Time to Receipt	Cash Flow	PV	Weight	Time to Receipt × Weight
			100.3920	1.0000	7.8624
			Annualized MacDur (years)		3.9312

When the Macaulay duration of a bond is longer than the investor's investment horizon (three years), price risk dominates and the investor's primary downside concern is rising interest rates.

3. Consider a bond that has five years remaining to maturity, a coupon of 0.5% paid annually, and a yield-to-maturity of –0.20%. The bond's annualized Macaulay duration is *closest* to:

   A. 2.4758.

   B. 4.9515.

   C. 5.3130.

   Solution:

   B is correct.

Period	Time to Receipt	CF	PV	Weight	Time to Receipt × Weight
1.0000	1.0000	0.5000	0.5010	0.0048	0.0048
2.0000	2.0000	0.5000	0.5020	0.0048	0.0097
3.0000	3.0000	0.5000	0.5030	0.0049	0.0146
4.0000	4.0000	0.5000	0.5040	0.0049	0.0195
5.0000	5.0000	100.5000	101.5111	0.9806	4.9029
			103.5211	1.0000	4.9515

4. Consider a bond that has five years remaining to maturity, a coupon of 0.5% paid annually, and a yield-to-maturity of –0.20%. Assume it is 91 days into the first coupon period and a 30/360 basis. The bond's annualized Macaulay duration is *closest* to:

   A. 4.2371.

   B. 4.5054.

   C. 4.6987.

   Solution:

   C is correct.

Period	Time to Receipt	Cash Flow	PV	Weight	Time to Receipt × Weight
1.0000	0.7472	0.5000	0.5007	0.0048	0.0036
2.0000	1.7472	0.5000	0.5018	0.0048	0.0085
3.0000	2.7472	0.5000	0.5028	0.0049	0.0133
4.0000	3.7472	0.5000	0.5038	0.0049	0.0182

Period	Time to Receipt	Cash Flow	PV	Weight	Time to Receipt × Weight
5.0000	4.7472	100.5000	101.4597	0.9806	4.6550
			103.4687	1.0000	4.6987

Note that a straightforward way to calculate Macaulay duration using a spreadsheet between coupon periods is to set the first cash flow's time to receipt as $1 - t/T$ (here = 1 – 91/360) and subsequent times to receipt as the prior plus 1.

PRACTICE PROBLEMS

1. Assuming no capital gain or loss when the bond is sold, an investor's horizon yield is equal to a bond's yield-to-maturity at the time of investment if coupons are reinvested at a rate:

   A. lower than the bond's yield-to-maturity at investment.

   B. equal to the bond's yield-to-maturity at investment.

   C. higher than the bond's yield-to-maturity at investment.

2. An investor purchases an eight-year, 6.4% annual coupon eurobond priced at par (settlement: 15 June 2031; maturity: 15 December 2039) and sells it after six years. Assuming interest rates rise by 100 bps immediately after purchase, the investor's rate of return at the end of six years is:

   A. lower than 6.4%.

   B. equal to 6.4%.

   C. higher than 6.4%.

3. The carrying value of a bond purchased at a price below par is equal to the original purchase price:

   A. minus the accumulated premium amortization.

   B. minus the accumulated discount amortization.

   C. plus the accumulated discount amortization.

4. The duration gap at which reinvestment risk and price risk are equal is:

   A. less than zero.

   B. equal to zero.

   C. greater than zero.

5. When an investor's investment horizon is less than a bond's Macaulay duration, the investor faces downside risk if, after the purchase of the bond, interest rates:

   A. decrease.

   B. increase.

   C. either decrease or increase.

6. An investor purchases a 12-year, 5.8% annual bond and intends to sell it after 10 years. The Macaulay duration of the bond is 8.97 years. If interest rates fall by 75 bps immediately after the purchase of the bond, the investor faces:

   A. negative reinvestment risk.

   B. no reinvestment risk.

   C. positive reinvestment risk.

7. Consider a bond that has three years remaining to maturity, a coupon of 4% paid semiannually, and a yield-to-maturity of 4.60%. Assuming it is 12 days into the first coupon period and a 30/360 basis, the bond's annualized Macaulay duration is *closest* to:

   A. 1.8764 years.

   B. 2.8386 years.

   C. 2.8553 years.

8. Hightest Capital purchases a seven-year, 6.4% coupon bond and has an intended investment horizon of four years. The Macaulay duration of the bond is 5.86 years. If interest rates increase by 50 bps immediately after buying the bond, Hightest Capital faces:

   A. negative price risk.

   B. negative reinvestment risk.

   C. positive price risk.

SOLUTIONS

1. B is correct. For the horizon yield to match the original yield-to-maturity of the bond, two conditions must be met:

   (1) The coupon payments are reinvested at the original yield-to-maturity.

   (2) The bond is sold at the constant-yield price trajectory, implying no capital gain or loss when the bond is sold.

   Since there is no gain or loss when the bond is sold, the horizon yield will be equal to the yield-to-maturity if the first condition is met (i.e., the coupons are reinvested at the original yield-to-maturity).

   A is incorrect because the horizon yield will be lower than the yield-to-maturity if the coupons are reinvested at a lower rate than the original yield-to-maturity, assuming no capital gain or loss on sale of the bond.

   C is incorrect because the horizon yield will be higher than the yield-to-maturity if the coupons are reinvested at a higher rate than the original yield-to-maturity, assuming no capital gain or loss on sale of the bond.

2. A is correct. The future value of reinvested coupon interest is

   $= FV(0.074,6,6.4,0,0) = 46.245.$

   The sale price of the bond at the end of six years is

   $= PV(0.054,2,6.40,100,0) = 98.202,$

   which results in a six-year horizon yield of 6.32%, which is lower than 6.40%:

   $$r = \left(\frac{FV}{PV}\right)^{\frac{1}{T}} - 1.$$

   $$r = \left(\frac{46.245 + 98.202}{100}\right)^{\frac{1}{6}} - 1.$$

   $r = 0.0632 = 6.32\%.$

   B and C are incorrect, because interest rates have risen and the investor's investment horizon is not long enough to offset the price decline with additional reinvestment return.

3. C is correct. A bond purchased at a discount will have its price "pulled to par" as it approaches maturity. Its carrying value at time t is equal to its purchase price plus the accumulated discount amortization.

   A is incorrect because a bond purchased below par is purchased at a discount, not a premium.

   B is incorrect because the accumulated discount amortization is added, not subtracted, from the purchase price to calculate carrying value.

4. B is correct. Reinvestment risk and price risk equally offset each other when an investor's investment horizon equals a bond's Macaulay duration. This is when the duration gap is zero.

   A is incorrect because a duration gap of less than zero means that Macaulay duration is less than the investor's investment horizon and that reinvestment risk is higher than price risk.

   C is incorrect because when the duration gap is greater than zero, the Macaulay duration is greater than the investor's investment horizon, so price risk is higher than reinvestment risk.

5. B is correct. If the investment horizon is less than the bond's Macaulay duration, then the investor's risk is higher interest rates. For such an investor, the market price risk dominates the coupon reinvestment risk.

   A is incorrect because an investor faces risk due to a lower interest rate when the investment horizon is greater than the bond's Macaulay duration.

   C is incorrect because when the investment horizon is less than the Macaulay duration, the investor faces risk due to higher interest rates, not lower interest rates.

6. A is correct. The investor has an investment horizon of 10 years, which is greater than the Macaulay duration of 8.97 years. Therefore, reinvestment risk dominates price risk.

   B is incorrect because the investor faces reinvestment risk because the investment horizon is higher than the Macaulay duration.

   C is incorrect because the investor faces negative coupon reinvestment risk, not positive coupon reinvestment risk, since the coupons will be reinvested at a lower interest rate.

7. B is correct.

Period	Time to Receipt	Cash Flow	PV	Weight	Time to Receipt × Weight
1.0000	0.9333	2.0000	1.9580	0.0199	0.0186
2.0000	1.9333	2.0000	1.9140	0.0194	0.0376
3.0000	2.9333	2.0000	1.8709	0.0190	0.0557
4.0000	3.9333	2.0000	1.8289	0.0186	0.0730
5.0000	4.9333	2.0000	1.7878	0.0182	0.0896
6.0000	5.9333	102.0000	89.1261	0.9050	5.3695
			98.4856	1.0000	5.6439
				Annualized MacDur	2.8220

8. A is correct. Hightest Capital's investment horizon is four years, which is less than the bond's Macaulay duration of 5.86 years. Therefore, price risk dominates reinvestment risk and Hightest Capital faces price risk from rising interest rates.

   B is incorrect because the increase in interest rates is beneficial for coupon reinvestment. Therefore, Hightest Capital has positive reinvestment risk.

   C is incorrect because Hightest Capital faces the risk that the price of the bond will fall as a result of the 50 bp increase in interest rates and therefore has negative price risk.

LEARNING MODULE

11

Yield-Based Bond Duration Measures and Properties

LEARNING OUTCOMES

Mastery	The candidate should be able to:
☐	define, calculate, and interpret modified duration, money duration, and the price value of a basis point (PVBP)
☐	explain how a bond's maturity, coupon, and yield level affect its interest rate risk

INTRODUCTION

1

Prior lessons explored two sources of interest rate risk—reinvestment risk and price risk—and demonstrated how holding a bond for its Macaulay duration balances them. This lesson and those that follow extend that discussion by introducing measures of price risk. Two broad categories of such measures exist: those that assume underlying bond cash flows are certain and measure price sensitivity to changes in a bond's *own yield*, which are covered in these lessons, and those that introduce the possibility of a bond default and that measure price sensitivity to changes in a *benchmark* yield curve, which are covered in later lessons. This lesson will illustrate how the interest rate risk of a bond is a function of its features, including its time-to-maturity, coupon rate, and yield.

Most of the examples and exhibits used throughout the reading can be downloaded as a Microsoft Excel workbook. Each worksheet in the workbook is labeled with the corresponding example or exhibit number in the text.

LEARNING MODULE OVERVIEW

- Duration is a quantitative measure of interest rate risk. There are several duration measures, including those that measure a bond's price sensitivity to changes in its own yield-to-maturity and assume underlying cash flows are certain (yield duration) and those that measure changes in a benchmark yield curve, with less certain underlying cash flows (curve duration).

- Macaulay duration, modified duration, money duration, and the price value of a basis point (PVBP) are yield duration measures.
- Modified duration is the slope or first derivative of the price of a bond with respect to its yield-to-maturity, measuring the sensitivity of a bond's price to changes in its yield-to-maturity. Modified duration can be calculated using a bond's Macaulay duration and yield or through approximation.
- Money duration is an extension of modified duration and incorporates the size of the bond position in currency terms. Related to this measure is the price value of a basis point, which is an estimate of the change in the price of a bond for a 1 bp change in the bond's yield.
- Duration can be used to estimate the change in the price of a bond in response to a change in yield, but it assumes a linear relationship between price and yield even though, in fact, the relationship is nonlinear. This is most evident when estimating price changes for large changes in yield and for bonds with certain features.
- A bond's features, including its time-to-maturity, coupon rate, and yield-to-maturity, determine its duration. Duration, for a given bond, is not static and decreases as the bond approaches maturity.
- All else equal, a longer (shorter) time-to-maturity, a lower (higher) coupon rate, or a lower (higher) yield-to-maturity results in higher (lower) duration or higher (lower) interest rate risk.

LEARNING MODULE SELF-ASSESSMENT

These initial questions are intended to help you gauge your current level of understanding of the learning module.

1. Match each of the following descriptions with the appropriate term:

Description	Term
Present-value-weighted average time-to-receipt of a bond's cash flows	i. Money duration
Used to estimate the percentage change in a bond's price for a given change in the bond's yield-to-maturity	ii. Price value per basis point
The product of the annualized modified duration and the full price of a bond	iii. Macaulay duration
Change in the full price of a bond for a 1 bp change in yield	iv. Modified duration

Solution:

Present value weighted average time-to-receipt of a bond cash flows matches with iii. Macaulay duration.

Used to estimate the percentage change in a bond's price for a given change in the bond's yield-to-maturity matches with iv. Modified duration.

The product of the annualized modified duration and the full price of a bond matches with i. Money duration.

Change in the full price of a bond for a 1 bp change in yield matches with ii. Price value per basis point.

2. If all other characteristics of a bond are held constant, an increase in the bond's yield-to-maturity will *most likely* result in:

   A. a decrease in the bond's modified duration.

   B. no change in the bond's modified duration.

   C. an increase in the bond's modified duration.

   Solution:

   A is correct. An increase in the bond's yield-to-maturity will result in a lower modified duration because future cash flows are discounted at a higher rate, which reduces the present-value-weighted average of their time to receipt.

   B is incorrect because duration is affected by the present value of the bond's cash flows, which, in turn, is affected by the bond's yield.

   C is incorrect because an increase in the bond's yield-to-maturity reduces the present value of each cash flow and hence reduces the bond's duration.

3. Consider a bond with an annualized modified duration of 4, a coupon of 5%, and a price of 95. The expected change in the price of the bond, per 100 of par value, for a 50 bp increase in the bond's yield-to-maturity is *closest* to:

   A. 4.75.

   B. 3.80.

   C. 1.90.

   Solution:

   C is correct. The money duration is 380:

   $$MoneyDur = AnnModDur \times PV^{Full}.$$

   $$MoneyDur = 4.0 \times 95.$$

   $$MoneyDur = 380.$$

   This results in a change in price of –1.90 for a 50 bp increase in the bond's yield:

   $$\Delta PV^{Full} \approx -MoneyDur \times \Delta Yield.$$

   $$\Delta PV^{Full} \approx -380 \times 0.005.$$

   $$\Delta PV^{Full} \approx -1.90.$$

   The change in price is negative for the increase in the yield-to-maturity.

4. Two bonds, Bond X and Bond Y, are identical except that Bond X has a lower coupon rate than Bond Y. Therefore:

   A. the bonds will have identical modified duration.

   B. Bond X will have a lower modified duration compared to Bond Y.

   C. Bond Y will have a lower modified duration compared to Bond X.

   Solution:

   C is correct. If two bonds are identical in all other respects (e.g., time-to-maturity, yield, etc.), the bond with the lower coupon rate will have the higher modified duration. This is because, compared to Bond Y, the present value of each of Bond X's coupon cash flows will make up less of the bond's price, while the contribution to the price of the bond from the face value will be greater.

5. Estimating the price value per basis point by dividing the difference in the price of a bond for a 0.0001 decrease and a 0.0001 increase by 2 ignores:

   A. convexity of the bond's price–yield relationship.

   B. concavity of the bond's price–yield relationship.

   C. symmetry in the bond's price–yield relationship.

   Solution:

   A is correct. This formulation of the price value of a basis point does not include an adjustment for convexity. This is important because the price change for increases and decreases in yields is asymmetric, owing to the convex relationship between price and yield.

6. The change in the price of a bond when its yield increases by 100 bps is best described as:

   A. less than the change in price for a decrease in its yield by 100 bps.

   B. the same as the change in price for a decrease in its yield by 100 bps.

   C. greater than the change in price for a decrease in its yield by 100 bps.

   Solution:

   A is correct. The price–yield relationship for most bonds is convex, such that the increase in the price of a bond is greater for yield decreases than a decrease in the price for the same yield increase.

2 MODIFIED DURATION

☐ define, calculate, and interpret modified duration, money duration, and the price value of a basis point (PVBP)

Recall from prior lessons that the price of a bond moves inversely with its yield. We can illustrate this by pricing bonds at varying yields-to-maturity. Exhibit 1 shows prices for three bonds introduced in prior lessons at yields ranging from 0% to 10%. Assume all the bonds are denominated in the same currency.

- 1-year, zero-coupon Australian government bond,
- 5-year, 3.2% semiannual coupon Bright Wheels Automotive Corporation (BRWA) bond, and
- 30-year, 4.625% annual coupon Romanian government bond.

Exhibit 1: Three Bond Prices at Varying Yields-to-Maturity

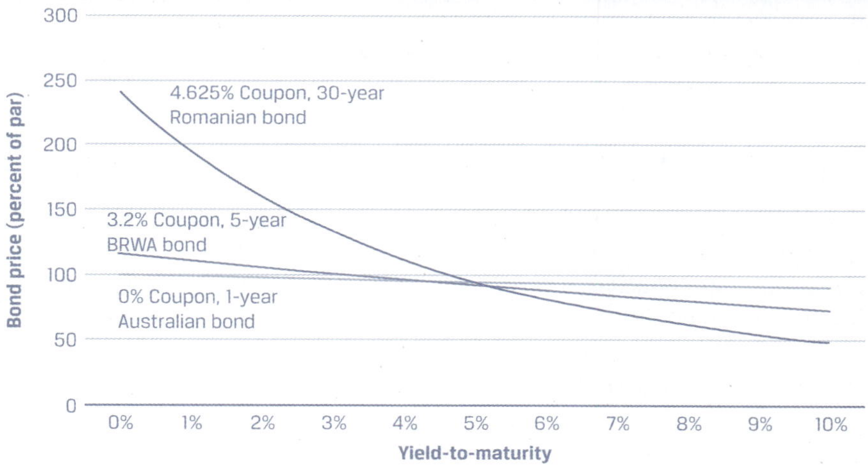

Notice how each line shows a different price–yield relationship. The line for the zero-coupon, 1-year Australian government bond is nearly flat, while the line for the 30-year Romanian bond is steep and downward sloping. If an investor held all three bonds and each bond's yield increased from 2% to 3%, the changes in price for each would be starkly different:

YTM	Price of 1-Year Australian Bond	Price of 5-Year BRWA Bond	Price of 30-Year Romanian Bond
2%	98.039	105.683	158.791
3%	97.087	100.922	131.851
Change in Price as YTM 2% → 3%	−1%	−5%	−17%

While graphs of the price–yield relationship can help in visualizing different bonds' interest rate risk, numbers are more useful so that investors can rank bonds by their price sensitivity to changes in yield.

A logical numerical expression for a bond's interest rate risk is the slope, or first derivative, of its price–yield line. We would expect the slope of the line for the one-year Australian bond, for example, to be relatively low, since the line is nearly flat. But we would expect the slope of the line for the 30-year Romanian bond to be high since that line is relatively steep. While candidates are not responsible for using calculus, we show the steps required to find the first derivative of the price–yield line to illustrate the logic behind the equations.

Recall that the price, PV, of an option-free bond is the present value of the bond's cash flows.

$$PV = \frac{PMT}{(1+r)^1} + \frac{PMT}{(1+r)^2} + \ldots + \frac{PMT}{(1+r)^N} + \frac{FV}{(1+r)^N}.$$

First, we take the derivative with respect to r, the yield-to-maturity:

$$\frac{dPV}{dr} = \frac{(-1)PMT}{(1+r)^2} + \frac{(-2)PMT}{(1+r)^3} + \ldots + \frac{(-N)PMT}{(1+r)^{N+1}} + \frac{(-N)FV}{(1+r)^{N+1}}.$$

Then, we factor out $-\frac{1}{(1+r)}$ to get

$$\frac{dPV}{dr} = -\frac{1}{(1+r)}\left[\frac{(1)PMT}{(1+r)^1} + \frac{(2)PMT}{(1+r)^2} + \ldots + \frac{(N)PMT}{(1+r)^N} + \frac{(N)FV}{(1+r)^N}\right].$$

While this gives us the change in a bond's price for a change in yield, it does so in terms of *PV*, but *percentage* change in price would be more useful. To get percentage change, we divide by *PV* (price):

$$\frac{\frac{dPV}{dr}}{PV} = \frac{-\frac{1}{(1+r)}\left[\frac{(1)PMT}{(1+r)^1} + \frac{(2)PMT}{(1+r)^2} + \ldots + \frac{(N)PMT}{(1+r)^N} + \frac{(N)FV}{(1+r)^N}\right]}{PV}.$$

Look closely at the term in brackets. Each $\frac{\frac{PMT}{(1+r)}}{PV}$ is the present value of that cash flow expressed as a percentage of the bond price, which is then multiplied by the time to receipt of that cash flow. In other words, the term in brackets divided by *PV* is the Macaulay duration, *MacDur*, introduced in prior lessons. We can substitute *MacDur* in the equation to obtain

$$\frac{\frac{dPV}{dr}}{PV} = -\frac{1}{(1+r)} \times MacDur,$$

or

$$\frac{\frac{dPV}{dr}}{PV} = -\frac{MacDur}{(1+r)}. \quad (1)$$

Without the negative sign, this is known as a bond's **modified duration**, or *ModDur*:

$$ModDur = \frac{MacDur}{(1+r)}. \quad (2)$$

ModDur can be annualized, like Macaulay duration, by dividing by the number of coupon periods per year for the bond.

Since *ModDur* captures the relationship between a bond's price and its yield, we can use it to estimate the percentage price change for a bond given a change in its yield-to-maturity, if we substitute –*AnnModDur* for the right side of Equation 1 and multiply both sides by *dr*, or the change in annualized yield-to-maturity:

$$\%\Delta PV^{Full} \approx -AnnModDur \times \Delta AnnYield. \quad (3)$$

For example, if a bond's modified duration is 5, its price will decrease by an estimated 5% for a 100 bp increase in yield: –5 × 0.01 = –5%. Therefore, the higher a bond's modified duration, the steeper its price–yield relationship line is and the more sensitive its price is to changes in yield.

The percentage price change refers to the full price, which includes accrued interest. The ≈ sign indicates that this calculation is an estimation because it is a linear approximation of the nonlinear relationship between price and yield, which will be covered in detail in a later lesson. The negative sign indicates that bond prices and yields-to-maturity move inversely with one another.

Modified duration can also be obtained directly using the MDURATION function in Microsoft Excel or Google Sheets. The inputs are the same as the DURATION function to calculate Macaulay duration:

= MDURATION(*Settlement*, *Maturity*, *Coupon*, *Yld*, *Frequency*, [*Basis*]).

EXAMPLE 1

Modified Duration for the BRWA Bond

We can use Equation 2 to calculate modified duration for the five-year BRWA bond for settlement at issuance and for 57 days after issuance.

Coupon	3.20%
Coupon frequency per year	2

Price per 100 par value	100
Yield-to-maturity	3.20%
Issuance date	15 Oct. 2025
Maturity	15 Oct. 2030
Years to maturity	5

Period	Time to receipt	Cash flow	*PV*	Weight	Time × Weight
1	1.0000	1.6	1.5748	0.0157	0.0157
2	2.0000	1.6	1.5500	0.0155	0.0310
3	3.0000	1.6	1.5256	0.0153	0.0458
4	4.0000	1.6	1.5016	0.0150	0.0601
5	5.0000	1.6	1.4779	0.0148	0.0739
6	6.0000	1.6	1.4546	0.0145	0.0873
7	7.0000	1.6	1.4317	0.0143	0.1002
8	8.0000	1.6	1.4092	0.0141	0.1127
9	9.0000	1.6	1.3870	0.0139	0.1248
10	10.0000	101.6	86.6875	0.8669	8.6688
			100.0000	1.0000	9.3203

At issuance, the Macaulay duration is 9.3203.

To solve for modified duration, we use Equation 2:

$$ModDur = \frac{MacDur}{(1 + r)}.$$

$$ModDur = \frac{9.3203}{1 + \left(\frac{0.032}{2}\right)}.$$

$ModDur = 9.17351; AnnModDur = 4.58676.$

For settlement 57 days after issuance, the Macaulay duration is 9.0036.

Coupon	3.20%
Coupon frequency per year	1
Price per 100 par value	100
Yield-to-maturity	3.20%
Settlement date	11 Dec. 2025
Maturity	15 Oct. 2030
Years to maturity	10

Period	Time to receipt	Cash flow	*PV*	Weight	Time × Weight
1	0.6833	1.6	1.5827	0.0157	0.0108
2	1.6833	1.6	1.5578	0.0155	0.0261
3	2.6833	1.6	1.5333	0.0153	0.0409
4	3.6833	1.6	1.5091	0.0150	0.0553

Period	Time to receipt	Cash flow	*PV*	Weight	Time × Weight
5	4.6833	1.6	1.4854	0.0148	0.0692
6	5.6833	1.6	1.4620	0.0145	0.0827
7	6.6833	1.6	1.4390	0.0143	0.0957
8	7.6833	1.6	1.4163	0.0141	0.1083
9	8.6833	1.6	1.3940	0.0139	0.1204
10	9.6833	101.6	87.1244	0.8669	8.3942
			100.5039	1.0000	9.0036

To solve for modified duration, we use Equation 2:

$$ModDur = \frac{MacDur}{(1 + r)}.$$

$$ModDur = \frac{9.0036}{1 + \left(\frac{0.032}{2}\right)}.$$

$ModDur = 8.86184; AnnModDur = 4.43092.$

If the annual yield on BRWA's five-year, 3.2% semiannual coupon bond, settling on 15 October 2025 and maturing on 15 October 2030, were to instantaneously (right after issuance) *increase* by 80 bps, to 4.00%, the estimated change in price would be –3.67%.

$$\%\Delta PV^{Full} \approx -4.58676 \times 0.0080 = -0.0366941.$$

If the yield-to-maturity were to instantaneously (right after issuance) *decrease* by 80 bps, to 2.40%, the estimated change in price would be +3.67%.

$$\%\Delta PV^{Full} \approx -4.58676 \times -0.0080 = 0.0366941.$$

Notice that the estimates for price changes are equal (in absolute value) for both an increase and a decrease in the yield-to-maturity. However, as we saw in Exhibit 1, the price–yield relationship is not a straight line but, rather, a curved or "convex" line. In a later lesson, we will add a "convexity adjustment" to account for this and improve the accuracy of price change estimations.

Approximate Modified Duration

While modified duration for a fixed-rate bond can be easily obtained if the Macaulay duration is already known, an alternative approach is to *approximate* modified duration by estimating the slope of the line tangent to the price–yield curve of a bond, as shown in Exhibit 2. This approach is useful for bonds with unknown Macaulay duration, owing to contingency features or default risk, which will be shown in later lessons.

Exhibit 2: Approximating Modified Duration

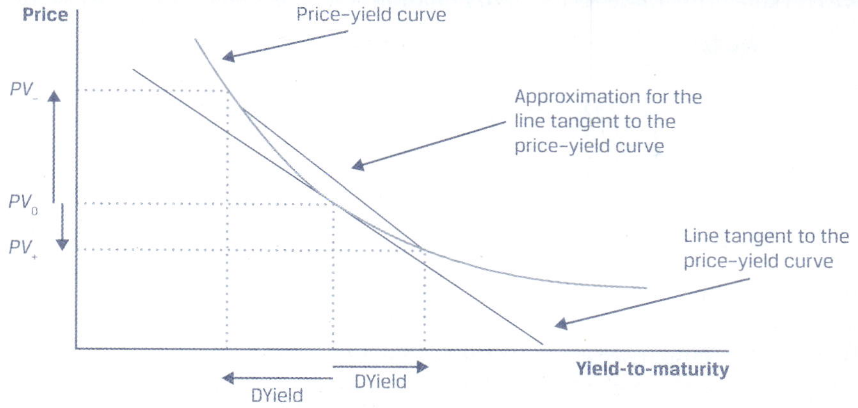

The quoted full price of the bond is denoted PV_0. To estimate the slope, the yield-to-maturity is changed up and down by the same amount—the ΔYield—and is used to calculate corresponding bond prices PV_+ and PV_-. We can use these variables to find the slope of the line tangent to the price–yield curve: the difference between PV_+ and PV_- divided by twice the assumed change in the yield-to-maturity. To find the slope in terms of percentage change in PV_0, we further divide by PV_0. This is shown as Equation 4.

$$AnnModDur \approx \frac{(PV_-)-(PV_+)}{2 \times (\Delta Yield) \times (PV_0)}. \quad (4)$$

This equation approximates *annualized* modified duration; the frequency of coupon payments and the periodicity of the yield-to-maturity are included in the bond price calculations. The following example illustrates the accuracy of this approximation.

EXAMPLE 2

Approximate Modified Duration for the BRWA Bond

Consider BRWA's 3.2% semiannual coupon payment bond for settlement 15 October 2025, maturing 15 October 2030 and yielding 3.2%. The full price (PV_0) is par or 100.00.

We can raise the annual yield-to-maturity by 5 bps, from 3.20% to 3.25% (denoted r_+), to obtain PV_+ of 99.771.

$$PV_+ = \frac{PMT}{(1+r_+)^1} + \frac{PMT}{(1+r_+)^2} + \ldots + \frac{PMT}{(1+r_+)^N} + \frac{FV}{(1+r_+)^N}.$$

$$PV_+ = \frac{1.6}{(1+0.01625)^1} + \frac{1.6}{(1+0.01625)^2} + \ldots + \frac{1.6}{(1+0.01625)^{10}} + \frac{100}{(1+0.01625)^{10}}.$$

$PV_+ = 99.771.$

And we can lower the annual yield-to-maturity by 5 bps, from 3.20% to 3.15% (denoted r_-), to obtain PV_- of 100.230.

$$PV_- = \frac{PMT}{(1+r_-)^1} + \frac{PMT}{(1+r_-)^2} + \ldots + \frac{PMT}{(1+r_-)^N} + \frac{FV}{(1+r_-)^N}.$$

$$PV_- = \frac{1.6}{(1+0.01575)^1} + \frac{1.6}{(1+0.01575)^2} + \ldots + \frac{1.6}{(1+0.01575)^{10}} + \frac{100}{(1+0.01575)^{10}}.$$

$PV_{-} = 100.230.$

We can substitute these results into Equation 4 for the 5 bp change in the annual yield-to-maturity, or $\Delta Yield$ = 0.0005:

$$AnnModDur \approx \frac{(PV_{-}) - (PV_{+})}{2 \times (\Delta Yield) \times (PV_0)}.$$

$$AnnModDur \approx \frac{100.230 - 99.771}{2 \times 0.0005 \times 100}.$$

$$AnnModDur \approx 4.587.$$

The "exact" annual modified duration we calculated for this BRWA bond was 4.58675, and the "approximation" is 4.586765—virtually identical results. Therefore, although duration can be calculated using the Macaulay duration approach, it can also be estimated quite accurately.

The Macaulay duration also can be approximated by multiplying the approximate modified duration by 1 plus the yield per period.

$$AnnMacDur \approx AnnModDur \times (1 + r) \quad (5)$$

QUESTION SET

1. Suppose a 4%, semiannual coupon bond has an annualized Macaulay duration of 3.589. The anticipated percentage change in the bond's full price if the bond's yield rises from 5% to 6% is *closest* to:

   A. 3.485%.

   B. 3.502%.

   C. 3.589%.

   Solution:

   B is correct. The Macaulay duration in years is 3.589; therefore, the annualized modified duration is 3.502%:

   $$ModDur = \frac{MacDur}{(1 + r)}.$$

   $$ModDur = \frac{3.589}{(1 + 0.025)}.$$

   $$ModDur = 3.502.$$

   This results in an estimated percentage change in price for a 100 bp increase in yield of –3.502%:

   $$\%\Delta PV^{Full} \approx -AnnModDur \times \Delta AnnYield.$$

   $$\%\Delta PV^{Full} \approx -3.502 \times 0.01.$$

   $$\%\Delta PV^{Full} \approx -3.502\%.$$

2. True or false: Duration measures are used to measure the sensitivity of flat bond prices to changes in yields.

   A. True

B. False

Solution:

B is correct. Duration measures are used to measure the sensitivity of full prices to changes in yields. Also known as the dirty price of a bond, full prices include the appropriate time value of each cash flow, whereas the flat price does not include accrued interest.

3. Bond C has a coupon rate of 1%, paid semiannually, and matures in five years. If its yield-to-maturity is –0.5%, its Macaulay duration is *most likely*:

   A. less than its modified duration.

   B. the same as its modified duration.

   C. greater than its modified duration.

Solution:

A is correct. Recall that a bond's modified duration is equal to its Macaulay duration divided by 1 plus its yield-to-maturity:

$$ModDur = \frac{MacDur}{(1+r)}.$$

If the yield, r, is negative, the denominator will be less than 1, which results in a *MacDur* less than the modified duration.

4. Consider a zero-coupon bond that matures in five years and is priced to yield 3%. The modified duration of this bond is:

   A. less than five years.

   B. five years.

   C. more than five years.

Solution:

A is correct. The Macaulay duration of a zero-coupon bond is its time-to-maturity, because a zero-coupon bond has a single cash flow with a present value weight of 1.0. The modified duration of this zero-coupon bond is less than its Macaulay duration because its yield is positive.

Questions 5–7 relate to the following information.

Deepak Chowdhury, a bond analyst, is evaluating the BRWA bond, the 1-year Australian government bond, and the 30-year Romanian government bond. Assuming that all three bonds were issued on 15 October 2025 and it is currently 15 January 2026, 92 days into the first coupon period, Chowdhury has compiled the following data:

	BRWA	Australian	Romanian
Coupon	3.200%	0.000%	4.625%
Coupon frequency	2	1	1
Yield-to-maturity	3.200%	1.000%	4.250%
Maturity	15 October 2030	15 October 2026	15 October 2055

5. Complete the following table:

	BRWA	Australian	Romanian
Full price (per 100 of par value)			
Macaulay duration			

	BRWA	Australian	Romanian
Modified duration			
Full price, assuming 5 bp YTM increase			
Full price, assuming 5 bp YTM decrease			
Approx. modified duration			

Solution:

	BRWA	Australian	Romanian
Full price (per 100 of par value)	100.815	99.262	107.429
Annualized Macaulay duration	4.405	0.744	16.939
Annualized modified duration	4.335	0.737	16.248
Full price, assuming 5 bp YTM increase	100.596	99.225	106.561
Full price, assuming 5 bp YTM decrease	101.033	99.299	108.307
Approx. annualized modified duration	4.335	0.737	16.249

The calculations are shown in tabular form. Please refer to the candidate learning ecosystem online for a spreadsheet in the downloadable Microsoft Excel workbook. Note that while solutions are rounded to three decimal places, other quantities are unrounded but shown only to three decimal places for presentation purposes.

BRWA Bond: Full Price and Duration

YTM (periodic)	0.01600

Period	Time to Receipt	Cash Flow	PV	Weight	Time × Weight
1	0.489	1.600	1.588	0.016	0.008
2	1.489	1.600	1.563	0.016	0.023
3	2.489	1.600	1.538	0.015	0.038
4	3.489	1.600	1.514	0.015	0.052
5	4.489	1.600	1.490	0.015	0.066
6	5.489	1.600	1.466	0.015	0.080
7	6.489	1.600	1.443	0.014	0.093
8	7.489	1.600	1.421	0.014	0.106
9	8.489	1.600	1.398	0.014	0.118
10	9.489	101.600	87.394	0.867	8.226
			100.815	1.000	8.809
			Annualized Macaulay Duration		4.405
			Modified Duration		8.670
			Annualized Modified Duration		4.335

BRWA Bond: Full price, assuming 5 bp YTM increase

YTM (periodic)	0.01625

BRWA Bond: Full price, assuming 5 bp YTM decrease

YTM (periodic)	0.01575

Period	Time to Receipt	Cash Flow	PV+	Period	Time to Receipt	Cash Flow	PV-
1	0.489	1.600	1.587	1	0.489	1.600	1.588
2	1.489	1.600	1.562	2	1.489	1.600	1.563
3	2.489	1.600	1.537	3	2.489	1.600	1.539
4	3.489	1.600	1.513	4	3.489	1.600	1.515
5	4.489	1.600	1.488	5	4.489	1.600	1.492
6	5.489	1.600	1.465	6	5.489	1.600	1.468
7	6.489	1.600	1.441	7	6.489	1.600	1.446
8	7.489	1.600	1.418	8	7.489	1.600	1.423
9	8.489	1.600	1.395	9	8.489	1.600	1.401
10	9.489	101.600	87.190	10	9.489	101.600	87.598
			100.596				101.033

BRWA Bond: Approx. Ann. Modified Duration	
PV0	100.815
PV+	100.596
PV-	101.033
Approximate Ann. ModDur	4.335

Australian Bond: Full Price and Duration	
YTM (periodic)	0.010

Period	Time to Receipt	Cash Flow	PV	Weight	Time × Weight
1	0.744	100.000	99.262	1.000	0.744
			99.262	1.000	0.744
				Annualized Macaulay Duration	0.744
				Modified Duration	0.737
				Annualized Modified Duration	0.737

Australian Bond: Full price, assuming 5 bp YTM increase		Australian Bond: Full price, assuming 5 bp YTM decrease	
YTM (periodic)	0.0105	YTM (periodic)	0.0095

Period	Time to Receipt	Cash Flow	PV+	Period	Time to Receipt	Cash Flow	PV-
1	0.744	100.000	99.225	1	0.744	100.000	99.299
			99.225				99.299

Australian Bond: Approx. Ann. Modified Duration	
PV0	99.262
PV+	99.225
PV-	99.299
Approximate Ann. ModDur	0.737

Romanian Bond: Full Price and Duration	
YTM (periodic)	0.0425

Period	Time to Receipt	Cash Flow	PV	Weight	Time × Weight
1	0.744	4.625	4.484	0.042	0.031
2	1.744	4.625	4.301	0.040	0.070
3	2.744	4.625	4.126	0.038	0.105
4	3.744	4.625	3.958	0.037	0.138
5	4.744	4.625	3.796	0.035	0.168
…	…	…	…	…	…
29	28.744	4.625	1.398	0.013	0.374
30	29.744	104.625	30.337	0.282	8.400
			107.429	1.000	16.939
				Annualized Macaulay Duration	16.939
				Modified Duration	16.248
				Annualized Modified Duration	16.248

Romanian Bond: Full price, assuming 5 bp YTM increase		Romanian Bond: Full price, assuming 5 bp YTM decrease	
YTM (periodic)	0.0430	YTM (periodic)	0.0420

Period	Time to Receipt	Cash Flow	PV+	Period	Time to Receipt	Cash Flow	PV-
1	0.744	4.625	4.482	1	0.744	4.625	4.485
2	1.744	4.625	4.297	2	1.744	4.625	4.305

Period	Time to Receipt	Cash Flow	PV+	Period	Time to Receipt	Cash Flow	PV-
3	2.744	4.625	4.120	3	2.744	4.625	4.131
4	3.744	4.625	3.950	4	3.744	4.625	3.965
5	4.744	4.625	3.788	5	4.744	4.625	3.805
…	…	…	…	…	…	…	…
29	28.744	4.625	1.379	29	28.744	4.625	1.417
30	29.744	104.625	29.907	30	29.744	104.625	30.773
			106.561				108.307

Romanian Bond: Approx. Ann. Modified Duration	
PV0	107.429
PV+	106.561
PV-	108.307
Approx. ModDur	16.249

6. Of these three bonds, identify which has the most and least interest rate risk. Justify your answers.

Solution:

The Romanian bond has the most interest rate risk, reflected in the bond's Macaulay and modified durations, which are nearly four times that of the BRWA bond.

The Australian bond has the least interest rate risk, because its Macaulay and modified durations are less than a quarter of that of the BRWA bond.

7. Chowdhury's portfolio manager expects interest rates to decrease from current levels. Which of these three bonds would *most likely* perform best in that environment, all else equal? Justify your answer.

Solution:

The Romanian bond would perform best. A decrease in interest rates would increase bond prices, with those having the greatest interest rate risk or duration having the highest increase.

MONEY DURATION AND PRICE VALUE OF A BASIS POINT 3

☐ define, calculate, and interpret modified duration, money duration, and the price value of a basis point (PVBP)

Modified duration is used to measure the *percentage price change* of a bond given a change in its yield-to-maturity. A related statistic is **money duration**. The money duration of a bond is a measure of the price change in *currency units*. The money duration can be stated per 100 of par value or in terms of the actual position size. In the United States, money duration is commonly called "dollar duration."

Money duration (*MoneyDur*) is the product of the annualized modified duration and the full price (PV^{Full}) of the bond, in either percent of par or the currency value of the position.

$$MoneyDur = AnnModDur \times PV^{Full}. \tag{6}$$

The estimated change in the bond price in currency units is very similar to Equation 4. The difference is that for a given change in the annual yield-to-maturity ($\Delta Yield$), modified duration estimates the percentage price change while money duration estimates the change in currency units.

$$\Delta PV^{Full} \approx -MoneyDur \times \Delta Yield \tag{7}$$

BRWA's five-year, 3.2% semiannual coupon bond, maturing 15 October 2030, is priced to yield 3.2%. Assume it is purchased by an institutional investor for settlement on 11 December 2025, so 57 days into the first coupon period (t/T = 57/180).

The full price of the bond is 100.504 per 100 of par value, and the annualized modified duration is 4.43092. Suppose the investor has a position in the bond for a par value of USD100,000,000. Consequently,

- the market value of the investment is USD100,503,921, and
- the money duration of the investment is USD445,324,719 (= 4.43092 × USD100,503,921).

Therefore, if the yield-to-maturity rises by 100 bps—from 3.20% to 4.20%—the expected loss is approximately USD4,453,247 (= –USD445,324,719 × 0.0100).

A similar measure is the **price value of a basis point (PVBP)**, an estimate of the change in the full price of a bond given a 1 bp change in its yield-to-maturity. The PVBP can be calculated using a formula like that for approximating modified duration. Equation 8 is the formula for the PVBP. PV_- and PV_+ are the full prices calculated by decreasing and increasing the yield-to-maturity by 1 bp.

$$\text{PVBP} = \frac{(PV_-) - (PV_+)}{2}. \tag{8}$$

The PVBP is also called the "PV01," standing for the "price value of an 01" or "present value of an 01," where "01" means 1 bp. In the United States, it is commonly called the "DV01" for the "dollar value" of 1 bp. The PVBP is particularly useful for bonds for which future cash flows are uncertain, such as callable bonds. A related statistic called a "basis point value" (BPV) is simply the money duration times 0.0001 (1 bp).

For a numerical example of the PVBP calculation, again consider BRWA's five-year, 3.2% semiannual coupon bond, maturing 15 October 2030 and priced to yield 3.2%, purchased by the institutional investor for settlement on 11 December 2025, so 57 days into the first coupon period (t/T = 57/180).

To determine the PVBP of this bond, calculate the new prices by increasing and decreasing the yield-to-maturity. First, increase the yield by 1 bp (0.01%), from 3.20% to 3.21%, to solve for a PV_+ of 100.459400.

$$PV_+ = \left[\frac{1.60}{(1.01605)^1} + \ldots + \frac{101.60}{(1.01605)^{10}}\right] \times (1.01605)^{57/180} = 100.459400.$$

Then, decrease the yield-to-maturity by 1 bp, from 3.20% to 3.19%, to solve for a PV_- of 100.548465.

$$PV_- = \left[\frac{1.60}{(1.01595)^1} + \ldots + \frac{101.60}{(1.01595)^{10}}\right] \times (1.01595)^{57/180} = 100.548465.$$

The PVBP is obtained by substituting these results into Equation 8.

$$\text{PVBP} = \frac{100.548465 - 100.459400}{2} = 0.044532.$$

Exhibit 3 provides a summary of the various yield duration statistics. To recap, they measure the instantaneous change in a bond's price for a given change in its own yield-to-maturity, assuming all other variables (especially, time-to-maturity) are unchanged and the underlying cash flows are certain.

Exhibit 3: Summary of Yield-Based Duration Statistics

Measure	Calculation	Use
Macaulay duration	Average time to receipt of promised cash flows, weighted by shares of the full price corresponding to each promised future cash flow	Holding period that would balance reinvestment and price risks for an investor
Modified duration	First derivative of price with respect to yield; Macaulay duration divided by 1 + yield per period	Estimate the percentage price change for a bond given a change in its yield-to-maturity
Money duration	Modified duration multiplied by full price of bond or bond position	Estimate price change in bond investment for a given yield change
Price value of a basis point	Difference in price of a 1 bp yield decrease and a 1 bp yield increase, divided by 2	Estimate of the change in the bond price given a 1 bp change in the yield-to-maturity

Yield Duration of Zero-Coupon and Perpetual Bonds

Because zero-coupon bonds have a single payment, the face value at maturity, the present weighted-average time to receipt of cash flows is the same as the time-to-maturity because that single cash flow has a present value weight of 1.0. Therefore, the Macaulay duration of a zero-coupon bond is its time-to-maturity, and modified duration is its time-to-maturity divided by 1 plus its yield.

A perpetuity or perpetual bond is a bond that does not mature, so there is no face or maturity value received at time *T*. The investor receives a fixed coupon payment forever unless the bond is called. Non-callable perpetuities are rare, but they have an interesting Macaulay duration:

$$MacDur = (1 + r)/r. \quad (9)$$

Duration of Floating-Rate Notes and Loans

As described in an earlier lesson, interest on floating-rate instruments varies depending on the level of a market reference rate (MRR) plus a quoted margin. At predetermined dates, payment amounts are reset to reflect changes in the MRR. Therefore, interest rate risk arises only *between* reset dates, because at the next reset date, coupon payments will adjust to the new MRR. Therefore, the Macaulay duration for a floating-rate note or bond is simply the fraction of a period remaining until the next reset date:

$$MacDur_{Floating} = \frac{(T-t)}{T}. \tag{10}$$

If there are 180 days in the coupon period and 57 days have passed since the last coupon, the Macaulay duration is

$$MacDur_{Floating} = \frac{(180-57)}{180} = 0.683333.$$

Floating-rate instruments typically have very low duration because coupon periods are typically less than six months in length. As a result, they are commonly used by investors to reduce duration in fixed-income portfolios.

KNOWLEDGE CHECK

An analyst is comparing the interest rate risk of the BRWA 3.2% bond maturing 15 October 2030 to a floating-rate note (FRN) that also matures 15 October 2030 and has its coupon reset semiannually.

At the last reset, 15 October 2027, the coupon rate of the FRN was 3.2%. The BRWA bond was priced to yield 3.2% at that same date.

1. Why would you expect the FRN to have a lower duration than the BRWA fixed-rate bond?

   Solution:

   A floating-rate instrument has a Macaulay duration that reflects the time to the next coupon reset date, while a fixed-rate instrument has a Macaulay duration that primarily reflects time-to-maturity but also its coupon rate, yield, and fraction of the coupon period that has passed. The maximum Macaulay duration the FRN would have is six months, while the BRWA bond has a Macaulay duration slightly lower than its maturity (five years).

2. Complete the following table:

	Macaulay duration	
	BRWA	FRN
15-Oct-2027		
15-Nov-2027		
15-Dec-2027		
15-Jan-2028		
15-Feb-2028		
15-Mar-2028		
15-Apr-2028		

   Solution:

	Macaulay duration	
	BRWA	**FRN**
15-Oct-2027	2.8843	0.0000
15-Nov-2027	2.8002	0.8306
15-Dec-2027	2.7169	0.6667
15-Jan-2028	2.6336	0.4973
15-Feb-2028	2.5502	0.3279
15-Mar-2028	2.4669	0.1694
15-Apr-2028	2.4221	0.0000

For example, for 15 December 2027, the number of days since the next coupon is 61 days. The number of days in the coupon period is 183, calculated using Microsoft Excel or Google Sheets as

= COUPDAYS(DATE(2027,12,15),DATE(2028,4,15),2,1).

Therefore, the Macaulay duration is $(183 - 61) \div 183 = 0.6667$.

QUESTION SET

Deepak Chowdhury is evaluating a USD30 million investment in par value terms in the BRWA, Australian, and Romanian bonds. Assume all bonds are denominated in the same currency and that all three bonds were issued on 15 October 2025.

Chowdhury is evaluating the bonds on 15 January 2026, 92 days into the first coupon period. Chowdhury has compiled the following data.

Characteristic	BRWA	Australian	Romanian
Coupon	3.200%	0.000%	4.625%
Coupon frequency	2	1	1
Yield-to-maturity	3.200%	1.000%	4.250%
Maturity	15 October 2030	15 October 2026	15 October 2055
Full price	100.815	99.262	107.429
Ann. Macaulay duration	4.405	0.744	16.939
Ann. modified duration	4.335	0.737	16.248

As part of his analysis, Chowdhury is evaluating the potential change in the prices of the bond investments for 1 bp and 100 bp changes in yields.

1. Complete the following table:

	Effect on a USD30 million investment		
	BRWA	**Australian**	**Romanian**
Price value per basis point			
Market value of investment (USD)			

	Effect on a USD30 million investment		
	BRWA	Australian	Romanian
Money duration (percent of par)			
Expected loss from a 100 bp YTM increase (USD)			

Solution:

	Effect on a USD30 million investment		
	BRWA	Australia	Romania
Price value per basis point	0.044	0.007	0.175
Market value of investment (USD)	30,244,381	29,778,597	32,228,627
Money duration (percent of par)	437.054	73.163	1745.518
Expected loss from a 100 bp YTM increase (USD)	−1,311,163	−219,490	−5,236,553

The calculations are shown in tabular form. Please refer to the candidate learning ecosystem online for a spreadsheet in the downloadable Microsoft Excel workbook. Note that while solutions are rounded to three decimal places, other quantities are unrounded but shown only to three decimal places for presentation purposes.

BRWA Bond: Full price, assuming 1 bp YTM increase

YTM (periodic)	0.01605		
Period	**Time to Receipt**	**Cash Flow**	**PV+**
1	0.489	1.600	1.588
2	1.489	1.600	1.563
3	2.489	1.600	1.538
4	3.489	1.600	1.514
5	4.489	1.600	1.490
6	5.489	1.600	1.466
7	6.489	1.600	1.443
8	7.489	1.600	1.420
9	8.489	1.600	1.398
10	9.489	101.600	87.353
			100.771

BRWA Bond: Full price, assuming 1 bp YTM decrease

YTM (periodic)	0.01595		
Period	**Time to Receipt**	**Cash Flow**	**PV-**
1	0.489	1.600	1.588
2	1.489	1.600	1.563
3	2.489	1.600	1.538
4	3.489	1.600	1.514
5	4.489	1.600	1.490
6	5.489	1.600	1.467
7	6.489	1.600	1.444
8	7.489	1.600	1.421
9	8.489	1.600	1.399
10	9.489	101.600	87.435
			100.858

BRWA Bond

PV+	100.771	Full price	100.815
PV-	100.858	Par	30,000,000
PVBP	0.044	Market value	30,244,381
AnnModDur	4.335	MoneyDur	437.054

BRWA Bond

Full price	100.815	MV	30,244,381
MoneyDur	437.054	ChgYield	0.01
		Exp. Loss	(1,311,163)

Australian Bond: Full price, assuming 1 bp YTM increase		**Australian Bond: Full price, assuming 1 bp YTM decrease**	
YTM (periodic)	0.0101	YTM (periodic)	0.0099

Period	Time to Receipt	Cash Flow	PV+	Period	Time to Receipt	Cash Flow	PV-
1	0.744	100.000	99.255	1	0.744	100.000	99.269
			99.255				99.269

Australian Bond

PV+	99.255	Full price	99.262
PV-	99.269	Par	30,000,000
PVBP	0.007	Market value	29,778,597
AnnModDur	0.737	MoneyDur	73.163
Full price	99.262	MV	29,778,597
MoneyDur	73.163	ChgYield	0.01
		Exp. Loss	(219,490)

Romanian Bond: Full price, assuming 1 bp YTM increase		**Romanian Bond: Full price, assuming 1 bp YTM decrease**	
YTM (periodic)	0.0426	YTM (periodic)	0.0424

Period	Time to Receipt	Cash Flow	PV+	Period	Time to Receipt	Cash Flow	PV-
1	0.744	4.625	4.484	1	0.744	4.625	4.484
2	1.744	4.625	4.300	2	1.744	4.625	4.302
3	2.744	4.625	4.125	3	2.744	4.625	4.127
4	3.744	4.625	3.956	4	3.744	4.625	3.959
5	4.744	4.625	3.794	5	4.744	4.625	3.798
...	...	...	...	...	...	...	...
29	28.744	4.625	1.394	29	28.744	4.625	1.402
30	29.744	104.625	30.251	30	29.744	104.625	30.424
			107.254				107.604

Romanian Bond

PV+	107.254	Full price	107.429
PV-	107.604	Par	30,000,000
PVBP	0.175	MV	32,228,627
AnnModDur	16.248	MoneyDur	1745.518
Full price	107.429	MV	32,228,627
MoneyDur	1745.518	ChgYield	0.01
		Exp. Loss	(5,236,553)

2. If the client believes that interest rates will rise in the future, with all else held constant, which bond investment would *most likely* perform best?

Solution:

The Australian bond would perform best. Since it has the lowest duration and PVBP, the expected loss on the investment from an increase in its yield is lower than the BRWA and Romanian bonds. The expected loss from a 100 bp increase in yield on the BRWA bond, for example, is almost six times that for the Australian bond (USD219,490 versus USD1.3 million).

4 PROPERTIES OF DURATION

☐ explain how a bond's maturity, coupon, and yield level affect its interest rate risk

The Macaulay and modified yield duration statistics for a traditional fixed-rate bond are primarily functions of the bond's features: its time-to-maturity, its coupon rate, its yield-to-maturity, and the fraction of the current coupon period that has elapsed. The closed-form formula for Macaulay duration, presented in a prior lesson and again here, is useful in demonstrating the characteristics of duration (the same characteristics hold for modified duration, money duration, and price value of basis point).

$$MacDur = \left\{\frac{1+r}{r} - \frac{1+r+[N\times(c-r)]}{c\times\left[(1+r)^N-1\right]+r}\right\} - \frac{t}{T}$$

The relationship between a bond's duration and its features (r, c, N, and t/T) are summarized in Exhibit 4.

Exhibit 4: Properties of Yield Duration Statistics

	Effect on duration (interest rate risk) from an *increase* in feature
Coupon rate, c	↓ (Inverse relationship)
Yield to maturity, r	↓ (Inverse relationship)

	Effect on duration (interest rate risk) from an *increase* in feature
Time-to-maturity, T	↑ (Direct relationship)
Fraction of current coupon period that has elapsed, t/T	↓ (Inverse relationship)

Exhibit 5 illustrates the relationships between Macaulay duration and time-to-maturity for premium, discount, zero-coupon, and perpetual bonds (the same characteristics hold for modified duration, money duration, and price value of basis point).

Exhibit 5: Properties of Macaulay Duration

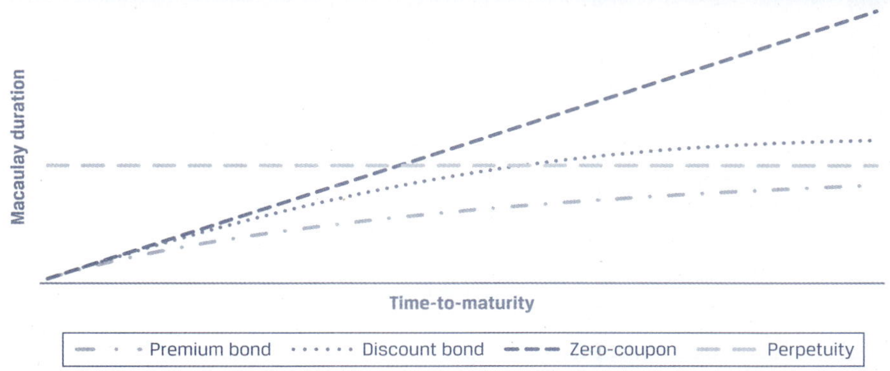

All else being equal,

- *a lower-coupon bond has a higher duration and more interest rate risk than a higher-coupon bond.*

The same pattern holds for the yield-to-maturity, so,

- *a lower yield-to-maturity increases the weighted average of the time to receipt of cash flow and thus increases duration.*

The reason is that lower coupons and lower yields increase the weight of the maturity value or final cash flow and reduce the weight of nearer-term cash flows in the bond price.

- *Longer times-to-maturity typically correspond to higher duration.*

This pattern always holds for bonds trading at par or at a premium. In the closed-form formula, the second expression within brackets is positive for premium and par bonds, because the coupon rate (c) is greater than or equal to the yield-to-maturity (r), so $(c - r) \geq 0$, whereas the denominator is always positive. Therefore, the Macaulay duration is always less than $(1 + r)/r$, and it approaches that threshold from below as the time-to-maturity increases.

A curious result is illustrated in Exhibit 5 for *discount bonds*: at some point, when the time-to-maturity is high enough, the Macaulay duration will exceed $(1 + r)/r$, reach a maximum, and then decrease. This pattern develops when the number of periods (N) is large and the coupon rate is below the yield-to-maturity, so $(c - r) < 0$. Then, the numerator of the second expression within braces can become negative. The implication is that for long-dated bonds trading at a discount to par, interest rate risk could be lower than that of a shorter-term bond.

For a constant yield-to-maturity (r), the expression in braces in the closed-form formula is unchanged as time passes *during the period*. Therefore, the Macaulay duration decreases smoothly as time passes and then jumps upward after the coupon is paid, which creates a "saw-tooth" pattern. This pattern for the BRWA bond with a constant yield-to-maturity is illustrated in Exhibit 6. As time passes, the Macaulay duration decreases smoothly but jumps upward by a small amount on coupon dates.

Exhibit 6: Macaulay Duration between Coupon Payments with Constant Yield-to-Maturity for the BRWA 3.2% Bond

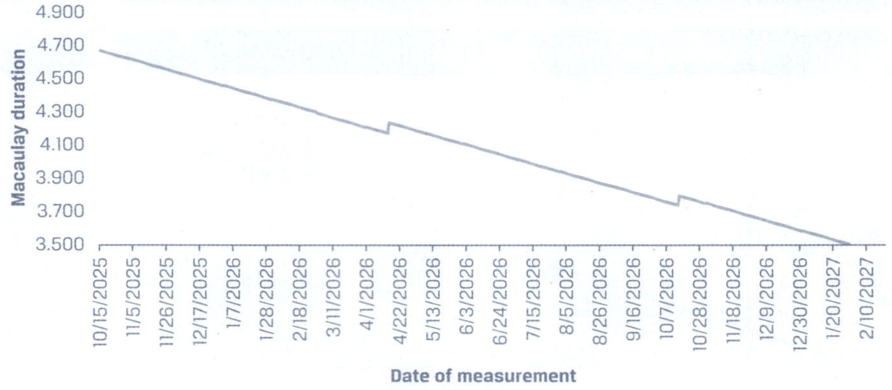

QUESTION SET

1. For each pair of bonds, indicate the bond that *most likely* has greater interest rate risk:

<table>
<tr><th>First bond</th><th>Second bond</th><th>Which has greater interest rate risk?</th></tr>
<tr><td rowspan="4">4% coupon, paid semiannually, and five years to maturity, priced to yield 6%</td><td>5% coupon, paid semiannually, and five years to maturity, priced to yield 6%</td><td></td></tr>
<tr><td>4% coupon, paid semiannually, and six years to maturity, priced to yield 6%</td><td></td></tr>
<tr><td>5% coupon, paid semiannually, and five years to maturity, priced to yield 8%</td><td></td></tr>
<tr><td>4% coupon, paid semiannually, and five years to maturity, priced to yield 8%</td><td></td></tr>
</table>

Solution:

First bond	Second bond	Which has greater interest rate risk?
4% coupon, paid semiannually, and five years to maturity, priced to yield 6%	5% coupon, paid semiannually, and five years to maturity, priced to yield 6%	First bond
	4% coupon, paid semi-annually, and six years to maturity, priced to yield 6%	Second bond
	5% coupon, paid semiannually, and five years to maturity, priced to yield 8%	First bond
	4% coupon, paid semiannually, and five years to maturity, priced to yield 8%	First bond

2. A bond analyst is comparing Bond D, a perpetual bond with a coupon of 5%, with Bond E, a zero-coupon bond maturing in five years. If both bonds are priced to yield 6%, Bond D has:

   A. lower interest rate risk.

   B. the same interest rate risk.

   C. higher interest rate risk.

   Solution:

   C is correct. The Macaulay duration for Bond D is 1.06/0.06 = 17.667. The Macaulay duration for Bond E is five years. The perpetual bond, Bond D, has higher interest rate risk.

3. The graph depicts the price–yield relationships for three bonds, Bond X, Bond Y, and Bond Z. The three bonds have the same coupon rate, 5%.

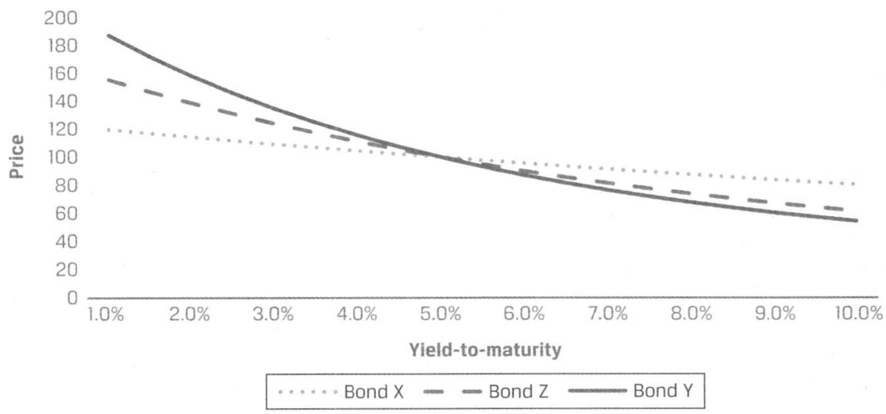

   Which of the three bonds *most likely* has the longest time to maturity?

   A. Bond X

   B. Bond Y

C. Bond Z

Solution:

B is correct. Bond Y has the steepest price-yield line, indicating that it has the greatest modified duration and, most likely, the longest time-to-maturity.

4. Between coupon payments, if the yield-to-maturity does not change, the Macaulay duration of a bond:

   A. decreases throughout the coupon period.

   B. is constant throughout the coupon period.

   C. increases throughout the coupon period.

   Solution:

   A is correct. During the coupon period, the Macaulay duration declines smoothly until the next coupon period, at which time it jumps. This is illustrated in Exhibit 6.

5. Two bonds have the same time-to-maturity and yield-to-maturity, but one is trading at a premium to par and the other at a discount. The Macaulay duration for the premium bond is *most likely*_________ that of the discount bond.

   A. lower than

   B. the same as

   C. higher than

   Solution:

   A is correct. If two bonds have the same maturity and the same yield-to-maturity but one trades at a premium and one trades at a discount to par, the premium bond must have a higher coupon rate. Therefore, the premium bond has the lower Macaulay duration.

PRACTICE PROBLEMS

1. *True or false:* Curve duration is a type of yield duration.

   A. True

   B. False

The following information relates to questions 2-7

A portfolio manager is assessing the interest rate risk of three bonds as she considers making an investment of USD50 million. All three bonds are issued on 1 June 2026 and mature on 1 June 2030, and they have the following characteristics:

Characteristic	Bond One	Bond Two	Bond Three
Coupon (semiannual)	7%	3%	5%
Yield-to-maturity	3%	7%	5%

2. The Macaulay duration, in years, for Bond One is *closest* to:

   A. 3.54.

   B. 3.59.

   C. 3.78.

3. The modified duration for Bond Two is *closest* to:

   A. 3.59.

   B. 3.65.

   C. 3.78

4. Relative to a five-year zero-coupon bond priced to yield 5%, Bond Three has a modified duration that is *best* described as:

   A. lower than the zero-coupon bond's modified duration.

   B. the same as the zero-coupon bond's modified duration.

   C. greater than the zero-coupon bond's modified duration.

5. If the yields-to-maturity for all three bonds were to increase by 100 bps, which bond has the greatest anticipated decrease in price?

   A. Bond One

   B. Bond Two

   C. Bond Three

6. Which bond has the highest price value of a basis point?

   A. Bond One

   B. Bond Two

   C. Bond Three

7. The portfolio manager is interested in comparing the interest rate risk of Bond Three to that of Bond Four, a floating-rate note that resets every six months. On 1 June 2026, both bonds were priced to yield 5%. If the yield changes from 5% to 5.25% halfway through the first coupon period, which bond has the greater Macaulay duration?

   A. Bond Three

   B. Bond Four

   C. Neither: The Macaulay duration is the same for both bonds.

SOLUTIONS

1. B is correct. The Macaulay, modified, and money duration measures, as well as the price value of a basis point, are all types of yield duration. The curve duration is not classified as a type of yield duration.

2. B is correct.

Period	Time to receipt	Cash flow	Present value	Weight	Time to receipt × weight
1	1.0000	3.5	3.44828	0.02999	0.02999
2	2.0000	3.5	3.39732	0.02955	0.05910
3	3.0000	3.5	3.34711	0.02911	0.08734
4	4.0000	3.5	3.29764	0.02868	0.11473
5	5.0000	3.5	3.24891	0.02826	0.14129
6	6.0000	3.5	3.20090	0.02784	0.16704
7	7.0000	3.5	3.15359	0.02743	0.19200
8	8.0000	103.5	91.87810	0.79914	6.39308
			114.97185	1.00000	7.18458
Annualized Macaulay duration					3.59229

3. B is correct.

Period	Time to receipt	Cash flow	Present value	Weight	Time to receipt × weight
1	1.0000	1.5	1.44928	0.01680	0.01680
2	2.0000	1.5	1.40027	0.01623	0.03247
3	3.0000	1.5	1.35291	0.01569	0.04706
4	4.0000	1.5	1.30716	0.01516	0.06062
5	5.0000	1.5	1.26296	0.01464	0.07321
6	6.0000	1.5	1.22025	0.01415	0.08488
7	7.0000	1.5	1.17899	0.01367	0.09568
8	8.0000	101.5	77.08027	0.89366	7.14930
			86.25209	1.00000	7.56003
Annualized Macaulay duration					3.780016
Modified duration					3.652190

4. A is correct. No calculation is necessary, as we know that a five-year zero-coupon bond has a Macaulay duration of 5, which is greater than that of a coupon bond like Bond three. Since they have the same yields, the bond's modified durations will have the same relationship as their Macaulay duration.

   Alternatively, we can calculate Bond Three's modified duration of 3.585:

Period	Time to receipt	Cash flow	Present value	Weight	Time to receipt × weight
1	1.0000	2.5	2.43902	0.02439	0.02439
2	2.0000	2.5	2.37954	0.02380	0.04759
3	3.0000	2.5	2.32150	0.02321	0.06964
4	4.0000	2.5	2.26488	0.02265	0.09060
5	5.0000	2.5	2.20964	0.02210	0.11048
6	6.0000	2.5	2.15574	0.02156	0.12934
7	7.0000	2.5	2.10316	0.02103	0.14722
8	8.0000	102.5	84.12652	0.84127	6.73012
			100.00000	1.00000	7.34939
			Annualized Macaulay duration		3.6747
			Modified duration		3.5851

The zero-coupon's modified duration is 5/(1 + 0.05) = 4.7619.

5. B is correct.

	Bond One	Bond Two	Bond Three
Full price (percent of par)	114.972	86.252	100.000
Modified duration	3.539	3.652	3.585
Investment (in USD millions)	50	50	50
Money duration	176.960	182.609	179.253
Change in value (in USD millions)	−1.770	−1.826	−1.793

6. A is correct.

	Bond One	Bond Two	Bond Three
Price	114.972	86.252	100.000
Price + 1 bp	114.931	86.221	99.964
Price – 1 bp	115.013	86.284	100.036
PVBP	0.04069	0.03150	0.03585

7. A is correct. The Macaulay duration for Bond Three is 3.6747. The Macaulay duration for Bond Four is 0.5 because there is exposure to interest rate changes for one-half of the coupon period.

LEARNING MODULE

12

Yield-Based Bond Convexity and Portfolio Properties

LEARNING OUTCOMES

Mastery	The candidate should be able to:
☐	calculate and interpret convexity and describe the convexity adjustment
☐	calculate the percentage price change of a bond for a specified change in yield, given the bond's duration and convexity
☐	calculate portfolio duration and convexity and explain the limitations of these measures

INTRODUCTION

1

While duration is a linear approximation of the sensitivity of a bond's price to changes in yield, the true relationship between a bond's price and its yield-to-maturity is a curved (convex) line. We introduce convexity as a complementary risk measure to improve bond price change estimates based on modified duration alone to account for this non-linear relationship. The convexity adjustment becomes more important when considering larger moves in yield-to-maturity and longer-maturity bonds. These lessons will also show how to estimate duration and convexity for a portfolio of bonds, as well as highlight limitations due to underlying assumptions.

Most of the examples and exhibits used throughout the reading can be downloaded as a Microsoft Excel workbook. Each worksheet in the workbook is labeled with the corresponding example or exhibit number in the text.

LEARNING MODULE OVERVIEW

- Convexity is a complementary risk metric that measures the second-order (non-linear) effect of yield changes on price for an option-free fixed-rate bond. The convexity adjustment adds to the linear price estimate provided by modified duration.

- Convexity is always positive for an option-free fixed-rate bond, such that estimated price increases from a decline in yields are higher than duration alone would suggest and estimated price decreases from an increase in yields are lower than duration alone would suggest. Therefore, convexity is valuable to investors.
- Convexity has the same relationship with bond features as duration: a fixed-rate bond will have greater convexity the longer its time-to-maturity, the lower its coupon rate, and the lower its yield-to-maturity.
- Money convexity expresses convexity in terms of currency units or percent of par for a position in a bond because it is the product of a bond's annual convexity and its full price.
- Portfolio duration and convexity can be calculated (1) as the weighted average of time to receipt of the aggregate cash flows or (2) by using the weighted averages of the durations and convexities of the individual bonds that make up the portfolio.
- While the first method is theoretically correct, it is difficult to use in practice. The second method is commonly used by portfolio managers but implicitly assumes parallel shifts in the yield curve, which are rare.

LEARNING MODULE SELF-ASSESSMENT

These initial questions are intended to help you gauge your current level of understanding of the learning module.

1. The annualized convexity of a four-year, 2.8% (semiannual) coupon bond priced at par at issuance on 1 August 2035 and maturing on 1 August 2039 is *closest* to:

   A. 7.624.

   B. 16.413.

   C. 65.651.

   Solution:

   B is correct.

Four-Year, 2.8% Semiannual Bond at Issuance

Fixed Coupon (%)	2.80
Periods p.a.	2
Price (per 100 Par Value)	100
Yield-to-Maturity (%)	2.8000

(1)	(2)	(3)	(4)	(5)	(6) = (2) × (5)	(7) = Col. 2 × (Col. 2 + 1) × Col. 5 × (1 + YTM/2)$^{-2}$
Period	**Time to Receipt**	**Cash Flow**	**Present Value**	**Weight**	**Time to Receipt × Weight**	**Convexity of Cash Flows**
1	1.0	1.4	1.380671	0.01381	0.01381	0.02686
2	2.0	1.4	1.361608	0.01362	0.02723	0.07946
3	3.0	1.4	1.342809	0.01343	0.04028	0.15672
4	4.0	1.4	1.324269	0.01324	0.05297	0.25759
5	5.0	1.4	1.305985	0.01306	0.06530	0.38105
6	6.0	1.4	1.287954	0.01288	0.07728	0.52611
7	7.0	1.4	1.270171	0.01270	0.08891	0.69179
8	8.0	101.4	90.726533	0.90727	7.25812	63.53176
			100.0000	**1.00000**	**7.62391**	**65.65133**
Annualized Macaulay Duration and Convexity					**3.81195**	**16.41283**

Annualized convexity is 16.41283 and results from the sum of Column 7 (65.65133) divided by the square of the periods per year (two periods per year: $2^2 = 4$).

2. Identify which of the following statements is true. The convexity adjustment:

   A. is always negative for an option-free fixed-rate bond.

   B. accounts for the first-order effect of yield changes on a bond.

   C. is added to the bond price change estimate provided by modified duration.

   Solution:

   C is correct. The convexity adjustment is added to the price change estimate provided by modified duration for a given change in yield-to-maturity:

$$\%\Delta P\, V^{Full} \approx (-AnnModDur \times \Delta Yield) + \left[\frac{1}{2} \times AnnConvexity \times (\Delta Yield)^2\right].$$

   A is incorrect because convexity is always positive for an option-free fixed-rate bond.

   B is incorrect because convexity accounts for the second-order effect of yield changes on a bond's price and duration accounts for the first-order effect.

Questions 3 and 4 relate to the following information.

An investor holds a GBP50,000,000 position in a 10-year, 3.50% fixed-coupon bond (semiannual) trading at par value. Annualized modified duration is 8.376, and annualized convexity is 81.701. The investor expects interest rates to decline by 100 bps.

3. The expected percentage change in the price of the bond is *closest* to:

   A. 7.97%.

   B. 8.01%.

   C. 8.78%.

   Solution:

   C is correct. The expected price change is calculated as follows:

$$\%\Delta PV^{Full} \approx (-AnnModDur \times \Delta Yield) + \left[\tfrac{1}{2} \times AnnConvexity \times (\Delta Yield)^2\right].$$

$$\%\Delta PV^{Full} \approx (-8.376 \times -0.01) + \left[\tfrac{1}{2} \times 81.701 \times (-0.01)^2\right].$$

$$\%\Delta PV^{Full} \approx 0.0878 = 8.78\%$$

4. The addition of money convexity to the estimated change in the value of the bond position using money duration alone is *closest* to:

   A. GBP204,252.

   B. GBP408,503.

   C. GBP4,188,220.

   Solution:

   A is correct. This question is asking for the money convexity adjustment. First we calculate money convexity:

   $$MoneyCon = AnnConvexity \times PV^{Full}.$$

   $$MoneyCon = 81.701 \times \text{GBP}50{,}000{,}000.$$

   $$MoneyCon = \text{GBP}4{,}085{,}033{,}604.$$

   Then we calculate the money convexity adjustment:

   $$MoneyConv.Adjustment \approx \left[\tfrac{1}{2} \times MoneyConvexity \times (\Delta Yield)^2\right].$$

   $$MoneyConv.Adjustment \approx \left[\tfrac{1}{2} \times \text{GBP}4{,}085{,}033{,}604 \times (-0.01)^2\right].$$

   $$MoneyConv.Adjustment \approx \text{GBP}204{,}252.$$

5. A EUR100 million bond portfolio contains the following bonds:

Bond	Maturity (yrs.)	YTM (%)	Market Value	Annualized Modified Duration	Annualized Convexity
A	3	2.80%	EUR40,000,000	2.858	9.752
B	10	3.50%	EUR60,000,000	8.376	81.701

   The expected percentage price change of the bond portfolio given a 50 bp increase in yield-to-maturity is *closest* to:

   A. 3.018%.

   B. 3.085%.

   C. 3.151%.

   Solution:

   A is correct. The weights of Bond A and Bond B are 40% and 60%, respectively. As a result, the portfolio weighted-average duration and convexity measures are 6.169 and 52.921, respectively. The expected portfolio percentage price change given a 50 bp increase in YTM is calculated as follows:

   $$\%\Delta PV^{Full} \approx (-AnnModDur \times \Delta Yield) + \left[\tfrac{1}{2} \times AnnConvexity \times (\Delta Yield)^2\right].$$

$$\%\Delta PV^{Full} \approx (-6.169 \times 0.005) + \left[\frac{1}{2} \times 52.921 \times (0.005)^2\right].$$

$$\%\Delta PV^{Full} \approx -3.018\%$$

6. Using weighted-average duration and convexity measures to estimate bond portfolio interest rate risk:

   A. is difficult in practice.

   B. is the theoretically correct approach.

   C. assumes a parallel shift in the yield curve.

   Solution:

   C is correct. Using the weighted-average duration and convexity measures to estimate bond portfolio interest rate risk is easy in practice, but it is not the theoretically correct approach (using the weighted average of time to receipt of the aggregate cash flows is theoretically correct). It does, however, implicitly assume a parallel shift in the yield curve.

BOND CONVEXITY AND CONVEXITY ADJUSTMENT 2

☐ calculate and interpret convexity and describe the convexity adjustment

Interest rate risk, or the sensitivity of a bond's price to changes in yield, is an important concept used to analyze fixed-income exposures. As a key risk metric, modified duration measures the first-order (linear) effect on a bond's price change given a yield-to-maturity change. **Convexity** is a complementary risk metric that measures the second-order (non-linear) effect of yield changes on price for an option-free fixed-rate bond, as shown in Exhibit 1.

Exhibit 1: Convexity of an Option-Free Fixed-Rate Bond

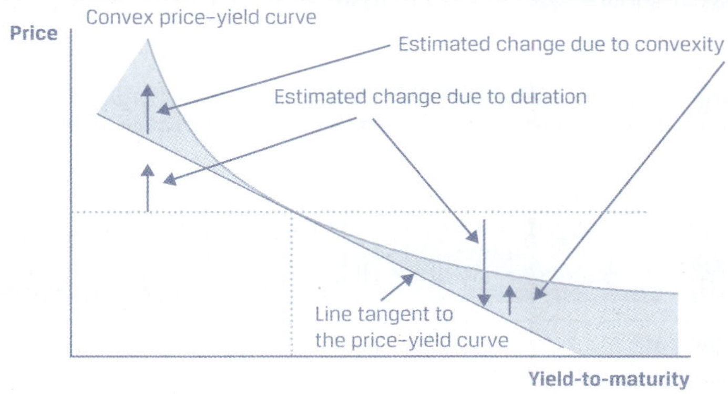

The true relationship between a bond's price and its yield-to-maturity is the curved (convex) line that shows the actual bond price given its market discount rate. Duration (i.e., money duration) estimates the change in the bond price along the straight line tangent to the curved line. For small yield-to-maturity changes, there is little difference between the lines.

However, for larger yield changes, the difference becomes significant and duration alone is an insufficient risk measure. In such cases, a proper assessment requires capturing the non-linear price effect of convexity. By considering duration and convexity metrics together for relatively large yield changes, the estimated bond prices are substantially closer to the actual bond prices. That is, when including convexity, bond prices rise more when yields decrease and fall less when yields increase than when estimated using duration alone.

As shown in Equation 1, convexity adds to the estimate of the percentage (full) price change provided when using modified duration by itself, which was used in prior lessons.

$$\%\Delta PV^{Full} \approx (-AnnModDur \times \Delta Yield) + \left[\frac{1}{2} \times AnnConvexity \times (\Delta Yield)^2\right]. \quad (1)$$

The first expression in parentheses is the effect from modified duration. The expression in brackets is the **convexity adjustment**: the annual convexity statistic, *AnnConvexity*, times one-half times the change in the yield-to-maturity *squared.* This term is always positive for an option-free fixed-rate bond, so, as noted, the bond price is higher for either an increase or decrease in yield (see Exhibit 1).

Similar to Macaulay and modified durations, *AnnConvexity* can be calculated in several ways: (1) using a Microsoft Excel spreadsheet, (2) using an approximation method, and (3) using a closed-form equation derived from calculus. We will now demonstrate methods 1 and 2.

Consider once again BRWA's five-year, 3.2% (semiannual) coupon bond priced at par for settlement on 15 October 2025 and maturity on 15 October 2030. Exhibit 2 is an interactive spreadsheet in the downloadable Microsoft Excel workbook that shows the calculation of *AnnConvexity* for this bond; notice that it is very similar to the one used to calculate duration. The difference is the inclusion of a new column (Col. 7) for the following operation (where *CF* means cash flow) to calculate convexity:

(Time to receipt of *CF*) × (Time to receipt of *CF* + 1) × (Weight of *CF*) × (1 + Periodic *YTM*)$^{(-\text{Periods per year})}$.

Note that the intermediate result of multiplying the first two terms introduces non-linearity (Time to receipt of CF^2). Dividing the sum of Column 7 (96.95578) by periods per year squared (2^2=4) results in an annualized convexity (*AnnConvexity*) statistic of 24.2389.

Exhibit 2: Convexity Calculation for an Option-Free Fixed-Rate Bond

BRWA Corporation Five-Year, 3.2% Semiannual Bond at Issuance	
Principal	$300,000,000
Fixed Coupon (%)	3.20
Periods p.a.	2
Price (per 100 Par Value)	100
Yield-to-Maturity (%)	3.20

Col. 1	Col. 2	Col. 3	Col. 4	Col. 5	Col. 6 = Col. 2 × Col. 5	Col. 7 = Col. 2 × (Col. 2 + 1) × Col. 5 × (1 + YTM/2)^-2
Period	**Time to Receipt**	**Cash Flow**	**Present Value**	**Weight**	**Time to Receipt × Weight**	**Convexity of Cash Flows**
1	1.0	1.6	1.5748	0.0157	0.0157	0.0305
2	2.0	1.6	1.5500	0.0155	0.0310	0.0901
3	3.0	1.6	1.5256	0.0153	0.0458	0.1774
4	4.0	1.6	1.5016	0.0150	0.0601	0.2909
5	5.0	1.6	1.4779	0.0148	0.0739	0.4295
6	6.0	1.6	1.4546	0.0145	0.0873	0.5919
7	7.0	1.6	1.4317	0.0143	0.1002	0.7767
8	8.0	1.6	1.4092	0.0141	0.1127	0.9829
9	9.0	1.6	1.3870	0.0139	0.1248	1.2093
10	10.0	101.6	86.6875	0.8669	8.6688	92.3766
			100.0000	**1.0000**	**9.3203**	**96.9558**
Annualized Macaulay Duration and Convexity					**4.6601**	**24.2389**

Exhibit 2 can also be viewed as a spreadsheet on the candidate learning ecosystem online in the downloadable Microsoft Excel workbook.

Alternatively, Equation 2 can be used to approximate annualized convexity (*ApproxCon*). This approach is useful for bonds with uncertain cash flows, such as those with contingency features and default risk, which will be explored in later lessons. Note that this equation uses the same inputs as approximating modified duration.

$$ApproxCon = \frac{(PV_-) + (PV_+) - [2 \times (PV_0)]}{(\Delta Yield)^2 \times (PV_0)}. \quad (2)$$

For BRWA's bond, first raise the annual yield-to-maturity by 5 bps, from 3.20% to 3.25%, and determine PV_+. Next, lower it by 5 bps, to 3.15%, and determine PV_-. These are the new full prices (original price is PV_0 = 100.00). Using Excel's PRICE function,

PRICE(*settlement, maturity, rate, yield, redemption, frequency, [basis]*),

we have the following:

PV_+ = PRICE(DATE(2025,10,15),DATE(2030,10,15),0.032,0.0325,100,2,0)
= 99.770965.

PV_- = PRICE(DATE(2025,10,15),DATE(2030,10,15),0.032,0.0315,100,2,0)
= 100.229641.

Applying Equation 2, *ApproxCon* is estimated to be 24.23896, which is a very close approximation to the bond's *AnnConvexity* of 24.23895 we calculated in Exhibit 2.

$$ApproxCon = \frac{100.229641 + 99.770965 - (2 \times 100.00)}{(0.0005)^2 \times 100.00} = 24.23896.$$

Bond features that lead to greater convexity are the same as for duration. A fixed-rate bond will have greater convexity:

- the *longer* its time-to-maturity,

- the *lower* its coupon rate, and
- the *lower* its yield-to-maturity.

Another factor is the dispersion of cash flows, meaning the degree to which payments are spread out over time. For two bonds with the same duration, the one with the greater dispersion of cash flows has greater convexity. The positive attributes of convexity for an investor are shown in Exhibit 3.

Exhibit 3: Positive Attributes of Bond Convexity on an Option-Free Bond

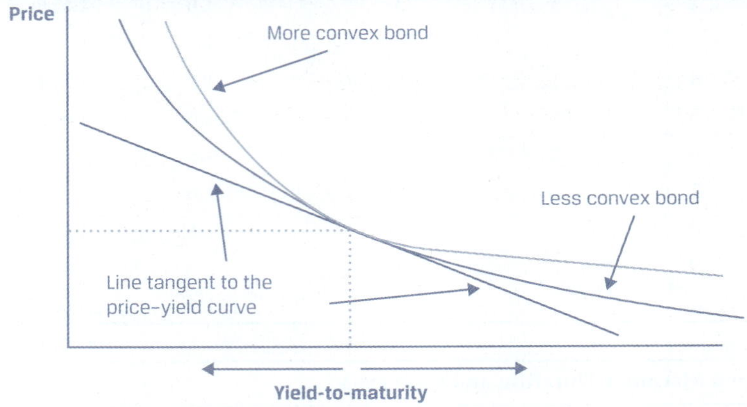

The two bonds depicted in Exhibit 3 are assumed to have the same price, maturity, yield-to-maturity, and modified duration, so they share the same line tangent to their price–yield curves. The benefit of greater convexity arises when their yields change significantly. For the same decrease in yield-to-maturity, the more convex bond *appreciates more* in price, while for the same increase in yield-to-maturity, the more convex bond *depreciates less* in price. Consequently, the more convex bond outperforms the less convex bond in both falling and rising yield environments, so it is less risky for investors.

This conclusion assumes the difference in convexity is not reflected in the price of the more convex bond. If it is priced in, the more convex bond would have a higher price (and lower yield-to-maturity). The key point is that convexity is valuable to investors for risk reduction, so they must pay for it.

EXAMPLE 1

Duration and Convexity of 30-Year Romanian Bond

A 30-year bond issued by the government of Romania has a coupon rate of 4.625% (paid annually) and currently trades at a yield-to-maturity of 4.75% on 15 October 2025, with a maturity date of 15 October 2055.

1. Use Excel's PRICE function to calculate *ApproxModDur* and *ApproxCon* using a 5 bp increase and decrease in yield-to-maturity.
2. Compare and interpret the duration and convexity measures of the 30-year Romanian bond and BRWA's 5-year bond.

To find *ApproxModDur* and *ApproxCon*, we must first calculate PV_0 and then, using a 5 bp increase and decrease in YTM, calculate PV_+ and PV_-:

PV_0 = PRICE(DATE(2025,10,15),DATE(2055,10,15),0.04625,0.0475,100,1,0)

= 98.022448.

PV_+ = PRICE(DATE(2025,10,15),DATE(2055,10,15),0.04625,0.0480,100,1,0)
= 97.247386.

PV_- = PRICE(DATE(2025,10,15),DATE(2055,10,15),0.04625,0.0470,100,1,0)
= 98.806567.

$$ApproxModDur = \frac{98.806567 - 97.247386}{2 \times (0.0005) \times 98.022448} = 15.90637.$$

$$ApproxCon = \frac{98.806567 + 97.247386 - (2 \times 98.022448)}{(0.0005)^2 \times 98.022448} = 369.58881.$$

Duration and Convexity Comparison: Romanian and BRWA Bonds

Bond	Maturity (Years)	Coupon (%)	YTM (%)	*Approx-ModDur*	*ApproxCon*
Romanian	30	4.625 Annual Pay	4.75	15.90637	369.64203
BRWA	5	3.20 Semi-Annual	3.20	4.58676	24.23896

The duration and convexity of the Romanian bond are significantly higher than BRWA's bond primarily due to its much longer time-to-maturity (30 years versus 5 years), which outweighs the Romanian bond's higher coupon rate and YTM, features that decrease duration and convexity.

QUESTION SET

Questions 1–5 relate to the following information.

Bond	Issuance Date	Maturity	Annual Pay Coupon (%)	YTM (%)
Bond X	7/15/25	7/15/34	2.25	2.25
Bond Y	7/15/25	7/15/35	5.33	2.34

1. Calculate the modified duration and convexity for Bond X at issuance.

   Solution:

Bond X	
Fixed Coupon (%)	2.25
Periods p.a.	1
Price (per 100 Par Value)	100
Yield-to-Maturity (%)	2.25

Col. 1	Col. 2	Col. 3	Col. 4	Col. 5	Col. 6 = Col. 2 × Col. 5	Col. 7 = Col. 2 × (Col. 2 + 1) × Col. 5 × (1 + YTM)$^{-1}$
Period	Time to Receipt	Cash Flow	Present Value	Weight	Time to Receipt × Weight	Convexity of Cash Flows
1	1.0	2.25	2.200489	0.02200	0.02200	0.04304
2	2.0	2.25	2.152067	0.02152	0.04304	0.12628
3	3.0	2.25	2.104711	0.02105	0.06314	0.24701
4	4.0	2.25	2.058398	0.02058	0.08234	0.40262
5	5.0	2.25	2.013103	0.02013	0.10066	0.59064
6	6.0	2.25	1.968805	0.01969	0.11813	0.80870
7	7.0	2.25	1.925481	0.01925	0.13478	1.05454
8	8.0	2.25	1.883111	0.01883	0.15065	1.32601
9	9.0	102.25	83.693835	0.83694	7.53245	73.66694
			100.0000	**1.00000**	**8.24718**	**78.26579**
Annualized Macaulay Duration and Convexity					**8.24718**	**78.26579**
Modified Duration					**8.06571**	—

2. Calculate *ApproxModDur* and *ApproxCon* for Bond Y using a 5 bp increase and decrease in the yield-to-maturity.

Solution:

To find *ApproxModDur* and *ApproxCon* for Bond Y, we must first calculate PV_0, PV_+, and PV_-.

PV_0 = PRICE(DATE(2025,7,15),DATE(2035,7,15),0.0533,0.0234,100,1,0) = 126.386358.

$PV+$ = PRICE(DATE(2025,7,15),DATE(2035,7,15),0.0533,0.0239,100,1,0) = 125.877943.

$PV\_$ = PRICE(DATE(2025,7,15),DATE(2035,7,15),0.0533,0.0229,100,1,0) = 126.897325.

$$ApproxModDur = \frac{126.897325 - 125.877943}{2 \times (0.0005) \times 126.386358} = 8.06560.$$

$$ApproxCon = \frac{126.897325 + 125.877943 - (2 \times 126.386358)}{(0.0005)^2 \times 126.386358} = 80.76704.$$

3. Compare and interpret the risk measures from Questions 1 and 2 relative to a small anticipated change in yield-to-maturity.

Solution:

For a small change in YTM, modified duration is a reasonable estimate of the price change risk of a bond. Since the modified duration (or *Approx-ModDur*) values of Bond X and Bond Y are virtually identical (8.06571 and 8.06560, respectively), the estimated price change based on a small change in YTM (either positive or negative) would be nearly identical for each bond.

4. Compare and interpret the risk measures from Questions 1 and 2 relative to a large anticipated change in yield-to-maturity.

Solution:

For a large change in YTM, duration alone does not capture the expected price change of a bond. The convexity adjustment accounts for the non-linear nature of the relationship of price to YTM. Since both bonds have virtually the same duration, the higher convexity of Bond Y should result in a smaller percentage drop given a large increase in YTM and a larger percentage increase given a large decrease in YTM. In either case, Bond Y should perform better than Bond X for a large change in YTM.

5. Compare and interpret each of the following features for its effect on the convexity of Bond X versus Bond Y:

a. Maturity

b. Coupon rate

c. YTM

Solution:

a. Bond Y has a longer maturity than Bond X (10 years versus 9 years), which would increase Bond Y's convexity relative to Bond X.

b. Bond X has a lower coupon rate compared to Bond Y (2.25% versus 5.33%), which would increase Bond X's convexity relative to Bond Y.

c. Bond X has a lower YTM compared to Bond Y (2.25% versus 2.34%), which would increase Bond X's convexity relative to Bond Y.

3 BOND RISK AND RETURN USING DURATION AND CONVEXITY

☐ calculate the percentage price change of a bond for a specified change in yield, given the bond's duration and convexity

We now show how to estimate the percentage price change of a bond for a specified yield change, given the bond's duration and convexity. As we will show, such an estimate is substantially closer to the bond's actual price change than if estimated using duration alone, allowing for more efficient risk management.

Continuing with our focus on BRWA's five-year, 3.2% (semiannual) coupon bond priced at par for settlement on 15 October 2025 and maturity on 15 October 2030, if its yield-to-maturity changes by ±100 bps from 3.20%, then the actual prices, using Excel's PRICE function, would be as follows:

PV_+ = PRICE(DATE(2025,10,15),DATE(2030,10,15),0.032,0.0420,100,2,0) = 95.53212.

PV_- = PRICE(DATE(2025,10,15),DATE(2030,10,15),0.032,0.0220,100,2,0) = 104.71035.

So, the actual price–yield relationship for this bond is as follows:

- 100 bp increase in yield (4.20%): Price = 95.53212; $\%\Delta PV^{Full} = -4.46788\%$.
- 100 bp decrease in yield (2.20%): Price = 104.71035; $\%\Delta PV^{Full} = 4.71035\%$.

The modified duration for this bond was previously found to be 4.58676, so a 100 bp increase (decrease) in yield-to-maturity results in $\%\Delta PV^{Full} \approx -4.58676\%$ (4.58676%).

We now show the enhanced precision and risk reduction achieved by adding the convexity adjustment to the duration estimate when determining the BRWA bond's percentage price changes. Using Equation 1 and the *AnnConvexity* metric, for ±100 bp changes in yield-to-maturity (from 3.20%), we have the following:

$$\%\Delta PV^{Full} \approx (-4.58676 \times 0.0100) + [\tfrac{1}{2} \times 24.23895 \times (0.0100)^2] = -4.46556\%.$$

$$\%\Delta PV^{Full} \approx (-4.58676 \times -0.0100) + [\tfrac{1}{2} \times 24.23895 \times (-0.0100)^2] = 4.70795\%.$$

Exhibit 4 compares the estimated percentage changes in BRWA's bond prices for ±100 bp changes in yield using duration alone and using duration plus convexity against the exact changes from Excel's PRICE function. It is clear that enhanced precision is achieved by adding the convexity adjustment, because the percentage price difference is less than ¼ of a basis point by adding convexity versus about 12 bps with duration alone. Note that this difference would be substantially greater for larger changes in yield or for longer-maturity or lower-coupon bonds.

Exhibit 4: Using Duration and Convexity to Estimate Bond Price Changes

Change in Bond Yield	Actual $\%\Delta PV^{Full}$	Estimated $\%\Delta PV^{Full}$ Using *ModDur*	Difference from Actual Change	Estimated $\%\Delta PV^{Full}$ Using *ModDur* + Convexity	Difference from Actual Change
+ 100 bps	−4.46788	−4.58676	−0.11887	−4.46556	0.00232
− 100 bps	4.71035	4.58676	−0.12359	4.70795	−0.00239

Recall that money duration indicates the first-order effect on the full price of a bond in currency units given a change in yield-to-maturity. **Money convexity** (*MoneyCon*) captures the second-order effect in currency terms and is the annual convexity multiplied by the full price, as in Equation 3.

$$MoneyCon = AnnConvexity \times PV^{Full}. \tag{3}$$

Similar to estimating the percentage change in a bond's full price, MoneyDur and MoneyCon are combined to achieve a more accurate, thus less risky, estimate of the change in a bond's full price, as shown in Equation 4.

$$\Delta PV^{Full} \approx -(MoneyDur \times \Delta Yield) + \left[\frac{1}{2} \times MoneyCon \times (\Delta Yield)^2\right]. \tag{4}$$

For a money convexity example, consider again BRWA's five-year, 3.2% semiannual coupon bond, settling 15 October 2025, maturing 15 October 2030, and yielding 3.2%—thus, priced at par. We saw previously that annual modified duration and annual convexity for this bond are 4.58676 and 24.23895, respectively.

Suppose the investor has a position in the bond with a par value of USD100 million and the yield-to-maturity increases by 100 bps. We saw earlier that the bond's price declines to 95.53212, so the market value of the position decreases to $95,532,116 (= $100,000,000 × 0.9553212), a decline of $4,467,884.

Estimating the market value change using *MoneyDur* alone results in a larger decline, $4,586,759 (= $458,675,875 × 0.0100), a difference of $118,875.

However, using Equation 3, the *MoneyCon* for this position is \$2,423,894,503 (= 24.23895 × \$100,000,000), and if we apply Equation 4, which uses both *MoneyDur* and *MoneyCon*, to estimate the market value change, the result is a decline of –\$4,465,564, as follows:

$$-\$4,465,564 \approx -(\$458,675,875 \times 0.01) + \left[\frac{1}{2} \times 2,423,894,503 \times (0.01)^2\right].$$

By using both MoneyDur and MoneyCon, the difference in the estimated versus the actual changes in bond position value is only \$2,320. Exhibit 5 summarizes these results and shows the estimated and actual changes in position value for a 100 bp decrease in yield.

Exhibit 5: Using Money Duration and Money Convexity to Estimate Bond Price Changes

Change in Bond Yield	Actual ΔPV^{Full}	Estimated ΔPV^{Full} Using *MoneyDur*	Difference from Actual Change	Estimated ΔPV^{Full} Using *MoneyDur* + *MoneyCon*	Difference from Actual Change
+ 100 BPS	–\$4,467,884	–\$4,586,759	\$118,875	–\$4,465,564	–\$2,320
– 100 BPS	\$4,710,348	\$4,586,759	–\$123,590	4,707,953	–\$2,395

KNOWLEDGE CHECK

An investor holds a position in five-year, zero-coupon Federal Republic of Germany bonds settling 11 May 2025 and maturing 11 April 2030. The yield-to-maturity is –0.72%, stated as an effective annual rate on an Act/Act basis. There are five annual periods, and settlement is 30 days into the 365-day year.

1. Calculate the full price of the bond per 100 of par value.

   Solution:

   Because Excel's PRICE function does not work for negative yields, the equation for *PV* of a zero-coupon bond must be used. There are five annual periods, settlement is 30 days into the 365-day year, and because 1 + *r* = 1 + (–0.0072) = 0.9928, the full price of the bond is 103.6175 per 100 of par value:

   $$PV_0 = \left[\frac{100}{(0.9928)^5}\right] \times (0.9928)^{\frac{30}{365}}$$

   $PV_0 = 103.617526.$

2. Calculate *ApproxModDur* and *ApproxCon* using a 1 bp increase and decrease in the yield-to-maturity.

   Solution:

   $PV_+ = 103.566215$, and $PV_- = 103.668868$:

   $$PV_+ = \left[\frac{100}{(0.9929)^5}\right] \times (0.9929)^{\frac{30}{365}}$$

   $PV_+ = 103.566215.$

$$PV_- = \left[\frac{100}{(0.9927)^5}\right] \times (0.9927)^{\frac{30}{365}}$$

$PV_- = 103.668868.$

The approximate modified duration is 4.9535:

$$ApproxModDur = \frac{103.668868 - 103.566215}{2 \times (0.0001) \times 103.617526} = 4.9535.$$

The approximate convexity is 29.918:

$$ApproxCon = \frac{103.668868 + 103.566215 - (2 \times 103.617526)}{(0.0001)^2 \times 103.617526} = 29.918.$$

3. Calculate the estimated convexity-adjusted percentage price change resulting from a 100 bp increase in the yield-to-maturity.

Solution:

The convexity-adjusted percentage price change from a 100 bp increase in yield-to-maturity is estimated as –4.80391%. Modified duration alone estimates the change as –4.9535%. The convexity adjustment adds 14.96 bps.

$$\%\Delta PV^{Full} \approx (-AnnModDur \times \Delta Yield) + \left[\frac{1}{2} \times AnnConvexity \times (\Delta Yield)^2\right].$$

$$\%\Delta PV^{Full} \approx (-4.9535 + 0.01) + \left[\frac{1}{2} \times 29.918 \times (0.01)^2\right]$$

$$\%\Delta PV^{Full} \approx -0.048039 = -4.8039\%.$$

4. Compare the estimated percentage price change with the actual change, assuming the yield-to-maturity jumps 100 bps, to 0.28%, on the settlement date.

Solution:

The new full price if the yield-to-maturity jumps from –0.72% to 0.28% on the settlement date is 98.634349:

$$PV^{Full} = \left[\frac{100}{(1.0028)^5}\right] \times (1.0028)^{\frac{30}{365}}$$

$PV^{Full} = 98.634349$

The actual percentage change in the bond price is –4.80920% (98.634349/103.617526 – 1). The convexity-adjusted estimate is –4.80391%, whereas the estimated change using modified duration alone is –4.95350%.

QUESTION SET

Questions 1–4 relate to the following information.

An investor purchases a €10 million semi-annual 2.95% coupon bond with a yield-to-maturity of 2.95%, settling 30 June 2025 and maturing 30 June 2032.

1. Calculate *ApproxModDur* and *ApproxCon* for the bond using a 1 bp increase and decrease in yield-to-maturity.

Solution:

PV_+ = PRICE(DATE(2025,6,30),DATE(2032,6,30),0.0295,0.0296,100,2,0)

$= 99.937.$

PV_{-} = PRICE(DATE(2025,6,30),DATE(2032,6,30),0.0295,0.0294,100,2,0)
= 100.063.

$$ApproxModDur = \frac{100.063 - 99.937}{2 \times (0.0001) \times 100} = 6.283.$$

$$ApproxCon = \frac{100.063 + 99.937 - (2 \times 100)}{(0.0001)^2 \times 100} = 44.965.$$

2. Calculate *MoneyDur* and *MoneyCon* for the bond position using the results from Question 1.

Solution:

$MoneyDur \approx 6.283 \times$ EUR10,000,000 = EUR62,829,180.

$MoneyCon \approx 44.965 \times$ EUR10,000,000 = EUR449,647,660.

3. Calculate the estimated price change in the investor's position in the bond using *MoneyDur* and *MoneyCon* for a 50 bp decrease in yield-to-maturity.

Solution:

$\Delta PV^{Full} \approx -(\text{EUR}62{,}829{,}180 \times -0.005) + [½ \times \text{EUR}449{,}647{,}660 \times (-0.005)^2]$
= EUR319,767.

4. Calculate the difference between the estimated price change and the actual price change given a 50 bp yield-to-maturity decrease.

Solution:

PV^{Full} = PRICE(DATE(2025,6,30),DATE(2032,6,30),0.0295,0.0345,100,2,0)
= 103.198.

The actual increase in the bond price is 3.1984%:

$\Delta PV^{Full} = 3.1984\% \times \$10{,}000{,}000$ = EUR319,840.

The difference between the actual and the estimated price change is EUR73 (= 319,840 – 319,767).

PORTFOLIO DURATION AND CONVEXITY

4

☐ calculate portfolio duration and convexity and explain the limitations of these measures

Just as duration and convexity provide measures of the interest rate risk of a single bond, these metrics can also be used to measure the interest rate risk of a portfolio of bonds. There are two ways to calculate the duration and convexity of a bond portfolio:

1. Using the weighted average of time to receipt of the *aggregate* cash flows

2. Using the weighted averages of the durations and convexities of the individual bonds that make up the portfolio

The first method is the theoretically correct approach, but it is difficult to use in practice. Our focus will be the second method since it is commonly used by fixed-income portfolio managers. We will also highlight its limitations.

Suppose an institutional investor holds a two-bond portfolio consisting of $50 million par value each of the BRWA five-year bond and a government of Romania 30-year bond, with details as shown in Exhibit 6. Assume that both bonds are denominated in US dollars.

Exhibit 6: Inputs for Determining Portfolio Duration and Convexity

Bond	Maturity (Years)	Coupon (%)	Price	Yield (%)	Duration	Convexity
BRWA	5	3.200	100.000	3.200	4.58676	24.23896
Romania	30	4.625	98.022	4.750	15.90637	369.64203

Bond	Par Value	Market Value	Portfolio Weight
BRWA	50,000,000	50,000,000	0.5050
Romanian	50,000,000	49,011,224	0.4950

The total market value for the portfolio is $99,011,224, and the portfolio is nearly evenly weighted in terms of market value between the two bonds. As noted previously, duration and convexity for a portfolio are calculated as the weighted average of the statistics for the individual bonds, with the shares of overall portfolio market value as the weights. This weighted average approximates the theoretically correct portfolio duration and convexity and becomes more accurate when differences in the yields-to-maturity on the bonds are smaller and when the yield curve is flat.

Given the portfolio weights in this simple example, portfolio duration and convexity are calculated as follows:

Weighted-average modified duration = (4.58676 × 0.5050) + (15.90637 × 0.4950) = 10.19004.

Weighted-average convexity = (24.23896 × 0.5050) + (369.64203 × 0.4950) = 195.21581.

The main advantage of this weighted-average approach is that it is easily used as a measure of interest rate risk. For instance, if yields-to-maturity on each of the bonds in the portfolio increase by 100 bps, then the estimated decline in the portfolio value is 9.214%.

$$\%\Delta PV^{Full} \approx (-10.19004 \times 0.0100) + [\tfrac{1}{2} \times 195.21581 \times (0.0100)^2] = -9.21396\%.$$

However, this approach also comes with a limitation: These measures of portfolio duration and convexity implicitly assume that yields of all maturities change by the same amount in the same direction, a **parallel shift** in the yield curve. In reality, pure parallel shifts are rare; rather, we frequently observe a steepening, flattening, or even twisting yield curve.

EXAMPLE 2

Portfolio Duration and Convexity

An institutional investor considers adding a new USD50 million par value position in a 10-year US Treasury bond to its existing portfolio of BRWA and government of Romania bonds. The relevant data are shown in Exhibit 7.

Exhibit 7: Inputs for Determining Portfolio Duration and Convexity

Bond	Maturity (Years)	Coupon (%)	Price	Yield (%)	Duration	Convexity
BRWA	5	3.200	100.000	3.200	4.58676	24.23896
Romanian	30	4.625	98.022	4.750	15.90637	369.64203
US Treasury	10	1.500	98.168	1.700	9.23693	93.87376

Bond	Par Value (USD)	Market Value (USD)	Portfolio Weight
BRWA	50,000,000	50,000,000	0.33762
Romania	50,000,000	49,011,224	0.33094
US Treasury	50,000,000	49,083,948	0.33144

1. Calculate the weighted-average duration and convexity for the proposed portfolio.

   Solution:

   Given the data in Exhibit 7, the weighted-average modified duration and convexity are calculated as follows:

   Weighted-average modified duration = (4.58676 × 0.33762) + (15.90637 × 0.33094) + (9.23693 × 0.33144)

   = 9.87415.

   Weighted-average convexity = (24.23896 × 0.33762) + (369.64203 × 0.33094) + (93.87376 × 0.33144)

   = 161.62749.

2. Compare and interpret duration and convexity for the proposed portfolio versus the current portfolio.

   Solution:

   Adding the US Treasury position would *decrease* both the portfolio duration (from 10.19004 to 9.87415) and convexity (from 195.21581 to 161.62749). The reduction in duration would reduce the price risk of the portfolio against an upward parallel shift in the yield curve, but due to the lower convexity, this reduction in risk would be lessened for large shifts.

3. Recommend whether the US Treasury bond position should be added if the investor expects a 100 bp parallel shift downward in yields.

Solution:

Given an expected 100 bp parallel shift down in yields, the investor should not add the position in US Treasury bonds. Adding the position lowers both the portfolio duration and convexity, which would also reduce the expected increase in the value of the portfolio. Given the investor's yield curve view, it should seek to increase both portfolio duration and convexity.

QUESTION SET

Questions 1–4 relate to the following information.

An investor purchases EUR10 million par value of a 5-year, zero-coupon bond and a 10-year, fixed-rate semiannual coupon bond. Details of the bonds are shown below.

Two-Bond Portfolio

Bond	Maturity (Years)	Coupon (%)	Price	YTM (%)	Duration	Convexity
Zero	5	0.00	83.18777	3.750	4.81928	27.87052
Semi- annual	10	5.50	105.91556	4.750	7.71210	72.54897

1. Calculate the weighted-average modified duration for the portfolio.

Solution:

The market value of the bonds are as follows:

Zero-coupon: €10,000,000 × 83.18777/100 = €8,318,777.

Semi-annual: €10,000,000 × 105.91556/100 = €10,591,556.

Therefore, the weights are 43.991% for the zero-coupon bond and 56.009% for the semi-annual bond. As a result, the weighted-average modified duration is

$$(4.81928 \times 0.43991) + (7.71210 \times 0.56009) = 6.43953.$$

2. Calculate the weighted-average convexity for the portfolio.

Solution:

Using the weights calculated previously,

$$\text{Weighted-average convexity} = (27.87052 \times 0.43991) + (72.54897 \times 0.56009) = 52.89463.$$

3. Calculate the estimated percentage price change of the portfolio given a 100 bp increase in yield-to-maturity on each of the bonds.

Solution:

$$\%\Delta PV^{Full} \approx (-6.43953 \times 0.0100) + [½ \times 52.89463 \times (0.0100)^2] = -6.1751\%.$$

4. Based on rising inflation and tightening monetary policy, the investor expects interest rates to rise. Given that view, which bond should the investor consider replacing the 10-year bond with?

   A. A 20-year bond

   B. A 15-year floating-rate bond

   C. A 10-year bond with a lower coupon

   Solution:

   B is correct. With interest rates expected to rise, the investor should choose a bond with lower interest rate risk. Both the 20-year bond and the 10-year bond with a lower coupon should have higher durations than the current 10-year bond, all else equal, and would be expected to experience a larger percentage price decrease if interest rates increase. Floating-rate bonds, however, have low interest rate risk because coupon payments adjust to changing interest rates.

PRACTICE PROBLEMS

1. A 5.5% semiannual-pay fixed-coupon bond is issued at par on 1 May 2025 and matures on 1 May 2029. For a 50 bps increase and decrease in yield-to-maturity, PV_+ and PV_- are 99.82283 and 100.177546, respectively. The approximate convexity is *closest* to:

   A. 3.548.

   B. 15.045.

   C. 101.793.

2. A bond pays a semiannual fixed coupon of 4.70%. It trades at par on its coupon date of 16 December 2025 and matures on 16 December 2033. The bond's annualized convexity statistic is *closest* to:

   A. 51.670.

   B. 53.231.

   C. 206.681.

3. For changes in yield-to-maturity, the convexity adjustment is *most* needed to account for the:

   A. first-order effect on bond prices.

   B. bond price risk due to small changes in yield-to-maturity.

   C. non-linear relationship of bond prices and yield to maturity.

The following information relates to questions 4-9

A bond portfolio consists of the following three option-free, fixed-rate bonds:

Bond	Market Value (£)	Annual Modified Duration	Annual Convexity
X	5,000,000	3.6239	16.2513
Y	5,000,000	9.0036	91.0278
Z	10,000,000	12.7512	179.8591

4. If the yield-to-maturity of Bond X increases by 50 bps, the expected percentage price change of Bond X is *closest* to:

   A. 1.792%.

   B. 1.812%.

   C. 1.832%.

5. Given a 75 bps change in the yields-to-maturity for Bonds Y and Z, the convexity adjustment for Bond Z would be greater than the convexity adjustment of Bond

Y:

A. if the YTM change is positive.

B. if the YTM change is negative.

C. regardless of the direction of the change in YTM.

6. For a 100 bps increase in yield-to-maturity and using money duration and money convexity, the estimated change in Bond Y's full price is *closest* to:

   A. GBP472,937.

   B. GBP450,180.

   C. GBP427,423.

7. For a 100 bps increase in yield-to-maturity and using the weighted average duration and convexity, the expected percentage price change for the bond portfolio is *closest* to:

   A. 7.981%.

   B. 8.949%.

   C. 9.533%.

8. The bond portfolio's benchmark is a fixed-income index with a duration of 9.5325 and convexity of 103.0677. Based on the weighted-average portfolio duration and convexity, the portfolio should outperform its benchmark in which of the following scenarios?

   A. Only when interest rates are rising

   B. Only when interest rates are falling

   C. Both when interest rates are rising and falling

9. The method of using weighted-average portfolio duration and convexity measures to assess price risk of a bond portfolio is *best* characterized as:

   A. being theoretically correct.

   B. being commonly used by portfolio managers.

   C. accommodating non-parallel shifts in the yield curve.

SOLUTIONS

1. B is correct.

$$ApproxCon = \frac{100.177546 + 99.82283 - (2 \times 100)}{(0.005)^2 \times 100} = 15.04.$$

2. A is correct.

Eight-Year, 4.70% Semiannual Bond	
Fixed Coupon (%)	4.70
Periods p.a.	2
Price (per 100 Par Value)	100
Yield-to-Maturity (%)	4.70

Col. 1	Col. 2	Col. 3	Col. 4	Col. 5	Col. 6 = Col. 2 × Col. 5	Col. 7 = Col. 2 × (Col. 2 + 1) × Col. 5 × $(1 + YTM/2)^{-2}$
Period	**Time to Receipt**	**Cash Flow**	**Present Value**	**Weight**	**Time to Receipt × Weight**	**Convexity of Cash Flows**
1	1.0	2.35	2.296043	0.02296	0.02296	0.04384
2	2.0	2.35	2.243325	0.02243	0.04487	0.12849
3	3.0	2.35	2.191817	0.02192	0.06575	0.25108
4	4.0	2.35	2.141492	0.02141	0.08566	0.40886
5	5.0	2.35	2.092323	0.02092	0.10462	0.59920
6	6.0	2.35	2.044282	0.02044	0.12266	0.81962
7	7.0	2.35	1.997344	0.01997	0.13981	1.06774
8	8.0	2.35	1.951484	0.01951	0.15612	1.34129
9	9.0	2.35	1.906677	0.01907	0.17160	1.63811
10	10.0	2.35	1.862899	0.01863	0.18629	1.95617
11	11.0	2.35	1.820126	0.01820	0.20021	2.29351
12	12.0	2.35	1.778336	0.01778	0.21340	2.64827
13	13.0	2.35	1.737504	0.01738	0.22588	3.01871
14	14.0	2.35	1.697610	0.01698	0.23767	3.40315
15	15.0	2.35	1.658632	0.01659	0.24879	3.80002
16	16.0	102.35	70.580104	0.70580	11.29282	183.26330
			100.0000	**1.00000**	**13.51910**	**206.68136**
Annualized Convexity						**51.67034**

3. C is correct. The convexity adjustment is a complementary risk measure to duration. It accounts for the second-order (non-linear) effect of yield changes on price. It is most useful for large yield changes, because duration provides a good approximation for small yield changes.

4. A is correct. The expected price change is calculated as follows:

$$\%\Delta PV^{Full} \approx (-3.6239 \times 0.005) + [½ \times 16.2513 \times (0.005)^2]$$

$= -1.79164\% \approx -1.792\%.$

5. C is correct. Since the convexity adjustment uses the square of the change in yield, it is always positive regardless of the direction of the change in yield-to-maturity. As a result, the convexity adjustment for Bond Z will always be greater than the convexity adjustment for Bond Y, given the same change in yields-to-maturity.

6. C is correct.

   $MoneyDur \approx 9.0036 \times 5{,}000{,}000 = 45{,}018{,}000$

   $MoneyCon \approx 91.0278 \times 5{,}000{,}000 = 455{,}139{,}000$

   $\Delta PV^{Full} \approx -(45{,}018{,}000 \times 0.01) + [\tfrac{1}{2} \times 455{,}139{,}000 \times (0.01)^2] = -\text{GBP}427{,}423.$

7. B is correct. The portfolio weights for Bonds X, Y, and Z are 0.25, 0.25, and 0.50, respectively. The weighted average duration and convexity measures are calculated as follows:

   Weighted-average duration = $(0.25 \times 3.6239) + (0.25 \times 9.0036) + (0.50 \times 12.7512)$

   $= 9.5325.$

   Weighted-average convexity = $(0.25 \times 16.2513) + (0.25 \times 91.0278) + (0.50 \times 179.8591)$

   $= 116.7493.$

   $\%\Delta PV^{Full} \approx (-9.5325 \times 0.01) + [\tfrac{1}{2} \times 116.7493 \times (0.01)^2] = -8.9487\% \approx -8.949\%.$

8. C is correct. The portfolio has a weighted-average duration of 9.5325, which is identical to the benchmark's duration. However, the portfolio has higher convexity (116.7493) compared to the benchmark (103.0677). All else equal, the portfolio should outperform the lower convexity benchmark portfolio in both rising and falling interest rate environments.

9. B is correct. The weighted-average portfolio duration and convexity method is easy to calculate and apply in practice and is commonly used by portfolio managers to assess bond portfolio price risk. It does, however, implicitly assume parallel shifts in the yield curve. Using the weighted average of time to receipt of the aggregate cash flows is the theoretically correct method to calculate portfolio duration and convexity, but it is difficult to use in practice.

LEARNING MODULE

13

Curve-Based and Empirical Fixed-Income Risk Measures

LEARNING OUTCOMES

Mastery	The candidate should be able to:
☐	explain why effective duration and effective convexity are the most appropriate measures of interest rate risk for bonds with embedded options
☐	calculate the percentage price change of a bond for a specified change in benchmark yield, given the bond's effective duration and convexity
☐	define key rate duration and describe its use to measure price sensitivity of fixed-income instruments to benchmark yield curve changes
☐	describe the difference between empirical duration and analytical duration

INTRODUCTION

1

Having covered yield-based duration and convexity measures, we now introduce curve-based measures of a bond's price sensitivity to changes in a benchmark yield curve and when cash flows are uncertain. We show how the change in a bond's full price is estimated by combining curve-based duration and convexity sensitivity measures, discuss uses of these approximate measures by issuers and investors, and explain their benefits and limitations. We also introduce key rate duration as a measure of interest rate risk across the term structure. Finally, we show that benchmark yield changes and credit spreads for issuers of lower credit quality are negatively correlated, especially during periods of market distress, establishing the benefit of an empirical versus analytical approach.

LEARNING MODULE OVERVIEW

- Yield duration and convexity estimates of interest rate risk are useful only for small changes in yields. Effective duration and effective convexity are valid for both small and large changes in yields.
- Effective duration and effective convexity are useful for gauging the interest rate risk of bonds whose future cash flows are uncertain.
- Effective duration and effective convexity can be used to estimate the percentage change in a bond's full price for a given shift in the benchmark yield curve.
- A key rate (or partial) duration is a measure of a bond's sensitivity to a change in the benchmark yield at a specific maturity. Key rate duration data, along with forecasted shifts in the benchmark curve, allow a portfolio to be rebalanced to improve its return.
- The sum of weighted key rate durations of the bonds in a portfolio are equal to the effective duration of the entire portfolio.
- Analytical duration and convexity are estimated duration and convexity statistics using mathematical formulas. Empirical duration and convexity are estimated using historical data that incorporate various factors affecting bond prices.
- When deciding whether to use an empirical or analytical measure, the correlation between benchmark yields and credit spreads must be considered.

LEARNING MODULE SELF-ASSESSMENT

These initial questions are intended to help you gauge your current level of understanding of the learning module.

1. For which of the following-fixed income instruments would an investor *most likely* use yield duration and convexity to measure interest rate risk rather than effective duration and effective convexity?

   A. 30-year fixed-rate bond

   B. Callable bond

   C. Mortgage-backed security

   Solution:

   A is correct. The callable bond and mortgage-backed security have embedded options, which yield duration and convexity cannot account for. The 30-year fixed-rate bond does not, so either method could be applied.

2. Calculate the effective duration of a bond given the following:

   - PV_0 = 102.208.
   - Price with the benchmark yield curve shifted up 25 bps: $PV+$ = 100.004.
   - Price with the benchmark yield curve shifted down by 25 bps: $PV\_$ = 103.891.

   Solution:

$$EffDur = \frac{(PV_-) - (PV_+)}{2 \times (\Delta Curve) \times (PV_0)}$$

$$EffDur = \frac{(103.891) - (100.004)}{2 \times (0.0025) \times (102.208)}$$

$$EffDur = 7.606$$

3. Calculate the effective convexity of a bond given the following:

- $PV_0 = 102.208$.
- Price with the benchmark yield curve shifted up 25 bps: $PV+ =$ 100.004.
- Price with the benchmark yield curve shifted down by 25 bps: $PV\_ =$ 103.891.

Solution:

$$EffCon = \frac{[(PV_-) + (PV_+)] - [2 \times (PV_0)]}{(\Delta Curve)^2 \times (PV_0)}$$

$$EffCon = \frac{[(103.891) + (100.004)] - [2 \times (102.208)]}{(0.0025)^2 \times (102.208)}$$

EffCon = −815.592

4. If the benchmark yield curve shifted by 50 bps, what would be the percentage change in the full price of a bond if its effective duration is 6.094 and its effective convexity is −230.097?

Solution:

$$\%\Delta PV^{Full} \approx (-EffDur \times \Delta Curve) + \left[\frac{1}{2} \times EffCon \times (\Delta Curve)^2\right]$$

$$\%\Delta PV^{Full} \approx (-6.094 \times 0.005) + \left[\frac{1}{2} \times -230.097 \times (0.005)^2\right]$$

$$\%\Delta PV^{Full} \approx 3.33\%$$

5. The table below contains forecasts of expected changes in the benchmark yield curve by tenor.

Maturity	**1 year**	**5 years**	**10 years**	**20 years**	**30 years**
Curve shift at maturity	+100 bps	+150 bps	+200 bps	+250 bps	+300 bps

Your portfolio contains equally sized positions in Bond A and Bond B, which have the following key rate durations.

	Tenor	Key Rate Duration
Bond A	5 years	1.706
Bond B	10 years	3.195

Given the information and expected changes in yields, identify the bond that could be sold to improve returns.

Solution:

Bond B, because its expected price decline from the expected change in benchmark yields is more than twice that of Bond A.

For Bond A, $\Delta PV/PV = -1.706 \times 0.015 = -2.56\%$.

For Bond B, $\Delta PV/PV = -3.195 \times 0.020 = -6.39\%$.

6. Explain why yield duration and convexity are less useful for bonds with contingency features, such as callable bonds.

Solution:

Yield duration and convexity assume cash flows are received on scheduled dates. Cash flows from bonds with contingency features may *not* be received on scheduled dates—if, for example, a callable bond is called by the issuer following a decrease in interest rates. Therefore, yield duration and convexity would not correctly measure the price sensitivity to interest rates.

7. When comparing analytical duration versus empirical duration, which of the following statements is correct?

A. Analytical duration and convexity are estimated duration and convexity statistics using mathematical formulas.

B. Empirical duration and convexity are estimated using historical data in non-statistical models that incorporate various factors affecting bond prices.

C. Both A and B

Solution:

A is correct. Analytical duration and convexity are estimated duration and convexity statistics using mathematical formulas.

B is incorrect because statistical models are primarily used to determine empirical duration and convexity.

C is incorrect because B is incorrect.

8. True or false: Analytical duration is superior to empirical duration for bonds with credit risk.

Solution:

False. If government bond yields are driven lower in a market stress scenario, the "flight to safety" will also cause credit spreads to widen because of an increase in expected default risk. Since credit spreads and benchmark yields are negatively correlated under this scenario, wider credit spreads will partially or fully offset the decline in government benchmark yields, resulting in lower empirical duration estimates than analytical duration estimates. Therefore, empirical duration estimates are a more accurate method of forecasting bond price changes for bonds with credit risk.

CURVE-BASED INTEREST RATE RISK MEASURES

2

☐ explain why effective duration and effective convexity are the most appropriate measures of interest rate risk for bonds with embedded options

Yield duration and convexity assume a bond's cash flows are certain. However, if a bond has contingency features, such as embedded options, as with a callable (or puttable) bond, then future cash flows are *uncertain* since option exercise depends on the level of market interest rates relative to coupon interest being paid (or received). For example, the duration of a callable bond does *not* reflect the sensitivity of the bond price to a change in the yield-to-worst, since this represents only one of several possible outcomes based on future interest rates.

Consequently, bonds with embedded options do not have well-defined yields-to-maturity, so Macaulay and modified durations are not appropriate interest rate risk measures for such bonds. Rather, the appropriate measure of interest rate risk is the sensitivity of the bond's price to a change in a *benchmark yield curve*—for example, the government par curve—known as **effective duration**, a *curve* duration rather than a *yield* duration statistic.

Exhibit 1 shows the impact of an instantaneous change in the benchmark yield curve ($\Delta Curve$) on the price of a callable bond compared with that on a comparable non-callable bond. The two bonds have the same features (i.e., coupon rate, payment frequency, time-to-maturity, and credit risk). Note that the horizontal axis is a benchmark yield—a point on the par curve for government bonds.

Exhibit 1: Interest Rate Risk Characteristics of a Callable Bond

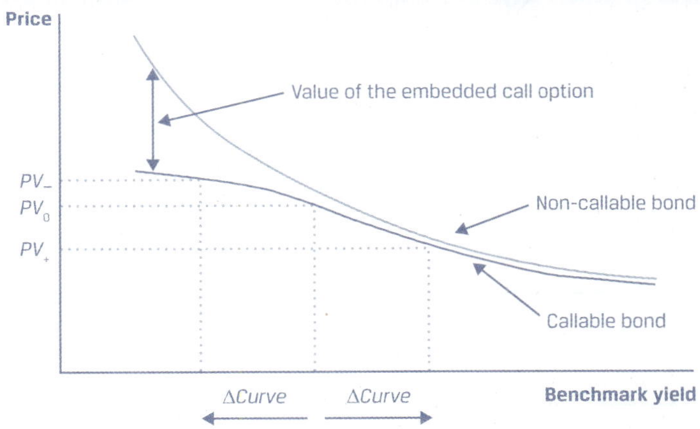

The price of the non-callable bond is always greater than that of the comparable callable bond. The difference is the value of the embedded call option, which is held by the bond issuer (not the investor). When interest rates are high relative to the coupon rate, the value of the call option is low. When rates are low, the value of the call option is high since the issuer is more likely to exercise the option to refinance the debt at the lower prevailing rates. The investor bears the "call risk" since if the bond is called, the investor must reinvest the proceeds at a lower interest rate.

Exhibit 1 shows that, given parallel shifts in the benchmark yield curve, when benchmark yields are high ($\Delta Curve$ is positive), the *effective durations* of the callable and non-callable bonds are very similar. But when interest rates are low ($\Delta Curve$ is negative), the effective duration of the callable bond is lower than that of the otherwise comparable non-callable bond, since the callable bond price does not increase as much when benchmark yields fall; the presence of the call option limits price appreciation. Thus, an embedded call option reduces the effective duration of the bond, especially when interest rates are falling and the bond is more likely to be called. The lower effective duration can be interpreted as a shorter expected life—a reduced weighted average of time to receipt of cash flow.

Analogous to effective duration, the second-order effect of a parallel shift in the benchmark yield curve is measured by **effective convexity**, a *curve convexity* statistic. In Exhibit 1, as the benchmark yield declines, the slope of the line tangent to the curve for the non-callable bond steepens, indicating positive convexity. But the slope of the line tangent to the callable bond flattens as the benchmark yield declines and reaches an inflection point, after which the effective convexity becomes negative.

When the benchmark yield is high and the value of the embedded call option is low, the callable and the non-callable bonds experience very similar effects from interest rate changes and both have positive convexity. But as the benchmark yield declines, the curves diverge, and at some point, the callable bond moves into the range of negative convexity, since the embedded call option has more value to the issuer and is more likely to be exercised. This situation further limits the potential price appreciation of the bond arising from lower benchmark yields.

Exhibit 2 shows characteristics of a bond with an embedded put option.

Exhibit 2: Interest Rate Risk Characteristics of a Putable Bond

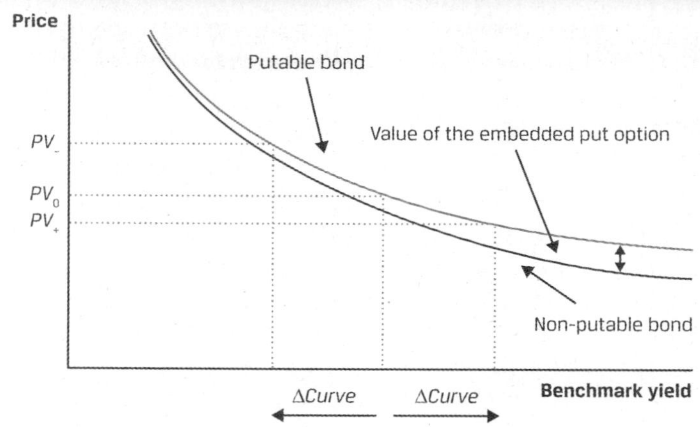

A putable bond allows the investor to sell the bond back to the issuer before maturity, usually at par value, protecting the investor from higher benchmark yields that would otherwise drive the bond's price below par. So, the price of a putable bond is always higher than that of an otherwise comparable non-putable bond, the price difference being the value of the embedded put option.

An embedded put option reduces the effective duration of the bond, especially when rates are rising. Given a parallel shift in the benchmark yield curve, if interest rates are low compared to the coupon rate, the value of the put option is low and the impact of a change in the benchmark yield on the bond's price is very similar to that for a non-putable bond. But when benchmark interest rates rise, the put option becomes more valuable to the investor, since the ability to sell the bond back to the issuer at par limits the price depreciation as rates rise. Importantly, putable bonds always have positive effective convexity.

Effective duration and effective convexity are also relevant for mortgage-backed securities (MBSs), which arise from a residential (or commercial) loan portfolio securitization and are covered in later lessons. MBS cash flows are contingent on homeowners' ability to refinance or pay off an existing mortgage with the proceeds from a new mortgage. Refinancing is a common feature of mortgages in the United States and some other jurisdictions that borrowers tend to exercise if interest rates fall.

Calculating effective duration (*EffDur*) is very similar to calculating approximate modified duration, as shown in Equation 1.

$$EffDur = \frac{(PV_{-})-(PV_{+})}{2 \times (\Delta Curve) \times (PV_0)} \tag{1}$$

The formula for calculating effective convexity (*EffCon*) is also very similar to the formula for approximate convexity, as shown in Equation 2.

$$EffCon = \frac{[(PV_{-})+(PV_{+})]-[2 \times (PV_0)]}{(\Delta Curve)^2 \times (PV_0)} \tag{2}$$

The differences are that $\Delta Curve$ is in the denominator—since effective duration is a *curve duration* statistic, it measures interest rate risk in terms of a parallel shift in the benchmark yield curve—and that PV_{-} and PV_{+} are calculated using option pricing models. These models are covered in more detail in later modules but include such inputs as (1) the length of the call protection period, (2) the schedule of call prices and call dates, (3) an assumption about credit spreads over benchmark yields (which also includes any liquidity spread), (4) an assumption about future interest rate volatility, and (5) the level of market interest rates (e.g., the government par curve). The analyst holds the first four inputs constant and then raises and lowers the fifth input (i.e., parallel shifts) to derive PV_{+} and PV_{-}, respectively.

Although effective duration and effective convexity are the appropriate interest rate risk measure for bonds with embedded options, they may also be useful with option-free bonds to supplement yield duration. Importantly, small differences may arise between a bond's effective duration and its modified duration because when the government par curve is shifted in the model, the government spot (i.e., zero) curve is also shifted, but not in the same parallel manner. Thus, the change in the bond price is not the same as it would be if its yield-to-maturity changed by the same amount as the change in the par curve.

In general, modified duration and effective duration on an option-free bond are not identical. However, the difference narrows when the yield curve is flatter, the time-to-maturity is shorter, and the bond is priced closer to par value; the difference disappears only in the rare circumstance of a flat yield curve.

For example, consider BRWA's five-year, 3.2% (semiannual) coupon bond priced at par for settlement on 15 October 2025 and maturity on 15 October 2030. Using PV_0 = 100.00 and $\Delta Yield$ = 0.0005, in an earlier lesson, we found

$PV_{+} = 99.771$ and $PV_{-} = 100.230$,

resulting in yield duration and convexity statistics as follows:

$ApproxModDur = 4.587$ and $ApproxCon = 24.239$.

Instead of a change in the bond's yield-to-maturity, assume there is an upward and downward shift of the benchmark government par curve ($\Delta Curve$) by 5 bps, which causes spot rates to move in a slightly non-parallel manner. Using PV_0 = 100.00 and $\Delta Curve$ = 0.0005 and assuming the following new prices,

$PV_{+} = 99.760$ and $PV_{-} = 100.241$,

then using Equation 1, effective duration is 4.816:

$$EffDur = \frac{(PV_-) - (PV_+)}{2 \times (\Delta Curve) \times (PV_0)}$$

$$EffDur = \frac{(100.241) - (99.760)}{2 \times (0.0005) \times (100)}$$

$$EffDur = 4.816$$

Using the same inputs in Equation 2, effective convexity is 40.000:

$$EffCon = \frac{[(PV_-) + (PV_+)] - [2 \times (PV_0)]}{(\Delta Curve)^2 \times (PV_0)}$$

$$EffCon = \frac{[(100.241) + (99.760)] - [2 \times (100)]}{(0.0005)^2 \times (100)}$$

$$EffCon = 40.000$$

EXAMPLE 1

Effective Duration and Convexity

The portfolio manager asks you, the analyst on a fixed-income team, to determine the interest rate sensitivity of a callable bond she is considering. The portfolio manager is seeking to invest in a bond with a duration between 7.0 and 8.0 and positive convexity.

Suppose the full price of the callable bond is 101.060 per 100 of par value. When the government par curve is raised and lowered by 25 bps, the new full prices for this callable bond from your option valuation model are 99.050 and 102.891, respectively. Therefore,

- $PV_0 = 101.060$,
- $PV_+ = 99.050$,
- $PV_- = 102.891$, and
- $\Delta Curve = 0.0025$.

You determine effective duration and effective convexity for this callable bond as follows:

$$\text{EffDur} = \frac{(PV_-) - (PV_+)}{2 \times (\Delta \text{Curve}) \times (PV_0)}.$$

$$\text{EffDur} = \frac{(102.891) - (99.050)}{2 \times (0.0025) \times (101.060)}.$$

$$EffDur = 7.601.$$

$$\text{EffCon} = \frac{[(PV_-) + (PV_+) - 2 \times (PV_0)]}{(\Delta \text{Curve})^2 \times (PV_0)}.$$

$$\text{EffCon} = \frac{[(102.891) + (99.050)] - [2 \times (101.060)]}{(0.0025)^2 \times (101.060)}.$$

$$EffCon = -283.$$

You recommend that the portfolio manager not buy this callable bond. While its effective duration meets her criteria, the bond has negative effective convexity.

QUESTION SET

1. Match each scenario to the interest rate risk measures below.

Scenario	Interest rate risk measure
A. Bond's percentage price change given a change in its yield-to-maturity	Money duration
B. Linear approximation of the bond's price change in currency, given a 1% change in yield	Modified duration
C. Callable bond	Effective duration

Solution:

The match for A is modified duration. Modified duration is used to estimate the percentage price change given a change in yield-to-maturity.

The match for B is money duration. Money duration expresses modified duration in currency units, which can be used to estimate the currency unit change in the position of a bond.

The match for C is effective duration. Callable bonds have uncertain future cash flows with respect to future interest rates. Therefore, a curve duration statistic, such as effective duration, would be best to measure interest rate risk.

Questions 2–5 relate to the following information:

As a member of a fixed-income team, you are asked to examine pricing data for a Viviyu Inc. callable bond. The current full price, the price assuming the benchmark yield curve shifts up 25 bps, and the price assuming the benchmark yield curve shifts down by 25 bps, are as follows:

- $PV_0 = 102.208$,
- $PV_+ = 100.004$, and
- $PV_- = 103.891$.

2. Calculate the effective duration of the Viviyu Inc. callable bond.

Solution:

$$\text{EffDur} = \frac{(PV_-) - (PV_+)}{2 \times (\Delta\text{Curve}) \times (PV_0)}.$$

$$\text{EffDur} = \frac{(103.891) - (100.004)}{2 \times (0.0025) \times (102.208)}.$$

$$EffDur = 7.6061.$$

3. In an audit of the data, it was determined that PV_+ was incorrect and that the correct value of PV_+ is 100.50426. All other data values were correct.

Explain whether the updated data would increase or decrease the value of effective duration.

Solution:

There is no need to recalculate the effective duration. Since the updated PV_+ value is larger than the prior one, with all else constant, the numerator would be lower; thus, effective duration would decrease.

4. Calculate the effective convexity of the Viviyu Inc. callable bond using the following:

   - PV_0 = 102.208,
   - PV_+ = 98.504,
   - PV_- = 103.891, and
   - $\Delta Curve$ = 0.0025.

   Solution:

   $$\text{EffCon} = \frac{[(PV_-) + (PV_+)] - [2 \times (PV_0)]}{(\Delta\text{Curve})^2 \times (PV_0)}.$$

   $$\text{EffCon} = \frac{[(103.891) + (98.504)] - [2 \times (102.208)]}{(0.0025)^2 \times (102.208)}.$$

   $EffCon = -3{,}164.$

5. In Question 4, the effective convexity was negative, not positive as it was for the effective duration. Explain what negative effective convexity implies.

   Solution:

   Negative effective convexity implies that the bond price will decline by a greater amount with an upward shift in benchmark yield than it will increase with a decline in the benchmark yield.

3 BOND RISK AND RETURN USING CURVE-BASED DURATION AND CONVEXITY

☐ calculate the percentage price change of a bond for a specified change in benchmark yield, given the bond's effective duration and convexity

As we have seen, effective duration and effective convexity are curve-based metrics that are useful for gauging the interest rate risk of complex instruments—such as those with embedded contingency provisions—whose future cash flows are uncertain. These metrics are typically determined from bond prices derived using an option valuation model, given specific (parallel) changes in the underlying benchmark government yield curve.

Just as with yield-based interest rate risk measures, effective duration and effective convexity can be used to estimate the percentage change in a bond's full price for a given shift in the benchmark yield curve ($\Delta Curve$), as shown in Equation 3.

$$\%\Delta PV^{Full} \approx (-EffDur \times \Delta Curve) + \left[\frac{1}{2} \times EffCon \times (\Delta Curve)^2\right]. \quad (3)$$

Let's return to BRWA's five-year, 3.2% (semiannual) coupon bond priced at par for settlement on 15 October 2025 and maturity on 15 October 2030. Using Equation 3 and previously derived effective duration and effective convexity,

$EffDur = 4.816$ and $EffCon = 26.723$,

the percentage changes in the bond's full price for ±100 bp shifts in the benchmark government par curve are estimated as follows:

$$\%\Delta PV^{Full} \approx (-4.816 \times 0.01) + [½ \times 26.723 \times (0.01)^2] = -4.68\%.$$

$$\%\Delta PV^{Full} \approx (-4.816 \times -0.01) + [½ \times 26.723 \times (-0.01)^2] = 4.95\%.$$

These bond price changes compare with the previously derived estimates of −4.47% and 4.71% for this BRWA bond when using *ApproxModDur* alone and *ApproxModDur* and *ApproxCon*, respectively, with yield-to-maturity changes of ±100 bps.

As noted earlier, the differences in results using the curve-based measures versus the yield-based interest rate risk measures are due to slightly different bond prices (PV_+ and PV_-) and, therefore, *EffDur* and *EffCon* metrics (versus *ApproxModDur* and *ApproxCon* metrics) since a parallel shift in the government par curve produces a non-parallel shift in spot (zero) rates and one-year forward rates.

Curve-based interest rate risk measures are important for both issuers and investors. For example, as noted previously, for a callable bond, when the benchmark curve shifts downward and interest rates are low relative to the bond's coupon rate, effective duration declines and effective convexity may even turn from positive to negative. From an investor's perspective, these results severely limit the bond's price appreciation in a declining interest rate environment. From the issuer's perspective, the bonds can be bought back at the call price and refinanced at lower market rates.

As for a putable bond, when the benchmark curve shifts upward and interest rates are high relative to the bond's coupon rate, both effective duration and effective convexity decline (but effective convexity always remains positive), which, from an investor's perspective, limits the bond's price depreciation in a rising interest rate environment. This is because the investor can sell the bonds back to issuer at the put price (typically par), rather than at a discounted price, and reinvest the proceeds at the higher prevailing market rates.

A practical consideration in using effective duration and effective convexity is setting the change in the benchmark yield curve. With approximate modified duration, accuracy is improved by choosing a smaller yield-to-maturity change. The pricing models used for more complex securities, such as callable bonds issued by corporations and asset-backed securities (ABSs), include assumptions about the behavior of corporate issuers or the borrowers whose loans make up the underlying ABS assets under different interest rate scenarios. For example, a corporate issuer's decision to call a bond and refinance depends in part on issuer-specific credit spreads. For mortgage borrowers, changes in the value of the underlying asset financed will affect the decision to refinance a mortgage and therefore call an MBS bond. Therefore, estimates of interest rate risk using effective duration and effective convexity are not necessarily improved by choosing a smaller change in benchmark rates. Curve-based interest rate risk measures have become an important tool in the financial analysis of not only traditional bonds but also financial liabilities.

EXAMPLE 2

Using Effective Duration and Convexity to Estimate Bonds' Price Changes Given Benchmark Rate Changes

Continuing from Example 1, to bolster your recommendation that the portfolio manager (PM) not buy the callable bond trading at 101.060, you want to demonstrate the price impact of the bond's negative effective convexity. You assume the benchmark government par curve increases and decreases by 100 bps and use Equation 3, with *EffDur* and *EffCon* estimates based on bond prices from your option valuation model, to derive the following results:

- $\%\Delta PV^{Full} \approx (-7.601 \times 0.01) + [½ \times -285.168 \times (0.0100)^2] = -9.03\%$.
- $\%\Delta PV^{Full} \approx (-7.601 \times -0.01) + [½ \times -285.168 \times (-0.0100)^2] = 6.17\%$.

In discussing these results with the PM, you conclude that the negative effective convexity adds to the bond's price decline when benchmark rates increase and subtracts from the bond's price rise when benchmark rates decrease. If the PM's forecast is an equal probability that the benchmark par curve will increase or decrease, the PM would not invest. However, if the PM's forecast is that the probability for the benchmark decreasing is greater, such that expected gain is greater than zero, she may decide to invest in the bond.

QUESTION SET

Questions 1–5 relate to the following information:

As a fixed-income analyst, you are asked to consider the impact of the benchmark government par curve shifting upward by 200 bps on two bonds, as part of an internal stress scenario. From a bond pricing model, the following information on effective duration and effective convexity were obtained.

Bond A: Effective duration = 9.369; Effective convexity = −353.752.

Bond B: Effective duration = 8.517; Effective convexity = −321.756.

1. Calculate the estimated percentage change in the full price of bond A for the 200 bps curve shift.

Solution:

$$\%\Delta PV^{Full} \approx (-EffDur \times \Delta Curve) + \left[\frac{1}{2} \times EffCon \times (\Delta Curve)^2\right].$$

$$\%\Delta PV^{Full} \approx (-9.369 \times 0.02) + \left[\frac{1}{2} \times -353.752 \times (0.02)^2\right].$$

$$\%\Delta PV^{Full} \approx -25.81\%.$$

2. Calculate the estimated percentage change in the full price of Bond B for the 200 bps curve shift.

Solution:

$$\%\Delta PV^{Full} \approx (-EffDur \times \Delta Curve) + \left[\frac{1}{2} \times EffCon \times (\Delta Curve)^2\right].$$

$$\%\Delta PV^{Full} \approx (-8.517 \times 0.02) + \left[\frac{1}{2} \times -321.756 \times (0.02)^2\right].$$

$$\%\Delta PV^{Full} \approx -23.47\%.$$

3. Based on Questions 1 and 2, if both bonds were in a portfolio and a decision to sell one of them had to be made in light of a forecast of sharply rising interest rates, recommend Bond A or Bond B to sell. Justify your answer.

Solution:

Sell Bond A since it has the more negative percentage change in the full price of the bond. For every 200 bps increase in the benchmark curve, the full price of the bond drops 25.81%.

4. If you were forecasting the benchmark yield curve to shift downward by 200 basis points, recommend Bond A or Bond B to add to the portfolio in anticipation of the curve shift. Justify your answer.

Solution:

Add Bond A, since when you calculate the percentage change in the full price for Bonds A and B, Bond A has the higher positive percentage change.

$\%\Delta PV^{Full}$ Bond A $\approx (-9.369 \times -0.02) + [½ \times -353.752 \times (-0.0200)^2]$

$= 11.66\%$.

$\%\Delta PV^{Full}$ Bond B $\approx (-8.517 \times -0.02) + [½ \times -321.756 \times (-0.0200)^2]$

$= 10.60\%$.

5. Explain why the estimated percentage change in the price of the bond from a 200 bps upward shift in the benchmark yield curve is more than twice the estimated percentage change in the price of the bond from a 200 bps downward yield curve shift.

Solution:

Because effective convexity is negative, an upward shift in the yield curve results in a higher absolute price change than a downward shift in the yield curve. For the upward shift, the duration contribution is positive and convexity contribution is negative, offsetting each other.

KEY RATE DURATION AS A MEASURE OF YIELD CURVE RISK 4

☐ define key rate duration and describe its use to measure price sensitivity of fixed-income instruments to benchmark yield curve changes

As we have seen, effective duration measures a bond's sensitivity to changes in the benchmark yield curve if all yields change by the same amount. Key rate duration provides further insight into a bond's sensitivity to *non-parallel* benchmark yield curve changes. **Key rate duration** (or partial duration) is a measure of a bond's sensitivity to a change in the benchmark yield at a specific maturity. Such a measure is important to isolate the price responses of bonds to changes in the rates of key maturities on the benchmark yield curve.

Key rate durations define a security's price sensitivity over a set of maturities along the yield curve, with the sum of key rate durations being equal to the effective duration, as shown in Equation 4 and Equation 5:

$$KeyRateDur_k = -\frac{1}{PV} \times \frac{\Delta PV}{\Delta r_k}; \tag{4}$$

$$\sum_{k=1}^{n} KeyRateDur_k = EffDur, \tag{5}$$

where r_k represents the *k*th key rate. In contrast to effective duration, key rate durations help identify "shaping risk" for a bond—that is, a bond's sensitivity to changes in the shape of the benchmark yield curve (e.g., the yield curve becoming steeper or flatter or twisting).

The procedure for the calculation of key rate durations is similar to that used in the calculation of effective duration, but instead of shifting the entire benchmark yield curve, only key points on the curve are shifted, one at a time, as shown in Exhibit 3. The *k*th key rate, which could be a 0.5-, 2-, 5-, 10-, 20-, or 30-year rate, is shifted up (as shown in Exhibit 3) and down by 1 bp, and then new bond prices are generated (PV_+ and PV_-) and the key rate duration at that specific maturity is calculated using Equation 4. Thus, the effective duration for each maturity point shift is calculated in isolation.

Exhibit 3: Key Rate Shift

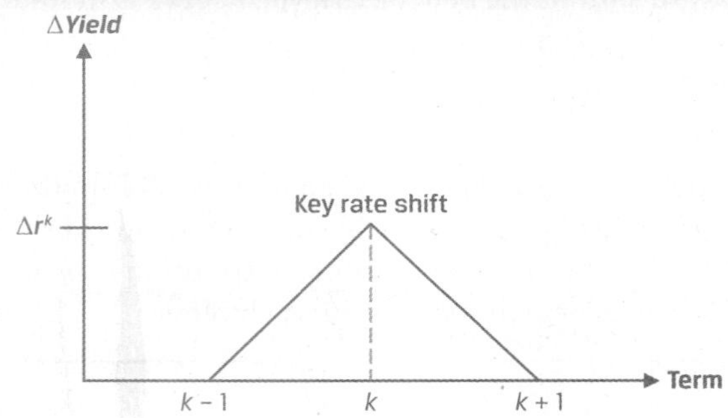

Exhibit 4 depicts the process of successively shifting the benchmark rate up and down at each of the key maturities along the benchmark yield to generate the key rate duration at maturity.

Exhibit 4: Key Rate Shifts across the Benchmark Yield Curve

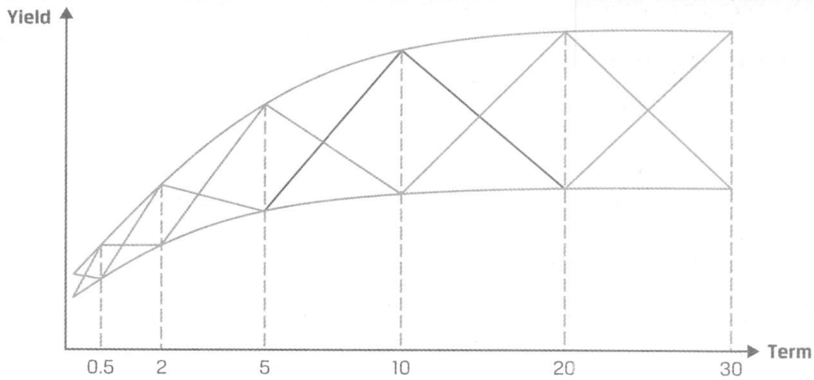

As for practical uses of key rate duration, the analyst may want to know how the price of a callable bond is expected to change if short-term benchmark rates—for example, the rate on the two-year Treasury note, with modified duration of 1.99—rise by 25 bps but longer-maturity benchmark rates remain unchanged. Given that the yield curve is upward sloping, this scenario represents a flattening of the curve.

Equation 6 rearranges terms from Equation 4 to solve for $\Delta PV/PV$ (or $\%\Delta PV^{Full}$):

$$\frac{\Delta PV}{PV} = -KeyRateDur_k \times \Delta r_k. \quad (6)$$

Using Equation 6, the expected estimated price change would be -0.4975%:

$$\Delta PV/PV = -1.99 \times 0.0025.$$

Now, consider the simple portfolio of government bonds shown in Exhibit 5.

Exhibit 5: Simple Government Bond Portfolio

Tenor (Years)	Coupon	Annualized Yield (%)	Price	Position Size	Modified Duration	Key Rate Duration
2	0.00	0.50	99.006	$99,006,219	1.990	0.711
5	0.00	1.25	93.960	$93,959,580	4.938	1.675
10	0.00	1.75	84.010	$84,009,625	9.828	2.981
				$276,975,424	5.368	5.368

Assume the portfolio is weighted by the prices of the respective 2-, 5-, and 10-year bonds for a total portfolio value of $277 million, or $1 million × (99.006 + 93.96 + 81.01). The portfolio's modified duration is calculated as

$$5.368 = [1.990 \times (99.006/277)] + [4.938 \times (93.96/277)] + [9.828 \times (84.01/277)].$$

Alternatively, we could calculate each key rate duration by maturity. For example, the two-year key rate duration ($KeyRateDur_2$) is

$$0.711 = 1.990 \times (99.006/277).$$

Note that the three key rate duration values sum to the portfolio duration value of 5.368.

If we assume this portfolio represents an "index," then a manager attempting to outperform the index could vary (or tilt) the key rate durations to capitalize on her view of expected changes in the shape of the benchmark yield curve, as demonstrated in the following example.

EXAMPLE 3

Using Key Rate Duration Estimate Interest Rate Risk for Bonds in a Portfolio

Continuing from Example 2, the portfolio manager asks you to determine if the bond portfolio may need rebalancing to improve overall return, given the tenor of the portfolio's bonds, key rate duration information, and forecasted benchmark government par curve shifts at the various maturities. All four bonds have the same benchmark government par curve. Current information for the bonds are as follows:

Bond	Tenor	Position Size	Key Rate Duration
A	1 year	$200,565,245	0.645
B	5 years	$201,042,132	1.483
C	10 years	$202,673,298	2.158
D	20 years	$202,588,801	2.982

Information on the forecasted benchmark government par curve changes at the various maturities are as follows:

Maturity	1 year	5 years	10 years	20 years
Expected change	–23 bps	–25 bps	–18 bps	–10 bps

If we take the product of the key rate duration and curve shift at a certain maturity, we can forecast the change in the price of the bond. For example, for the one-year maturity, this would be –0.645 × –0.0023 = 0.148%. The calculation for all the bonds is shown below:

Maturities	1 year (Bond A)	5 years (Bond B)	10 years (Bond C)	20 years (Bond D)
% change in bond price	0.148%	0.371%	0.388%	0.298%

Therefore, since the forecasted price change in the bonds favor Bonds B and C, it would be advisable to increase the weightings for these bonds, taking more from the Bond A position than the Bond D position, since Bond A is forecasted to give the least gain of all the bonds.

QUESTION SET

Questions 1–3 relate to the following information.

The analysis you performed previously on the consideration of the impact of the benchmark government par curve increasing by 200 bps on two bonds has now been expanded for a more complicated scenario. You are asked to consider the scenario of a non-parallel shift in the benchmark government par curve, where a steepening of the curve is occurring at longer maturities. Below are the details on non-parallel shifts to the benchmark government par curve:

Maturity	1 year	5 years	10 years	20 years	30 years
Expected change	+100 bps	+150 bps	+200 bps	+250 bps	+300 bps

Relevant details on the two bonds are as follows:

	Tenor	Key Rate Duration
Bond A	5 years	2.702
Bond B	10 years	3.953

1. Based on the information above, identify which bond will have a greater percentage change in its price due to the benchmark par curve shift.

Solution

Bond B.

For Bond A, $\Delta PV/PV = -2.702 \times 0.015 = -4.05\%$.

For Bond B, $\Delta PV/PV = -3.953 \times 0.020 = -7.91\%$.

2. If the values in the table above on the non-parallel yield curve shifts were forecasts and your portfolio contains equal positions in the two bonds, which of the following would be the best course of action?

A. Sell Bond A.

B. Sell Bond B.

C. Sell both Bond A and Bond B.

Solution

C is correct. Sell both Bonds A and B, since both are expected to see price declines.

3. Explain why key rate durations might be useful for a portfolio manager even though key rate duration values of the bonds in a portfolio sum to the portfolio duration.

Solution

Knowing the portfolio duration and overall movement of the benchmark yield curve can provide a quick estimate of gains or losses; however, by using key rate durations, a portfolio manager can over- or underweight specific tenors to maximize risk-adjusted return.

EMPIRICAL DURATION 5

☐ describe the difference between empirical duration and analytical duration

The approaches taken so far to estimate duration and convexity statistics using mathematical formulas is often referred to as **analytical duration**; the measures we have covered are summarized in Exhibit 6. Importantly, estimates of the impact of benchmark yield changes on bond prices using analytical duration implicitly assume that government bond yields and spreads are independent variables and are uncorrelated. Analytical duration offers a reasonable approximation of the price–yield relationship in many situations.

Exhibit 6: Curve-Based and Empirical Duration Measures

Measure	Definition	Interpretation
Approximate Modified Duration	Estimates the slope of the line tangent to a bond's price–yield curve	Yield-based method to estimate modified duration
Effective Duration	Sensitivity of a bond's price to a change in a benchmark yield curve	Curve-based method to estimate modified duration for complex bonds with uncertain cash flows
Key Rate	Measures bond sensitivity to a benchmark yield change for a specific maturity	Partial duration statistic that gauges a bond's sensitivity to non-parallel benchmark yield curve changes
Empirical	Measure using historical data in statistical models and incorporating factors affecting bond prices to determine the price–yield relationship	Statistical estimate that accounts for correlation between yield spreads and benchmark yield-to-maturity changes under different economic scenarios

However, in practice, there is another important type of duration: Fixed-income professionals often use historical data in statistical models that incorporate various factors affecting bond prices to calculate **empirical duration** estimates (see Exhibit 6). These estimates are calculated over time and in different interest rate environments to inform the fixed-income portfolio decision-making process.

For instance, during crises, investors typically sell risky assets and purchase government bonds. Such a "flight to quality" can cause government benchmark yields to fall while credit spreads widen. Exhibit 7 depicts the flight to quality during the onset of the COVID-19 pandemic at the end of February 2020.

Exhibit 7: 10-Year US Treasury Yield vs. US Corporate BB Credit Spread, Q1 2020

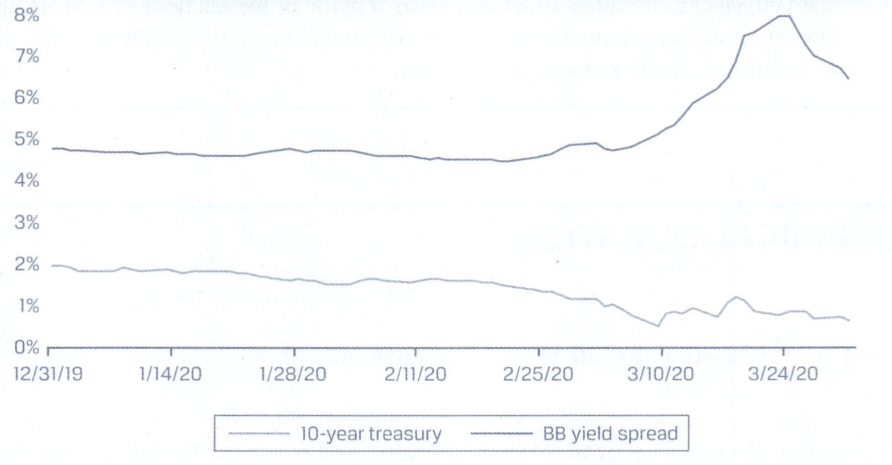

During such periods, we might expect analytical and empirical duration estimates to differ. For a government bond with little or no credit risk, we would expect analytical and empirical duration to be similar because benchmark yield changes largely drive bond prices. Conversely, credit spreads (and liquidity spreads) would widen because of an increase in expected default risk. Since credit spreads and benchmark yields are negatively correlated under this scenario, wider credit spreads will partially or fully offset the decline in government benchmark yields, resulting in lower empirical duration estimates than analytical duration estimates (in other words, the expected *increase* in a bond's price from declining government benchmark yields is offset by a *decrease* in price from widening credit spreads). Analysts must consider the correlation between benchmark yields and credit spreads when deciding whether to use empirical or analytical duration estimates.

EXAMPLE 4

Viswan Family Office's Corporate Bond Portfolio—Empirical vs. Analytical Duration

In addition to equity holdings, the Viswan Family Office (VFO) manages a government bond portfolio and a corporate bond portfolio. Positions in the government bond portfolio are mainly medium-term US Treasury securities but also include debt of other highly rated developed-market sovereign issuers. About half of the corporate bond portfolio is invested in investment-grade issues, and the other half consists of high-yield issues, with a mix of maturities and a mix of North American, European, and Asian companies.

Explain why empirical duration is likely to be a more relevant interest rate risk measure for VFO's corporate bond portfolio than for its government bond portfolio.

Solution:

The government bond portfolio includes debt securities of the US government and other highly rated developed-market sovereign issuers. Since benchmark yields are the primary driver of changes in overall bond yields in this portfolio, the results of analytical duration and empirical duration should be broadly similar.

The corporate bond portfolio includes a wide variety of debt securities with varying levels of credit quality and liquidity risk and, therefore, different credit and liquidity spreads.

Correlations between benchmark yield changes and the sizes of the credit and liquidity spreads are negative, particularly during stressed market conditions, such that during such times, lower benchmark yields are more than offset by higher credit and liquidity spreads. So, for the lower-quality corporate bonds, yields increase, which makes their empirical duration significantly lower than their analytical duration.

Consequently, empirical duration, not analytical duration, is the more accurate interest rate risk measure for the corporate bond portfolio.

QUESTION SET

1. When comparing analytical duration and empirical duration, which of the following statements is correct?

   A. Empirical duration and convexity are estimated duration and convexity statistics using mathematical formulas.

B. Analytical duration and convexity are estimated using historical data in non-statistical models that incorporate various factors affecting bond prices.

C. Neither A nor B

Solution:

C is correct.

A is incorrect because it is *analytical*, not empirical, duration and convexity that are measured using mathematical formulas.

B is incorrect because it is *empirical*, not analytical, duration and convexity that are estimated using historical data in non-statistical models that incorporate various factors affecting bond prices.

2. True or false: Empirical duration estimates provide better estimates than the analytical duration estimates for bonds that have credit risk.

Solution:

True. Macroeconomic factors drive government bond yields lower in a market stress scenario, and the flight to safety will cause high-yield bond credit spreads to widen because of an increase in expected default risk. Since credit spreads and benchmark yields are negatively correlated under this scenario, wider credit spreads will partially or fully offset the decline in government benchmark yields. Analytical duration, however, assumes that benchmark yields and spreads are uncorrelated. Empirical duration estimates are a more accurate method of forecasting for bonds with credit risk.

3. Identify some of the challenges that may be encountered in estimating empirical duration.

Solution:

Empirical duration estimation utilizes historical data based on multiple factors. What factors to use and not use, what weight to give the factors, and how to weight current data versus older data (e.g., the time period to measure duration) are some challenges.

PRACTICE PROBLEMS

The following information relates to questions 1-8

An investor's well-diversified portfolio has $200,000 in cash. The investor aims to invest in short-term, one-year Large-Cap Company bonds, prior to using the cash to invest in an upcoming IPO. There are currently two Large-Cap Company bonds on the market to purchase, both with one-year maturities. One of the bonds, Bond A, is a non-callable bond, while Bond B is a callable bond. As a fixed-income analyst, you are asked to conduct an analysis.

1. For the two bonds offered by Large-Cap Company, which duration calculation would be the *most* appropriate to use to measure interest rate risk?

   A. Modified duration

   B. Macaulay duration

   C. Effective duration

2. For Bond B, as the benchmark yield curve declines, the slope of the line tangent to the bond flattens as the benchmark yield declines and reaches an inflection point, after which the effective convexity becomes:

   A. positive.

   B. negative.

   C. neither positive nor negative.

3. The following information on Bonds A and B was obtained:

Bond	Effective Duration	Effective Convexity
A	7.48621	29.35972
B	7.23852	−321.75618

   Compare the interest rate risk of Bond A and Bond B.

   A. Bond A is riskier than Bond B.

   B. Bond B is riskier than Bond A.

   C. Bond A and Bond B have approximately the same interest rate risk.

4. For the percentage price change for Bond A, given a 200 bp increase in benchmark yield, what part of the price change is of the most concern?

   A. Duration

   B. Convexity

   C. Not able to determine with given information

5. A colleague asks whether you also considered looking at the key rate durations when comparing the interest rate risks of Bond A and Bond B. Would research into key rate durations for Bond A and Bond B help you make a better decision about the interest rate risk of the two bonds?

   A. Yes

   B. No

   C. Inconclusive

6. The investor's portfolio is diversified, and the fixed-income component of the portfolio has bonds of various maturities, with a duration of 7.48621. What would happen to the effective duration of the fixed-income component of the investor's portfolio if Bond A is added to the portfolio?

   A. It would increase.

   B. If would decrease.

   C. It would stay the same.

7. For the two bonds under consideration, would analytical duration estimates or empirical duration estimates be *most* appropriate in conducting your analysis?

   A. Analytical duration estimates

   B. Empirical duration estimates

   C. Either type of estimate would be appropriate.

8. What impact would a "flight to safety" (i.e., government bond yields falling and credit spreads widening) have on the analytical duration estimate of Bond A?

   A. Decreased duration

   B. Increased duration

   C. No impact

SOLUTIONS

1. C is correct. Since Bond B is callable, it has an embedded option, and effective duration is the most appropriate duration measure. Effective duration also works on bonds without embedded options and would allow the analyst to compare the interest rate risk of the two bonds.

2. B is correct. Since the bond is callable, after a certain point on the yield curve, the issuer will exercise the call and the owner will not be able to realize additional gains from declines in the benchmark yield curve.

3. B is correct. Bond B is riskier since the 100 bps upward shift in the yield curve results in a greater percentage price decrease, owing to its negative effective convexity:

   $\%\Delta PV^{Full}$ Bond A $\approx (-7.48621 \times 0.0200) + [\frac{1}{2} \times 29.35972 \times (-0.0200)^2]$
   $= -7.33941\%$.

   $\%\Delta PV^{Full}$ Bond B $\approx (-7.23853 \times 0.0200) + [\frac{1}{2} \times -321.75618 \times (0.0200)^2]$
   $= -8.84730\%$.

4. A is correct. Typically, the effect of duration is much larger than the effect of convexity.

   $\%\Delta PV^{Full}$ Bond A, Duration $\approx -7.48621 \times 0.0200 = -14.97242\%$.

   $\%\Delta PV^{Full}$ Bond A, Convexity Adjustment $\approx \frac{1}{2} \times 29.35972 \times (-0.0200)^2$
   $= -0.58719\%$.

5. B is correct. Since both bonds mature in one year, key rate duration analysis would not give you any additional insight, since both bonds would undergo the same shift in the curve.

6. C is correct. Bond A has the same effective duration as the portfolio effective duration.

7. B is correct. Since both Bond A and Bond B are corporate bonds, they have credit risk, and as such, empirical duration would be the most appropriate because benchmark yields and credit spreads may not be positively correlated.

8. C is correct. There would be no impact on the analytical duration estimate. However, an empirical duration estimate would be impacted. A flight to safety would result in an increase in the bond price due to the falling benchmark yield being offset by widening credit spread. This would lead to a lower empirical duration than analytical duration.

LEARNING MODULE

14

Credit Risk

LEARNING OUTCOMES	
Mastery	*The candidate should be able to:*
☐	describe credit risk and its components, probability of default and loss given default
☐	describe the uses of ratings from credit rating agencies and their limitations
☐	describe macroeconomic, market, and issuer-specific factors that influence the level and volatility of yield spreads

INTRODUCTION

1

Credit analysis plays a critical role in fixed-income markets. Proper evaluation and pricing of credit risk facilitates the efficient allocation of capital. This is a dynamic process as credit risk components are continuously re-evaluated and fixed-income instruments repriced according to market conditions. This learning module covers the basic principles of credit analysis. First, we introduce the concepts of credit risk and expected loss and interpret what credit ratings mean. We compare bond issuer creditworthiness within a given industry as well as across industries, and we explore how financial markets price credit risk. This lesson focuses primarily on the analysis of credit risk, while subsequent lessons discuss credit analysis of sovereign and non-sovereign government issuers as well as corporate debt

LEARNING MODULE OVERVIEW

- Credit risk is the risk of economic loss resulting from borrower failure to make full and timely payments of interest and principal. The key components of credit risk are the probability of default and the loss given default, and their product is expected loss.
- Chief sources of credit risk include adverse macroeconomic conditions, a financing mismatch between resources and obligations, and issuer-specific factors in corporate and sovereign debt markets.

- Nearly every bond issue in developed debt markets carries credit ratings classifying creditworthiness. Credit ratings enable comparisons of the credit risk of debt issues and issuers within and across industries.
- Bonds or issuers with an investment-grade (IG) credit rating pose the lowest risk of default and are rated Baa3 by Moody's and BBB– or higher by S&P and Fitch. In contrast, non-investment-grade or high-yield (HY) bonds or issuers are rated BB+ or lower by S&P/Fitch and Ba1 or less by Moody's and represent substantial to very high credit risk.
- Pitfalls of relying solely on credit ratings in making investment decisions include that rating agency decisions may lag market pricing of credit risk, overlook key financial risks, and/or involve miscalculations or unforeseen changes not fully captured in a rating agency's forward-looking analysis.
- The premium, or yield spread, at which corporate bonds trade relative to default risk-free assets widens when credit risk rises and narrows if credit risk falls.
- Credit spread changes affect holding period returns via two primary factors: a) the basis point spread change and b) the sensitivity of price to yield as reflected by end-of-period modified duration and convexity. Spread narrowing increases holding period returns.

LEARNING MODULE SELF-ASSESSMENT

These initial questions are intended to help you gauge your current level of understanding of this learning module.

1. Credit risk is:

   A. activated upon a borrower's default.

   B. the spread an investor receives above the risk-free rate.

   C. experienced in several ways by lenders.

   Solution:

   The correct answer is C. Lenders are impacted by credit risk in several ways, including failure to receive principal and interest payments in a timely manner, the inability to sell collateral at a market price sufficient to meet an issuer's obligations in the case of secured debt, or the potential incurrence of legal or other costs to collect debt. A is incorrect because while a borrower default initiates a realized loss, expected loss exists prior to the occurrence of any actual loss. B is incorrect because it refers to the credit spread, which compensates investors for assuming credit risk.

2. A EUR500,000 loan has the following characteristics:

   - Probability of default 5%
   - Recovery rate 90%
   - Expected exposure EUR400,000

   The expected loss for this loan is:

   A. EUR1,500

B. EUR2,000

C. EUR20,000

Solution:

The correct answer is B. We solve for expected loss (EL) as follows:

EL = POD × LGD = POD × EE × (1 – RR).

Since probability of default (POD) is 5%, expected exposure (EE) is EUR400,000, and the recovery rate (RR) is 90%:

EL = EUR2,000 = 0.05 × (400,000) × (1 – 0.9).

A is incorrect as it fails to reduce the expected exposure by the collateral, while C is incorrect as it simply multiplies EE and POD.

3. Credit ratings are:

   A. developed on behalf of investors.

   B. a symbol-based measure of the potential default risk of a bond issue or issuer.

   C. measures of credit risk that are used to determine bond market pricing.

Solution:

The correct answer is B: Credit ratings are a symbol-based measure of the potential default risk of a bond issue or issuer. A is incorrect because credit ratings are developed on behalf of the issuer. C is incorrect because credit ratings are not used to determine bond prices.

4. Which of the following statements best describes risks that are difficult to capture in credit ratings?

   A. Environmental risks are captured by ESG ratings rather than credit ratings.

   B. Debt-financed acquisitions are usually captured in credit ratings.

   C. Split ratings demonstrate that credit rating agencies may view complex risks very differently.

Solution:

The correct answer is C. A is incorrect as environmental risks may affect credit ratings. B is incorrect since debt-financed acquisitions are difficult to anticipate.

5. *Determine the correct answers to fill in the blanks:* Spreads are __________ at or near the top of the credit cycle, when market participants perceive credit risk to be at its lowest; they are __________ at or near the bottom of the credit cycle, when financial markets believe credit risk has reached its peak.

Solution:

Spreads are **narrowest (or lowest)** at or near the top of the credit cycle, when market participants perceive credit risk to be at its lowest; they are **widest (or highest)** at or near the bottom of the credit cycle, when financial markets believe credit risk has reached its peak.

6. A portfolio manager assessing a downside case believes that HY bond spreads will rise 100 bps in a recession. If an observed HY bond has modi-

fied duration of 4.5 and reported convexity of 0.23, the expected change in the HY bond's price under this scenario would be *closest to*:

A. 4.5%.

B. 4.385%.

C. 4.615%.

Solution:

The correct answer is B. Bond price changes based upon modified duration, convexity, and the spread change are calculated as follows:

$$\%\Delta PV^{Full} = -(AnnModDur \times \Delta Spread) + \tfrac{1}{2}AnnConvexity \times (\Delta Spread)^2.$$

With AnnModDur = 4.5 and reported convexity of 0.23, rescaling convexity to 23 and substituting values to solve for spread results in

$$\Delta PV^{Full} = -(4.5 \times 1.00\%) + \tfrac{1}{2}(23) \times (1.00\%)^2$$

$$\Delta PV^{Full} = -4.385\%.$$

2 SOURCES OF CREDIT RISK

☐ describe credit risk and its components, probability of default and loss given default

Fixed-income investors face credit risk, a form of performance risk in a contractual relationship. A borrower that fails to meet its promised interest and/or principal payment obligations under a bond or loan contract is said to be in **default**. A fixed-income investor seeks compensation for the expected economic loss under a potential borrower default over the life of the contract known as **credit risk**.

Credit risk depends upon specific factors related to the borrower itself as well as general economic conditions and is subject to change over the life of the contract. Credit risk exposes the lender or investor to potential losses and underperformance.

Traditionally, many analysts evaluated creditworthiness based on what are often called the "Cs of credit analysis," as shown in Exhibit 1:

Exhibit 1: The Cs of Credit Analysis

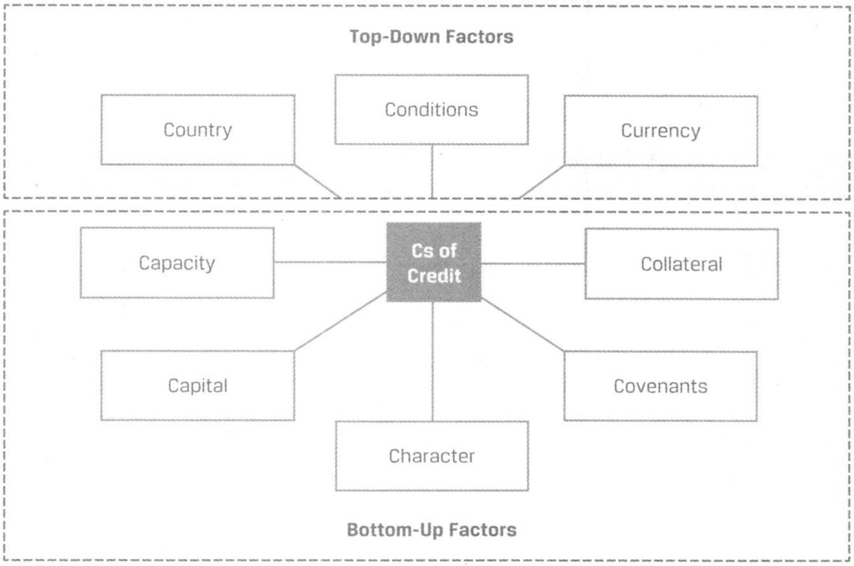

Five of these criteria—capacity, capital, collateral, covenants, and character—are related to the specific bottom-up factors applicable to an individual borrower. **Capacity** refers to the ability of the borrower to make its debt payments on time. **Capital** addresses other company resources available that reduce reliance on debt. **Collateral** refers to the quality and value of the assets supporting the issuer's indebtedness, while **covenants** are the legal terms of debt agreements that an issuer must comply with. **Character** refers to the quality of management and the willingness of repay indebtedness.

While capacity and capital are generally quantitative metrics based on financial statements, collateral, covenants, and character are largely qualitative measures that analysts assess based on historical company performance, credit relationships and the reputation of current management.

The remaining three criteria—conditions, country, and currency—involve general top-down factors that apply to all borrowers to a greater or lesser extent. **Conditions** refers to the general economic, competitive, and business environment faced by all borrowers that may affect their ability to service or refinance debt. **Country** involves the geopolitical environment as well as the legal and political system faced by all issuers in a jurisdiction that may affect debt payment. **Currency** affects issuers whose cash flows are affected by exchange rate changes or who borrow in a currency outside of their jurisdiction, such as sovereign issuers with foreign currency debt.

A borrower's inability to make timely payments may be due to several underlying and contributing factors, but it ultimately results from a lack of sufficient cash available to make a current debt payment. Lenders, as fixed-income investors, are impacted by credit risk. They may lose some or all of the principal and interest due, suffering a capital loss or income shortfall. This disruption to their cash flows may impact their own ability to repay debt, and payment delays as well as increased legal and collection costs may further reduce their income and margins.

Sources of Credit Risk

Changes in credit risk due to issuer-based or overall economic conditions are affected by the source of repayment, which differs among issuer types. Exhibit 2 shows the main sources of repayment for corporate and sovereign bonds.

Exhibit 2: Sovereign and Corporate Bond Sources of Repayment

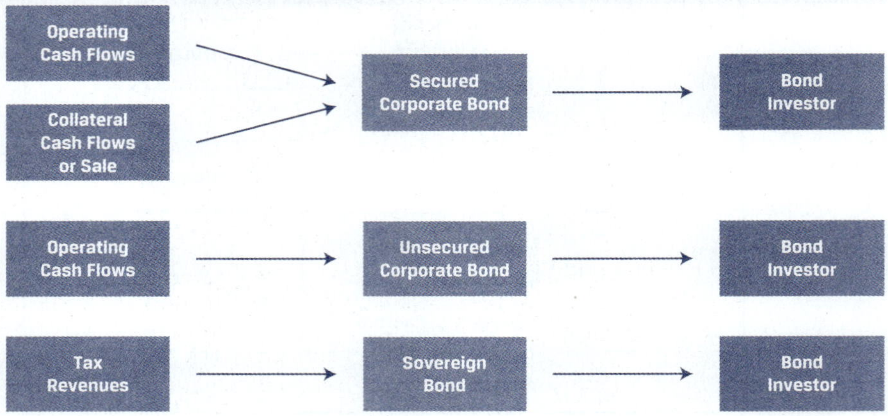

A corporation may not generate sufficient cash flow from its operations, financing activities, and investments to make timely payments on its debt, increasing the risk of default. Similarly, a sovereign borrower may not generate sufficient revenue through taxes, incomes, and fees to make timely payments.

Borrowers that lack the resources to meet debt obligations as they come due are often described as illiquid. An illiquid borrower is unable to raise the necessary funds to fulfill a debt obligation. They may not be able to tap credit lines, sell assets, or otherwise raise funding to make a timely debt payment. That is different from an *insolvent* borrower whose assets are worth less than its liabilities. An illiquid borrower just does not have, or is unable to secure, the liquidity needed to make timely payment.

Credit risk analysis focuses on understanding how a borrower generates cash, how and when cash is used, and what events and risks may impede the borrower's ability to repay the debt. In earlier lessons, we encountered *unsecured* debt, where the primary source of repayment is the cash flow generated by the business. In the case of *secured* debt, the primary source of repayment remains the firm's cash flows, but it is also supported by collateral pledged by the company. The following example involves an investor considering an unsecured bond versus a secured bond.

EXAMPLE 1

Risk Comparison of BRWA and VIVU Notes

The hypothetical car manufacturer Bright Wheel Automotive (BRWA) is an investment-grade (IG) issuer with ready access to unsecured debt, while Vivivyu Inc. (VIVU) is a hypothetical high-yield (HY) issuer that borrows on a secured basis. Let us compare 3.2% senior unsecured and unsubordinated BRWA notes to 6.5% secured unsubordinated VIVU notes. Consider BRWA's debt profile:

BRWA Corporation Debt Profile

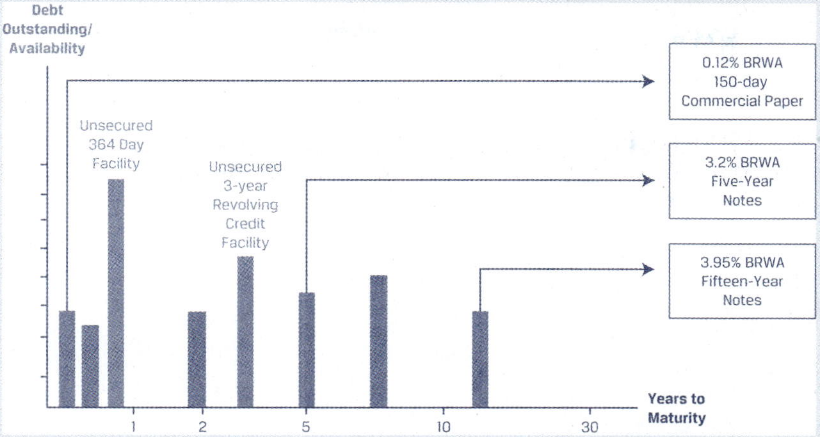

If BRWA fails to make an interest or principal payment on the note, BRWA is in default. Since its bonds are unsecured and unsubordinated obligations with pari passu and cross-default language in its bond indenture, failure to repay unsecured indebtedness means that all its debt obligations are in default and investors must rely on BRWA's general asset pool to satisfy their obligations, as shown below.

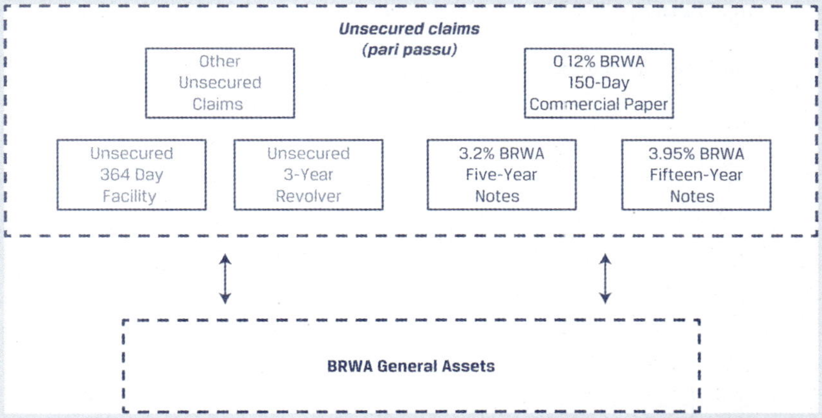

As an HY issuer, on the other hand, VIVU is limited to secured debt market access, as shown in its debt profile.

VIVU Debt Profile

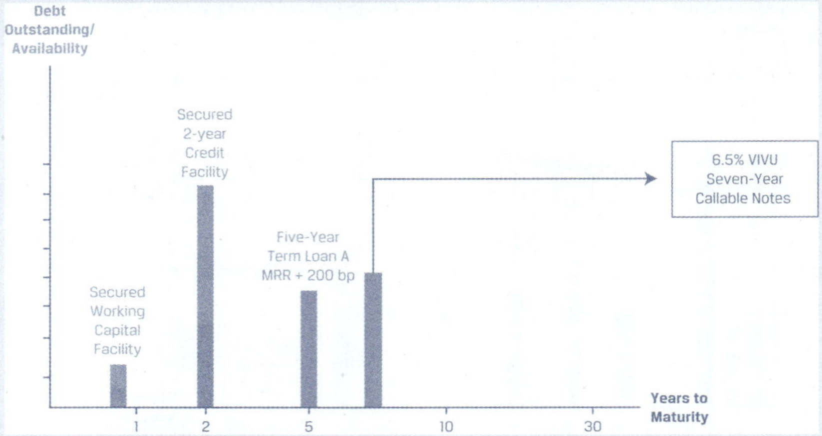

Note: MRR stands for market reference rate.

VIVU's failure to make timely payments due on the note will also result in default. The pari passu clause and cross-default language in its bond indenture with other unsecured indebtedness also sends all VIVU debt obligations into default. While *all* of VIVU's debt investors have access to any unpledged assets, specific pledged assets serve as a secondary source of repayment for specific debt, as shown below.

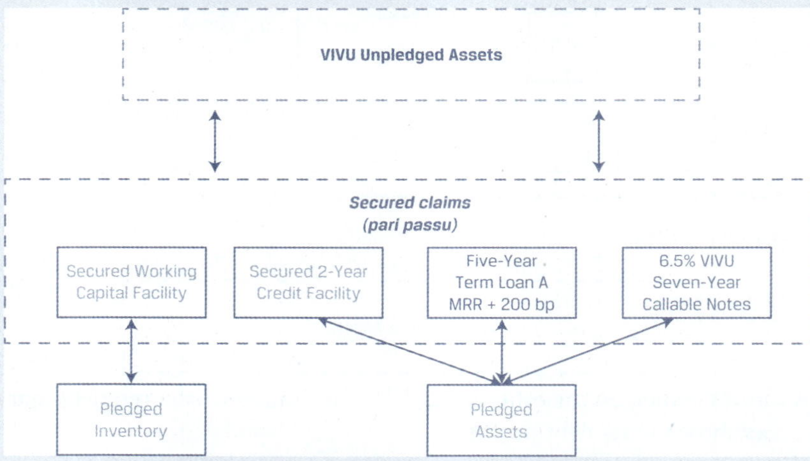

In this example, VIVU's secured claims include its working capital facility secured by short-term assets (in this case inventory), while its long-term secured debt including the callable notes are backed by a claim to specific long-term assets pledged. As a secondary source of repayment, only when the value of the pledged assets falls below the total amount of pari passu secured debt will VIVU noteholders begin to suffer a credit loss.

While the *likelihood of default* for investment-grade borrowers, such as BRWA, is typically well below that of a high-yield issuer such as VIVU, the investor's *loss in the event of a default* for secured debt is usually lower than unsecured debt due to the secondary source of repayment for secured bonds.

We encountered the Government of Romania's EUR1.95 billion 30-year debt issue in an earlier lesson. For a sovereign government, the right to tax economic activity within its borders means that the sources of repayment are the personal and corporate income taxes, sales taxes, and other revenue generated by the government. In the specific case of Romania's EUR-denominated debt, the government's ability to generate reserve currency cash flows based upon its institutional and economic profile, use of monetary and fiscal policy, and exchange rate regime are additional considerations.

The main borrower types and their primary sources of repayment and credit risk are listed in Exhibit 3.

Exhibit 3: Borrower Types, Sources of Repayment, and Sources of Credit Risk

Borrower Type	Primary Source of Cash Flow Generation	Secondary Source of Cash Flow Generation	Sources of Credit Risk
Corporate	▪ Business operations ▪ Investment and financing activities	▪ Asset sales ▪ Divestitures ▪ Additional debt issuance ▪ Equity issuance	▪ Economic contraction ▪ Strategic shifts in the business and market environment ▪ Increased competition ▪ Reduced pricing power ▪ Shrinking operating margins, increased losses ▪ Excessive debt service needs
Sovereign or public entity	▪ Corporate and personal income taxes, sales tax and VAT revenue, capital gains and wealth-based taxes ▪ Tariffs, fees, and other government revenue	▪ Newly issued debt ▪ Sale of public assets, privatization	▪ Economic contraction ▪ Political uncertainty ▪ Excessive debt service needs ▪ Expansionary economic policies ▪ Budget deficits ▪ Tax cuts ▪ Limited ability to collect taxes

While many factors affect the primary and secondary sources of repayment for different fixed-income issuers, investors seek to measure and compare credit risk among different borrowers for similar maturities as well as across maturities for the same borrower.

For example, consider the comparison of BRWA and VIVU notes in Example 1. If we set aside both the VIVU maturity difference and call feature (which the issuer may exercise any time from year three through maturity in year seven) by assuming a similar expected maturity to the BRWA bond for the time being, compare the 6.5% VIVU debt coupon to the 3.2% fixed rate of the BRWA bond. How can we assess whether the additional 3.3% (= 6.5% – 3.2%) in interest adequately compensates an investor for the additional risk? We turn to measures of credit risk, which help answer this question in the next section.

Measuring Credit Risk

Fixed-income investors face credit risk, or the risk that an issuer does not make promised interest and principal payments. This probability-weighted shortfall known as the **expected loss (EL)** for a given period has two components, as shown in Exhibit 4.

Exhibit 4: Components of Credit Risk

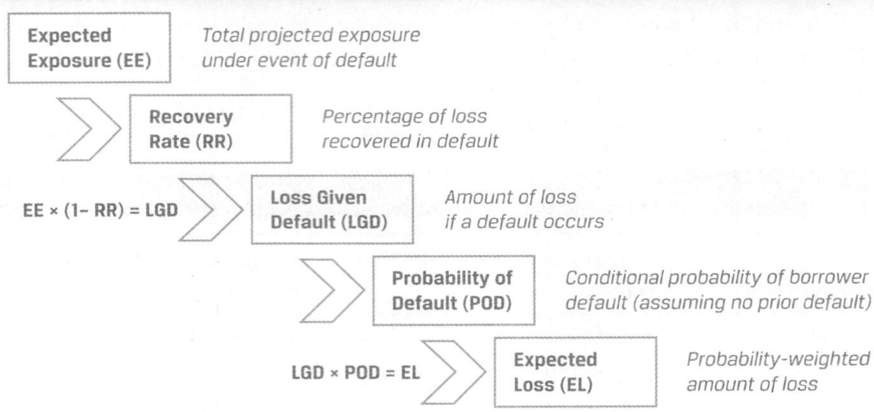

The first is known as the **probability of default (POD)**, which is the likelihood that an issuer fails to make full and timely payments of principal and interest. The probability of default is typically an annualized measure.

The second component is the **loss given default (LGD)**, or the investor's loss conditional on an issuer event of default. The loss given default combines the severity of loss under a default scenario with the amount of the investor's claim at the time of default. The **recovery rate (RR)** represents the percentage of an outstanding debt claim recovered when an issuer defaults, while the **loss severity** of (1 – RR) represents the unrecovered portion of the claim. The size of the investor's claim at the time of default is known as the **expected exposure (EE)** or **exposure at default (EAD)**. This is the amount an investor may expect to lose in the case of default, which is usually equal to the loan or bond face value plus accrued interest less the current market value of available collateral. In most instances, in the event of default, bondholders will usually recover some proportion of their investment.

The expected loss is shown in Equation 1:

$$EL = POD \times LGD, \quad (1)$$

where $LGD = EE \times (1 - RR)$.

The LGD can be expressed either in currency terms (e.g., EUR450,000) or as a percentage of principal (e.g., 45%). The latter form of expression is more useful for analysis since it allows comparison across borrowers and investments of different sizes.

One way to interpret the expected loss on a fixed-income security for a given period is to compare it to the compensation an investor expects for taking on the credit risk of a borrower over that period, which is the credit spread. Recall from an earlier lesson that the G-spread is equal to yield spread in basis points over an actual or interpolated government bond. This approximation may be expressed as follows:

$$\text{Credit Spread} \approx POD \times LGD. \quad (2)$$

Therefore, we can say that the investor is fairly compensated if the expected loss is equal to the credit spread for a given period. The following example uses this information to assess the expected loss versus compensation for the BRWA and VIVU bonds from Example 1.

EXAMPLE 2

Comparing Expected Loss and Credit Spreads

Recall from Example 1 that Bright Wheel Automotive (BRWA) issued an unsecured five-year bond with a 3.2% fixed coupon. The yield-to-maturity difference between BRWA's five-year bond and the comparable US Treasury bond is 90 bps (= 3.2% – 2.3%), which reflects BRWA's credit spread over Treasuries, known as the G-spread. Vivivyu Inc. (VIVU) issued a 6.5% fixed-rate bond, which the issuer has the right to call at a fixed price any time from three years from the issuance date until final maturity in seven years.

1. Assuming the BRWA bond has a probability of default of 1% and a loss given default of 80%, estimate whether BRWA bond investors are adequately compensated for assuming BRWA credit risk.

   Solution:

   Using Equation 1, we may solve for BRWA's expected loss in percentage terms as follows:

   EL = POD × LGD, or 0.8% = [0.01 × 80%].

   Given BRWA's credit spread of 0.9%, we may conclude based upon the approximation in Equation 2 that BRWA investors are fairly compensated for assuming the credit risk since:

   Credit Spread > POD × LGD.

   Investors earn a 90 bps spread per year and have an expected loss of 80 bps per year.

2. If we assume that VIVU has issued a five-year non-callable bond, as in the case of BRWA, with a probability of default of 6% and a loss given default of 50%, compare investor compensation for assuming the credit risk of the 6.5% VIVU debt coupon to that of the 3.2% fixed rate of the BRWA bond.

   Solution:

   Using Equation 1, we may solve for VIVU's expected loss in percentage terms as follows:

   EL = POD × LGD, or 3.0% = [0.06 × 50%].

   We may calculate VIVU's five-year credit spread by subtracting its 6.5% coupon from the 2.3% five-year US Treasury to solve for a G-spread of 4.2%. Based upon the approximation in Equation 2, we may conclude that VIVU investors are fairly compensated for assuming the credit risk since:

   Credit Spread > POD × LGD.

   Investors earn a 420 bps per year spread and have an expected loss of 300 bps per year.

3. How would the determination of the spread as well as investor's view of the risk versus compensation for the VIVU bond change from Question 2 if we

consider the VIVU bond's *actual* maturity and call feature with the original 6.5% coupon?

Solution:

VIVU investors face both call risk and greater maturity risk on the original bond terms versus a five-year, non-callable bond. As described in earlier lessons, bonds callable at a fixed price prior to maturity are advantageous to issuers and disadvantageous to investors, so investors expect to be compensated via a higher yield versus a similar non-callable bond given the uncertain maturity and limited price appreciation known as call risk. This option-adjusted yield is the required market discount rate for which the bond's price is adjusted for the value of the embedded option. Investors would also expect to be compensated for a longer time to maturity with a higher credit spread.

We may further consider the drivers of expected loss for BRWA's unsecured investment-grade debt as compared to VIVU's secured high-yield debt in Example 2. The POD is driven by an issuer's ability to service debt based on both qualitative and quantitative factors, including:

- Profitability: Stable, predictable cash flows and profits;
- Coverage: Sufficient cash flows/profits to make debt payments; and
- Leverage: Relative reliance on debt financing.

Higher profitability (as measured, for example, by EBIT margin) and higher coverage (EBIT to interest expense) coupled with lower leverage (debt to earnings or cash flow ratios, such as debt/EBITDA or cash flow to net debt) are associated with lower POD and higher credit quality. While financial ratios are one of several factors used to assess credit risk, and their relative level by rating category varies widely across industries and over time, Exhibit 5 provides a generic example of these relationships.

Exhibit 5: Key Financial Ratios for Corporate Credit Risk and Ratings

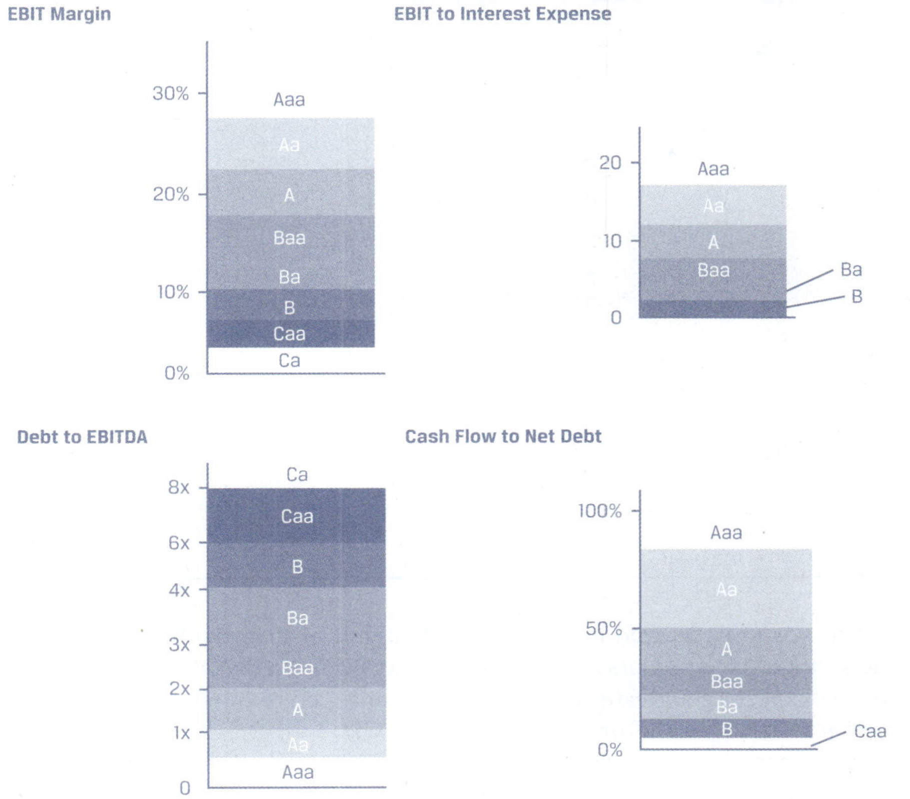

As Exhibit 5 shows, changes in profitability (EBIT margin), coverage (EBIT to interest expense), and leverage (debt/EBITDA and cash flow to net debt) ratios over time may result in ratings upgrades or downgrades as well as changing credit spreads. The LGD for a given exposure, on the other hand, is largely a function of the nature and seniority of a creditor's claim in a default scenario, as shown in Exhibit 6:

Exhibit 6: Seniority and LGD

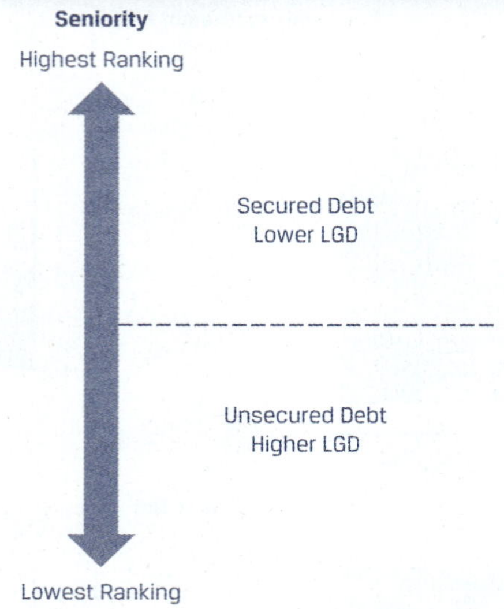

For investors in unsecured investment-grade bonds or loans with a high LGD, the greatest risk of expected loss arises due to a rise in POD. On the other hand, high-yield investors expecting a greater likelihood of default seek to minimize EL by seeking covenant restrictions and/or security to lower LGD.

QUESTION SET

1. *Determine the correct answers to fill in the blanks:* The two components of credit risk are the ________________, typically measured over a 12-month horizon, and the ________________, which together with the recovery rate determine the ________________.

   Solution:

   The two components of credit risk are the **probability of default**, typically measured over a 12-month horizon, and the **exposure at default (or expected exposure)**, which together with the recovery rate determine the **loss given default**.

2. Which of the following statements best describes the difference between unsecured and secured debt obligations in the event of issuer default?

   A. Unsecured debtholders only have access to issuer cash flows, while secured debtholders only have access to specific pledged assets.

   B. Both unsecured and secured debtholders have access to unpledged assets, while only secured debtholders have access to specific pledged assets as a secondary repayment source.

   C. Only unsecured debtholders have access to pledged assets, while only secured debtholders have access to specific pledged assets.

   Solution:

   B is correct. While all debtholders receive interest and principal payments from issuer cash flows, in an event of default both unsecured and secured debtholders have access to unpledged assets, while only secured debtholders have access to specific pledged assets as an additional repayment source.

3. Which of the following factors are associated with a lower probability of default and higher credit quality for a corporate issuer?

   A. Higher profitability, higher coverage, and higher leverage

   B. Higher profitability, lower coverage, and lower leverage

   C. Higher profitability, higher coverage, and lower leverage

   Solution:

   C is correct. Higher profitability, higher coverage, and lower leverage are associated with a lower probability of default and higher credit quality for a corporate issuer.

4. A bond investor analyzing Broadvue Corporation's unsecured debt estimates a POD of 2% and an LGD of 80%. Using this information to approximate the annual credit spread and observing an actual credit spread of 200 bps per year, which of the following statements is correct?

   A. An investor would be fairly compensated for assuming Broadvue's credit risk.

   B. An investor would be less than fairly compensated for assuming Broadvue's credit risk.

   C. An investor would be more than fairly compensated for assuming Broadvue's credit risk.

   Solution:

   C is correct. Since POD × LGD = 1.60% and the credit spread is 2.00%, Credit Spread > POD × LGD and the investor would expect to be more than fairly compensated for assuming Broadvue's credit risk.

CREDIT RATING AGENCIES AND CREDIT RATINGS 3

☐ describe the uses of ratings from credit rating agencies and their limitations

The three major credit rating agencies—Moody's Investors Service ("Moody's"), Standard & Poor's ("S&P"), and Fitch Ratings ("Fitch")—play a central role in the credit markets. The rating agencies independently assess issuer credit risk on a forward-looking basis using quantitative and qualitative analysis. For most outstanding corporate and sovereign bonds, at least two of the agencies provide **credit ratings**, a symbol-based measure of the potential risk of default of a particular bond or issuer of debt.

Many bond investors use credit ratings to provide direct and easy comparability of the relative creditworthiness of all bond issuers, within and across industries and bond types, although there is some debate about ratings comparability across the types of bonds. Changes in credit ratings provide a broad overview of changing credit market conditions. In individual bond or issuer cases, they may trigger covenants, changes to debt pricing for step-up bonds, or other contractual clauses. **Credit migration risk**, or downgrade risk, is the risk that a bond issuer's creditworthiness deteriorates, or migrates to a lower rating, leading investors to believe the risk of default is higher. Credit ratings are also widely used to satisfy regulatory, statutory, and contractual requirements.

Ratings are issued on behalf of the issuer. To issue a rating, the rating agencies often meet with the issuer and in some cases receive access to material non-public information, such as financial projections unavailable to public investors. Rating agencies monitor the ongoing performance of debt issuers once a rating is issued, adjusting ratings higher as credit risk decreases or lower if a default is deemed more likely. In addition, credit agencies may issue a positive or negative outlook as creditworthiness improves or deteriorates but a rating change is not yet warranted.

A rating agency's forward-looking analysis may overlook or underestimate key financial risks. For example, rating agencies were widely criticized for contributing to the Global Financial Crisis of 2008–2009 given what came to be seen as overly optimistic ratings on subprime mortgage-backed securities following the sharp decline in housing prices. This led to regulatory attempts to reduce the dominant role of the major credit rating agencies. As a result of these new rules, regulations, and legislation, credit rating agencies have become more transparent and reduced their conflicts of interest. Additional credit rating agencies have emerged both globally and locally. Some credit rating agencies are well-established in their home markets but are less well-known globally, such as Dominion Bond Rating Service (DBRS) in Canada and Japan Credit Rating Agency (JCR) in Japan. The market dominance of the largest credit rating agencies and the prevalence of the "issuer pay" model, however, remain largely intact and unchallenged.

Credit Ratings

The three major global credit rating agencies use similar, symbol-based ratings that assess a bond issue's risk of default and the potential loss the investor may suffer. Exhibit 7 compares their long-term rating scale ranked from highest to lowest. These are ratings for bonds with a maturity exceeding one year. Ratings on short-term debt follow a similar logic but are not shown here.

Exhibit 7: Long-Term Rating Matrix: Investment Grade vs. Non-Investment Grade

		Moody's	S&P	Fitch	Rating Grade Description
Investment Grade	High-Quality Grade	Aaa	AAA	AAA	Highest credit quality, lowest level of credit risk
		Aa1	AA+	AA+	Very high credit quality with very low level of credit risk
		Aa2	AA	AA	
		Aa3	AA–	AA–	
	Upper-Medium Grade	A1	A+	A+	High credit quality with low level of credit risk
		A2	A	A	
		A3	A–	A–	
	Low-Medium Grade	Baa1	BBB+	BBB+	Good credit quality with moderate level of credit risk
		Baa2	BBB	BBB	
		Baa3	BBB–	BBB–	

		Moody's	S&P	Fitch	Rating Grade Description
Non-Investment Grade ("Junk" or "High Yield")	Low Grade or Speculative Grade	Ba1	BB+	BB+	Speculative with substantial credit risk
		Ba2	BB	BB	
		Ba3	BB–	BB–	
		B1	B+	B+	Highly speculative with high credit risk
		B2	B	B	
		B3	B–	B–	
		Caa1	CCC+		Substantial credit risk with default as a real possibility
		Caa2	CCC	CCC	
		Caa3	CCC–		
		Ca	CC	CC	Very high levels of credit risk with default either occurring or about to occur
		Ca	C	C	Default or default-like process has begun
	Default	C	D	D	In default (entered bankruptcy filings, administration, receivership, liquidation, or other formal winding-up procedure) with little prospect for recovery of principal or interest

Aaa or AAA rated bonds are triple-A and are "of the highest quality, subject to the lowest level of credit risk." Bonds rated Baa3/BBB– or higher are called "investment grade." Bonds rated Ba1 or lower by Moody's and BB+ or lower by S&P and Fitch, respectively, are considered speculative credit and increasingly higher default risk. These types of bonds are also referenced as: "low grade," "speculative grade," "non-investment grade," "below investment grade," "high yield," and more colloquially to specifically emphasize their inherent riskiness, "junk bonds." The D rating is reserved for securities that are already in default in S&P's and Fitch's scales. For Moody's, bonds rated C are likely, but not necessarily, in default. Issuers of bonds rated investment grade are generally more consistently able to issue debt and can borrow at lower interest rates than those rated below investment grade.

In comparison to high-yield bonds, investment-grade bonds have a lower risk profile, are less negatively affected by adverse economic and market conditions, and are more appropriate for institutional portfolios that face quality restrictions.

Credit Rating Considerations

While credit rating agencies perform a useful market function by classifying bonds based upon relative credit risk, market participants usually conduct their own analysis rather than exclusively relying on ratings when choosing investments. Sole reliance on credit ratings in making investment decisions includes pitfalls, such as the potential for rating agency decisions to lag market pricing of credit risk, overlook relevant financial risks, or involve miscalculations or unforeseen changes not fully captured in a rating agency's forward-looking analysis. It is important for investors to perform their own research and draw their own conclusions regarding the credit risk of a given debt issue or issuer, particularly for investors in high-yield bonds or bonds that face a potential downgrade.

Credit ratings tend to be sticky and lag market pricing of credit risk.

- Bond prices and credit spreads often move faster than rating agencies change their ratings (or ratings outlook) in response to changes in perceived creditworthiness. Credit spreads change daily, whereas bond ratings, appropriately, change less frequently. Even over long time periods, however, credit ratings may lag changes in bond prices. Moreover, particularly for certain speculative-grade credits, two bonds with similar ratings may trade at very different credit spreads. This may result from the fact that credit ratings seek primarily to assess the expected loss, whereas for distressed debt, pricing is focused more on default timing and expected recovery rates.
- While ratings outlooks suggesting a possible future upgrade or downgrade are more closely aligned with market conditions, bond investors who wait for rating changes before making buy and sell decisions may underperform other investors who make portfolio decisions in advance of rating agency changes.

Some risks are difficult to capture in credit ratings.

- Examples include litigation risk, environmental risk, and natural disasters. Leveraged transactions, such as debt-financed acquisitions (i.e., changes in the capital structure through large stock buybacks), are often difficult to anticipate and thus to capture in credit ratings. Rating agencies may view complex risks very differently, resulting in divergent or **split ratings** between the agencies. For example, when WeWork Inc., a US-based real estate private start-up company with an asset light business model and negative cash flow, issued unsecured debt for the first time in 2018, it was rated BB– by Fitch, B+ by S&P, and Caa1 by Moody's.

Ratings may involve miscalculations or unforeseen changes not fully captured in a rating agency's forward-looking analysis.

- As mentioned earlier, credit rating agency analyses failed to anticipate the sharp decline in housing prices that led to the default of highly rated subprime mortgage bonds during the Global Financial Crisis of 2008–2009. Historical examples of complex accounting fraud that supported high issuer credit ratings for companies that subsequently defaulted, include Enron and WorldCom in the United States and Wirecard AG in Germany.

Example 3 highlights these considerations using the example of Wirecard AG.

EXAMPLE 3

Wirecard AG Ratings and Bond Prices

Wirecard AG is a German payments firm that issued unsecured debt in 2019 and was subsequently declared insolvent in June 2020 due to complex accounting fraud described in detail later in the curriculum. The price of Wirecard's bonds from issuance until insolvency is shown below:

Wirecard 0.5% Coupon 2024 Maturity Bond Price (% of Par)

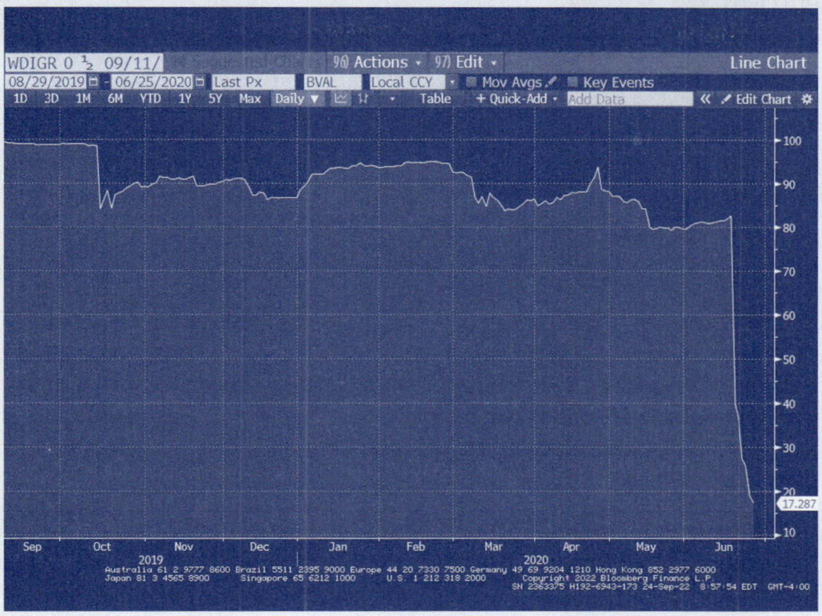

Source: Bloomberg.

Moody's initiated its coverage of Wirecard AG by issuing a Baa3 long-term issuer rating in August 2019. The company's debut public bond offering of EUR500 million in five-year senior unsecured debt with a fixed annual coupon of 0.5% was priced just below par in early September 2019.

On 15 October 2019, Wirecard's bond price fell below 85% of par following a *Financial Times* report alleging fraud and false accounting practices at the company. While Wirecard denied the claims and subsequently hired an independent auditor, doubts remained among debt and equity investors. Despite changes at the company's supervisory board and reports of a strategic investment from Japanese investment firm Softbank, the release of a critical independent audit in April 2020, delays in reporting audited financial results, and other irregularities contributed to ongoing investor concerns.

With Wirecard AG's bonds trading at a price near 80, Moody's placed the company on review for downgrade on 2 June 2020, citing these concerns but retaining an IG issuer rating. Two weeks later, Wirecard AG bond prices plunged to 40 as claims of fraud and missing cash balances were confirmed in mid-June. On 19 June 2020, Moody's downgraded the issuer to a sub-investment-grade B3 rating with a negative outlook and withdrew its credit rating altogether three days later, citing insufficient information to support the maintenance of a rating. The company filed for insolvency on 25 June 2020, and its bond price fell to below 20% of par value.

Investors who bought and held Wirecard AG bonds until 19 June 2020 solely on the basis of its IG credit rating suffered a substantial loss. The Wirecard example highlights the challenges faced by credit rating agencies in evaluating expected loss and adjusting credit ratings given a rapidly evolving series of events.

QUESTION SET

1. Which of the following choices properly ranks ratings from the three major credit rating agencies from the lowest to highest credit risk?

   A. B1, Ba2, Baa3

   B. BBB+, Ba3, B–

   C. Baa1, BB, Baa3

   Solution:

   B is correct.

2. *Determine the correct answers to fill in the blanks:* In comparison to high-yield bonds, investment-grade bonds have a __________ risk profile and are __________ negatively affected by adverse economic and market conditions.

   Solution:

   In comparison to high-yield bonds, investment-grade bonds have a **lower** risk profile and are **less** negatively affected by adverse economic and market conditions.

3. Which of the following statements most accurately characterizes best practices for the use of credit ratings among analysts?

   A. Analysts can generally rely on credit ratings and ratings outlooks to predict the market price of credit risk.

   B. Analysts must incorporate credit ratings into their analysis to meet regulatory requirements.

   C. Analysts should conduct their own credit analysis, as sole reliance on credit ratings to make investment decisions has several pitfalls.

   Solution:

   C is correct. A is incorrect since credit ratings tend to lag rather than predict the market price of credit risk.

4. Which of the following statements best describes the relationship between credit ratings and market pricing of credit risk?

   A. Credit ratings primarily seek to assess expected loss, while market pricing of credit risk for investment-grade bonds is primarily focused on default timing and expected recovery rates.

   B. Credit rating outlooks tend to be more closely aligned with market conditions than credit ratings.

   C. Credit ratings usually capture the market pricing of credit risk associated with debt-financed acquisitions.

   Solution:

   The correct answer is B. A is incorrect, as while credit ratings primarily seek to assess expected loss, the market pricing of credit risk for distressed bonds is primarily focused on default timing and expected recovery rates.

FACTORS IMPACTING YIELD SPREADS

4

☐ describe macroeconomic, market, and issuer-specific factors that influence the level and volatility of yield spreads

Corporate bonds and other "credit-risky" debt instruments typically trade at a yield premium, or spread, to bonds that have been considered "default-risk free," such as US Treasury bonds or German government bonds. Credit spreads, expressed in basis points, widen based on issuer-specific factors, such as a decline in creditworthiness, sometimes referred to as credit migration or downgrade risk, or market-based factors, such as a greater risk aversion during periods of financial distress. **Credit spread risk** is the risk of greater expected loss due to changes in credit conditions as a result of macroeconomic, market, and/or issuer-related factors.

Macroeconomic Factors

Changing macroeconomic conditions and changes in the credit cycle often go in lockstep: As the business cycle improves, credit spreads narrow and investors are willing to assume more credit risk. A deteriorating credit cycle will cause credit spreads to widen. Spreads are narrowest at or near the top of the credit cycle, when market participants perceive credit risk to be at its lowest; they are widest at or near the bottom of the credit cycle, when financial markets believe credit risk has reached its peak. Beyond the higher coupons typically offered by high-yield bonds to compensate for their greater risk, reasons for investing in HY bonds include the following:

- *Portfolio diversification* – HY bonds often have lower correlation with IG bonds and default risk-free interest rates. Their inclusion in a fixed-income portfolio may therefore increase diversification and risk-adjusted return.
- *Capital appreciation* – Economic recovery, or improved issuer-specific performance, often has a more sizeable positive impact on HY than IG bond prices. In addition to improved cash flow, other issuer-specific events that may drive capital appreciation include rating upgrades, mergers or acquisitions, or favorable management changes.
- *Equity-like return with lower volatility* – While HY bond and equity prices tend to fluctuate in a similar way over the economic cycle, HY bond returns typically exhibit more stability given their larger income component versus stocks. Some empirical studies suggest that HY bonds offer a more attractive risk–return profile than equities over the long term. They may also be preferable for yield-seeking investors with a limited ability to assume equity volatility.

Credit ratings estimate expected loss by considering not only the POD but also the LGD, establishing a clear relationship between credit ratings and bond yields. The relationship between credit ratings and composite bond yields of different ratings and maturities are shown in Exhibit 8.

Exhibit 8: U.S. Composite Bond Yields by Rating and Tenor

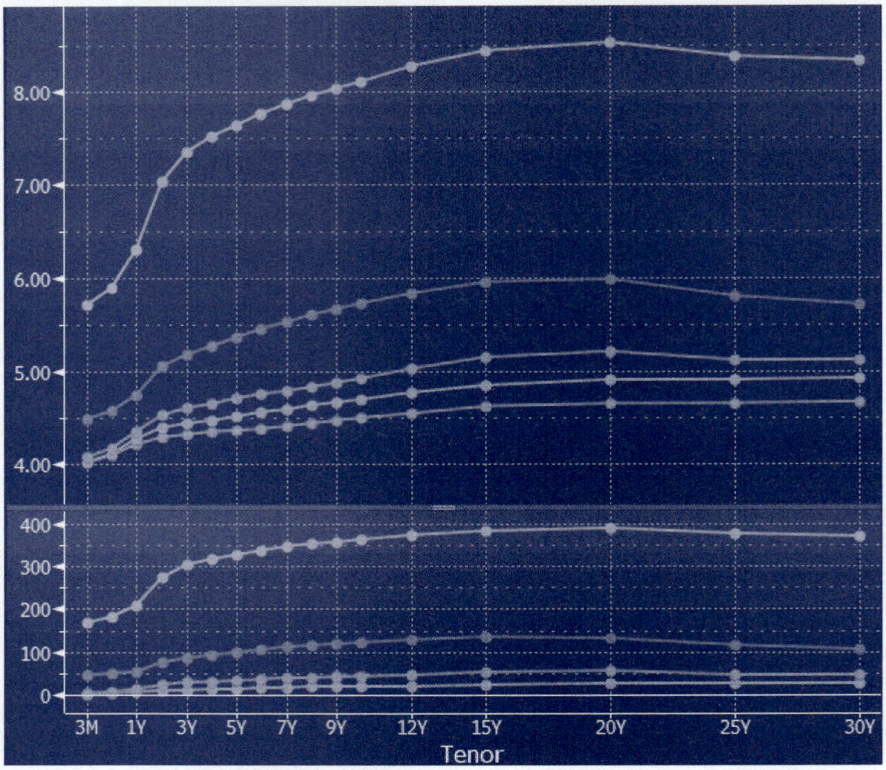

Source: Bloomberg as of 23 September 2022.

Exhibit 8 shows three important relationships. First, the higher the credit rating, the lower the yield for a given maturity. Investors require less compensation for the risk of higher rated bonds with lower default risk. Second, in general, the longer the maturity, the higher the yield, as default risk tends to rise for longer maturities. Third, the yield spread difference between IG bond ratings is generally narrower than the difference between IG and HY.

Over the cycle, HY bond spreads are more susceptible to widening under adverse market conditions when investors tend to sell riskier assets and buy default risk-free assets, known as a "flight to quality." In addition, HY bonds may face liquidity risk, which also widens bid–offer spreads in times of financial stress. The benefits and considerations of adding HY bonds to a portfolio are addressed in Example 4.

EXAMPLE 4

Benefits and Considerations of High-Yield Bond Investments

A pension fund manager made the economic forecasts for the following year:

	Last Year (Actual)	This Year (Forecast)
Economic growth	2.5%	3.2%
Long-term interest rate	1.5%	2.0%

	Last Year (Actual)	This Year (Forecast)
High-yield default rate	3.3%	2.1% (Historical low)
Financial market volatility	16.5%	20.0%

Despite improving economic and market conditions, financial market volatility is expected to increase.

1. Describe the benefits and considerations of adding high-yield bonds to the investment portfolio under this scenario.

   Solution:

   Benefits: Investing in high-yield bonds should improve the risk-adjusted return of the overall portfolio in an expected environment of:

   - accelerating economic growth,
   - rising interest rates, and
   - falling HY default risk to a historical low.

   Considerations: The additional market risk arising from higher expected market volatility may temper the diversification benefit. In times of heightened volatility, HY bonds may also be exposed to market liquidity risk when cash is needed from the portfolio (for example, to meet regular pension payments).

Exhibit 9 presents a stylized view of these credit spread curve level and shape changes for investment-grade (IG) and high-yield (HY) issuers over the economic cycle moving clockwise across the four scenarios shown. The spread change in spread for IG bonds is narrower than that for HY bonds. HY bonds are more sensitive to changing macroeconomic and credit conditions.

Exhibit 9: Credit Spread Curves over the Economic Cycle

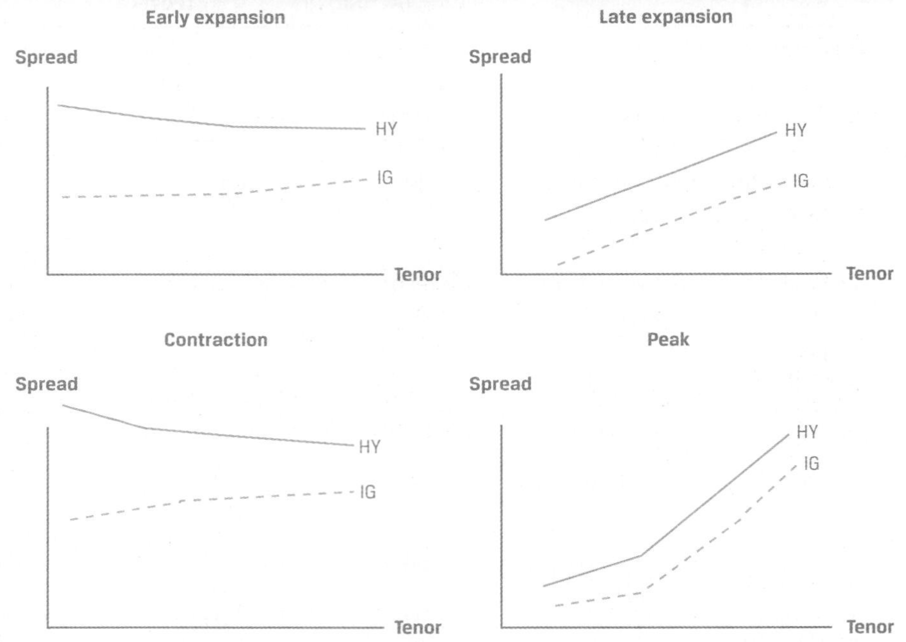

There may be other systematic reasons why spreads change. Corporate bonds trade primarily over the counter using broker–dealers who must commit their own capital for market-making purposes. Tighter financial regulations increase the cost of holding capital for trading in credit-risky bonds, particularly for large global banks that are the most dominant market participants. Funding stresses also naturally translate into wider credit spreads. The availability of funding is related to overall macroeconomic and credit cycle conditions but may also be driven by market sentiment, such as the willingness to take on risk. Additionally, in periods of heavy new issue supply, credit spreads will widen if there is insufficient demand. In periods of high demand for bonds, spreads will move tighter.

Market Factors

For the most liquid bonds with the lowest default risk, such as developed market sovereign debt, the yield for a given maturity is a combination of real interest rates plus an expected inflation rate premium. The yield spread on corporate bonds includes an additional risk premium that compensates investors for credit and liquidity risks as well as the potential tax impact of investing in a specific bond. Changes in any of these components will alter the yield, price, and return on the bond. The total yield spread over the government benchmark bond captures these risk components.

Market liquidity risk refers to the transaction costs associated with selling a bond. This is the risk that the price at which investors can actually transact may differ from the price indicated in the market through bid–ask spreads. The ability and willingness of broker–dealers to make markets, as reflected in the bid–ask spread, is an important determinant of market liquidity and associated risks to transact in the market.

Two main issuer-specific factors affect market liquidity risk. First, issuer size, or more specifically the aggregate value of publicly traded debt an issuer has outstanding, is an important liquidity factor. Second, the issuer's credit quality is critical. In general, the less debt an issuer has outstanding and the less frequently its debt trades, the higher the market liquidity risk and the bid–ask spread. The lower the credit quality of an issuer, the higher the market liquidity risk. To compensate investors for the risk that there may not be sufficient market liquidity for them to buy or sell bonds in the quantity they desire, the spread or yield premium on corporate bonds includes both a market liquidity and a credit risk component.

Typically, a bond that trades more frequently and with higher volume provides investors more opportunity to purchase or sell the security and thus has less liquidity risk. The difference between the *bid* (or purchase) and the *offer* (or sale) price depends on the type of bond, the size of the transaction, and the time of execution, among other factors. For instance, the most liquid government bonds often trade at a fraction of a basis point between the purchase and sale prices, while less liquid corporate bonds can have a much wider difference between the bid and offer prices.

During times of financial stress or crisis, market liquidity can decline sharply, causing bond prices to fall and yield spreads on corporate and other spread-based debt to widen significantly. In most crises, not only does credit deterioration result in wider bid–ask spreads, but it also may cause spillover effects from one fixed-income market segment to others. For example, risk aversion among HY bond investors may lead to significant spread widening among lower rated IG bonds as well.

Issuer-Specific Factors

Beyond macroeconomic and market factors, the expected financial performance of individual issuers has a significant effect on both the level and volatility of yields and yield spreads.

In particular, factors common to all issuers include debt coverage and leverage. Debt coverage refers to the sufficiency of a borrower's resources or cash flows to make necessary interest and principal payments, while leverage measures a borrower's relative reliance on debt versus other sources of financing. The source of repayment and use of proceeds differ among issuer types. Corporate issuers typically invest in long-term assets and repay debt from operating cash flow, while sovereign borrowers conduct fiscal policy and provide public goods while collecting tax revenue as a primary source of repayment. These factors are evaluated in detail for sovereign and non-sovereign government as well as corporate issuers in later lessons.

Investors often evaluate the yield and yield spread of a specific issuer's bond using a comparison to bonds within the same credit rating category, within the same sector due to similar performance drivers, or to companies with a similar business model or other common features. Example 5 illustrates the use of such a comparison to allow an investor to distinguish between macroeconomic and issuer-specific factors.

EXAMPLE 5

WeWork Yields versus B-Rated Corporates

WeWork is a US-based real estate company that leases commercial properties to provide co-working spaces for firms and individuals. The company enjoyed a meteoric rise during its first several years of existence as a rapidly expanding office space lessee financed by private equity capital. Despite its asset light business model and negative cash flow, WeWork issued debt in April 2018, a privately placed USD700 million seven-year senior unsecured bond with a fixed coupon of 7.875% priced at par and rated Caa1 by Moody's, B+ by S&P, and BB– by Fitch. The following diagram shows the relationship between the average five-year yield of corporate bonds with high credit risk with a similar maturity and WeWork's bond yield following the issuance.

WeWork 7.875% 2025 Bond Yield versus Five-Year B Corporate Yield

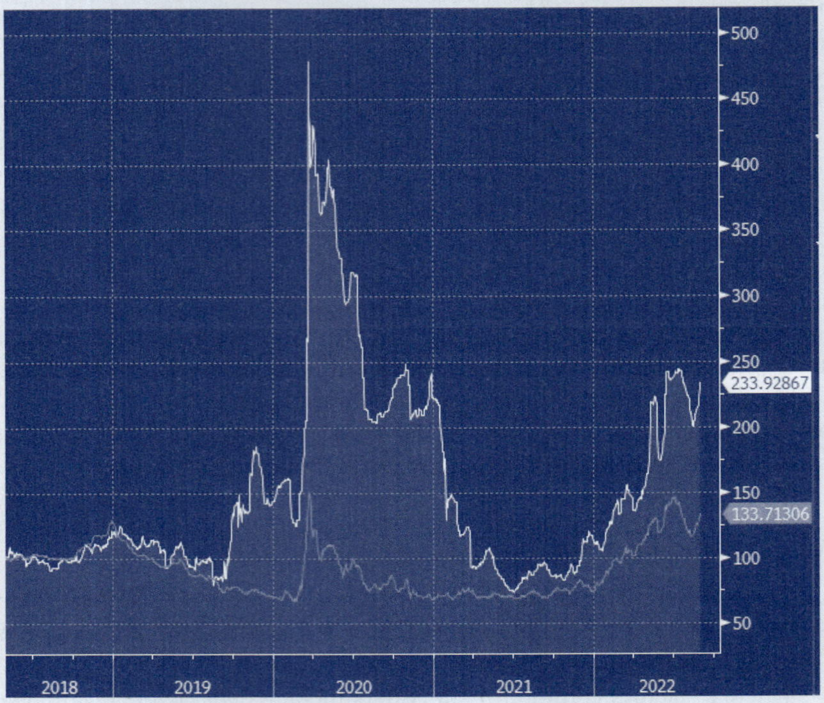

Source: Bloomberg, Normalized Yields with April 2018 = 100.

We see that B-rated corporate bond yields fluctuated between 75% and 150% of their April 2018 levels over the period, but WeWork's bond yield exhibited far greater volatility, reaching a yield nearly five times that of April 2018 in early 2020. While a detailed analysis is beyond the scope of this example, three noteworthy issuer-specific events may be used to explain the relative yield relationship over the period:

WeWork's Failed IPO (September 2019): The failure of WeWork's widely anticipated IPO was caused by weak governance and inflated growth and earnings expectations, which resulted in a company valuation of USD50 billion. As the failure increased WeWork's relative reliance on existing debt versus anticipated new equity, its bond yield nearly doubled, while average B-rated corporate bond yields fell in a favorable macroeconomic environment through 2019.

COVID-19 Pandemic (March 2020): Economic shutdowns and work-from-home policies had a disproportionately negative effect on WeWork's co-working business model and expected cash flows as compared to other HY issuers. The company's bonds traded at distressed prices as low as 35% of par value and were downgraded to CCC+ (negative outlook) by S&P, the only credit rating agency that had retained a B rating for WeWork to date.

Recovery and WeWork's IPO (October 2021): The decline in WeWork's bond yields was disproportionately large in 2021 as compared to B-rated corporate yields as the economy reopened and employees returned to work. This improved outlook allowed the company to revisit its plans to issue equity at a more realistic valuation. News of a possible second IPO attempt in mid-2021 caused WeWork bond yields to decline. Its bonds traded at a premium when the IPO was completed via a combination with special purpose acquisition company

(SPAC) BowX, which valued WeWork at USD9 billion and raised USD1.3 billion in cash. WeWork's reduced reliance on debt and improved cash flow caused its bond yields to trade close to those of B-rated bonds, despite its lower rating.

This simplified WeWork example ignores duration differences and compares bonds across sectors within a ratings category rather than within the commercial real estate sector or among comparable asset light, negative cash companies, such as Uber. Later fixed-income lessons will introduce greater detail in comparing issuer-specific, macroeconomic, and market factors.

The Price Impact of Spread Changes

In an earlier module, we explained how bond duration and convexity are used to approximate a bond's price change given a change in yield-to-maturity. We now address the *source* of the yield-to-maturity change. Since the yield-to-maturity on a corporate bond consists of a government *benchmark* yield and a *spread*, a change in the bond's yield-to-maturity can originate in either component or a combination of the two. The key point is that for an option-free fixed-rate bond, the same duration and convexity statistics that apply for a change in benchmark yield also apply for a change in spread.

Importantly, the modified duration and convexity measures give an approximate change in the full price of a bond for a change in yield-to-maturity, regardless of the *source* of the change. However, changes in the yield-to-maturity components do not occur in isolation. In practice, the analyst is concerned with the *interaction* between benchmark yield and spread changes, between changes in expected inflation and the expected real rate, and between changes in credit and liquidity risk. For example, a "flight to quality" described earlier can cause government benchmark yields to fall as credit spreads widen and liquidity declines for bonds of low credit-quality issuers.

Example 6 shows the risk/return components of a bond via a hypothetical spread decomposition.

EXAMPLE 6

Decomposition of a Romanian Eurobond Yield

In 2019, the Government of Romania issued its first-ever 4.625% 30-year Eurobond, which was priced at a spread of 411.4 bps over the 1.25% Federal Republic of Germany bond maturing 15 August 2048. The initial yield spread indicated the combined credit and liquidity risk of the bond. The 4.625% Romania bond subsequently traded in a wide price range, reflecting the prevailing market assessment of its credit risk and yield spread as well as the benchmark German yield, as shown in the chart below:

Source: Bloomberg.

Suppose that two years after issuance, the bond was traded at 122.25/125.75 (bid/offer). This meant that a buyer would have to pay the offer price of 125.75 for the bond and a seller would receive the bid price of 122.25.

Bond mid-market price = (122.25 + 125.75)/2 = 124.00.

With 28 years remaining to maturity, the Romanian bond yield based on its mid-market price is equivalent to 3.2988%:

$$124.00 = \sum_{n=1}^{28} \frac{4.625}{(1+r)^n} + \frac{100}{(1+r)^{28}}$$

$r \approx 3.2988\%$.

Assume we observe a Federal Republic of Germany benchmark bund yield of 0.2350% on the same day. The current spread of the Romania bond may be shown as:

= 3.2988% – 0.2350%

= 3.0638% or 306.38 bps.

To further break down this spread, we can compute the liquidity spread using the bid/offer prices. At the offer price, the yield is equivalent to 3.2396%:

$$125.25 = \sum_{n=1}^{28} \frac{4.625}{(1+r)^n} + \frac{100}{(1+r)^{28}}$$

$r \approx 3.2396\%$.

At the bid price, the yield is equivalent to 3.3588%:

$$122.75 = \sum_{n=1}^{28} \frac{4.625}{(1+r)^n} + \frac{100}{(1+r)^{28}}$$

$r \approx 3.3588\%$.

Therefore: Liquidity spread = 3.3588% – 3.2396% = 0.1192% or 11.92 bps.

Credit spread = 306.38 bps – 11.92 bps = 294.46 bps.

These "building blocks" of the Romania bond yield are summarized below:

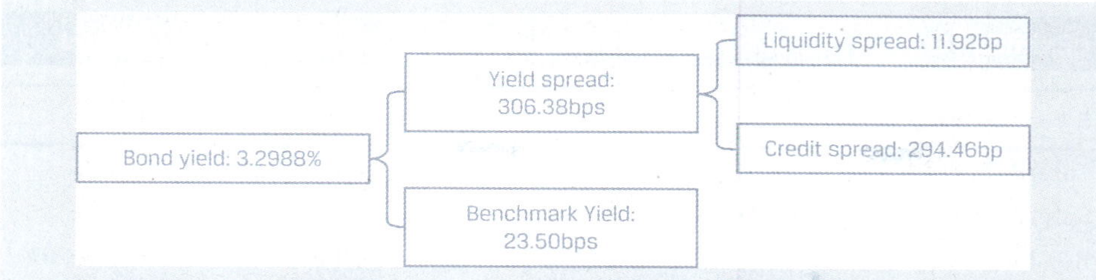

While IG debt investors are less likely to be impacted by default, they are more focused on **spread risk**—that is, the effect on prices and returns from changes in spreads. The price impact from spread changes is driven by two main factors: (1) the modified duration of the bond and (2) the magnitude of the spread change. The effect on return to the bondholder depends on the holding period used to calculate the return.

In the case of a small, instantaneous change in yield spread, the price impact can be approximated, as shown in Equation 3, by

$$\%\Delta PV^{Full} = -AnnModDur \times \Delta Spread, \qquad (3)$$

where AnnModDur is the annualized modified duration and PV^{Full} is the bond's full price. Note that lower (higher) spreads have a positive (negative) impact on bond prices and thus returns.

For larger spread changes, the effect of convexity needs to be incorporated into the approximation, as seen in Equation 4:

$$\%\Delta PV^{Full} = -(AnnModDur \times \Delta Spread) + \tfrac{1}{2} AnnConvexity \times (\Delta Spread)^2, \qquad (4)$$

where AnnConvexity is annualized convexity. Care is required to ensure convexity is properly scaled to be consistent with how the spread change is expressed. For option-free bonds, convexity should be scaled so it has the same order of magnitude as duration squared and the spread change is expressed as a decimal. For example, if a bond has duration of 5.0 and reported convexity of 0.235, then first re-scale convexity to 23.5, and then apply the formula. For a 1% increase in spread, the result would be

$$\%\Delta PV^{Full} = (-5.0 \times 0.01) + \tfrac{1}{2} \times 23.5 \times (0.01)^2 = -0.048825 \text{ or } -4.8825\%.$$

The price impact of instantaneous spread changes is illustrated in Exhibit 10 using the two semiannual coupon BRWA bonds with a price of par highlighted in the preceding lessons:

Exhibit 10: Price Impact of Instantaneous Spread Changes

Tenor and Coupon	Settlement	Maturity	Modified Duration	Convexity
5-year, 3.20%	15 October 2025	15 October 2030	4.58676	24.23895
10-year, 6.20%	15 October 2025	15 October 2035	7.29085	68.74440

From the initial spread, in increments of 50 bps and for both wider and narrower spreads, the new price and actual return for each spread change are calculated. Moreover, the estimated returns without and then with the convexity term are presented. As shown, the approximation using only duration is reasonably accurate for small spread changes, but for larger changes, the convexity term generally provides a meaningful improvement, as in Exhibit 11.

Exhibit 11: Price Impact of Duration & Convexity for Given Spread Change

5-Year BRWA Bond			Scenarios		
Spread (bps)	−100	−50	0	50	100
Spread over 5-year UST (bps)	0	50	100	150	200
Bond yield	2.20%	2.70%	3.20%	3.70%	4.20%
Actual bond price	104.71	102.32	100.00	97.73	95.53
Actual return	4.71%	2.32%	—	−2.26%	−4.46%
Approx. return: duration only	4.58%	2.29%	—	−2.29%	−4.59%
Approx. return: duration & convexity	4.70%	2.32%	—	−2.26%	−4.46%

10-Year BRWA Bond			Scenarios		
Spread (bps)	−100	−50	0	50	100
Spread over 10-Year UST (bps)	100	150	200	250	300
Bond yield	5.20%	5.70%	6.20%	6.70%	7.20%
Actual bond price	107.72	103.77	100.00	96.39	92.95
Actual return	7.72%	3.77%	—	−3.60%	−7.04%
Approx return: duration only	7.29%	3.64%	—	−3.64%	−7.29%
Approx return: duration & convexity	7.63%	3.73%	—	−3.55%	−6.94%

(*Note:* Assume 5-year UST: 2.20%, 10-year UST: 4.20% on the bond settlement date.)

Note the price change for a given spread change is higher for the longer-duration bond than for the shorter-duration bond. As with yield changes, longer-duration corporate bonds have "higher spread sensitivity," meaning their prices, and returns, are more volatile with respect to spread changes.

Additionally, investors must be compensated for greater uncertainty about an issuer's future creditworthiness in longer-dated bonds. An investor might be confident in assessing issuer default risk in the near term; however, investor uncertainty grows over time due to factors that are increasingly difficult to forecast (e.g., poor management strategy or execution, technological obsolescence, natural or man-made disasters, corporate leveraging events).

Example 7 shows the impact on price of a bond due to changes in credit quality or liquidity. Here we apply the methodology from an earlier lesson to approximate modified duration and convexity. We estimated the modified duration by increasing and decreasing the yield-to-maturity by the same amount (ΔYield) to calculate corresponding bond prices PV_+ and PV_- for a given initial price (PV_0), as shown in Equation 5:

$$\text{Annualized ModDur} \approx \frac{(PV_-) - (PV_+)}{2 \times (\Delta\text{Yield}) \times (PV_0)}. \quad (5)$$

This approximate *annualized* modified duration (or ApproxModDur) includes the frequency of coupon payments and the periodicity of the yield-to-maturity in the bond price calculations. Recall that approximate annualized convexity (ApproxCon) uses similar inputs and may be calculated as follows.

$$\text{ApproxCon} = \frac{(PV_-) + (PV_+) - [2 \times (PV_0)]}{(\Delta\text{Yield})^2 \times (PV_0)}. \quad (6)$$

EXAMPLE 7

Bond Price Sensitivity to Spread Changes

Show the price impact on the 4.625% 30-year Romania Eurobond versus a new shorter-term Romania bond (details below) if the spread changes due to changes in credit quality and/or liquidity. Show estimated price and return changes (using modified duration and convexity), approximate modified duration and convexity versus actual price changes and returns (using the Excel PRICE function), and discuss the results.

On 13 July 2021, Romania issued another EUR2 billion 1.75% Eurobond:

- Coupon: 1.75% (annual)
- Priced at 99.95% of par
- Yield: 1.756%
- Maturity date: 13 July 2030
- Settlement date: 13 July 2021
- Benchmark 10-year German bund yield: –0.292%

(*Note:* ApproxModDur: 8.2600; ApproxCon: 79.2963.)

The modified duration and convexity of this bond are computed using the approximation shown above. The spread sensitivity to changes in credit quality and/or bond liquidity on the settlement date are listed in the table below:

2030 Bond	Scenarios				
Spread change (bps)	–100	–50	0	50	100
Spread (bps)	105	155	205	255	305
Yield	0.7561%	1.2561%	1.7561%	2.2561%	2.7561%
Actual clean price	108.617	104.179	99.950	95.919	92.077
Actual return	8.67%	4.23%	0.00%	–4.03%	–7.88%
Estimated price: ApproxModDur & ApproxCon	108.602	104.177	99.950	95.921	92.090
Estimated return: ApproxModDur & ApproxCon	8.66%	4.23%	0.00%	–4.03%	–7.86%

In contrast, the 4.625% 30-year Eurobond has greater spread sensitivity as reflected by its higher modified duration and convexity:

- Coupon: 4.625% (annual)
- Traded at 125.13% of par
- Yield: 3.2373%
- Maturity date: 3 April 2049
- Settlement date: 13 July 2021
- Benchmark 30-year German bund yield: 0.206%

(*Note:* ApproxModDur: 17.2569; ApproxCon: 389.1376.)

2049 Bond	Scenarios				
Spread change (bps)	−100	−50	0	50	100
Spread (bps)	203	253	303	353	403
Yield	2.2373%	2.7373%	3.2373%	3.7373%	4.2373%
Actual clean price	148.923	136.332	125.130	115.147	106.236
Actual return	19.01%	8.95%	0.00%	−7.98%	−15.10%
Estimated price: ApproxModDur & ApproxCon	149.158	136.535	125.130	114.942	105.971
Estimated return: ApproxModDur & ApproxCon	19.20%	9.11%	0.00%	−8.14%	−15.31%

There are two main observations from the tables above:

a. The estimated price changes and returns using modified duration and convexity are quite close to actual price changes and returns, especially for the shorter-duration 2030 bond. *The longer a bond's duration, the greater the discrepancy between estimated and actual price changes.*

b. The 2049 bond is far more sensitive to spread changes than the 2030 bond. *The longer the duration, the more sensitive a bond's price is to changes in credit quality and bond liquidity.*

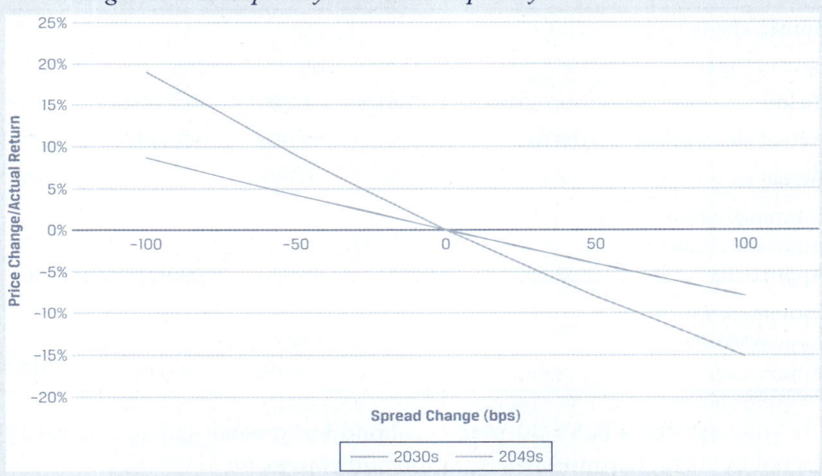

Taking on more default risk in fixed income offers higher potential return but at the cost of higher volatility and less certainty of earning that return. The lower the credit quality, the higher the quoted yield. The realized yield, or return, will almost always differ because of changes in interest rates, coupon re-investment rates, holding period changes, and the credit-related risks discussed earlier. Additionally, the volatility of returns will vary by rating. Example 8 shows the impact on bond prices due to a credit downgrade.

EXAMPLE 8

Changes in BRWA Bond Price Following a Credit Downgrade

The 3.2% BRWA senior unsecured five-year note was originally offered with few covenants. Suppose that BRWA is downgraded by one notch by the rating agencies due to rising technological and environmental risk and BRWA's focus on the legacy technology of internal combustion engines. Based on the current market environment, the differences in credit spread in the same industry due to the one-notch lower rating, applicable to the 2030 and 2035 bond tenors, are observed to be 1.0% and 2.2%, respectively.

Assume that when the rating downgrade happens:

	Modified Duration	Convexity
3.20% 2030s	3.82250	20.22640
6.20% 2035s	6.57882	58.43082

Using Equation 3, the price impact on the 3.20% BRWA 2030 bond can be estimated as:

$$\%\Delta PV^{Full} = -(\text{AnnModDur} \times \Delta\text{Spread}) + \tfrac{1}{2}\text{AnnConvexity} \times (\Delta\text{Spread})^2$$

$$= -(3.82250 \times 0.01) + \tfrac{1}{2}(20.2264) \times (0.01)^2$$

$$= -0.037214 \text{ or } -3.7214\%.$$

For the 6.20% BRWA 2035 bond, the price impact is estimated as:

$$\%\Delta PV^{Full} = -(6.57882 \times 0.022) + \tfrac{1}{2}(58.43082) \times (0.0220)^2$$

$$= -0.130594 \text{ or } -13.0594\%.$$

As in the earlier examples, the negative price impact on the longer-duration bond is expected to be much larger due to credit migration.

QUESTION SET

1. Which of the following statements best describes the relative performance of HY bonds over the economic cycle?

   A. HY bonds often have lower correlation with IG bonds and default risk-free interest rates.

   B. HY bond and equity prices tend to fluctuate similarly over the economic cycle, but HY bond returns exhibit more stability given their smaller income component versus stocks.

   C. Economic recovery or improved issuer-specific performance often has a similar positive impact on HY and IG bond prices.

   Solution:

   A is correct. B is incorrect since HY exhibit more stability due to a higher income component versus stocks. C is incorrect since economic recovery or improved issuer-specific performance usually has a greater positive impact on HY versus IG bond prices.

2. A bond investor observes a bid/offer quote for a 5-year French government zero-coupon bond of 93.75/93.775. The bond's liquidity spread is closest to:

   A. 25 bps.

   B. 5 bps.

   C. 0.54 bps.

   Solution:

   C is correct. We first calculate the respective bid and offer yields as follows:

   $$\text{Bid yield: } 93.75 = \frac{100}{(1+r)^5}$$

   $$r_{\text{bid}} = 1.2991\%$$

   $$\text{Offer yield: } 93.7755 = \frac{100}{(1+r)^5}$$

   $$r_{\text{offer}} = 1.2937\%$$

   The liquidity spread of 0.54 bps (0.0054%) is equal to the difference in the bid yield and the offer yield (= 1.2991% – 1.2937%).

3. *Determine the correct answers to fill in the blanks:* The longer a bond's duration, the __________ the discrepancy between estimated and actual price changes and the __________ sensitive a bond's price is to changes in credit quality and bond liquidity.

   Solution:

   The longer a bond's duration, the **greater** the discrepancy between estimated and actual price changes and the **more** sensitive the bond's price is to changes in credit quality and bond liquidity.

4. For a bond with a modified duration of 4 and a convexity of 0.25, which of the following changes in credit spread would result in a price decrease closest to 7.5%?

   A. 1% decrease

   B. 1% increase

   C. 2% increase

   Solution:

   The correct answer is C, as shown by solving for ΔSpread in Equation 4:

   $$\%\Delta PV^{\text{Full}} = -(\text{AnnModDur} \times \Delta\text{Spread}) + \tfrac{1}{2}\text{AnnConvexity} \times (\Delta\text{Spread})^2$$

   $$-(4 \times 0.02) + \tfrac{1}{2}(25) \times (0.02)^2 = -0.075 \text{ or } -7.5\%.$$

   The spread change is inversely related to the price effect, with a spread increase leading to a fall in bond price. Note that since duration was 4, we had to rescale the convexity from 0.25 to 25.

PRACTICE PROBLEMS

1. *Determine the correct answers to fill in the blanks:*____________ is the risk that a bond issuer's creditworthiness deteriorates, leading investors to believe the risk of default is __________ and causing the yield spreads on the issuer's bonds to _________ and the price of its bonds to _______.

2. An uncollateralized USD200,000 note has the following characteristics:

   Recovery rate 95%

   Exposure at default USD150,000

   If the note's expected loss in the event of default is USD2,500, its probability of default is *closest to:*

   A. 15%.

   B. 25%.

   C. 33%.

3. *Determine the correct answers to fill in the blanks:* While the likelihood of default for IG borrowers is typically __________ that of an HY issuer, an investor's loss in the event of a default for secured debt is usually __________ than unsecured debt due to the secondary source of repayment.

4. A bond investor is considering the credit risk components and observed yield spreads for two IG bonds of similar maturity and liquidity:

	POD	LGD	Yield Spread
Bond 1	1.25%	75%	100 bps
Bond 2	1.1%	85%	95 bps

   Which of the following conclusions about the relationship between these bonds is most correct?

   A. An investor should be indifferent between purchasing Bond 1 and Bond 2, since Bond 1's higher spread is sufficient compensation for the higher POD versus Bond 2.

   B. An investor should prefer Bond 2 over Bond 1, since they may earn a spread that is more than sufficient for assuming the credit risk.

   C. An investor should prefer Bond 1 over Bond 2, since it offers the highest spread relative to the expected loss.

5. Pitfalls of relying solely on credit ratings when making bond investment decisions may be best described as the following:

   A. Rating agencies may change their rating in response to changing market and credit conditions for a given issuer.

   B. Credit agencies may issue a positive or negative outlook for an issuer as credit risk rises or falls, but a rating change is not yet warranted.

   C. Ratings may involve miscalculations or unforeseen changes not fully captured in a rating agency's forward-looking analysis.

6. An investment-grade bond with modified duration of 7 and reported convexity of 0.51 increases in price by 9.93% after a yield spread change. The value of the spread change would be *closest to:*

   A. −1.5%.

   B. 0.15%.

   C. 1.5%.

SOLUTIONS

1. Credit migration risk (or downgrade risk) is the risk that a bond issuer's creditworthiness deteriorates, leading investors to believe the risk of default is higher and causing the yield spreads on the issuer's bonds to widen and the price of its bonds to fall.

2. The correct answer is C.

   Here we may use Equation 1 to solve for POD:

   EL = POD × (EE – Collateral) × (1 – RR).

   Substituting in the values provided:

   USD2,500 = POD × (USD150,000)×(1 – 0.95)

   POD = USD2,500/(USD150,000 ×0.05) = 0.33 = 33%.

3. While the likelihood of default for IG borrowers is typically **below** that of an HY issuer, an investor's loss in the event of a default for secured debt is usually **lower** than unsecured debt due to the secondary source of repayment.

4. C is correct. We can compare Bond 1 and Bond 2 by calculating the expected loss for each and comparing it to the annual spread:

   EL = POD × LGD

   Credit Spread ≈ POD × LGD

   Bond 1: EL = 0.938% (= 1.25% × 75%)

   Spread − EL = 6.2 bps (= 1.00% − 0.938%).

   Bond 2: EL = 0.935% (= 1.1% × 85%)

   Spread − EL = 1.5 bps (=0.95% − 0.935%).

   An investor should therefore choose Bond 1 given its higher expected return versus credit risk. A is incorrect as it fails to take the LGD into account. B is incorrect as although Bond 1 earns a 1.5 bps spread above the expected annual loss, it is less than the additional 6.2 bps spread above the expected loss earned by purchasing Bond 1.

5. The correct answer is C. While answers A and B are both true, they are not a pitfall of sole reliance on credit ratings when making bond investments.

6. The correct answer is A. Equation 4 estimates bond price changes based on duration, convexity, and changes in spread:

   $\%\Delta PV^{Full} = -(\text{AnnModDur} \times \Delta\text{Spread}) + \frac{1}{2}\text{AnnConvexity} \times (\Delta\text{Spread})^2$.

   With ModDur = 7 and reported convexity 0.51, making the necessary convexity re-scaling and substituting in values to solve for spread results in

   $0.0993 = -(7 \text{ x } \Delta\text{Spread}) + \frac{1}{2}\,(51)\,(\Delta\text{Spread})^2$

   $\Delta\text{Spread} = -0.0135 = -1.35\%$.

   Lower spreads make the first expression in the equation positive, along with the equation's second convexity-based term. The answer must therefore involve a decline in spreads as in answers A and B.

LEARNING MODULE

15

Credit Analysis for Government Issuers

LEARNING OUTCOMES	
Mastery	***The candidate should be able to:***
□	explain special considerations when evaluating the credit of sovereign and non-sovereign government debt issuers and issues

INTRODUCTION

1

This learning module explores special considerations for the credit evaluation of sovereign and other public issuers that often access fixed-income markets to finance their activities.

A major difference between corporate and sovereign issuers is the use of proceeds and source of repayment of debt obligations. In contrast to corporations that fund working capital and fixed assets to generate profits, sovereign and other government issuers use debt to conduct fiscal policy, supply public goods and services, and fund other government expenditures. While companies primarily rely on operating cash flow to repay debt, governments use tax revenues and other government revenues, such as tariffs and fees, to pay interest and principal.

We analyze sovereign bonds using a combination of qualitative and quantitative factors to assess their ability and willingness to pay. Sovereign defaults are not uncommon, particularly as countries transition from emerging to advanced economies. However, in contrast to corporate issuers, sovereign bondholders are generally unable to force governments to declare bankruptcy and liquidate assets. Non-sovereign issuers, such as certain local governments or quasi-government entities, also issue debt to finance their expenditures or develop infrastructure. This debt is backed by their ability to levy local taxes or generate specific project revenue.

LEARNING MODULE OVERVIEW

- Governments borrow in public markets to conduct fiscal policy and meet budgetary needs, such as the provision of public goods.

- A sovereign government's ability to tax private economic activity causes these bonds to normally have the lowest credit risk of any issuer in a specific country. In advanced economies, sovereign debt is often considered default risk-free.
- A combination of qualitative and quantitative factors is used to analyze a sovereign issuer's ability and willingness to pay.
- Greater central bank independence from the sovereign issuing entity reduces the likelihood that a national government will simply increase the money supply by purchasing domestic debt.
- A key distinction for sovereign creditworthiness is whether its domestic currency is considered to be a reserve currency, that is, one that is fully convertible and held by foreign central banks and other investors.
- Non-sovereign government debt is issued by local governments or quasi-government entities, backed by their tax revenue or specific project revenue.
- The credit analysis of non-sovereign debt backed by tax revenue has similar considerations to sovereign bonds, while project-based revenue bonds are typically evaluated based upon the cash flows associated with the underlying project.

LEARNING MODULE SELF-ASSESSMENT

These initial questions are intended to help you gauge your current level of understanding of this learning module.

1. Identify the debt type that corresponds to the correct example:

   A) sovereign debt, B) non-sovereign debt, C) corporate debt

1. Issued by an entity backed by cash flow from its business operations	
2. Issued by a country's government, backed by its ability and willingness to tax	
3. Issued by a local government or entity, backed by its ability and willingness to tax, or revenue from a specific public project	

Solution:

1. C is correct. Corporate debt is issued by non-government corporations to finance business operations, and payments are made from operating cash flow.

2. A is correct. Sovereign debt is issued by national governments to conduct fiscal policy and finance their budgets. This debt is paid based on the government's ability and willingness to collect taxes from within a jurisdiction.

3. B is correct. Non-sovereign debt is issued by sub-sovereign or local governments and related entities. These bonds are supported by the local taxing authority of the issuer or specific public project revenue.

2. The principle of sovereign immunity is related to the sovereign government's:

   A. ability to pay.

   B. ability to tax.

   C. willingness to pay.

   Solution:

   C is correct. Under the principle of sovereign immunity, national laws limit investors' ability to force a sovereign government into bankruptcy or liquidate its assets to settle debt claims as would be the case for a corporate issuer.

3. The creditworthiness of sovereign and other government borrowers is based upon qualitative and quantitative factors. Which of the following is *not* a quantitative factor?

   A. External stability

   B. Economic growth and flexibility

   C. Fiscal strength

   Solution:

   B is correct. The quantitative factor is actually economic growth and stability, not flexibility.

4. Which of the following statements best describes characteristics of external strength associated with higher credit quality?

   A. A government that is able to impose and enforce capital controls

   B. A government that has established free trade agreements with neighboring countries

   C. A government whose central bank issues a reserve currency

   Solution:

   C is correct. A key distinction for sovereign creditworthiness is whether its domestic currency is considered to be a reserve currency, fully convertible and frequently held by foreign central banks and other investors. A is incorrect as capital controls may not support debt capacity. B is incorrect since free trade is a necessary, but not a sufficient, condition for establishing external strength.

5. Match the following debt issuances to the correct issuer type:

   A) agency bonds, B) general obligation bonds, C) revenue bonds

1. Bonds issued for building a regional highway toll road	
2. Bonds issued by the national mortgage finance corporation, under national law.	
3. Bonds issued by a state government to fund a pension deficit	

   Solution:

   1. C is correct. Revenue bonds are issued to finance a specific public benefit project, mostly supported by the local/regional government. The revenue

from the project supported by the economic base for utilization of the project determines its credit worthiness.

2. A is correct. Agencies are quasi-government entities whose primary activities are to fulfill a government-sponsored mission to provide public services that are often based upon a specific sovereign law or statute. In many cases, either the law or statute creating the entity authorizes it to finance its activities using debt.

3. B is correct. General obligation (GO) bonds are unsecured bonds backed by the general revenues of the issuing non-sovereign government. These bonds are supported by the taxing authority of the issuer, rather than the revenue from a specific project.

6. Which of the following is a relevant qualitative factor for assessing the sovereign rating for a country's debt issue?

   A. Natural resources

   B. Trading partnership with a strong economy

   C. Economic diversification

Solution:

C is correct. One of the key factors for assessing the creditworthiness of a sovereign issuer's debt is the degree of economic diversification, as well as growth potential. The economies in countries with the highest-rated sovereign borrowers typically have an advanced and highly diversified domestic economy with strong, sustainable growth prospects. Emerging or frontier market economies, on the other hand, often depend upon a single industry or commodity and/or fewer trading partners, causing the tax revenues available to these sovereign borrowers to be more susceptible to an economic downturn, key commodity price fluctuations, and/or trade interruptions.

2 SOVEREIGN CREDIT ANALYSIS

☐ explain special considerations when evaluating the credit of sovereign and non-sovereign government debt issuers and issues

As outlined in earlier lessons, both sovereign and non-sovereign governments issue debt to finance their activities. In contrast to corporate debt, this debt is used to conduct fiscal policy and meet budgetary needs, such as providing public goods and services including infrastructure, health care, and education. The primary source of repayment for sovereign debt is usually taxes and other government revenue, which can include fees, tariffs, and in some cases the profits of state-owned enterprises. A sovereign government's ability to tax all private economic activity under its jurisdiction is the primary reason why such bonds usually have the lowest credit risk of any issuer within a specific country. While sovereign bonds in the most advanced economies are often considered default risk-free, those issued by emerging and frontier market governments involve greater default risk.

Bond investors evaluate the creditworthiness of both corporate and public issuers by the stability and predictability of issuer cash flows, the sufficiency of those cash flows to meet required interest and principal payments, and the issuer's relative reliance on debt financing versus other available resources. The creditworthiness of sovereign and other government borrowers is based upon qualitative and quantitative factors unique to the public sector, as shown in the following sections.

Qualitative Factors

Sovereign government policies affecting the macroeconomy and financial markets include monetary and fiscal policies that typically seek to create an economic environment with positive, stable growth and stable, low inflation. Domestic and foreign investors evaluate the creditworthiness of a sovereign issuer by considering a government's taxation and spending policies and the underlying economy as a primary source of tax revenue for repayment. Qualitative factors included in this assessment are shown in Exhibit 1.

Exhibit 1: Qualitative Factors in Sovereign Creditworthiness

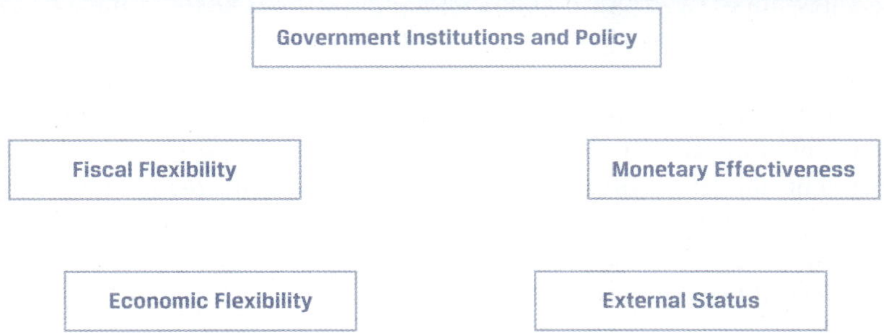

Government Institutions & Policy: This factor addresses the role of sovereign government institutions and policies in fostering political and economic stability. From an economic standpoint, these policies range from basic legal protections, such as maintaining the rule of law and the enforcement of property rights, to promoting a culture of debt repayment, transparency, the consistency of financial data reporting, and the relative ease of doing business within a jurisdiction. Political factors include stability of domestic political institutions and the absence of conflict with neighboring countries. These factors are often captured using a relative ranking or scoring approach.

In addition to a sovereign government's ability to pay, we must also consider its *willingness* to pay. Willingness to pay is important for sovereign issuers because of the principle of **sovereign immunity**, under which investors face limitations in forcing a sovereign government to declare bankruptcy or liquidate its assets to settle debt claims as would be the case for a corporate issuer. Sovereign immunity limits the legal recourse of bondholders in many instances, preventing external creditors from fully enforcing debt claims. In most cases, given the involvement of multiple lenders and multilateral agencies such as the International Monetary Fund (IMF), investors agree to restructure debt to provide extended terms and/or favorable interest rates for a specified period to recover their investment, as in the following example.

EXAMPLE 1

Uruguay's 2003 Sovereign Debt Exchange

After years of economic stagnation compounded by a banking crisis resulting from large deposit withdrawals first by neighboring Argentines and then by its own residents, Uruguay was forced to float its currency in June 2002. This caused a large depreciation of the Uruguayan peso (UYI) which, together with the fiscal cost of the banking crisis, led to a sharp rise in debt that pushed the country to the brink of default. With the support of the IMF, in March 2003 the authorities announced their intention to carry out a market-friendly debt restructuring to moderate short-term liquidity pressures and improve the medium-term servicing profile of foreign currency-denominated sovereign debt. A debt exchange to extend Uruguay's bond maturities by five years was successfully agreed to in May 2003 with the consent of 90% of bondholders. Although the transaction was voluntary, it was deemed by analysts to be a default in substance given a lack of sufficient bondholder compensation for the delayed debt payment as well as the subordination of bondholders who did not participate in the exchange.

Fiscal Flexibility: Sovereign governments are also evaluated on how well they establish and maintain fiscal discipline over time and under different economic conditions. The management of public finances extends from the enforceability of tax collection to the prudent allocation of government budget expenditures on public goods to managing sovereign debt outstanding relative to economic activity. This assessment is based upon past experience in adjusting spending over economic cycles and the expected effect of fiscal policy changes, as in the following example.

EXAMPLE 2

Government of Romania's Improved Ratings Outlook

In October 2021, Moody's Investors Service changed its ratings outlook on the Government of Romania from negative to stable with a Baa3 issuer and senior unsecured debt rating. In addition to solid economic growth prospects, Moody's cited an expectation of consistent and sustained fiscal consolidation as a reason for the improved outlook. As part of Romania's goal to become a full-fledged member state after joining the EU in 2007, the government was expected to prepare and implement fiscal reforms to reduce its annual deficit to below 3% of GDP within three years. The incentive to reduce the deficit was strengthened by the possible suspension of EU structural and investment grants in the case of non-compliance.

Monetary Effectiveness: Monetary policy involves central bank activity directed toward influencing the quantity of money and credit in an economy. Central banks establish short-term interest rates and reserve requirements, and they buy and sell sovereign bonds using open market operations—all to encourage stable and sustainable growth amid relative price stability. At one extreme, central banks may implement policy almost completely independent of government interference and influence; at the other extreme, they may simply act as the agent of the government. Central bank independence from the public Treasury reduces the likelihood that a sovereign government will monetize their domestic debt, driving domestic inflation higher and reducing the external value of the domestic currency.

Economic Flexibility: The economic activity under a sovereign government's jurisdiction available to tax and service debt is usually the primary source of debt repayment. Key factors important in gauging creditworthiness include not only the size of an economy and level of per capital income, but also the degree of economic diversification and growth potential.

Economies in countries with the highest-rated sovereign borrowers typically have an advanced and highly diversified domestic economy with strong, sustainable growth prospects. Emerging or frontier market economies, on the other hand, often depend upon a single industry or commodity or have fewer trading partners, causing the tax revenues available to these sovereign borrowers to be more susceptible to an economic downturn, key commodity price fluctuations, and/or trade interruptions. In many cases, such countries have a sizable informal economy or face challenges in collecting tax revenue.

External Status: External status or governance refers to how a sovereign government's international trade, capital, and foreign exchange policies influence its ability to support and service outstanding debt. Monetary policy credibility and the exchange rate regime have a significant effect on international capital flows. A key distinction for the creditworthiness of a sovereign government is whether its domestic currency is considered to be a **reserve currency**, that is, one that is fully convertible and frequently held by foreign central banks and other investors as a portion of their foreign exchange reserves. When foreign investors are able and willing to hold assets in a country's currency in the form of cash, sovereign bonds, and other investments, it greatly expands the government's ability to access foreign investors using domestic currency debt. This greater flexibility minimizes the likelihood of sovereign default and increases a government's ability to sustain structural budget deficits and a higher level of debt.

In contrast, many emerging and frontier market countries have exchange rate restrictions, capital controls, and/or a lack of full convertibility that constrains their ability to borrow from foreign entities by issuing bonds in foreign currencies. In cases where such debt markets are unavailable, these countries are more likely to access foreign currency funding from supranational organizations, such as the IMF, in order to meet development needs or implement economic reforms.

While a country's internal and external strength are usually determined by its economic growth dynamics, competitiveness, and diversification, geopolitical risk is also often a factor to consider, as in the following example.

EXAMPLE 3

Moldova's IMF Credit Facility

Russia's military invasion of Ukraine in February 2022 caused a deterioration in the creditworthiness of several East European countries due to heightened political and economic risk. Given its proximity to the conflict and the influx of far more refugees on a per capita basis than its neighbors, the Republic of Moldova faced the greatest adverse economic impact. Rising inflation, stagnant growth, and a higher current account deficit due to falling exports and rising energy prices led Moldovan authorities to request and receive permission from the IMF to partially draw down an extended credit facility to meet immediate external obligations, such as energy purchases, in May 2022. The Moldovan government received IMF approval for the temporary funding by both submitting a budget to meet immediate fiscal needs due to the crisis and reinforcing its commitment to pursue structural economic reforms in order to avert a default.

The combinations of qualitative institutional (including fiscal and monetary policy), economic, and external factors used to evaluate sovereign creditworthiness are shown in detail in Exhibit 2.

Exhibit 2: Detailed Qualitative Factors in Sovereign Creditworthiness

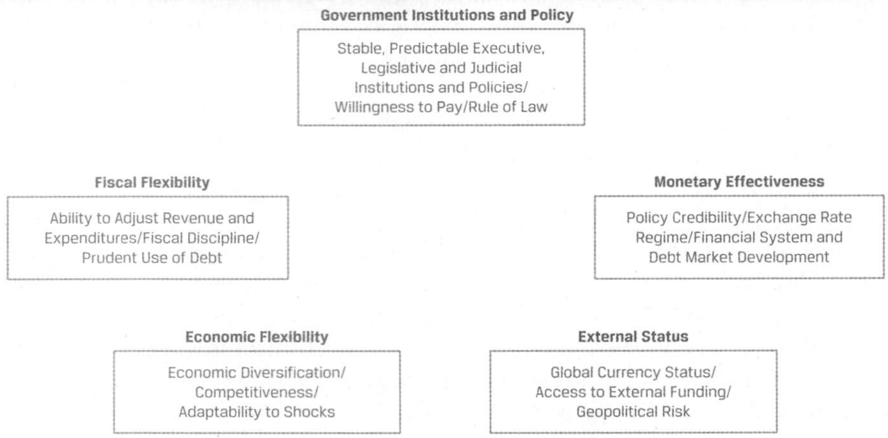

In practice, many of these qualitative factors are interrelated; for example, a weak legal system often goes hand in hand with a limited ability to collect taxes due or enforce debt contracts. The use of these qualitative factors in assessing creditworthiness is best understood using an example, such as the following country comparison.

EXAMPLE 4

Moldova and Romania

Three decades after emerging from central planning to a market economy, Romania and Moldova share linguistic, cultural, and historical ties as well as a common border, but they have different sovereign credit risk profiles. Romania is an investment-grade sovereign issuer (rated Baa3 by Moody's, and BBB– by S&P and Fitch), while Moldova is a non-investment-grade issuer (rated B3 by Moody's, and B– by S&P and Fitch) based in part upon the following factors:

Government Institutions & Policy: While both Romania and Moldova established representative democracies following one-party rule under socialism, Romania signed an Association Agreement with the EU in 1992 and formally joined in 2007, codifying its access to European markets and economic integration. Moldova's political transition was slower, and its government is still considered by many analysts to be an unstable democracy, with weak governance and institutions and widespread corruption. Moldova faces economic and political hurdles in joining the EU, including an unresolved conflict within the Transnistria region as well as internal resistance to EU membership. It did not formally apply to join the EU until 2022.

Given its aspiration to join the euro currency area, Romania's fiscal and monetary policy is focused on meeting strict EU convergence criteria, including limiting fiscal deficits and government debt outstanding, stabilizing exchange rates, and managing inflation and long-term interest rates. Romania has a financial and banking system with an active, but small, domestic currency government and corporate bond market. Moldova's financial system is less well developed, and it faces near-term fiscal and monetary challenges compounded by the Ukraine conflict as outlined above. Moldova's domestic currency government debt issuance is concentrated in short-term maturities, and its ability to borrow is limited, while domestic inflation is well above the central bank's target despite its monetary tightening measures.

Economy: Romania has a much larger, more diversified, and competitive industrial economy due to the influx of foreign direct investment from EU countries since its transition to a market economy as well as abundant natural resources. Moldova in contrast was slower to privatize its economy following socialism, facing a limited ability to attract capital over the transition period with a high degree of dependence on Russia for energy imports. The domestic economy remains dependent upon agriculture and food processing (which comprise 40% of GDP).

External Status: While both countries increased access to foreign currency bond markets after emerging from socialism, Moldova rescheduled its foreign currency debt in 2002 to avoid default and remains dependent upon IMF credit facilities as outlined earlier. In contrast, Romania has maintained access to international capital markets, issuing foreign currency (EUR and USD) bonds both before and after the 2022 invasion of Ukraine. As Moldova is more dependent on regional trading partners, has less well diversified exports and fewer trading partners, it has faced greater trade disruption due to the war in Ukraine.

Quantitative Factors

Quantitative credit analysis seeks to estimate the likelihood that an issuer can meet its fixed debt obligations. Unlike corporations that issue periodic financial statements based upon generally accepted accounting principles, sovereign credit analysts must rely on government economic data, which varies in terms of quality and timing, lacks comparability across countries and over time, and faces periodic revision as well as political considerations. As a result, detailed public sector financial balance sheets tend to be of limited use in forecasting creditworthiness, with analysts focusing on a top-down, macroeconomic approach based upon the quantitative factors shown in Exhibit 3.

Exhibit 3: Quantitative Factors in Sovereign Creditworthiness

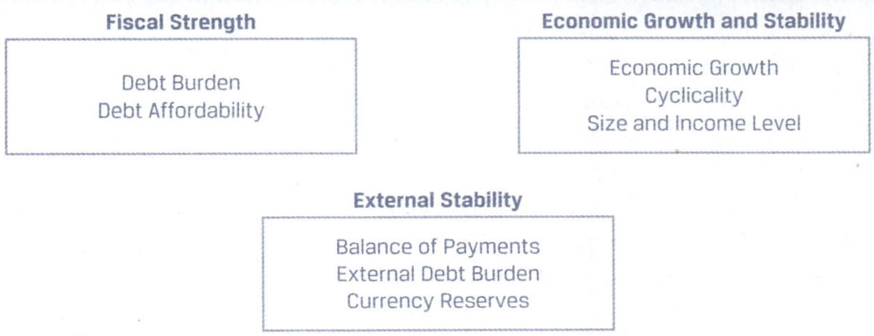

Financial ratios allow the comparison across sovereign issuers and over time in a similar way as for corporate issuers. While the relevant numerator for such ratios is often debt size or the level of periodic fixed payments as for corporate issuers, the denominator is not total sales or total assets but often either government revenue or domestic GDP as the primary measure of economic activity subject to taxation.

Fiscal Strength: Measuring a sovereign issuer's relative fiscal strength depends upon both its current and expected future debt burden, as well as the relative reliance on debt versus other financial resources. Some of the key financial ratios that measure sovereign fiscal strength are shown in Exhibit 4.

Exhibit 4: Key Financial Ratios to Measure Fiscal Strength

Fiscal Strength

Debt Burden	Debt Affordability
Debt to GDP: $\frac{\text{General Government Debt}}{\text{GDP}}$	*Interest to GDP:* $\frac{\text{Government Interest Payments}}{\text{GDP}}$
Debt to Revenue: $\frac{\text{General Government Debt}}{\text{Revenue}}$	*Interest to Revenue:* $\frac{\text{Government Interest Payments}}{\text{Revenue}}$

Debt burden measures are similar to leverage and provide an indication of a government's solvency. In each case, a higher debt burden ratio is associated with lower credit quality. In addition, annual fiscal surpluses or deficits as a percentage of GDP are often used to measure fiscal discipline and to determine whether a country's debt burden is improving or deteriorating over time. Debt affordability, on the other hand, provides a measure of debt coverage, with a higher ratio also a sign of lower credit quality.

EXAMPLE 5

Fiscal Deficits and Debt-to-GDP in the Eurozone Crisis

The European debt crisis of 2010 arose as several European Union member states (including Greece, Portugal, Ireland, Spain, and Cyprus) were no longer able to meet their financial obligations without the assistance of other EU member states, the European Central Bank, and/or the International Monetary Fund. The situation stemmed largely from the aftermath of the Global Financial Crisis of 2008–09, as governments provided financial assistance to failing domestic banks while their domestic economies stalled and tax revenue fell. As members of the euro currency zone under the direction of the European Central Bank, these countries were prevented from using monetary policy tools, such as devaluing the domestic currency, in response to the crisis. As shown in the following figures, relatively high pre-existing debt-to-GDP ratios coupled with rising fiscal deficits caused sovereign credit spreads among these countries relative to Germany, the largest and most creditworthy member of the EU, to widen dramatically. Later, some of these EU members adopted austerity measures to improve their fiscal governance and obtain support from stronger EU member states, which resulted in tighter sovereign credit spreads over time.

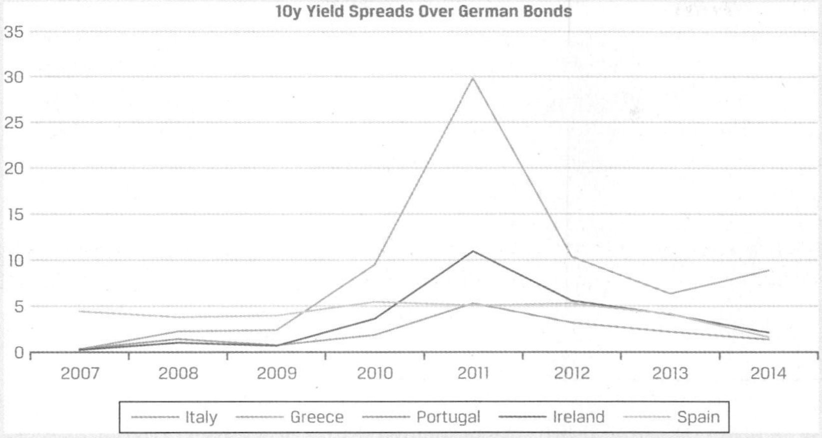

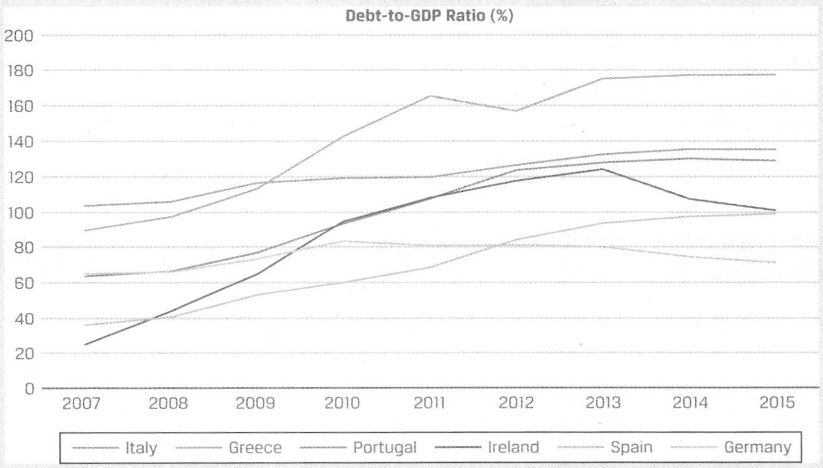

Source: Bloomberg.

The ratios in Exhibit 4 are used by rating agencies to gauge a country's relative debt burden and debt affordability in a similar manner to corporate financial ratios. Exhibit 5 shows how these fiscal strength metrics align to Moody's sovereign ratings, for example. In the case of Moody's and other rating agencies, these and other financial metrics are not considered in isolation but rather are weighted and combined with other factors in a comprehensive credit analysis.

Exhibit 5: Debt Burden and Debt Affordability

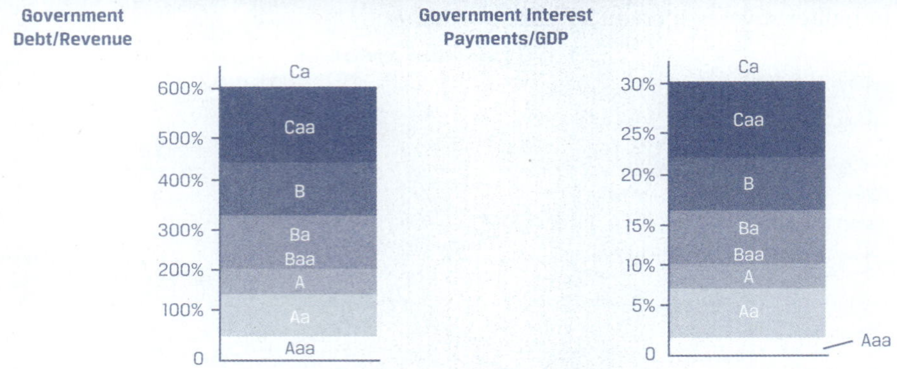

Economic Growth and Stability: As larger, wealthier economies are better positioned to achieve sustainable growth and withstand economic and political shocks, the economy's size as measured by GDP as well as its per capita income are important factors in gauging a country's economic prospects. Historical and projected future real economic growth levels as well as their variability are also key quantitative measures, which are summarized in Exhibit 6.

Exhibit 6: Key Financial Measures of Economic Growth and Stability

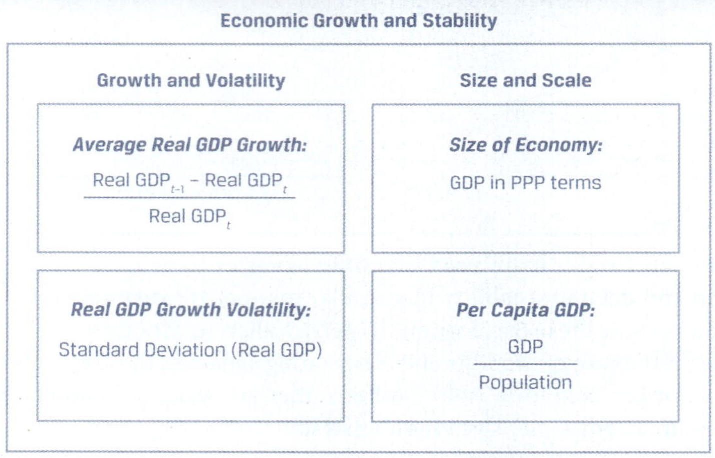

EXAMPLE 6

Sovereign Credit Risk of Southeast Asian Economies

A junior analyst is conducting a comparative credit analysis of several upper-medium to non-investment-grade Southeast Asian sovereign issuers (Malaysia, Thailand, Indonesia, Vietnam, and the Philippines) in the aftermath of the COVID-19 pandemic. As a first step, she compares the relative size of these five economies based on GDP as well as per capita GDP:

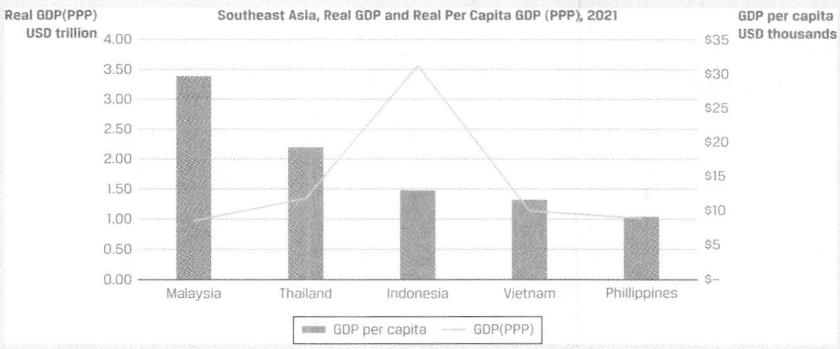

Source: World Bank (data.worldbank.org).

While Indonesia is the largest economy in Southeast Asia in terms of GDP on a purchasing power parity (PPP) basis, Malaysia has the smallest economy but by far the highest per capita GDP. Despite its size relative to its neighbors, the Malaysian economy is a relatively high-growth, competitive export-based economy focused on high technology products, such as electronics and health care. Malaysia's growth, competitiveness, and stability are among the economic factors that have earned it the highest credit rating among the five countries (A3 from Moody's and A from S&P).

GDP growth rates over the past decade and volatility are key indicators of relative trends among economies, as shown in the following comparison over the past decade:

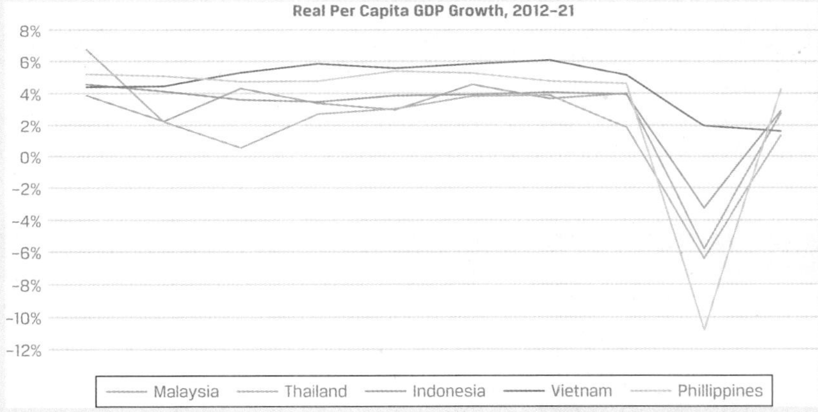

Source: World Bank (data.worldbank.org).

While Vietnam is among the smallest of the five economies with the second-lowest per capita GDP, it enjoyed the highest growth rate over the decade and was the only Southeast Asian economy that grew in 2020. The following summarizes average GDP growth and volatility (as measured by standard deviation of annual GDP changes):

Despite being the lowest rated of the five countries (rated Ba3 by Moody's and BB+ by Standard & Poor's), Vietnam's stable and high growth relative to its neighbors contributed to a positive outlook from Moody's and ratings upgrades from BB– to BB+ over the past decade from S&P.

External Stability: A country's external stability depends critically upon whether foreign investors are able and willing to hold assets in a country's currency. Countries with actively traded currencies where foreign entities are significant investors in domestic currency assets or those whose domestic currency is held in reserve by other countries tend to exhibit greater external stability.

Key factors influencing whether a sovereign government with a non-reserve currency can meet external debt obligations include its external liquidity and solvency, that is, the short- and long-term ability to generate sufficient, stable foreign currency cash inflows that may be used to meet interest and principal payments on external debt as well as other obligations to foreign investors.

Exhibit 7: Key Financial Ratios to Measure External Stability

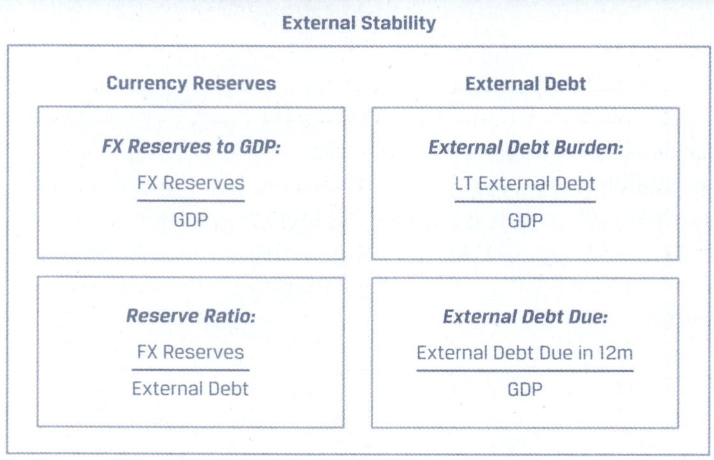

Quantitative measures of external stability focus on the relative size of external debt as compared to available sources of repayment. These sources include broad measures, such as GDP, as well as foreign currency balances (i.e., reserves), or foreign currency cash flows, often measured as currency account receipts. Current account deficits and surpluses based on the international trade of goods and services offset changes in a country's capital account through capital inflows or outflows from abroad. Many countries with FX reserves accumulate such balances through a current account surplus with developed countries, while others benefit from foreign currency remittances from citizens working abroad. Declining or volatile foreign currency balances or cash flows reduce a sovereign borrower's ability to service foreign currency debt. While quantitative ratios provide a basis for comparison, it is important to consider a number of factors, as outlined in the following example.

EXAMPLE 7

FX Reserves of Southeast Asian Economies

Country	Reserve Ratio	FX Reserves to GDP
Malaysia	54%	11.9%
Thailand	102%	16.4%
Indonesia	31%	3.9%
Vietnam	84%	9.9%
Philippines	96%	10.3%

Source: Bloomberg, FYE 2020.

A cursory comparison of ratios based upon currency reserves among the five Southeast Asian countries shown above suggests that Thailand should have the highest external creditworthiness among the five countries. In fact, Malaysia's greater economic competitiveness and lower reliance on foreign currency-denominated debt actually results in higher external creditworthiness as measured by rating agencies (with a Moody's external long-term foreign currency rating of A3 versus Baa1 for Thailand). Despite Thailand's higher FX reserves to GDP, its foreign currency credit rating is the same as that for the Philippines. This is due in large part to the far greater proportion of Philippine workers abroad sending foreign currency to the country, which in 2020 comprised nearly 10% of GDP in the Philippines versus less than 2% in Thailand.

In the case of emerging and frontier market countries where commodity exports generate the bulk of foreign currency reserves, commodity demand and prices can be primary factors driving sovereign creditworthiness. While countries facing strong, stable commodity demand, such as oil-producing nations, often accumulate substantial reserves and establish sovereign wealth funds to increase economic diversification, adverse commodity price fluctuations can contribute to sovereign default, as in the following case.

EXAMPLE 8

Zambia's Default in 2020

The Republic of Zambia defaulted on a USD42.5 million Eurobond payment in November 2020, the first sovereign default following the COVID-19 pandemic. Zambia is Africa's second-largest producer of copper, which comprises 60% of its exports. An economic slowdown due to COVID-19 accelerated a decline in copper prices beginning in 2014. By November 2020, Zambia's annual inflation rate climbed to 17.4%, its highest level in four years. Additionally, the national currency, the kwacha (ZMK), depreciated 33% against the US dollar in 2020, creating more pain for Zambian consumers. Zambia's total external debt had more than doubled in just five years, increasing from USD4.8 billion, or 18% of gross domestic product, at the end of 2014 to USD11.2 billion, or 48% of GDP, in 2019. At the same time, external reserves fell from over 50% of external debt to just 5% due to falling prices for its copper exports. This led to the inevitable default on external debt and the consequent restructuring.

QUESTION SET

1. Which of the following statements best describes debt burden versus debt affordability measures?

   A. Debt burden measures are similar to leverage, indicating a government's relative solvency, while debt affordability measures provide a measure of debt coverage.

   B. A higher interest-to-GDP measure is associated with higher credit quality, while a lower debt-to-GDP ratio signals less credit risk.

   C. Higher debt to revenue is associated with greater credit risk, while a higher interest-to-revenue ratio signals higher credit quality.

   Solution: A is correct. B is incorrect, since a higher interest-to-GDP measure is associated with *lower* credit quality, while a lower debt-to-GDP ratio signals less credit risk. C is incorrect, as higher debt to revenue is associated with greater credit risk, while a higher interest-to-revenue ratio signals *lower* credit quality.

2. **Determine the correct answers to fill in the blanks:** A key distinction for the creditworthiness of a sovereign government is whether its domestic currency is considered to be a __________ currency, that is, one that is fully convertible and held by foreign central banks and other investors. When foreign investors are able and willing to hold assets in a country's currency, it greatly ___________ the government's ability to access foreign investors using domestic currency debt.

   Solution:

   A key distinction for the creditworthiness of a sovereign government is whether its domestic currency is considered to be a *reserve* currency, that is, one that is fully convertible and held by foreign central banks and other investors. When foreign investors are able and willing to hold assets in a country's currency, it greatly *expands* the government's ability to access foreign investors using domestic currency debt.

3. Which of the following is a key ratio to measure the fiscal strength of a sovereign government?

   A. FX reserves to GDP

   B. Government interest payments to GDP

   C. GDP to population

   Solution:

   B is correct. Measuring a sovereign issuer's relative fiscal strength depends upon both its current debt burden as well as the relative reliance on debt versus other financial resources. Debt burden measures provide an indication of a government's solvency, one of which is the level of government interest payments as a percentage of GDP.

A is incorrect. Although FX reserves to GDP is a key ratio in determining the creditworthiness of a sovereign government, it is an external stability ratio, that is, a measure of foreign currency available to service foreign currency debt payments.

C is incorrect. GDP to population is a key ratio in determining the creditworthiness of a sovereign government, but it is related to economic growth and stability rather than fiscal strength.

4. Match the following indicators to the respective factors in sovereign credit assessment:

A. Monetary governance

B. Fiscal governance

C. External governance

D. Economic and political governance

1. Government budget deficit/GDP	
2. Long-term external debt/GDP	
3. International competitiveness ranking	
4. Central Bank policy independent of public treasury	

Solution:

1. Government budget deficit/GDP	B. Fiscal governance
2. Long-term external debt/GDP	C. External governance
3. International competitiveness ranking	D. Economic and political governance
4. Central Bank policy independent of public treasury	A. Monetary governance

NON-SOVEREIGN CREDIT RISK 3

☐ explain special considerations when evaluating the credit of sovereign and non-sovereign government debt issuers and issues

Non-Sovereign Government Debt

While sovereign issuers comprise the largest issuers of government debt, a number of non-sovereign government issuers, such as government agencies or regional governments, issue debt to finance their activities as well. In the case of government agencies, investors typically face very similar credit risk to the sovereign given either implicit government backing in the form of a sovereign law creating the entity and granting it powers to raise debt, or explicit backing in the form of a guarantee. In the case of sub-sovereign issuers with their own taxation and income-generating powers, such as regional government issuers, they benefit from the economic and political governance as well as monetary and fiscal policies of the sovereign as they fall under its jurisdiction; still, they have a number of features that may cause their creditworthiness to vary significantly from that of the sovereign issuer.

The main types of non-sovereign government issuers include agencies, public banks, supranationals, and regional governments.

Agencies

Agencies are quasi-government entities whose primary activities are to fulfill a government-sponsored mission to provide public services, often based upon a specific sovereign law or statute. In many cases, either the law or statute creating the entity authorizes it to finance its activities using debt. As quasi-government entities, investors usually assume a high likelihood of sovereign government support, and rating agencies typically grant the same rating to these entities as the sovereign entity.

An example of a perpetual bond issued by a government entity is as follows:

EXAMPLE 9

Airport Authority Hong Kong SAR (AAHK) Perpetual Bonds

AAHK is a statutory body owned by the Hong Kong SAR government responsible for operating and developing Hong Kong International Airport (HKIA), one of the world's busiest cargo airports and a major passenger hub connecting to over 200 global destinations. In late 2020, following a sharp decline in passenger volume during the COVID-19 pandemic, AAHK announced a two-part, USD1.5 billion perpetual bond issuance to fund construction of a third runway and for general corporate purposes. The issuance was evenly split between bonds with a 2.10% fixed coupon, which AAHK has the right to buy back after 5.5 years, and those with a 2.40% fixed coupon, which AAHK can repurchase after 7.5 years. The bonds were rated AA, one notch down from the long-term issuer rating of AAHK, which was AA+ due to the buyback option. The long-term issuer rating of AAHK was based on equalization with the Hong Kong SAR government sovereign rating of AA+. The assumption supporting this rating is the implicit support for AAHK expected from the Hong Kong SAR government in case of any financial distress of AAHK.

Government Sector Banks and Development Financing Institutions

Sovereign governments often sponsor the establishment of specialized financial intermediaries to operate in a specific market or to promote specific sovereign political, economic, social, or other growth and policy objectives. Similar to agencies, these institutions are usually created or supported by the sovereign government and enjoy a similar rating, as in the following example:

EXAMPLE 10

Kreditanstalt für Wiederaufbau (KfW)

Established in 1948 in the Federal Republic of Germany, KfW is the largest national development bank (80% owned by the German federal government and 20% by the federal states). It benefits from explicit and direct statutory guarantee and institutional liability by the Federal Republic of Germany. It is regulated by the "Law concerning KfW," exempt from corporate taxes, and supervised by the German Federal Ministry of Finance and the German Federal Financial Supervisory Authority, better known as "BaFin." KfW bonds receive a zero risk weighting under bank capital rules. Its bonds are rated AAA and "Prime" ESG rating. During 2020 its ESG commitment was to originate at least 33% new business in environment and climate protection initiatives and 48% of new domestic business volume from small and medium-sized enterprises. To fund this business, KfW has been the most active issuer of Green Bonds in the international capital markets. It issued its first Green Bond in 2013, and it raised 20% of its new debt through Green Bonds (EUR16.2 billion in 2021), with total Green Bond issuance totaling EUR47.1 billion by 2021. The proceeds of Green Bond issuance are deployed in projects mitigating climate change in the categories of renewable energies and energy efficiency.

Supranational Issuers

So-called supranational entities are organizations that are established and owned by sovereign governments that join as members to pursue a common objective. For example, the World Bank and its affiliates, such as the International Bank for Reconstruction and Development (IBRD), issue debt to assist developing countries with projects aimed at combating poverty and pursuing sustainable economic growth. Examples of supranational entities with a regional focus include the Asian Development Bank (ADB) and the Development Bank of Latin America (Corporacion Andina de Fomento, or CAF) in Latin America. Another example of a supranational entity is provided in Example 11.

EXAMPLE 11

Indonesia Infrastructure Finance (IIF)

The Indonesia Infrastructure Finance (IIF) was established by the Government of the Republic of Indonesia (30% shareholding) along with World Bank (20% shareholding), ADB (20% shareholding), and other multilateral institutions, like KfW (15% shareholding) and Sumitomo Mitsui Banking Corporation (15% shareholding). IIF was established in January 2010 to help accelerate and improve private participation in infrastructure development in Indonesia. IIF provides fund-based products, such as long-term loans, and non-fund-based products, such as guarantees and other services relating to infrastructure projects. IIF applies international social and environmental protection standards to ensure sustainability of infrastructure development in Indonesia. IIF's credit rating is BBB, equivalent to the sovereign rating of the Government of Indonesia, based on its strategic importance as well as the implicit support and share ownership of global development institutions.

Regional Government Issuers

These include provincial, state, and local governments, referred to as municipal bonds in the US and most often as local authority bonds elsewhere, within a specific sovereign jurisdiction. Local government finance varies widely across countries. In some cases, such as the Netherlands, the federal government has established a public financial institution that offers financing to municipalities while establishing a structure that grants them the same credit rating as the federal government. Other countries use a tax revenue sharing system across sovereign and local governments to ensure that local authorities are able to meet their obligations. In contrast, in the United States, municipal issuers, such as state and local governments, are rated individually and typically issue either general obligation or revenue bonds.

General Obligation Bonds

General obligation (GO) bonds are unsecured bonds that are backed by the general revenues of the issuing non-sovereign government. These bonds are supported by the taxing authority of the issuer. Revenue bonds are issued for specific project financing—for example, financing for a new sewer system, a toll road, bridge, hospital, or sports arena.

The credit analysis of GO bonds has some similarities to sovereign debt analysis (e.g., the ability to levy and collect taxes and fees to service debt) but also some differences. The attractiveness of the local business climate, presence of major industries and employers to establish a diversified, stable corporate tax base, implicit national government support in some cases, as well as the prudent management of state or local government budgets all play an important role in establishing the relative creditworthiness of the issuer. That said, non-sovereign governments have limited jurisdictional powers and no control over sovereign economic and monetary institutions, as is the case for sovereign issuers. Non-sovereign issuers may face greater exposure to technological change, such as declining industries, and demographic changes, as in the case of the largest US municipal bankruptcy filing presented in Example 12.

EXAMPLE 12

City of Detroit Bankruptcy Filing

The City of Detroit became the largest US municipal bankruptcy filing in 2013 following a decades-long decline in automotive industry employment and a shift in manufacturing jobs to lower-wage Southern states. The result was a demographic shift—causing the city's population to decline from 2 million to 700,000—and increased racial tensions that accelerated a population shift out of the city to the suburbs. The resulting declines in the property and income tax base left Detroit with a shortfall in meeting payments on its estimated USD18 billion in debt outstanding. The city was unable to reach an agreement with lenders, unions, and pensioners, forcing it to file for Chapter 9 bankruptcy protection. After a 17-month negotiation period with its creditors, Detroit emerged from bankruptcy after selling and pledging assets and offering concessions, with pensioners retaining approximately 85% of their benefits and general obligation unlimited tax bondholders recovering 74 cents on the dollar for their investments.

Revenue Bonds

Revenue bonds, which are issued to finance a specific project, have a higher degree of risk than GO bonds because their cash flows are dependent upon a single source of revenue. The analysis of these bonds is a combination of an analysis of the project and the finances around the particular project. The project analysis focuses on the need and projected utilization of the project, as well as on the economic base supporting the project. This analysis has similarities to that of a corporate bond in that it is focused on operating results, cash flow, liquidity, capital structure, and the issuer's ability to service and repay its debt based upon cash flow projections. Similar to corporate debt, a key credit measure for revenue-backed non-sovereign government bonds is the **debt service coverage ratio**, a measure of revenue available to cover principal and interest payments after operating expenses. The higher the coverage ratio, the stronger the creditworthiness. Minimum coverage ratio covenants are a common feature of revenue bonds. Coverage and other financial ratios are covered in greater detail in the next learning module on corporate credit risk.

In analyzing these bonds, the inherent riskiness of the cash flows becomes increasingly important. Hence, not only are the underlying capacity and ability to raise revenue through taxes and fees material, which is important for the sovereign bond evaluation, but also an understanding of other repayment sources. This becomes particularly material for various non-sovereign government infrastructure bonds, which may be issued either by supranational entities or other quasi-governmental issuers, such as airport authorities or public utility companies (for which the national government may be a secondary implicit source of repayment in the event of a revenue shortfall). An example of a non-sovereign government infrastructure project is described below.

EXAMPLE 13

Lima Metro Line 2 Finance Limited

Lima Metro Line 2 Finance Limited (Lima Metro 2) is one of the largest infrastructure debt offerings in Latin America and the largest RPI-CAO-backed offering to date. RPI-CAOs (Retribución por Inversión – Certificado de Avance de Obras) are a milestone payment, government-sponsored mechanism characteristic of the Peruvian infrastructure financing program.

The RPI-CAO regime is a payment mechanism under which the concessionaire, Metro de Lima Línea 2 S.A., obtains the right to receive systematic payments as compensation for construction costs incurred for a project. RPI-CAOs are obtained after construction milestones are achieved and progress reports are submitted to, and approved by, the Ministry of Transport and Communications of Peru. These USD-denominated compensation rights are guaranteed by the Ministry and payable to the concessionaire following a specified installment schedule. RPI-CAOs are not direct sovereign obligations, but investors have recourse to the Peruvian government if the Ministry fails to make interest and principal payments.

The bonds were issued to finance the construction of two routes of the subway system in the city of Lima, Peru, along with the related electromechanical equipment. The project involved the construction of 35 subway stations and approximately 35 kilometers of tunnels and courtyards. In April 2014, the Ministry entered into a concession agreement with Metro de Lima Línea 2 S.A. (a consortium comprised of ACS Iridium, Vialia [FCC], Salini Impregilo, AnsaldoBreda, Ansaldo STS, and COSAPI, and the project equity sponsors) for the construction and operation of two underground railway lines.

In June 2015, Lima Metro 2 issued USD1,150MM in 144A/Reg S senior secured notes at 5.875%. The 19.1-year notes had an average life at issuance of 12.8 years and are rated Baa1 (Moody's); BBB (S&P); and BBB (Fitch). The notes drew significant interest from asset managers and local Peruvian investors, with these investor bases comprising the majority of the final order book.

5.875% Lima Metro Line 2 Finance Limited
Brief Summary of Terms

Issuer:	Lima Metro Line 2 Finance Limited
Issuance Date:	June 2015
Maturity Date:	July 2034
Issuance Amount	USD1,150MM
Use of Proceeds	Finance construction of a metro line project in the city of Lima
Credit Ratings	Baa1 (Moody's); BBB (S&P); BBB (Fitch)
Country	Peru
Project Type	Transportation, Rail
Project Sponsor	A consortium comprised of ACS Iridium, Vialia (FCC), Salini Impregilo, AnsaldoBreda, Ansaldo STS, and COSAPI
Source of Payment	RPI-CAO payment regime

QUESTION SET

1. Which of the following statements best describes the relationship between local government and sovereign creditworthiness?

   A. Local governments have limited jurisdictional powers and no control over economic and monetary institutions.

   B. All sovereign governments use a tax revenue sharing system across sovereign and local governments to ensure that local authorities are able to meet their obligations.

   C. Local governments with the power to attract and retain major industries and employers are often more creditworthy than their sovereign government.

   Solution:

   A is correct. Local governments have limited jurisdiction and no control over national fiscal and monetary policy. B is incorrect, as some, not all, sovereign governments use tax revenue sharing. C is incorrect. Since local governments are subject to the economic and monetary policy of the sovereign, their rating is typically equal or below that of the sovereign government.

2. Ile-de-France, the regional government of Paris, issued a green bond, the proceeds of which are to be used for investments including ecofriendly construction and renovation of buildings, public transport to support sustainable mobility, and renewable energy projects. The bond is backed by the tax and other revenue of Ile-de-France. This bond is an example of:

   A. a general obligation (GO) bond.

   B. a revenue bond.

   C. an agency bond.

   Solution:

   A is correct. Though the proceeds of the bond are used for specific green infrastructure development, interest and principal payments are backed by the tax and other revenue of the local government rather than any specific project revenue.

3. Danainfra Nasional Berhad, a special purpose vehicle of the Government of Malaysia, issued retail bonds for the purpose of financing mass rapid transport infrastructure in Kuala Lumpur. Interest and principal payments are supported by the cash flows of the mass rapid transport system and a credit guarantee of the Government of Malaysia. This bond is an example of:

   A. a general obligation (GO) bond.

   B. a revenue bond.

   C. an agency bond.

Solution:

B is correct. The funding is for the development of a specific mass rapid project for Kuala Lumpur, and the repayment is supported by the revenue of the mass rapid transport line. While the bonds also have a sovereign guarantee to provide credit enhancement, the primary source of repayment is mass transit revenue.

4. A key credit measure for revenue-backed non-sovereign government bonds is:

   A. the debt service coverage ratio.

   B. level of unemployment in the local area.

   C. the tax base (depth, breadth, diversification, stability).

Solution:

A is correct. A key credit measure for revenue-backed non-sovereign government bonds is the debt service coverage ratio, which measures how much revenue is available to cover debt payments (principal and interest) after operating expenses. This is because the repayment ability for the bond is directly linked to the revenue of the specific underlying project, rather than the general tax revenue of the state. Many revenue bonds have a minimum ratio covenant; the higher the debt service coverage ratio, the stronger the creditworthiness.

PRACTICE PROBLEMS

1. Which of the following statements best characterizes higher creditworthiness for a non-reserve currency emerging market sovereign government?

   A. A country with a government budget surplus, current account surplus with high economic growth, and a freely floating currency.

   B. A country with a government budget deficit, a current account deficit with moderate economic growth and a fixed exchange rate regime

   C. A country with a government budget deficit, a current account deficit, low economic growth, and a fixed exchange rate regime.

2. Match the indicators below to the impact (positive or negative) on the creditworthiness of a general obligation bond issued by a state government:

   - Positive
   - Negative

A. Low unemployment	
B. Low per capita income	
C. Low per capita debt	
D. Low tax base	
E. High dependence on sales tax	
F. High post-retirement obligations	

3. Based upon the following data, which country is expected to be assigned the lowest sovereign credit rating?

	Country		
Economic Statistics	**Costa Rica**	**Dominican Republic**	**El Salvador**
Long-term external debt/GDP (%)	39.6	35.7	57.0
GDP growth (%)	2.06	5.07	2.39
Currency reserves (% of GDP)	13.9	8.1	12.4

   A. Costa Rica

   B. Dominican Republic

   C. El Salvador

4. Gulf Investment Corporation (GIC) is an investment company incorporated in Kuwait as a Gulf Shareholding Company. GIC is equally owned by the governments of the six member states of the Gulf Cooperation Council (GCC). GIC was formed to foster economic growth, economic diversification, and capital market development across the GCC region. The credit rating for GIC should be assessed based on its status as a:

   A. sovereign agency.

B. supranational issuer.

C. specialized financial intermediary or public bank.

5. Which of the following statements best characterizes external strength for a non-reserve currency sovereign country?

   A. The ability to impose and enforce strict capital controls

   B. The establishment of a fixed exchange rate regime

   C. The ability to generate sufficient stable foreign currency cash inflows

6. Agora is an emerging market economy with restricted capital convertibility (domestic to foreign exchange is not freely convertible). It is significantly dependent on income from the tourism sector and repatriation of income by its citizens living in foreign countries. It also has a high percentage of external debt to GDP. Which of the following is the most important factor that may result in an improvement in its sovereign creditworthiness?

   A. Diversification of its foreign currency inflows

   B. Reducing foreign currency reserves as a percentage of GDP

   C. Devaluation of its exchange rate versus major reserve currencies

SOLUTIONS

1. A is correct. This country exhibits fiscal stability as evidenced by its government budget surplus, high economic growth, and external strength given its current account surplus and freely floating currency.

2.

A. Low unemployment	Positive
B. Low per capita income	Negative
C. Low per capita debt	Positive
D. Low tax base	Negative
E. High dependence on sales tax	Negative
F. High post-retirement obligations	Negative

A. Positive, as low unemployment indicates a more productive and income-generating population with potential for higher tax revenue.

B. Negative, as low per capita income reduces the potential for tax collection and any potential tax raise.

C. Positive, as low per capita debt suggests a higher debt service ratio and greater capacity for additional debt, if required.

D. Negative, a low tax base limits the potential for tax collection and significantly weakens the potential for state revenue to meet expenses and service its debt.

E. Negative, as the more diversified the state's revenue stream, the higher its credit quality. Overreliance on a single revenue stream creates the potential for volatility in case of any economic disruption.

F. Negative, as high post-retirement obligations indicate further state indebtedness, reducing its ability to service its debt.

3. C is correct. El Salvador is expected to have the lowest credit rating due to its high long-term external debt-to-GDP ratio. While the Dominican Republic has lower currency reserves than El Salvador, it also has a lower external debt burden and higher economic growth.

4. B is correct. GIC is a supranational issuer, as it is sponsored and owned by multiple sovereigns. Its credit rating would be assessed as a supranational based on weighted sovereign ratings of the sponsoring countries and the nature of their implicit support in case of financial distress.

5. C is correct. A key factor influencing whether a non-reserve currency sovereign government can meet external debt obligations is external liquidity and solvency, or the ability to generate sufficient, stable foreign currency cash inflows to meet interest and principal payments on external debt. A is incorrect, as capital controls may restrict the ability to generate FX inflows. B is incorrect, as a fixed exchange rate regime may cause instability in the case of currency devaluation.

6. A is correct. Since Agora has high external debt to GDP and is very dependent on foreign currency inflows, it should seek to diversify its sources of foreign currency to avoid financial distress in case of disruption in tourism revenue or immigrant repatriation. B is incorrect, as maintaining or increasing foreign currency reserves is important for debt service rather than reducing FX reserves. C is incorrect. While the devaluation of Agora's exchange rate versus foreign reserve currencies may make it a more affordable tourist destination, it may also

reduce the rationale for income repatriation, leading to lower foreign inflows and a reduced ability to service external debt.

LEARNING MODULE

16

Credit Analysis for Corporate Issuers

LEARNING OUTCOMES

Mastery	*The candidate should be able to:*
☐	describe the qualitative and quantitative factors used to evaluate a corporate borrower's creditworthiness
☐	calculate and interpret financial ratios used in credit analysis
☐	describe the seniority rankings of debt, secured versus unsecured debt and the priority of claims in bankruptcy, and their impact on credit ratings

INTRODUCTION

1

In this learning module, we focus on the relative creditworthiness of non-financial corporate borrowers, building on earlier learning modules on corporate issuers as well as the earlier fixed-income module on credit risk and its components.

In particular, we assess a company's activities, or its business model, and how this affects the company's ability to meet its debt obligations. While a company's probability of default (POD) and loss given default (LGD) are not directly observable, in the first lesson we consider qualitative and quantitative factors that affect these credit risk components. Financial statement analysis and cash flow projections are important tools used to conduct corporate credit analysis. The second lesson applies these tools to calculate and interpret a variety of financial ratios, including profitability, leverage, and coverage metrics, to assess an issuer's probability of default. The seniority rankings of specific debt issues and use of collateral are of particular importance in determining credit ratings for a corporate issue and assessing the LGD in an event of default, which is addressed in the third and final lesson.

LEARNING MODULE OVERVIEW

- The credit risk of a borrower can be evaluated using qualitative and quantitative criteria that affect a company's likelihood of default and the investor's loss in the event of a default.

- Qualitative factors important in gauging creditworthiness include a company's business model, its industry, and its competitive position and business risks, as well as its corporate governance
- Quantitative factors in measuring creditworthiness involve financial statement analysis and forecasts, which use profitability, liquidity, leverage, and coverage measures to gauge a company's ability to meet its fixed debt obligations.
- Financial ratios are a critical tool used to assess the financial health of a company, identify trends over time, and compare companies within and across industries.
- Seniority rankings determine the priority of claims on an issuer's assets and are important determinants of the loss given default for a specific issue. Rating agencies typically provide both issuer and issue ratings for corporate credit.
- While an issuer credit rating captures the probability of default or expected loss of the issuer's senior unsecured bonds, an issue rating refers to specific financial obligations of an issuer and takes such factors as seniority into account.

LEARNING MODULE SELF-ASSESSMENT

1. Which of the following is *not* a characteristic of higher corporate creditworthiness?

   A. Lower leverage

   B. Higher coverage

   C. Lower liquidity

   Solution:

   The correct answer is C. All else held equal, a company with higher liquidity has a greater ability to meet its short-term obligations, including debt interest and principal.

2. All else being equal, a borrower will have higher capacity to repay its debt in an industry where the:

   A. barriers to entry are higher.

   B. threat of substitutes is higher.

   C. bargaining power of buyers is higher.

   Solution:

   The correct answer is A. An industry with higher barriers to entry tend to have lower threat of new entrants and lower competition. All else being equal, a borrower in such an industry has higher capacity to support its debt.

3. Identify the key credit metrics used in credit analysis:

   EBIT margin.

   Debt/EBITDA.

EBIT/interest expense.

1. Coverage metric	
2. Leverage metric	
3. Profitability metric	

Solution:

1. Coverage metric	**C. EBIT/interest expense**
2. Leverage metric	**B. Debt/EBITDA**
3. Profitability metric	**A. EBIT margin**

4. Companies X, Y, and Z belong to the same industry with the following financial ratios:

	Company X	Company Y	Company Z
EBITDA margin	15%	18%	18%
Free cash flow (FCF) after dividends/ debt	10%	10%	8%
Debt/EBITDA	1.5	1.5	1.8
Debt/capital	35%	35%	38%
EBITDA/interest	5.6	6.2	6.2

Based on the following financial ratios only, which company has the lowest credit risk?

A. Company X

B. Company Y

C. Company Z

Solution:

The correct answer is B. Compared to Company X, Company Y has similar leverage metrics but better profitability and coverage. Compared to Company Z, Company Y has similar profitability and coverage but better leverage ratios. Also, when viewing all the metrics, Company Y has either the same value or better than the other two companies. Therefore, Company Y has the lowest credit risk among the three companies.

5. Rank the recovery rate of the following bonds in the capital structure of a company in bankruptcy from the highest to the lowest:

- Junior subordinated debt
- Senior unsecured debt
- Subordinated debt
- Second lien debt
- First lien debt

Solution:

1. First lien debt
2. Second lien debt
3. Senior unsecured debt

4. Subordinated debt
5. Junior subordinated debt

6. Two senior unsecured bonds of the same issuer of different maturities have the same:

   A. issue credit rating only.
   B. issuer credit rating only.
   C. issuer and issue credit rating.

Solution:

The correct answer is C. An issuer rating usually applies to its senior unsecured debt and is meant to address an obligor's overall creditworthiness.

All senior unsecured bonds are treated as one class and rank pari passu irrespective of maturity. Therefore, both the issuer and the issue credit ratings are the same.

2 ASSESSING CORPORATE CREDITWORTHINESS

☐ describe the qualitative and quantitative factors used to evaluate a corporate borrower's creditworthiness

A company's creditworthiness depends primarily on its ability to generate profits and cash flow sufficient to meet interest and principal payments. Analysts rely on both qualitative and quantitative factors to evaluate both the likelihood of corporate default as well as an investor's loss in the event of a default. While several different analytical models measure credit risk, here we focus on broad qualitative and quantitative factors.

Qualitative Factors

Earlier Corporate Issuer learning modules covered many of the key qualitative factors used to gauge a company's ability to satisfy its debt obligations, which include a company's business model and the industry within which it operates, as well as the competitive forces and business risks it faces. These factors are summarized in Exhibit 1.

Exhibit 1: Qualitative Factors in Corporate Creditworthiness

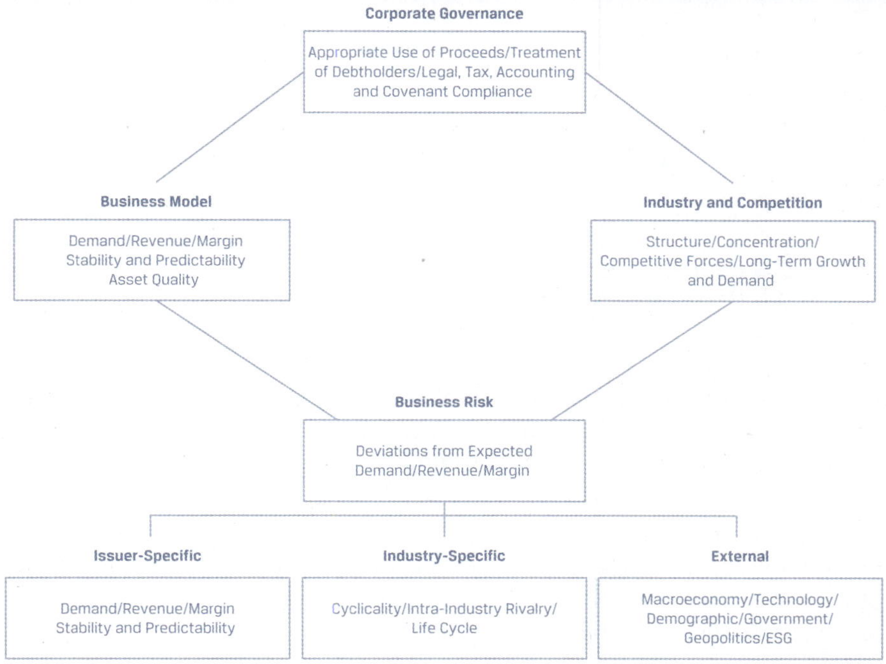

Financial analysts evaluating a company's business model, its industry, and its competitive position and business risks from a debtholder's perspective must not only consider whether a firm generates an acceptable return over its cost of capital, but also whether the timing and size of cash flows are sufficient to adequately cover debt obligations.

Established firms with a business model characterized by stable and predictable cash flows, low business risk, and less-competitive pressures have a higher capacity to use debt in their capital structure and a lower likelihood of default than those firms with lower and less stable cash flows, higher business risk, and/or greater competition. In contrast to an equity analyst's valuation of all future cash flows, fixed-income analysts often focus on how a company's creditworthiness may change over time given the finite nature of short- and long-term debt claims, as shown in the following example.

EXAMPLE 1

Qualitative Factors Affecting BRWA Creditworthiness

Bright Wheel Automotive (BRWA), a hypothetical auto manufacturing firm mentioned in an earlier lesson, has a product line based on traditional internal combustion engine ("ICE") technology. Having introduced its first electric vehicle (EV) two years ago, which comprises 5% of current revenue, BRWA's management has ambitious plans to convert over half of its models to all-electric over the coming decade, while adopting hybrid (ICE and electric) technology for its remaining fleet over the same period. BRWA's debt profile as an investment-grade corporate issuer is as follows:

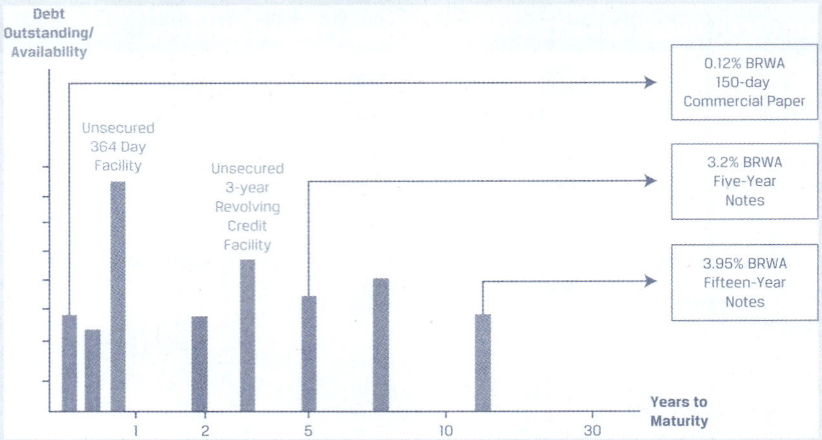

Qualitative factors, including BRWA's business model, industry, and competition and business risk, affect the creditworthiness of its outstanding 150-day commercial paper, five-year notes and fifteen-year notes.

BRWA's planned shift to a mostly EV-based product line over the next decade mirrors changes announced by other global automobile producers as policymakers seek to reduce vehicle emissions in the wake of climate change. The impact of BRWA's business model, industry, and competitive forces and business risk on its outstanding debt may be described as follows:

Business Model: BRWA's established customer base and acclaimed ICE vehicle lineup have enabled it to maintain stable revenue growth and profitability to date, but the company's technology and products must evolve over time to meet EV market demand. This business model change results in higher business risk.

Industry and Competitive Environment: BRWA faces growing competition within a fragmented global auto industry, with some competitors moving faster in establishing EV market share. Competition will intensify as other traditional ICE producers pursue a similar EV strategy amid potentially lower barriers to entry for pure EV companies, such as Tesla and software technology companies.

Business Risk: The execution risk of the EV strategy significantly increases BRWA's business risk. This is because the EV technology platform is not based on ICE technology, but rather on the integration of batteries, hardware, and software, increasing the bargaining power of BRWA's supplier base.

Consider BRWA's debt outstanding as follows:

Commercial Paper: Commercial paper investors face little to no exposure to BRWA's long-term business strategy given the very short tenor of this debt. Investors will primarily focus on the company's liquidity position based upon its existing ICE revenue base when assessing credit risk.

Five-Year Notes: Investors in BRWA's medium-term bonds face growing exposure to the greater competitive pressures and business risk associated with BRWA's EV strategy, but the company expects to generate most of its revenue from its traditional ICE customer base when the bond matures.

Fifteen-Year Notes: Investors in BRWA's long-term bonds face the greatest risk to the company's EV strategy and the associated competitive pressures and elevated business risk, as the company will make later interest and principal payments from cash flows that depend upon a successful EV transition.

The BRWA debt issues highlighted in Example 1 are for general, unsecured claims where company cash flows are the primary source of repayment. Secured debt, on the other hand, designates specific company assets as collateral as a secondary source of interest and principal payments. While the quality of a company's assets is an important factor for both unsecured and secured debt, secured lenders prefer to have tangible (or hard collateral) rather than intangible (or soft collateral) assets promised or pledged to secure debt. The value of collateral is most relevant for companies with lower credit quality and of greatest importance to creditworthiness when a borrower's POD rises to a level where the collateral is necessary to protect the exposure. Tangible assets are identifiable physical assets like property, plant and equipment, inventory, cash, and marketable securities, whereas intangible assets include patents, intellectual property rights, and goodwill. The use of collateral and secured debt can either reduce the cost of borrowing versus unsecured alternatives or offer corporate issuers access to debt markets that may otherwise not be available at all, as in the case of the following example.

EXAMPLE 2

Royal Caribbean Cruise Lines Secured Debt

In the wake of the COVID-19 pandemic, Royal Caribbean Cruises Ltd. (RCL) suspended its cruise operations in March 2020. Given the uncertainty surrounding the length and severity of the health crisis, RCL took immediate steps to enhance liquidity, preserve cash, and obtain additional financing.

The first of several RCL financings in that year took place in May 2020, when the company initiated a private offering of $3.3 billion in senior secured notes due in 2023 and 2025. The notes were secured by 28 of Royal Caribbean's fleet of over 60 vessels and also included material intellectual property of the company. RCL used the proceeds of the bond to repay a $2.35 billion 364-day senior secured term loan agreement, with the remainder of the bond proceeds available for general corporate purposes. While the continued suspension of cruises due to the ongoing pandemic led to subsequent RCL convertible bond and equity issuances later in the year, the initial issuance of secured debt at the outset of the COVID-19 crisis represented a cost-effective alternative for the company to preserve liquidity and financial flexibility in the near term by pledging its tangible assets as collateral. Despite the increase in RCL's POD due to the pandemic, investors were willing to provide debt financing in part due to the reduced LGD of the secured notes.

Corporate governance is an important qualitative factor to consider when evaluating corporate creditworthiness. While the assessment of an individual borrower's character is a common element of consumer credit analysis, it is more difficult in practice to evaluate management's character and the expected treatment of debtholders for a publicly owned corporation or one that is privately held by investors and private equity firms. Unlike equity investors with voting rights on important company matters, debtholders seek to specify the use of debt proceeds as well as any borrower restrictions at the time of issuance.

Highly rated issuers of unsecured debt are usually able to raise debt proceeds for general corporate purposes with few restrictions that usually include affirmative covenants only, such as compliance with applicable laws and regulations, maintaining current lines of business, insuring and maintaining company assets, and paying taxes. Credit analysts must evaluate management signals to make appropriate judgments about the treatment of debtholders versus shareholders and the potential for dilution.

For high-yield issuers of secured debt, investors usually impose additional restrictions to protect bondholders if an issuer's financial condition deteriorates, including covenants restricting dividends or additional debt as well as financial covenants. Management's past track record in the treatment of bondholders is an important consideration. For example, if management pursued business or financial strategies that resulted in major credit rating downgrades—such as an overleveraged debt-financed acquisition, a large debt-financed special dividend to shareholders, or a major debt-financed stock buyback program—credit analysts should look closely at the borrower's character.

As in the case of equity analysts, credit analysts should also evaluate accounting policies. Aggressive accounting policies mask the performance and the risk of the underlying business and are potential warning flags to the true character of the business and its leaders. Examples may include the use of significant off-balance-sheet financing, the preference for capitalizing versus immediately expensing items, and early and premature revenue recognition. Perhaps the most important red flag is changing auditors or CFOs frequently. These potential warning flags, as well as any evidence of fraud or malfeasance, may signal other behaviors or actions that may adversely impact an issuer's creditworthiness. A well-known example of accounting fraud is provided below in Example 3.

EXAMPLE 3

Wirecard AG's Accounting Fraud

Wirecard AG, a German payments firm that processed credit card and online payments, enjoyed a meteoric rise following its 2005 listing on the Frankfurt Stock Exchange. It joined the DAX index of the 30 most valuable companies in Germany and reached a peak market capitalization of over EUR27 billion in 2018 before filing for insolvency in June 2020.

A qualitative analysis of its management strategy and accounting policy in the years prior to insolvency raises the following red flags about the company's character:

After Wirecard received a banking license in 2006, it showed a significant revenue growth and a rapid international expansion through acquiring legitimate existing businesses, such as Citibank's Asia-Pacific credit card processing arm.

Wirecard's opaque and overly complex business model masked rapidly rising revenue and profit figures, giving rise to market rumors of suspicious transactions and money laundering.

While the company claimed thousands of small and medium-sized business customers and dozens of partners globally as sources of revenue growth, just three third-party partner companies provided a large share of Wirecard's reported revenue and most of its profits. Additionally, many of the firm's assets were held through external offshore trust accounts.

Wirecard used its bank subsidiary as a lender to fintech partner companies, as evidenced by the following excerpt from its half-year financial report dated 30 June 2019:

"Wirecard does not only provide risk management, technology, and banking services (to its fintech partner companies) but also sometimes provides the financing based on detailed individual assessments and suitable security measures – often in the form of cash securities. This enables the Group, on the one hand, to increase the added value from its cooperation with FinTech companies and, on the other, to also significantly increase interest income."

The company filed for insolvency in June 2020 when auditors could not confirm the existence of EUR1.9 billion in cash, which comprised the bulk of Wirecard's profits. It was later discovered that Wirecard's revenue was deposited in escrow accounts held by third-party trustees, rather than paid to the company itself.

After Wirecard was declared insolvent with debts of EUR3.2 billion, its share price immediately fell by over 70% and the price of its unsecured bonds fell to 20 cents per EUR. CEO Markus Braun was arrested and later charged with fraud, breach of trust, and accounting manipulation following a criminal investigation. It was the biggest accounting fraud and bankruptcy in Germany's post-World War II corporate history.

Quantitative Factors

Financial statement modeling and forecasting are a quantitative expression of analyst expectations for a company's future performance. Model inputs are based on an understanding of a company's fundamental business drivers and an assessment of future risks and opportunities. These inputs are derived using a top-down, macroeconomic or a bottom-up, issuer-specific approach at the company level. In contrast to equity models, which seek to value a firm's stock based upon all cash flows available to shareholders, quantitative credit analysis aims to estimate the likelihood that a company can meet its debt obligations in the future. Exhibit 2 summarizes key quantitative factors used to measure a corporate issuer's credit risk.

Exhibit 2: Quantitative Approaches in Corporate Credit Risk Assessment

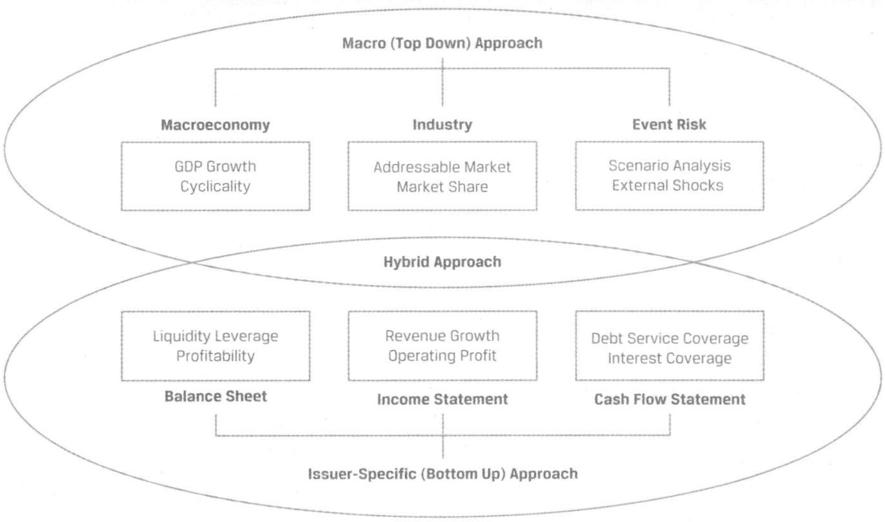

Top-down analysis typically begins with a macroeconomic forecast, gauging a company's growth relative to GDP, addressing a firm's addressable market and market share, and assessing the likelihood and impact of possible adverse events that may be incorporated in a scenario analysis. For example, the economic cycle has a relationship with the timing and severity of the credit cycle; thus, the credit cycle's expected impact on a specific company or industry is commonly used to gauge credit risk on a macro level. Bottom-up analysis involves forecasting key revenue drivers and balance sheet positions, while a hybrid approach might combine expected cyclicality with changing bottom-up features to forecast a company's cash flows. The goal of quantitative analysis is to identify key factors that drive a corporate issuer's POD and how they change over the credit cycle. These include the following factors:

Profitability: Strong and stable earnings are important in generating the cash flows that are a primary source of debt repayment. Analysts gauging a company's ability to make periodic fixed debt payments typically focus on operating profits and recurring revenues as opposed to non-recurring or one-time gains. Macro factors, such as an expected economic downturn for cyclical companies or a declining market share, can adversely impact future profitability.

Leverage: Financial leverage measures a company's relative reliance on debt financing in its operations. Measures of leverage typically compare the total level of debt to a firm's resources as gauged by assets, capital, or a measure of profitability or cash flow. Given the fixed nature of debt claims, debt investors prefer lower leverage—that is, more resources per unit of debt—while equity investors usually benefit from more debt and higher financial leverage.

Coverage: Lenders gauge creditworthiness by comparing periodic income measures or cash flows to debt service (interest and principal), interest, or debt-like payments, which include leases. Greater coverage means that debt investors benefit from higher income or cash flows from which fixed debt obligations can be paid.

Liquidity: Debtholders evaluating near-term debt obligations for issuers with less stable cash flows often consider the availability of short-term resources to pay interest or principal. While a firm may be solvent (i.e., have assets in excess of liabilities and equity), it may nevertheless fail to meet its fixed obligations if it lacks cash or assets that can be readily converted into cash, such as marketable securities. Measures of liquidity also include committed bank facilities if a corporate borrower has the contractual right to draw down cash for the period in question.

The calculation and interpretation of these quantitative factors using financial ratios is addressed in the next lesson. While investors in senior unsecured investment-grade debt are almost solely focused on POD, high-yield investors in companies that use subordination in their debt structure and/or collateral as a secondary source of repayment also consider historical LGD rates and other factors in assessing credit risk, which is the subject of the third lesson.

QUESTION SET

1. Match the key quantitative factors:

- Coverage
- Leverage
- Liquidity

Relative reliance on debt to finance operations	
Borrower ability to meet short-term obligations	
Comparison of periodic earnings or cash flow to debt service	

Solution:

Relative reliance on debt to finance operations	**Leverage**
Borrower ability to meet short-term obligations	**Liquidity**
Comparison of periodic earnings or cash flow to debt service	**Coverage**

2. **Determine the correct answers to fill in the blanks:** Secured lenders prefer to have _______ assets (or _____ collateral) rather than _______ assets (or _____ collateral) promised or pledged to secure debt.

Solution:

Secured lenders prefer to have *tangible* assets (or *hard* collateral) rather than *intangible* assets (or *soft* collateral) promised or pledged to secure debt.

3. Which of the following statements about shareholders and debtholders is not true?

A. Both shareholders and debtholders benefit from higher profitability.

B. Shareholders generally benefit from higher leverage, while debtholders prefer lower leverage.

C. Both shareholders and debtholders benefit from lower coverage.

Solution:

The correct answer is C. Both shareholders and debtholders benefit from higher coverage, which is the income or cash flow available to pay debt service.

4. **Determine the correct answers to fill in the blanks:** Firms with a business model characterized by stable and predictable cash flows, _____ business risk, and _____ competitive pressures have a higher capacity to use debt in their capital structure and a lower likelihood of default.

Solution:

Firms with a business model characterized by stable and predictable cash flows, *low* business risk, and *less* competitive pressures have a higher capacity to use debt in their capital structure and a lower likelihood of default.

FINANCIAL RATIOS IN CORPORATE CREDIT ANALYSIS 3

☐ calculate and interpret financial ratios used in credit analysis

The use of financial ratios based upon the quantitative factors outlined in the prior lesson allows credit analysts to assess the relative financial health of a company, identify trends over time, and compare companies within and across industries with a focus on profitability, coverage, and leverage. Common financial ratios used to evaluate a corporate issuer's credit risk are outlined in Exhibit 3.

Exhibit 3: Key Financial Ratios for Corporate Creditworthiness

Profitability

EBIT Margin:

$$\frac{\text{Operating Income}}{\text{Revenue}}$$

Coverage

EBIT to Interest Expense:

$$\frac{\text{Operating Income}}{\text{Interest Expense}}$$

Leverage

Debt to EBITDA:

$$\frac{\text{Debt}}{\text{EBITDA}}$$

RCF to Net Debt:

$$\frac{\text{Retained Cash Flow (RCF)}}{\text{Debt} - \text{Cash and Marketable Securities}}$$

In general, credit risk analysis using profitability, coverage, and leverage ratios seeks to establish a firm's ability to service cash flows from operating activities, as opposed to asset disposals or financing activities. Cash flow measures used in credit analysis, such as free cash flow (FCF, or net income less working capital increases, investment in fixed assets, and net interest paid), funds from operations (FFO, or net income from continuing operations, depreciation and amortization, deferred income tax, and other non-cash items), or retained cash flow (RCF, or net cash flow from operating activities less dividends paid) are more conservative than others because they make certain adjustments for cash used in managing and maintaining the business or distributed to shareholders. Debt and interest expense measures used in credit analysis also may be adjusted for operating leases, debt-like fixed lease payments, and/or other fixed off-balance-sheet obligations that impact a company's ability to service its debt.

These measures and the ratios developed based upon these measures are non-IFRS in the sense that they do not have official IFRS definitions; the concepts, names, and definitions given should be viewed as one usage among several possible, in most cases.

EBIT Margin: Credit analysts focus on EBIT (earnings before interest and taxes) to determine a company's operating performance prior to capital costs and taxes, since interest expense is paid before income taxes are calculated. In some cases, EBITDA (or earnings before interest, taxes, depreciation, and amortization expense) is used as a broader measure, which adds back (non-cash) depreciation and amortization expense. Higher EBIT margins increase profits available to service debt.

EBIT to Interest Expense: This measures the degree to which operating profit covers periodic interest payments, with a higher coverage ratio representing less credit risk. In some cases, the numerator is changed to include depreciation and amortization (EBITDA) as well as rental expense (EBITDAR), while the denominator may be increased to include lease payments or reduced by interest earned on marketable securities and cash.

Debt to EBITDA: Leverage ratios are often expressed with debt either in the numerator or denominator, so care must be taken to reflect whether a greater or lesser number reflects increased leverage. For example, a higher debt-to-EBITDA ratio represents higher leverage, and debt may be adjusted to reflect operating leases or off-balance-sheet commitments. Rating agencies often use it as a trigger for rating actions, and banks reference it in loan covenants. A higher ratio indicates more leverage and thus higher credit risk. Note that this ratio can be very volatile for companies with high cash flow variability, such as those in cyclical industries and with high operating leverage (fixed costs).

Retained Cash Flow (RCF) to Net Debt: Use of cash flow rather than earnings measures is also common in measuring leverage, while here the debt measure is reduced by available cash. A higher RCF to net debt measure implies lower leverage.

While financial ratios used in credit analysis vary across industries, the values of financial ratios themselves for a given rating or level of credit quality may also range widely across industries due to different business models, competitive pressures, and other factors.

Credit analysts use financial modeling to evaluate how these ratios might change over time as revenue drivers change, as in the following example:

EXAMPLE 4

Bowstream Corporation Credit Risk Assessment

A credit analyst has created a financial statement model to evaluate the credit risk of Bowstream Corporation, a mid-sized, investment-grade consumer durables company. While Bowstream's most recent financial results show a solid 10% sales growth and a robust 35% operating profit margin, the analyst would like to assess Bowstream's performance under a downside scenario where the company's production and interest costs rise due to inflation amid slower sales growth. Model assumptions used for Bowstream's sales growth, cost of goods sold as a percentage of sales, interest rates, and debt growth over the next five years are as follows:

	Reported Year 0	Projected Year 1	Year 2	Year 3	Year 4	Year 5
Sales growth	10%	5%	5%	5%	5%	5%
Cost of goods sold/Sales	65%	70%	75%	80%	85%	85%
Interest rate on debt	6%	7%	7%	7%	8%	8%
Debt growth rate	10%	10%	10%	10%	10%	10%

Selected financial data and projections from these three-statement model results based on these assumptions and stable ratios of balance sheet and other positions to sales are as follows:

Income Statement	Year 0	Year 1	Year 2	Year 3	Year 4	Year 5
Sales	**5,225**	**5,486**	**5,761**	**6,049**	**6,351**	**6,669**
Cost of goods sold	(3,396)	(3,840)	(4,320)	(4,839)	(5,398)	(5,668)
Gross profit	**1,829**	**1,646**	**1,440**	**1,210**	**953**	**1,000**
Gross profit (%)	35%	30%	25%	20%	15%	15%
Selling, general, and administrative	(499)	(524)	(550)	(577)	(606)	(637)
Interest payments on debt	(38)	(46)	(51)	(56)	(72)	(83)
Interest earned on cash and mktable sec	12	12	12	12	12	12
Depreciation	(400)	(467)	(517)	(547)	(559)	(552)

Income Statement	Year 0	Year 1	Year 2	Year 3	Year 4	Year 5
Profit before tax	**905**	**621**	**335**	**41**	**(273)**	**(259)**
Taxes	(317)	(217)	(117)	(14)	95	90
Net income	**588**	**404**	**218**	**27**	**(177)**	**(168)**
Net income (% of sales)	11%	7%	4%	0%	−3%	−3%
Dividends	(118)	(81)	(44)	(5)	—	—
Retained earnings	**470**	**323**	**174**	**21**	**(177)**	**(168)**

Balance Sheet	Year 0	Year 1	Year 2	Year 3	Year 4	Year 5
Cash and marketable securities	400	400	400	400	400	400
Current assets	627	658	691	726	762	800
Fixed assets						
Cost basis	5,993	6,840	7,594	8,233	8,735	9,256
Accumulated depreciation	(2,400)	(2,867)	(3,383)	(3,931)	(4,490)	(5,042)
Net fixed assets	3,593	3,973	4,211	4,303	4,244	4,214
Total assets:	**4,620**	**5,032**	**5,302**	**5,428**	**5,407**	**5,414**
Current liabilities	523	549	576	605	635	667
Debt	627	690	759	835	960	1,104
Stock (225 shares issued @ 10)	2,250	2,250	2,250	2,250	2,250	2,250
Accumulated retained earnings	1,220	1,543	1,718	1,739	1,562	1,394
Total liabilities and equity	**4,620**	**5,032**	**5,302**	**5,428**	**5,407**	**5,414**

Consolidated Statement of Cash Flows	Year 0	Year 1	Year 2	Year 3	Year 4	Year 5
Net cash from operating activities	978	866	729	568	376	377
Net cash used in investing activities	(918)	(847)	(754)	(639)	(501)	(521)
Net cash from financing activities	(61)	(18)	25	71	125	144

The analyst uses data from these three-statement model results to solve for recent and projected profitability, coverage, and leverage ratios in Exhibit 3:

	Year 0	Year 1	Year 2	Year 3	Year 4	Year 5
EBIT	1,330	1,122	890	632	346	364
EBITDA	1,730	1,589	1,407	1,180	906	916
FFO (Net cash from operating activities)	978	866	729	568	376	377
RCF (FFO − Dividends)	861	785	685	563	376	377
EBIT margin	25%	20%	15%	10%	5%	5%
EBIT to Interest expense	51.9	32.9	23.0	14.4	5.8	5.2

	Year 0	Year 1	Year 2	Year 3	Year 4	Year 5
Debt to EBITDA	0.36	0.43	0.54	0.71	1.06	1.21
RCF to Net debt	379%	271%	191%	130%	67%	54%

Under this scenario, Bowstream faces declining profitability (as EBIT margin falls), weaker debt coverage (lower EBIT-to-interest expense), and increased leverage (a higher debt to EBITDA and lower RCF to net debt), which is likely to lead to wider credit spreads and a potential ratings downgrade.

In order to measure these changes, analysts often compare existing and projected ratios to industry and credit rating peers to determine expected future credit quality changes as categorized by expected rating. For example, consider the following comparisons based upon Moody's ratings methodology and these ratios for consumer durables:

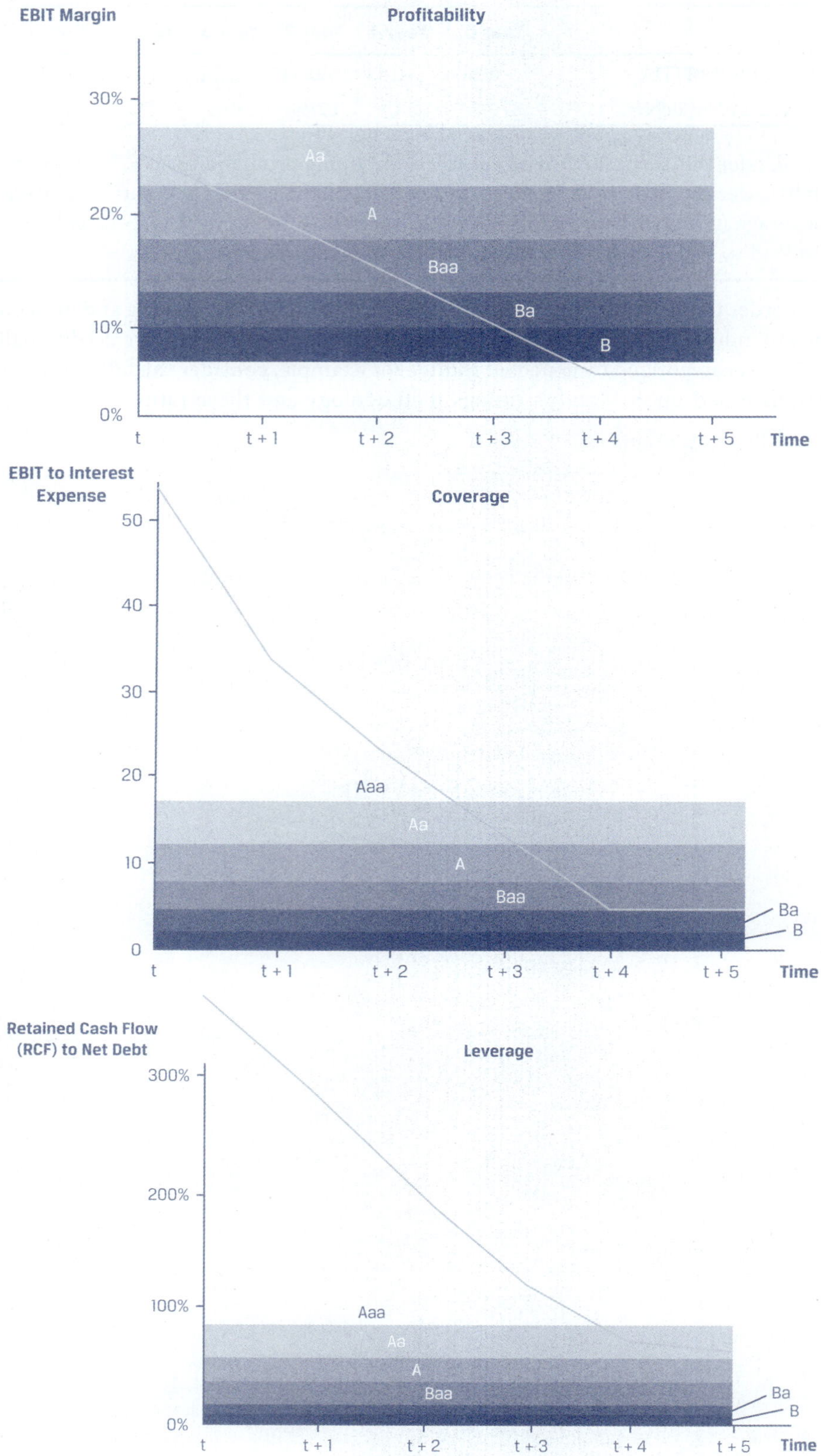
EBIT Margin
Profitability
30%
20%
10%
0%
Aa
A
Baa
Ba
B
t
t + 1
t + 2
t + 3
t + 4
t + 5
Time
EBIT to Interest Expense
Coverage
50
40
30
20
10
0
Aaa
Aa
A
Baa
Ba
B
t
t + 1
t + 2
t + 3
t + 4
t + 5
Time
Retained Cash Flow (RCF) to Net Debt
Leverage
300%
200%
100%
0%
Aaa
Aa
A
Baa
Ba
B
t
t + 1
t + 2
t + 3
t + 4
t + 5
Time

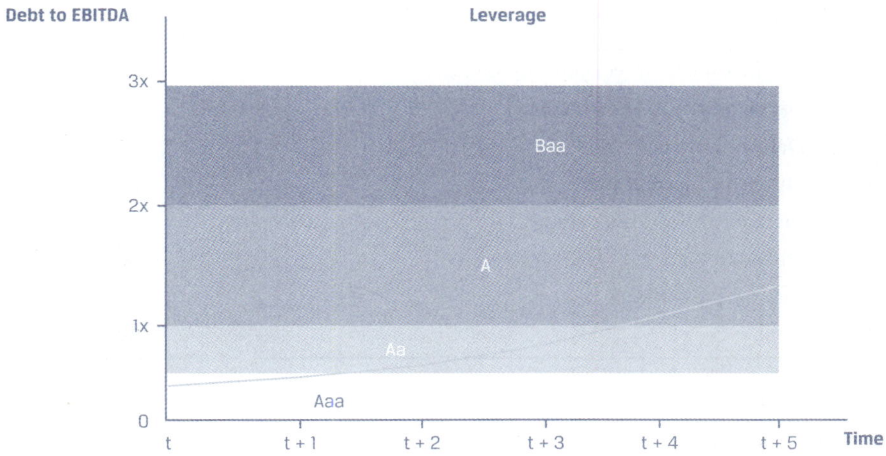

Source: Moody's Investors Service, "Methodology Announcement: Moody's Updates Its Methodology for Rating Consumer Durables Companies" (10 September 2021).

QUESTION SET

1. Identify the key credit analysis ratios that correspond to the types of metrics:

   A. RCF/Debt
   B. EBITDA/Interest Expense
   C. Debt/Capital
   D. EBITDA
   E. Debt/EBITDA
   F. FCF
   G. EBIT/Interest Expense

   1. Profitability and cash flow metrics
   2. Leverage metrics
   3. Coverage metrics

   Solution:

   1. Profitability and cash flow metrics: D, F
   2. Leverage metrics: A, C, E
   3. Coverage metrics: B, G

2. State true or false to the following statement and explain your reasoning: The higher the coverage ratios, the higher the credit risk of the borrower.

   Solution:

   False. Coverage ratios measure an issuer's ability to cover its interest payments. The higher the coverage ratios, the *lower* the credit risk of the borrower.

3. Calculate FFO/debt based on the following financial information:

Net income from continuing operations	180
Depreciation & amortization	30
Deferred income taxes	18
Other non-cash items	28
Increase in working capital	(52)
Dividend paid	(60)
Capital expenditure	(100)
Debt	1,280

Solution:

FFO = Net income from continuing operations + Depreciation & amortization + Deferred income taxes + Other non-cash items = 180 + 30 + 18 + 28 = 256.

FFO/debt = 256/1,280 = 0.2 or 20%.

4. Company X and Company Y operate in the same industry. Based on the financial information below, which company has lower credit risk?

	Company X	Company Y
EBITDA margin	15%	15%
FCF	(20)	20
FCF before dividends	(45)	18
Debt/EBITDA	2.5	1.6
EBITDA/interest expense	3.0	3.5

Solution:

Company Y has lower credit risk. While Company X and Company Y have the same EBITDA margin, Company Y has positive FCF and FCF before dividends, a lower leverage ratio, and a higher coverage ratio than Company X.

4 SENIORITY RANKINGS, RECOVERY RATES, AND CREDIT RATINGS

☐ describe the seniority rankings of debt, secured versus unsecured debt and the priority of claims in bankruptcy, and their impact on credit ratings

The debt obligations of a corporate borrower often have different seniority rankings. Some companies and industries have straightforward capital structures, with all the debt equally ranked and issued by one main operating entity. Other companies and industries, due to acquisitions and divestitures (e.g., media companies or conglomerates) or regulation (e.g., banks and utilities), have more complex debt structures. Firms in these industries often have many different subsidiaries, or operating companies, that have their own debt outstanding and parent holding companies that also issue debt with different seniority levels.

Seniority Rankings

A seniority ranking refers to the priority of payment, with the most senior or highest-ranking debt having the first claim on the cash flows and assets of the issuer. The level of seniority affects the value of an investor's claim in the event of default and restructuring. Secured debt involves a debtholder claim—a pledge from the issuer—to certain assets and their associated cash flows. This collateral reduces the lender's potential loss in the event of default, as the lender may take possession of and sell these assets to offset their losses. Seniority rankings involving secured and unsecured debt are shown in Exhibit 4.

Exhibit 4: Seniority Rankings

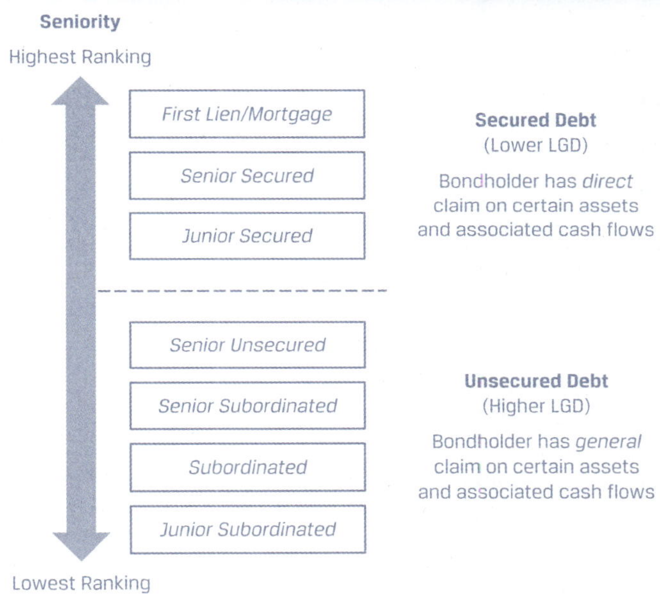

Secured versus Unsecured Debt

First mortgage and first lien debt are ranked highest among secured creditors in terms of priority of repayment. **First mortgage debt** or loan refers to the pledge of specific property (e.g., a power plant for a utility). **First lien debt** or loan refers to a pledge of certain assets that could include buildings but might also include property and equipment, licenses, patents, brands, or inventory. As the name implies, *second lien* secured debt has a secured interest in the pledged assets that ranks below first lien debt in both collateral protection and priority of payment. Most second lien loans are senior secured obligations of the borrower, which rank above junior secured obligations.

Unsecured bondholders have only a general claim on an issuer's assets and cash flows. In the event of default, unsecured debtholders' claims rank below (i.e., get paid after) those of secured creditors under what is known as the **priority of claims**.

The highest-ranked unsecured debt is **senior unsecured debt**. It is the most common type of corporate bond, ranking below senior secured debt but above subordinated debt. Other, lower-ranked debt includes **subordinated debt** and junior subordinated debt. Among the various creditor classes, these obligations have the lowest priority of claims and frequently have little or no recovery in the event of default (i.e., an LGD of 100%).

Different seniority rankings satisfy the needs and demands of both issuers and investors. Issuers seek to optimize their cost of capital—in some cases offering secured debt to meet investor requirements, as in the earlier Royal Caribbean example, and in other cases offering subordinated debt, which is less costly than equity and non-dilutive. The seniority of debt drives decisions in the case of bankruptcy or liquidation. Senior creditors with a secured claim have the right to the value of specific assets before any other claim. If the value of the pledged property is less than the amount of the claim, then the difference becomes a senior unsecured claim. Senior unsecured creditors take priority over all subordinated creditors, who in turn have the right to be paid in full before shareholders receive any compensation. Example 5 shows differences in repayment seniority.

EXAMPLE 5

VIVU Bond

The 6.5% VIVU seven-year callable notes were introduced earlier in the curriculum.

6.5% Vivivyu Inc. (VIVU) 7-Year Callable Notes

Issuer:	Vivivyu Incorporated
Maturity Date:	7 Years
Principal Amount:	USD400 million
Interest:	6.5% fixed coupon
Interest Payment:	Semi-annual
Seniority:	The Notes are secured and unsubordinated obligations of VIVU and rank pari passu with all other secured and unsubordinated debt.
Security:	The Notes are secured by a pledge of certain assets as identified in the Indenture.

Assume VIVU also has a 10-year subordinated bond outstanding with the following terms:

10.0% Vivivyu Inc. (VIVU) 10-Year Subordinated Notes

Issuer:	Vivivyu Incorporated
Maturity Date:	10 years
Principal Amount:	USD300 million
Interest:	10.0% fixed coupon
Interest Payment:	Semi-annual
Seniority:	The Notes will constitute direct, unsecured, and subordinated obligations of the Issuer and shall rank pari passu and without any preference among themselves.
Security:	None

While the 6.5% notes are senior secured debts, the 10.0% notes are unsecured subordinated debt.

In an insolvency or a restructuring event, the 6.5% notes rank highest in the payment priority as they are backed by certain specified assets as a secondary source of repayment. If the value of the collateral falls short of the total amount of pari passu secured debt, the balance will rank pari passu with senior unsecured creditors in insolvency or restructuring.

The 10.0% subordinated notes rank below senior secured and senior unsecured debt in the priority of claims, but above junior subordinated debts (if any) and shareholders. These notes have among the lowest priority of claims in an event of default and often have the lowest recovery rate.

Recovery Rates

All creditors at the same debt seniority level are treated as one class; thus, a senior unsecured bondholder whose debt is due in 30 years has the same pro rata (pari passu) claim in bankruptcy as one whose debt matures in six months. Defaulted debt often continues to trade near the expected recovery rate for bonds expected to enter bankruptcy or liquidation. Recovery rates vary by seniority ranking based upon the priority of claims.

Historical default data provide statistically meaningful recovery rates by seniority ranking. Exhibit 5 shows recovery rates by seniority ranking for North American non-financial companies. For example, as shown in Exhibit 5, investors recovered 45.9% of the value of defaulted senior secured debt in 2019 but only 31.3% of defaulted senior unsecured issues that year.

Exhibit 5: Average Corporate Debt Recovery Rates (%)

	Emergence Year			Default Year		
Priority Position	**2020**	**2019**	**1987–2020**	**2020**	**2019**	**1987–2020**
Term Loans*	48.5	58.1	72.6	50.1	52.7	86.3
Senior Secured Bonds	34.8	45.9	61.4	34.8	44.6	61.4
Senior Unsecured Bonds	8.6	31.3	46.9	8.6	40.5	46.9
Subordinated Bonds	0.9	24.7	27.9	0.9	24.7	27.9

* *Includes all types of term loans:* first, second-lien, unsecured.
Notes: Emergence year is typically the year the defaulted company emerges from bankruptcy. Default year data refer to the recovery rate of debt that defaulted in that year (i.e., 2019 and 2020) or range of years (i.e., 1987–2020). Data are for North American nonfinancial companies.
Source: Moody's Investors Service, "Default Trends — Global: Annual Default Study: Following a Sharp Rise in 2020, Corporate Defaults Will Drop in 2021" (28 January 2021).

Recovery rates:

1. vary widely by industry,
2. vary depending on when they occur in the cycle, and
3. represent averages across industries and companies.

Companies entering bankruptcy in industries in secular decline usually have lower recovery rates than those merely facing cyclical economic downturn. Exhibit 6 shows the distribution of selected recovery rates between 1983 and 2020 across industries and debt seniority levels.

Exhibit 6: Recovery Rates across Selected Industries, 1983–2020, Measured by Trading Prices before Default (%)

Industry Groups	1st Lien Bond	Senior Unsecured Bond	Subordinated Bond
Automotive	57.94	46.08	49.46
Capital Equipment	62.34	36.69	45.48
Energy: Electricity	81.48	58.24	39.45
Energy: Oil & Gas	56.55	36.33	39.10
Environmental	13.00	29.73	5.44
Finance	47.60	45.68	27.80
High-Tech Industries	53.51	33.08	23.71
Retail	57.78	36.30	21.68
Services: Business	71.14	46.83	46.22
Telecommunications	56.80	26.22	31.61
Average recovery rate*	53.04	41.80	34.69
Highest recovery rate*	96.25	92.00	63.56
Lowest recovery rate*	7.00	22.18	1.47

* *Calculated for all the 33 industries identified by Moody's.*
Note: Average defaulted corporate bond and loan recoveries by selected industries, 1983–2020.
Source: Moody's Investors Service, "Default Trends — Global: Annual Default Study: Following a Sharp Rise in 2020, Corporate Defaults Will Drop in 2021" (28 January 2021).

Recovery rates also vary depending upon when they occur in the credit cycle. When the economy is strong or improving, robust markets exist for the resale of collateral and recovery rates are therefore higher. Conversely, when the economy is weak or weakening, lenders' ability to liquidate assets at or near the original value is diminished and recovery rates fall.

Importantly, these recovery rates are averages, with high variability across industries and companies within a given industry. Factors include the composition and proportion of debt across an issuer's capital structure. An abundance of secured debt will lead to smaller recovery rates on lower-ranked debt. Understanding recovery rates is important because they are a key component of credit analysis and risk, as shown in the following knowledge check.

KNOWLEDGE CHECK: EXPECTED LOSS

1. The one-year forward default rate for an issuer in the automotive industry is expected to be 0.8%. What is the expected percentage credit loss of the issuer's bonds under the historical recovery rate assumptions (see Exhibit 5)?

Senior secured bond	58%
Senior unsecured bond	46%
Subordinated bond	23%

Solution:

Recall from an earlier lesson that:

Expected loss (EL) = POD × LGD

Senior secured bond: EL = 0.008 × (1 – 0.58) = 0.00336 = 0.336%

Senior unsecured bond: EL = 0.008 × (1 – 0.46) = 0.00432 = 0.432%

Subordinated bond: EL = 0.008 × (1 – 0.23) = 0.00616 = 0.616%

The priority of claims in bankruptcy under which the highest-ranked creditors get paid out first, followed by the next level, and so on, is a well-established legal standard. However, creditors with lower seniority and even shareholders may receive consideration without more senior creditors being satisfied in full, since bankruptcy resolution takes time. By compensating subordinated debt holders, senior debt holders can accelerate the bankruptcy process.

During bankruptcy, legal and accounting fees can be substantial, and the company value may decline as key employees and customers leave and competitors actively gain market share. Claimants therefore have an incentive to negotiate and compromise, leading to creditors with lower seniority and other claimants receiving more consideration than they are legally entitled to.

While a bias in the United States toward reorganization and recovery of companies in bankruptcy exists, elsewhere it is more common to liquidate companies in bankruptcy and maximize value to bank lenders and other senior creditors. Since bankruptcy and bankruptcy laws are very complex and can vary greatly by country, it is difficult to generalize how creditors will fare under a default scenario.

Issuer and Issue Ratings

Rating agencies typically provide both issuer and issue ratings for corporate debt. Terminology used to distinguish between issuer and issue ratings includes corporate family rating (CFR) and corporate credit rating (CCR), or issuer credit rating and individual issue credit rating. An **issuer rating** usually applies to its senior unsecured debt and addresses an obligor's overall creditworthiness. On the other hand, an individual **issue rating** refers to specific financial obligations of an issuer and takes such factors as seniority into account. While the probability of default (POD) for an issuer and its issues may be the same due to cross-default provisions, issuer ratings may differ due to loss given default (LGD) differences because of seniority, subordination, and sources of repayment. This rating adjustment methodology is known as **notching**.

EXAMPLE 6

Royal Caribbean Unsecured Debt

As the COVID-19 pandemic began to subside and Royal Caribbean (RCL) announced its resumption of cruise operations in 2021, the company once again approached the debt markets in March, this time with a $1.5 billion 7-year unsecured note issuance used primarily to repay existing debt and to raise cash for other debt maturities. At the time of issuance, RCL had a Moody's B1 corporate family rating (CFR), while the new unsecured debt issue was rated B2. The company's senior secured notes, on the other hand, were rated three notches higher, or Ba2, due to the vessels and intellectual property used as collateral, as described in Example 2.

While POD and LGD are the primary factors in assigning ratings, another factor considered by rating agencies is **structural subordination**, which can arise when a corporation with a holding company structure has debt at both its parent holding company and operating subsidiaries. Operating subsidiary debt is serviced by the cash flow and assets of the subsidiaries before funds can be passed ("upstreamed") to the holding company to service parent level debt.

Different payment priorities and possible higher (or lower) LGDs give rise to a rating agency notching process where issue credit ratings are moved up or down from the issuer rating. Generally, the higher the senior unsecured rating, the smaller the notching adjustment due to a lower perceived risk of default. That is, the need to "notch" the rating to capture the potential difference in loss severity is greatly reduced. For lower-rated credits, however, the risk of default is greater and thus the potential LGD difference in loss from a lower (or higher) priority ranking carries greater weight in assessing an issue's credit riskiness. Thus, the rating agencies will typically apply larger rating adjustments. Rating agencies differ in their approaches, as discussed in Example 7 below.

EXAMPLE 7

Different Approaches to Credit Ratings

While all the major rating agencies consider POD and EL in assigning their credit ratings, which ultimately reflect the agencies' forward-looking opinion of the relative level of credit risk, nuanced differences exist between credit rating agencies.

For example, Moody's defines credit risk as "the risk that an entity may not meet its contractual financial obligations as they come due and any estimated financial loss in the event of default or impairment." In so doing, the rating agency considers recovery as a rating factor in evaluating the creditworthiness of debt (especially for speculative-grade debt). In other words, its rating scale principally reflects EL.

On the other hand, S&P Global Ratings assigns credit ratings that primarily reflect POD. The agency issues separate recovery ratings in addition to rating specific debt issues. These recovery ratings consider the relative seniority and loss severity of particular issues in the event of default. S&P may also consider recovery ratings in making its notching adjustments.

Fitch Ratings takes a similar approach to S&P. Fitch assigns Issuer Default Ratings ("IDRs") reflecting a POD view. Notching adjustments then apply to issue ratings by considering recovery expectations for specific issues.

(Sources: Moody's, S&P, and Fitch.)

QUESTION SET

1. A company with the following simplified balance sheet faces impairment on its net current assets (other than cash) of USD90. Identify the potential recovery of the company's debt according to the priority of claims in an event of default:

Assets	USD	Liabilities & Equity	USD
Cash	40	Secured bank loans (secured by cash collateral)	30
Net Current Assets (other than Cash)	100	Unsecured bonds	90
Net Fixed Assets	60	Subordinated bonds	10
		Common shares	40
		Retained earnings	30
Total Assets	**200**	Total Liabilities & Equity	**200**

A. Shareholders and subordinated debtholders receive zero recovery, while unsecured bondholders receive partial recovery.

B. Unsecured debtholders receive zero recovery as the impairment equals the amount of unsecured debt outstanding.

C. Subordinated and unsecured bondholders both face partial recovery, as the impairment is greater than the sum of these bonds outstanding.

Solution:

A is correct. The seniority ranking of the capital structure is as follows:

Secured bank loans > Unsecured bonds > Subordinated bonds > Equity

The USD90 impairment will initially be absorbed by the company's most junior claim, equity (including common shares and retained earnings), with a total equity value of USD70 (40 + 30 = 70).

The remaining USD20 (USD90 – USD70) impairment balance will be borne by the next junior claim, subordinated bonds. As subordinated bonds total just USD10, they have zero recovery.

The remaining USD10 impairment is allocated to the unsecured bonds. The USD10 impairment reduces the recovery to USD80 (USD90 – USD10). The USD30 bank loans secured by cash collateral are unaffected, as the cash collateral value of USD40 fully covers this loan.

2. State true/false to the following statement and explain your reasoning: Notching is the rating adjustment process whereby the credit rating of a corporate issuer can be moved up or down from the sovereign credit rating.

Solution:

False. Notching is the rating adjustment process whereby the credit rating of a *bond* can be moved up or down from the *issuer* credit rating.

3. Why is the probability of default likely to be the same for all unsubordinated bonds of an issuer?

   Solution:

   Cross-default provisions exist where an event of default on one bond triggers default on all outstanding debt, implying the same default probability for all issues. However, issue ratings may differ due to LGD differences.

4. An issuer credit rating assigned by the rating agencies reflects the:

   A. recovery rate of a specific debt of the issuer.

   B. expected credit loss of all the issuer's outstanding debt.

   C. probability of default of the issuer's senior unsecured debt.

   Solution:

   The correct answer is C. An issuer credit rating usually applies to the issuer's senior unsecured debt and is meant to address the issuer's overall creditworthiness in the form of probability of default (and for some rating agencies, both probability of default and expected recovery).

PRACTICE PROBLEMS

The following information relates to questions 1-9

The following questions are related to Mojofon Holdings:

Mojofon Holdings specializes in the design, manufacturing, and marketing of its own branded smartphones. An evolving sector, the smartphone market is dominated by few large firms who together have close to 70% of the global market. Mojofon's global market share is consistently around 3%, and it is positioned as a niche player.

An industry assessment leads to the following observations:

- Competition of the smartphone industry is intense, driven by consistent technology upgrades and new models with short product life cycles. The large investment and marketing budgets of dominant players have sustained high industry concentration.
- New entrants positioned as niche producers of "cult" models like Mojofon consistently compete for market share.
- Customers are "price-takers," as smartphones are seen as a necessity. Pricing is usually set by the top three producers, and small firms have little pricing power. Surveys show that customers defer new phone purchases unless they have damaged their phones or there is a leap in technology.
- Core mobile phone technology, such as semiconductor chips and mobile operating licenses, are concentrated among few key suppliers that command large profit margins at the expense of phone manufacturers.
- Smartphone shipment has seen low growth in recent years due to market saturation and high penetration, limited technological advancement, and an economic slowdown. There are signs the sector is maturing. Industry concentration is increasing, with the top five firms accounting for 60–70% of global shipment and industry profit.

1. Based on her smartphone industry assessment, the credit analyst concludes that Mojofon's debt service capacity is low because:

   A. the threat of substitutes is low.

   B. the threat of new entrants and bargaining power of customers are low.

   C. the industry rivalry and the bargaining power of suppliers are high.

2. Based on the overall industry assessment, the credit analyst concludes that the credit conditions for Mojofon will *most likely*:

   A. tighten because the sector is maturing, and industry concentration is increasing.

   B. remain unchanged because Mojofon's market share is constant despite low industry growth.

C. expand since niche market entrants are consistently seizing market share from dominant firms.

3. Which of the following will *most likely* reduce Mojofon's near-term default risk?

   A. A new policy to increase dividends on a steady basis

   B. A three-year strategy to pursue acquisitions funded by debt

   C. Proactive management of debt maturity by issuing longer-term bonds

4. The credit analyst studies the key financial information of Mojofon and that of its peers below:

	Mojofon		Peer Average Current Year
Key Credit Metrics	**Prior Year**	**Current Year**	
EBITDA	27	20	55
Revenue	121	100	305
FCF	9	−5	40
FCF after dividends	5	−7	32
Interest expense	5	8	10
Total debt	100	100	150
Total equity	120	100	250

   Debt/capital for Mojofon for the current year is *closest* to:

   A. 37.5%.

   B. 50.0%.

   C. 100.0%.

5. The outstanding bonds of Mojofon contain a covenant that requires its EBITDA/Interest coverage ratio to be above 3.0. Based on coverage ratio analysis, Mojofon *most likely*:

   A. has improved its coverage ratio.

   B. is in breach of this bond covenant.

   C. has lower credit risk than its peers.

6. Based on the financial information, Mojofon's credit risk is:

   A. below that of its peers.

   B. similar to that of its peers.

   C. above that of its peers.

7. Mojofon's capital structure consists of the following:

Type	**Amount**
Senior secured bonds (pledged by collateral valued at 60)	50
Senior unsecured bonds	35

Type	Amount
Subordinated bonds	15
Common equity	100

Mojofon's bonds all contain a cross-default provision. If the company is to default on one of its senior unsecured bonds:

A. the secured bonds are likely to have full recovery.

B. the credit loss on senior unsecured bonds will be the same as that on subordinated bonds.

C. the subordinated bonds will rank below shareholders, who may dictate how recovery is to be distributed.

8. Half of Mojofon's senior unsecured bonds are issued by its major operating subsidiary, which contributes over 90% of the group's cash flow and assets, and the remainder of the group's senior unsecured bonds are issued by the holding company that relies on dividend upstreamed by its subsidiaries. There is no cross-guarantee between the holding company and the subsidiary. In an event of default, it is *most likely* that:

A. the unsecured bonds issued by the holding company will have a higher recovery rate.

B. the unsecured bonds issued by the operating subsidiary will have a higher recovery rate.

C. the recovery rate will be the same for all senior unsecured bonds since they rank pari passu with each other.

9. Mojofon's S&P issuer credit rating is B+. Its S&P subordinated bond issue rating is *most likely*:

A. BB –.

B. B+.

C. B –.

SOLUTIONS

1. The correct answer is C. Based on the industry assessment:

Competitive Forces	Intensity	Capacity to Support Debt
Threat of new entrants	Low	High
Bargaining power of suppliers	High	Low
Bargaining power of customers	Low	High
Threat of substitutes	Low	High
Industry rivalry	High	Low

   Industry rivalry and bargaining power of suppliers are all high intensity, implying low capacity to support debt.

2. The correct answer is A. If the industry is maturing with low growth and the market becomes further concentrated among a few dominant firms, credit conditions for smaller smartphone producers will most likely tighten.

3. The correct answer is C. Extending debt maturity proactively will help extend Mojofon's debt maturity profile and reduce near-term default risk. B is incorrect, as debt-funded acquisitions reduce future cash flow certainty and increase credit risk. A is incorrect since increasing the dividend is a shareholder-friendly action that increases leverage and credit risk.

4. The correct answer is B. Debt/capital = Debt / (Debt + Equity)
   = 100/(100 + 100) = 0.5 or 50% for Mojofon for the current year.

5. The correct answer is B. EBITDA/Interest coverage for Mojofon for the current year = 20/8 = 2.5. The corresponding ratio for the prior year = 27/5 = 5.4. Therefore, Mojofon's coverage ratio has deteriorated, and the company has breached its coverage ratio covenant (>= 3.0). On the other hand, EBITDA/Interest among its peers = 55/10 = 5.5, which is much better than that of Mojofon. Based on coverage ratio analysis, Mojofon has higher, not lower, credit risk than its peers.

6. The correct answer is C. Despite the better profit measure, EBITDA margin, versus its peers, Mojofon's cash flow measures, leverage, and coverage ratios are all considerably worse than its peers. Therefore, it has higher credit risk.

7. The correct answer is A. Senior secured bonds rank the highest in the priority of claims, and their recovery depends on the value of the asset collateral. Since the value of asset collateral (60) exceeds the amount of secured bonds outstanding (50), the secured bonds are likely to have full recovery in an event of default. Senior unsecured bonds have higher priority over subordinated bonds, which in turn have higher priority over common equity in insolvency.

8. The correct answer is B. Senior unsecured bonds issued by the holding company are said to be structurally subordinated to those issued by the major operating subsidiary. Debt at the operating subsidiary will be serviced by the cash flow and assets of the subsidiary first before any funds can be upstreamed to the holding company to service debt at that level.

   Since the operating subsidiary accounts for over 90% of the group's cash flow and assets but only half of the group's senior unsecured debt, the holding company debt can only be serviced after the operating subsidiary debt is paid in full. The unsecured bonds issued by the subsidiary will most likely have higher recovery.

9. The correct answer is C. An issuer credit rating is the rating applied to a company's senior unsecured debt. The rating agency will usually apply a notching adjustment to the lower-ranked subordinated debt, whose rating should therefore be lower than that of the senior unsecured debt.

LEARNING MODULE

17

Fixed-Income Securitization

LEARNING OUTCOMES

Mastery	The candidate should be able to:
☐	explain benefits of securitization for issuers, investors, economies, and financial markets
☐	describe securitization, including the parties and the roles they play

INTRODUCTION

1

Asset-backed securities (ABS) are securities backed by and repaid from a pooled group of loans or receivables. Creating securities that are repaid from particular types of loans or receivables transfers risk, provides flexibility to issuers and investors, and efficiently allocates capital. In a securitization, cash flows from a designated pool of assets are redistributed by a special purpose issuer to pay interest and principal to investors in a predetermined manner. Thus, ABS transactions create an entire new subordination structure on the designated pool of assets. Securitization takes place around the world — in the Americas, Asia, and Europe. This first of three Fixed-Income Learning Modules describes the benefits of securitization, the securitization process, and typical securitization structures.

LEARNING MODULE OVERVIEW

- Securitization benefits investors by redistributing payment risks, enhancing the predictability of payments, diminishing the impact of unexpected changes in payment patterns (such as defaults, prepayments, or payment extensions), helping investors match risk, return and maturity needs, and reducing risk through various credit enhancements.
- Securitization enables issuers to operate more efficiently on a risk-adjusted basis by removing assets and lending risks from their balance sheets (thereby reducing their leverage), expanding their capacity to originate loans and to secure lower funding costs.
- Securitization enhances financial market efficiency, improving overall liquidity in the financial system and reducing liquidity risk.

- Several parties participate in a securitization, including the original corporate issuers of the assets (for example, loans, receivables, leases, or debt) to be securitized; a special purpose entity (SPE) created to buy/own these corporate assets, create new assets from them, and sell the new assets to investors; the servicer of the underlying loans or debt; and other (third-party) entities (for example, accountants, attorneys, and underwriters).
- When an original issuer elects to securitize assets, it first establishes an SPE to which it sells the assets. The SPE then issues and sells to investors securities backed by these assets. Interest and principal payments on the assets are used to pay the investors in the new securities.
- The separate legal entity structure of the SPE is designed to protect the underlying assets from any claims by creditors of the issuer should the issuer go into financial distress. However, ABS investors should evaluate the legal considerations of the actual jurisdiction where they purchase an ABS, since legal frameworks vary by country.

LEARNING MODULE SELF-ASSESSMENT

These initial questions are intended to help you gauge your current level of understanding of this learning module.

1. Which of the following asset-backed securities (ABS) is *most* complex?

   A. Covered bonds

   B. Pass-through securities

   C. Collateralized mortgage obligations

   Solution

   C is correct. Collateralized mortgage obligations enhance the predictability of payment patterns of pass-through securities by redistributing the cash flows in the pool across the different tranches according to a preset schedule. A is incorrect because covered bonds are the simplest securitization structure. The issuer segregates (but retains) the underlying loans/assets and then uses the segregated loans/assets as collateral for the covered bonds it issues. B is incorrect because pass-through securities, while true securitizations (meaning that the pool of assets is removed from the balance sheet and transferred into a separate and independent legal entity), are not as complex as collateralized mortgage obligations.

2. Which of the following legal documents in the securitization process describes the structure of the securitization, including the priority of payments and the credit enhancements to be used?

   A. Prospectus

   B. Notes issued by the SPE

   C. Purchase agreement between the seller of the collateral and the SPE

   Solution

   The correct answer is A. The prospectus describes the structure of the securitization, including the priority and amount of payments to be made to the servicer, administrators, and the ABS holders, as well as the credit enhancements used in the securitization. B is incorrect because the notes issued by the SPE are the actual asset-backed-securities (ABS), not legal documents supporting the securitization process. C is incorrect because the purchase agreement between the seller of the collateral and the SPE outlines the representations and warranties that the seller makes about the assets sold.

3. Identify the role that corresponds to each of the following participants in a securitization:

1. Seller	A. The entity that issues the ABS
2. Servicer	B. The entity that wishes to increase liquidity, lower funding costs, and operate more efficiently on a risk-adjusted basis
3. SPE	C. The entity that collects payments from borrowers

Solution

1. B is correct. By removing assets and lending risks from their balance sheet, the seller can operate more efficiently on a risk-adjusted basis. And, by selling the assets to an SPE, investors can rely on the default risk associated with collecting payments from customers, rather than the seller's credit quality and default risk. As a result, in aggregate, the funding cost of a securitization may be lower than that of a corporate bond issue.
2. C is correct. Loan servicing refers to administering any aspect of a loan, including collecting payments from borrowers, notifying borrowers who may be delinquent, and recovering and disposing of the underlying asset if the borrower does not make the payments as scheduled.
3. A is correct. The SPE purchases the assets from the seller and then issues and sells ABS backed by the pool of securitized assets.

4. Identify the benefit of securitization that corresponds most closely to each of the following parties: (A. Economies and Financial Markets, B. Issuers, C. Investors):

1. By removing assets and lending risks from their balance sheet, _________ can operate more efficiently on a risk adjusted basis. Ultimately, securitization enables ___________ to expand lending origination beyond their balance sheets.	
2. Securitization allows __________ to tailor interest rate and credit risk exposures to suit their specific risk, return, and maturity needs.	
3. Securitization creates tradable securities with higher liquidity than that of the original, thereby making ___________ more efficient, improving overall liquidity and reducing liquidity risk	

Solution

1. By removing assets and lending risks from their balance sheet, _________ can operate more efficiently on a risk adjusted basis. Ultimately, securitization enables __________ to expand lending origination beyond their balance sheets.	B. Issuers
2. Securitization allows __________ to tailor interest rate and credit risk exposures to suit their specific risk, return, and maturity needs.	C. Investors
3. Securitization creates tradable securities with higher liquidity than that of the original, thereby making __________ more efficient, improving overall liquidity and reducing liquidity risk	A. Economies and Financial Markets

1. B is correct. By removing assets and lending risks from their balance sheet, *issuers* can operate more efficiently on a risk adjusted basis. Ultimately, securitization enables *issuers* to expand lending origination beyond their balance sheets.
2. C is correct. Securitization allows *investors* to tailor interest rate and credit risk exposures to suit their specific risk, return, and maturity needs.
3. A is correct. Securitization creates tradable securities with higher liquidity than that of the original, thereby making *economies and financial markets* more efficient, improving overall liquidity and reducing liquidity risk.

2 THE BENEFITS OF SECURITIZATION

☐ explain benefits of securitization for issuers, investors, economies, and financial markets

The securitization process pools and transfers the ownership of cash flow generating assets, such as loans or receivables, from the original lender into a specially created legal entity. The pool of assets are the securitized assets, also called the reference portfolio or collateral. In turn, that legal entity issues securities backed by these pooled assets to investors and uses the cash flows to pay interest and repay the principal to investors. Securitization creates a direct link between investors and borrowers for many types of loans and receivables, and it provides benefits for issuers and investors as well as economies and financial markets. The steps of the securitization process are outlined in Exhibit 1.

Exhibit 1: The Securitization Process

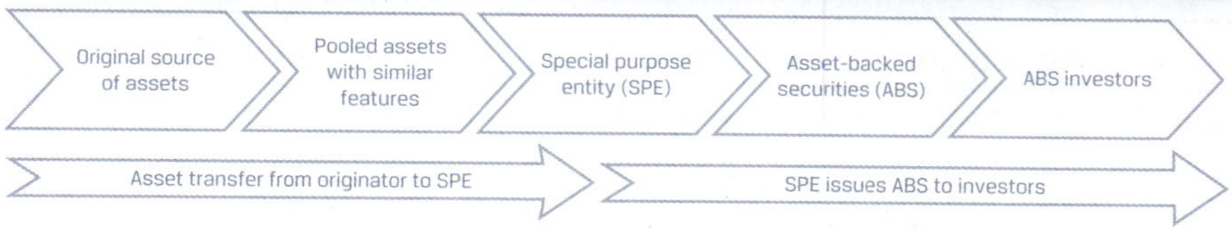

There are several different types of securitized products. In order of increasing complexity, the following products are examples of ABS.

- Covered bonds are the simplest securitization structure. The issuers, mainly European banks, create a specific pool of mortgage loans on the balance sheet of the bank and segregate it from other bank assets. This pool then serves as collateral ("cover") for bonds issued by the bank. Should the issuing bank default on a covered bond issue, investors can use the collateral underlying the pool to receive payment. Covered bonds are not considered full securitizations because the underlying assets are not transferred to a separate independent SPE but rather remain on the issuing bank's balance sheet. Moreover, covered bond investors receive payment directly from the bank and not from the cash flow generated by the specific pool of mortgage loans.
- Pass-through securities are true securitizations: The specific pool of assets is removed from the balance sheet and transferred into a separate and independent legal entity. That legal entity then issues securities backed by these pooled assets. The investors in these securities receive the principal and interest payments from the assets (often loans) in the pool as they are "passed through" the legal entity. Pass-through securities pass through the payments proportionally across the different tranches and redistribute the payment risks to investors seeking differing levels of risk exposures. The payments investors receive vary and depend directly on the overall credit risk of the pool and payment patterns.
- Bonds with structural enhancements enhance the predictability of payment patterns of pass-through securities by redistributing the cash flows in the pool across specified tranches according to a preset schedule. The set payment schedule mitigates the impact of unexpected changes in payment patterns, such as defaults, prepayments, or extended repayment periods. Additionally, tranches are subordinated with lower tranches assuming greater risks of defaults and changes in repayment patterns than higher tranches. They may further mitigate and redistribute the potential credit risk of a risky pool of securitized loans by adding various types of credit enhancements to further reduce the risk investors are exposed to.
- Mortgage-backed securities (MBS) are ABS backed by a pool of mortgages. A distinction is sometimes made between MBS and ABS backed by non-mortgage assets. This distinction is common in the United States and is shown in Exhibit 2.

Exhibit 2: Pass-Through Securities

Pass-Through Securities	Subgroup
Mortgage-backed securities	▪ Residential Mortgage-Backed Securities (RMBS) ▪ Commercial Mortgage-Backed Securities (CMBS) ▪ Collateralized Mortgage Obligation (CMO)
Non-Mortgage-backed securities	▪ Collateralized Debt Obligation (CDO) ▪ Collateralized Loan Obligation (CLO) ▪ Collateralized Bond Obligation (CBO) ▪ Collateralized Debt Obligation Squared (CDO Squared)

Exhibit 3: Securitization Structure and Tranche Cash Flows

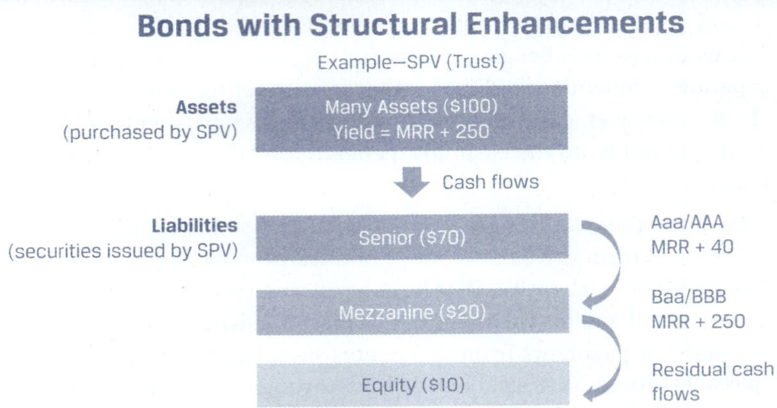

Subordination, or tranching, in the securitization transaction involves creating more than one bond class or tranche, and the bond classes differ in how they receive cash flows from the underlying pool of assets. The bond classes are classified as senior bond classes or subordinated bond classes, and this structure is also referred to as a senior/subordinated structure as seen in Exhibit 3. The subordinated bond classes are sometimes called "non-senior bond classes" or "junior bond classes." Since all investors in a securitization are paid from the same underlying cash flow pool, the tranching dictates the order of payments made to investors and the order in which losses are absorbed by the investors.

Benefits to Issuers

Traditionally, banks underwrite loans to allow borrowers to finance various purchases and direct investments. These bank loans, which typically remain on the balance sheet of the bank until the loans are fully repaid, are relatively illiquid.

Banks act as the intermediary between borrowers and investors. If they can separate loan origination from loan financing, they can improve their profitability, earning origination fees and reducing capital requirements for loans that are sold to investors, as shown in Exhibit 4. As we learned in the example on asset-backed commercial paper (ABCP) in an earlier learning module, by removing assets and lending risks from their balance sheet, banks sell illiquid assets and operate more efficiently on a risk-adjusted basis. Selling assets also generates fee income. Ultimately, securitization enables banks to expand lending origination beyond their balance sheets.

Exhibit 4: Banks and Securitization

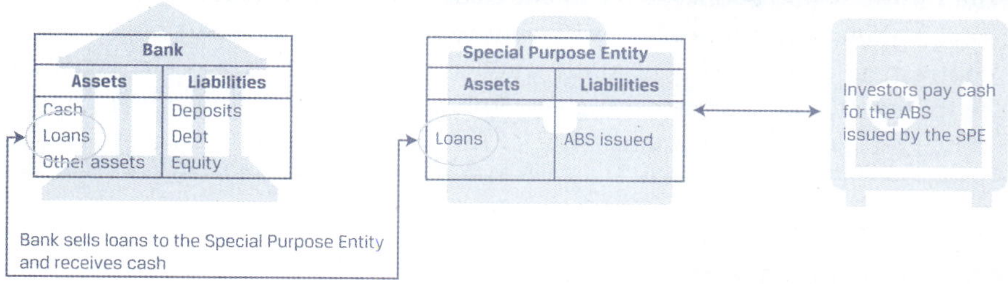

Without ABS as an investment instrument, investors wanting to gain exposure to private debts would have to directly underwrite loans, hold some combination of bank debt and common equity, or purchase loans from bank outright. Direct debt underwriting requires specialized skills in credit evaluation, origination, underwriting, and servicing, and one has to assume the operational costs and business risks of banking. ABS investment breaks down the wide range of skills and risks and redistributes them to appropriate parties.

Benefits to Investors

Securitization provides a direct conduit between borrowers and investors, allowing investors to tailor interest rate and credit risk exposures to suit their specific risk, return, and maturity needs. Securitization transactions allow issuers to design risk–return characteristics to satisfy the risk tolerance of investors.

Although few institutional or individual investors have the specialized resources and expertise needed to originate, monitor, and collect the payments from the underlying loans and receivables, many can invest in securities backed by such loans or receivables. The ABS that are created by pooling these loans and receivables have characteristics similar to those of a standard bond.

For example, a pension fund with a long-term horizon can use securitized debt to achieve higher returns, match asset maturities to anticipated liability payout dates, and increase diversity in its asset pool while maintaining the option to adjust holdings quickly and cost-effectively. Thus, holding securitized debt helps pension fund investors increase exposure to the risk–return characteristics of a wider range of underlying assets.

EXAMPLE 1

Benefits of Securitized Debt for Long-term Investors

Pawas Singhvi, an investment manager for a defined benefit pension fund at a large manufacturer, is discussing investment options and expectations with a new associate, Kevin Epstein. Epstein asks why Singhvi holds a significant portion of fund assets in securitized debt. Singhvi explains that a number of parameters and expectations influence the investments selected for the pension fund, starting with asset and income diversification. The fund seeks safe, diversified assets and income streams, which offer low risk. Anticipated pension payments or outflows from the fund drive the need for liquid and stable investments, which mature or can be sold easily to match the timing of required cash outflows. Any fund investments must be highly rated.

Because pension payouts take place over many years into the future, pension assets must be invested long-term, too. And the fund's assets must grow over time in order to produce promised pension payments at the levels required in the future. While public, government-issued debt is highly rated and typically safe, it alone may not produce sufficient returns to meet future obligations. By contrast, holding investment-grade, publicly traded, securitized debt, which can be traded, allows us to garner higher returns and to respond quickly to changes in market sentiment, risk sensitivity, or funding needs at low transaction costs.

Benefits to Economies and Financial Markets

Securitization creates tradable securities with higher liquidity than that of the original loans on the bank's balance sheet, and trading securities in the secondary market allows investors to determine equilibrium prices—thereby making financial markets more efficient. Securitization also improves overall liquidity in the financial system and reduces liquidity risk.

An important benefit of securitization is that it provides an alternative means of funding business operations beyond traditional financing tools, such as bonds, preferred equity, and common equity. Companies can use securitization to reduce their funding costs by pooling securitizable assets (often receivables and loans), which increases their return on capital versus borrowing though traditional financing methods.

Securitization is beneficial to financial markets. Corporate issuers can facilitate the process of selling their products by extending credit to their customers, usually through their financing subsidiary. These subsidiaries specialize in financing and leasing and often issue much of the corporation's consolidated debt, selling receivables either to a bank or directly to an SPE. The company can then securitize these loans, receiving cash from the SPE that then sells them to investors. A company can use these proceeds to fund financing for new customers and sell even more of their product. If the company instead kept these loans to customers on their own balance sheet, they would have to issue additional debt. That would increase their leverage, increase their overall financing and funding costs, and reduce their credit quality. Securitizing loans for their products allows companies to directly tap the financial markets and move loans off their balance sheet. They can thus capture the benefits of a cheaper source of funding without reducing the company's overall credit quality.

Securitizations may involve any number of revenue-generating assets owned by companies from a variety of industries. Securitization provides efficiencies to the entire system, benefiting many parties. Manufacturers are able to outsource debt servicing, consumers benefit from reduced costs, and investors benefit from diversified investment opportunities. The following are some interesting examples of securitizations.

EXAMPLE 2

Examples of Securitizations

Notes securitized by music royalties and licensing agreements (which allow places such as restaurants or retail stores to play popular music) have been issued. In 2019, the performing-rights company, SESAC, issued securitized bonds backed by its music royalties and licensing agreements with more than 30,000 artists, including Adele, Bob Dylan, Kesha, Gabriel Mann, and R.E.M. The largest piece of the securitization was a fixed-rate note, worth $530 million with a weighted average life of 6.7 years. The note offered a yield of 5.25%. The smaller portion of the deal was a floating-rate note, worth $30 million with a weighted average life of 4.9 years, which was not publicly offered. This type of offering is known as a "whole-business securitization." This type of bond usually is backed by such assets as restaurant franchise agreements or other unusual assets and typically pays higher rates than more traditional ABS tied to consumer debt.

In 2021, Yum! Brands, the parent company of such fast-food chains as KFC, Pizza Hut, and Taco Bell, issued USD2.3 billion in notes securitized by cash flows from franchised Taco Bell locations through a special purpose subsidiary, Taco Bell Funding.

Although securitization brings many benefits to economies, it is not without risks. Broadly, these risks fall into two categories: risks that relate primarily to the timing of the ABS's cash flows, such as contraction risk and extension risk, and risks related to the inherent credit risk of the loans and receivables backing the ABS. Later modules will address how securitization structures reduce these risks. Some of these risks are widely attributed to have precipitated the turmoil in financial markets during 2007–2009.

QUESTION SET

1. Identify three benefits of securitization to issuers of ABS.

   Solution

   1. By removing assets and lending risks from their balance sheet, banks can sell illiquid assets and *operate more efficiently* on a risk-adjusted basis.
   2. Selling assets also *generates fee income.*
   3. Ultimately, securitization enables banks to *expand lending origination beyond their balance sheets.*

2. Identify two benefits of securitization to investors.

   Solution

   1. Securitization allows investors to tailor interest rate and credit risk exposures to suit their specific risk, return, and maturity needs.
   2. Securitization allows investors to gain exposure to a wider range of imperfectly correlated assets to build more efficient and diversified portfolios.

3. Matching asset maturities to anticipated liability payout dates and increasing diversity in an asset pool while maintaining the option to adjust holdings quickly and cost-effectively is *most likely* a benefit to:

   A. issuers.

   B. investors.

   C. economies and financial markets.

   Solution

   The correct answer is B. Matching asset maturities to anticipated liability payout dates and increasing diversity in an asset pool while maintaining the option to adjust holdings quickly and cost-effectively is most likely a benefit to investors. For example, a pension fund with a long-term horizon can use securitized debt gains to achieve higher returns, match asset maturities to anticipated liability payout dates, and increase diversity in its asset pool while maintaining the option to adjust holdings quickly and cost-effectively.

4. Determine if the following events associated with an ABS are *more likely* to result in a benefit or a risk and identify for whom (issuers, investors, financial markets):

Event	Benefit or Risk	For Whom
A. Change in the timing of the cash flows		
B. Change in the credit worthiness of the associated ABS loans		
C. Selling illiquid assets		
D. Securitizing assets		

Solution

Event	Benefit or Risk	For Whom
A. Change in the timing of the cash flows	Risk	Investors – Prepayment risk, the uncertainty that cash flows will differ from the schedule set forth in the initial loan agreement, can result either when interest rates decline and borrowers pay off part or all of their loans early or when borrowers experience financial duress and slow down their loan payments.
B. Change in the credit worthiness of the associated ABS loans	Risk	Investors – If the borrowers default on their loans, then the SPE may not be able to make cash payments to the security holders. On the other hand, if the borrowers' credit worthiness improves, there is no direct benefit to the investors.
C. Selling illiquid assets	Benefit	Issuer
D. Securitizing assets	Benefit	Issuer, Investors Financial Markets

3 THE SECURITIZATION PROCESS

☐ describe securitization, including the parties and the roles they play

Securitization requires that several legal and regulatory conditions are satisfied and involves multiple parties to facilitate the transaction and ensure that these conditions are met. This section describes a typical securitization process, the parties, and their roles.

An Example of a Securitization

Let's revisit Bright Wheel Automotive (BRWA), the hypothetical car manufacturer introduced earlier. BRWA's financing company subsidiary provides loans to BRWA customers with the vehicles serving as collateral. These fixed-rate loans represent an asset to the company with maturities averaging four years. They are fully amortizing with the principal repaid in 48 monthly payments (12 months × 4 years). The borrowers make equal payments each month consisting of interest payment and principal repayment, as shown in Exhibit 5.

Exhibit 5: Bright Wheel Automotive Securitization

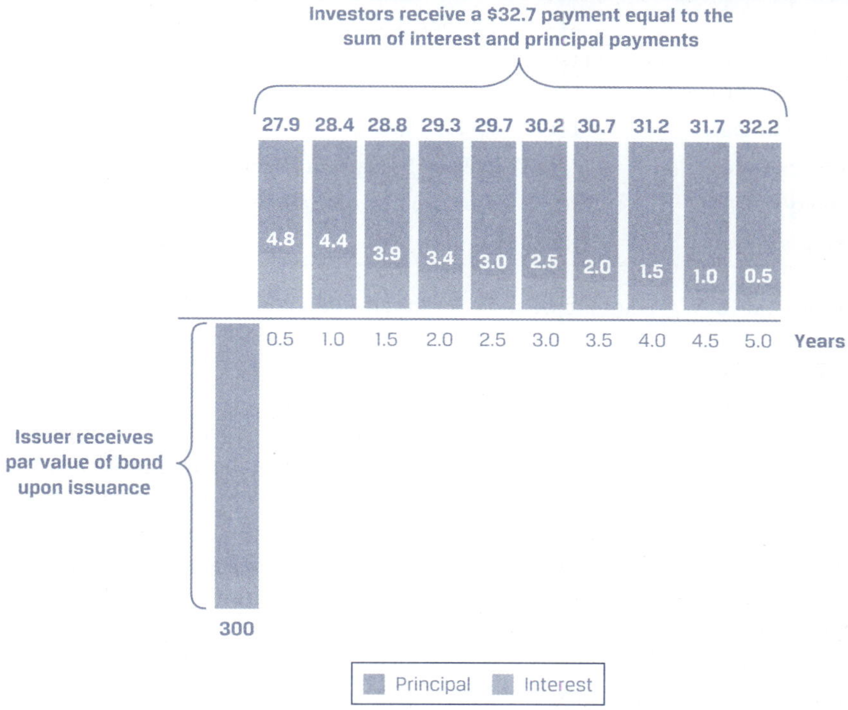

BRWA's financing subsidiary decides whether to extend credit to customers, and it also services the loans. Loan servicing refers to administering any aspect of a loan, including collecting payments from borrowers, notifying borrowers who may be delinquent, and recovering and disposing of a vehicle if the borrower does not make the payments as scheduled. If a customer defaults, BRWA can seize the car and sell it to recoup the remaining principal on the loan. The role of the servicer can vary: In this example, the issuer continues to service the loan, but at other times, the servicing may be provided by another entity.

The following is an illustration of how these loans can be securitized. In this simplified example, the costs and fees associated with the securitization are ignored. Exhibit 6 shows a summary of the terms for a securitization transaction where BRWA sold car loans to a hypothetical SPE named Car Loan Trust (CLT), which then uses the loans as collateral for ABS it issues.

Exhibit 6: Notes Issued by Car Loan Trust Collateralized by Car Loans – Brief Summary of Terms

Four-Year Asset-Backed Notes — Car Loan Trust	
Issuer:	Car Loan Trust (CLT), a special purpose entity.
Underlying Assets/ Collateral:	Portfolio of loans by which new cars and vehicles are financed.
Description:	Car finance receivables originated by Bright Wheel Automotive (BRWA), sold by BRWA to CLT, purchased by CLT, and fully transferred from BRWA to CLT. There are 45,000 loans in the outstanding pool, with an average balance of EUR22,222.
Outstanding Principal Balance of the Pool:	EUR1,000 million
Settlement Date:	[T + 3 Business Days]
Maturity Date:	[Four Years from Settlement Date]
Security:	The Notes are secured obligations of CLT.
Business Days:	Frankfurt.

Assume that BRWA wants to raise EUR1,000 million and faces two choices. One is to issue a four-year corporate bond; the other is to issue an ABS backed by the car loans. BRWA seeks to achieve the lowest possible interest rate relative to its benchmark interest rate, where the difference is the credit spread.

Unlike banks and finance companies, car manufacturers are more capital-intensive. Tying up capital on their balance sheet to finance car purchases may be a suboptimal use of their capital. Selling off loans frees up capital and recognizes profits that can finance the core business.

First, BRWA sets up a separate legal entity called Car Loan Trust (CLT), a **special purpose entity (SPE)**, sometimes also called a special purpose vehicle (SPV) or a special purpose company, to which it sells the EUR1,000 million worth of car loans. CLT, a legally independent and bankruptcy-remote entity from BRWA, acquires these loans from BRWA and becomes the ultimate owner of the loans. The separate legal entity structure ensures that if BRWA, the originator of the loans, files for bankruptcy, the loans backing the ABS that are issued by BRWA are secure within CLT, the SPE, and BRWA's creditors cannot have any claim on them. Creating the required separate and bankruptcy-remote legal structures for the SPE and fully transferring the loans from the issuer to the SPE can be a complicated process that varies across jurisdictions.

Exhibit 7 reflects BRWA's business: (1) selling cars financed by loans, (2) BRWA sells to CLT EUR1,000 million worth of car loans, and (3) BRWA receives from CLT EUR1,000 million in cash.

Exhibit 7: Setting up the Securitized Pool

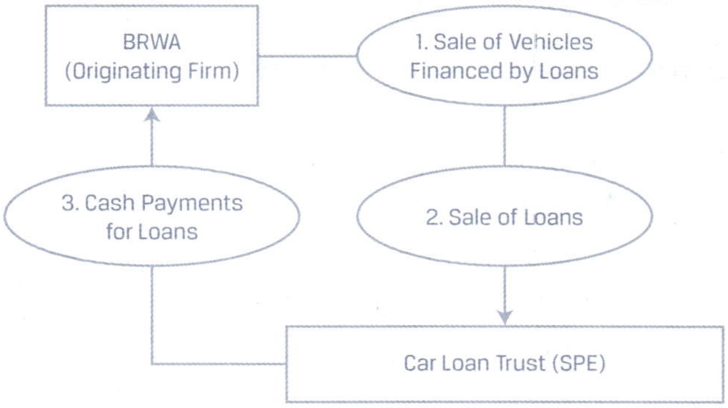

Exhibit 8 shows how CLT then (4) issues and sells securities that are backed by the pool of securitized loans and (5) receives cash from investors. These securities are the ABS mentioned earlier with the EUR1,000 million in car loans representing the collateral.

Exhibit 8: Issuing the ABS

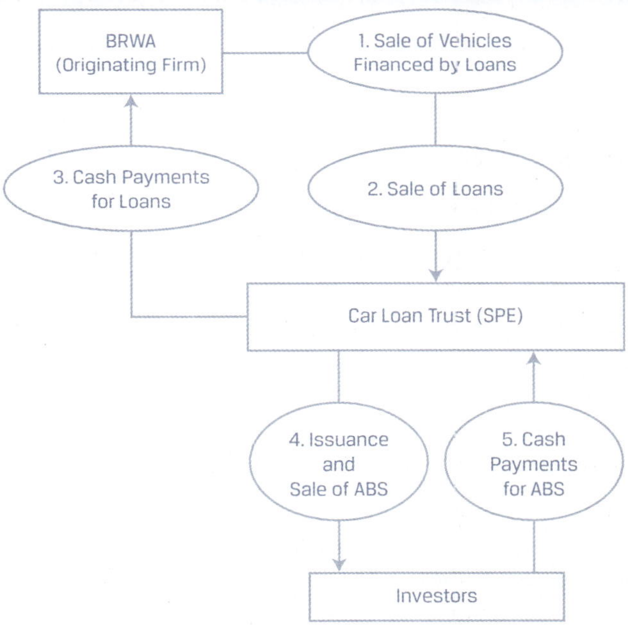

Exhibit 9 shows (6) how the monthly payments made by BRWA's customers, which include both interest payment and principal repayment, go to the special purpose entity CLT, which then (7) directs the agreed periodic cash payments to the investors in the ABS. Exhibit 9 also summarizes the full set of steps in a typical securitization. It shows the parts played by all parties, including the company wanting to securitize its assets, the issuer (SPE), as well as customers and investors.

Exhibit 9: Periodic Payments on the ABS

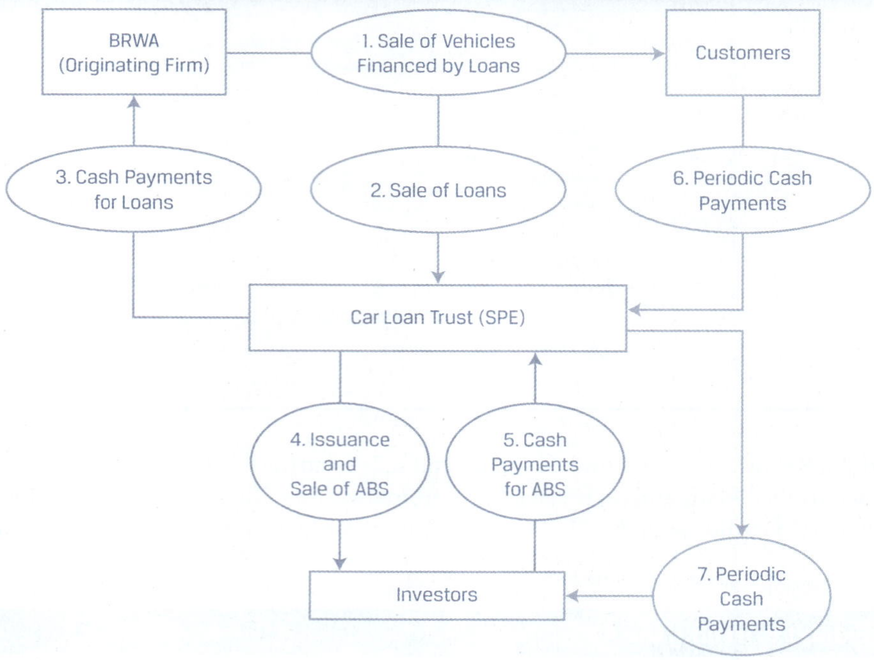

Parties to a Securitization

The three main parties to a securitization are:

- the *seller* of the collateral, sometimes called the depositor (BRWA in our example);
- the *SPE* that purchases the loans or receivables and uses them as collateral to issue the ABS, CLT in our example (the SPE is often referred to as the issuer in the prospectus because it is the entity that issues the securities); and
- the *servicer* of the loans (BRWA's financing subsidiary in our example).

Other parties, such as independent accountants, lawyers/attorneys, trustees, underwriters, rating agencies, and sometimes financial guarantors, are also involved in these transactions. Since these parties are different from the seller of the collateral, they are referred to as third parties to the securitization.

Besides the standard bond indenture and its covenants, two additional legal documents play an important role in the securitization process. One is the **purchase agreement** between the seller of the collateral (the original lender) and the SPE, which outlines the representations and warranties that the seller makes about the assets sold. These representations and warranties assure investors about the quality of the assets, an important consideration when assessing the risks associated with the ABS. The other is the **prospectus**, which describes the structure of the securitization, including the priority and amount of payments to be made to the servicer, administrators, and the ABS holders, as well as the credit enhancements used in the securitization.

A trustee or trustee agent is known as a "disinterested trustee" and is typically a financial institution that safeguards the assets after they have been sold to the SPE, holds the funds due to the ABS holders until they are paid, and provides periodic cash flow reports to ABS holders as agreed to in the terms of the prospectus. These reports are the only source of information for investors to update the credit standing of the ABS.

The Role of the SPE

The legal protection the SPE creates for the originator or issuer and the investors in an ABS transaction plays a pivotal role in securitization. Without an SPE, securitizations would not be possible. Securitization can be a cheaper way to raise funds than a corporate bond issue secured by the same collateral because the SPE is not affected by the bankruptcy of the seller of the collateral.

In a securitization, the courts in most jurisdictions have no discretion to change seniority because the bankruptcy of the originating company does not affect the SPE. Hence removing assets from the balance sheet into an SPE is an important decoupling of the credit risk of the entity needing funds from the SPE and the bond classes issued by it. This explains why the SPE is structured as a bankruptcy-remote entity and why the legal separation from the issuer and the SPE is critical.

The only credit risk that the investors face is the risk that the borrowers whose loans are included in the SPE default on their loans. The SPE's ability to make cash payments to the security holders remains intact if the borrowers make the interest payments and/or the principal repayments on their loans.

In many countries, the creditors are protected in the recognition of the securitization as a true sale, where all rights of the lender are irrevocably, unqualifiedly, and fully transferred to the SPE according to the laws of the jurisdiction. The SPE has full legal ownership of the securitized assets, which are de-recognized from the seller's balance sheet. Note that it is possible that transfers made to bankruptcy-remote vehicles, such as an SPE, can be challenged as fraudulent transactions or conveyances in court and if so determined, potentially unwound.

It is also important to note that not all countries have the same legal framework. Impediments with respect to ABS issuance have arisen in some countries where the concept of trust law is less well developed. Thus, investors should evaluate the legal considerations that apply in the jurisdictions where they purchase ABS.

QUESTION SET

Questions 1 to 4 are based on the following example:

Ahbaling Industries (Ahbaling), a manufacturer of industrial machine tools based in Johor, Malaysia, has SGD500 million of corporate bonds outstanding. These bonds have a credit rating below investment grade. Ahbaling has SGD400 million of receivables on its balance sheet that it would like to securitize. The receivables represent payments Ahbaling expects to receive for machine tools it has sold to various customers in Europe. Ahbaling's finance subsidiary sells the receivables to Ahbaling Trust, an SPE. Ahbaling Trust then issues ABS, backed by the pool of receivables, with the following structure:

Bond Class	Par Value (SGD millions)
A (senior)	280
B (subordinated)	60
C (subordinated)	60
Total	400

1. Identify the correct order for the following steps related to securitizing receivables of Ahbaling Industries:

	A. Investors buy securities based on their preferred level of risk and return.
	B. Ahbaling pools SGD400 million in receivables.
	C. Ahbaling sells machine tools on credit.
	D. ABS are issued.
	E. Segregated receivables are sold to Ahbaling Trust.

Solution

Step 1	C. Ahbaling sells machine tools on credit.
Step 2	B. Ahbaling pools SGD400 million in receivables.
Step 3	E. Segregated receivables are sold to Ahbaling Trust.
Step 4	D. ABS are issued.
Step 5	A. Investors buy securities with their preferred level of risk and return.

2. If Ahbaling Industries issues SGD400 million in corporate bonds one year from now:

   A. the new bonds will be senior to the ABS.

   B. the ABS will be senior to the new bonds.

   C. seniority will not apply between the new bonds and the ABS.

   Solution

   The correct answer is C. Since the new bonds are issued by Ahbaling Industries and the ABS are issued by Ahbaling Trust, two distinct entities, seniority will not apply.

3. Investors considering the purchase of the ABS bonds will rely most on:

   A. the financial health of Ahbaling Trust.

   B. the financial health of Ahbaling Industries.

   C. the default risk associated with collecting payments from Ahbaling customers.

   Solution

   The correct answer is C. As long as Ahbaling's customers make the interest payments and/or principal repayments on their loans, Ahbaling Trust will be able to make cash payments to the ABS investors. The legal implication of setting up Ahbaling Trust is that investors contemplating the purchase of any ABS backed by the cash flows from the pool of Ahbaling receivables will evaluate the default risk associated with collecting the payments from the machine tool customers. The credit quality and default risk of Ahbaling Industries are no longer directly relevant.

4. Identify the *most important* reason why the ABS issued by Ahbaling Trust offers a lower interest rate than the existing Ahbaling Industries corporate bonds outstanding.

   A. Ahbaling Industries' existing bonds are rated below investment grade.

B. Ahbaling Trust would not be affected if Ahbaling Industries files for bankruptcy.

C. The ABS issued by Ahbaling Trust are secured by collateral, the receivables purchased from Ahbaling Industries.

Solution

The correct answer is C. A secured bond is secured by collateral and is considered less risky than an unsecured bond without collateral backing, and accordingly, has a lower credit spread than an unsecured bond. A is incorrect because the credit rating on Ahbaling Industries' existing bonds does not dictate the interest rate on the ABS issued by Ahbaling Trust. B is incorrect because even though Ahbaling Trust, as a separate legal entity, would not be affected if Ahbaling Industries files for bankruptcy, this is not the *most important* reason that the ABS require a lower interest rate.

PRACTICE PROBLEMS

1. Which of the following benefits of securitization is most likely to be important for investors?
   A. Increased efficiency
   B. Reduced liquidity risk
   C. The ability to tailor interest rate and credit risk exposures

The following information relates to questions 2-4

AR&C Limited leases private jets to corporations in North America for a fixed term of five years. AR&C retains ownership of the jets. The corporations make equal interest payments each month. If a customer defaults, AR&C can repossess the jet. AR&C has been in business for approximately fifteen years and has a B3 credit rating, meaning that its debt is non-investment grade. AR&C has CAD500 million in leases on its balance sheet, which it wants to securitize into ABS.

2. Determine which of the following is the *best* next step for AR&C.
   A. AR&C issues and sells securities backed by the pool of leases.
   B. AR&C sets up a separate legal entity to which it sells the CAD500 million in leases.
   C. AR&C discontinues servicing the leases, shifting this responsibility to a special purpose company.

3. Which shape *best* represents the cash payments for the Leases?

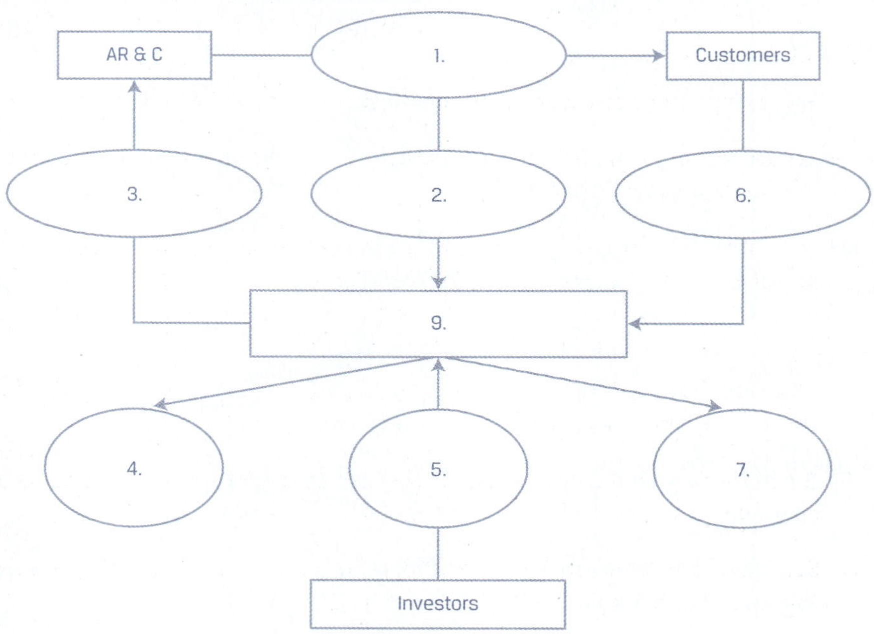

A. Shape 2

B. Shape 3

C. Shape 5

4. Which of the following *best* describes the entity shown in shape 9?

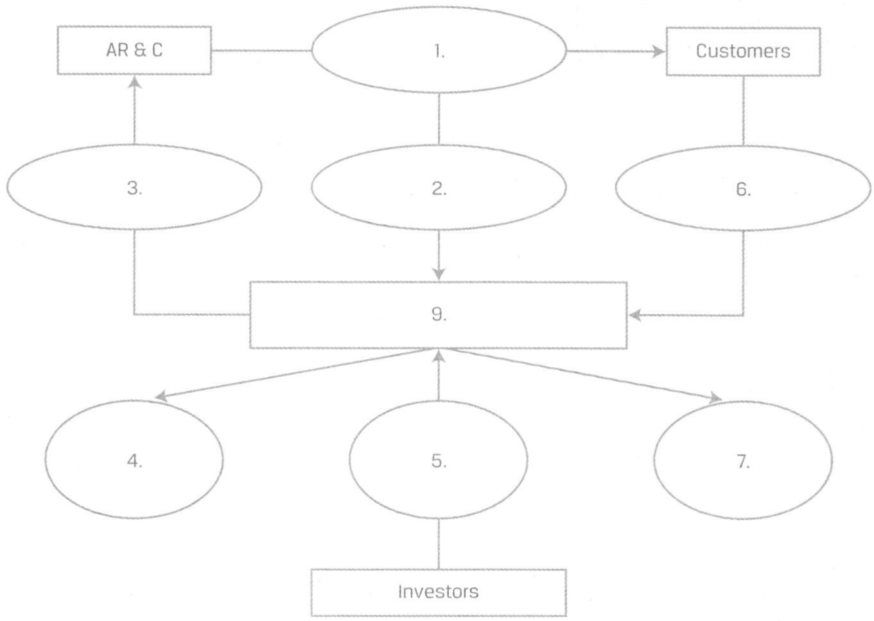

The entity in shape 9 is the:

A. seller of the collateral.

B. servicer of the leases.

C. SPE that purchases the leases and uses them as collateral for the ABS.

---

5. Which of the following statements about securitization's impact on economies and financial markets is correct?

A. Securitization decreases overall liquidity in the financial system.

B. Securitization provides an alternative means of funding business operations beyond traditional financing.

C. Securitization allows companies to directly access the financial markets and purchase loans that will be held on their balance sheet.

6. Which of the following statements about securitization is incorrect?

A. The ABS that are created by securitization have characteristics similar to those of equity investments.

B. Buying securitized debt helps investors increase exposure to the risk–return characteristics of a wider range of underlying assets.

C. Securitization transactions allow issuers to create risk–return characteristics to satisfy the risk tolerance of different investors.

7. In the event of a bankruptcy of the originator in a loan securitization, the investors would *most likely* experience:

   A. gains.

   B. losses.

   C. no impact.

8. In a securitization, the party that purchases the loans or receivables and uses them as collateral to issue ABS is the:

   A. SPE.

   B. seller.

   C. servicer.

SOLUTIONS

1. The correct answer is C. Securitization provides a direct conduit between borrowers and investors. It also allows investors to tailor interest rate and credit risk exposures to suit their specific risk, return, and maturity needs. A is incorrect because securitization creates efficiency for issuers and financial markets more directly than for investors. Securitization allows issuers to sell illiquid assets and operate more efficiently on a risk-adjusted basis. Moreover, because securitization creates tradable securities with higher liquidity than the original underlying assets, it makes financial markets more efficient. B is incorrect because securitization improves overall liquidity in the financial system and reduces liquidity risk, which benefits participants in financial markets.

2. The correct answer is B. In order for these assets (leases) to be securitized, they must be held in a separate legal entity structure distinct from AR&C. The separate legal entity structure ensures that if AR&C, the originator of the leases, files for bankruptcy, the leases backing the ABS that are issued by the separate legal entity are secure there, thus AR&C's creditors cannot have any claim on them. A is incorrect because if AR&C issues the securities, the leases remain on AR&C's balance sheet and thus could still be accessible to AR&C's creditors in the event of a bankruptcy. C is incorrect because servicing the leases must continue whether or not by AR&C or another entity, but servicing the leases is separate from securitizing them.

3. The correct answer is B. As shown in the diagram below, the SPE (in rectangle 9 above), pays AR&C for the leases (as noted in shape 3 above). A is incorrect because shape 2 above represents the sale of the leases (as shown in the diagram below), not the payment for them, and C is incorrect because shape 5 above represents payments from the investors for the ABS sold by the SPE (as shown in the diagram below).

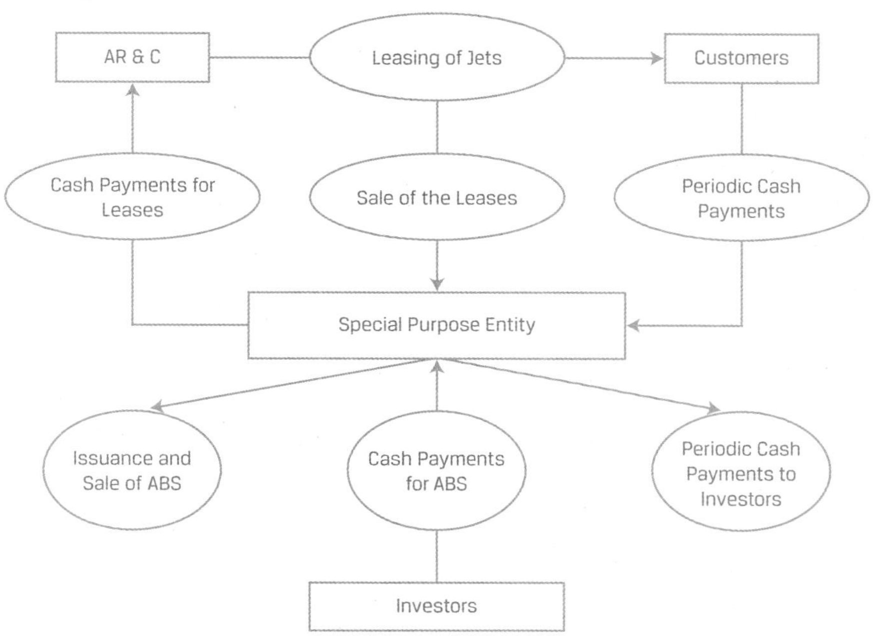

4. The correct answer is C. The SPE purchases the leases from AR&C and uses them as collateral for the ABS, which it issues and sells to the investors. A is incorrect because AR&C is the seller of the collateral, not the SPE. C is incorrect because

the diagram does not show clearly who services the leases, but it does show that the entity in shape 9 is the SPE.

5. The correct answer is B. An important benefit of securitization is that it provides an alternative means of funding business operations beyond traditional financing tools, such as bonds, preferred equity, and common equity. A is incorrect because securitization improves overall liquidity in the financial system and reduces liquidity risk. C is incorrect because securitization allows companies to directly access the financial markets and move loans off their balance sheet.

6. The correct answer is A. The ABS that are created by pooling loans and receivables have characteristics similar to those of a standard bond. B is incorrect because it is a correct statement. Holding securitized debt helps pension fund investors increase exposure to the risk–return characteristics of a wider range of underlying assets. C is incorrect because it is a correct statement. Securitization transactions allow issuers to design risk–return characteristics to satisfy the risk tolerance of different investors.

7. The correct answer is C. Since the SPE, which owns the loans, is bankruptcy remote from the seller of the collateral, the bankruptcy of the seller of the collateral will not affect the holders of securities issued by the SPE and backed by the collateral. The only credit risk that the investors face is the risk that the borrowers whose loans are included in the SPE default on their loans.

8. The correct answer is A. The SPE is often referred to as the issuer in the prospectus because it is the entity that issues the securities to investors. B is incorrect because the seller of the collateral, also called the depositor, is the party that originally aggregated the assets and sold them to the SPE. C is incorrect because the servicer has an administrative function and is the entity that collects payments from borrowers.

LEARNING MODULE

18

Asset-Backed Security (ABS) Instrument and Market Features

LEARNING OUTCOMES

Mastery	The candidate should be able to:
☐	describe characteristics and risks of covered bonds and how they differ from other asset-backed securities
☐	describe typical credit enhancement structures used in securitizations
☐	describe types and characteristics of non-mortgage asset-backed securities, including the cash flows and risks of each type
☐	describe collateralized debt obligations, including their cash flows and risks

INTRODUCTION

1

Prior Learning Modules have shown the funding technique of securitization can be backed by diverse types of assets, including loans and receivables as well as residential or commercial mortgages. A unifying principle in all asset-backed security (ABS) structures is that their underlying cash flows can be reconfigured into various tranches, each with its particular payment pattern to investors and associated risks. The advantage of this targeted partitioning includes a reduction in the variability of cash flows and the reallocation of risks, such as default and early repayment across specific tranches, with associated returns. Overall, ABS securitization provides risk transfer, flexibility to issuers and investors, and efficiency of capital allocation.

LEARNING MODULE OVERVIEW

- Covered bonds are issued by financial institutions as senior debt obligations. Backed by a segregated pool of assets typically consisting of commercial or residential mortgages, or public sector assets, these assets remain on the issuer's balance sheet.

- Non-mortgage ABS are securitizations that remove the pool of assets from the original issuer's balance sheet. They are generally collateralized by non-amortizing loans, such as credit card receivables, that retain their original loan value during a specific period of their life before the stated maturity date, known as the lockout or revolving period. During this time, principal that is repaid is reinvested to replenish the collateral pool.
- Collateralized debt obligation (CDO) is a generic term describing securitization backed by diversified collateral pools of non-mortgage debt (such as bonds or loans) that redistribute segmented cash flows to investors. The CDO's tranches receive the cash flows according to an order of priority, with senior claims having lower bond-like payouts and junior claims receiving potentially higher but more variable returns.
- The most common CDO structure is a collateralized loan obligation (CLO) and is subject to uniquely complex non-linear risks in cases of collateral defaults.
- Credit tranching, which involves creating distinct senior and subordinated bond classes ("tranches"), offers credit protection for the more senior bond classes in a securitization. Senior bond classes are paid from the underlying asset pool before subordinated tranches; subordinated bond classes absorb any cash flow losses resulting from defaults in the asset pool before senior tranches.
- Creating a set of bond classes allows investors to choose the level of risk, expected maturity, and the associated returns they prefer. Each bond class created in a securitization is typically rated based on both the quality of the underlying collateral and the seniority of the class.

LEARNING MODULE SELF-ASSESSMENT

1. Which of the following types of descriptive information is typically excluded from an ABS term sheet?

   A. Conditions for early amortization

   B. Market values of the tranche notes

   C. Aggregate amount of collateral pool assets

   Solution:

   The correct answer is B. The term sheet typically provides the face value of the tranche notes at the time of the transaction, not their market value. Both A and C are incorrect as these items are typically included in the term sheet.

2. After the lockout period for ABS with non-amortizing collateral, how are the cash flows for loan repayments directed?

   A. All of the principal is reinvested to acquire additional loans.

   B. Part of the principal is reinvested if the collateral pool is depleted.

   C. No principal is reinvested, and all is distributed to different tranches.

   Solution:

   The correct answer is C. When the lockout period is over and the amortization period starts, any principal that is repaid will not be reinvested in new loans but will be distributed to the different tranches.

3. The prevailing CDO structure is the:

   A. CLO.

   B. CMO.

   C. Structured finance CDO.

Solution:

The correct answer is A. Collateralized loan obligations (CLOs) have a collateral pool composed of loans. B is incorrect because while similar, CMOs are based on mortgages. C is incorrect because it is based on a portfolio of other CDOs.

4. Which of the following statements about CLOs is accurate?

   A. The CLO replicates the firm's capital structure.

   B. Purchases of a CLO's collateral are funded by issuing equity.

   C. A CLO's junior tranche earns a potentially higher yield than comparable corporate bonds.

Solution:

The correct answer is A. Fundamentally, a CLO replicates the capital structure of the firm. B is incorrect because CLO collateral purchases rely on funds obtained from the issuance of debt. C is incorrect because it is the senior of mezzanine tranches that earn a potentially higher yield than comparable corporate bonds.

5. Which of the following aspects of their transaction structures is *most likely* shared by solar ABS, CLOs, and covered bonds?

   A. A pre-funding period

   B. An unstable collateral pool

   C. A diversity of default exposures

Solution:

The correct answer is B. All these ABS lack a stable initial asset pool and require ongoing collateral management. A is incorrect because a pre-funding period is used by solar ABS post transaction to acquire additional qualifying assets that meet certain eligibility criteria. C is incorrect because covered bonds have only one bond class with its associated default exposure in its cover pool.

6. Which internal credit enhancement involves creating bond classes that differ in how they share any losses resulting from defaults in the collateral pool?

   A. Subordination

   B. Overcollateralization

   C. Cash collateral accounts

Solution:

The correct answer is A. Subordination or credit tranching in the securitization transaction involves creating more than one bond class or tranche, and the bond classes differ in how they share any losses resulting from defaults in the collateral pool. B is incorrect because overcollateralization is an internal credit enhancement in which the collateral underlying the transaction is larger than the face value of the issued bonds, so that even if defaults are in the pool, the transaction has sufficient cushion to continue paying principal and interest payments on the bonds. C is incorrect because it is a type of external, not internal, credit enhancement.

7. Which of the following statements about covered bonds is *incorrect*?

   A. The LTV on the mortgages included in the transactions must meet certain standards to be eligible for inclusion in the pool.

   B. Covered bond transactions typically involve collateral underlying the transaction that is less than the face value of the issued bonds.

   C. Redemption regimes exist to align the covered bond's cash flows with the original maturity schedule in the event of default of a covered bond's sponsor.

Solution:

The correct answer is B. Covered bond transactions typically involve collateral underlying the transaction, which exceeds the face value of the issued bonds referred to as overcollateralization. A is incorrect because it is a correct statement. The loan to value (LTV) on the mortgages included in the transactions must meet certain standards to be eligible for inclusion in the pool. If a mortgage fails to meet the LTV criteria, it is replaced with another mortgage that meets the criteria. C is incorrect because it is a correct statement. Redemption regimes exist to align the covered bond's cash flows as closely as possible with the original maturity schedule in the event of default of a covered bond's financial sponsor.

8. Which of the following bonds experiences a bond default and accelerated bond payments if payments are not made according to the original schedule?

   A. Soft-bullet covered bonds

   B. Hard-bullet covered bonds

   C. Conditional pass-through covered bonds

Solution:

The correct answer is B. For hard-bullet covered bonds, if payments do not occur according to the original schedule, a bond default is triggered and bond payments are accelerated. A is incorrect because soft-bullet covered bonds delay the bond default and payment acceleration of bond cash flows until a new final maturity date, which is usually up to a year after the original maturity date. C is incorrect because conditional pass-through covered bonds convert to pass-through securities after the original maturity date if all bond payments have not been made.

2 COVERED BONDS

☐ describe characteristics and risks of covered bonds and how they differ from other asset-backed securities

Covered bonds, which we touched on in earlier readings, are senior debt obligations issued by a financial institution and backed by a segregated pool of assets that typically consist of commercial or residential mortgages, or public sector assets. Covered bonds that are backed by ships and commercial aircraft have also been issued.

The covered bond (or *Pfandbrief* in German) originated over 250 years ago in Prussia and has been adopted by issuers in Europe, Asia, and Australia. Each country or jurisdiction specifies eligible collateral and structures permissible in the covered bond market, and the European Union is taking steps to harmonize these elements among its member states. Exhibit 1 provides a typical structure for a covered bond transaction.

Exhibit 1: Covered Bond Transaction Structure

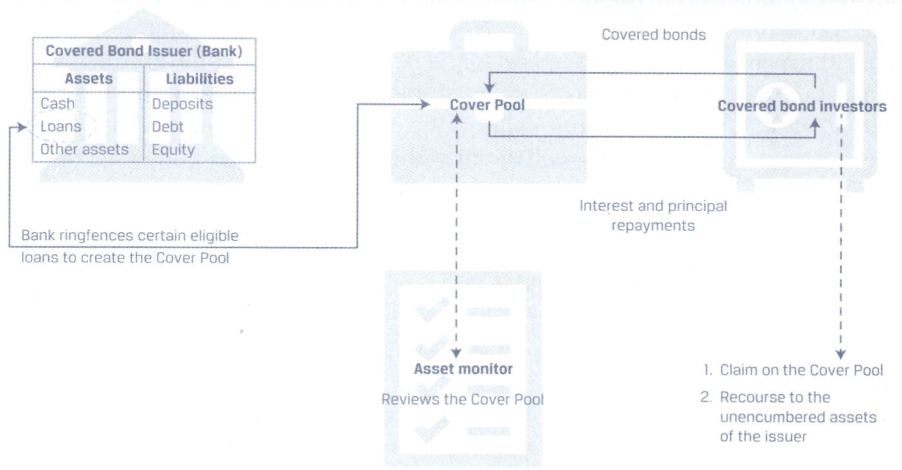

Covered bonds are similar to ABS. However, the loans remain on the issuer's balance sheet and are ringfenced into a separate cover pool. The investors in the covered bonds have dual recourse in case of bankruptcy: first on the ringfenced loans in the cover pool that underlie the covered bond transaction, and second on the unencumbered assets of the issuing institution.

Covered bond transactions financing environmental remediation projects and investments in renewable energy production and infrastructure are increasingly popular. The cover pools for these green covered bonds are largely made up of mortgages to green buildings, which can be identified through various green building certification standards.

Typical covered bond terms issued by Commercial Finance Partners are found in Exhibit 2. The mortgages underlying the transaction remain on its balance sheet.

Exhibit 2: Covered Bond Term Sheet

Issue of EUR30 Million 2.00% Prospectus Summary	
Issuer:	Commercial Finance Partners AG
Issue Size:	EUR30,000,000
Tranche Size:	EUR30,000,000
Interest Rate:	2.00%, payable annually on June 30.

Settlement Date:	[T + 3 Business Days]
Maturity Date:	[Twenty Years from Settlement Date]
The Collateral:	Security in a pool of prime, fully amortizing mortgages.
LTV Cut-off:	80%
Format:	Soft bullet

Covered bonds usually consist of one bond class per cover pool. Another important feature lies in the dynamic nature of the cover pool. The assets in the pool are monitored by a third party for performance and adherence to underwriting standards. Moreover, the covered bond issuer must replace any prepaid or non-performing assets (i.e., assets that do not generate the promised cash flows) to ensure sufficient cash flows until the maturity of the covered bond.

Covered bonds offer two additional tools to mitigate the risks of investors. First, covered bond transactions typically involve collateral underlying the transaction which exceeds the face value of the issued bonds, referred to as **overcollateralization**. For instance, Germany requires that all covered loan collateral pools are overcollateralized by at least 2% of the economic value of the outstanding covered bonds and some German issuers voluntarily overcollateralize their covered bond issues. Second, the loan to value (LTV) on the mortgages included in the transactions must meet certain standards to be eligible for inclusion in the pool. If a mortgage fails to meet the LTV criteria, it is replaced with another mortgage that meets the criteria.

Redemption regimes exist to align the covered bond's cash flows as closely as possible with the original maturity schedule in the event of default of a covered bond's financial sponsor. For example, in the case of **hard-bullet covered bonds**, if payments do not occur according to the original schedule, a bond default is triggered and bond payments are accelerated. **Soft-bullet covered bonds** delay the bond default and payment acceleration of bond cash flows until a new final maturity date, which is usually up to a year after the original maturity date. **Conditional pass-through covered bonds**, in contrast, convert to pass-through securities after the original maturity date if all bond payments have not yet been made.

Covered bonds have remained a relatively stable and reliable source of funding over time because of their dual recourse nature, strict eligibility criteria, dynamic cover pool, and redemption regimes in the event of sponsor default. As a result, covered bonds usually carry lower credit risks and offer lower yields than otherwise similar ABS.

EXAMPLE 1

Comparing Covered Bonds and ABS at Banks

"Ultimately, covered bonds and ABS are complements, not substitutes. ABS are a vehicle for packaging and selling exposure to private credit risk, with the promise of the higher returns that holding such risk entails. Covered bonds are a means for banks to raise long-term funding at a lower cost than if they issued unsecured debt. The assets underlying a covered bond simply enhance the issuer's promise to pay back the loan and are not intended to offer exposure to the underlying pool of assets. "These differences between the two instruments are reflected in their payment structure: ABS typically pay floating interest rates and pass through any early payments; covered bonds typically pay a fixed interest rate and mature on a fixed date, like any other type of bond.

"Although there may be disadvantages to banks selling the loans that they originate, there are also advantages. Securitization increases the financial system's capacity to lend in a way that covered bonds do not. By moving loans off the originating bank's balance sheet, securitization reduces the amount of capital (reserves) that the bank must hold to back its loans. As a result, banks can make more loans with the same amount of capital. Covered bonds, which keep the loans on the banks' balance sheets, do not offer this benefit."

Source: Brett W. Fawley and Luciana Juvenal, "Coming to America: Covered Bonds?" Federal Reserve Bank of St. Louis *Economic Synopses* 20 (July 2012). https://research.stlouisfed.org/publications/economic-synopses/2012/07/27/coming-to-america-covered-bonds/.

QUESTION SET

1. *Determine whether the following statement is true or false, and explain your reasoning.*

   In covered bond transactions, loans in the cover pool stay on the issuer's balance sheet.

   Solution:

   True. While covered bonds are similar to ABS, the loans composing the covered bond collateral remain on the issuer's balance sheet and are ringfenced into a separate cover pool.

2. *Determine the correct answers to fill in the blanks:* To further _______ investor risks, covered bond transactions are typically _______ to some _______ percentage of their cover pool's economic value.

   Solution:

   To further *reduce* investor risks, covered bond transactions are typically *overcollateralized* to some *greater* percentage of their cover pool's economic value.

3. Identify the covered bond type that corresponds to its correct characteristic:

   i. New form with payment lapse

   ii. Quickest triggering of defaults

   iii. New maturity date with payment lapse

A. Hard-bullet	
B. Soft-bullet	
C. Conditional pass-through	

Solution:

A. Hard-bullet	ii. Quickest triggering of defaults
B. Soft-bullet	iii. New maturity date with payment lapse
C. Conditional pass-through	i. New form with payment lapse

A. ii is correct. With hard-bullet bonds, if payments do not occur according to the original schedule, a bond default is triggered and bond payments are accelerated.

B. iii is correct. Soft-bullet bonds delay the bond default and payment acceleration of bond cash flows until a new final maturity date, which is usually up to a year after the original maturity date.

C. i is correct. Conditional pass-through bonds convert to pass-through securities after the original maturity date if all bond payments have not yet been made.

4. Which of the following statements about covered bonds is correct?

A. Covered bonds have a single recourse nature.

B. Covered bonds have lower credit risk and offer lower yields than otherwise similar ABS.

C. Covered bonds are removed from the issuer's balance sheet and are ringfenced into a separate cover pool.

Solution:

The correct answer is B. Covered bonds have remained a relatively stable and reliable source of funding over time because of their dual recourse nature, strict eligibility criteria, dynamic cover pool, and redemption regimes in the event of sponsor default. As a result, covered bonds usually carry lower credit risks and offer lower yields than otherwise similar ABS.

A is incorrect because covered bonds have a dual recourse nature. The investors in the covered bonds have dual recourse in case of bankruptcy: first on the ringfenced loans in the cover pool that underlie the covered bond transaction, and second on the unencumbered assets of the issuing institution. C is incorrect because the loans remain on the issuer's balance sheet and are ringfenced into a separate cover pool.

3 ABS STRUCTURES TO ADDRESS CREDIT RISK

☐ describe typical credit enhancement structures used in securitizations

A simple securitization transaction may involve the sale of only one class of ABS: Let us call this class Bond Class A. Returning to the Bright Wheel Automotive (BRWA) and Car Loan Trust (CLT) hypothetical example, CLT may raise EUR1,000 million by issuing 1,000,000 certificates for ABS Bond Class A with a par value of EUR1,000 per certificate. Thus, each certificate holder is entitled to 1/1,000,000 of the payments from the collateral, after payment of servicing and other administrative fees. In this case, the investors will be exposed directly to the default risk of the assets of the pool as well as other risks that impact the payments to the pool. There are different credit enhancement approaches the SPE can pursue to mitigate the impact of these risks on the investors.

These are achieved by creating securitization structures with multiple classes of ABS debt issued.

Credit Enhancement

Most securitization structures involve multiple different tranches where each of the tranches plays a different role; often, one tranche assumes risk from other tranches. Credit risk is a core risk that securitization structures seek to mitigate through **credit**

enhancement, a type of financial support that absorbs losses from defaults on the underlying loans. Three main types of **internal credit enhancements** are widely used in securitization transactions:

As introduced in Lesson 1 on covered bonds, overcollateralization involves a provision that a bond's collateral value exceeds the face value of the issued bonds. Even if there are defaults in the pool, the transaction has sufficient cushion to continue paying principal and interest payments on the bonds. Revisiting our previous example of the notes issued by Car Loan Trust, if the value of the loans and leases underlying the EUR1,000 million securitization is EUR1,200 million, there is EUR200 million overcollateralization. If the car loans perform poorly, let's say 10% default, there is still EUR1,080 million collateral to cover losses from other defaults. This additional cushion makes both the senior and subordinated tranches more attractive to potential investors.

Excess spread is the difference between the coupon on the underlying collateral and the coupon paid on the securities. For example, if the average loan in the CLT example generates 8% but the securities issued from the pool earn 6%, then the excess spread of 2% can absorb collateral shortfall or be used to build up reserves.

Subordination or **credit tranching** in the securitizationtransaction involves creating more than one bond class or tranche, and the bond classes differ in how they share any losses resulting from defaults in the collateral pool. The bond classes are classified as senior bond classes or subordinated bond classes; this structure is also referred to as a senior/subordinated structure. The subordinated bond classes are sometimes called "non-senior bond classes" or "junior bond classes." Since all investors in a securitization are paid from the same underlying cash flow pool, the tranching dictates the order of payments made to investors and the order in which losses are absorbed by the investors.

There are also **external credit enhancements**, such as financial guarantees by banks or insurance companies, letters of credit, and cash collateral accounts, which we do not cover here.

EXAMPLE 2

Overcollateralization

In November 2013, SolarCity, a predecessor organization of Tesla Energy, issued the first-ever US public solar ABS (SOCTY 2013-1) backed by USD54.425 million of bundled cash payments. This ABS allowed SolarCity to access a relatively cheap source of funding. Normal monthly payments by customers purchasing solar power from SolarCity generated the income stream used to pay ABS investors. The collateral comprised 5,033 photovoltaic (PV) systems located across 14 states, 143 counties, and 53 utility service territories. The bonds had a weighted average life of 7.05 years and a BBB+ credit rating from S&P, and they provided a 4.8% annual return to investors through 2026. The investment-grade rating meant pension funds and other regulated investment vehicles could own the ABS.

The ABS were overcollateralized versus the face value of the bonds, which meant that the ABS buyers received more collateral in case of default than the USD54.425 million purchase value. This overcollateralization was one of the reasons that the ABS received an investment-grade credit rating (BBB+ by S&P). The overcollateralization was also significant in facilitating the offering's 4.8% interest rate, which was a low cost of capital for solar developers. The 4.8% interest rate was only about 0.50% higher than the 30-year fixed-rate mortgage at that time. Lastly, the high amount of overcollateralization was required given that this was the first publicly known solar ABS, and investors needed to be comfortable in purchasing a new structured finance product.

SolarCity's 10-K for the fiscal year ending 31 December 2014 describes the assets backing these securities, as follows:

> In November 2013, we pooled and transferred qualifying solar energy systems and the associated customer contracts into a special purpose entity, or SPE, and issued $54.4 million in aggregate principal of Solar Asset-backed Notes, Series 2013-1, backed by these solar assets to certain investors. The SPE is wholly owned by us and is consolidated in our financial statements. Accordingly, we did not recognize a gain or loss on the transfer of these solar assets. As of December 31, 2014, these solar assets had a carrying value of $143.9 million and are included under solar energy systems, leased and to be leased — net, in our consolidated balance sheets.

Thus, collateral for these ABS was worth approximately 2.7 times the value of the ABS themselves, calculated as follows:

Total collateral USD143.9 million/Total value of ABS USD54.4 million

= 2.66 times.

Solar ABS securities such as this one can offer an attractive risk/reward profile for fixed-income investors. The securities are typically well-structured, with high levels of collateralization and credit enhancement, relatively low risk of default, and an attractive spread.

Credit Tranching

Subordination functions as credit protection for the more senior bond classes; that is, losses are realized by the subordinated bond classes before any losses are realized by the senior bond classes. This type of protection is also commonly referred to as a "waterfall" structure because of the cascading flow of payments between bond classes in the event of default, as shown in Exhibit 3.

Exhibit 3: Waterfall and Capital Structure

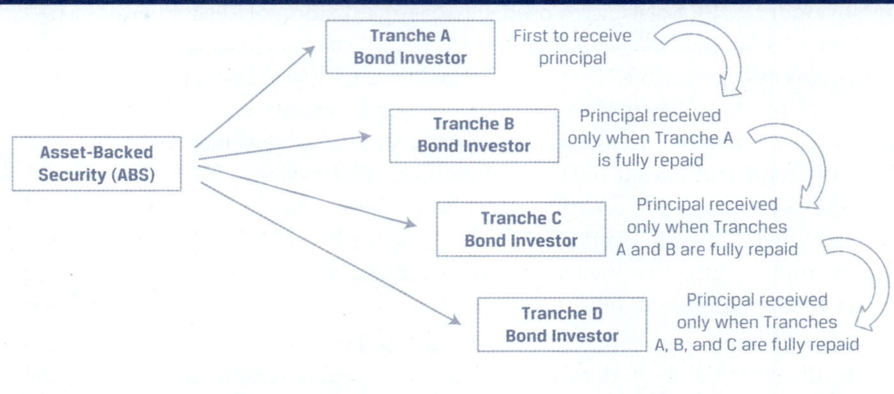

Let's revisit the BRWA securitization from an earlier module. In this case, CLT, the SPE, acquired the pool of car loans from BRWA. Assume that CLT then issues four bond classes with a total par value of EUR1,000 million: Bond Class A, the senior tranche, with a par value of EUR825 million; Bond Class B, the mezzanine tranche, with a par value of EUR100 million; Bond Class C, the junior tranche, with a par value of EUR50 million; and Bond Class D, a junior tranche that is subordinated to all the other bond classes and has a value of EUR25 million. In this structure, the four bond classes determine the capital structure of the securitization transaction.

In the securitization structure shown in Exhibit 4, there is a prioritization of payments that determines the timing of interest and principal cash flows to the different tranches. The most senior investor tranche, with the highest ranking in the capital structure, Class A, receives principal payments first, carries the lowest risk, and offers the lowest return. The mezzanine tranche, Class B, assumes a slightly higher degree of risk but offers higher returns. Class D absorbs losses first and has the highest risk, with potentially the highest yield. The lowest tranche is sometimes referred to as the "equity" tranche because of the residual nature of its claims to cash flows from the asset pool.

The four tranches carry different yields and degrees of risk, and they are impacted differently in case of default. The specific terms and conditions are outlined in Exhibit 4. This structure is typical of securitizations.

Exhibit 4: Overview of Notes Issued by Car Loan Trust – Brief Summary of Terms

	Four-Year Asset-Backed Notes Issued by CLT	
Issuer:	Car Loan Trust (CLT)	
Tranches:	Tranche A Notes	
	Face value:	EUR825 million
	Interest rate:	MRR + 0.50%
	Credit enhancement features:	Subordination of the Class B Notes, the Class C Notes, and the Class D Notes
	Tranche B Notes	
	Face value:	EUR100 million
	Interest rate:	MRR + 1.50%
	Credit enhancement features:	Subordination of the Class C Notes and the Class D Notes
	Tranche C Notes	
	Face value:	EUR50 million
	Interest rate:	MRR + 2.50%
	Credit enhancement features:	Subordination of the Class D Notes
	Tranche D Notes	
	Face value:	EUR25 million
	Interest rate:	Variable (higher spread than Tranche C)
	Credit enhancement features:	None
Status and Ranking of Payments:	The Class A Notes are senior to the Class B, C, & D Notes. The Class B Notes are senior to the Class C & D Notes and junior to the Class A Notes. The Class C Notes are senior to the Class D Notes and junior to the Class A & B Notes. The Class D Notes are junior to the Class A, B, & C Notes.	

Four-Year Asset-Backed Notes Issued by CLT	
Interest Payment:	Monthly commencing 30 days from [Settlement Date] to be paid each month, with final payment on [Maturity Date]
Seniority:	The Notes are secured obligations of CLT
Business Days:	Frankfurt

This senior/subordinated structure is an example of **credit tranching**. The most junior tranche, Class D, will absorb all losses up to EUR25 million. Should the credit losses exceed that threshold, Bond Class C will absorb all losses beyond the first EUR25 million, up to an additional EUR50 million. Consequently, Bond Class B will absorb losses beyond EUR75 million and up to an additional EUR100 million. Thus, if defaults in the CLT pool do not exceed EUR175 million, Bond Class A will be fully repaid its EUR825 million.

For example, if the total loss on the collateral in CLT is EUR70 million, then Class D Notes absorb the first EUR25 million of losses and are wiped out, and the Class D investors lose their investment. Then Bond Class C absorbs an additional EUR45 million of losses, and the Class C investors are repaid only the remaining EUR5 million. However, both Bond Class A and B continue to receive payments from the pool as agreed: They do not realize any loss in this scenario. Clearly, Bond Class A realizes a loss only if the total loss on the collateral exceeds EUR175 million and all the more junior tranches are wiped out.

This waterfall structure redistributes the credit risk associated with the collateral. The creation of a set of bond classes allows investors to choose the level of risk that they prefer to bear and receive a return accordingly. Moreover, by adjusting the features of the various tranches, investors can pick an appropriate combination of maturity, risk, and return characteristics.

EXAMPLE 3

Waterfall Calculation for ABS of Car Loan Trust

Similarly, if market reference rate (MRR) is 4.0%, an investor who purchased the following ABS issued by CLT would receive the following interest payments in the order shown.

Investor's Initial CLT ABS Purchases		Interest Paid If No Defaults in the CLT Pool	Interest Paid If Defaults in the CLT Pool Are EUR20 Million	Interest Paid If Defaults in the CLT Pool Are EUR90 Million
Class A Notes	EURC million			
Class B Notes	EUR3 million	EUR165 thousand	EUR165 thousand	EUR140 thousand
Class C Notes	EUR2 million	EUR130 thousand	EUR130 thousand	EUR0 thousand
Class D Notes	EUR0 million			
Total	EUR5 million	EUR295 thousand	EUR295 thousand	EUR140 thousand

Risk ratings are assigned to each bond class created in the securitization, and these ratings depend on both the quality of the collateral and the seniority of the class. The risk ratings reflect the credit risk of the pool of securitized loans or receivables as well as the priority of how they absorb losses. In our example, the two subordinated classes would be considered risker than the senior class and would carry a much higher credit spread, with the Class D bonds carrying a higher spread than the Class C bonds. Depending on the structure of the securitization, each bond class in the transaction receives a risk rating that reflects its credit risk, and some of the bond classes may have a better credit rating than the company that is seeking to raise funds because of collateralization or credit enhancement.

QUESTION SET

1. *Determine the correct answers to complete the following sentences:*

   It is common for securitizations to include a form of internal credit enhancement called ______________, also referred to as ______________. In such a structure, there is more than one bond class, and the bond classes differ as to how they will share any losses resulting from defaults of the borrowers whose loans are in the collateral.

   Solution:

   It is common for securitizations to include a form of internal credit enhancement called subordination, also referred to as credit tranching. In such a structure, there is more than one bond class, and the bond classes differ as to how they will share any losses resulting from defaults of the borrowers whose loans are in the collateral.

For Questions 2 and 3, please refer to the additional information below regarding the ABS issued by Ahbaling Trust.

Bond Class	Par Value (SGD millions)	Interest Rate	When Principal Is Repaid If No Prepayments in the Pool	Credit Enhancement Features
A (senior)	280	MRR + 1.0%	One year, per ABS terms	Subordination of the Class B and the Class C Notes
B (subordinated)	60	MRR + 2.0%	Two years, per ABS terms	Subordination of the Class C Notes
C (subordinated)	60	MRR + 4.0%	Three years, per ABS terms	None
Total	400			

2. Calculate the value for each of the three bond classes *if* SGD140 million of the securitized receivables backing the ABS default.

   Solution:

Bond Class	Initial Value (SGD millions)	After Default (SGD millions)
A (senior)	280	260
B (subordinated)	60	0
C (subordinated)	60	0

   The rules for the distribution of losses are as follows. All losses on the collateral are absorbed by Bond Class C before any losses are realized by Bond Class B and then Bond Class A. Consequently, if the losses on the collateral are SGD140 million, then the entire SGD60 million par value of Bond Class C is lost, as is the entire SGD60 million par value of Bond Class B. Bond Class A loses SGD20 million of its original SGD280 million par value.

3. Identify the new maturity dates for the three bond classes if economic conditions worsen, driving up interest rates in year three.

Solution:

Bond Class	When Principal Is Repaid If No Prepayments in the ABS Pool	When Principal Is Repaid If Interest Rates Increase, Causing Some Borrowers to Slow Their Payments
A (senior)	One year, per ABS terms	One year, per ABS terms
B (subordinated)	Two years, per ABS terms	Two years, per ABS terms
C (subordinated)	Three years, per ABS terms	Potentially more than three years

If an increase in interest rates results in financial distress for borrowers, some of them may slow down the speed of their payments. Since this takes place in year three, Class A and Class B bondholders already would have been repaid their principal. Only Class C bondholders would be impacted in this instance.

4. *Determine the correct answers to complete the following sentences:*

There are three main types of internal credit enhancements that are widely used in securitization transactions. _______________ is a provision that the collateral underlying the transaction is larger than the face value of the issued bonds, providing a cushion for continued payments even with defaults in the pool. Excess spread is the difference between the coupon on the underlying collateral and the coupon paid on the securities, which can absorb collateral shortfall or build up reserves. With _______________ or _______________, the securitization transaction involves creating more than one bond class or tranche, and the bond classes differ in how they share any losses resulting from defaults in the collateral pool. The ___________ determines the order of payments made to investors and the order losses are absorbed by the investors.

Solution:

There are three main types of internal credit enhancements that are widely used in securitization transactions. Overcollateralization is a provision that the collateral underlying the transaction is larger than the face value of the issued bonds, providing a cushion for continued payments even with defaults in the pool. Excess spread is the difference between the coupon on the underlying collateral and the coupon paid on the securities, which can absorb collateral shortfall or build up reserves. With subordination or credit tranching, the securitization transaction involves creating more than one bond class or tranche, and the bond classes differ in how they share any losses resulting from defaults in the collateral pool. The tranching determines the order of payments made to investors, and the order losses are absorbed by the investors.

5. Which of the following statements about credit tranching is *incorrect*?

   A. The waterfall structure redistributes the credit risk associated with the underlying collateral.

   B. Some of the bond classes may have a better credit rating than the company that is seeking to raise funds.

C. Risk ratings are based on the market risk of the pool of securitized loans or receivables as well as the priority of how they absorb losses.

Solution:

The correct answer is C. Risk ratings are based on the credit risk (not market risk) of the pool of securitized loans or receivables as well as the priority of how they absorb losses.

A is incorrect because it is a correct statement. The waterfall structure redistributes the credit risk associated with the collateral. The creation of a set of bond classes allows investors to choose the level of risk that they prefer to bear and receive return accordingly. B is incorrect because it is a correct statement. Each bond class in the transaction receives a risk rating that reflects its credit risk, and some of the bond classes may exhibit a better credit rating than the company that is seeking to raise funds because of collateralization or credit enhancement.

NON-MORTGAGE ASSET-BACKED SECURITIES 4

☐ describe types and characteristics of non-mortgage asset-backed securities, including the cash flows and risks of each type

As we have seen earlier, non-mortgage assets, such as auto loans, have been used as collateral in securitization. Securitizations can also involve credit card receivables, personal loans, receivables, and commercial loans.

ABS can be categorized whether the collateral is amortizing or non-amortizing. Traditional residential mortgages and auto loans are examples of amortizing loans, where the periodic payments include both principal and interest. In amortizing ABS, as the loans are paid off, the investors receive the scheduled principal repayments, and any prepayments will be distributed to the bond classes based on the payment rule. Over time as loans mature, the number of loans and their total value shrinks.

In contrast, **non-amortizing loans**, such as credit card debt, do not involve scheduled principal repayments. For a non-amortizing collateral pool, the situation is different. Over time, some of these loans will be repaid before the stated maturity date of the ABS. If the loans are paid off during the **lockout or revolving period**, then the principal repaid is reinvested to acquire additional loans with a principal equal to the principal repaid. This reinvestment during the lockout period replenishes the collateral pool. At the end of the lockout period, the amortization period starts, and any principal that is repaid will not be reinvested in new loans but will be distributed to the ABS holders.

A large variety of assets can be securitized as non-mortgage ABS. This module focuses on a credit card receivable ABS and a residential solar ABS.

Credit Card Receivable ABS

Credit cards, issued by banks, credit card companies, retailers, and travel and entertainment companies, provide a convenient way to pay and extend credit. When a purchase is made on a credit card, the issuer of the credit card (the lender) extends credit to the cardholder (the borrower). The cardholder agrees to repay the amount borrowed plus any applicable finance charges. From the lender's perspective, the borrowed amount is a receivable. These receivables can be pooled and used as the underlying collateral for credit card receivable ABS.

A term sheet for a typical credit card ABS can be found in Exhibit 5. In this particular securitization, Commercial Finance Partners AG (CFP), a European bank, pools credit card receivables denominated in CHF. Credit card issuers, such as CFP, benefit from credit card securitization. First, it removes the credit card receivables from their balance sheet, which provides both capital efficiency and reduces the cost of funding. Second, it reduces the cost of default risk from credit card debt. Third, it generates additional fee income.

This particular ABS has a 3-year revolving period when the pool uses balance repayments to purchase new credit card receivables, and this is followed by a 6-year amortization period.

Exhibit 5: Credit Card ABS Term Sheet Summary

Nine-Year Credit Card-Backed Notes Issued by Commercial Finance Partners AG Prospectus Summary

Issuer:	Commercial Finance Partners AG	
Issue Size:	CHF900,000,000	
Maturity Date:	[Nine Years from Settlement Date]	
Revolving Period	[Starts on the Settlement Date and Ends Three Years from Settlement Date]	
Amortization Period:	[Starts Three Years and One Business Day After the Settlement Date and Ends Nine Years from Settlement Date]	
The Collateral:	Portfolio comprises credit card loan receivables originated in, and to individuals in, Switzerland. Aggregate receivables are CHF925 million, with an average principal balance of CHF2,300, with a weighted average interest rate of 12%.	
Tranches	Tranche A Notes	
	Face value:	EUR400 million
	Interest rate:	7.00%
	Credit enhancement features:	Subordination of the Class B, C, & D Notes
	Tranche B Notes	
	Face value:	EUR300 million
	Interest rate:	8.00%
	Credit enhancement features:	Subordination of the Class C & D Notes
	Tranche C Notes	
	Face value:	EUR150 million
	Interest rate:	10.50%
	Credit enhancement features:	Subordination of the Class D Notes
	Tranche D Notes	
	Face value:	EUR50 million
	Interest rate:	Variable

Nine-Year Credit Card-Backed Notes Issued by Commercial Finance Partners AG Prospectus Summary	
	Credit enhancement features: None
Interest Payment:	Monthly commencing 30 days from [Settlement Date] to be paid each month, with final payment on [Maturity Date]

For a pool of credit card receivables, the cash flows consist of finance charges collected, fees, and principal repayments. Finance charges collected are the periodic interest rate the lender charges the borrower on the unpaid balance on the credit card. That interest rate may be fixed or floating. Typically, the floating rate is capped: There is an upper limit of how much the lender can charge the borrower. The fees the lender collects from the borrower include late payment fees and any annual membership fees.

As credit cards are non-amortizing loans, during the revolving period––in this case the first 3 years of the structure––the security holders receive only payments from the finance charges and fees the lender collects. The impact of the revolving period and the amortization period on the cash flows that noteholders receive from ABS that securitizes receivables are depicted in Exhibit 6.

Exhibit 6: Cash Flows from a Credit Card ABS

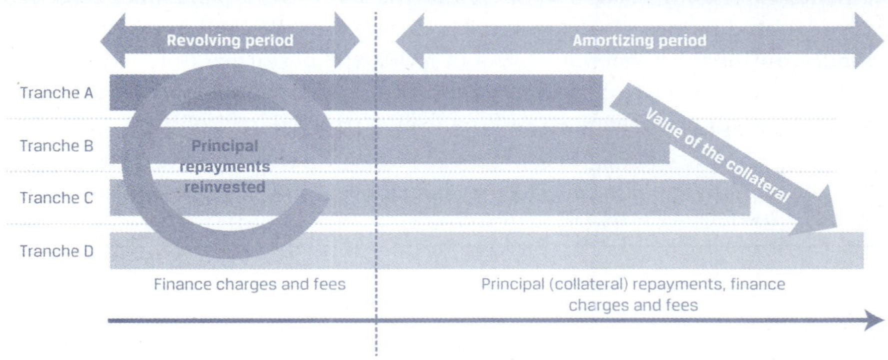

Some provisions in credit card receivable ABS may require early principal amortization if specific events occur. Such provisions are referred to as early amortization or **rapid amortization provisions** and are included to safeguard the credit quality of the issue, particularly during the revolving period. If the repayments during the revolving periods are not sufficient to replenish the pool, or if the defaults significantly alter the pool, the economics of the transaction may no longer be there. This triggers a rapid amortization clause that accelerates and alters principal cash flows. Noteholders will receive their investments earlier, which they can then reallocate to other investments offering more attractive risk/return characteristics. These rapid amortization clauses can be particularly beneficial to investors during periods when there are growing uncertainties about the macroeconomic environment.

Moreover, credit card ABS typically combine various sources of credit enhancements to support the various tranches. ABS structures normally provide credit enhancements through subordination. For instance, in the CFP example, there are four tranches in addition to the overcollateralization (CHF25 million), the rapid amortization provision, and other tools to support investor appetite for an appropriate risk/

return trade-off. In this particular case, losses from the pool have to exceed CHF75 million, or 8.33% of the face value of the ABS issue, before holders of the Tranche C Notes are impacted by the collateral losses.

EXAMPLE 4

Contrasting Non-Mortgage ABS: Credit Card Receivable ABS vs. Auto Loan ABS

For credit card receivable ABS, the collateral is a pool of non-amortizing loans. During the lockout period, the cash proceeds from principal repayments are reinvested in additional credit card receivables. During this period, there is no prepayment risk and potential default risk is generally limited or is absorbed by credit enhancements. When the lockout period is over, principal repayments are used to pay off the outstanding principal on the ABS.

For auto loan-backed securities, the collateral is a pool of amortizing loans and occasionally leases. Security holders receive regular principal repayments. As a result, the outstanding principal balance declines over time. Additionally, the investors in the pool are exposed to both prepayment and default risk from the inception of the pool.

US credit card ABS ratings performed strongly through both the Global Financial Crisis of 2008–09 (GFC) and the COVID-19 pandemic: Less than 2% of related ratings were downgraded during the GFC, and none were downgraded during the pandemic's onset in 2020. ABS performance is supported by the consistent quality of securitized assets and structural features that protect against weaker performance resulting from a stressed environment.

Source: Fitch Ratings, "US Auto, Credit Card ABS Performed Well Through Crises," Fitch Wire (7 April 2021). https://www.fitchratings.com/research/structured-finance/us-auto-credit-card-abs-performed-well-through-crises-07-04-2021.

Solar ABS

With an increasing number of homeowners installing solar energy systems and other home energy efficiency improvements, many specialty finance companies have begun to offer specialized home improvement financing options: solar loans or solar leases. Solar loans allow consumers to borrow the cost of purchasing and the system from an installer. Solar leases involve renting the solar equipment directly from a solar company.

Switching to solar energy not only improves environmental sustainability, but it also reduces overall household utility and electricity expenses. The economics are straightforward: The utility cost savings from switching to solar energy are expected to typically exceed the costs of investing in solar energy systems. Institutional investors have become interested in purchasing solar ABS as these structures offer the opportunity to contribute to sustainability while generating attractive risk-adjusted yields.

Al-Shims Enterprises decides to securitize its solar energy systems loans via its financing subsidiary using a solar ABS. The solar ABS issues EUR300 million notes secured by 10,000 sustainable, residential, home improvement loans with a face value of EUR320 million. The average loan balance of the home improvement loans is EUR32,500, paying a weighted average rate of 7.5% with a weighted average maturity of 17 years. All loans are amortizing. The net proceeds of the offering will be allocated, in whole or in part, to the purchase and installation of residential solar energy systems, which are eligible green projects.

From Al-Shims' perspective, the securitization transaction removes receivables from its balance sheet, increases capital efficiency, and generates fee income.

An additional feature of the solar ABS transaction is that the proceeds are directed to financing green or environmentally friendly projects. Because solar loans facilitate environmentally sustainable benefits through the installation of a renewable and efficient energy source, they may qualify as green bonds. For institutional investors looking for environmental, social, and governance (ESG) or climate finance investment alternatives, solar ABS can offer an attractive investment alternative.

The precise legal structure of the solar ABS transaction and its collateral depend on the jurisdiction. Normally, ABS are collateralized by the underlying debt: mortgages, loans, or receivables. The loans can be further collateralized by a lien pledged on the installed systems, on the property itself, or both. When the solar energy system loans are structured as residential home improvement loans, the solar ABS effectively securitizes a subordinated (junior) mortgage on the property.

That is why solar ABS investors look for this type of debt: Usually, solar loan borrowers are prime borrowers that own their homes and have good payment records. Additionally, solar ABS investors are typically protected through overcollateralization, subordination, and excess spreads. Collectively, these features further reduce the default risk in these securitizations.

Finally, many solar ABS contain a **pre-funding period**, which allows the trust to acquire during a certain period of time after the close of the transaction additional qualifying transactions that meet certain eligibility criteria.

EXAMPLE 5

Potential Investment Strengths of Solar ABS

Solar ABS can offer an attractive risk/reward profile for fixed income investors. The securities are typically well-structured, with high levels of collateralization and credit enhancement, relatively low risk of default, and an attractive spread. Solar ABS are collateralized by the underlying PV systems, with credit enhancement consisting of (i) overcollateralization, (ii) subordinate bonds, (iii) general reserve account, (iv) inverter replacement reserve account, and (v) excess spread. Additionally, to date, all solar ABS transactions through 2019 have been comprised of pools of consumers with weighted-average FICO consumer credit scores above 700.[a]

Solar lease or loan payments often displace a consumer's former energy payment thus losses in this sector will likely remain low. Defaulting on a solar loan is unlikely to reduce a consumer's overall payment obligation as they need to purchase energy in some form, and defaulting on a solar loan could revert them to paying higher monthly energy expenses. While this asset class has not been through a full credit cycle (the first solar ABS was issued in November 2013 by SolarCity), a combination of a higher credit quality consumer and the desire for a budget-saving power source may reduce the risk of default/loss on the underlying loan/lease payment.[a]

With a focus on combatting climate change, consumers and utilities are continuing to shift away from traditional fossil fuels and are moving towards renewable energy sources such as solar, wind, and geothermal. Unlike coal, petroleum, and other fossil fuels, solar power contributes to a more sustainable environment as a clean, carbon-free form of green energy. Solar ABS directly supports a sustainable future by offering solar energy providers a term funding source. Solar loan/lease payments primarily displace the homeowner's former energy bill, with the average system generally sized to provide more than 90% of the home's current usage.[a]

Solar ABS may offer opportunities for institutions to accomplish dual investment goals of furthering sustainability as part of their ESG initiatives and generating incremental yield.[b]

[a] *Institutional Investor, "Solar ABS:* A Growing Sector Offered Sunny Side Up" (17 September 2019). https://www.institutionalinvestor.com/article/b1h4mybwwjy5p7/Solar-ABS-A-Growing-Sector-Offered-Sunny-Side-Up.

[b] *Tim Zawacki, "Solar Securitizations Present Yield, ESG Play for Institutional Investors," S&P Global Market Intelligence (16 December 2020).https:*//www.spglobal.com/marketintelligence/en/news-insights/latest-news-headlines/solar-securitizations-present-yield-esg-play-for-institutional-investors-61756315.

QUESTION SET

1. *Determine the correct answers to fill in the blanks:* During the ___________ of a credit card receivable ABS, the security holders receive only ________________________________.

   Solution:

   During the revolving period of a credit card receivable ABS, the *security holders* receive only *payments from the finance charges and fees the lender collects.*

2. Describe institutional investor motivations for investing in solar ABS.

   Solution:

   Institutional investors have become interested in purchasing solar ABS as these structures offer the opportunity to contribute to sustainability while generating attractive risk-adjusted yields. Solar loans have clear environmentally sustainable benefits through the installation of renewable energy and energy efficiency, which can make them appropriate for investors seeking ESG or climate finance investment alternatives.

3. Explain the potential investment advantage from including a pre-funding period into the structure of a solar ABS.

   Solution:

   A Solar ABS that includes a pre-funding period allows its underlying trust to acquire during a certain period of time after the close of the transaction additional qualifying transactions that meet certain eligibility criteria for sustainable investment. This enhances the overall environmental benefit. In addition, there is a direct investor benefit due to diversification benefits from a broader pool.

4. Describe a similarity of solar ABS and green covered bonds.

   Solution:

   Both types of securities are popular means of financing environmental investments in infrastructure. Solar ABS have clear environmentally sustainable benefits through the installation of renewable energy and energy efficiency. The cover pool for green covered bonds are largely made up of mortgages to green buildings, identified through various green building certification standards.

5. Which of the following statements about credit card securitization is correct?

   A. Additional fee income is generated for the issuer.

   B. The credit card receivables are kept on the issuer's balance sheet.

   C. The cost of default risk from credit card debt to the issuer increases.

   Solution:

   The correct answer is A. Credit card securitization generates additional fee income for the issuer. B is incorrect because the credit card receivables are removed from the issuer's balance sheet, which provides both capital efficiency and reduces the cost of funding. C is incorrect because the cost of default risk from credit card debt is reduced.

COLLATERALIZED DEBT OBLIGATIONS 5

☐ describe collateralized debt obligations, including their cash flows and risks

Collateralized debt obligations (CDOs) issue securities backed by a diversified pool of one or more debt obligations. CDOs can be backed by a broad range of debt. CDOs backed by corporate and emerging market bonds are **collateralized bond obligations (CBOs)**; those backed by leveraged bank loans are **collateralized loan obligations (CLOs)**; those backed by other CDOs are structured finance CDOs; and those backed by a portfolio of credit default swaps for other structured securities are synthetic CDOs. The prevailing CDO structure is the CLO structure, where the collateral pool is made up of leveraged bank loans.

Exhibit 7 summarizes features of CDOs, covered bonds, mortgage-backed securities (MBS), and non-mortgage ABS:

Exhibit 7: Overview of CDOs and Other Securitized Products

	Covered Bonds	CDO	MBS	Non-Mortgage ABS
Collateral	Commercial or residential mortgages, or public sector assets	Leveraged bank loans (CLOs)	Commercial and residential mortgage loans	Credit card receivables (non-amortizing) and Solar lease/loan payments
Impact on Issuer Balance Sheet	Collateral remains on the balance sheet and ringfenced into a separate cover pool	Collateral removed from balance sheet	Collateral removed from balance sheet	Collateral removed from balance sheet
Number of Bond Classes	One bond class with its associated default exposure in its cover pool	Typically several	Typically several	Typically several

	Covered Bonds	CDO	MBS	Non-Mortgage ABS
Collateral Pool	Unstable with ongoing collateral management	Unstable with ongoing collateral management	Stable	Unstable with ongoing collateral management; a pre-funding period is used by solar ABS post-transaction
Recourse	Dual recourse nature: first on the ringfenced loans in the cover pool and second on the unencumbered assets of the issuing institution	Single recourse nature	Single recourse nature	Single recourse nature

Similar to the ABS structures discussed earlier, the CDO structures redistribute the cash flows the underlying collateral pool generates and redistribute them to the tranches. For the majority of CDOs, the collateral pools are not static, so there is a need for a **collateral manager** that buys and sells debt obligations for and from the CDO's collateral pool to generate sufficient cash flows to meet the obligations to the CDO bondholders. Otherwise, the steps and the structure of the securitization process are largely the same. The structure of a generic CDO transaction is shown in Exhibit 8.

Exhibit 8: The Structure of a Generic CDO Transaction

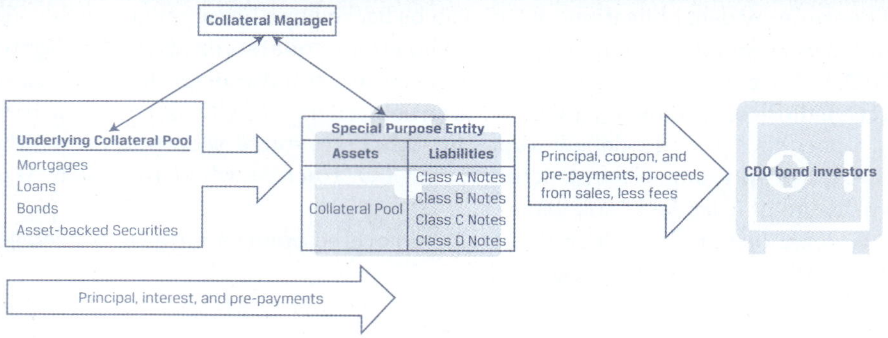

The proceeds to pay the CDO bond classes can come from interest payments from collateral assets, maturing of collateral assets, and sale of collateral assets. The basic economics of these CDO transactions is to ensure that the return on the collateral pool is higher than the funding costs, the aggregate cost of the bond classes issued to finance the transaction. Holders of senior and mezzanine bonds earn fixed returns, while the equity tranche holders and the CDO manager earn more equity-like returns. Essentially, a CDO is a leveraged transaction, where equity tranche holders use borrowed funds (the bond classes issued) to generate a return above the funding cost.

The CDO market has changed significantly since the 2003–2007 period. The collateral today is primarily leveraged bank loans (i.e., CLOs), while during the 2003–2007 period, it consisted of a wide range of products, including different types of real estate debt and commercial mortgage-backed securities (CMBS). While subsequent regulatory and legal changes made arranging and investing in CDOs less attractive, the underlying securitization framework remains similar today. It can be best explored through CLOs, collateralized by senior secured bank loans creating a diversified portfolio of company loans.

Generic CLO Structure

The capital structure of a generic CLO transaction is shown in Exhibit 9. The funds to purchase the collateral assets for a CLO are obtained from the issuance of debt obligations. These tranches include senior, mezzanine, and subordinated/junior/equity tranches.

Investors in senior or mezzanine bond classes earn a potentially higher yield than comparable corporate bonds offer, or they gain exposure to debt products that they may not otherwise be able to acquire. Investors in equity tranches take on equity-like risks with the potential to earn returns comparable to equities. Moreover, the residual tranche plays a key role in whether a CLO is viable or not; the CLO structure has to offer competitive returns for this tranche.

CLOs come in multiple flavors. These are the most common:

- Cash Flow CLOs, where the cash flows from interest payments and principal repayments are redistributed across the tranches. This is the most common CLO structure.
- Market Value CLOs, where the value accruing to the tranches depends on the market value of the portfolio.
- Synthetic CLOs, where the collateral pool is created synthetically through credit derivatives.

Exhibit 9: The Capital Structure of a Generic CLO Transaction

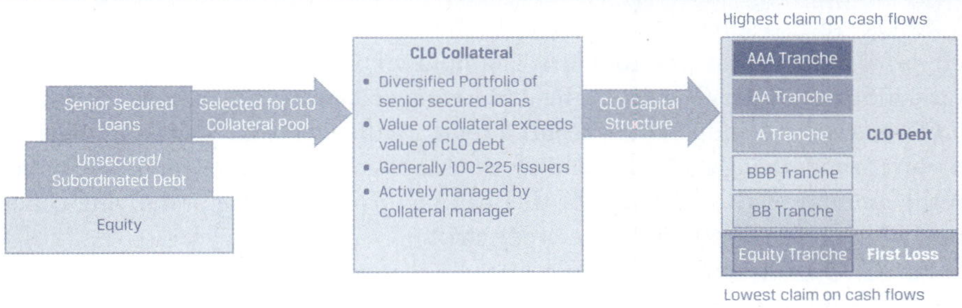

The ability of the manager to make the interest payments and principal repayments depends on collateral performance. The collateral manager must continually meet various performance tests and collateral limits for the underlying collateral. If the manager fails pre-specified tests, a provision is triggered that requires the payoff of the principal to the senior bond class until the tests are met. This process effectively deleverages the CLO because the cheapest funding source for the CLO, the senior bond class, is reduced.

A typical feature of CLO transactions is that the collateral portfolio is not finalized until after the transaction closes. While the collateral manager acquires most of the loans before the transaction closes, there is a subsequent ramp-up period when additional assets are added to the collateral pool. After this period, the manager may replace loans in the portfolio as long as the new asset meets the portfolio selection criteria. The final phase of the CLO lifecycle is when the underlying loans mature and the collateral manager uses the proceeds to pay off the tranches according to the order of payments. Recourse is typically limited to the collateral pool, with minimal recourse to the original issuers.

The cash flow waterfall, in connection with performance-based tests, provides varying degrees of protection to the CLO's debt tranches. The most senior and highest-rated AAA tranche has the lowest yield but enjoys the highest claim on the cash flow distributions and is the most loss-remote. Mezzanine tranches pay higher coupons but are more exposed to loss and have lower ratings. The most junior tranche, equity, is the riskiest, is not rated, and does not have a set coupon. Instead, the equity tranche represents a claim on all excess cash flows once the obligations for each debt tranche have been met.

CLOs face a series of coverage tests to help ensure the cash flows generated by the underlying bank loan collateral meet the distribution obligations in the various CLO tranches. One such test is an overcollateralization test, which helps to keep the principal value of a CLO's underlying bank loan pool above the total principal value of the notes issued by the various CLO debt tranches as long as the CLO debt remains outstanding. If the principal value declines below the overcollateralization test trigger value, cash will be diverted away from equity and junior CLO debt tranches toward senior debt tranche investors.

Consider a hypothetical CLO created with USD700 million of principal promised to the owners of its various debt tranches. To meet this USD700 million obligation, investors and rating agencies may require that the CLO manager use the capital raised from the CLO's debt and equity issuance to purchase USD840 million of bank loans. This would result in an overcollateralization ratio of 1.20.

Each CLO debt tranche has its own targeted overcollateralization ratio. The overcollateralization ratios for each tranche act as covenants and, when tripped, redirect cash flows to purchase additional bank loan collateral or repay the senior-most CLO debt tranche.

CLOs are also subject to a variety of other tests that act in concert in an effort to help protect debt investors from loss. Examples of these tests include a measurement of the industry diversification in the underlying collateral pool of bank loans and the CLO's exposure to non-senior secured loans. Other tests consider the diversity of borrowers underlying each CLO and set single obligor limits. There are also limitations on the amount of CCC-rated debt that can be included in the underlying collateral pool, which help contain negative credit drift.

For CLO transactions, the role of the collateral manager is key. The skill the manager displays in selecting, managing, and exchanging assets in the pool directly impacts the performance of the CLO. In a way, the collateral manager acts as an active bond portfolio manager by determining the asset mix and the risk and exposures in the collateral pool.

EXAMPLE 6

CLOs and Systematic Risk

Institutional investors, such as banks, insurance companies, hedge funds, mutual funds, and pension plans, are the primary buyers in the CLO market. Each of these investors targets different CLO tranches. Due to regulations, many banks almost exclusively buy the AAA-rated tranche. Other investors, such as hedge funds and endowments, may be more speculative and thus take more risk to earn higher returns. Current CLO structures are typically simpler than the CDO structures that played a pivotal role in the GFC. Structured finance CDOs, which are made up of other CDOs, are no longer common, and even synthetic CLOs that use derivatives are less prevalent.

After the GFC, the underlying asset quality of CLOs has received more scrutiny than was previously common. This is a reflection of the need to understand the unique characteristics of the complex asset pool in a CLO.

QUESTION SET

1. Describe how a CDO is distinguished from a CMO by the function of the CDO's collateral manager.

   Solution:

   While CDOs are similar to CMOs in that both issue securities backed by a diversified pool of one or more debt obligations, CDO collateral pools usually are not static. Their volatility generates a need for a collateral managerthat buys and sells debt obligations for and from the CDO's collateral pool to generate sufficient cash flows to meet the obligations to the CDO bondholders.

2. Identify the CLO type that corresponds to its correct characteristic:

   i. Relies on OTC contracts

   ii. Most common CLO structure

   iii. Sizes of tranches have greatest variability

A. Cash flow CLO	
B. Market value CLO	
C. Synthetic CLO	

Solution:

A. Cash flow CLO	ii. Most common CLO structure
B. Market value CLO	iii. Sizes of tranches have greatest variability
C. Synthetic CLO	i. Relies on OTC contracts

A. ii is correct. Cash flow CLOs are the most common CLO structure.

B. iii. is correct. For market value CLOs, the value accruing to the tranches depends on the market value of the portfolio and thus cannot be stated with certainty.

C. i is correct. The collateral pool of synthetic CLOs are created synthetically through credit derivatives, which are financial contracts traded OTC.

3. Explain why a CDO's equity tranche holders are *most likely* to earn the highest returns when the CDO works as designed.

   Solution:

   The basic economics of CDO transactions is to ensure the return on the collateral pool is higher than the funding costs, the aggregate cost of the bond classes issued to finance the transaction. Holders of senior and mezzanine tranches earn fixed returns, while the equity tranche holders and the CDO manager earn more equity-like returns. The equity tranche represents a claim on all excess cash flows once the obligations for each debt tranche have been met, so it is the riskiest tranche and should earn the highest return. Essentially, a CDO is a leveraged transaction, where equity tranche holders use borrowed funds (the bond classes issued) to generate a return above the funding cost.

4. Describe the effect of collateral performance test failure on a CLO's financial structure.

Solution:

In making interest and principal payments, a CLO collateral manager must continually meet various performance tests and collateral limits for the underlying collateral. Upon a test failure, a provision is triggered requiring payoff of the principal to the senior bond class until the tests are met. This effectively deleverages the CLO because the cheapest funding source for the CLO, the senior bond class, is reduced.

5. In certain CLOs, the motivation is to capture a spread between the potential collateral return and the funding cost. An additional risk of this type of securitization relative to an investment in an asset-backed security is:

   A. the default risk on the collateral assets.

   B. the risk that the CLO manager will fail to earn a return sufficient to pay off the investors in the senior and the mezzanine tranches.

   C. the risk due to the mismatch between the collateral making fixed-rate payments and the bond classes making floating-rate payments.

Solution:

B is correct. In addition to the risks associated with investments in ABS, such as the default risk on the collateral assets (answer A) and the risk due to the potential mismatch between the collateral making fixed-rate payments and the bond classes making floating-rate payments (answer C), investors in CLOs face the risk that the CLO manager will fail to earn a return sufficient to pay off the investors in the senior and the mezzanine tranches. With an ABS, the cash flows from the collateral are used to pay off the holders of the bond classes without the active management of the collateral—that is, without a manager altering the composition of the debt obligations in the pool that is backing the securitization. In contrast, in a CLO, the manager buys and sells debt obligations with the dual purpose of not only paying off the holders of the bond classes but also generating an attractive/competitive return for the equity tranche and for the manager.

6. Which of the following statements about collateralized loan obligations (CLOs) is *incorrect*?

   A. Recourse is limited to the collateral pool, with minimal recourse to the original issuers.

   B. Investors in senior or mezzanine bond classes typically earn a lower yield than comparable corporate bonds.

   C. After the ramp-up period, the collateral manager may replace loans in the portfolio as long as the new asset meets the portfolio selection criteria.

Solution:

The correct answer is B. Investors in senior or mezzanine bond classes earn a potentially *higher* yield than comparable corporate bonds offer. A is incorrect because it is a correct statement. Recourse is limited to the collateral pool, with minimal recourse to the original issuers. C is incorrect because it is a correct statement. The collateral manager acquires most of the loans before the transaction closes. In the subsequent ramp-up period, additional assets are added to the collateral pool. After this ramp-up period, the manager may replace loans in the portfolio as long as the new asset meets the portfolio selection criteria.

PRACTICE PROBLEMS

1. Which of the following statements regarding securitized products is correct?

   A. Credit tranching offers credit protection for the equity tranche in a securitization.

   B. Pass-through securities are the simplest securitized structure and involve issuers retaining the underlying assets.

   C. In a true securitization, the underlying pool of assets is removed from the balance sheet and transferred into an independent legal entity that issues securities backed by these assets.

2. Upon a bankruptcy affecting a covered bond, the first available safeguards to protect against potential losses are the:

   A. ringfenced loans.

   B. unencumbered assets of the issuer.

   C. assets added by the collateral manager during ramp-up.

3. Consider the following potential reasons to explain why covered bonds usually carry lower credit risks and offer lower yields than otherwise similar ABS:

   1. Eligibility criteria
   2. Dynamic cover pool
   3. Redemption regime in event of sponsor default

   Which of the following factors accurately explain(s) this result?

   A. Reason 1 only

   B. Reasons 1 and 2 only

   C. Reasons 1, 2, and 3

4. Select the internal credit enhancement that seeks to improve the overall credit quality of a risky pool of securitized loans.

   A. Letters of credit

   B. Overcollateralization

   C. Cash collateral accounts

5. For an issuer, which of the following outcomes is *most likely* afteroffering a credit card ABS?

   A. Increased cost of funding

   B. Increased income from fees

   C. Increased cost of default risk

6. An action affecting the cash flow received by a credit card ABS holder during its

revolving period is the:

A. early repayment of principal by cardholders.

B. card's floating-rate cap exceeding the periodic rate.

C. triggering of an ABS rapid amortization provision.

7. A characteristic of solar loans that makes them attractive to potential solar ABS investors is their:

A. universal availability to any homeowners.

B. ability to combine multiple liens to mitigate default risk.

C. flexibility in allowing either purchase or rental of solar systems.

8. Which investor tranche plays a key role in determining CLO viability?

A. Senior

B. Equity

C. Mezzanine

9. The inclusion of assets into a CLO collateral pool is completed:

A. during a subsequent ramp-up period.

B. prior to the close of the CLO transaction.

C. between ramp-up and loan maturity on meeting certain requirements.

10. When a CLO transaction experiences a collateral pool default:

A. senior tranche holders are guaranteed full repayment.

B. call features embedded in bonds likely affect junior tranches.

C. losses are distributed proportionately across all the tranches.

11. The feature of a covered bond transaction *most likely* shared with both CDOs and non-mortgage ABS is its:

A. specified LTV cutoff.

B. multiple tranches for the cover pool.

C. distinct maturity and settlement dates.

12. Which of the following statements about CDOs is correct?

A. The collateral pools for CDOs are static.

B. The proceeds to pay the CDO bond classes can only come from interest payments from collateral assets.

C. A CDO is a leveraged transaction, where equity tranche holders use borrowed funds to generate a return above the funding cost.

SOLUTIONS

1. The correct answer is C. In a true securitization, the specific pool of assets is removed from the balance sheet and transferred into a separate and independent legal entity that then issues securities backed by these pooled assets. A is incorrect because credit tranching offers credit protection for the more senior bond classes in a securitization not the equity tranche. B is incorrect because covered bonds, not pass-through securities, are the simplest securitization structure, which involves the issuer retaining the underlying assets on its balance sheet.

2. The correct answer is A. In the case of bankruptcy covered bond investors, they have dual recourse with the first safeguard being the ringfenced loans in the cover pool that underlie the covered bond transaction. B is incorrect because while investors also have recourse to the unencumbered assets of the issuer, those serve as a subsequent safeguard. C is incorrect because this post-transaction contribution is characteristic of the non-amortizing structure of a CDO (collateralized debt obligation).

3. The correct answer is C. All three of the listed reasons explain this comparative result, which has made covered bonds a relatively stable and reliable source of funding over time.

4. The correct answer is B. Overcollateralization, one of the three main types of internal credit enhancements used in securitization transactions, is a provision that the collateral underlying the transaction is larger than the face value of the issued bonds. The extra collateral provides a cushion to cover losses from defaults in the underlying pool of collateral. A and C are incorrect because both are types of external, not internal, credit enhancements.

5. The correct answer is B. A credit card ABS generates additional fee income. A is incorrect because by removing the credit card debt from the balance sheet, ABS issuance improves capital efficiency and lowers the cost of funding. C is incorrect as the ABS also reduces the cost of default risk from credit card debt.

6. The correct answer is C. Triggering rapid amortization provisions accelerates and alters principal cash flows. Noteholders will receive their investments earlier, which they can then reallocate to other investments offering more attractive risk/return characteristics. A is incorrect because typically during the revolving period, as credit cards are non-amortizing loans, the security holders receive only payments from the finance charges and fees the lender collects. Returned principal is reinvested in the collateral pool. B is incorrect because when floating-rate cap exceeds the rate cardholders must pay, there is no related binding limit on finance payments.

7. The correct answer is B. Default risk minimization adds to investment appeal, and solar loans provide opportunities for overcollateralization. Normally, solar ABS are collateralized by the underlying debt: mortgages, loans, or receivables. These loans can be further collateralized by a lien pledged on the installed systems, on the property itself, or both. A is incorrect as solar loans are typically extended only to prime borrowers who own their homes and have good payment records. C is incorrect as the loans enable property owner purchase of installed systems instead of rental that is transacted through solar leases.

8. The correct answer is B. Investors in equity tranches take on equity-like risks with the potential to earn returns comparable to equities. Moreover, these

residual tranche investors play a key role in whether a CLO is viable or not; the CLO structure has to offer competitive returns for this tranche. Facing these risk/return possibilities puts them in the position of the marginal, price-setting investors. A and C are incorrect because they are promised fixed returns without reference to the underlying performance of the collateral pool. They are also exposed to less risk in having seniority payoff preference in case of default.

9. The correct answer is C. After the ramp-up period but before underlying collateral pool loans mature, the collateral manager may replace loans in the portfolio as long as the new asset meets the portfolio selection criteria. A is incorrect because while additional assets are added to the collateral pool during a subsequent ramp-up period, loan replacements can still occur after the ramp-up period. B is incorrect because a typical feature of CLO transactions is that the collateral portfolio is not finalized until after the transaction closes.

10. The correct answer is B. A complicating factor of a default can be the call features embedded in bonds. While exercising call options on debt would replenish the collateral pool, distributing these proceeds to the senior and mezzanine tranches would shrink the size of the collateral pool, further narrowing the earnings potential with junior tranches receiving the least cash flow. A is incorrect because senior tranches are then in danger of not receiving some or any payments, depending on the size of the default. C is incorrect because losses would first be absorbed by junior tranche investors, with remaining losses realized by the other tranches in order of repayment seniority.

11. The correct answer is C. As illustrated by their respective term sheets, all three types of ABS transactions have timing milestones designating due dates for investments (settlement date) and the end of their terms (maturity date). A is incorrect because in contrast to their non-amortizing counterparts, covered bonds are backed by a segregated pool of assets that typically consist of commercial or residential mortgages, for which an LTV cutoff is applicable. B is incorrect because while other ABS often use credit tranching to create bond classes with different borrower default exposures, covered bonds usually consist of one bond class per cover pool.

12. The correct answer is C. A CDO is a leveraged transaction, where equity tranche holders use borrowed funds (i.e., the bond classes issued) to generate a return above the funding cost. A is incorrect because unlike MBS, the pools in a CDO are not static; so, there is a need for a collateral manager that buys and sells debt obligations for and from the CDO's collateral pool to generate sufficient cash flows to meet the obligations to the CDO bondholders. B is incorrect because the proceeds to pay the CDO bond classes can come from interest payments from collateral assets, maturing of collateral assets, and sale of collateral assets.

LEARNING MODULE

19

Mortgage-Backed Security (MBS) Instrument and Market Features

LEARNING OUTCOMES	
Mastery	***The candidate should be able to:***
☐	define prepayment risk and describe time tranching structures in securitizations and their purpose
☐	describe fundamental features of residential mortgage loans that are securitized
☐	describe types and characteristics of residential mortgage-backed securities, including mortgage pass-through securities and collateralized mortgage obligations, and explain the cash flows and risks for each type
☐	describe characteristics and risks of commercial mortgage-backed securities

INTRODUCTION

1

This module builds on the prior ones that provided an overview of asset-backed securities (ABS) and described the benefits of securitization, the securitization process, and typical securitization structures. This module focuses on the largest ABS market in the world, mortgage-backed securities (MBS). It introduces mortgage loans and their characteristic features; discusses residential MBS (RMBS), including mortgage pass-through securities and collateralized mortgage obligations (CMOs); and describes commercial MBS (CMBS). It shows how to measure, mitigate, and share securitization-related risks across different tranches and their characteristics, and it examines MBS cash flows and risks.

LEARNING MODULE OVERVIEW

- Prepayment risk is the risk that the borrower does not repay the principal (or a portion of the principal) as scheduled. Contraction risk occurs when the borrower repays the principal faster than anticipated, while extension risk occurs when the borrower repays the principal more slowly than planned.
- Mortgage-backed securities (MBS) are bonds created from securitizing mortgage loans. Mortgage loans provide borrowers the funds to purchase property and require borrowers to repay lenders on a mutually agreed schedule, otherwise the lender has the right to seize the property.
- MBS can be created based on either residential or commercial mortgages. Bonds created from the securitization of mortgages backed by residential properties are residential mortgage-backed securities (RMBS).
- Because both scheduled principal repayments and unscheduled prepayments are made over the life of an MBS, the contractual maturity for an MBS does not reveal its actual payments and prepayments. The weighted average life is a measure widely used to assess when an MBS can be expected to be paid off.
- A mortgage pass-through security is a security created when mortgage lenders pool mortgages together and use them to back securities that they sell to investors. The cash flows of a mortgage pass-through security depend on the monthly cash flows of the underlying pool of mortgages.
- Collateralized mortgage obligations (CMOs) securitize mortgage pass-through securities or multiple pools of loans and are structured to redistribute the cash flows to different bond classes or tranches, thereby creating securities that have different exposures to prepayment risk.
- The tranching structure of a CMO can redistribute prepayment risk across the different tranches; the more senior a tranche is, the less exposure it has to prepayment risk and default risk.
- Commercial mortgage-backed securities (CMBS) can consist of just a few underlying commercial mortgages, and so one default in a CMBS pool may significantly impact the CMBS investors. Investors must evaluate this unique concentration risk by analyzing the individual loans and properties backing the CMBS, the owners of the commercial properties themselves, as well as the CMBS structure.
- Unlike RMBS, CMBS offer investors call protection at either the structural or individual loan level and thus trade more like corporate bonds than RMBS. However, commercial mortgages often include a large balloon payment at maturity, making CMBS more vulnerable to a type of extension risk, balloon risk.

SELF-ASSESSMENT

1. Which of the following statements regarding the loan-to-value ratio (LTV) is *most* accurate?

   A. The LTV for a given mortgage remains static for the life of the loan.

   B. The higher the LTV, the more protection a lender has in the event of default.

   C. LTV serves as a key measure in both residential and commercial mortgages.

   Solution:

   The correct answer is C. LTV serves as a key measure both in residential and commercial mortgages. LTV is calculated as the ratio of the amount of the mortgage to the property's value. A is incorrect because over time, the LTV changes: As the borrower makes mortgage payments, including principal repayments, the outstanding balance on the loan is reduced and also, fluctuations in the market value of the property cause the borrower's equity to change. B is incorrect because the higher the LTV, the less protection a lender has in the event of default.

2. Which of the following statements regarding mortgage-backed securities (MBS) is *most accurate*? MBS:

   A. must be backed or guaranteed by a government or a quasi-government entity.

   B. can be created by securitizing mortgages backed by residential or by commercial properties.

   C. that use credit enhancements to reduce credit risk for securities backed by residential mortgages typically are agency RMBS.

   Solution:

   The correct answer is B. The mortgages in MBS can either be residential mortgages or commercial mortgages. A is incorrect because MBS do not have to be guaranteed by the government or a quasi-government entity. But, when these mortgages or the securities issued backed by these mortgages are guaranteed by the government, there is a credit support. MBS backed by residential mortgages that are issued by private entities and not guaranteed by a federal agency or a government-sponsored enterprise (GSE) are called "non-agency RMBS." C is incorrect because non-agency RMBS, not agency RMBS, typically use credit enhancements, such as insurance, letters of credit, guarantees, or subordinated interests, to mitigate the credit risk and improve the overall quality of the mortgage pool. These securities include credit enhancements because they are not guaranteed or insured by a government agency or by a GSE.

3. When a mortgage is used as collateral for a mortgage pass-through security, the mortgage is *most likely* said to be:

   A. enhanced.

   B. securitized.

C. subordinated.

Solution:

The correct answer is B. When a mortgage is used as collateral for a mortgage pass-through security, the mortgage is said to be securitized. A and C are incorrect because a mortgage that is used as collateral for a mortgage pass-through security is said to be *securitized,* not enhanced or subordinated.

4. Which of the following structures is created through time tranching?

   A. Z-tranches

   B. Floating-rate tranches

   C. Principal-only (PO) securities

Solution:

The correct answer is A. Z-tranches and residual tranches are created through time tranching, which means they do not pay interest payments until a pre-set date. B is incorrect because floating-rate tranches carry interest rates that are linked to an index or a market reference rate (MRR) and are used to hedge interest rate risk in portfolios. C is incorrect because principal-only (PO) securities pay only the principal repayments from the pool and can be created either from mortgage pass-throughs or as a tranche in a CMO.

5. Which of the following risks *most likely* explains why the maturity of an MBS declines when interest rates decline?

   A. Balloon risk

   B. Extension risk

   C. Contraction risk

Solution:

The correct answer is C. Contraction risk is the risk that the borrower might pay back the money borrowed more quickly than anticipated, reducing the amount of future payments the investor receives. When interest rates decline, actual prepayments will be higher than forecasted because homeowners will be more likely to refinance their mortgages. A is incorrect because balloon risk occurs when the borrower fails to make the balloon payment at the maturity of a loan with a balloon payment; it is a form of extension risk. B is incorrect because extension risk is the risk that the borrower might pay back the money borrowed more slowly than anticipated, extending rather than shortening the time of repayment and the maturity of the bond.

6. Which of the following statements related to mortgage-backed securities (MBS) is true?

   A. The contractual maturity for an MBS accurately predicts future payments and prepayments.

   B. A measure widely used by market participants for MBS is the weighted average life, or simply the average life, of the MBS.

C. A 30-year, option-free corporate bond and an MBS with a 30-year legal maturity with the same coupon rate offer equivalent interest rate risk.

Solution:

The correct answer is B. A measure widely used by market participants for MBS is the weighted average life, or simply the average life, of the MBS. This measure gives investors an indication of how long they can expect to hold the MBS before it is paid off, assuming interest rates stay at current levels and thus expected prepayments are realized. A is incorrect because the contractual maturity for an MBS does *not* reveal its actual payments and prepayments. Unscheduled principal repayments will shorten the maturity of an MBS, but the pattern of repayments is driven by shifts in interest rates that are not known with certainty. C is incorrect because a 30-year, option-free corporate bond would not have the same prepayments/prepayment rates as an MBS with a 30-year legal maturity with the same coupon rate and thus would not offer equivalent interest rate risk.

7. A major difference between residential and commercial mortgage-backed securities is that:

A. CMBS securitize conforming mortgages and are collateralized by homogeneous properties as compared to properties backing an RMBS.

B. investors must evaluate the individual loans and properties backing a CMBS as well as the owners of the commercial properties themselves.

C. a CMBS pool may consist of thousands of mortgages from various parts of a country, while an RMBS may consist of a few homogenous residential mortgages.

Solution:

The correct answer is B. CMBS can consist of a few underlying commercial mortgages, whereas an RMBS pool may consist of thousands of mortgages from various parts of a country. Thus, one default in a CMBS pool may have a significant impact on the CMBS investors. Investors in the CMBS must consider explicitly this unique concentration risk by not only analyzing the CMBS structure but also the individual loans and properties backing the CMBS as well as the owners of the commercial properties themselves. A is incorrect because RMBS, not CMBS, securitize conforming mortgages and are collateralized by homogeneous (single-family) residential properties. C is incorrect because an RMBS pool, not a CMBS pool, may consist of thousands of mortgages from various parts of a country, while CMBS can consist of a few underlying commercial mortgages.

8. Which of the following statements related to the debt service coverage (DSC) ratio, a key indicator of potential credit performance in commercial real estate lending, is *most accurate*? A DSC ratio:

A. is equal to the property's annual net operating income (NOI) divided by its debt service.

B. is calculated as the ratio of the amount of the loan to the underlying property's value.

C. that exceeds 1.0 indicates that the cash flows from the property are insufficient to cover the debt service while maintaining the property in its initial state of repair.

Solution:

The correct answer is A. The DSC ratio is equal to the property's annual NOI divided by its debt service. NOI is defined as the rental income reduced by cash operating expenses and a replacement reserve. Debt service is the annual amount of interest payments and principal repayments. B is incorrect because the ratio of the amount of the loan to the underlying property's value is the LTV ratio, another key indicator of potential credit performance, not the DSC. C is incorrect because a DSC ratio that exceeds 1.0 indicates that the cash flows from the property are sufficient, not insufficient, to cover the debt service while maintaining the property in its initial state of repair.

2 TIME TRANCHING

☐ define prepayment risk and describe time tranching structures in securitizations and their purpose

ABS and MBS pass-through security cash flows are uncertain because scheduled and actual payments frequently differ. Borrower behavior, such as the early payment of interest and principal as well as payment delinquencies over the life of a loan, depends upon a number of factors, including the income of the borrower (household income or cash flows for a corporation), the terms and conditions of the loan (such as the original interest rate versus current rates and any prepayment penalties), and the sale of the underlying asset being financed. To correctly value these securities, investors make certain assumptions about the predicted contractual payments after factoring in prepayment risk. **Prepayment risk** is the risk that the principal or a proportion of the principal is paid back at a different pace from the contractually agreed scheduled payment plan by the borrower. Prepayment risk has two components: contraction risk and extension risk, both of which reflect changes in the general level of interest rates.

Prepayment Risk

When interest rates decline, actual prepayments for fixed-rate mortgages will be higher than forecasted because homeowners will refinance at lower interest rates. Mortgage refinancing is particularly common in the US given the absence of loan prepayment penalties, which are more prevalent in other countries. Thus, the maturity of an MBS will be shorter than what was anticipated at the time of purchase. **Contraction risk** is the risk that the borrower repays the principal or a portion of the principal in a shorter period of time than the contractually agreed scheduled payment, reducing the amount of future payments the investor receives. For investors, this has two adverse consequences. First, investors must reinvest the proceeds at lower interest rates. Second, the prepayment option reduces the potential price appreciation for the bond.

When interest rates increase, actual prepayments will be lower than forecasted because homeowners will become less likely to refinance their mortgages and may even delay new home purchases. Thus, the maturity of an MBS will be longer than what was anticipated at the time of purchase. **Extension risk** is the risk that the borrower repays the principal or a proportion of the principal in a longer time period than the contractually agreed scheduled payment. For investors, this has adverse consequences: Higher interest rates reduce the value of the cash flows investors receive. Therefore, payments the investors receive will be discounted at a higher interest rate, and the extension stretches out the payments the investors receive.

The structure of a securitization may also allow the redistribution of "prepayment risk" among bond classes. An approach for reducing this risk is to create bond classes that possess different expected maturities. This is referred to as **time tranching**. For instance, a securitization pool may contain sequential tranching, where the principal repayments flow first to one tranche until the principal is fully repaid for that tranche and then to the sequential tranche until the principal is repaid for that tranche.

EXAMPLE 1

Time Tranching with Waterfall for RLT MBS

If the Residential Loan Trust (RLT) had issued the MBS with different expected maturities by bond class, rather than all the MBS being due in four years, the MBS investors also could select bonds based on their expected maturity. However, the investors could face prepayment or extension risk in this instance. The specific maturity dates are noted in Exhibit 1.

Exhibit 1: Overview of Notes Issued by Residential Loan Trust – Brief Summary of Maturity Terms

Maturity of Mortgage-Backed Notes Issued by the Residential Loan Trust	
Issuer:	Residential Loan Trust (RLT)
Status and Ranking of Payments	**Tranches**
Class A Notes rank senior to the Class B, C, & D Notes.	Tranche A Notes Face value: EUR825 million Interest rate: MRR + 0.50% Maturity: One year
Class B Notes rank senior to Class C & D Notes and rank junior to Class A Notes.	Tranche B Notes Face value: EUR100 million Interest rate: MRR + 1.50% Maturity: Two years
Class C Notes rank senior to the Class D Notes and rank junior to Class A & B Notes.	Tranche C Notes Face value: EUR50 million Interest rate: MRR + 2.50% Maturity: Three years
Class D Notes will rank junior to Class A, B, & C Notes.	Tranche D Notes Face value: EUR25 million Interest rate: Variable Maturity: Four years
Principal Payment:	To be paid on [Maturity Date]
Seniority:	The Notes are secured obligations of RLT.
Business Days:	Frankfurt

For the investor purchasing EUR5 million across Tranche B and Tranche C notes, loan prepayments could impact principal repayment as noted below:

		Timing of Principal Repaid	
Investor's Initial RLT MBS Purchases		When principal is repaid if no prepayments in the RLT collateral pool	When principal is repaid if interest rates decline early in year two, thereby driving immediate prepayments in the RLT pool
Class A Notes	EUR0 million	One year, per MBS terms	One year, per MBS terms
Class B Notes	EUR3 million	Two years, per MBS terms	Less than two years
Class C Notes	EUR2 million	Three years, per MBS terms	Less than three years
Class D Notes	EUR0 million	Four years, per MBS terms	Less than four years

We would require additional information about the value of all prepayments and their exact timing to identify the exact principal repayment date.

As seen in Exhibit 1, it is possible and quite common for a securitization to have structures with both credit tranching (subordinated structures) and time tranching (different expected maturities).

EXAMPLE 2

Volkswagen Emissions Scandal

Investors are exposed to certain types of idiosyncratic risks when buying asset-backed securities (ABS). For buyers of auto ABS, major automaker recalls are a known risk to bond investors. In 2015, the US Securities and Exchange Commission (SEC) accused Volkswagen (VW), one of the world's largest carmakers, and its CEO Martin Winterkorn with defrauding American investors during an emissions scandal (the "Dieselgate" scandal). Volkswagen later admitted that it cheated on diesel emission tests, and this admission wiped billions of euros from the company's market value and led to the resignation of Winterkorn. The emissions scandal that rocked Volkswagen also impacted ABS tied to car loans and leases. Sales of auto ABS were booming in the years just prior to the scandal as investors sought higher-yielding products given the low interest-rate environment.

About USD5.6 billion worth of VW auto ABS were outstanding in 2015, with USD4.39 billion coming from bonds backed by loans and leases. Volkswagen, facing potential fines and litigation, found its ability to attract new business temporarily crimped, forcing down the values of the cars backing such loans. There were USD1.25 billion worth of bonds that were backed by car dealer inventories of VW cars, known as dealer floorplan ABS. For dealer floorplan ABS, the ABS trust benefits from VW financing assistance, including but not limited to VW's pledge to repurchase unsold new vehicles and inventory. Car dealers, told to immediately halt sales of popular 2015 and 2016 models, including Volkswagen's Jetta and Beetle convertible, were saddled with unsalable product. Dealers had a number of cars that they could not sell, so inventory did not turn over as rapidly. The ABS most adversely affected by VW's sales stoppage of certain 2015 and 2016 diesel models was the dealer floorplan securitization.

Debt investors were demanding greater compensation from Volkswagen after the company said its emissions-cheating scandal would cost the firm more than EUR6.5 billion. Volkswagen, a frequent issuer in Europe's asset-backed securities market, said that EUR2.6 billion of loans or leases for vehicles built with engines using cheating software were packaged into its securitizations.

Late in 2015, Volkswagen was marketing a new auto ABS with a yield premium that was three times bigger than a similar deal earlier that year. The German carmaker was offering to pay about 60 bps to 65 bps more than benchmark rates for top-ranking notes of the securitization of auto leases. In comparison, Volkswagen paid a spread of 20 bps over the one-month euro interbank offered rate for similar debt in April 2015.

QUESTION SET

1. Creating bond classes that possess different expected maturities is referred to as:

   A. subordination.

   B. time tranching.

   C. credit tranching.

   Solution:

   The correct answer is B. An approach for reducing "prepayment risk" or "extension risk" among bond classes is to create bond classes that possess different expected maturities. This is referred to as time tranching. A and C are incorrect because subordination, also commonly referred to as a "waterfall" structure, involves directing losses to the subordinated bond classes before the senior bond classes, not creating bond classes that possess different expected maturities.

2. Identify which of the following statements regarding securitized products is most accurate:

   A. With time tranching, the tranches of a CMO amortize over time and all tranches mature at the same time.

   B. Pass-through securities are the simplest securitized structure and involve issuers retaining the underlying assets.

   C. In a true securitization, the underlying pool of assets is removed from the balance sheet and transferred into an independent legal entity that issues securities backed by these assets.

   Solution:

   The correct answer is C. In a true securitization, the specific pool of assets is removed from the balance sheet and transferred into a separate and independent legal entity that then issues securities backed by these pooled assets. A is incorrect because time tranching is an approach to reduce prepayment or extension risk by creating bond classes that possess different expected maturities. B is incorrect because covered bonds, not pass-through securities, are the simplest securitization structure; they involve the issuer retaining the underlying assets on its balance sheet.

3. Issuing the collateralized bond classes with different expected maturities is *most likely* designed to mitigate:

   A. credit risk.

   B. default risk.

   C. prepayment risk.

Solution:

The correct answer is C. Prepayment risk is the uncertainty that the cash flows will be different from the scheduled cash flows as set forth in the lease agreement because of the lessors' ability to alter payments. The creation of bond classes with different expected maturities, referred to as time tranching, allows prepayment risk to be redistributed among bond classes. A is incorrect because credit risk pertains to the risk of default in the assets backing the collateralized bonds, not to the timing of payments, and B is incorrect because default risk again pertains to the risk of default in the assets backing the collateralized bonds.

4. *Determine the correct answers to complete the following sentences:*

_______ is the risk that the borrower might pay back the money borrowed more quickly than anticipated, reducing the amount of future payments the investor receives. _______ is the risk that the borrower might pay back the money borrowed more slowly than anticipated, extending the time of repayment and the maturity of the bond.

Solution:

Contraction risk is the risk that the borrower might pay back the money borrowed more quickly than anticipated, reducing the amount of future payments the investor receives. *Extension risk* is the risk that the borrower might pay back the money borrowed more slowly than anticipated, extending the time of repayment and the maturity of the bond.

3 MORTGAGE LOANS AND THEIR CHARACTERISTIC FEATURES

☐ describe fundamental features of residential mortgage loans that are securitized

This lesson describes fundamental features of mortgage loans, the building block of the largest ABS market, the **mortgage-backed securities (MBS)** market. MBS are bonds created from the securitization of mortgages. A **mortgage loan** is secured by the collateral of a specified real estate property that obliges the borrower to make a predetermined series of payments to the lender. The mortgage lender has a **first lien** and security interest in the property, which gives the lender the right to seize the collateral if the borrower does not pay as agreed. Upon a **default** on the mortgage loan, the lender can potentially foreclose on the property. The **foreclosure** would allow the lender to take possession of the property and ultimately sell the property to recover funds toward satisfying the outstanding debt obligation.

Typically, the amount of the loan advanced to buy the property is less than the property's purchase price: The difference is the down payment. The ratio of the amount of the mortgage to the property's value is called the **loan-to-value ratio (LTV)**. The lower the LTV, the higher the borrower's equity. From the lender's perspective, the higher the borrower's equity, the less likely the borrower is to default. Moreover, the lower the LTV, the more protection the lender has if the borrower does default and the lender repossesses and sells the property. When the loan is first taken out, the borrower's equity in the property is equal to the down payment. Over time, the LTV changes: As the borrower makes mortgage payments, including principal repayments, the outstanding balance on the loan is reduced and as the market value of the property changes, the borrower's equity also changes. LTV serves as a key measure both in residential and commercial mortgages.

The capacity to sustain debt payments is another consideration. For residential lending, the metric is the **debt-to-income ratio (DTI)**, which compares an individual's monthly debt payments to their monthly pre-tax, gross income. Lenders, including mortgage lenders, use the DTI to measure an individual's ability to manage monthly payments and repay debts. A low DTI shows a balance between income and debt and suggests that the borrower could sustain additional debt. A high DTI ratio signals that the borrower may carry too much debt for the amount of income earned each month. Typically, lenders want to see low DTI ratios before extending loans to a potential borrower.

EXAMPLE 3

LTV and DTI Calculation

A borrower wishes to secure a mortgage loan to purchase a house. Information regarding the house, the desired loan, and the buyer's finances is shown below:

- House Price: EUR800,000
- Desired Loan Amount: EUR600,000
- Annual interest rate: 4.50%
- Loan term: 20 years/240 months
- Borrower's annual pre-tax gross income EUR141,000

The associated loan-to-value ratio (LTV) can be calculated using the desired loan value and the anticipated house price, as shown here:

$$LTV = \frac{Loan\ Amount}{House\ Price}$$

$$LTV = \frac{EUR\ 600,000}{EUR\ 800,000} = 75\%.$$

To calculate the debt-to-income ratio (DTI), we use the monthly debt payment and the borrower's monthly pre-tax gross income:

Month	Total Monthly Payment	Monthly Interest Payment	Monthly Principal Payment	Remaining Principal
1	3,795.90	2,250.00	1,545.90	598,454.10
2	3,795.90	2,244.20	1,551.69	596,902.41
3	3,795.90	2,238.38	1,557.51	595,344.90
4	3,795.90	2,232.54	1,563.35	593,781.55
5	3,795.90	2,226.68	1,569.22	592,212.33
236	3,795.90	70.38	3,725.52	15,042.30

Month	Total Monthly Payment	Monthly Interest Payment	Monthly Principal Payment	Remaining Principal
237	3,795.90	56.41	3,739.49	11,302.81
238	3,795.90	42.39	3,753.51	7,549.30
239	3,795.90	28.31	3,767.59	3,781.71
240	3,795.90	14.18	3,781.71	(0.00)

We calculate the monthly debt payment, with the first five and final five monthly payments of the 20-year mortgage. Putting the borrower's monthly pre-tax gross income and the monthly mortgage payment into the DTI formula provides the following DTI ratio:

$$DTI = \frac{Monthly\ Debt\ Payment}{Monthly\ pre - tax\ gross\ income}$$

$$DTI = \frac{EUR\ 3,795.90}{(EUR\ 141,000/12)} = 32.31\%.$$

In the United States, market participants typically identify two types of mortgages based on the credit quality of the borrower: prime loans and subprime loans. **Prime loans** have borrowers of high credit quality with strong employment and credit histories, a low DTI, substantial equity in the underlying property, and a first lien on the mortgaged property serving as the collateral for the loan. **Subprime loans** have borrowers with lower credit quality, high DTI, and/or are loans with higher LTV, and include loans that are secured by second liens otherwise subordinated to other loans.

Agency and Non-Agency RMBS

The mortgages in MBS can either be residential mortgages or commercial mortgages. The bonds created from the securitization of mortgages backed by residential properties are residential mortgage-backed securities (RMBS).

In the United States, Canada, Japan, and South Korea, there is a distinction between RMBS that are guaranteed by the government or a quasi-government entity and RMBS that are not. In the United States, securities backed by residential mortgages are divided into three sectors:

1. Guaranteed by a federal agency;
2. Guaranteed by government-sponsored enterprises (GSEs); and
3. Issued by private entities and thus not guaranteed by a federal agency or a GSE.

The first two sectors are referred to as **agency RMBS**, and the third sector is referred to as **non-agency RMBS**. Agency RMBS include securities issued by government agencies. These RMBS carry the full faith and credit of the government, essentially a guarantee with respect to timely payment of interest and repayment of principal. Agency RMBS also include RMBS issued by GSEs. RMBS issued by GSEs do not carry the full faith and credit of the government, but rather the GSEs' guarantee of the timely payment of interest and principal for the securities. The GSE's charge a fee for this guarantee.

Due to changing regulatory guidance and increased scrutiny, non-agency-RMBS all but disappeared after the global financial crisis. They were issued by banks, financial institutions, and other private businesses and were not beneficiaries of government guarantees. These private pass-throughs or private label MBS gained credit enhancement through pool insurance, letters of credit, guarantees, or subordination.

Non-agency RMBS securitized mortgages were collateralized by non-conforming mortgages, or by subprime, highly risky mortgages. Some residential home improvement loans, such as solar ABS discussed in an earlier lesson, that are subordinated to primary mortgage liens are now securitized in increasing volume.

Mortgage Contingency Features

Mortgages contain certain features that give the borrower and the lender certain rights throughout the contract. The most important right a borrower has is the option to prepay a mortgage by making any payment on the principal that exceeds the scheduled principal repayment. The **prepayment option** or an **early repayment option** may entitle the borrower to prepay all or part of the outstanding mortgage principal prior to maturity. This creates a risk from the lender's or investor's viewpoint: the cash flow amounts and timing cannot be known with certainty. This prepayment risk affects all mortgages that allow prepayment, not only the level-payment, fixed-rate, fully amortizing mortgages.

Lenders reduce this risk by stipulating a monetary penalty for prepayment that compensates the lender for the difference between the contract rate and the prevailing mortgage rate if the borrower prepays when interest rates decline. It is an effective mechanism that provides some certainty for the lender and reduces the incentive to prepay a mortgage. Prepayment penalty mortgages are quite common in Europe, while in the United States few mortgages have prepayment penalties.

When the borrower fails to make the contractual loan payments as stipulated in the note and loan documents, it may trigger a default on the mortgage loan that would allow the lender to potentially foreclose on the property and sell it. But the proceeds received from the sale of the property may be insufficient to recoup the losses. In a **recourse loan**, the lender has a claim against the borrower for the shortfall (deficiency) between the amount of the outstanding mortgage balance and the proceeds received from the sale of the property. In a **non-recourse loan**, the lender does not have such a claim against the borrower and thus can look only to the property to recover the outstanding mortgage balance. In the United States, recourse is typically determined by the state, and residential mortgages are non-recourse loans in many states. In contrast, residential mortgages in most European countries are recourse loans.

The recourse/non-recourse feature of a mortgage has implications for projecting the likelihood of defaults by borrowers, particularly for mortgages where the LTV exceeds 100%—sometimes referred to as "underwater mortgages."

EXAMPLE 4

Underwater Mortgages during the 2008–09 Global Financial Crisis

A mortgage is said to be in negative equity, or "underwater," when a home is valued for less than the amount their owners owe the banks holding their mortgage loans. Being underwater is typically a precursor to foreclosure.

The most extreme example of widespread underwater mortgages occurred during the Global Financial Crisis of 2008–09 (GFC). At the end of 2009, almost 10.7 million, or 23% of, US residential properties were underwater. An additional 2.3 million mortgages were approaching negative equity, meaning they had less than 5% equity.

This phenomenon existed primarily because of loose credit underwriting standards and inflated home prices from 2004–06, followed by declining home prices and high leverage on non-recourse mortgage loans provided by banks and other debt capital providers.

The distribution of negative equity was heavily concentrated in five states: Nevada (65%), followed by Arizona (48%), Florida (45%), Michigan (37%), and California (35%). Among the top five states, the average negative equity share was 40%, compared to 14% for the remaining states.

The rise in negative equity is closely tied to increases in pre-foreclosure activity. At one end of the spectrum, borrowers with equity tend to have very low default rates. At the other end, investors tend to more commonly default on their mortgages once in negative equity, as their default rate is typically 2% to 3% higher than owner-occupied homes with similar degrees of negative equity. For the highest level of negative equity, investors and owners behave very similarly and default at similar rates. Strategic default on the part of the owner occupier becomes more likely at such high levels of negative equity, especially when the mortgage loan is non-recourse.

If the mortgage is non-recourse, the borrower may have an incentive to strategically default on an underwater mortgage and allow the lender to foreclose on the property, even if the borrower has resources available to continue to make mortgage payments. Although there are negative consequences to a "strategic default," such as lower credit scores and a reduced ability to borrow in the future, some borrowers may make use of this approach. Where mortgages are recourse loans, a strategic default is less likely because the lender can recover the shortfall from the borrower's other assets and/or income.

QUESTION SET

1. *Determine the correct answers to complete the following sentences:*

   ___________ are bonds created from the securitization of mortgages. A ___________ is secured by the collateral of some specified real estate property that obliges the borrower to make a predetermined series of payments to the lender.

   Solution:

   MBS are bonds created from the securitization of mortgages. A *mortgage loan* is secured by the collateral of some specified real estate property that obliges the borrower to make a predetermined series of payments to the lender.

2. A borrower procures a JPY33,165,000 loan for a JPY36,850,000 house in Tokyo. Calculate the LTV for this transaction and explain why the lender uses this measure.

   Solution:

   The LTV (loan-to-value ratio) is the ratio of the amount of the mortgage to the property's value.

$$LTV = \frac{\text{Amount of the mortgage}}{\text{Property's value}}$$

$$LTV = \frac{33,165,000}{36,850,000}$$

$LTV = 90.0\%$.

The lender uses the LTV ratio to assess the likelihood that a borrower will default. The lower the LTV, the higher a borrower's equity. The higher the borrower's equity, the less likely a default.

3. Identify the mortgage feature below that corresponds to its description. (Matching)

1. Maturity	A. The contract or note rate
2. Mortgage Interest Rate	B. The right of a borrower to pay more than the scheduled principal required
3. Amortization	C. The rights of a lender when the borrower fails to make required loan payments
4. Right to Prepay	D. The typical term
5. Rights in a Foreclosure	E. The set schedule for repayment of the mortgage

Solution:

1. D is correct. Maturity is the typical term or number of years to maturity of a mortgage.
2. A is correct. The interest rate on a mortgage is called the mortgage rate, contract rate, or note rate, and it varies among countries.
3. E is correct. Amortization pertains to the pace at which the balance of a loan is gradually reduced over time according to a set schedule.
4. B is correct. A prepayment option (or early repayment option) may entitle the borrower to prepay all or part of a mortgage's outstanding principal prior to maturity.
5. C is correct. When a borrower fails to make the contractual loan payments, the lender's rights in a foreclosure allow foreclosure and sale of the property.

4. A real estate investor has obtained a recourse mortgage loan on a shopping center from a bank. The loan has an outstanding balance of USD7,000,000, while the property is valued at only USD5,000,000. In the event of a default on the loan, the bank has a claim on:

   A. the property.

   B. the borrower's personal assets.

   C. both the property and the borrower's personal assets.

Solution:

The correct answer is C. In a recourse loan, the lender has a claim against the borrower for the shortfall (deficiency) between the amount of the outstanding mortgage balance and the proceeds received from the sale of the property. A is incorrect because in a non-recourse loan, the lender has a claim against only the property for any shortfall between the amount of the outstanding mortgage balance and the proceeds received from the sale of the property. B is incorrect because mortgage lending entails a first lien and security interest in the property, which is the lender's collateral.

4 RESIDENTIAL MORTGAGE-BACKED SECURITIES (RMBS)

- [ ] describe types and characteristics of residential mortgage-backed securities, including mortgage pass-through securities and collateralized mortgage obligations, and explain the cash flows and risks for each type

This section starts with a discussion of different RMBS types, to continue with an overview of mortgage pass-through securities and non-agency RMBS. It concludes with collateralized mortgage obligations.

A **mortgage pass-through security** is a security created when mortgage lenders pool mortgages together and sell securities to investors. The cash flow from the mortgage pool––monthly payments of principal, interest, and prepayments––are "passed through" to the security holders. A pool can consist of several thousand or only a few mortgages. When a mortgage is used as collateral for a mortgage pass-through security, the mortgage is said to be securitized.

Mortgage Pass-Through Securities

The cash flows of a mortgage pass-through security depend on the monthly cash flows of the underlying pool of mortgages. The amount and the timing of the cash flows from the pool of mortgages cover both the cash flow passed through to the security holders and administrative charges for servicing the pool; the structure is depicted in Exhibit 2.

Exhibit 2: Mortgage Pass-Through

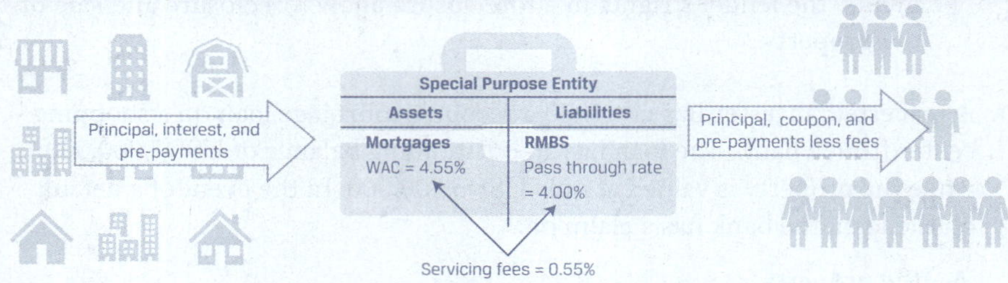

Note: WAC = weighted average coupon rate.

These administrative charges include collecting monthly payments from borrowers, forwarding proceeds to owners of the loan, sending payment notices to borrowers, maintaining records of the outstanding mortgage balance, initiating foreclosure proceedings if necessary, and providing tax information to borrowers when applicable. Additionally, the issuer or financial guarantor of the mortgage pass-through security may charge fees for guaranteeing the issue. All these fees are typically calculated as a portion of the mortgage rate.

A comparison of MBS and RMBS can be found in Exhibit 3.

Exhibit 3: Comparison of MBS and RMBS

	Mortgage-Backed Securities (MBS)	Residential Mortgage-Backed Securities (RMBS)
Underlying collateral	Residential or commercial mortgages	Residential mortgages and/or mortgage pass-through securities
Subtype	▪ RMBS ▪ CMBS	▪ Mortgage pass-through securities ▪ Collateralized mortgage obligations (CMOs), including sequential pay, planned amortization class (PAC), and support tranches ▪ Agency RMBS ▪ Non-Agency RMBS

A mortgage pass-through security's coupon rate is called the **pass-through rate** and is lower than the weighted average mortgage rate earned on the underlying pool of mortgages because of administrative charges. The pass-through rate that the investor receives is said to be "net interest" or "net coupon."

The mortgages in a securitization pool are heterogeneous: outstanding principal, interest rates, and maturities vary across the mortgages. Consequently, for each mortgage pass-through security, a **weighted average coupon rate (WAC)** and a **weighted average maturity (WAM)** are determined. The WAC is calculated by weighting the mortgage rate of each mortgage in the pool by the percentage of the outstanding mortgage balance relative to the outstanding amount of all the mortgages in the pool. Similarly, the WAM is calculated by weighting the remaining number of months to maturity of each mortgage in the pool by the outstanding mortgage balance relative to the outstanding amount of all the mortgages in the pool.

Exhibit 4 shows the five mortgages underlying a specific mortgage-backed security.

Exhibit 4: Weighted Average Coupon Rate and Weighted Average Maturity

Mortgage	Interest rate (*i*)	Beginning Balance (BB)	Current Balance (CB)	Original Term (months)	Number of Months to Maturity (MM)
A	2.50%	EUR300,000	EUR238,000	240	180
B	3.30%	EUR420,000	EUR380,000	600	480
C	2.80%	EUR100,000	EUR87,000	288	240
D	4.00%	EUR280,000	EUR132,000	360	120
E	3.70%	EUR350,000	EUR312,000	384	312
		EUR1,450,000	EUR1,149,000		

The weighted average coupon rate for this MBS is calculated as follows:

$$WAC = i_A\left(\frac{CB_A}{\sum_{CB}}\right) + i_B\left(\frac{CB_B}{\sum_{CB}}\right) + i_C\left(\frac{CB_C}{\sum_{CB}}\right) + i_D\left(\frac{CB_D}{\sum_{CB}}\right) + i_E\left(\frac{CB_E}{\sum_{CB}}\right)$$

$$WAC = 2.50\%\left(\frac{238,000}{1,149,000}\right) + 3.30\%\left(\frac{380,000}{1,149,000}\right) + 2.80\%\left(\frac{87,000}{1,149,000}\right)$$
$$+4.00\%\left(\frac{132,000}{1,149,000}\right) + 3.70\%\left(\frac{312,000}{1,149,000}\right)$$

$$WAC = 3.29\%.$$

The weighted average maturity for this MBS is calculated as follows:

$$WAM = MM_A\left(\frac{CB_A}{\sum_{CB}}\right) + MM_B\left(\frac{CB_B}{\sum_{CB}}\right) + MM_C\left(\frac{CB_C}{\sum_{CB}}\right)$$
$$+MM_D\left(\frac{CB_D}{\sum_{CB}}\right) + MM_E\left(\frac{CB_E}{\sum_{CB}}\right)$$

$$WAM = 180\left(\frac{238,000}{1,149,000}\right) + 480\left(\frac{380,000}{1,149,000}\right) + 240\left(\frac{87,000}{1,149,000}\right)$$
$$+120\left(\frac{132,000}{1,149,000}\right) + 312\left(\frac{312,000}{1,149,000}\right)\text{month}$$

$$WAM = 313 \text{ months.}$$

Collateralized Mortgage Obligations (CMOs)

Collateralized mortgage obligations securitize mortgage pass-through securities or multiple pools of loans. CMOs are structured to redistribute the cash flows to different bond classes or tranches and create securities that have different exposures to prepayment risk. Exhibit 5 depicts a simplified CMO structure where the cash flows are pooled and redistributed across the different tranches.

Exhibit 5: Collateralized Mortgage Obligation (CMO)

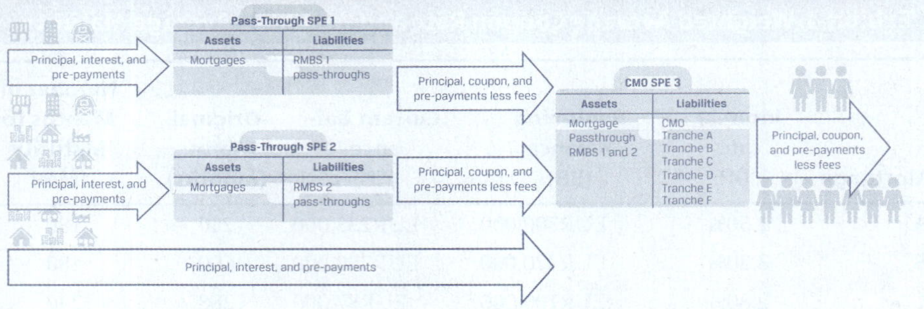

The tranching structure in the CMOs cannot eliminate prepayment risk, but it can redistribute the prepayment risk across the different tranches, insulating some tranches more than others. The CMO tranche structures reduce the uncertainties of the size and timing of payments investors receive. The features of these tranches are designed to specifically meet the various needs of institutional investors. Across the range of CMO structures, the more senior a tranche is, the less exposure it has to prepayment risk and default risk.

Sequential-Pay CMO

In sequential-pay CMO structures, each tranche would be retired sequentially. This is an example of time tranching. One class begins to receive principal payments from the underlying securities only after the principal on any previous class has been completely paid off and retired. All principal payments are made to Tranche A until the principal balance for Tranche A is zero. After Tranche A is paid off, the principal payments go to Tranche B until the principal balance for Tranche B is zero. This continues until all the tranches are repaid.

To illustrate a sequential-pay CMO, let us use a hypothetical transaction with the terms outlined above. The collateral for this CMO is the mortgage pass-through security described in Exhibit 2, where the total par value of the collateral is USD100 million, the pass-through coupon rate is 4%, the WAC is 4.55%, and the WAM is 360 months (about 30 years). From this collateral, three tranches are created, as shown in Exhibit 6. The coupon rate varies with the differences in maturity and reflects the term structure of interest rates, among other factors. Exhibit 6 shows the resulting structure.

Exhibit 6: Sequential-Pay CMO

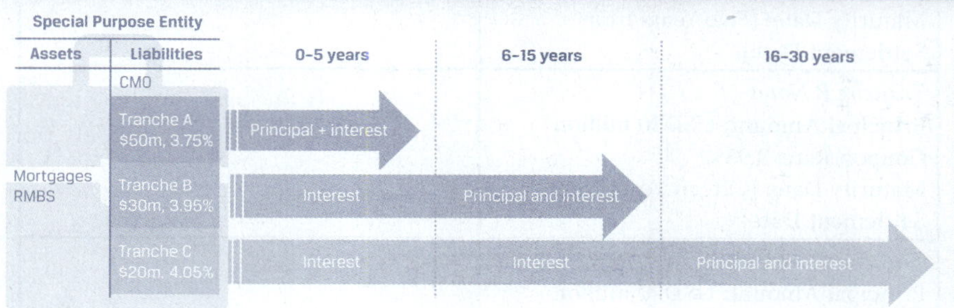

Some protection against prepayment risk is provided for each tranche. The protection arises because prioritizing the distribution of principal (that is, establishing the payment rule for the principal repayment) effectively protects the shorter-term tranche (A in this structure) against extension risk. This protection comes from the longer-term tranches B and C. At the same time, Tranches B and C benefit because they are provided protection against contraction risk from Tranche A. Thus, the sequential-pay CMO structure allows investors concerned about extension risk to invest in Tranche A, and those concerned about contraction risk to invest in Tranches B and C.

Although the payment rules for the distribution of the principal repayments are known, the actual principal repayment amount in each month is not, as it depends on the actual prepayment rate of the collateral. In the sequential-pay CMO structure, the tranches have average lives that are shorter or longer than the collateral, thereby attracting investors who have preferences for different average lives. A pension fund that expects a significant increase in the number of retirements after several years may opt for a tranche with a longer average life, such as Tranche B. An endowment that looks to finance large building projects over the next few years may choose a tranche with lower average life, such as Tranche A. And long-term investors willing to assume more risk may select Tranche C.

KNOWLEDGE CHECK

1. Referring to the sequential-pay CMO in Exhibit 6, match each investor type to the tranche that *most closely* fits its needs.

Investor Types:

a. A pension fund looking for higher returns in exchange for accepting more risk

b. A mutual fund seeking safe returns for a small portion of its portfolio.

c. An insurance company that sells annuities to clients expected to retire starting in approximately fifteen years

Tranche	Investor Type
Tranche A Notes Principal Amount: USD50 million Coupon Rate: 3.75% Maturity Date: [Five Years from Settlement Date]	
Tranche B Notes Principal Amount: USD30 million Coupon Rate: 3.95% Maturity Date: [Fifteen Years from Settlement Date]	
Tranche C Notes Principal Amount: USD20 million Coupon Rate: 4.05% Maturity Date: [Thirty Years from Settlement Date]	

Solution:

Tranche	Investor Type
Tranche A Notes Principal Amount: USD50 million Coupon Rate: 3.75% Maturity Date: [Five Years from Settlement Date]	b) A mutual fund seeking safe returns for a small portion of its portfolio.
Tranche B Notes Principal Amount: USD30 million Coupon Rate: 3.95% Maturity Date: [Fifteen Years from Settlement Date]	c) An insurance company that sells annuities to clients expected to retire starting in approximately fifteen years.
Tranche C Notes Principal Amount: USD20 million Coupon Rate: 4.05% Maturity Date: [Thirty Years from Settlement Date]	a) A pension fund looking for higher returns in exchange for accepting more risk.

Other CMO Structures

The cash flows from an underlying mortgage pool can be structured in additional ways. The structures below describe various tranches that are created through time tranching (Z-tranche and residual tranche) or by splitting up cash flows from the pool.

- *Z-Tranches* do not pay interest payments until a pre-set date, when both principal and accrued interest payments start. During the accrual period at each payment date, the principal value of the Z-tranche is credited by the stated coupon rate. Typically, Z-tranches are the last tranche in a series of sequential or PAC and companion tranches. A Z-tranche benefits the other tranches because it frees up cash flows that other tranches can distribute. At the same time, holders of the Z-tranche do not face reinvestment risk when market yields decline. Z-tranches usually have average lives in excess of 20 years. This makes these tranches risky and hard to value. Z-tranches are also known as accretion bonds or accrual bonds.
- *Principal-Only (PO) securities* pay only the principal repayments from the pool. These securities can be created either from mortgage pass-throughs or as a tranche in a CMO. Because PO investors receive the face value of their securities through scheduled principal payments and prepayments, the value of these securities is very sensitive to prepayment rates and interest rates. With falling interest rates or when prepayments accelerate, the value of the PO will increase.
- *Interest-Only (IO) securities* pay their holders only the interest payments from the pool. IO securities are a companion of the PO securities in a CMO transaction. These securities have no face or par value. With increased prepayments, the cash flows paid to the IO investors decline. That is why investors use IOs to hedge their portfolios against interest rate risk.
- *Floating-Rate tranches* carry interest rates that are linked to an index or a market reference rate. The interest rates are variable and are often subject to both a cap and a floor rate. These tranches are impacted by how interest rate movements affect prepayment rates. Floating-rate tranches can also be structured as inverse floaters, where the interest paid changes in the opposite direction of the change in interest rates. They are used to hedge interest rate risk in portfolios.
- *Residual tranches* collect any remaining cash flow from the pool after all the obligations to the other tranches are met. These investments are appropriate for investors that can assume the risk and hedge it. Such investors include hedge funds and long-term institutional investors. Banks typically avoid such investments due to capital requirements.
- A further evolution of the sequential pay CMO are CMOs that include Planned Amortization Class (PAC) tranches, occasionally accompanied by support tranches. PAC tranches offer greater predictability and stability of the cash flows. These tranches make scheduled and fixed principal payments over a predetermined time period to their investors if the prepayment levels in the pool are within a certain maximum and minimum range. If the prepayment rate is within the specified range, all prepayment risk is absorbed by the support tranche.

QUESTION SET

The following table is used for questions 1, 2, and 3:

Shown below are five mortgages that comprise the entire pool in a mortgage-backed security.

Mortgage	Interest Rate (i)	Beginning Balance (BB)	Current Balance (CB)	Original Term (Months)	Number of Months to Maturity
A	2.00%	CAD200,000	CAD83,000	420	140
B	3.00%	CAD300,000	CAD193,000	360	192
C	4.00%	CAD400,000	CAD315,000	360	240
D	5.00%	CAD500,000	CAD357,000	240	144
E	6.00%	CAD600,000	CAD548,000	420	324
		CAD2,000,000	CAD1,496,000		

1. The WAC for this security is *closest* to:

A. 4.00%.

B. 4.50%.

C. 4.73%.

Solution:

The correct answer is C. The weighted average coupon is calculated by weighting the mortgage rate of each mortgage in the pool by the percentage of the outstanding mortgage balance relative to the outstanding amount of all the mortgages in the pool, as shown in the equation below.

$$WAC = i_A\left(\frac{CB_A}{\sum_{CB}}\right) + i_B\left(\frac{CB_B}{\sum_{CB}}\right) + i_C\left(\frac{CB_C}{\sum_{CB}}\right) + i_D\left(\frac{CB_D}{\sum_{CB}}\right) + i_E\left(\frac{CB_E}{\sum_{CB}}\right)$$

$$WAC = 2.00\%\left(\frac{83,000}{1,496,000}\right) + 3.00\%\left(\frac{193,000}{1,496,000}\right) + 4.00\%\left(\frac{315,000}{1,496,000}\right)$$
$$+5.00\%\left(\frac{357,000}{1,496,000}\right) + 6.00\%\left(\frac{548,000}{1,496,000}\right)$$

$$WAC = 4.73\%.$$

A is incorrect because it is calculated as a straight average of the five interest rates of the five mortgages in the pool.

B is incorrect because it is calculated by weighting the mortgage rate of each mortgage in the pool by its percentage of the pool's total beginning mortgage balance, not by its percentage of the pool's current mortgage balance.

2. Referring to the Summary of Terms for the Sequential-Pay CMO Structure with Three Tranches Government Housing Trust, pool 917-37 shown in Exhibit 3, identify the investor *most likely* to select each tranche.

Investor	Tranche
1. A fund that is expected to provide retirement benefits beginning in about ten years	A. Tranche A
2. A long-term fund seeking high returns	B. Tranche B
3. A foundation that expects to award sizeable grants for medical research within the next few years and wants to avoid extension risk	C. Tranche C

Solution:

1. B is correct. A fund that expects to provide retirement benefits in about ten years may opt for a tranche, such as Tranche B. (In the sequential-pay CMO structure, the tranches have average lives that are shorter or longer than the underlying collateral, thereby attracting investors who have preferences for different average lives.)
2. C is correct. A long-term fund seeking high returns would *most likely* be willing to assume more risk in order to achieve those higher returns. Tranche C has the longest term and is the riskiest of the three tranches.
3. A is correct. A foundation that requires funding within the next few years and thus wants to avoid extension risk (the risk that borrowers will slow down payments and not meet scheduled payment timelines) *most likely* would opt for Tranche A.

3. *Determine the correct answers to complete the following sentences:*

The tranching structure in the CMOs cannot eliminate ________________ but can redistribute it across the different tranches, insulating some more than others. Across the range of CMO structures, the more senior a tranche is, the less exposure it has to ____________________ and ________________.

Solution:

The tranching structure in the CMOs cannot eliminate *prepayment risk* but can redistribute it across the different tranches, insulating some more than others. Across the range of CMO structures, the more senior a tranche is, the less exposure it has to *prepayment risk* and *default risk.*

5 COMMERCIAL MORTGAGE-BACKED SECURITIES (CMBS)

☐ describe characteristics and risks of commercial mortgage-backed securities

Commercial mortgage-backed securities (CMBS) are backed by a pool of commercial mortgages on income-producing property, such as multifamily properties (e.g., apartment buildings), office buildings, industrial properties (including warehouses), shopping centers, hotels, and health care facilities (e.g., senior housing care facilities). Repayment can be made from leases and other revenue the property generates. The collateral is a pool of commercial loans that were originated either to finance a commercial property acquisition or to refinance a prior mortgage obligation. Exhibit 7 provides an example of a CMBS structure where the mortgages on several properties owned by the hypothetical car manufacturer Bright Wheel Automotive (BRWA), used in previous lessons, are securitized.

Exhibit 7: Sequential Pay CMBS, Summary of Terms

CMBS SPE
Commercial Finance Partners

Assets	Liabilities
WAC = 4.66% WAM = 88 mos.	GBP 100 million
Office Bldg: GBP 21m FMV: GBP 27m, 4.0% Maturity: 5 Yrs	**Tranche A: GBP 25m** 2.5%, Maturity 3 Yrs
Factory Bldg: GBP 32m FMV: GBP 40m, 6.0% Maturity: 5 Yrs	**Tranche B: GBP 25m** 4.25%, Maturity 10 Yrs
Office Bldg: GBP 30m FMV: GBP 36m, 3.5% Maturity: 10 Yrs	**Tranche C: GBP 25m** 4.75%, Maturity 10 Yrs
Warehouse: GBP 17m FMV: GBP 20m, 5.0% Maturity: 10 Yrs	**Tranche D: GBP 25m** 5.75%, Maturity 10 Yrs

In this specific transaction, properties valued at GBP123 million serve as collateral for GBP100 million mortgages, giving an LTV of 81.3%, which provides GBP23 million excess collateral for the mortgage lender. The lender then transfers the GBP100 million mortgages to an independent entity, Commercial Finance Associates, which then through the securitization process issues securities backed by the mortgages. Effectively, the weighted average proceeds from the mortgages (WAMP) are 4.66% and the weighted coupon payment 4.075%, where the spread provides compensation for arranging the securitization. For simplicity, all the mortgages are fully amortizing; in practice, commercial mortgages are balloon loans and not fully amortizing.

An additional feature of this transaction is that the cash flows do not immediately match across time horizons, including a Tranche A that is repaid in 3 years and carries a lower interest rate than any of the mortgages. However, the pool generates sufficient cash flows to make these payments, and the mortgages do not allow any prepayment during their first 5 years.

CMBS transactions are common in many markets. In the United States, CMBS transactions pool a larger number of commercial mortgages. Some transactions focus on mortgages on specific property types (such as warehouses and multi-family residential) or specific geographic areas (such as the Northeast or the Southwest United States). Others pool commercial mortgages from one lender. A small, but sizable, portion of the US market focuses on securitizing a single loan backed typically by one high value, marquee property in a major city. Akin to these single asset deals are single borrower deals where the CMBS transaction securitizes multiple commercial mortgage loans from one borrower.

Outside the United States, the volume of CMBS transactions is growing, particularly in Europe. European CMBS transactions have some structural differences reflecting differences in legal standards, commercial credit conventions, and bankruptcy. For instance, many European CMBS securitize a few loans in each transaction, but these loans can originate from different European countries. This introduces legal risk to the transaction because in the event of foreclosure or bankruptcy, the sale of the property must follow local rules that can be vastly different across Europe. Typically, European CMBS carry a floating rate, but that rate may be capped, while US CMBS usually pay a fixed rate and only occasionally offer a floating rate. Overall, CMBS deals require more direct understanding of the legal, financial, and commercial structures underlying each mortgage in the securitization transaction.

CMBS Structure

Both the CMBS and RMBS securitization processes and securitization structures, respectively are highly similar. However, two features specific to CMBS structures are worth mentioning: the presence of call protection and the balloon maturity provision.

Call Protection

A critical investment feature that distinguishes CMBS from RMBS is the protection against early prepayments. Call protection is available to investors in CMBS, which results in CMBS trading more like corporate bonds than RMBS. The call protection comes either at the structure level or at the loan level.

Structural call protection is achieved through sequential-pay tranches in the CMBS: A lower-rated tranche cannot be paid down until the higher-rated tranche is completely retired. Principal losses are always borne by the junior tranches first.

Call protection on the individual loan level relies on three mechanisms, usually through covenants. The first is prepayment lockout, a contractual agreement that prohibits any prepayments during a specified period. Second, the loan agreement can also stipulate prepayment penalty points, predetermined penalties that a borrower who wants to refinance must pay to the CMBS SPE. A point is equal to 1.00% of the outstanding loan balance.

Third, **defeasance** is a mechanism that allows prepayment, but the borrower must purchase a portfolio of government securities that fully replicates the cash flows of the remaining scheduled principal and interest payments, including the balloon loan balance, on the loan. When the last obligation is paid off, the value of the portfolio is zero (that is, no funds remain). The cost of assembling such a portfolio is the cost of defeasing the loan that must be paid by the issuer.

Balloon Maturity Provision

Another material difference lies in the structure of commercial mortgages. Unlike most residential mortgages, which are self-amortizing, commercial real estate loans are not fully amortizing. They usually pay interest payments and some principal repayments throughout the loan with the balance of the unamortized principal repaid at maturity through a large "balloon" payment. At loan maturity (e.g., the end of year 5 or year 10), the borrower must make the remaining balloon payment to pay down the principal.

Many commercial loans backing CMBS are balloon loans that require a substantial principal repayment at the maturity of the loan. There are several reasons why a borrower may fail to make the balloon payment at maturity. First, the borrower may not be able to refinance the existing mortgage to roll the balloon loan into a new loan due to the borrower's deteriorating debt service coverage or LTV ratios. Lenders also may not be able to extend the terms of the existing loan given the economic environment. Finally, the borrower may not be able to sell the property to generate sufficient funds to pay off the outstanding principal balance.

Balloon risk is the risk that the borrower fails to make the balloon payment at maturity and is in default. In this case, the lender may extend the loan over a period known as the "workout period," and modify the original terms of the loan during the workout period. Because the life of the loan is extended by the lender during the workout period, balloon risk is a type of extension risk.

CMBS Risks

Another significant difference between RMBS and CMBS is that a RMBS pool may consist of thousands of mortgages from various parts of a country, while CMBS can consist of a few underlying commercial mortgages. With RMBS collateralized by relatively homogeneous single-family residential properties, individual defaults can be frequent but have minimal impact on security holders due to the small size of any one mortgage in the RMBS pool. A single default in a CMBS pool, on the other hand, can have a significant impact on the CMBS investors. Investors in the CMBS must explicitly consider this unique concentration risk by not only analyzing the CMBS structure but also by analyzing the individual loans and properties backing the CMBS and the owners of the commercial properties themselves.

In commercial real estate lending, the key indicators of potential credit performance are the loan-to-value ratio (LTV), which was discussed earlier, and the debt service coverage ratio (DSCR or DSC ratio), like the debt-to-income ratio. The **DSC ratio** is equal to the property's annual net operating income (NOI) divided by the debt service.

$$DSC = \frac{Net\ Operating\ Income}{Debt\ Service}$$

NOI is defined as the rental income reduced by cash operating expenses and a non-cash replacement reserve reflecting the depreciation of the property over time.

$$NOI = (Rental\ income - cash\ operating\ expenses) - replacement\ reserves.$$

NOI excludes principal and interest payments on loans, capital expenditures, depreciation, and amortization.

Note that debt service is the annual amount of interest payments and principal repayments. A DSC ratio that exceeds 1.0× indicates that the cash flows from the property are sufficient to cover the debt service while maintaining the property in its initial state of repair. The higher the DSC ratio, the more likely it is that the borrower will be able to meet debt-servicing requirements from the property's cash flows.

EXAMPLE 5

Debt Service Coverage Ratio Calculation

The first property listed in Exhibit 7 has an estimated fair market value of GBP27 million. Its net operating income is GBP7,590,000 million. With annual debt service of GBP4,717,169 its DSC ratio is 1.61×, as shown below. This DSC level indicates that the property's cash flows are more than sufficient to cover the debt service while maintaining the property in its initial state of repair.

$$DSC = \frac{GBP\ 7,590,000}{GBP\ 4,717,169} = 1.61\times.$$

Lenders must evaluate the cash flow generating capacity of the property closely because commercial mortgages are non-recourse loans, where the lenders can look only to the income-producing property serving as collateral for the loan to satisfy the debt in foreclosure.

Exhibit 8 compares representative aspects of CMBS and RMBS.

Exhibit 8: CMBS vs. RMBS

	CMBS	RMBS
Underlying assets	From one to a pool of commercial mortgages on income-producing property	A pool of mortgages backed by residential properties or a pool of RMBS
Issuer	▪ Lenders, commercial banks, investment banks, or syndicates of banks	▪ A government or a quasi-government entity or by a bank, financial institution, or other private business
Rate for security	▪ Europe – Floating rate; may be capped ▪ US – typically fixed rate	▪ Either fixed or floating rate
Risk aspect: Credit Risk	▪ May be high, since the assets backing the CMBS can be concentrated in one mortgage or a small number (as compared to the number backing an RMBS)	▪ Agency RMBS – Issued and fully guaranteed by the government or a quasi-government entity ▪ Non-agency RMBS – Issued by banks, financial institutions, or other private businesses that use credit enhancements to reduce credit risk

	CMBS	RMBS
Risk aspect: Prepayment Risk	▪ *contraction risk* – Low No prepayment risk since commercial loans either do not offer a prepayment option or make prepayment uneconomical ▪ *extension risk* - High Balloon risk – Many commercial loans backing CMBS are balloon. If balloon payment not made, the lender may extend the life of the loan, leading to extension risk	▪ *contraction risk* – High Particularly during periods of declining or persistently low interest rates, or when the value of the underlying properties increase. ▪ *extension risk* – High Particularly during periods of increasing interest rates or high interest rates, or when the value of the underlying properties stays stable or declines.
Risk aspect: Default Risk	Depends on: ▪ Security held: Pool based on few mortgages (high) or RMBS pools (lower) ▪ Concentration of pool: Pool of few mortgages (high) vs. a diversified pool (lower)	▪ Aggregate risk may be lower due to diversification from many small, uniform underlying mortgages.

QUESTION SET

1. *Determine the correct answers to complete the following sentences:*

   A critical investment feature that distinguishes CMBS from RMBS is the protection against early prepayments. Call protection is available to investors in _______, which results in the securities trading more like corporate bonds than _______.

   Solution:

   A critical investment feature that distinguishes CMBS from RMBS is the protection against early prepayments. Call protection is available to investors in *CMBS*, which results in the securities trading more like corporate bonds than *RMBS*.

2. Using the information below for a 3,000 square foot warehouse and its loan, determine if the debt service coverage (DSC) ratio in year 5 is *most likely*:

5.0%, Ten-Year CAD450,000 Loan with Twenty Year Amortization	
Rental Rate	USD20/square foot/year
Rental Income	USD60,000
Cash Operating Expenses	
▪ Property Taxes	USD6,000
▪ Insurance	USD2,000
▪ Property Maintenance	USD1,500
Depreciation	USD10,000

5.0%, Ten-Year CAD450,000 Loan with Twenty Year Amortization

Annual payment (principal & interest) – years 1–10	USD36,110

A. above 1.

B. 1.

C. below 1.

Solution:

The correct answer is A. The debt service coverage ratio (DSC) is calculated as:

$$DSC = \frac{Net\ Operating\ Income}{Debt\ Service}$$

$$DSC = \frac{(Rental\ Income - Cash\ Operating\ Expenses\ )}{Annual\ Debt\ Service\ (principal + interest\ payments)}$$

$$DSC = \frac{(60,000 - 9,500\ )}{36,110}$$

$$DSC = \frac{USD\ 50,500}{36,110} = 1.3985\times.$$

B and C are incorrect because the calculated DSC ratio is above 1.0×, not equal to or below 1.

3. Which of the following mechanisms is *least likely* to offer investors protection from default on the individual loan level?

A. Defeasance

B. Balloon payment structure

C. Prepayment penalty points

Solution:

The correct answer is B. Typically, commercial real estate loans are not fully amortizing and thus require the unamortized principal to be repaid at maturity through a large "balloon" payment. If the borrower fails to make the balloon payment at maturity and is in default, then balloon risk results. Thus, the balloon payment structure increases risk to investors, rather than protecting against it. A is incorrect because defeasance, a mechanism that requires the borrower to purchase a portfolio of government securities that replicates the cash flows of the remaining scheduled principal and interest payments remaining on the loan, protects the investor. C is incorrect because prepayment penalty points (i.e., predetermined penalties that a borrower who wants to refinance must pay to the lender) offer investors call protection on the individual loan level.

4. Relative to RMBS loan pools, CMBS loan pools exhibit less:

A. credit risk.

B. prepayment risk.

C. concentration risk.

Solution:

The correct answer is B. CMBS loans exhibit less prepayment risk because commercial loans either do not offer prepayment options or make prepayment uneconomical. Conversely, RMBS loans are freely prepayable, thus prepayment risk is higher. A is incorrect because CMBS loans have higher credit risk because the assets backing the CMBS can be concentrated in one mortgage or a small number of mortgages (as compared to the large number backing an RMBS). In addition, agency RMBS are issued and fully guaranteed by the government or a quasi-government entity, and non-agency RMBS are issued by banks, financial institutions, or other private businesses, which use credit enhancements to reduce credit risk. C is incorrect because CMBS loan pools exhibit more concentration risk than RMBS loan pools. CMBS loan pools exhibit a fewer number of loans and will have some larger loans that create concentration risk.

PRACTICE PROBLEMS

The following information relates to questions 1-2

Please refer to the information below to answer questions 1 and 2 regarding the bonds securitized by the AR&C leases.

AR&C Limited Securitization of Private Jet Leases

AR&C Limited leases private jets to corporations in North America for a fixed term of five years. AR&C retains ownership of the jets. The corporations make equal interest payments each month. If a customer defaults, AR&C can repossess the jet. AR&C has been in business for approximately fifteen years and has a B3 credit rating, meaning that its debt is non-investment grade. AR&C has CAD500 million in leases on its balance sheet that it wants to securitize into ABS.

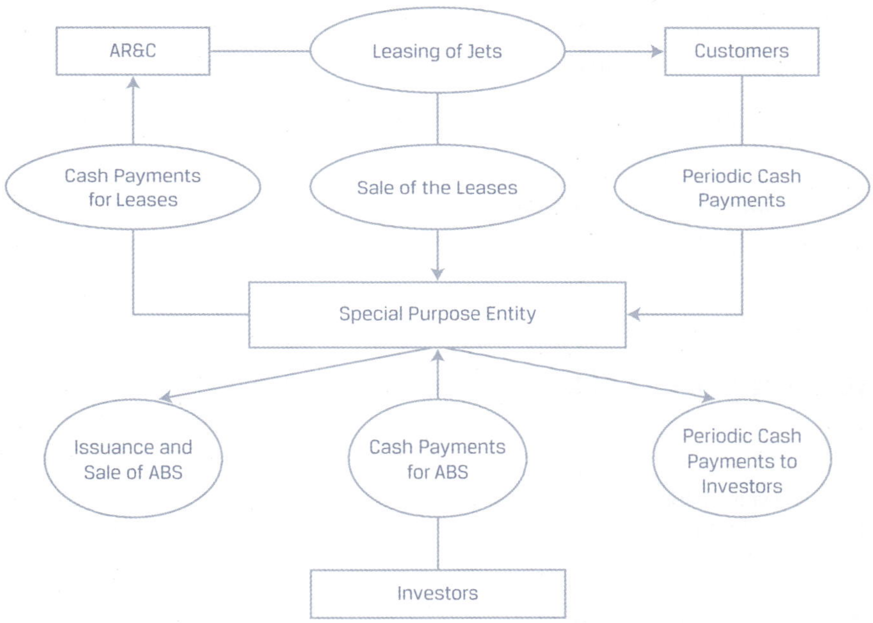

Bond Class	
A (senior)	*Tranche A Notes* Face value: CAD250 million Interest rate: MRR + 1.00% Maturity: One year
B (subordinated)	*Tranche B Notes* Face value: CAD100 million Interest rate: MRR + 2.00% Maturity: Two years
C (subordinated)	*Tranche C Notes* Face value: CAD100 million Interest rate: MRR + 3.00% Maturity: Three years

Bond Class	
D (subordinated)	*Tranche D Notes* Face value: CAD50 million Interest rate: MRR + 4.00% Maturity: Four years
Total	CAD500 million

1. Compare the credit rating of the Class A bonds issued by the SPE and the un-collateralized bonds issued directly by AR&C. The Class A bonds are *most likely* rated:

   A. lower than AR&C bonds.

   B. the same as AR&C bonds.

   C. higher than AR&C bonds.

2. Select which of the following statements related to the collateralized bonds issued directly by the SPE is *most* accurate.

   A. This senior/subordinated structure is an example of time tranching.

   B. Losses are realized by the subordinated bond classes before any losses are realized by Class A bonds.

   C. In a waterfall structure such as this one, losses are shared proportionally across all subordinated bond classes.

The following information relates to questions 3-4

A borrower wishes to procure a mortgage loan to purchase a property. Information regarding the property, the desired loan, and the buyer's finances is shown below:

- Property price: CAD750,000
- Desired loan amount: CAD525,000
- Annual interest rate: 5.00%
- Loan term: 30 years/360 months
- Monthly payment: CAD2,818.31
- Borrower's annual pre-tax gross income: CAD210,000

3. The loan-to-value (LTV) ratio is *closest to*:

   A. 54%.

   B. 66%.

   C. 70%.

4. The debt-to-income (DTI) ratio is *closest to*:

   A. 1.30%.

   B. 16.10%.

   C. 250.00%.

---

5. For a CMO that includes Planned Amortization Class (PAC) tranches, if the prepayment rate is within the anticipated range, which of the following tranches *most likely* protects investors from prepayment risk?

   A. PAC tranche

   B. Senior tranche

   C. Support tranche

6. Which of the following approaches redistributes prepayment risk?

   A. Tranching

   B. Excess spread

   C. Overcollateralization

7. Shown below are five mortgages that comprise the entire pool in a mortgage-backed security.

Mortgage	Interest Rate (*i*)	Beginning Balance (BB)	Current Balance (CB)	Original Term (months)	Number of Months to Maturity
A	2.00%	CAD200,000	CAD83,000	420	140
B	3.00%	CAD300,000	CAD193,000	360	192
C	4.00%	CAD400,000	CAD315,000	360	240
D	5.00%	CAD500,000	CAD357,000	240	144
E	6.00%	CAD600,000	CAD548,000	420	324
		CAD2,000,000	**CAD1,496,000**		

   The WAM for this security is *closest* to:

   A. 208 months.

   B. 224 months.

   C. 236 months.

8. Which of the following adverse consequences is most likely associated with extension risk?

   A. Investors must reinvest the proceeds at lower interest rates.

   B. Higher interest rates reduce the value of the cash flows investors receive.

   C. The prepayment option reduces the potential price appreciation for the bond.

The following information relates to questions 9-11

Use the following information for questions 9, 10, and 11:

Shown below are three properties whose mortgages are securitized to create a sequential-pay CMBS and information related to the four tranches comprising the CMBS.

Property Information

Property Type	Fair Market Value	Mortgaged Amount	Coupon Rate	Maturity	Repayment
Office Building	35,000,000	27,000,000	4.00%	Four years from settlement date	Fully amortizing
Office Building	60,000,000	44,000,000	3.00%	Four years from settlement date	Fully amortizing
Warehouse	15,000,000	12,000,000	5.00%	Eight years from settlement date	Fully amortizing

Prepayment: No prepayment on the underlying mortgages is allowed in the first 5 years.

Tranche Information

Tranche	Coupon Rate	Principal Value
A	2.00%	20,000,000
B	3.00%	22,000,000
C	4.00%	23,000,000
D	5.00%	18,000,000

9. The associated loan to value ratio is *closest to*:

   A. 0.75.

   B. 0.77.

   C. 0.80.

10. The weighted average coupon payment is *closest to*:

    A. 3.47%.

    B. 3.50%.

    C. 3.61%.

11. The weighted average proceeds from the mortgages is *closest to*:

    A. 3.47%.

    B. 3.50%.

C. 3.61%.

---

12. Which of the following would *most likely* increase balloon risk for a commercial mortgage loan that is maturing?
    A. High DSCR
    B. Low LTV ratio
    C. Lack of property buyers in market

13. Which of the following provides call protection for CMBS investors at the structural level?
    A. Defeasance
    B. Prepayment lockout
    C. Sequential-pay tranches

SOLUTIONS

1. The correct answer is C. The Class A bonds issued by the SPE are backed by collateral, the leases sold by AR&C to the SPE, and they are the most senior of the bonds issued by the SPE. A secured bond is secured by collateral and is considered less risky than a bond without collateral backing. The Class A bonds issued by the SPE would *most likely* be rated higher than any unsecured corporate bonds issued directly by AR&C.

2. The correct answer is B. Losses are realized by the subordinated bond classes before any losses are realized by the senior Class A bonds. A is incorrect because this senior/subordinated structure is an example of credit tranching, not time tranching. C is incorrect because in a waterfall structure such as this one, the most junior tranche, Class D, will absorb all losses up to its full CAD50 million par value first. Then, if credit losses exceed that threshold, Bond Class C will absorb all losses up to its full CAD100 million par value. The losses are not shared proportionally across all subordinated bond classes; instead, they are absorbed by the most junior classes first and subsequently by the more senior ones up to the value of the loss.

3. The correct answer is C. The loan-to-value ratio (LTV) is the ratio of the amount of the loan/mortgage to the property's value.

   $$LTV = \frac{Amount\ of\ the\ loan/mortgage}{Property's\ value}$$

   $$LTV = \frac{525,000}{750,000}$$

   $$LTV = 70\%.$$

   A is incorrect because it was calculated as the monthly payment divided by the beginning loan value, not the loan to property value, as follows:

   $$\frac{2,818.31}{525,000} = 0.54\%.$$

   Note: This is 0.54%, not 54%. Choice A was adjusted to 54% to make the correct answer less obvious.

   B is incorrect because it was calculated as the monthly payment for a 20-year loan, not a 30-year loan, divided by the beginning loan value, not the loan to property value, as follows:

   $$\frac{3,464.77}{525,000} = 0.66\%.$$

   Note: This is 0.66%, not 66%. Choice B was adjusted to 66% to make the correct answer less obvious.

4. The correct answer is B. The DTI is calculated using the monthly debt payment and the borrower's monthly pre-tax gross income, as follows:

   $$DTI = \frac{Monthly\ Debt\ Payment}{Monthly\ pre-tax\ gross\ income}$$

   $$DTI = \frac{CAD\ 2,818.31}{(CAD\ 210,000/12)} = 16.10\%.$$

   A is incorrect because it was calculated as the monthly payment divided by the annual pre-tax gross income, as follows:

$$\frac{2{,}818.31}{210{,}000} = 1.30\%.$$

C is incorrect because it was calculated as the starting loan value divided by the annual pre-tax gross income, as follows:

$$\frac{525{,}000}{210{,}000} = 250.00\%.$$

5. The correct answer is C. If the prepayment rate is within the specified range, all prepayment risk is absorbed by the support tranche. This provides greater predictability of the size and timing of cash flows paid to investors in the PAC tranches.

   A is incorrect because in a CMO that includes a PAC tranche, the PAC tranche is protected from prepayment risk because all prepayment risk is absorbed by the support tranche.

   B is incorrect because in a CMO that includes a PAC tranche, the senior (PAC) tranche is protected from prepayment risk because all prepayment risk is absorbed by the support tranche.

6. The correct answer is A. The tranching structure in CMOs cannot eliminate prepayment risk, but it can redistribute prepayment risk across the different tranches, insulating some tranches more than others. CMO tranche structures reduce the uncertainties of the size and timing of payments investors receive.

   B and C are incorrect because excess spread and overcollateralization are both common forms of credit enhancement, but they do not redistribute prepayment risk.

7. The correct answer is C. The weighted average maturity is calculated by weighting the number of months to maturity for each mortgage in the pool by the percentage of the outstanding mortgage balance relative to the outstanding amount of all the mortgages in the pool, as shown in the following equation:

$$WAM = MM_A\left(\frac{CB_A}{\sum_{CB}}\right) + MM_B\left(\frac{CB_B}{\sum_{CB}}\right) + MM_C\left(\frac{CB_C}{\sum_{CB}}\right) + MM_D\left(\frac{CB_D}{\sum_{CB}}\right) + MM_E\left(\frac{CB_E}{\sum_{CB}}\right)$$

$$WAM = 140\left(\frac{83{,}000}{1{,}496{,}000}\right) + 192\left(\frac{193{,}000}{1{,}496{,}000}\right) + 240\left(\frac{315{,}000}{1{,}496{,}000}\right) + 144\left(\frac{357{,}000}{1{,}496{,}000}\right) + 324\left(\frac{548{,}000}{1{,}496{,}000}\right)$$

$WAM = 236$ months.

   A is incorrect because it is calculated by averaging the months to maturity for the five mortgages, rather than calculating their weighted average.

   B is incorrect because it is calculated by weighting the number of months to maturity for each mortgage in the pool by the percentage of the beginning mortgage balance relative to the beginning amount of all the mortgages in the pool, not by the current balances.

8. The correct answer is B. Extension risk is the risk that the borrower might pay back the money borrowed more slowly than anticipated, extending the time of repayment and the maturity of the bond. For investors, this has one adverse consequence: Higher interest rates reduce the value of the cash flows investors receive. The payments the investors receive will be discounted at a higher interest

rate, and the extension stretches out the payments the investors receive.

A is incorrect because contraction risk (the risk that the borrower might pay back the money borrowed more quickly than anticipated, reducing the amount of future payments the investor receives), not extension risk, has the adverse consequence that investors must reinvest the proceeds at lower interest rates.

C is incorrect because contraction risk (the risk that the borrower might pay back the money borrowed more quickly than anticipated, reducing the amount of future payments the investor receives), not extension risk, has the adverse consequence that the prepayment option reduces the potential price appreciation for the bond.

9. The correct answer is A. The associated loan to value ratio is calculated as the total value of all loans (mortgages) divided by the total value of the properties associated with the mortgages, as follows:

$$LTV = \frac{Total\ value\ of\ all\ loans\ (mortgages)}{Total\ value\ of\ all\ properties\ mortgaged}$$

$$LTV = \frac{83,000,000}{110,000,000} = 0.75.$$

B is incorrect because 0.77 is the value of just the mortgage on the first property (27,000,000) divided by the first property's total value (35,000,000).

C is incorrect because 0.80 is the value of just the mortgage on the third property (11,400,000) divided by the third property's total value (15,000,000).

10. The correct answer is A. The weighted average coupon payment is calculated as the value of each tranche's coupon rate weighted by the principal value of that tranche as a percentage of the total value of all tranches:

$$WAC = i_A\left(\frac{PV_A}{\sum PV}\right) + i_B\left(\frac{PV_B}{\sum PV}\right) + i_C\left(\frac{PV_C}{\sum PV}\right) + i_D\left(\frac{PV_D}{\sum PV}\right)$$

$$WAC = 2.00\%\left(\frac{20,000,000}{83,000,000}\right) + 3.00\%\left(\frac{22,000,000}{83,000,000}\right)$$
$$+4.00\%\left(\frac{23,000,000}{83,000,000}\right) + 5.00\%\left(\frac{18,000,000}{23,000,000}\right)$$

$$WAC = 3.47\%.$$

B is incorrect because 3.50% is calculated as a straight average of the four coupon rates (of the four tranches), rather than a weighted average.

C is incorrect because 3.61% is the weighted proceeds from the three mortgages, not the weighted average coupon payment.

11. The correct answer is C. The weighted average proceeds from the mortgages ($WAMP$ shown below) is calculated as the coupon rate of each mortgage weighted by that mortgage's value/amount as a percentage of the total value of all the mortgages:

$$WAMP = i_A\left(\frac{MA_A}{\sum MA}\right) + i_B\left(\frac{MA_B}{\sum MA}\right) + i_C\left(\frac{MA_C}{\sum MA}\right)$$

$$WAMP = 4.00\%\left(\frac{27,000,000}{83,000,000}\right) + 3.00\%\left(\frac{44,000,000}{83,000,000}\right) + 5.00\%\left(\frac{12,000,000}{83,000,000}\right)$$

$$WAMP = 3.61\%.$$

A is incorrect because 3.47% is the weighted average coupon payment for the four tranches, not the weighted average proceeds from the mortgages.

B is incorrect because 3.50% is calculated as a straight average of the four coupon rates (of the four tranches), not the weighted average proceeds from the mortgages.

12. The correct answer is C. A lack of property buyers in the market will make it challenging for a borrower to sell a property to generate sufficient funds to pay off the outstanding principal balance. A is incorrect because a high DSCR would reduce the balloon risk. B is incorrect because a low LTV ratio would also reduce the balloon risk of a maturing loan.

13. The correct answer is C. Structural call protection is achieved through sequential-pay tranches in the CMBS as a lower-rated tranche cannot be paid down until the higher-rated tranche is completely retired. A is incorrect because defeasance provides call protection at the individual loan level. Defeasance allows prepayment, but the borrower must purchase a portfolio of government securities that fully replicates the cash flows of the remaining scheduled principal and interest payments, including the balloon loan balance, on the loan. B is incorrect because prepayment lockout provides call protection at the individual loan level. Prepayment lockout is a contractual agreement that prohibits any prepayments during a specified period.

Glossary

Abandonment option The option to terminate an investment at some future time if the financial results are disappointing.

Abnormal return The amount by which a security's actual return differs from its expected return, given the security's risk and the market's return.

Absolute dispersion The amount of variability present without comparison to any reference point or benchmark.

Accelerated book build An offering of securities by an investment bank acting as principal that is accomplished in only one or two days.

Accounting profit Income as reported on the income statement, in accordance with prevailing accounting standards, before the provisions for income tax expense. Also called *income before taxes* or *pretax income.*

Accredited investors Investors that meet certain minimum regulatory net worth or other requirements in order to invest in certain types of alternative assets.

Accrued interest The amount of interest in currency or par value terms of a fixed-income instrument that accumulates from the last coupon payment until the trade settlement date. The amount is paid by the buyer to the seller.

Action lag Delay from policy decisions to implementation.

Active investment An approach to investing in which the investor seeks to outperform a given benchmark.

Active return The return on a portfolio minus the return on the portfolio's benchmark.

Activist Short for "activist shareholder." Managers secure sufficient equity holdings to allow them to seek a position in a company's board and influence corporate policies or direction.

Activity ratios Ratios that measure how well a company is managing key current assets and working capital over time.

Ad hoc committee A small group of lenders or bondholders who negotiate with an issuer on debt restructuring and refinancing before the issuer submits a final proposal to the wider group of all lenders and bondholders.

Add-on pricing A pricing approach based on high-margin optional features, customizations, and additional content.

Add-on rate A yield or pricing convention for money market instrument quotations. It is the interest earned on an instrument, derived from the difference between the price and face value, expressed as a percentage of the price and multiplied by the periodicity of the annual rate.

Agency costs Direct and indirect costs borne by the principal in a principal-agent relationship owing primarily to information asymmetries. Agency costs include the costs of monitoring and assessing the agent as well as missed opportunities.

Agency RMBS Securities created by the pooling of residential mortgage-backed securities in the United States by either the Federal National Mortgage Association (Fannie Mae) or the Federal Home Loan Mortgage Corporation (Freddie Mac). These RMBS carry the full faith and credit of the government, essentially a guarantee with respect to timely payment of interest and repayment of principal.

All-or-nothing (AON) orders An order that includes the instruction to trade only if the trade fills the entire quantity (size) specified.

Allocationally efficient A characteristic of a market, a financial system, or an economy that promotes the allocation of resources to their highest value uses.

Altcoin A cryptocurrency other than Bitcoin.

Alternative data Data that are generated from non-traditional sources, such as social media and sensor networks.

Alternative hypothesis The hypothesis that is accepted if the null hypothesis is rejected.

Alternative investment markets Market for investments other than traditional securities investments (i.e., traditional common and preferred shares and traditional fixed income instruments). The term usually encompasses direct and indirect investment in real estate (including timberland and farmland) and commodities (including precious metals); hedge funds, private equity, and other investments requiring specialized due diligence.

Alternative trading systems Trading venues that function like exchanges but that do not exercise regulatory authority over their subscribers except with respect to the conduct of the subscribers' trading in their trading systems. Also called *electronic communications networks* or *multilateral trading facilities.*

American depository receipt A US dollar-denominated security that trades like a common share on US exchanges.

American depository share The underlying shares on which American depository receipts are based. They trade in the issuing company's domestic market.

American options Options that may be exercised at any time from contract inception until maturity.

American-style Type of option contract that can be exercised at any time up to the option's expiration date.

Amortization The process of allocating the cost of intangible long-term assets having a finite useful life to accounting periods; the allocation of the amount of a bond premium or discount to the periods remaining until bond maturity.

Amortizing debt A loan or bond with a payment schedule that calls for the complete repayment of principal over the instrument's time to maturity.

Analysis of variance (ANOVA) A table that presents the sums of squares, degrees of freedom, mean squares, and F-statistic for a regression model.

Analytical duration Estimates of duration using mathematical formulas. Estimates of the impact of yield changes on bond prices using analytical duration implicitly assume that benchmark yields and spreads are independent variables and are uncorrelated.

Anchoring and adjustment bias An information-processing bias in which the use of a psychological heuristic influences the way people estimate probabilities.

Annual general meeting (AGM) A yearly meeting of the corporate board of directors and shareholders, typically held in person and digitally, during which votes on directors, compensation plans, shareholder resolutions, and any other matters properly brought forward at the meeting are held. Issuer management may also make presentations and hold events.

Anomalies Apparent deviations from market efficiency.

Antidilutive With reference to a transaction or a security, one that would increase earnings per share (EPS) or result in EPS higher than the company's basic EPS—antidilutive securities are not included in the calculation of diluted EPS.

Arbitrage (1) The simultaneous purchase of an undervalued asset or portfolio and sale of an overvalued but equivalent asset or portfolio in order to obtain a riskless profit on the price differential. Taking advantage of a market inefficiency in a risk-free manner. (2) The condition in a financial market in which equivalent assets or combinations of assets sell for two different prices, creating an opportunity to profit at no risk with no commitment of money. In a well-functioning financial market, few arbitrage opportunities are possible (3) A risk-free operation that earns an expected positive net profit but requires no net investment of money.

Arbitrageurs Traders who engage in arbitrage. See *arbitrage*.

Arithmetic mean The sum of the observations divided by the number of observations.

Artificial intelligence (AI) Computer systems that are capable of performing tasks that previously required human intelligence. AI methods are sometimes better suited to identify complex, non-linear relationships than are traditional quantitative and statistical methods.

Ask The price at which a dealer or trader is willing to sell an asset, typically qualified by a maximum quantity (ask size). See *offer*.

Ask size The maximum quantity of an asset that pertains to a specific ask price from a trader. For example, if the ask for a share issue is $30 for a size of 1,000 shares, the trader is offering to sell at $30 up to 1,000 shares.

Asset allocation The process of determining how investment funds should be distributed among asset classes.

Asset class A group of assets that have similar characteristics, attributes, and risk–return relationships.

Asset utilization ratios Ratios that measure how efficiently a company performs day-to-day tasks, such as the collection of receivables and management of inventory.

Asset-backed commercial paper Secured form of commercial paper issuance. Loans or receivables are sold to a special purpose entity that issues the ABCP and makes interest and principal payments to investors from asset cash flows.

Asset-backed securities (ABS) A type of bond issued by a legal entity called a special purpose entity created solely to own assets such as loans, receivables, and mortgages and to distribute cash flows to ABS investors. Generally, ABS backed by mortgages are known as mortgage-backed securities (MBS) while ABS refer to non-mortgage ABS.

Asset-backed token A token that represents the ownership of a physical asset that does not exist on the blockchain and whose value is based on the underlying asset.

Asset-based valuation models Valuation based on estimates of the market value of a company's assets.

Asymmetric information Also known as *information asymmetry*; the differential of information between corporate insiders and outsiders regarding the company's performance and prospects. Managers typically have more information about the company's performance and prospects than owners and creditors.

At-the-money Describes a unique situation in which the price of the underlying is equal to an option's exercise price. Like an out-of-the-money option, the intrinsic value is zero.

Auction/reverse auction models Pricing models that establish prices through bidding (by sellers in the case of reverse auctions).

Autarky Countries seeking political self-sufficiency with little or no external trade or finance. State-owned enterprises control strategic domestic industries.

Automatic stabilizer A countercyclical factor that automatically comes into play as an economy slows and unemployment rises.

Availability bias An information-processing bias in which people take a heuristic approach to estimating the probability of an outcome based on how easily the outcome comes to mind.

Available-for-sale Under US GAAP, debt securities not classified as either held-to-maturity or held-for-trading securities. The investor is willing to sell but not actively planning to sell. In general, available-for-sale debt securities are reported at fair value on the balance sheet, with unrealized gains included as a component of other comprehensive income.

Average revenue (AR) Total revenue divided by quantity sold.

Backfill Bias A problem whereby certain surviving hedge funds may be added to databases and various hedge fund indexes only after they are initially successful and start to report their returns. Also see *survivorship bias*.

Backup line of credit A type of credit enhancement provided by a bank to an issuer of commercial paper to ensure that the issuer will have access to sufficient liquidity to repay maturing commercial paper if issuing new paper is not a viable option.

Backwardation A downward-sloping, or inverted, forward curve in a futures market.

Balance sheet ratios Financial ratios involving balance sheet items only.

Balanced With respect to a government budget, one in which spending and revenues (taxes) are equal.

Balloon payment A large payment required at maturity to retire a bond's outstanding principal amount.

Base rates The reference rate on which a bank bases lending rates to all other customers.

Base-rate neglect A type of representativeness bias in which the base rate or probability of the categorization is not adequately considered.

Basic EPS Net earnings available to common shareholders (i.e., net income minus preferred dividends) divided by the weighted average number of common shares outstanding.

Basis risk The possibility that the expected value of a derivative differs unexpectedly from that of the underlying.

Basket of listed depository receipts (BLDR) An exchange-traded fund (ETF) that represents a portfolio of depository receipts.

Bayes' formula The rule for updating the probability of an event of interest—given a set of prior probabilities for the event, information, and information given the event—if you receive new information.

Bearer bonds Bonds for which ownership is not recorded; only the clearing system knows who the bond owner is.

Behavioral finance A field of finance that examines the psychological variables that affect and often distort the investment decision making of investors, analysts, and portfolio managers.

Behind the market Said of prices specified in orders that are worse than the best current price; e.g., for a limit buy order, a limit price below the best bid.

Benchmark A bond used to compare against another bond to discern attributes, often a government bond with the same or similar time-to-maturity as the bond under analysis.

Benchmark spread The difference in yield-to-maturity between a bond and that of a benchmark bond.

Best bid The highest bid in the market.

Best effort offering An offering of a security using an investment bank in which the investment bank, as agent for the issuer, promises to use its best efforts to sell the offering but does not guarantee that a specific amount will be sold.

Best offer The lowest offer (ask price) in the market.

Best-in-class An ESG implementation approach that seeks to identify the most favorable companies and sectors based on ESG considerations. Also called *positive screening*.

Beta A measure of the sensitivity of a given investment or portfolio to movements in the overall market.

Bid The price at which a dealer or trader is willing to buy an asset, typically qualified by a maximum quantity.

Bid size The maximum quantity of an asset that pertains to a specific bid price from a trader.

Big data The vast amount of information being generated by both traditional sources—for example, stock exchanges, companies, governments—and non-traditional sources—for example, electronic devices, social media, sensor networks, and company exhaust.

Bilateralism The conduct of political, economic, financial, or cultural cooperation between two countries. Countries engaging in bilateralism may have relations with many different countries but in one-at-a-time agreements without multiple partners. Typically, countries exist on a spectrum between bilateralism and multilateralism.

Bimodal A distribution that has two most frequently occurring values.

Bitcoin A cryptocurrency using blockchain technology that was created in 2009.

Bivariate correlation Also known as Pearson correlation. A parametric measure of the relationship between two variables.

Black swan risk An event that is rare and difficult to predict but has an important impact.

Block brokers A broker (agent) that provides brokerage services for large-size trades.

Blockchain A type of digital ledger in which information is recorded sequentially and then linked together and secured using cryptographic methods.

Blue chip Widely held large market capitalization companies that are considered financially sound and are leaders in their respective industry or local stock market.

Board of directors A body or individual selected by a limited company's member(s) or shareholder(s), in a manner determined by the company's charter, that manages the company. Typically, for larger companies, boards of directors appoint and oversee executive management.

Bond equivalent yield A money market interest rate quoted on a 365-day add-on rate basis.

Bond indenture A legal document between a bond issuer and investors that governs each party's rights and responsibilities.

Bond market vigilantes Bond market participants who might reduce their demand for long-term bonds, thus pushing up their yields.

Bondholders Investors in an entity's securitized debt claims, such as commercial paper, notes, and bonds. Common types of bondholders include investment funds and institutional investors.

Bonds Contractual agreements between an issuer and bondholders.

Bonus issue of shares A type of dividend in which a company distributes additional shares of its common stock to shareholders instead of cash.

Book building Investment bankers' process of compiling a "book" or list of indications of interest to buy part of an offering.

Book value Shareholders' equity (total assets minus total liabilities) minus the value of preferred stock; common shareholders' equity.

Boom An expansionary phase characterized by economic growth "testing the limits" of the economy.

Bootstrap A resampling method that repeatedly draws samples with replacement of the selected elements from the original observed sample. Bootstrap is usually conducted by using computer simulation and is often used to find standard error or construct confidence intervals of population parameters.

Bottom-up analysis An investment selection approach that focuses on company-specific circumstances rather than emphasizing economic cycles or industry analysis.

Box and whisker plot A graphic for visualizing the dispersion of data across quartiles. It consists of a box with "whiskers" connected to the box.

Breakeven point Represents the price of the underlying in a derivative contract in which the profit to both counterparties would be zero.

Bridge financing Interim financing that provides funds until permanent financing can be arranged.

Broker An agent who executes orders to buy or sell securities on behalf of a client in exchange for a commission.

Brokered market A market in which brokers arrange trades among their clients.

Broker–dealer A financial intermediary (often a company) that may function as a principal (dealer) or as an agent (broker) depending on the type of trade.

Brownfield investments The third stage of development of an infrastructure asset. Brownfield investments involve expanding existing facilities and may involve privatization of public assets or a sale leaseback of completed greenfield projects. They are characterized by a shorter investment period with immediate cash flows and an operating history.

Budget surplus/deficit The difference between government revenue and expenditure for a stated fixed period of time.

Bullet bond A bond whose principal repayment is made entirely at maturity.

Bundling A pricing approach that refers to combining multiple products or services so that customers are incentivized or required to buy them together.

Business cycles Are recurrent expansions and contractions in economic activity affecting broad segments of the economy.

Business model A concise description of how a business works and makes revenues and profits, including its customers, products or services, channels for reaching customers, and pricing.

Businesses Organization entities formed and managed for the purpose of providing a return or economic benefits to its investors and owners.

Buy-side firm An investment management company or other investor that uses the services of brokers or dealers (i.e., the client of the sell side firms).

Buyback A transaction in which a company buys back its own shares. Unlike stock dividends and stock splits, share repurchases use corporate cash.

Cabotage The right to transport passengers or goods within a country by a foreign firm. Many countries—including those with multilateral trade agreements—impose restrictions on cabotage across transportation subsectors, meaning that shippers, airlines, and truck drivers are not allowed to transport goods and services within another country's borders.

Call market A market in which trades occur only at a particular time and place (i.e., when the market is called).

Call money rate The interest rate that buyers pay for their margin loan.

Call option The right to buy an underlying.

Call period The time during which the issuer of a callable bond can exercise the call option.

Call price The price at which the issuer of a callable bond has the right to purchase the bond from investors.

Call protection period The time during which the issuer of a callable bond is not allowed to exercise the call option.

Call risk The uncertain maturity and limited price appreciation associated with callable bonds.

Callable bond A bond containing an embedded call option that gives the issuer the right to buy the bond back from the investor at specified prices on predetermined dates.

Cannibalization A transfer of sales or market share from one product to another product owned by the same company. It tends to occur when the two products are actual or perceived substitutes.

Capacity The ability of the borrower to make its debt payments on time.

Capital Other company resources available that reduce reliance on debt.

Capital allocation The process that companies use for decision making on capital investments—those projects with a life of one year or longer.

Capital allocation line (CAL) A graph line that describes the combinations of expected return and standard deviation of return available to an investor from combining the optimal portfolio of risky assets with the risk-free asset.

Capital asset pricing model (CAPM) An equation describing the expected return on any asset (or portfolio) as a linear function of its beta relative to the market portfolio.

Capital expenditure Expenditure on physical capital (fixed assets).

Capital investments An expenditure for an asset or resource with a useful life of more than one year.

Capital market expectations (CME) Expectations concerning the risk and return prospects of asset classes.

Capital market line (CML) The line with an intercept point equal to the risk-free rate that is tangent to the efficient frontier of risky assets; represents the efficient frontier when a risk-free asset is available for investment.

Capital market securities Fixed-income securities with original maturities greater than one year.

Capital markets Financial markets that trade securities of longer duration, such as bonds and equities.

Capital restrictions Controls placed on foreigners' ability to own domestic assets and/or domestic residents' ability to own foreign assets.

Capital structure The mix of debt and equity that a company uses to finance its business; a company's specific mix of long-term financing.

Capital-indexed bond A type of index-linked bond for which changes in the index are captured with adjustments to the principal. A common example is Treasury Inflation Protected Securities (TIPS) issued by the United States government.

Capital-intensive businesses Companies or business activities that are characterized by a relatively low fixed asset turnover, a high percentage of capital expenditures to sales, or a high net-working-capital-to-sales ratio.

Capital-light businesses Also known as *asset light businesses*, companies or business activities characterized by relatively high fixed asset turnover, a low percentage of capital expenditures to sales, or a low net-working-capital-to-sales ratio.

Carried interest A performance fee (also referred to as an incentive fee, or carry) that is applied based on excess returns above a hurdle rate.

Carrying Investing and holding an asset for a period of time.

Carrying amount The amount at which an asset or liability is valued according to accounting principles.

Carrying value Of a fixed-income instrument is the purchase price plus (minus) the amortized amount of the discount (premium) if the bond is purchased at a price below (above) par value.

Cartel Participants in collusive agreements that are made openly and formally.

Cash conversion cycle The amount of time between an issuer paying its suppliers in cash and receiving cash from its customers.

Cash flow additivity principle The principle that dollar amounts indexed at the same point in time are additive.

Cash flow from operations A cash profit measure over a period for an issuer's primary business activities. It includes cash from customers as well as interest and dividends received from financial investments, less cash paid to employees and suppliers as well as taxes paid to governments and interest paid to lenders.

Cash flow hedge Refers to a specific **hedge accounting** classification in which a derivative is designated as absorbing the variable cash flow of a floating-rate asset or liability, such as foreign exchange, interest rates, or commodities.

Cash markets Markets in which specific assets are exchanged at current prices. Cash markets are often referred to as **spot markets**.

Cash prices The current prices prevailing in **cash markets**.

Cash ratio A measure of liquidity that is the ratio of cash and marketable securities to current liabilities.

Catch-up clause A clause in an agreement that favors the GP. For a GP who earns a 20% performance fee, a catch-up clause allows the GP to receive 100% of the distributions above the hurdle rate *until* she receives 20% of the profits generated, and then every excess dollar is split 80/20 between the LPs and GP.

CDS credit spread Reflects the credit spread of a credit default swap (CDS) derivative contract. As with cash bonds, CDS credit spreads depend on the probability of default (POD) and the loss given default (LGD).

Central bank digital currencies (CBDCs) A tokenized version of the currency issued by the central bank, such as a digital bank note or coin, and a digital liability of the central bank.

Central bank funds market The market in which deposit-taking banks that have an excess reserve with their national central bank can lend money to banks that need funds for maturities ranging from overnight to one year. Called the federal or fed funds market in the United States.

Central bank funds rate The interest rate at which central bank funds are bought (borrowed) and sold (lent) for maturities ranging from overnight to one year. Called federal or fed funds rate in the United States.

Central clearing mandate A requirement instituted by global regulatory authorities following the 2008 global financial crisis that most **over-the-counter (OTC)** derivatives be **cleared** by a **central counterparty (CCP)**.

Central counterparty (CCP) An economic entity that assumes the **counterparty credit risk** between derivative **counterparties**, one of which is typically a financial intermediary. CCPs provide **clearing** and **settlement** for most **derivative contracts**.

Central limit theorem The theorem that states the sum (and the mean) of a set of independent, identically distributed random variables with finite variances is normally distributed, whatever distribution the random variables follow.

Certificate of deposit (CD) An instrument that represents a specified amount of funds on deposit with a bank for a specified maturity and interest rate. CDs are issued in various denominations and can be negotiable or non-negotiable.

Channels Venues where a company markets and/or delivers its products and services.

Character The quality of a debt issuer's management.

Checking accounts Bank deposits with no stated maturity available for transactional purposes that pay little or no interest. Also known as a *demand deposit*.

Circuit breaker A pause in intraday trading for a brief period if a price limit is reached.

Classical cycle Refers to fluctuations in the level of economic activity when measured by GDP in volume terms.

Clawback A requirement that the general partner return any funds distributed as incentive fees until the limited partners have received their initial investment and a percentage of the total profit.

Clearing An exchange's process of verifying the execution of a transaction, exchange of payments, and recording of participants.

Clearing instructions Instructions that indicate how to arrange the final settlement ("clearing") of a trade.

Clearinghouse An entity associated with a futures market that acts as middleman between the contracting parties and guarantees to each party the performance of the other.

Closed-end fund A mutual fund in which no new investment money is accepted. New investors invest by buying existing shares, and investors in the fund liquidate by selling their shares to other investors.

Cluster sampling A procedure that divides a population into subpopulation groups (clusters) representative of the population and then randomly draws certain clusters to form a sample.

Co-investing In co-investing, the investor invests in assets *indirectly* through the fund but also possesses rights (known as co-investment rights) to invest *directly* in the same assets. Through co-investing, an investor is able to make an investment *alongside* a fund when the fund identifies deals.

Code of ethics An established guide that communicates an organization's values and overall expectations regarding member behavior. A code of ethics serves as a general guide for how community members should act.

Coefficient of determination (R^2) The percentage of the variation of the dependent variable that is explained by the independent variable. It is a measure of goodness of fit of a regression model.

Coefficient of variation The ratio of a set of observations' standard deviation to the observations' mean value.

Cognitive cost The effort involved in processing new information and updating beliefs.

Cognitive dissonance The mental discomfort that occurs when new information conflicts with previously held beliefs or cognitions.

Cognitive errors Behavioral biases resulting from faulty reasoning; cognitive errors stem from basic statistical, information-processing, or memory errors.

Coincident economic indicators Turning points that are usually close to those of the overall economy; they are believed to have value for identifying the economy's present state.

Collateral Assets or financial guarantees underlying a debt obligation that are above and beyond the issuer's promise to pay.

Collateral manager Buys and sells debt obligations for and from the CDO's collateral pool to generate sufficient cash flows to meet the obligations to the CDO bondholders.

Collateralized bond obligations (CBOs) CDOs backed by high-yield corporate and emerging market bonds.

Collateralized debt obligations (CDOs) Securities backed by a diversified pool of one or more debt obligations. CDOs can be backed by a broad range of debt.

Collateralized loan obligations (CLOs) Investment vehicle with exposure to a portfolio of leveraged loans separated into tranches with different cash flow claims and exposure to losses based on a waterfall.

Collateralized mortgage obligations Securitize mortgage pass-through securities or multiple pools of loans. CMOs are structured to redistribute the cash flows to different bond classes or tranches and create securities that have different exposures to prepayment risk.

Commercial paper (CP) Short-term, negotiable, unsecured promissory note that represents a debt obligation of the issuer.

Committed (regular) lines of credit Bank commitments to extend credit; the commitment is considered a short-term liability and is usually in effect for 364 days (one day short of a full year).

Committed capital The amount that the limited partners have agreed to provide to the private equity fund.

Commodities A product or service from a firm that is indistinguishable from products or services of competing firms, usually conforming to a common standard or grade imposed by convention or regulation.

Commoditization A process by which competing products become less differentiated over time and become interchangeable "commodities" in the eyes of customers. This process is typically associated with declining profitability for the selling firms.

Commodity producers A firm that makes and/or sells commodities.

Commodity swap A type of swap involving the exchange of payments over multiple dates as determined by specified reference prices or indexes relating to commodities.

Common market Level of economic integration that incorporates all aspects of the customs union and extends it by allowing free movement of factors of production among members.

Common shares A type of security that represents an ownership interest in a company. Also called *common stock*.

Common stock A type of security that represents an ownership interest in a company. Also called *common shares*.

Common-size analysis The restatement of financial statement items using a common denominator or reference item that allows one to identify trends and major differences; an example is an income statement in which all items are expressed as a percent of revenue.

Companies Organization entities formed and managed for the purpose of providing a return or economic benefits to its investors and owners.

Company research report A document that presents an analyst's investment recommendation on an issuer and its securities, supported by financial modeling, industry overviews and competitive analyses, valuation scenarios, ESG considerations, and investment risks.

Complete markets Informally, markets in which the variety of distinct securities traded is so broad that any desired payoff in a future state-of-the-world is achievable.

Concession agreement A contractual arrangement under which an entity (also known as a grantor) establishes terms and conditions with a developer or operator (referred to as a concessionaire) to plan, build, operate, finance, and maintain an infrastructure asset for a specific period.

Conditional expected value The expected value of a stated event given that another event has occurred.

Conditional pass-through covered bonds Convert to pass-through securities after the original maturity date if all bond payments have not yet been made.

Conditional variances The variance of one variable, given the outcome of another.

Conditions The general economic, competitive, and business environment faced by all borrowers that may affect their ability to service or refinance debt.

Confidence level The complement of the level of significance.

Confirmation bias A type of cognitive bias that makes individuals view information that confirms beliefs they already hold as more salient.

Consensus protocol A set of rules governing how blocks can join the blockchain that is designed to resist attempts at malicious manipulation up to a certain level of security; it can be either a proof of work or a proof of stake.

Conservatism bias A belief perseverance bias in which people maintain their prior views or forecasts by inadequately incorporating new information.

Constant yield-price trajectory A graphical depiction of the relationship between time to maturity and a bond price, assuming no default, that shows that a bond price approaches par as time passes.

Constituent securities With respect to an index, the individual securities within an index.

Contango Refers to spot price below forward price in a futures market.

Contingency provision Clause in a legal document that allows for some action if a specific event or circumstance occurs.

Contingency table A table of the frequency distribution of observations classified on the basis of two discrete variables.

Contingent claim A type of derivative in which one of the *counterparties* determines whether and when the trade will settle. An *option* is a common type of contingent claim.

Contingent convertible bonds Bonds that automatically convert to equity if a specific event or circumstance occurs, such as the issuer's equity capital falling below the minimum requirement set by regulators.

Continuous trading market A market in which trades can be arranged and executed any time the market is open.

Continuously compounded return The natural logarithm of 1 plus the holding period return, or equivalently, the natural logarithm of the ending price over the beginning price.

Contract manufacturers Companies that make products for other companies that meet specific terms and specifications.

Contract size Amount(s) used for calculation to price and value the derivative. The contract size is often referred to as "notional amount or notional principal."

Contraction The period of a business cycle after the peak and before the trough; often called a *recession* or, if exceptionally severe, called a *depression*.

Contraction risk The risk of earlier repayment of a mortgage-backed security than expected.

Contractionary Tending to cause the real economy to contract.

Contractionary fiscal policy A fiscal policy that has the objective to make the real economy contract.

Contribution margin A profitability measure using variable costs: unit price less unit variable cost. It can also be expressed as a percentage of price or sales.

Controlling shareholder An individual or entity that owns a majority of the voting rights in a corporation.

Convenience sampling A procedure of selecting an element from a population on the basis of whether or not it is accessible to a researcher or how easy it is for a researcher to access the element.

Convenience yield A non-cash benefit of holding a physical commodity versus a derivative.

Conversion price Predetermined share price at which convertible debt may be fully exchanged for common shares during the conversion period.

Conversion ratio The number of common shares a convertible bond or noteholder may receive in exchange for a specific bond par value.

Conversion value The current contingency feature value derived by comparing a convertible bond's price with its value if a bondholder were to exchange bonds for shares.

Convertible bond A bond that gives the bondholder the right to exchange the bond for a specified number of common shares in the issuing company.

Convertible debt A fixed-income instrument which combines the features of debt with equity via a contingent feature, allowing debtholders to exchange their claim for common shares at a predetermined fixed price in the future.

Convertible preference shares A type of equity security that entitles shareholders to convert their shares into a specified number of common shares.

Convexity The second order, usually a positive change in the price of a bond for a given change in yield, which can be negative for a callable bond such as a high-yield bond.

Convexity adjustment A measure that is used to complement modified duration to capture the second-order effect of yield changes on a bond's price. It is equal to the annual convexity statistic times one-half times the given change in the yield-to-maturity squared.

Convexity bias Refers to the difference in price changes for a given change in yield between interest rate futures and interest rate forward contracts. That is, interest rate forwards exhibit a non-linear or convex relationship between price and yield, while the price–yield relationship is linear for interest rate futures.

Cooperation The process by which countries work together toward some shared goal or purpose. These goals may, and often do, vary widely—from strategic or military concerns, to economic influence, to cultural preferences.

Cooperative country A country that engages and reciprocates in rules standardization; harmonization of tariffs; international agreements on trade, immigration, or regulation; and allowing the free flow of information, including technology transfer.

Core real estate strategies Strategies with exposure to well-leased, high-quality commercial and residential real estate in the best markets, generally offered by open-end funds. Investors expect core real estate to deliver stable returns, primarily from income from the property.

Core-plus real estate strategies Value-add investments that require modest redevelopment or upgrades to lease any vacant space together with possible alternative use of the underlying properties. Compared to core real estate strategies, these may be appealing for investors seeking higher returns and willing to accept additional risks from development, redevelopment, repositioning, and leasing.

Corporate issuers Limited companies or corporations that seek financing in financial markets by, for example, issuing debt or equity securities.

Corporations Another term for limited companies, though often used to refer to public limited companies. See *limited company, private limited company*, and *public limited company*.

Correlation A measure of the linear relationship between two random variables.

Correlation coefficient A number between −1 and +1 that measures the consistency or tendency for two investments to act in a similar way. It is used to determine the effect on portfolio risk when two assets are combined.

Cost averaging The periodic investment of a fixed amount of money.

Cost of capital The cost of financing for a company; the rate of return that suppliers of capital require as compensation for their contribution of capital (also called *opportunity cost of funds*).

Cost of carry The net of the costs and benefits related to owning an underlying asset for a specific period.

Cost of debt The required return on debt financing for a company, such as when it issues a bond, takes out a bank loan, or leases an asset through a finance lease.

Cost of equity The return required by equity investors to compensate for both the time value of money and the risk. Also referred to as the required rate of return on common stock or the required return on equity.

Counterparty Legal entities entering a **derivative contract**.

Counterparty credit risk The likelihood that a **counterparty** is unable to meet its financial obligations under the contract.

Counterparty risk The risk that the other party to a contract will fail to honor the terms of the contract.

Country The geopolitical environment as well as the legal and political system faced by all issuers in a jurisdiction that may affect debt payment.

Coupon Periodic interest payments paid by a bond issuer to investors, typically expressed as a percentage of par on an annual basis.

Cournot assumption Assumption in which each firm determines its profit-maximizing production level assuming that the other firms' output will not change.

Covariance A measure of the co-movement (linear association) between two random variables.

Covenants The terms and conditions of lending agreements that the issuer must comply with; they specify the actions that an issuer is obligated to perform (affirmative covenant) or prohibited from performing (negative covenant).

Credit default swap (CDS) A type of credit derivative in which one party, the credit protection buyer who is seeking credit protection against a third party, makes a series of regularly scheduled payments to the other party, the credit protection seller. The seller makes no payments until a credit event occurs.

Credit enhancements Provisions or methods that allow a borrower improve their creditworthiness in a structured transaction.

Credit event An occurrence that triggers the settlement of a CDS contract, including failure to make a debt payment, debt restructuring, or a bankruptcy filing.

Credit facilities Loan agreements with pre-specified terms and limits but with fluctuating balances based on borrower-specific needs at different points in time, analogous to a credit card.

Credit migration risk The risk that a bond issuer's creditworthiness deteriorates, or migrates lower, leading investors to believe the risk of default is higher. Also called **downgrade risk**.

Credit rating Letter-grade, qualitative measures of an issuer's ability to meet its debt obligations based on both the probability of default and the expected loss under a default scenario.

Credit rating agencies Institutions that issue and maintain credit ratings. The three largest are Standard & Poor's, Moody's, and Fitch Ratings.

Credit risk The expected economic loss under a potential borrower default over the life of the contract.

Credit spread The compensation for the risk of default in a debt security, typically measured by the yield-to-maturity difference between a bond and a comparable government benchmark security.

Credit spread risk The risk of greater expected loss due to changes in credit conditions as a result of macroeconomic, market, and/or issuer-related factors.

Credit tranching Internal credit enhancement where cash flows into a senior/subordinate structure.

Credit-linked notes Bonds whose coupon changes when the bonds' credit rating changes.

Critical values Values of the test statistic at which the decision changes from fail to reject the null hypothesis to reject the null hypothesis.

Cross-default clause Covenant or contract clause that specifies borrowers are considered in default if they default on another debt obligation.

Cross-sectional analysis Analysis over a group as of a given time.

Crossing networks Trading systems that match buyers and sellers who are willing to trade at prices obtained from other markets.

Crowdsourcing A business model that enables users to contribute directly to a product, service, or online content.

Cryptocurrency An electronic medium of exchange that lacks physical form.

Cryptocurrency wallet A storage unit for public and/or private keys for cryptocurrency transactions. These wallets may be a physical device, program, or service.

Cryptography An algorithmic process to encrypt data, making the data unusable if received by unauthorized parties.

Cumulative preference shares Preference shares for which any dividends that are not paid accrue and must be paid in full before dividends on common shares can be paid.

Cumulative voting A voting process whereby shareholders can accumulate and vote all their shares for a single candidate in an election, as opposed to having to allocate their voting rights evenly among all candidates.

Currencies Monies issued by national monetary authorities.

Currency Money issued by national monetary authorities.

Currency swap A swap in which each party makes interest payments to the other in different currencies.

Current government spending With respect to government expenditures, spending on goods and services that are provided on a regular, recurring basis including health, education, and defense.

Current ratio A measure of liquidity that is the ratio of current assets to current liabilities.

Current yield The sum of the coupon payments received over the year divided by the flat price. Also called the income, interest yield, or running yield.

Customs union Extends the free trade area (FTA) by not only allowing free movement of goods and services among members, but also creating a common trade policy against nonmembers.

CVaR Conditional VaR, a tail loss measure. The weighted average of all loss outcomes in the statistical distribution that exceed the VaR loss.

Daily settlement A specific process of *mark-to-market* by a central clearing party in which the profits and losses of all counterparties to derivatives contracts are determined using settlement prices for each contract.

Dark pools Alternative trading systems that do not display the orders that their clients send to them.

Data mining The practice of determining a model by extensive searching through a dataset for statistically significant patterns. Also called *data snooping*.

Data science An interdisciplinary field that harnesses advances in computer science, statistics, and other disciplines for the purpose of extracting information from big data (or data in general).

Data snooping The subconscious or conscious manipulation of data in a way that produces a statistically significant result (i.e., the p-value is sufficiently small or the t-statistic sufficiently large to indicate statistical significance), such as by running multiple simulations and naively accepting the best result. Also known as p-hacking.

Day order An order that is good for the day on which it is submitted. If it has not been filled by the close of business, the order expires unfilled.

Days of inventory on hand (DOH) The average number of days it would take to sell the amount of inventory on hand. It is calculated as either the ending or average balance of inventories divided by (cost of goods sold/days in the period).

Days payable outstanding (DPO) The average number of days it takes a company to pay its suppliers. It is calculated as either the ending or average balance of accounts payable divided by (cost of goods sold/days in the period).

Days sales outstanding (DSO) The average number of days it takes for a company to receive payment from customers who purchase goods or services on credit. It is calculated as either the ending or average balance of accounts receivable divided by (revenues/days in the period).

Dealers Financial intermediaries, such as commercial banks or investment banks, who transact as **counterparties** with derivative end users.

Debt A claim against an entity to receive cash, stock, or other assets at a future date. From the perspective of the debtor or borrower, an obligation to pay cash, stock, or other assets at a future date. Generally, debt claims are unconditional and are senior to equity claims.

Debt service coverage ratio A key indicator of credit performance equal to the ratio of net operating income to debt service.

Debt tax shield The tax benefit from interest paid on debt being tax deductible from income, equal to the marginal tax rate multiplied by the value of the debt.

Debt-to-assets ratio A solvency ratio calculated as total debt divided by total assets.

Debt-to-capital ratio A solvency ratio calculated as total debt divided by total debt plus total shareholders' equity.

Debt-to-equity ratio A solvency ratio calculated as total debt divided by total shareholders' equity.

Debt-to-income ratio (DTI) Residential lending metric that compares an individual's monthly debt payments to their monthly pre-tax, gross income.

Debut issuer An issuer approaching the bond market for the first time.

Deciles Values that divide a distribution ranked smallest to largest into 10 equal parts.

Declaration date The day that the corporation issues a statement declaring a specific dividend.

Decreasing returns to scale When a production process leads to increases in output that are proportionately smaller than the increase in inputs.

Deductible temporary differences Temporary differences that result in a reduction of or deduction from taxable income in a future period when the balance sheet item is recovered or settled.

Deep learning An area of artificial intelligence in which a system uses neural networks to perform multistage, non-linear data processing to identify patterns. Also called *deep learning nets*.

Deep learning nets See *Deep learning*.

Deep-in-the-money option An option that is highly likely to be exercised.

Deep-out-of-the-money option An option that is highly unlikely to be exercised.

Default When a borrower on a mortgage loan fails to meet the obligations of the loan.

Default risk premium An extra return that compensates investors for the possibility that the borrower will fail to make a promised payment at the contracted time and in the contracted amount.

Defeasance Mechanism that allows prepayment on mortgage, but the borrower must purchase a portfolio of government securities that fully replicates the cash flows of the remaining scheduled principal and interest payments, including the balloon loan balance, on the loan.

Defensive interval ratio A liquidity ratio that estimates the number of days that an entity could meet cash needs from liquid assets; calculated as (cash + short-term marketable investments + receivables) divided by daily cash expenditures.

Deferred coupon bonds Bonds that pay no coupons for their first few years but then pay a higher coupon than they otherwise normally would for the remainder of their life. Also called *split coupon bonds.*

Deferred tax assets A balance sheet asset that arises when an excess amount is paid for income taxes relative to accounting profit. The taxable income is higher than accounting profit and income tax payable exceeds tax expense. The company expects to recover the difference during the course of future operations when tax expense exceeds income tax payable.

Deferred tax liabilities A balance sheet liability that arises when a deficit amount is paid for income taxes relative to accounting profit. The taxable income is less than the accounting profit and income tax payable is less than tax expense. The company expects to eliminate the liability over the course of future operations when income tax payable exceeds tax expense.

Defined benefit pension plans (DB plans) Plans in which the company promises to pay a certain annual amount (defined benefit) to the employee after retirement. The company bears the investment risk of the plan assets.

Defined contribution pension plans Individual accounts to which an employee and typically the employer makes contributions during their working years and expect to draw on the accumulated funds at retirement. The employee bears the investment and inflation risk of the plan assets.

Deflation Negative inflation.

Degree of financial leverage The ratio of percentage change in net income to percentage change in operating income over a period. It is a measure of how sensitive net income is to changes in operating income, driven by the firm's use of debt in its capital structure.

Degree of operating leverage The ratio of percentage change in operating income to percentage change in sales over a period. It is a measure of how sensitive operating income is to changes in sales, driven by the fixed and variable cost composition of operating expenses.

Delta The sensitivity of the derivative price to a small change in the value of the underlying asset.

Demand shock A typically unexpected disturbance to demand, such as an unexpected interruption in trade or transportation.

Dependent variable The variable that is explained by a regression model.

Depository bank A bank that raises funds from depositors and other investors and lends it to borrowers.

Depository institutions Commercial banks, savings and loan banks, credit unions, and similar institutions that raise funds from depositors and other investors and lend it to borrowers.

Depository receipt A security that trades like an ordinary share on a local exchange and represents an economic interest in a foreign company.

Depreciation The process of systematically allocating the cost of long-lived (tangible) assets to the periods during which the assets are expected to provide economic benefits.

Derivative A financial instrument that derives its value from the performance of an underlying asset or factor (e.g., stock price, interest rate, or exchange rate).

Derivative contract A legal agreement between counterparties with a specific **maturity**, or length of time, until the closing of the transaction, or **settlement**.

Derivative pricing rule A pricing rule used by crossing networks in which a price is taken (derived) from the price that is current in the asset's primary market.

Differentiated products A product or service from a firm that is distinguishable or distinct from those of competing firms. It is customers who determine and value whether a product is differentiated.

Diffuse prior The assumption of equal prior probabilities.

Diffusion index Reflects the proportion of the index's components that are moving in a pattern consistent with the overall index.

Digital assets The umbrella term covering assets that can be created, stored, and transmitted electronically and have associated ownership or use rights. Digital assets include a variety of assets, such as cryptocurrencies, tokens (security and utility), and digital collectables.

Diluted EPS The EPS that would result if all dilutive securities were converted into common shares.

Dilution An increase in the number of shares outstanding from share issuance that decreases the percentage of shares owned by existing shareholders.

Direct investing Occurs when an investor makes a direct investment in an asset without the use of an intermediary.

Direct lending Providing capital directly from private debt investors.

Direct listing Where the equity of a security is floated on the public markets directly, without underwriters, reducing the complexity and cost of the transaction.

Direct sales Marketing and/or delivering products and services to customers without an intermediary or third party between the customer and seller.

Direct taxes Taxes levied directly on income, wealth, and corporate profits.

Discount factor The price equivalent of a zero rate. Also may be stated as the present value of a currency unit on a future date.

Discount rate A yield or pricing convention for money market instrument quotations. It is the interest earned on an instrument, derived from the difference between the price and face value, expressed as a percentage of the face value and multiplied by the periodicity of the annual rate.

Discounted cash flow models Valuation models that estimate the intrinsic value of a security as the present value of the future benefits expected to be received from the security.

Discriminatory pricing rule A pricing rule used in continuous markets in which the limit price of the order or quote that first arrived determines the trade price.

Diseconomies of scale Increase in cost per unit resulting from increased production.

Dispersion The variability of a population or sample of observations around the central tendency.

Display size The size of an order displayed to public view.

Disposition effect A type of cognitive bias that makes individuals unwilling to sell their possessions at a loss.

Distressed debt Debt of mature companies in financial difficulty, in bankruptcy, or likely to default on debt.

Distressed/restructuring These strategies focus on securities of companies either in or perceived to be near bankruptcy. In one approach, hedge funds simply purchase fixed-income securities trading at a significant discount to par but that are still senior enough to be backed by sufficient corporate assets.

Distributed ledger A type of database that can be shared among entities in a network.

Distributed ledger technology (DLT) Technology based on a distributed ledger.

Diversification ratio The ratio of the standard deviation of an equally weighted portfolio to the standard deviation of a randomly selected security.

Dividend discount model (DDM) The model of the value of stock that is the present value of all future dividends, discounted at the required return on equity.

Dividend payout ratio The ratio of cash dividends paid to earnings for a period.

Dividends Distributions of profits and/or net assets from a corporation to its shareholders. While often in cash, dividends can be also be paid in stock or assets, such as property.

Divisor A number (denominator) used to determine the value of a price return index. It is initially chosen at the inception of an index and subsequently adjusted by the index provider, as necessary, to avoid changes in the index value that are unrelated to changes in the prices of its constituent securities.

Domestic bonds A type of bond for which the issuer's domicile and jurisdiction of issuance are the same.

Domestic content provisions Stipulate that some percentage of the value added or components used in production should be of domestic origin.

Double taxation Income is taxed twice.

Downside risk The potential for loss.

Drag on liquidity An action or event that reduces available funds or delays cash inflows.

Drivers Causative factors that explain the level of and changes in an output variable.

DSC ratio A property's annual net operating income (NOI) divided by the debt service.

Dual-class structure A capital structure that includes at least two classes of equity shares with unequal voting rights.

Dupont analysis An approach to decomposing return on investment, e.g., return on equity, as the product of other financial ratios.

Duration The first-order, linear change in a bond's price for a given yield change in yield, which is a negative or inverse relationship.

Duration gap the difference between a bond's Macaulay duration and its investor's investment horizon.

Dynamic pricing A pricing approach that charges different prices at different times. Specific examples include off-peak pricing, "surge" pricing, and "congestion" pricing.

Early repayment option May entitle the borrower to prepay all or part of the outstanding mortgage principal prior to maturity. This creates a risk from the lender's or investor's viewpoint because the cash flow amounts and timing cannot be known with certainty.

Earnings surprise The difference between reported EPS and expected EPS. Also referred to as *unexpected earnings*.

Economic indicators Economic statistics provided by government and established private organizations that contain information on an economy's recent past activity or its current or future position in the business cycle.

Economic infrastructure investments A category of infrastructure investments that support economic activity through transportation assets, information and communication technology assets, and utility and energy assets.

Economic stabilization Reduction of the magnitude of economic fluctuations.

Economic union Incorporates all aspects of a common market and in addition requires common economic institutions and coordination of economic policies among members.

Economies of scale A decline in costs per unit as output grows, generally resulting from having fixed costs in the cost structure that are spread over more units of output.

Economies of scope A decline in costs per unit as the number of product or business lines increases, generally resulting from having shared costs between the product lines.

Effective annual rate An interest rate with a periodicity of one.

Effective convexity An interest rate risk statistic that measures the non-linear/second-order effect of changes in the benchmark yield curve on a bond's price.

Effective duration The sensitivity of the bond's price to an instantaneous parallel shift in a benchmark yield curve—for example, the government par curve.

Efficient market A market in which asset prices reflect new information quickly and rationally. See also, *informationally efficient market*.

Either/or fee A custom fee arrangement whereby major investors are offered a structure where managers agree to charge *either* a lower management fee *or* a higher incentive fee, whichever is greater.

Electronic communications networks (ECNs) See *alternative trading systems* and *multilateral trading facilities*.

Embedded derivative A derivative within an underlying, such as a callable, putable, or convertible bond.

Embedded options Contingency provisions found in a bond's indenture representing rights that enable their holders to take advantage of interest rate movements. They can be exercised by the issuer, by the bondholder, or automatically depending on the course of interest rates.

Emotional biases Behavioral biases resulting from reasoning influenced by feelings; emotional biases stem from impulse or intuition.

Empirical duration Estimation of the price–yield relationship using historical bond market data in statistical models.

Employee stock ownership plan (ESOP) A type of employee benefit plan in which a company sets up a trust fund to receive contributions of newly issued shares or cash to buy existing shares. Contributions are tax deductible up to certain limits. Shares in the trust fund are allocated to individual employees based on relative pay or a formula.

Endowment bias An emotional bias in which people value an asset more when they hold rights to it than when they do not.

Enterprise risk management An overall assessment of a company's risk position. A centralized approach to risk management sometimes called firmwide risk management.

Enterprise value A measure of a company's total market value from which the value of cash and short-term investments have been subtracted.

Equal weighting An index weighting method in which an equal weight is assigned to each constituent security at inception.

Equity Ownership interest in an entity. A residual claim on the assets of an entity after more senior claims, such as debt, have been satisfied. Also known as *net assets*.

Equity swap A swap transaction in which at least one cash flow is tied to the return to an equity portfolio position, often an equity index.

Error term Represents the difference between the observed value of the independent variable and that expected from the true underlying population relation between the dependent and independent variable.

Estimated parameters In a simple linear regression, the estimated parameters are the intercept and slope of the fitted line.

Ether A programmable cryptocurrency created on the Ethereum blockchain in 2015 that allows for the execution of smart contracts.

Ethical principles Beliefs regarding what is good, acceptable, or obligatory behavior and what is bad, unacceptable, or forbidden behavior.

Ethics The study of moral principles or of making good choices. Ethics encompasses a set of moral principles and rules of conduct that provide guidance for our behavior.

Eurobonds A type of bond issued internationally, outside the jurisdiction of the country in whose currency the bond is denominated.

European options Options that may be exercised only at contract maturity.

European-style Said of an option contract that can only be exercised on the option's expiration date.

Event risk Risk that evolves around set dates, such as elections, new legislation, or other date-driven milestones, such as holidays or political anniversaries, known in advance. Example: Brexit referendum.

Ex-dividend date The first date that a share trades without (i.e., "ex") the right to receive the declared dividend for the period.

Excess kurtosis Degree of kurtosis (fatness of tails) relative to the kurtosis of the normal distribution.

Excess spread Surplus difference of yield remaining after payments to bondholders are made after expenses are made and losses are covered.

Exchange A rules-based, open access market venue where financial instruments are traded, with price and volume transparency accessible by issuers, investors, and their intermediaries.

Exchange-traded derivative (ETD) Futures, options, and other financial contracts available on exchanges.

Execution instructions Instructions that indicate how to fill an order.

Exercise The decision to transact the underlying by an option holder.

Exercise date The day that an option is exercised by its holder. For a call option, the day the strike price is paid and underlying is purchased. For a put option, when the strike price is received and the underlying is sold.

Exercise price The pre-agreed execution price specified in an option contract. Sometimes, this price is referred to as the strike price.

Exogenous risk A sudden or unanticipated risk that impacts either a country's cooperative stance, the ability of non-state actors to globalize, or both. Examples include sudden uprisings, invasions, or the aftermath of natural disasters.

Expansion The period of a business cycle after its lowest point and before its highest point.

Expansionary Tending to cause the real economy to grow.

Expansionary fiscal policy Fiscal policy aimed at achieving real economic growth.

Expected exposure (EE) The size of the investor's claim at the time of default.

Expected loss (EL) Default probability times loss severity given default.

Expected return on the portfolio Denoted as $(E(R_p))$. The weighted average of the expected returns (R_1 to R_n) on the component securities using their respective weights (w_1 to w_n).

Expected value of a random variable The probability-weighted average of the possible outcomes of a random variable.

Expert system A type of computer programming, often based on "if–then" rules, that attempts to simulate the knowledge base and analytical abilities of human experts in specific problem-solving contexts.

Export subsidy Paid by the government to the firm when it exports a unit of a good that is being subsidized.

Exposure at default (EAD) The size of the investor's claim at the time of default.

Extension risk The risk of later repayment of a mortgage-backed security than expected.

External credit enhancements Provisions or methods from a third party that allow a borrower improve their creditworthiness in a structured transaction.

External debt Sovereign debt owed to foreign creditors.

Extra dividend A dividend paid by a company that does not pay dividends on a regular schedule, or a dividend that supplements regular cash dividends with an extra payment.

Extraordinary general meetings (EGMs) Meetings besides an AGM of the corporate board and shareholders, typically held to deliberate and vote on urgent matters. Corporate charters and bylaws specify who can call an EGM and under what conditions.

Extreme value theory A branch of statistics that focuses primarily on extreme outcomes.

Face value The amount of principal on a bond, also known as par value.

Factoring arrangement When a company sells its accounts receivable to a lender (known as a factor) that assumes responsibility for the credit-granting and collection process.

Fair value A market-based measure of an investment based on observable or derived assumptions to determine a price that market participants would use to exchange an asset or liability in an orderly transaction at a specific time.

Fair value hedge Refers to a specific **hedge accounting** designation that applies when a derivative is deemed to offset the fluctuation in fair value of an asset or liability.

Fallen angels Formerly investment-grade-rated issuers whose bonds are downgraded to high yield due to credit deterioration.

Fat-Tailed Describes a distribution that has fatter tails than a normal distribution (also called leptokurtic).

Fed funds rate The US interbank lending rate on overnight borrowings of reserves.

Federal funds rate The US interbank lending rate on overnight borrowings of reserves. Also known as *Fed Funds rate*.

Fiat money Money that is not convertible into any other commodity.

Fiduciary call A combination of a purchased call option and investment in a risk-free bond with face value of the option's exercise price.

Fill or kill See *immediate or cancel order*.

Finance lease A type of lease which is more akin to the purchase or sale of the underlying asset.

Financial leverage The use of debt in the capital structure. Measured using ratios such as operating income to operating income less interest expense, total assets to total equity, or debt to equity.

Financial leverage ratio A measure of financial leverage calculated as average total assets divided by average total equity.

Financial risk The risk arising from a company's capital structure and, specifically, from the level of debt and debt-like obligations.

Fintech Technological innovation in the financial services industry, specifically with the design and delivery of financial services and products. It may also refer more broadly to companies involved in developing the new technologies and their applications, as well as the business sector that includes such companies.

Firm commitment A pre-determined amount (price and quantity) is agreed to be exchanged at settlement. Examples of firm commitments include forward contracts, futures contracts, and swaps.

First lien Also known as a priority lien, this investor protection grants a lender the right to take possession of property from a borrower which fails to repay debt.

First lien debt Debt secured by a pledge of certain assets that could include buildings, but it may also include property and equipment, licenses, patents, brands, etc.

First mortgage debt Debt secured by a pledge of a specific property.

Fiscal multiplier The ratio of a change in national income to a change in government spending.

Fiscal policy The use of taxes and government spending to affect the level of aggregate expenditures.

Fixed charge coverage A solvency ratio measuring the number of times interest and lease payments are covered by operating income, calculated as (EBIT + lease payments) divided by (interest payments + lease payments).

Fixed charge coverage ratio A measure of how well a company's earnings covers its fixed expenses, which may include debt payments, interest expense, and lease costs.

Fixed-income instruments Debt instruments such as loans or bonds.

Fixed-income securities Fixed-income instruments designed to be more easily tradeable than a loan, such as a bond.

Fixed-price call A contingency provision that grants an issuer the right to buy back a bond at a predetermined price in the future.

Fixed-rate payer The counterparty paying fixed cash flows in a swap contract. May also be referred to as the floating-rate receiver.

Flat price The full price of a bond minus accrued interest. Flat prices are usually quoted by bond dealers.

Float-adjusted market-capitalization weighting An index weighting method in which the weight assigned to each constituent security is determined by adjusting its market capitalization for its market float.

Floating-rate notes Notes on which interest payments are not fixed but instead vary from period to period depending on the current level of a reference interest rate. Also known as *floaters.*

Floating-rate payer The counterparty paying the variable cash flows in a swap contract. May also be referred to as the fixed-rate receiver.

Forecast object A variable on or related to an issuer's financial statements that an analyst makes a projection for. Examples include drivers of financial statements, financial statement lines, and summary measures like EBITDA.

Foreclosure Allows a lender to take possession of the property and ultimately sell the property to recover funds toward satisfying the outstanding debt obligation.

Foreign bonds A type of bond for which the issuer's domicile and jurisdiction of issuance are different.

Foreign currency reserves Holding by the central bank of non-domestic currency deposits and non-domestic bonds.

Foreign direct investments (FDI) Long-term investments in the productive capacity of a foreign country.

Foreign exchange gains (or losses) Gains (or losses) that occur when the exchange rate changes between the investor's currency and the currency that foreign securities are denominated in.

Forward contract A **derivative contract** for the future exchange of an **underlying** at a fixed price set at contract signing.

Forward price Represents the price agreed upon in a forward contract to be exchanged at the contract's maturity date, *T*. This price is shown in equations as $F_0(T)$.

Forward price-to-earnings ratio A P/E calculated on the basis of a forecast of EPS; a stock's current price divided by next year's expected earnings.

Forward rate agreement (FRA) An OTC derivatives contract in which counterparties agree to apply a specific interest rate to a future time period.

Founders class shares A way to entice early participation in startup funds whereby managers offer incentives that entitle investors to a lower fee structure and/or other favorable terms.

Framing bias An information-processing bias in which a person answers a question differently based on the way in which it is asked (framed).

Franchising A situation where an owner of an asset and associated intellectual property divests the asset and licenses intellectual property to a third-party operator (franchisee) in exchange for royalties. Franchisees operate under the constraints of a franchise agreement.

Free cash flow The actual cash that would be available to the company's investors after making all investments necessary to maintain the company as an ongoing enterprise (also referred to as free cash flow to the firm); the internally generated funds that can be distributed to the company's investors (e.g., shareholders and bondholders) without impairing the value of the company.

Free cash flow hypothesis The hypothesis that higher debt levels discipline managers by forcing them to make fixed debt service payments and by reducing the company's free cash flow.

Free float The portion of a listed company's equity securities that are not held by insiders, strategic investors, sponsors, founders, and so on, that are more freely available for trading.

Free trade areas One of the most prevalent forms of regional integration, in which all barriers to the flow of goods and services among members have been eliminated.

Free-cash-flow-to-equity models Valuation models based on discounting expected future free cash flow to equity.

Freemium business model A pricing approach that allows customers a certain level of usage or functionality at no charge. Those who wish to use more must pay.

Frequency table A representation of the frequency of occurrence of two discrete variables.

Full price The price of a bond including any accrued interest owed to the seller. It is the flat price plus accrued interest.

Fully amortizing loan A loan or bond with a payment schedule that calls for the complete repayment of principal over the instrument's time to maturity.

Fund investing In fund investing, the investor invests in assets indirectly by contributing capital to a fund as part of a group of investors. Fund investing is available for all major alternative investment types.

Fund of funds Funds that hold a portfolio of hedge funds; also called *funds of hedge funds.*

Fundamental analysis The examination of publicly available information and the formulation of forecasts to estimate the intrinsic value of assets.

Fundamental growth These strategies use fundamental analysis to identify companies expected to exhibit high growth and capital appreciation.

Fundamental long/short In this strategy, the hedge fund takes a long position in companies that are trading at inexpensive levels compared to their potential intrinsic value and shorts those that trade in the other direction, with the intention of reversing this trade to obtain alpha.

Fundamental value These strategies use fundamental analysis to identify undervalued and unloved companies for which there is a possibility that a corporate turnaround, with future revenue and cash flow growth, will result in higher valuations.

Fundamental weighting An index weighting method in which the weight assigned to each constituent security is based on its underlying company's size. It attempts to address the disadvantages of market-capitalization weighting by using measures that are independent of the constituent security's price.

Fungible Freely exchangeable, interchangeable, or substitutable with other things of the same type. Money and commodities are the most common examples.

Futures contract A variation of a forward contract that has essentially the same basic definition but with some additional features, such as a clearinghouse guarantee against credit losses, a daily settlement of gains and losses, and an organized electronic or floor trading facility.

Futures contract basis point value (BPV) The change in price of a futures contract given a 1 basis point (0.01%) change in yield.

Futures margin account An account held by an exchange clearinghouse for each derivatives counterparty. The funds in such an account are used to ensure that counterparties do not default on their contract obligation.

Futures price The pre-agreed price at which a futures contract buyer (seller) agrees to pay (receive) for the underlying at the maturity date of the futures contract.

FX swap The combination of a spot and a forward FX transaction.

G-spread Yield spread in basis points between a bond's yield-to-maturity and that of an actual or interpolated government bond. It represents the return for bearing risks relative to the government bond.

Game theory The set of tools decision makers use to incorporate responses by rival decision makers into their strategies.

Gamma A numerical measure of how sensitive an option's delta (the sensitivity of the derivative's price) is to a change in the value of the underlying.

Gate A provision that when implemented limits or restricts redemptions for a period of time.

General collateral repo Rather than involving a specific security, a repo that instead references a specific group of securities as eligible collateral (such as government bonds of a specific maturity).

General collateral repo rate The interest rate on a general collateral repo.

General obligation (GO) bonds Unsecured bonds issued by a non-sovereign government which are backed by the taxing authority of the issuer.

General obligation bonds Also known as GO bonds. Bonds issued by non-sovereign governments for general purposes and repaid from tax cash flows.

General partners (GPs) Private fund managers responsible for sourcing and deploying capital from limited partner investors over an investment life cycle and distributing returns to those investors over a finite investment holding period.

General partnership A business organizational form owned entirely by general partners.

Geophysical resource endowment Includes such factors as livable geography and climate as well as access to food and water, which are necessary for sustainable growth. Geophysical resource endowment is highly unequal among countries.

Geopolitics The study of how geography affects politics and international relations. These relations matter for investments because they contribute to important drivers of investment performance, including economic growth, business performance, market volatility, and transaction costs.

Gilts Bonds issued by the UK government.

Global depository receipt (GDR) A depository receipt that is issued outside of the company's home country and outside of the United States.

Global minimum-variance portfolio The portfolio on the minimum-variance frontier with the smallest variance of return.

Global registered share (GRS) A common share that is traded on different stock exchanges around the world in different currencies.

Globalization The process of interaction and integration among people, companies, and governments worldwide. It is marked by the spread of products, information, jobs, and culture across borders.

Gold standard With respect to a currency, if a currency is on the gold standard a given amount can be converted into a prespecified amount of gold.

Good-on-close An execution instruction specifying that an order can only be filled at the close of trading. Also called *market-on-close.*

Good-on-open An execution instruction specifying that an order can only be filled at the opening of trading.

Good-till-cancelled order An order specifying that it is valid until the entity placing the order has cancelled it (or, commonly, until some specified amount of time such as 60 days has elapsed, whichever comes sooner).

Goodwill An intangible asset that represents the excess of the purchase price of an acquired company over the value of the net identifiable assets acquired.

Governance tokens In permissionless networks, governance tokens serve as votes to determine how the particular network is run.

Government debt management Government policies that relate to the issuance of debt securities, typically handled by a treasurer or finance ministry.

Government equivalent yield Measures quoted using actual/actual day counts.

Grant date The day that terms of compensation are communicated by an issuer and accepted by an employee recipient.

Green bonds Bonds used to specifically finance environmental-related projects.

Greenfield investments New, "to-be-built" infrastructure projects and assets created to provide a specific essential service or to supply a public good.

Gross profit margin The ratio of gross profit to revenues.

Groupthink A behavioral bias that occurs when a team minimizes conflict and dissent in reaching and maintaining a consensus.

Growth cycle Refers to fluctuations in economic activity around the long-term potential trend growth level, focusing on how much actual economic activity is below or above trend growth in economic activity.

Growth option The option to make additional investments in a project at some future time if the financial results are strong. Also called an *expansion option.*

Growth rate cycle Refers to fluctuations in the growth rate of economic activity.

Haircut The difference between the market value of the security used as collateral and the value of the loan. Also called *repo margin.*

Halo effect An emotional bias that extends a favorable evaluation of some characteristics to other characteristics.

Hard commodities Traded natural resources, such as crude oil and metals, with markets often involving the physical delivery of the underlying upon settlement.

Hard hurdle rate Hurdle ratewhere the manager earns fees on annual returns in excess of the hurdle rate

Hard-bullet covered bonds Type of security where if payments do not occur according to the original schedule of a covered bond, a bond default is triggered and bond payments are accelerated.

Harmonic mean A type of weighted mean computed as the reciprocal of the arithmetic average of the reciprocals.

Hedge The **derivative contract** used in **hedging** an exposure.

Hedge accounting Accounting standard(s) that allow an issuer to offset a hedging instrument (usually a derivative) against a hedged transaction or balance sheet item to reduce financial statement volatility.

Hedge funds Private investment vehicles that may invest in public equities or publicly traded fixed-income assets, private capital, and/or real assets, but they are distinguished by their investment *approach* rather than by the investments themselves.

Hedge ratio The proportion of an underlying that will offset the risk associated with a derivative position.

Hedging The use of a derivative contract to offset or neutralize existing or anticipated exposure to an **underlying**.

Hegemony Countries that are regional or even global leaders and use their political or economic influence of others to control resources.

Held-to-maturity Debt (fixed-income) securities that a company intends to hold to maturity; these are presented at their original cost, updated for any amortisation of discounts or premiums.

Herding Clustered trading that may or may not be based on information.

Herfindahl-Hirschman Index (HHI) A measure of market concentration, calculated as the sum of the squares of competitor market shares. Antitrust regulators in some countries consider markets with an HHI between 1,500 and 2,500 moderately concentrated and consider markets with an HHI over 2,500 highly concentrated.

Heteroskedasticity Non-constant variance across all observations.

Hidden order An order that is exposed not to the public but only to the brokers or exchanges that receive it.

Hidden revenue business model Business models that provide services to users at no charge and generate revenues elsewhere.

High yield Bond issuers and issues rated BB+ (Ba1 on Moody's scale) or lower. Also known as speculative grade and junk.

High-water mark The highest value, net of fees, that a fund has reached in history. It reflects the highest cumulative return used to calculate an incentive fee.

Hindsight bias A type of cognitive bias that makes individuals misremember the past in ways that make them appear to have made better and more well-informed choices.

Holder-of-record date The date that a shareholder listed on the corporation's books will be deemed to have ownership of the shares for purposes of receiving an upcoming dividend.

Holding period return The single-period internal rate of return for a real estate property that includes property income and the change in property value over the period.

Home bias A preference for securities listed on the exchanges of one's home country.

Homogeneity of expectations The assumption that all investors have the same economic expectations and thus have the same expectations of prices, cash flows, and other investment characteristics.

Homoskedasticity Constant variance across all observations.

Horizon yield An investor's total rate of return on a fixed income instrument over their holding period, including reinvested coupon payments. It is an internal rate of return expressed as an annualized rate.

Hostile takeover When a potential acquirer seeks to acquire a company (the target) against the wishes of the target's board of directors. Typically, a tender offer is used to carry out the hostile takeover, against which a board might use a poison pill in its defense.

Household A person or a group of people living in the same residence, taken as a basic unit in economic analysis.

Human capital The present value of an individual's future expected labor income.

Hurdle rate Also called "preferred return." The minimum rate of return on investment that a fund must reach before a GP receives carried interest.

Hypothesis A proposed explanation or theory that can be tested.

Hypothesis testing The process of testing of hypotheses about one or more populations using statistical inference.

I-spread also known as interpolated spread, it is the yield spread for a bond over the standard swap rate in that currency of the same tenor.

Iceberg order An order in which the display size is less than the order's full size.

If-converted method A method for accounting for the effect of convertible securities on earnings per share (EPS) that specifies what EPS would have been if the convertible securities had been converted at the beginning of the period, taking account of the effects of conversion on net income and the weighted average number of shares outstanding.

Illusion of control bias A bias in which people tend to believe that they can control or influence outcomes when, in fact, they cannot.

Immediate or cancel order An order that is valid only upon receipt by the broker or exchange. If such an order cannot be filled in part or in whole upon receipt, it cancels immediately. Also called *fill or kill*.

Impact lag The lag associated with the result of actions affecting the economy with delay.

Implied forward rate An interest rate or yield over a future period implied by the current term structure of interest rates.

Import license Specifies the quantity of a good that can be imported into a country.

In-the-money Describes an option with a positive intrinsic value.

Income tax paid The actual amount paid for income taxes in the period; not a provision, but the actual cash outflow.

Income tax payable The income tax owed by the company on the basis of taxable income.

Increasing returns to scale When a production process leads to increases in output that are proportionately larger than the increase in inputs.

Incurrence test A financial ratio or other measurement taken prior to an action such as debt issuance, usually on a pro forma basis taking the action into account. Satisfaction of the test (e.g., leverage ratio below a certain value) is linked to covenants between the issuer and investors.

Indenture A written contract between a lender and borrower that specifies the terms of the loan, such as interest rate, interest payment schedule, or maturity.

Independent With reference to events, the property that the occurrence of one event does not affect the probability of another event occurring. With reference to two random variables X and Y, they are independent if and only if $P(X,Y) = P(X)P(Y)$.

Independent directors Members of a corporation's board of directors who do not have an employment or familial relationship with the company, nor do they have a relationship that would impair their independence such as an economic interest in a vendor or competitor of the company.

Independent variable An explanatory variable in a regression model.

Independently and identically distributed With respect to random variables, the property of random variables that are independent of each other but follow the identical probability distribution.

Index-linked bonds A bond whose coupon payments or principal repayment is linked to a specified index.

Indexing An investment strategy in which an investor constructs a portfolio to mirror the performance of a specified index.

Indicator variable A variable that takes on only one of two values, 0 or 1, based on a condition. In simple linear regression, the slope is the difference in the dependent variable for the two conditions. Also referred to as a *dummy variable*.

Indifference curve A curve representing all the combinations of two goods or attributes such that the consumer is entirely indifferent among them.

Indirect taxes Taxes such as taxes on spending, as opposed to direct taxes.

Inflation premium An extra return that compensates investors for expected inflation.

Inflation reports A type of economic publication put out by many central banks.

Inflation-linked bonds Debt instruments that link the principal and interest to inflation.

Information cascade The transmission of information from those participants who act first and whose decisions influence the decisions of others.

Information-motivated traders Traders that trade to profit from information that they believe allows them to predict future prices.

Informationally efficient market A market in which asset prices reflect new information quickly and rationally.

Infrastructure A type of real asset that is intended for public use and provides essential services. These assets are typically long-lived fixed assets, such as bridges and toll roads.

Initial coin offering (ICO) An unregulated process whereby companies raise capital by selling crypto-tokens to investors in exchange for fiat money or another agreed-upon cryptocurrency.

Initial margin The ratio of the price of collateral to the value of cash exchanged in a repo; a value over 1.0 or 100% indicates overcollateralization.

Initial margin requirement The margin requirement on the first day of a transaction as well as on any day in which additional margin funds must be deposited.

Initial public offering (IPO) The first issuance of common shares to the public by a formerly private corporation.

Inside directors Members of a corporation's board of directors who are not independent. Typically, inside directors are employees or founders (and their family) of the company.

Insolvency A situation in which an issuer's total liabilities exceed the market value of its assets.

Institution An established organization or practice in a society or culture. An institution can be a formal structure, such as a university, organization, or process backed by law; or it can be informal, such as a custom or behavioral pattern important to society. Institutions can, but need not be, formed by national governments. Examples of institutions include non-governmental organizations, charities, religious customs, family units, the media, political parties, and educational practice.

Intangible assets Assets without a physical form, such as patents and trademarks.

Interbank market The market of loans and deposits between banks for maturities ranging from overnight to one year.

Intercept The estimated value of the dependent variable when the independent variable is zero.

Interest coverage A solvency ratio calculated as EBIT divided by interest payments.

Interest coverage ratio A measure of an issuer's ability to service its debt, typically the ratio of operating income or EBIT to interest expense.

Interest rate A rate of return that reflects the relationship between differently dated cash flows; a discount rate.

Interest rate swap A swap in which the underlying is an interest rate. Can be viewed as a currency swap in which both currencies are the same and can be created as a combination of currency swaps.

Interest-indexed bond A type of index-linked bond for which changes in the index are captured with adjustments to interest payments.

Internal credit enhancements Provisions or methods a borrower initiates to improve their creditworthiness in a structured transaction, such as overcollateralization or excess spread.

internal rate of return The discount rate that makes net present value equal 0; the discount rate that makes the present value of an investment's costs (outflows) equal to the present value of the investment's benefits (inflows).

Internal rate of return (IRR) The uniform discount rate for a series of cash flows over n periods that returns a net present value of zero.

Internet of things The vast array of physical devices, home appliances, smart buildings, vehicles, and other items that are embedded with electronics, sensors, software, and network connections that enable the objects in the system to interact and share information.

Interquartile range The difference between the third and first quartiles of a dataset.

Intrinsic value The amount gained (per unit) by an option buyer if an option is exercised at any given point in time. May be referred to as the exercise value of the option.

Investment banks Financial intermediaries that provide advice to their mostly corporate clients and help them arrange transactions such as initial and seasoned securities offerings.

Investment grade Bond issuers and issues rated BBB- (Baa3 on Moody's scale).

Investment policy statement (IPS) A written planning document that describes a client's investment objectives and risk tolerance over a relevant time horizon, along with constraints that apply to the client's portfolio.

Issue rating A rating which seeks to capture the probability of default or expected loss of the issuer's senior unsecured bonds.

Issuer rating A rating which seeks to capture the credit risk of a specific financial obligation of an issuer which takes such factors as seniority into account.

J-curve effect Net income over a multiyear private investment holding period characterized by negative returns in an initial phase, followed by cash flow and income growth toward the end of the holding period.

Jackknife A resampling method that repeatedly draws samples by taking the original observed data sample and leaving out one observation at a time (without replacement) from the set.

January effect Calendar anomaly that stock market returns in January are significantly higher compared to the rest of the months of the year, with most of the abnormal returns reported during the first five trading days in January. Also called *turn-of-the-year effect*.

Joint probability function A function giving the probability of joint occurrences of values of stated random variables.

Judgmental sampling A procedure of selectively handpicking elements from the population based on a researcher's knowledge and professional judgment.

Junior debt Debt obligation with lower priority of payment than senior debt obligations.

Key rate duration Also known as partial duration, is a measure of a bond's sensitivity to a change in the benchmark yield at a specific maturity.

Keynesians Economists who believe that fiscal policy can have powerful effects on aggregate demand, output, and employment when there is substantial spare capacity in an economy.

Kurtosis The statistical measure that indicates the combined weight of the tails of a distribution relative to the rest of the distribution.

Lagging economic indicators Turning points that take place later than those of the overall economy; they are believed to have value in identifying the economy's past condition.

Law of one price A principle that states that if two investments have the same or equivalent future cash flows regardless of what will happen in the future, then these two investments should have the same current price.

Lead underwriter The lead investment bank in a syndicate of investment banks and broker–dealers involved in a securities underwriting.

Leading economic indicators Turning points that usually precede those of the overall economy; they are believed to have value for predicting the economy's future state, usually near-term.

Legal tender Something that must be accepted when offered in exchange for goods and services.

Lender of last resort An entity willing to lend money when no other entity is ready to do so.

Leptokurtic Describes a distribution that has fatter tails than a normal distribution (also called fat-tailed).

Lessee Tenant or property user that enters a lease with a property owner or lessor.

Lessor Property owner or manager that leases a property to a tenant or property user.

Level of significance The probability of a Type I error in testing a hypothesis.

Leverage A measure for identifying a potentially influential high-leverage point.

Leveraged buyout (LBO) A transaction in which a private acquiror uses equity and a high proportion of debt to acquire a public or private company in order to make changes to increase value over an investment period.

Leveraged loan Where private debt investor firms borrow money to make a direct loan to a borrower.

Leveraged loans Loans made to a borrower or issuer with relatively lower credit quality and/or higher leverage.

Liability-driven investing An investment industry term that generally encompasses asset allocation that is focused on funding an investor's liabilities in institutional contexts.

Licensing arrangements Rights to produce a product or have access to intangible assets using someone else's brand name in return for a royalty (often a percentage of revenues).

Lien A legal right or claim to property by a creditor.

Likelihood The probability of an observation, given a particular set of conditions.

Limit order Instructions to a broker or exchange to obtain the best price immediately available when filling an order, but in no event accept a price higher than a specified (limit) price when buying or accept a price lower than a specified (limit) price when selling.

Limit order book The book or list of limit orders to buy and sell that pertains to a security.

Limited company A business organizational form owned by shareholders or members with limited liability who elect a board of directors to appoint management. Generally, limited companies have indefinite life and easier transfer of ownership interests than limited partnerships.

Limited liability partnership (LLP) A business organizational form available in some jurisdictions owned entirely by limited partners with limited liability.

Limited partners (LPs) Outside investors in a private market fund who own a fractional interest in a limited, closed-end partnership managed by a general partner based on the investment commitment and other terms set out in a limited partner agreement.

Limited partnership Closed-end form of ownership frequently used in private market funds in which private market fund investors, or limited partners, commit capital that is invested, managed, and distributed by a private market fund manager, or general partner, over an investment holding period.

Limited partnership agreement (LPA) A legal document that outlines the rules of the partnership and establishes the framework that ultimately guides the fund's operations throughout its life.

lin-log model A functional form for transforming regression model data in which the dependent variable is linear but the independent variable is logarithmic.

Linear derivatives Firm commitment derivative contracts in which the contract's payoff/profit function is linear with respect to the price of the underlying.

Liquid market Said of a market in which traders can buy or sell with low total transaction costs when they want to trade.

Liquidity The extent to which a company is able to meet its short-term obligations using cash flows and those assets that can be readily transformed into cash.

Liquidity premium The compensation for liquidity risk that increases in proportion to the investment's illiquidity.

Liquidity ratios Financial ratios measuring the company's ability to meet its short-term obligations to creditors as they come due.

Liquidity risk The risk that an investment may not be readily sold at its true value.

Liquidity trap A condition in which the demand for money becomes infinitely elastic (horizontal demand curve) so that injections of money into the economy will not lower interest rates or affect real activity.

Load fund A mutual fund in which, in addition to the annual fee, a percentage fee is charged to invest in the fund and/or for redemptions from the fund.

Loan-to-value ratio (LTV) Ratio of the amount of the mortgage to the property's value. The lower the LTV, the higher the borrower's equity. From the lender's perspective, the higher the borrower's equity, the less likely the borrower is to default.

Loans Debt instruments agreed to between a borrower and lender, typically a bank.

Lockout or revolving period For an ABS with a non-amortizing collateral pool, such as credit card debt, is the period in which the cash proceeds from principal repayments are reinvested in additional loans with a principal equal to the principal repaid. During this period, there is no prepayment risk and potential default risk is generally limited. When the lockout period is over, principal repayments are used to pay off the outstanding principal on the ABS. Lockout period and revolving period are interchangeable.

Lockup period The minimum holding period before investors are allowed to make withdrawals or redeem shares from a fund. Its purpose is to allow the hedge fund manager the required time to implement and potentially realize a strategy's expected results.

log-lin model A functional form for transforming regression model data in which the dependent variable is logarithmic but the independent variable is linear.

log-log model A functional form for transforming regression model data in which both the dependent and independent variables are in logarithmic form.

Long A trading position in a **derivative contract** that gains value as the price of the **underlying** moves higher.

Long position A position in an asset or contract in which one owns the asset or has an exercisable right under the contract.

Long-run average total cost The curve describing average total cost when no costs are considered fixed.

Loss aversion The tendency of people to dislike losses more than they like comparable gains.

Loss given default (LGD) The amount a debtholder fails to recover if a default occurs, usually expressed as a percentage of par value.

Loss severity Portion of a bond's value (including unpaid interest) an investor loses in the event of default.

Loss-aversion bias A bias in which people tend to strongly prefer avoiding losses as opposed to achieving gains.

Low-cost producer A firm with lower production costs than its industry competitors.

M^2 A measure of what a portfolio would have returned if it had taken on the same total risk as the market index.

M^2 alpha Difference between the risk-adjusted performance of the portfolio and the performance of the benchmark.

Macaulay duration the present-value weighted average time to receipt of cash flows for fixed-income instrument, also the holding period needed to balance coupon reinvestment risk and price risk for a one-time instantaneous "parallel" shift in the yield curve once the bond purchase is settled. It is named after Frederick Macaulay, the Canadian economist who introduced the concept in 1938.

Machine learning (ML) Involves computer-based techniques that seek to extract knowledge from large amounts of data without making any assumptions about the data's underlying probability distribution. The goal of ML algorithms is to automate decision-making processes by generalizing, or "learning," from known examples to determine an underlying structure in the data.

Maintenance capital expenditures Investments in assets to keep them in operation or increase their efficiency without extending their useful lives.

Maintenance margin Minimum balance set below the initial margin that each contract buyer and seller must hold in the futures margin account from trade initiation until final settlement at maturity.

Maintenance margin requirement The margin requirement on any day other than the first day of a transaction.

Management buy-in A type of leveraged buyout where the current management team is replaced with the acquiring team involved in managing the company.

Management buyout A private sale to a strategic buyer that includes a company's existing management. The management team commits their own equity capital along with other investors as an incentive to grow the firm's cash flows and value.

Management guidance Management of public companies may publicly provide targets for earnings, revenues, and other measures (e.g., capital expenditures) for the next quarter, year, or longer term. Guidance can be detailed or rather directional and is often updated throughout the year. Initial guidance for next fiscal year might be provided during the fourth-quarter earnings call and updated for completed quarters, and new information provided at the first-, second-, and third-quarter earnings calls. Also known simply as *guidance*.

Margin call Request to a derivatives contract counterparty to immediately deposit funds to return the futures margin account balance to the initial margin.

Margin financing A financing arrangement whereby the prime broker lends shares, bonds, or derivatives and the hedge fund (or investment manager) deposits cash or other collateral into a margin account at the prime broker based on certain fractions of the investment positions.

Margin loan Money borrowed from a broker to purchase securities.

Marginal propensity to consume The proportion of an additional unit of disposable income that is consumed or spent; the change in consumption for a small change in income.

Marginal propensity to save The proportion of an additional unit of disposable income that is saved (not spent).

Mark to market (MTM) The practice in which a central clearing party assigns profits and losses to counterparties to derivative contracts. In exchange-traded markets, this practice takes place daily and is often referred to as daily settlement.

Market anomaly Change in the price or return of a security that cannot directly be linked to current relevant information known in the market or to the release of new information into the market.

Market bid–ask spread The difference between the best bid and the best offer.

Market discount rate The rate of return required by investors given the risk of the bond investment, also known as the required yield or required rate of return.

Market float The number of shares that are available to the investing public.

Market makers **Over-the-counter (OTC) dealers** who typically enter into offsetting bilateral transactions with one another to transfer risk to other parties.

Market model A regression model with the return on a stock as the dependent variable and the returns on a market index as the independent variable.

Market multiple models Valuation models based on share price multiples or enterprise value multiples.

Market neutral These strategies use quantitative, fundamental, and technical analysis to identify under- and overvalued equity securities. The hedge fund takes long positions in undervalued securities and short positions in overvalued securities, while seeking to maintain a market-neutral net position.

Market order Instructions to a broker or exchange to obtain the best price immediately available when filling an order.

Market reference rate (MRR) The interest rate underlying used in interest rate swaps. These rates typically match those of loans or other short-term obligations. Survey-based Libor rates used as reference rates in the past have been replaced by rates based on a daily average of observed market transaction rates. For example, the Secured Overnight Financing Rate (SOFR) is an overnight cash borrowing rate collateralized by US Treasuries. Other MRRs include the euro short-term rate (€STR) and the Sterling Overnight Index Average (SONIA).

Market risk Risk related to market movements, e.g., unexpected changes in share prices, interest rates, currency exchange rates, and commodity prices.

Market share A company's or product's revenue expressed as a percentage of its market size.

Market size Total sales for a good or service, which can be calculated on a global or more regional basis.

Market value The price at which an asset or security can currently be bought or sold in an open market.

Market-capitalization weighting An index weighting method in which the weight assigned to each constituent security is determined by dividing its market capitalization by the total market capitalization (sum of the market capitalization) of all securities in the index. Also called *value weighting*.

Market-on-close An execution instruction specifying that an order can only be filled at the close of trading.

Marketable limit order A buy limit order in which the limit price is placed above the best offer, or a sell limit order in which the limit price is placed below the best bid. Such orders generally will partially or completely fill right away.

Markowitz efficient frontier The graph of the set of portfolios offering the maximum expected return for their level of risk (standard deviation of return).

Master limited partnership (MLP) Has similar features to limited partnerships but is usually a more liquid investment that is often publicly traded.

Master repurchase agreement A legal document governing all repo trades between two parties.

Match funding Financing an asset with a source, such as a loan or bond, that is aligned with certain attributes of the asset, such as duration and the respective streams of income and financing costs.

Material (materiality) Refers to information that is decision-useful for a reasonable investor.

Matrix pricing An estimation process for financial instruments based on the prices of comparable instruments.

Maturity The date of a fixed-income instrument's final payment to investors.

Maturity premium An extra return that compensates investors for the increased sensitivity of the market value of debt to a change in market interest rates as maturity is extended.

Maturity structure of interest rates Also known as the term structure of interest rates, refers to the difference in interest rates or benchmark yields by time-to-maturity.

Mean absolute deviation With reference to a sample, the mean of the absolute values of deviations from the sample mean.

Mean square error (MSE) Calculated as the sum of squares error (SSE) divided by the degrees of freedom, which are the number of observations minus the number of independent variables minus one. Since simple linear regression has just one independent variable, the degrees of freedom calculation is the number of observations minus 2.

Mean square regression (MSR) Calculated as the sum of squares regression (SSR) divided by the number of independent variables in the regression model. In simple linear regression, there is only one independent variable, so MSR equals SSR.

Mean–variance analysis An approach to portfolio analysis using expected means, variances, and covariances of asset returns.

Measure of central tendency A quantitative measure that specifies where data are centered.

Measures of location Quantitative measures that describe the location or distribution of data. They include not only measures of central tendency but also other measures, such as percentiles.

Median The "middlemost" observation; i.e., in a set of observations that has been ranked from highest to lowest, the median will lie in the middle.
Meme coin A type of altcoin that is often inspired by a joke.
Mental accounting bias An information-processing bias in which people treat one sum of money differently from another equal-sized sum based on which mental account the money is assigned to.
Merger arbitrage Special situations investments related to business combinations in which investors seek to capitalize on price discrepancies of securities issued by the target company.
Mesokurtic Describes a distribution with kurtosis equal to that of the normal distribution, namely, kurtosis equal to three.
Mezzanine debt Refers to private credit subordinated to senior secured debt but senior to equity in the borrower's capital structure.
Mezzanine-stage financing Mezzanine venture capital that prepares a company to go public as it continues to expand capacity and enhance its growth trajectory. It represents the bridge financing needed to fund a private firm until it can execute an IPO or be sold.
Miner A validator of transactions on the blockchain that locks blocks of transactions into the blockchain and receives compensation for this process in the form of a digital asset.
Minimum efficient scale The smallest output that a firm can produce such that its long-run average total cost is minimized.
Minimum-variance portfolio The portfolio with the minimum variance for each given level of expected return.
Minority shareholder An individual or entity that owns less than a majority of the voting rights in a corporation.
Mode The most frequently occurring value in a distribution.
Modern portfolio theory (MPT) The analysis of rational portfolio choices based on the efficient use of risk.
Modified duration The first derivative of a bond's price with respect to its yield, this statistic is a measure of interest rate risk used to estimate the percentage price change for a given change in yield-to-maturity.
Monetarists Economists who believe that the rate of growth of the money supply is the primary determinant of the rate of inflation.
Monetary policy Actions taken by a nation's central bank to affect aggregate output and prices through changes in bank reserves, reserve requirements, or its target interest rate.
Monetary transmission mechanism The process whereby a central bank's interest rate gets transmitted through the economy and ultimately affects the rate of increase of prices.
Monetary union An economic union in which the members adopt a common currency.
Money convexity A measure that is used to complement modified duration to capture the second-order effect of yield changes on a bond's price, expressed in currency terms.
Money duration A measure of the price change of a fixed-income instrument in currency units from a change in yield-to-maturity. The money duration can be stated per 100 of par value or in terms of the actual position size. In the United States, money duration is commonly called "dollar duration."
Money market The market for short-term debt instruments (one-year maturity or less).
Money market securities Fixed-income securities with original maturities of one year or less.
Money-weighted return The internal rate of return on a portfolio, taking account of all cash flows.
Moneyness Expresses the relationship between an option's value and its exercise price across the full range of possible underlying prices.
Monopolistic competition Highly competitive form of imperfect competition; the competitive characteristic is a notably large number of firms, while the monopoly aspect is the result of product differentiation.
Monopoly In pure monopoly markets, there are no substitutes for the given product or service. There is a single seller, which exercises considerable power over pricing and output decisions.
Monte Carlo simulation A technique that uses the inverse transformation method for converting a randomly generated uniformly distributed number into a simulated value of a random variable of a desired distribution. Each key decision variable in a Monte Carlo simulation requires an assumed statistical distribution; this assumption facilitates incorporating non-normality, fat tails, and tail dependence as well as solving high-dimensionality problems.
Moral principles Beliefs regarding what is good, acceptable, or obligatory behavior and what is bad, unacceptable, or forbidden behavior.
Mortgage loan Agreement to finance real estate by the collateral of a specified property that obliges the borrower to make a predetermined series of payments to the lender.
Mortgage pass-through security Security created when mortgage lenders pool mortgages together and sell securities to investors. The cash flow from the mortgage pool––monthly payments of principal, interest, and prepayments––are "passed through" to the security holders.
Mortgage-backed securities (MBS) Debt obligations that represent claims to the cash flows from pools of mortgage loans, most commonly on residential property.
Multi-factor model A model that explains a variable in terms of the values of a set of factors.
Multi-market indexes Comprised of indexes from different countries, designed to represent multiple security markets.
Multilateral trading facilities See *alternative trading systems*.
Multilateralism The conduct of countries who participate in mutually beneficial trade relationships and extensive rules harmonization. Private firms are fully integrated into global supply chains with multiple trade partners. Examples of multilateral countries include Germany and Singapore.
Multiple of invested capital (MOIC) Also referred to as the multiple of money or total value to paid-in, this private market performance measure incorporates both the cumulative distributions received and the net asset value of a fund as a proportion of invested capital.
Multiple-price auction A debt securities auction in which bidders receive distinct prices based on their bids.
Multiplier models Valuation models based on share price multiples or enterprise value multiples.
Mutual fund A comingled investment pool in which investors in the fund each have a pro-rata claim on the income and value of the fund.
Nash equilibrium When two or more participants in a non-coop-erative game have no incentive to deviate from their respective equilibrium strategies given their opponent's strategies.
Nationalism The promotion of a country's own economic interests to the exclusion or detriment of the interests of other nations. Nationalism is marked by limited economic and

financial cooperation. These actors may focus on national production and sales, limited cross-border investment and capital flows, and restricted currency exchange.

Natural language processing (NLP) A field of research within the field of text analytics and at the intersection of computer science, AI, and linguistics that focuses on developing computer programs to analyze and interpret human language.

Natural resources These include commodities (hard and soft), agricultural land (farmland), and timberland.

Negative externalities A cost to a third party because of the production or consumption of a good or service.

Negative pledge clause Limitations on investments, the disposal of assets, or issuance of debt senior to existing obligations. Negative covenants seek to ensure that an issuer maintains the ability to make interest and principal payments.

Net cash An issuer's total debt less cash and marketable securities. When the balance is negative it is referred to as net cash.

Net debt An issuer's total debt less cash and marketable securities. When the balance is positive it is referred to as net debt.

Net investment hedge Refers to a specific **hedge accounting** designation that applies when either a foreign currency bond or a derivative, such as an FX swap or forward, is used to offset the exchange rate risk of the equity of a foreign operation.

Net present value (NPV) The present value of an investment's cash inflows (benefits) minus the present value of its cash outflows (costs).

Net profit margin An indicator of profitability, calculated as net income divided by revenue; indicates how much of each dollar of revenues is left after all costs and expenses. Also called *profit margin* or *return on sales*.

Net tax rate The tax rate net of transfer payments.

Net working capital Working capital excluding short-term items unrelated to business operations, such as cash, marketable securities, and short-term debt.

Network effects A business model that enables users to contribute directly to a product, service, or online content.

Neural networks A type of computer program design based on how the human brain learns and processes information.

Neutral rate of interest The rate of interest that neither spurs on nor slows down the underlying economy.

No-load fund A mutual fund in which there is no fee for investing in the fund or for redeeming fund shares, although there is an annual fee based on a percentage of the fund's net asset value.

Node Each value on a binomial tree from which successive moves or outcomes branch.

Non-agency RMBS MBS backed by residential mortgages that are issued by private entities and not guaranteed by a federal agency or a GSE.

Non-amortizing loans Type of debt where there are no scheduled principal repayments.

Non-cooperative country A country with inconsistent and even arbitrary rules; restricted movement of goods, services, people, and capital across borders; retaliation; and limited technology exchange.

Non-cumulative preference shares Preference shares for which dividends that are not paid in the current or subsequent periods are forfeited permanently (instead of being accrued and paid at a later date).

Non-financial risks Risks that arise from sources other than changes in the external financial markets, such as changes in accounting rules, legal environment, or tax rates.

Non-fungible token (NFT) A unique cryptographic token on the blockchain that cannot be replicated and is used to represent ownership of physical assets, such as artwork, real estate, or other assets.

Non-linear derivatives Derivatives, such as options or other contingent claims, with payoff/profit profiles that are non-linear (asymmetric) with respect to the price of the underlying.

Non-participating preference shares Preference shares that do not entitle shareholders to share in the profits of the company. Instead, shareholders are only entitled to receive a fixed dividend payment and the par value of the shares in the event of liquidation.

Non-probability sampling A sampling plan dependent on factors other than probability considerations, such as a sampler's judgment or the convenience to access data.

Non-recourse loan Loan in which the lender does not have a claim against the borrower and thus can look only to the property to recover the outstanding mortgage balance.

Non-state actors Those that participate in global political, economic, or financial affairs but do not directly control national security or country resources. Examples of non-state actors are non-governmental organizations (NGOs), multinational companies, charities, and even influential individuals, such as business leaders or cultural icons.

Nonparametric test A test that is not concerned with a parameter or that makes minimal assumptions about the population from which a sample comes.

Nonsystematic risk Unique risk that is local or limited to a particular asset or industry that need not affect assets outside of that asset class.

Normal distribution A continuous, symmetric probability distribution that is completely described by its mean and its variance.

Normalized earnings The expected level of mid-cycle earnings for a company in the absence of any unusual or temporary factors that affect profitability (either positively or negatively).

Notching Ratings adjustment methodology where specific issues from the same borrower may be assigned different credit ratings.

Notice period The length of time (typically 30–90 days) in advance that investors may be required to notify a fund of their intent to redeem some or all of their investment. This allows a fund manager to liquidate a position in an orderly fashion without magnifying losses.

Novation process A process that substitutes the initial **swap execution facility (SEF)** contract with identical trades facing the **central counterparty (CCP)**. The CCP serves as **counterparty** for both financial intermediaries, eliminating bilateral **counterparty credit risk** and providing **clearing** and **settlement** services.

Null hypothesis The hypothesis that is tested.

Off-the-run Seasoned government bonds that are often less liquid.

Off-the-run securities Sovereign debt securities outstanding other than on-the-sun securities. Off-the-run securities are less liquid than on-the-run securities.

Offer The price at which a dealer or trader is willing to sell an asset, typically qualified by a maximum quantity (ask size).

Official interest rate An interest rate that a central bank sets and announces publicly; normally the rate at which it is willing to lend money to the commercial banks. Also called *official policy rate* or *policy rate.*

Official policy rate An interest rate that a central bank sets and announces publicly; normally the rate at which it is willing to lend money to the commercial banks.

Oligopoly Market structure with a relatively small number of firms supplying the market.

Omnichannel Refers to a company selling its products or services in multiple channels, such as in store and online.

On-the-run Most recently issued, and liquid, government bonds.

On-the-run securities The most recently issued and liquid sovereign debt securities.

Open interest The number of outstanding contracts.

Open market operations The purchase or sale of bonds by the national central bank to implement monetary policy. The bonds traded are usually sovereign bonds issued by the national government.

Open-end fund A mutual fund that accepts new investment money and issues additional shares at a value equal to the net asset value of the fund at the time of investment.

Operating cycle The length of time between a company's acquisition of goods or raw materials and the collection of cash from sales to customers.

Operating efficiency ratios Ratios that measure how efficiently a company performs day-to-day tasks, such as the collection of receivables and management of inventory.

Operating leases A type of lease which is more akin to the rental of the underlying asset.

Operating leverage The sensitivity of a firm's operating profit to a change in revenues, determined by the composition of fixed and variable operating costs.

Operating profit margin A profitability ratio calculated as operating income (i.e., income before interest and taxes) divided by revenue. Also called *operating margin.*

Operational deposits Bank deposits generated by clearing, custody, and cash management activities.

Operational independence A bank's ability to execute monetary policy and set interest rates in the way it thought would best meet the inflation target.

Operational risk The risk that arises from inadequate or failed people, systems, and internal policies, procedures, and processes, as well as from external events that are beyond the control of the organization but that affect its operations.

Operationally efficient Said of a market, a financial system, or an economy that has relatively low transaction costs.

Opportunistic real estate strategies Include major redevelopment, repurposing of assets, taking on large vacancies, or speculating on significant improvement in market conditions. These may be appealing for investors seeking higher returns and willing to accept additional risks from development, redevelopment, repositioning, and leasing.

Opportunity cost Reflects the foregone opportunity of investing in a different asset. It is typically denoted by the risk-free rate of interest, *r*.

Optimal capital structure The capital structure at which the value of the company is maximized.

Option A primary example of a **contingent claim**. A **derivative contract** that provides the buyer the right, but not the obligation, to buy or sell an **underlying**.

Option contract See *option*.

Option premium An amount that is paid upfront from the option buyer to the option seller. Reflects the value of the option buyer's right to exercise in the future.

Option-adjusted price The sum of a bond's flat price and value of an embedded option.

Option-adjusted spread or OAS for a bond is its Z-spread adjusted for the value of an embedded option.

Option-adjusted yield A yield measure for a bond adjusted for embedded options.

Order A specification of what instrument to trade, how much to trade, and whether to buy or sell.

Order precedence hierarchy With respect to the execution of orders to trade, a set of rules that determines which orders execute before other orders.

Order-driven markets A market (generally an auction market) that uses rules to arrange trades based on the orders that traders submit; in their pure form, such markets do not make use of dealers.

Ordinary shares Equity shares that are subordinate to all other types of equity (e.g., preferred equity). Also called *common stock* or *common shares.*

Organizational form A legal and tax classification of a business, specific to a jurisdiction, that determines the organization's legal identity, owner–manager relationship, owner liability, taxation, and access to financing.

Out-of-the-money Describes an option with zero intrinsic value because the option buyer would not rationally exercise the option. An example of such would be the case in which the price of the underlying is less than the option's exercise price for a call option.

Over-the-counter (OTC) Refers to derivative markets in which **derivative contracts** are created and traded between derivatives end users and **dealers**, or financial intermediaries, such as commercial banks or investment banks.

Overcollateralization Credit enhancement technique where collateral underlying the transaction exceeds the face value of the issued bonds.

Overconfidence bias A bias in which people demonstrate unwarranted faith in their own intuitive reasoning, judgments, and/or cognitive abilities.

Overfitting When a machine learning model learns the input and target dataset too precisely, making the system more likely to discover false relationships or unsubstantiated patterns that will lead to prediction errors.

P-value The smallest level of significance at which the null hypothesis can be rejected.

Par rate A yield-to-maturity that makes the present value of a bond's cash flows equal to par.

Par swap rate The fixed swap rate that equates the present value of all future expected floating cash flows to the present value of fixed cash flows.

Par value The amount of principal on a bond, also known as face value.

Parallel shift When all maturities along a yield curve increase or decrease in yield in the same direction by the same magnitude. A parallel shift in the yield curve is implicitly assumed in analytical duration and convexity.

Parameter A descriptive measure computed from or used to describe a population of data, conventionally represented by Greek letters.

Parametric test Any test (or procedure) concerned with parameters or whose validity depends on assumptions concerning the population generating the sample.

Pari passu clause A covenant or contract clause that ensures a debt obligation is treated the same as the borrower's other senior debt instruments and is not subordinated to similar obligations.

Partially amortizing bond A loan or bond with a payment schedule that calls for partial repayment of principle over the life of the bond, with the remaining principal paid at maturity.

Participating preference shares Preference shares that entitle shareholders to receive the standard preferred dividend plus the opportunity to receive an additional dividend if the company's profits exceed a pre-specified level.

Pass-through businesses Businesses that, by virtue of their organizational form and/or other legal and regulatory attributes, do not pay entity-level taxes on income or loss; income or loss is passed through to owners, who pay personal taxes.

Pass-through rate The coupon rate of a mortgage pass-through security that is received by the investor after administrative charges. It is lower than the weighted average mortgage rate earned on the underlying pool of mortgages because of administrative charges. The pass-through rate that the investor receives is said to be "net interest" or "net coupon."

Passive investment A buy-and-hold approach in which an investor does not make portfolio changes based on short-term expectations of changing market or security performance.

Payable date The day that the company actually mails out (or electronically transfers) a dividend payment.

Payment date The day that the company actually mails out (or electronically transfers) a dividend payment.

Payment-in-kind A bond feature whereby coupon payments can be fully or partially paid in the form of additional issuance or added to the principal amount.

Payments system The system for the transfer of money.

Pearson correlation A parametric measure of the relationship between two variables.

Pecking order theory The theory that managers consider how their actions might be interpreted by outsiders and thereby order their preferences for various forms of corporate financing. Forms of financing that are least visible to outsiders (e.g., internally generated funds) are most preferable to managers, and those that are most visible (e.g., equity issuance) are least preferable.

Penetration pricing A discount pricing approach used when a firm willingly sacrifices margins in order to build scale and market share.

Percentiles Values that divide a distribution into 100 equal parts.

Perfect competition A market structure in which the individual firm has virtually no impact on market price, because it is assumed to be a very small seller among a very large number of firms selling essentially identical products.

Performance evaluation The measurement and assessment of the outcomes of investment management decisions.

Performance fee Fee paid to the general partner from the limited partner(s) based on realized net profits.

Period costs Costs (e.g., executives' salaries) that cannot be directly matched with the timing of revenues and which are thus expensed immediately.

Periodicity Number of periods in a year, used for compound interest. The periodicity of a fixed-income instrument usually matches the frequency of its coupon payments.

Permanent differences Differences between tax and financial reporting of revenue (expenses) that will not be reversed at some future date. These result in a difference between the company's effective tax rate and statutory tax rate and do not result in a deferred tax item.

Permissioned networks Networks that are fully open only to select participants on a DLT network.

Permissionless networks Networks that are fully open to any user on a DLT network.

Perpetual bonds Bonds with no stated maturity date.

Perpetuity A perpetual annuity, or a set of never-ending level sequential cash flows, with the first cash flow occurring one period from now.

PESTLE analysis A framework for analyzing factors that influence an industry's economic outcomes.

Pet projects A capital investment that is pursued by management but is not economically justifiable by a disinterested party. Motivations for pet projects include self-dealing and vanity.

Physical risks Economic and financial losses from the increase in the severity and frequency of extreme weather due to climate change—for example, the loss of coastal real estate from a storm.

PIPE (private investment in public equity) A private offering to select investors with fewer disclosures and lower transaction costs that allows the issuer to raise capital more quickly and cost effectively.

Platykurtic Describes a distribution that has relatively less weight in the tails than the normal distribution (also called thin-tailed).

Pledge A legal right or claim to property by a creditor. Also called a lien.

Poison pill Officially known as a shareholder rights plan, a poison pill is a hostile-takeover defense adopted by boards of directors according to rules specified in the corporate charter. There are several types of poison pills. Generally, they allow shareholders, *excluding* the shareholder making the hostile bid and their affiliates, to buy newly issued shares at a discounted price. The share issuance would dilute the bidder's ownership percentage, rendering it impossible for the bidder to attain control.

Policy rate An interest rate that a central bank sets and announces publicly; normally the rate at which it is willing to lend money to the commercial banks.

Portfolio companies The individual companies owned by a private equity firm.

Portfolio investment flows Short-term investments in foreign assets, such as stocks or bonds.

Portfolio planning The process of creating a plan for building a portfolio that is expected to satisfy a client's investment objectives.

Position The quantity of an asset that an entity owns or owes.

Posterior probability An updated probability that reflects or comes after new information.

Power of a test The probability of correctly rejecting the null—that is, rejecting the null hypothesis when it is false.

Pre-funding period Allows the trust to acquire during a certain period of time after the close of the transaction.

Preference shares A type of equity interest which ranks above common shares with respect to the payment of dividends and the distribution of the company's net assets upon liquidation. They have characteristics of both debt and equity securities. Also called *preferred stock.*

Preferred stock See *preference shares.*

Premium In the case of bonds, premium refers to the amount by which a bond is priced above its face (par) value. In the case of an option, the amount paid for the option contract.
Prepayment option May entitle the borrower to prepay all or part of the outstanding mortgage principal prior to maturity. This creates a risk from the lender's or investor's viewpoint because the cash flow amounts and timing cannot be known with certainty.
Prepayment risk The risk that the some or all of a mortgage-backed security's principal is repaid at a different speed than expected, either in the form of contraction risk (or earlier repayment than expected) or extension risk (later repayment).
Present value models Valuation models that estimate the intrinsic value of a security as the present value of the future benefits expected to be received from the security. Also called *discounted cash flow models.*
Pretax margin A profitability ratio calculated as earnings before taxes divided by revenue.
Price discrimination A pricing approach that charges different prices to different customers based on their willingness to pay.
Price index Represents the average prices of a basket of goods and services.
Price limits Establish a band relative to the previous day's settlement price within which all trades must occur.
Price multiple A ratio that compares the share price with some sort of monetary flow or value to allow evaluation of the relative worth of a company's stock.
Price priority The principle that the highest priced buy orders and the lowest priced sell orders execute first.
Price return Measures *only* the price appreciation or percentage change in price of the securities in an index or portfolio.
Price return index An index that reflects *only* the price appreciation or percentage change in price of the constituent securities. Also called *price index.*
Price stability In economics, refers to an inflation rate that is low on average and not subject to wide fluctuation.
Price takers Producers that must accept whatever price the market dictates.
Price value of a basis point (PVBP) An estimate of the change in the full price of a bond given a 1 bp change in its yield-to-maturity. The PVBP is also called the "PV01," standing for the "price value of an 01" or "present value of an 01," where "01" means 1 bp. In the United States, it is commonly called the "DV01" for the "dollar value" of 1 bp.
Price weighting An index weighting method in which the weight assigned to each constituent security is determined by dividing its price by the sum of all the prices of the constituent securities.
Price-setting option The option to adjust prices when demand or supply varies from what is forecast.
Price-to-earnings ratio (P/E) The ratio of share price to earnings per share.
Pricing power A company's ability to set prices and other economic terms with customers without affecting its sales volumes.
Primary bond markets Fixed-income markets comprised of issuers issuing bonds to investors to raise capital, often intermediated by a third-party such as an investment bank.
Primary capital markets (primary markets) The market where securities are first sold and the issuers receive the proceeds.
Primary dealer Financial institution that is authorized to deal in new issues of sovereign bonds and that serves primarily as a trading counterparty of the office responsible for issuing sovereign bonds.
Primary market The market where securities are first sold and the issuers receive the proceeds.
Prime broker A broker that provides services that commonly include custody, administration, lending, short borrowing, and trading.
Prime loans Lending made to borrowers of high credit quality with strong employment and credit histories, a low DTI, substantial equity in the underlying property, and a first lien on the mortgaged property serving as the collateral for the loan.
Principal The amount that an issuer agrees to repay the debtholders on the maturity date.
Principal-agent relationship An arrangement in which one party (the agent) has authority to act for or on behalf of another party (the principal). Such an arrangement imposes a duty on the agent to act in the principal's best interest.
Prior probabilities Probabilities reflecting beliefs prior to the arrival of new information.
Priority of claims Priority of payment, with the most senior or highest ranking debt having the first claim on the cash flows and assets of the issuer.
Private capital Funding provided to companies that is not sourced from the public markets.
Private company A company, typically a limited company, that does not list its equity securities on an exchange.
Private debt Capital extended to companies through a loan or other form of debt.
Private debtholders Investors in an entity's non-securitized debt claims, such as a loan or lease. The most common type of private debtholder is a bank.
Private equity Equity investment capital raised from sources other than public markets and traditional institutions.
Private equity fund A hedge fund that seeks to buy, optimize, and ultimately sell portfolio companies to generate profits. See *venture capital fund.*
Private equity securities Securities that are not listed on public exchanges and have no active secondary market. They are issued primarily to institutional investors via non-public offerings, such as private placements.
Private investment in public equity (PIPE) An investment in the equity of a publicly traded firm that is made at a discount to the market value of the firm's shares.
Private limited company A type of limited company in many jurisdictions with pass-through taxation but restrictions on the number of shareholders or members and on the transfer of ownership interest.
Private placement A sale of debt or equity securities to a small group of investors on an unregulated basis. The terms of the offering are negotiated by the issuer and investors.
Probability of default (POD) The likelihood that a borrower fails to make full and timely payments of principal and interest according to debt terms, usually expressed in annual percentage terms.
Probability sampling A sampling plan that allows every member of the population to have an equal chance of being selected.
Probability tree diagram A diagram with branches emanating from nodes representing either mutually exclusive chance events or mutually exclusive decisions.

Production flexibility option The option to alter production when demand varies from what is forecast.

Profession An occupational group that has specific education, expert knowledge, and a framework of practice and behavior that underpins community trust, respect, and recognition.

Profit margin An indicator of profitability, calculated as net income divided by revenue; indicates how much of each dollar of revenues is left after all costs and expenses.

Profitability ratios Ratios that measure a company's ability to generate profitable sales from its resources (assets).

Prospectus Legal document in securitization that describes the structure of the transaction, including the priority and amount of payments to be made to the servicer, administrators, and the ABS holders, as well as the credit enhancements used in the securitization.

Protective put A strategy of purchasing an underlying asset and purchasing a put on the same asset.

Proxy contest When a shareholder or group of shareholders campaigns for certain matters they have submitted to a shareholder vote, often a slate of directors who oppose the incumbent board and management. The incumbent board and management simultaneously campaign for their side.

Proxy voting A form of casting a ballot in an election in which a voter authorizes a representative to vote on their behalf according to instructions. In corporate elections, proxy ballots are cast by shareholders that direct a representative, typically the corporate secretary, to enter their votes as instructed.

Public (listed) company A company with its equity securities traded on an exchange.

Public limited companies A type of limited company in many jurisdictions with entity-level taxation but no restrictions on the number of shareholders or transferability of ownership interest; the most suitable organizational form for a company that seeks to go public.

Public–private partnership A long-term contractual relationship between the public and private sectors for the purpose of having the private sector deliver a project or service traditionally provided by the public sector. Infrastructure is increasingly being financed privately through public–private partnerships by local, regional, and national governments.

Public–private partnership (PPP) An agreement between the public sector and the private sector to finance, build, and operate public infrastructure, such as hospitals and toll roads.

Pull on liquidity An action or event that accelerates cash outflows.

Purchase agreement Legal document in a securitization transaction that outlines the representations and warranties that the seller makes about the assets sold.

Pure discount bonds Bonds that do not pay interest during their life. They are issued at a discount to par value and redeemed at par. Also called zero-coupon bonds.

Put An option that gives the holder the right to sell an underlying asset to another party at a fixed price over a specific period of time.

Put option The right to sell an underlying.

Putable bonds Bonds that give the bondholder the right to sell the bond back to the issuer at a predetermined price on specified dates.

Put–call forward parity Describes the no-arbitrage condition in which at $t = 0$ the present value of the price of a long forward commitment plus the price of the long put must equal the price of the long call plus the price of the risk-free asset (with face value of the exercise price of both the call and the put).

Put–call parity Describes the no-arbitrage condition in which at $t = 0$ the price of the long underlying asset plus the price of the long put must equal the price of the long call plus the price of the risk-free asset (with face value of the exercise price of both the call and the put).

Quantile A value at or below which a stated fraction of the data lies. Also referred to as a fractile.

Quantitative easing An expansionary monetary policy based on aggressive open market purchase operations.

Quartiles Quantiles that divide a distribution into four equal parts.

Quick ratio A measure of liquidity that is the ratio of cash, marketable securities, and receivables to current liabilities.

Quintiles Quantiles that divide a distribution into five equal parts.

Quota rents Profits that foreign producers can earn by raising the price of their goods higher than they would without a quota.

Quotas Government policies that restrict the quantity of a good that can be imported into a country, generally for a specified period of time.

Quote-driven market A market in which dealers acting as principals facilitate trading.

Quoted margin Specified spread of a floating rate instrument over a market reference rate or benchmark.

Range The difference between the maximum and minimum values in a dataset.

Rapid amortization provisions Provisions in receivable ABS that may require early principal amortization if specific events occur. Such provisions are referred to as early amortization and are included to safeguard the credit quality of the issue, particularly during the revolving period.

Razor, razorblade pricing A pricing approach that combines a low price on a piece of equipment and high-margin pricing on repeat-purchase consumables.

Real assets Generally, these are tangible physical assets, such as real estate, infrastructure, and natural resources, but they also include such intangibles as patents, intellectual property, and goodwill. Real assets generate current or expected future cash flows and/or are considered a store of value.

Real estate Includes borrowed or ownership capital in buildings or land. Developed land includes commercial and industrial real estate, residential real estate, and infrastructure.

Real option A right, but not an obligation, for management to make a decision with respect to a capital investment that alters future cash flows from the original forecasted scenario.

Real risk-free interest rate The single-period interest rate for a completely risk-free security if no inflation were expected.

Rebalancing Adjusting the weights of the constituent securities in an index.

Rebalancing policy The set of rules that guide the process of restoring a portfolio's asset class weights to those specified in the strategic asset allocation.

Recapitalization Recapitalization via private equity describes the steps a firm takes to increase or introduce leverage to its portfolio company and pay itself a dividend out of the new capital structure.

Recognition lag The lag in government response to an economic problem resulting from the delay in confirming a change in the state of the economy.

Recourse loan Loan in which the lender has a claim against the borrower for the shortfall (deficiency) between the amount of the outstanding mortgage balance and the proceeds received from the sale of the property.

Recovery rate (RR) The percentage of an outstanding debt claim recovered when an issuer defaults

Redemption fee A fee charged to discourage redemptions and to offset the transaction costs for remaining investors in the fund.

Refinancing rate A type of central bank policy rate.

Regionalism In between the two extremes of bilateralism and multilateralism. In regionalism, a group of countries cooperate with one another. Both bilateralism and regionalism can be conducted at the exclusion of other groups. For example, regional blocs may agree to provide trade benefits to one another and increase barriers for those outside of that group.

Registered bonds Bonds for which ownership is recorded by either name or serial number.

Regression analysis Allows us to test hypotheses about the relationship between two variables, by quantifying the strength of the relationship between the two variables, and to use one variable to make predictions about the other variable.

Regression coefficients The collective term for the intercept and slope coefficients in the regression model.

Regret The feeling that an opportunity has been missed; typically, an expression of *hindsight bias.*

Regret-aversion bias An emotional bias in which people tend to avoid making decisions that will result in action out of fear that the decision will turn out poorly.

Relative dispersion The amount of dispersion relative to a reference value or benchmark.

Reopening Issuing bonds by increasing the size of an existing bond issue with a price significantly different from par.

Replication A strategy in which a derivative's cash flow stream may be recreated using a combination of long or short positions in an underlying asset and borrowing or lending cash.

Repo rate The interest rate on a repurchase agreement.

Representativeness bias A belief perseverance bias in which people tend to classify new information based on past experiences and classifications.

Repurchase agreement (Repo) A form of collateralized loan involving the sale of a security with a simultaneous agreement by the seller to buy back the same security from the purchaser at an agreed-on price and future date. The party who sells the security at the inception of the repurchase agreement and buys it back at maturity is borrowing money from the other party, and the security sold and subsequently repurchased represents the collateral.

Repurchase date The date when the party who sold the security at the inception of a repurchase agreement buys back the security from the cash lending counterparty.

Repurchase price The price at which the party who sold the security at the inception of the repurchase agreement buys back the security from the cash lending counterparty.

Required margin Also known as discount margin. The market-determined yield spread over or under the market reference rate such that a floating-rate loan is priced at par on a rate reset date following issuance.

Required rate of return The rate of return required by investors given the risk of the bond investment, also known as the market discount rate or required yield.

Required yield The rate of return required by investors given the risk of the bond investment, also known as the market discount rate of required rate of return.

Required yield spread The difference in yield-to-maturity between a bond and that of a government benchmark bond with the same or similar time-to-maturity.

Resampling A statistical method that repeatedly draws samples from the original observed data sample for the statistical inference of population parameters.

Reserve currency A currency held by global central banks in significant quantities and widely used to conduct international trade and financial transactions.

Reserve requirement The requirement for banks to hold reserves in proportion to the size of deposits.

Residual The amount of deviation of an observed value of the dependent variable from its estimated value based on the fitted regression line.

Restricted domestic currency A currency with limited convertibility into other currencies due to illiquidity.

Return on assets (ROA) A profitability ratio calculated as net income divided by average total assets; indicates a company's net profit generated per dollar invested in total assets.

Return on equity (ROE) A profitability ratio calculated as net income divided by average shareholders' equity.

Return on invested capital (ROIC) A measure of the profitability of a company relative to the amount of capital invested by the equityholders and debtholders.

Return on sales An indicator of profitability, calculated as net income divided by revenue; indicates how much of each dollar of revenues is left after all costs and expenses. Also referred to as *net profit margin.*

Return-generating model A model that can provide an estimate of the expected return of a security given certain parameters and estimates of the values of the independent variables in the model.

Revenue bonds Bonds issued by non-sovereign governments related to a government sponsored project expected to generate future cash flow as a primary source of repayment.

Reverse repurchase agreement A repurchase agreement viewed from the perspective of the cash lending counterparty.

Reverse stock split A reduction in the number of shares outstanding with a corresponding increase in share price but no change to the company's underlying fundamentals.

Revolving credit agreements The most reliable form of short-term bank borrowing facilities; they are in effect for multiple years (e.g., three to five years) and can have optional medium-term loan features. Also known as *revolvers.*

Rho The change in a given derivative instrument for a given small change in the risk-free interest rate, holding everything else constant. Rho measures the sensitivity of the option to the risk-free interest rate.

Ricardian equivalence An economic theory that implies that it makes no difference whether a government finances a deficit by increasing taxes or issuing debt.

Risk Exposure to uncertainty. The chance of a loss or adverse outcome as a result of an action, inaction, or external event.

Risk averse The assumption that an investor will choose the least risky alternative.

Risk aversion The dislike for risk such that compensation is required in terms of higher expected returns for assuming higher risk.

Risk budgeting The establishment of objectives for individuals, groups, or divisions of an organization that takes into account the allocation of an acceptable level of risk.

Risk exposure The state of being exposed or vulnerable to a risk. The extent to which an organization is sensitive to underlying risks.

Risk governance The top-down process and guidance that directs risk management activities to align with and support the overall enterprise.

Risk management The process of identifying the level of risk an organization wants, measuring the level of risk the organization currently has, taking actions that bring the actual level of risk to the desired level of risk, and monitoring the new actual level of risk so that it continues to be aligned with the desired level of risk.

Risk management framework The infrastructure, process, and analytics needed to support effective risk management in an organization.

Risk premium An extra return expected by investors for bearing some specified risk.

Risk shifting Actions to change the distribution of risk outcomes.

Risk tolerance The level of risk an investor is willing and able to bear.

Risk transfer Strategies implemented to mitigate the impact of specific risks by transferring them to an insurance company.

Risk-neutral pricing A no-arbitrage derivative value established separately from investor views on risk that uses underlying asset volatility and the risk-free rate to calculate the present value of future cash flows.

Risk-neutral probability The computed probability used in binomial option pricing by which the discounted weighted sum of expected values of the underlying equal the current option price. Specifically, this probability is computed using the risk-free rate and assumed up gross return and down gross return of the underlying.

Rollover risk The likelihood that a property owner will lose an existing tenant and forgo income until a new one is found.

Safety-first rules Rules for portfolio selection that focus on the risk that portfolio value or portfolio return will fall below some minimum acceptable level over some time horizon.

Sample correlation coefficient A standardized measure of how two variables in a sample move together. It is the ratio of the sample covariance to the product of the two variables' standard deviations.

Sample covariance A measure of how two variables in a sample move together.

Sample excess kurtosis A sample measure of the degree of a distribution's kurtosis in excess of the normal distribution's kurtosis.

Sample mean The sum of the sample observations divided by the sample size.

Sample skewness A sample measure of the degree of asymmetry of a distribution.

Sample standard deviation The positive square root of the sample variance.

Sample variance The sum of squared deviations around the mean divided by the degrees of freedom.

Sample-size neglect A type of representativeness bias in which financial market participants incorrectly assume that small sample sizes are representative of populations (or "real" data).

Sampling distribution The distribution of all distinct possible values that a statistic can assume when computed from samples of the same size randomly drawn from the same population.

Sampling error The difference between the observed value of a statistic and the estimate resulting from using subsets of the population.

Sampling plan The set of rules used to select a sample.

Saving deposits Bank deposits typically held for non-transactional purposes that often have a stated term.

Scatter plot A two-dimensional graphical plot of paired observations of values for the independent and dependent variables in a simple linear regression.

Scenario analysis A variation of the valuation process combining a base case with alternative outcomes, allowing the incorporation of more favorable or adverse scenarios in the valuation process.

Scraping An automated, large-scale, algorithm-driven approach that retrieves otherwise unstructured data available on websites and creates data in a more structured format.

Seasoned offering An offering in which an issuer sells additional units of a previously issued security.

Secondary bond markets Fixed-income markets comprised of investors trading existing bonds amongst themselves.

Secondary market The market where securities are traded among investors.

Secondary precedence rules Rules that determine how to rank orders placed at the same time.

Secondary sale Sale of a private company stake to another private equity firm or group of financial buyers.

Secondary-stage investments The second stage of development of an infrastructure asset. Secondary-stage investments involve existing infrastructure facilities or fully operational assets that do not require further investment or development over the investment horizon. These assets generate immediate cash flow and returns expected over the investment period.

Sector indexes Indexes that represent and track different economic sectors—such as consumer goods, energy, finance, health care, and technology—on either a national, regional, or global basis.

Secured With collateral; secured debt is backed by the cash flows of the issuer and the collateral as a secondary source of repayment.

Secured loans Loans collateralized by an asset of the borrower.

Security Evidence of equity or debt interest or in an entity or a related right, such as a derivative. Often standardized to conform to security exchange requirements.

Security characteristic line A plot of the excess return of a security on the excess return of the market.

Security market index A portfolio of securities representing a given security market, market segment, or asset class.

Security market line The graphical representation of the CAPM formula, showing the relationship between expected return and beta.

Security selection The process of selecting individual securities; typically, security selection has the objective of generating superior risk-adjusted returns relative to a portfolio's benchmark.

Security tokens Digitizes the ownership rights associated with publicly traded securities.

Segmenting A process of identifying and grouping customers by decision-useful attributes.

Self-attribution bias A bias in which people take too much credit for successes (*self-enhancing*) and assign responsibility to others for failures (*self-protecting*).

Self-control bias A bias in which people fail to act in pursuit of their long-term, overarching goals because of a lack of self-discipline.

Self-investment limits With respect to investment limitations applying to pension plans, restrictions on the percentage of assets that can be invested in securities issued by the pension plan sponsor.

Sell-side firm A broker/dealer that sells securities and provides independent investment research and recommendations to their clients (i.e., buy-side firms).

Semi-strong-form efficient market A market in which security prices reflect all publicly known and available information.

Semiannual bond basis yield Also known as a semiannual bond equivalent yield, it is an annualized interest rate with a periodicity of two.

Semiannual bond equivalent yield Also known as a semiannual bond basis yield, it is an annualized interest rate with a periodicity of two.

Senior debt A debt obligation with higher priority of payment than junior debt obligations.

Senior unsecured debt The highest-ranked debt in an issuer's capital structure which is a general obligation of the borrower.

Seniority Priority of payment of various debt obligations.

Sensitivity analysis A form of analysis used to determine the impact of a change in one or more key variables affecting investment returns or valuation.

Separately managed account (SMA) An investment portfolio managed exclusively for the benefit of an individual or institution.

Service period The time between the grant and vesting dates for an employee share-based award, usually measured in years.

Settlement The closing date at which the counterparties of a derivative contract exchange payment for the underlying as required by the contract.

Settlement price The price determined by an exchange's clearinghouse in the daily settlement of the mark-to-market process. The price reflects an average of the final futures trades of the day.

Share class Types of equity securities that have different voting rights—for example, an issuer may issue Class A shares that carry one vote per share and Class B shares that carry ten votes per share.

Share repurchase A transaction in which a company buys back its own shares. Unlike stock dividends and stock splits, share repurchases use corporate cash.

Shareholder activism A range of actions by a corporation's shareholders that are intended to result in some change in the corporation, typically a change in the board of directors, management, or business strategy.

Shareholder derivative lawsuit A legal action by a shareholder on behalf of a company, not the shareholder personally, against a third party. Often, the third party is a director or manager who the shareholder believes has harmed the company.

Shareholder engagement Shareholder engagement reflects active ownership by investors in which the investor seeks to influence a corporation's decisions on ESG matters, either through dialogue with corporate officers or votes at a shareholder assembly (in the case of equity).

Shareholder theory of corporate governance Espoused by Milton Friedman in his famous 1970 essay, the shareholder theory holds that the objective of a business is to increase profits and shareholder value.

Shareholders Hold a direct equity position in a firm, and both individual persons and financial institutions can be shareholders. The term comes from the individual or investment firm literally having a share of the company. It is most commonly used when talking about the rights and responsibilities that come with being an "owner" of a company, such as stewardship, voting, and engagement. This differentiates it from a situation where an individual or an investment firm lends money or invests in a bond (in other words, they are not an equityholder of a company). Because bond investors do not have a share and are not owners of a company, they cannot vote. Nonetheless, expectations around engagement are increasing for those who invest in loans and bonds as well, making the difference between the two terms more subtle.

Shares Units of ownership interest in a limited company.

Sharpe ratio The ratio of mean excess return to standard deviation (excess return).

Shelf registration A type of public offering that allows the issuer to file a single, all-encompassing offering circular that covers a series of bond issues.

Short A trading position in a **derivative contract** that gains value as the price of the **underlying** moves lower.

Short biased These strategies use quantitative, technical, and fundamental analysis to short overvalued equity securities with limited or no long-side exposures.

Short position A position in an asset or contract in which one has sold an asset one does not own, or in which a right under a contract can be exercised against oneself.

Short selling A transaction in which borrowed securities are sold with the intention to repurchase them at a lower price at a later date and return them to the lender.

Short-run average total cost The curve describing average total cost when some costs are considered fixed.

Shortfall risk The risk that portfolio value or portfolio return will fall below some minimum acceptable level over some time horizon.

Shutdown point The point at which average revenue is equal to the firm's average variable cost.

Side letter A side agreement created between the GP and specific LPs. These agreements exist *outside* the LPA. These agreements provide additional terms and conditions related to the investment agreement.

Signpost An indicator, market level, data piece, or event that signals a risk is becoming more or less likely. An analyst can think of signposts like a traffic light.

Simple linear regression (SLR) An approach for estimating the linear relationship between a dependent variable and a single independent variable by minimizing the sum of the squared deviations between the fitted line and the observed values.

Simple random sample A subset of a larger population created in such a way that each element of the population has an equal probability of being selected to the subset.

Simple random sampling The procedure of drawing a sample to satisfy the definition of a simple random sample.

Simple yield The sum of the coupon payments plus the straight-line amortized share of the gain or loss divided by the bond's flat price. Simple yields are used mostly to quote JGBs.

Simulation A technique for exploring how a target variable (e.g. portfolio returns) would perform in a hypothetical environment specified by the user, rather than a historical setting.

Simulation trial A complete pass through the steps of a simulation.

Single-price auction A debt securities auction in which all bidders pay the same price

Sinking fund Provisions that reduce the credit risk of a bond issue by requiring the issuer to retire a portion of the bond's principal outstanding each year.

Situational influences External factors, such as environmental or cultural elements, that shape our behavior.

Skewed Not symmetrical.

Skewness A quantitative measure of skew (lack of symmetry); a synonym of skew. It is computed as the average cubed deviation from the mean standardized by dividing by the standard deviation cubed.

Slope coefficient The change in the estimated value of the dependent variable for a one-unit change in the value of the independent variable.

Small country A country that is a price taker in the world market for a product and cannot influence the world market price.

Smart beta Involves the use of simple, transparent, rules-based strategies as a basis for investment decisions.

Smart contracts Computer programs that are designed to self-execute on the basis of pre-specified terms and conditions agreed to by parties to a contract.

Social infrastructure investments A category of infrastructure investments that are directed toward human activities and include such assets as educational, health care, social housing, and correctional facilities, with the focus on providing, operating, and maintaining the asset infrastructure.

Soft commodities Standardized agricultural products, such as cattle and corn, with markets often involving the physical delivery of the underlying upon settlement.

Soft hurdle rate Hurdle rate where the fee is calculated on the entire return when the hurdle is exceeded. With a soft hurdle, GPs are able to catch up performance fees once the hurdle threshold is exceeded.

Soft power A means of influencing another country's decisions without force or coercion. Soft power can be built over time through actions, such as cultural programs, advertisement, travel grants, and university exchange.

Soft-bullet covered bonds Delay the bond default and payment acceleration of bond cash flows until a new final maturity date, which is usually up to a year after the original maturity date.

Solvency Refers to the condition in which firm value exceeds the face value of debt used to finance the firm's assets.

Solvency ratios Ratios that measure a company's ability to meet its long-term obligations.

Solvency risk The risk that an organization does not survive or succeed because it runs out of cash, even though it might otherwise be solvent.

Sophisticated investors Individuals or entities that are permitted in a jurisdiction to trade unregistered or, generally, less regulated securities, including shares of privately held companies; also called *accredited investors*.

Sovereign immunity A principle that limits legal recourse of lenders from forcing a sovereign borrower to declare bankruptcy or liquidate its assets to settle debt claims.

Spearman rank correlation coefficient A measure of correlation applied to ranked data.

Special dividend A dividend paid by a company that does not pay dividends on a regular schedule, or a dividend that supplements regular cash dividends with an extra payment.

Special purpose acquisition company A "blank check" company that exists solely for the purpose of acquiring an unspecified private company within a predetermined period or return capital to investors.

Special purpose entity (SPE) Also referred to as a special purpose vehicle (SPV), this legal entity is created for a specific economic purpose. In the case of a project SPV, the entity's sole purpose is to facilitate the construction, operation, and financing of an infrastructure asset over its contractual life.

Special purpose vehicle See *special purpose entity*.

Special situations An area of private capital investment which targets return by investing in stressed, distressed, or event-driven opportunities.

Split ratings Complex risks viewed very differently by rating agencies

Sponsored A type of depository receipt in which the foreign company whose shares are held by the depository has a direct involvement in the issuance of the receipts.

Spot curve Yields-to-maturity on a series of default-risk-free zero-coupon bonds.

Spot markets Markets in which specific assets are exchanged at current prices. Spot markets are often referred to as **cash markets**.

Spot prices The current prices prevailing in **spot markets**.

Spot rates Yields-to-maturity on default-risk-free zero-coupon bonds.

Spread The difference in yield-to-maturity between a bond and that of a another bond.

Spread risk Bond price risk arising from changes in the yield spread on credit-risky bonds; reflects changes in the market's assessment and/or pricing of credit migration (or downgrade) risk and market liquidity risk.

Spurious correlation Refers to: 1) correlation between two variables that reflects chance relationships in a particular dataset; 2) correlation induced by a calculation that mixes each of two variables with a third variable; and 3) correlation between two variables arising not from a direct relation between them but from their relation to a third variable.

Stablecoin A cryptocurrency that aims to maintain a stable value relative to a specified asset or to a pool or basket of assets.

Stackelberg model A prominent model of strategic decision making in which firms are assumed to make their decisions sequentially.

Staggered board A structure of board elections in which only part of the board is elected simultaneously—for example, only one-third of the board may be up for election each year, so the board can be replaced over three years, not in one year if all seats were elected annually. This structure fosters greater continuity of board members but is an obstacle for shareholders seeking to effect change.

Stakeholder theory of corporate governance An expansion of the shareholder theory of corporate governance under which the objective of a business is to maximize value for, and balance the interests of, a broad group of stakeholders, including shareholders, employees, society, and the non-human environment.

Stakeholders Any party with an interest, financial or non-financial, in an entity or its actions.

Standard deviation The positive square root of the variance; a measure of dispersion in the same units as the original data.

Standard error of the estimate A measure of the distance between the observed values of the dependent variable and those predicted from the estimated regression. The smaller this value, the better the fit of the model. Also known as the standard error of the regression and the root mean square error.

Standard error of the forecast Used to provide an interval estimate around the estimated regression line. It is necessary because the regression line does not describe the relationship between the dependent and independent variables perfectly.

Standard error of the slope coefficient Calculated for simple linear regression by dividing the standard error of the estimate by the square root of the variation of the independent variable.

Standardization The process of creating protocols for the production, sale, transport, or use of a product or service. Standardization occurs when relevant parties agree to follow these protocols together. It helps support expanded economic and financial activities, such as trade and capital flows that support higher economic growth and standards of living, across borders.

Standards of conduct Behaviors required by a group; established benchmarks that clarify or enhance a group's code of ethics.

Standing limit orders A limit order at a price below market and which therefore is waiting to trade.

State actors Typically national governments, political organizations, or country leaders that exert authority over a country's national security and resources. The South African President, Sultan of Brunei, Malaysia's Parliament, and the British Prime Minister are all examples of state actors.

Statement of cash flows A financial statement that details the movement of cash over a period. The statement is classified into operating, investing, and financing activities.

Static trade-off theory of capital structure A theory pertaining to a company's optimal capital structure; the optimal level of debt is found at the point where additional debt would cause the costs of financial distress to increase by a greater amount than the benefit of the additional tax shield.

Statistically significant A result indicating that the null hypothesis can be rejected; with reference to an estimated regression coefficient, frequently understood to mean a result indicating that the corresponding population regression coefficient is different from zero.

Status quo bias An emotional bias in which people do nothing (i.e., maintain the status quo) instead of making a change.

Statutory voting A common method of voting where each share represents one vote.

Step-up bonds Bonds for which the coupon, be it fixed or floating, increases by specified margins at specified dates.

Stock dividend A type of dividend in which a company distributes additional shares of its common stock to shareholders instead of cash.

Stock exchange An exchange in which equity securities are traded. See *exchanges*.

Stock split An increase in the number of shares outstanding with a consequent decrease in share price, but no change to the company's underlying fundamentals.

Stockholder overhang The downward pressure on the share price of stock as large blocks of shares are being sold on the open market.

Stop order An order in which a trader has specified a stop price condition. Also called *stop-loss order*.

Stop-loss order See *stop order*.

Stranded assets A resource that is no longer economically valuable owing to changes in demand, regulations, or availability of substitutes—for example, a newly discovered oil well that will not be brought into production.

Strategic asset allocation A long-term strategy that establishes target allocations for various asset classes and aims to optimize the balance between risk and reward by diversifying investments.

Stratified random sampling A procedure that first divides a population into subpopulations (strata) based on classification criteria and then randomly draws samples from each stratum in sizes proportional to that of each stratum in the population.

Street convention For yield measures on fixed-income instruments that assume payments are made on scheduled dates and ignore weekends and holidays.

Stress testing A specific type of scenario analysis that estimates losses in rare and extremely unfavorable combinations of events or scenarios.

Strong-form efficient market A market in which security prices reflect all public and private information.

Structural budget deficit Also known as the cyclically adjusted budget deficit. The deficit that would exist if the economy was at full employment (or full potential output).

Structural subordination Refers to the positioning of debt, which is issued by a legal entity, typically a holding company, which is separate and therefore one step removed from an operating company, which holds assets pledged under a security agreement to senior secured debtholders.

Structured notes A broad category of securities that incorporate the features of debt instruments and one or more embedded derivatives designed to achieve a particular issuer or investor objective.

Subordinated debt A class of unsecured debt that ranks below a firm's senior unsecured obligations.

Subordination A form of internal credit enhancement that relies on creating more than one bond tranche and ordering the claim priorities for ownership or interest in an asset between the tranches. The ordering of the claim priorities is called a senior/subordinated structure, where the tranches of highest seniority are called senior, followed by subordinated or junior tranches. Also called **credit tranching**.

Subprime loans Lending to borrowers with lower credit quality, high DTI, and/or are loans with higher LTV, and include loans that are secured by second liens otherwise subordinated to other loans.

Sum of squares error (SSE) A measure of the total deviation between observed and estimated values of the dependent variable. It is calculated by subtracting each estimated value $\hat{Y}_i$ from its corresponding observed value Y_i, squaring each of these differences, and then summing all of these squared differences.

Sum of squares regression (SSR) A measure of the explained variation in the dependent variable, calculated as the sum of the squared differences between the predicted value of the dependent variable, Y ^_i, based on the estimated regression line, and the mean of the dependent variable, $\bar{Y}$.

Sum of squares total (SST) A measure of the total variation in the dependent variable in a simple linear regression. It is calculated by subtracting the mean of the observed values $\bar{Y}$ from each of the observed values Y_i, squaring each of these differences, and then summing all of these squared differences.

Sunk costs A cost that has already been incurred.

Supervised learning A type of machine learning in which the system attempts to learn to model relationships based on labeled training data.

Supervisory board In some jurisdictions, a corporation's board of directors is formally composed of a supervisory board and a management board. The supervisory board appoints and oversees the management board and often includes representatives of employees and other non-shareholder stakeholders.

Supply chain The sequence of processes involved in the creation and delivery of a physical product to the end customer, both within and external to a firm, regardless of whether those steps are performed by a single firm.

Supply shock A typically unexpected disturbance to supply.

Survivorship bias Relates to the inclusion of only current investment funds in a database. As such, the returns of funds that are no longer available in the marketplace (have been liquidated) are excluded from the database. Also see *backfill bias*.

Swap A firm commitment involving a periodic exchange of cash flows.

Swap contract An agreement between two parties to exchange a series of future cash flows.

Swap execution facility (SEF) A swap trading platform accessed by multiple **dealers**.

Swap rate The fixed rate to be paid by the fixed-rate payer specified in a swap contract.

Syndicate A group of lenders, typically made up of banks.

Synthetic protective put The combination of a synthetic long underlying position (i.e., a long forward and risk-free borrowing) and a purchased put on the underlying.

Systematic risk Risk that affects the entire market or economy; it cannot be avoided and is inherent in the overall market. Systematic risk is also known as *non-diversifiable* or *market risk*.

Systematic sampling A procedure of selecting every *k*th member until reaching a sample of the desired size. The sample that results from this procedure should be approximately random.

Systemic risk Refers to risks supervisory authorities believe are likely to have broad impact across the financial market infrastructure and affect a wide swath of market participants.

Tactical asset allocation A proactive strategy that adjusts asset class allocations within a portfolio based on short-term market trends, economic conditions, or valuation changes to capitalize on temporary market inefficiencies or opportunities to improve returns or manage risk more effectively.

Target capital structure Management's desired proportions of debt and equity financing, usually stated on a book value basis or indirectly using a financial leverage metric, such as net or gross debt to EBITDA or credit rating.

Target independent A bank's ability to determine the definition of inflation that they target, the rate of inflation that they target, and the horizon over which the target is to be achieved.

Target semideviation A measure of downside risk, calculated as the square root of the average of the squared deviations of observations below the target (also called *target downside deviation*).

Tariffs Taxes that a government levies on imported goods.

Tax base The amount at which an asset or liability is valued for tax purposes.

Tax expense An aggregate of an entity's income tax payable (or recoverable in the case of a tax benefit) and any changes in deferred tax assets and liabilities. It is essentially the income tax payable or recoverable if these had been determined based on accounting profit rather than taxable income.

Taxable income The portion of an entity's income that is subject to income taxes under the tax laws of its jurisdiction.

Taxable temporary differences Temporary differences that result in a taxable amount in a future period when determining the taxable profit as the balance sheet item is recovered or settled.

Technical analysis A form of security analysis that uses price and volume data, often displayed graphically, in decision making.

Tender offer A solicitation by a current or prospective shareholder to other shareholders to acquire a substantial percentage, including 100%, of shares at a specified price. This action is usually undertaken by a potential acquirer whose bid was rejected by the issuer's board of directors, prompting the potential acquirer to appeal directly to shareholders.

Tenor Remaining time-to-maturity for a fixed-income instrument.

Term repos Repos with a maturity longer than one day.

Term structure of interest rates Also known as the maturity structure of interest rates, refers to the difference in interest rates or benchmark yields by time-to-maturity.

Terminal stock value The expected value of a share at the end of the investment horizon—in effect, the expected selling price. Also called *terminal value*.

Terminal value The expected value of a share at the end of the investment horizon—in effect, the expected selling price.

Test of the mean of the differences A statistical test for differences based on paired observations drawn from samples that are dependent on each other.

Text analytics Involves the use of computer programs to analyze and derive meaning typically from large, unstructured text- or voice-based datasets, such as company filings, written reports, quarterly earnings calls, social media, email, internet postings, and surveys.

Thematic risks Known risks that evolve and expand over a period of time. Climate change, pattern migration, the rise of populist forces, and the ongoing threat of terrorism fall into this category.

Thin-tailed Describes a distribution that has relatively less weight in the tails than the normal distribution (also called platykurtic).

Tiered pricing A pricing approach that charges different prices to different buyers, commonly based on volume purchased.

Timberland investment management organizations Entities that support institutional investors by managing their investments in timberland by analyzing and acquiring suitable timberland holdings.

Time tranching Structure of a securitization that allows for the redistribution of "prepayment risk" among bond classes by creating bond classes of different expected maturities.

Time value The difference between an option's premium and its intrinsic value.

Time value decay The process by which the time value of an option declines toward zero as the option's expiration date is approached.

Time-weighted rate of return The compound rate of growth of one unit of currency invested in a portfolio during a stated measurement period; a measure of investment performance that is not sensitive to the timing and amount of withdrawals or additions to the portfolio.

Tokenization The process of representing ownership rights to physical assets on a blockchain or distributed ledger.

Top-down analysis An investment selection approach that begins with consideration of macroeconomic conditions and then evaluates markets and industries based upon such conditions.

Total probability rule for expected value A rule explaining the expected value of a random variable in terms of expected values of the random variable conditional on mutually exclusive and exhaustive scenarios.

Total return Measures the price appreciation, or percentage change in price of the securities in an index or portfolio, plus any income received over the period.

Total return index An index that reflects the price appreciation or percentage change in price of the constituent securities plus any income received since inception.

Total working capital The difference between current assets and current liabilities.

Tracking error The standard deviation of the differences between a portfolio's returns and its benchmark's returns; a synonym of active risk.

Tracking risk The standard deviation of the differences between a portfolio's returns and its benchmarks returns. Also called *tracking error*.

Trade creation When regional integration results in the replacement of higher cost domestic production by lower cost imports from other members.

Trade diversion When regional integration results in lower-cost imports from non-member countries being replaced with higher-cost imports from members.

Trade sale A portion or division of a private company sold via either direct sale or auction to a strategic buyer interested in increasing the scale and scope of an existing business.

Trade settlement date The date when the buyer and seller transfer consideration and securities.

Traditional investment markets Markets for traditional investments, which include all publicly traded debts and equities and shares in pooled investment vehicles that hold publicly traded debts and/or equities.

Tranches A grouping of securities within an issue with characteristics that vary from other tranches, such as different credit quality and seniority.

Transfer payments Welfare payments made through the social security system that exist to provide a basic minimum level of income for low-income households.

Transition risks Economic and financial losses from the transition to a lower-carbon economy in response to climate change—for example, the abandonment of an oil well that is no longer economical.

Treasury Inflation-Protected Securities (TIPS) US Treasury bonds with a principal that is adjusted for changes in the Consumer Price Index. TIPS are issued in 5-, 10-, and 30-year maturities.

Treynor ratio A measure of risk-adjusted performance that relates a portfolio's returns in excess of the risk-free rate to a portfolio's beta.

Trimmed mean A mean computed after excluding a stated small percentage of the lowest and highest observations.

Triparty repo A repurchase agreement in which the transacting parties agree to use a third-party agent that provides access to a larger collateral pool and multiple counterparties, as well as valuation and safekeeping of assets.

True yield Measures on fixed-income instruments use actual payment dates, accounting for weekends and holidays. The true yield on an instrument is always lower than the street convention yield.

Turn-of-the-year effect Calendar anomaly that stock market returns in January are significantly higher compared to the rest of the months of the year, with most of the abnormal returns reported during the first five trading days in January.

Two-fund separation theorem The theory that all investors regardless of taste, risk preferences, and initial wealth will hold a combination of two portfolios or funds: a risk-free asset and an optimal portfolio of risky assets.

Two-way table A table of the frequency distribution of observations classified on the basis of two discrete variables. Also known as *Contingency table*.

Two-week repo rate The interest rate on a two-week repurchase agreement; may be used as a policy rate by a central bank.

Type I error The error of rejecting a true null hypothesis; a false positive.

Type II error The error of not rejecting a false null hypothesis; false negative.

Uncommitted lines of credit Sources of bank credit that a bank can refuse to honor. Uncommitted credit lines are made up to a certain principal amount for a pre-determined maximum maturity, charging a market reference rate plus an issuer-specific spread on only the principal outstanding for the period of use.

Underfitted When a machine learning model treats true parameters as if they are noise and is unable to recognize relationships in the training data, making the model more likely to fail to fully discover patterns that underlie the data.

Underlying The asset referred to in a **derivative contract**.

Underwritten offering A type of securities issue mechanism in which the investment bank guarantees the sale of the securities at an offering price that is negotiated with the issuer. Also known as *firm commitment offering*.

Unearned revenue A liability account for money that has been collected for goods or services that have not yet been delivered; payment received in advance of providing a good or service. Also called *deferred revenue* or *deferred income*.

Unimodal A distribution with a single value that is most frequently occurring.

Unit economics The expression of revenues and costs on a per-unit basis.

Unitranche debt A hybrid or blended loan structure combining different tranches of secured and unsecured debt into a single loan with a single, blended interest rate.

Unsecured Without collateral; unsecured debt is backed only by cash flows of the issuer.

Unsponsored A type of depository receipt in which the foreign company whose shares are held by the depository has no involvement in the issuance of the receipts.

Unsupervised learning A type of machine learning in which the system tries to learn the structure of unlabeled data.

Utility tokens Tokens that provide services within a network, such as paying for services and network fees.

Validity instructions Instructions which indicate when the order may be filled.

Value added resellers Businesses that distribute a product and also handle more complex aspects of product installation, customization, service, or support.

Value at risk A money measure of the minimum value of losses expected during a specified time period at a given level of probability.

Value chain The systems and processes in a firm that create value for its customers.

Value proposition The product or service attributes valued by a firm's target customer that lead those customers to prefer that firm's offering.

Value-add real estate strategies Strategies that involve larger-scale redevelopment and repositioning of existing assets and that may allow the investor to earn a higher return compared with core-plus real estate strategies.

Value-based pricing Pricing set primarily by reference to the value of the product or service to customers.

VaR See *value at risk*.

Variance The expected value (the probability-weighted average) of squared deviations from a random variable's expected value.

Variance of a random variable The expected value (the probability-weighted average) of squared deviations from a random variable's expected value.

Variation margin The difference between current margin required and the current collateral price in a repurchase agreement.

Vega A measure of the sensitivity of an option's price to changes in the underlying's volatility.

Velocity The pace at which geopolitical risk impacts an investor portfolio.

Venture capital Private equity investment in a startup or early-stage company involving high risk and a high rate of failure.

Venture capital fund A hedge fund that seeks to buy, optimize, and ultimately sell portfolio companies to generate profits. See *private equity fund*.

Venture debt Private debt funding that provides venture capital backing to start-up or early-stage companies that may be generating little or negative cash flow.

Vest To become unconditionally entitled to.

Vesting date The day that an employee becomes unconditionally entitled to compensation.

Vintage year The year in which a private capital fund makes its first investment.

Volatility The standard deviation of the continuously compounded returns on the underlying asset.

Vote by proxy A mechanism that allows a designated party—such as another shareholder, a shareholder representative, or management—to vote on the shareholder's behalf.

Voting rights The power of shareholders to cast votes in corporate elections for directors and other matters submitted to a shareholder vote.

Warrant Debt feature or security granting the right to purchase additional common equity shares issued by the company at a predetermined price for a given period.

Waterfall structures These represent the distribution order for cash flows and risk to different tranches in a financing structure.

Weak-form efficient market hypothesis The belief that security prices fully reflect all past market data, which refers to all historical price and volume trading information.

Weighted average coupon rate (WAC) Rate calculated for a mortgage pass-through security by weighting the mortgage rate of each mortgage in the pool by the percentage of the outstanding mortgage balance relative to the outstanding amount of all the mortgages in the pool.

Weighted average maturity (WAM) Calculated for a mortgage pass-through security by weighting the remaining number of months to maturity of each mortgage in the pool by the outstanding mortgage balance relative to the outstanding amount of all the mortgages in the pool.

Weighted-average cost of capital (WACC) A weighted average of the after-tax required rates of return on a company's equity, debt, preferred stock, and other long-term financing sources, where the weights are the fraction of each source of financing in the company's current market value or management's target capital structure.

Winsorized mean A mean computed after assigning a stated percentage of the lowest values equal to one specified low value and a stated percentage of the highest values equal to one specified high value.

Write-off/liquidation Refers to a transaction that has not gone well, and the investment is likely to lose value. The private equity firm revises the value of its investment downward or liquidates the portfolio company.

Yield curve A graphical depiction of yields-to-maturity of bonds from the same issuer across maturities.

Yield spread The difference in yield-to-maturity between a bond and that of a another bond.

Yield-to-call An internal rate of return on a fixed-income instrument's cash flows assuming cash flows are received on scheduled dates and the bond is called at a certain call price and date.

Yield-to-maturity Internal rate of return on a fixed-income instrument's cash flows assuming all cash flows are received on their scheduled dates.

Yield-to-worst The lowest among a fixed-income instrument's yields-to-call and yield-to-maturity. A commonly cited yield measure for fixed-rate callable bonds.

Z-spread or zero-volatility spread is a constant yield spread for a bond over a government or swap curve.

Zero-coupon bonds Bonds that do not pay interest during their life. They are issued at a discount to par value and redeemed at par. Also called pure discount bond.